Tolley's TAXWISE II
2006-07

Inheritance Tax
Taxation of Trusts
Taxation of Estates

Authors:
Keith Gordon MA (Oxon) ACA CTA Barrister
Peter Gravestock FCA CTA (Fellow) ATT
Sue Jones CTA TEP ATT BSc (Hons)

LexisNexis®
Tolley

Members of the LexisNexis Group worldwide

United Kingdom	LexisNexis Butterworths, a Division of Reed Elsevier (UK) Ltd, Halsbury House, 35 Chancery Lane, London, WC2A 1EL, and RSH, 1–3 Baxter's Place, Leith Walk Edinburgh EH1 3AF
Argentina	LexisNexis Argentina, Buenos Aires
Australia	LexisNexis Butterworths, Chatswood, New South Wales
Austria	LexisNexis Verlag ARD Orac GmbH & Co KG, Vienna
Benelux	LexisNexis Benelux, Amsterdam
Canada	LexisNexis Canada, Markham, Ontario
Chile	LexisNexis Chile Ltda, Santiago
China	LexisNexis China, Beijing and Shanghai
France	LexisNexis SA, Paris
Germany	LexisNexis Deutschland GmbH, Munster
Hong Kong	LexisNexis Hong Kong, Hong Kong
India	LexisNexis India, New Delhi
Italy	Giuffrè Editore, Milan
Japan	LexisNexis Japan, Tokyo
Malaysia	Malayan Law Journal Sdn Bhd, Kuala Lumpur
Mexico	LexisNexis Mexico, Mexico
New Zealand	LexisNexis NZ Ltd, Wellington
Poland	Wydawnictwo Prawnicze LexisNexis Sp, Warsaw
Singapore	LexisNexis Singapore, Singapore
South Africa	LexisNexis Butterworths, Durban
USA	LexisNexis, Dayton, Ohio

© Reed Elsevier (UK) Ltd 2006
Published by LexisNexis Butterworths

A CIP Catalogue record for this book is available from the British Library.

ISBN 10: 0 7545 2973 8

ISBN 13: 9 780754 529736

Typeset by Letterpart Ltd, Reigate, Surrey
Printed and bound in Great Britain by William Clowes Limited, Beccles, Suffolk
Visit LexisNexis Butterworths at www.lexisnexis.co.uk

About this book

For over 25 years Tolley's Taxwise II has provided practitioners with a practical means of keeping up to date with changing legislation relating to inheritance tax and trusts. This is achieved by way of worked examples, which have been updated annually to illustrate the major changes introduced by the Finance Act.

The publication is useful as a manual for staff, also acting as a training aid, as well as giving guidance as to the layout of computations. The examples are supplemented with explanatory notes explaining the law and practice relating to the issue illustrated.

The Taxwise publications are invaluable for students enabling them to apply their theoretical knowledge to practical examples of the types used by examiners in professional examinations.

Coverage

A selection of examples on inheritance tax, taxation of trusts and taxation of estates, based on the legislation current for 2006-07, complete with annotated solutions.

The examples are preceded by a summary on page (ix) of the relevant provisions of Finance Act 2006, which received Royal Assent on 19 July 2006.

The book is not an exhaustive work of reference but it shows the treatment of the points that are most likely to be encountered.

The contents list starting on page (v) shows the broad coverage of each example. In addition, there is a general index at the back of the book to assist in the location of specific points.

All statutory references in the inheritance tax sections of the book are to the Inheritance Tax Act 1984 unless otherwise stated.

References to ITTOIA 2005 are to the Income Tax (Trading and Other Income) Act 2005.

The authors

Keith Gordon, MA (Oxon), ACA, CTA, Barrister; Peter Gravestock, FCA, CTA (Fellow), ATT, Past President of the Association of Taxation Technicians, tax lecturer and author; Sue Jones, CTA, TEP, ATT, BSc (Hons), Technical Officer for the Low Incomes Tax Reform Group (LITRG), continuing the original work of Arnold Homer, FCA, CTA, TEP, and Rita Burrows, MBA, ACIS, CTA.

Companion publications

Tolley's Taxwise I 2006-07 (covering Income Tax and National Insurance, Corporation Tax, Capital Gains Tax and Stamp Duty)

Contents

v

INHERITANCE TAX – RATES FROM 15 MARCH 1988

Since 15 March 1988 there has been a single rate of inheritance tax of 40% (halved for some lifetime transfers), applicable where the gross cumulative chargeable transfers exceed a stipulated threshold:

Threshold	Fixed by	Applicable to following transfers
110,000	FA 1988	Between 15 March 1988 and 5 April 1989
118,000	Statutory Instrument	Between 6 April 1989 and 5 April 1990
128,000	Statutory Instrument	Between 6 April 1990 and 5 April 1991
140,000	Statutory Instrument	Between 6 April 1991 and 9 March 1992
150,000	F(No 2)A 1992, FA 1993 and FA 1994	Between 10 March 1992 and 5 April 1995
154,000	Statutory Instrument	Between 6 April 1995 and 5 April 1996
200,000	FA 1996	Between 6 April 1996 and 5 April 1997
215,000	FA 1997	Between 6 April 1997 and 5 April 1998
223,000	Statutory Instrument	Between 6 April 1998 and 5 April 1999
231,000	Statutory Instrument	Between 6 April 1999 and 5 April 2000
234,000	Statutory Instrument	Between 6 April 2000 and 5 April 2001
242,000	Statutory Instrument	Between 6 April 2001 and 5 April 2002
250,000	FA 2002	Between 6 April 2002 and 5 April 2003
255,000	Statutory Instrument	Between 6 April 2003 and 5 April 2004
263,000	Statutory Instrument	Between 6 April 2004 and 5 April 2005
275,000	Finance Act 2005 s 98	Between 6 April 2005 and 5 April 2006
285,000	Finance Act 2005 s 98	Between 6 April 2006 and 5 April 2007
300,000	Finance Act 2005 s 98	Between 6 April 2007 and 5 April 2008
312,000	Finance Act 2006 s 155	Between 6 April 2008 and 5 April 2009
325,000	Finance Act 2006 s 155	Between 6 April 2009 and 5 April 2010

INCOME TAX RATES

Individuals are charged to income tax on non-savings income at the following rates for 2005/06 and 2006/07:

| | 2005/06 | | 2006/07 | |
	£	Tax on full band	£	Tax on full band
10% starting rate on	2,090	209.00	2,150	215.00
22% basic rate on	30,310	6,668.20	31,150	6,853.00
40% (higher rate) over	32,400		33,300	

For both years, savings income other than dividends is taxed at the starting rate of 10% up to the starting rate limit, the lower rate of 20% up to the basic rate limit and 40% thereafter. Dividend income is taxed at 10% up to the basic rate limit and at 32.5% thereafter.

Rates for trusts and estates

Special trust rates

The 'rate applicable to trusts' applies to income of discretionary and accumulation and maintenance trusts. In addition it applies to trust capital gains or the capital gains of personal representatives.

The 2006-07 rate is 40%.

The 'dividend trust rate' applies to company dividends and other distributions (including share buy-backs) of discretionary and accumulation and maintenance trusts. In addition it applies to some dividend income received by all trusts.

The 2006-07 rate is 32.5%.

The special trust rates do not apply to the first £1,000 (£500 for 2005/06) of relevant income, instead that will be charged at the standard rate, ie the income tax rate applicable to that type of income.

Trust income not liable at special rates

Trustees of other trusts and personal representatives of deceased's estates are charged at the dividend rate of 10% on dividend income, the lower rate of 20% on savings income and the basic rate on non-savings income.

Trusts with vulnerable beneficiaries

Trusts with vulnerable beneficiaries are able to elect irrevocably for the income and gains of the trust to be taxed as if the income belonged to the vulnerable beneficiary. See question 45.

CAPITAL GAINS TAX

Total net gains of individuals for 2006/07 not exceeding £8,800 (2005/06 £8,500) are exempt. Gains in excess of the annual exemption are taxed at 10% to the extent that the individual's taxable income is less than the starting rate band, 20% to the extent of the unused part of the basic rate band and at 40% thereafter (unchanged from 2005/06).

Personal representatives are entitled to the annual exemption, currently £8,800 for the tax year of death and the next two tax years. Gains not covered by the exemption are taxed at 40% (unchanged from 2005/06).

Gains of trusts in which the settlor retains an interest are taxed as the settlor's gains. For other trusts, the trustees are entitled to an annual exemption (AE) of £4,400 (2005/06 £4,250), divided equally between trusts created by the same settlor after 6 June 1978, subject to a minimum exemption of £880 for each trust (2005/06 £850). Gains in excess of the exemption are charged at 40% for all types of trust (unchanged from 2005/06).

SUMMARY OF PROVISIONS OF FINANCE ACT 2006 RELATING TO INHERITANCE TAX AND TAXATION OF TRUSTS AND ESTATES

Finance Act 2006 reference

s 88 and Sch 12

In summary (main changes)

These amendments form part of the Trusts Modernisation programme.

The legislation provides for revision to TCGA 1992 with effect from 6 April 2006.

The main amendments are intended to define a settlor for most TCGA purposes, and include modification of when a settlement is settlor-interested. They also allow an election for a sub-fund of a settlement to be treated as a separate settlement.

From 6 April 2007 different rules will apply to determine the residence status of trustees for TCGA purposes.

It is intended that there is alignment for income tax and capital gains tax purposes of the definitions of 'settled property', and for most purposes the meanings of 'settlement', 'settlor' and the residence status of the trustees of a settlement.

Section 68 of TCGA is amended to provide a revised meaning of 'settled property'. The amendment comes into force on 6 April 2006 in relation to settlements whenever created.

Sections 68A to 68C are inserted into TCGA. These provisions have effect to determine whether a person is a settlor in relation to a settlement for TCGA purposes.

Sections 68A and 68B come into force on 6 April 2006, in relation to settlements whenever created.

Section 68C will have effect in relation to variations of wills or intestacies etc occurring on or after 6 April 2006, irrespective of the date of death of the deceased person in question.

Section 68A of TCGA: Meaning of 'settlor'

For the purposes of TCGA (except where the context otherwise requires) a person is a settlor in relation to a settlement if the settlement was made (or is treated for TCGA purposes as having been made) by that person.

A person is treated for TCGA purposes as having made a settlement if:

- he has made or entered into it, directly or indirectly, or

- the settlement arose on his death and any of the settled property is, or is derived from, property of which he was competent to dispose immediately before his death.

In particular, a person is treated for TCGA purposes as having made a settlement if

- he has provided property directly or indirectly for the purposes of the settlement, or

- he has undertaken to provide property, directly or indirectly, for the purposes of the settlement.

Where one person makes or enters into a settlement in accordance with reciprocal arrangements with another person, the legislation determines who is to be treated for TCGA purposes as having made the settlement in such circumstances.

A person who has been a settlor in relation to a settlement is treated for TCGA purposes as having ceased to be such if three conditions are met. The conditions are:

(a) no property of which he is a settlor is comprised in the settlement,

(b) he has not undertaken to provide property directly or indirectly for the purposes of the settlement in the future, and

(c) he has not made reciprocal arrangements with another person for that other person to enter into the settlement in the future.

For the purpose of ss 68A, 68B and 68C property is derived from other property:

(a) if it derives (directly or indirectly and wholly or partly) from that property or any part of it, and

(b) in particular, if it derives (directly or indirectly and wholly or partly) from income from that property or any part of it.

'Arrangements' includes any scheme, agreement or understanding, whether or not legally enforceable.

TCGA s 68B – Transfer between settlements: identification of settlor

Section 68B applies in relation to 'transfers of property' between settlements which are made for no consideration or for consideration of an amount less than full consideration. The section does not apply in any case where the transfer of property is made by way of a bargain at arm's length.

In s 68B, references to 'Settlement 1' are to the settlement from which the property is transferred, and references to 'Settlement 2' are to settlement to which it is transferred.

A 'transfer of property' for the purposes of s 68B is a disposal of property by the trustees of Settlement 1 and the corresponding acquisition of property by the trustees of Settlement 2. Transferred property is property acquired on the disposal by the trustees of Settlement 2. What is acquired by the trustees of Settlement 2 could be property which is created by the disposal. This would happen if, for example, the trustees of Settlement 1 were to hold a freehold interest in land and grant a leasehold interest in it to the trustees of Settlement 2.

Any person who is a settlor of the property disposed of by the trustees of Settlement 1 is, from the time of the disposal, treated for TCGA purposes (except where the context otherwise requires) as having made Settlement 2. In addition, any of the transferred property which was provided for the purposes of Settlement 1 (or which is derived from property that was so provided) is, from the time of the disposal, likewise treated as having been provided for the purposes of Settlement 2.

In any case where there is more than one settlor of the property disposed of by the trustees of Settlement 1, each person concerned is treated, in relation to Settlement 2, as the settlor of a proportionate part of the transferred property for TCGA purposes (except where the context otherwise requires).

The transferred property is treated for TCGA purposes (except where the context otherwise requires) as having been provided for the purposes of Settlement 2 if and to the extent that the property disposed of by the trustees of Settlement 1 was provided for the purposes of Settlement 1, or is derived from property provided for that purpose.

Where the property disposed of by the trustees of Settlement 1 was provided by, or is derived from property provided by, one person for the purposes of Settlement 1, he is treated as having provided the transferred property for the purposes of Settlement 2. Where the property disposed of by the trustees of Settlement 1 was provided by, or is derived from property provided by, two or more persons for the purposes of Settlement 1, each of them is treated as having provided a proportionate part of the transferred property for the purposes of Settlement 2.

The above three paragraphs will not apply if:

- the transfer occurs only by reason of the assignment or assignation by a beneficiary of Settlement 1 of an interest in that settlement to the trustees of Settlement 2, or

- the transfer occurs only because of the exercise of a general power of appointment, or

- s 68C(6) applies.

TCGA s 18(2) is to be disregarded for the purposes of determining whether s 68B applies in relation to a transfer of property. Section 18(2) applies where a person acquires an asset and the person making the disposal is connected with him (the rules which determine whether persons are 'connected persons' for TCGA purposes are given by TCGA s 286). The effect of s 18(2) is to treat, for TCGA purposes, the person making the disposal and the person making the acquisition as parties to a transaction which is not a bargain at arm's length. The significance of s 68B is that if the trustees of Settlement 1 and the trustees of Settlement 2 are connected persons, that fact will not cause an acquisition of an asset by the trustees of Settlement 2 and its disposal by the trustees of Settlement 1 which is actually transacted by way of a bargain at arm's length to be treated as having been transacted otherwise than by way of a bargain at arm's length.

TCGA s 68C – Variation of will or intestacy, identification of settlor

Section 68C applies where a disposition of property following a person's death is varied in circumstances where s 62(6) of TCGA applies. The main conditions for s 62(6) to apply in respect of a variation are that the variation is made within two years after the deceased person's death, and the instrument of variation contains a statement that the provision is to apply.

Where property becomes settled property in consequence of the variation, but would not otherwise have become settled property, provision is made for a person listed below to be treated for TCGA purposes (except where the context otherwise requires) as having made the settlement and as having provided the property for the purposes of the settlement.

Four categories of person are identified in this context:

- The first category comprises any person who, immediately before the variation, was entitled to the property (or to property from which it derives) absolutely as legatee. (The reference to derived property covers circumstances such as those where the person's entitlement, immediately before the variation, was to an interest in the property.)

- The second category comprises persons who would have become entitled to the property (or to property from which it derives) absolutely as legatee but for the variation.

- The other two categories comprise persons who would have fallen into either of the first two categories were they not to have been infants or other persons under a disability.

The legislation applies in any case where property which is not settled property immediately before the variation would have become comprised in a settlement (whether it is a settlement which arose on the deceased person's death or a pre-existing settlement), but the effect of the variation is that the property, or property derived from it, becomes comprised in a different settlement. In such circumstances, provision is made for the deceased person to be treated for TCGA purposes (except where the context otherwise requires) as having made that other settlement.

Where, immediately before the variation, property is comprised in a settlement and is property of which the deceased person is a settlor, and the effect of the variation is that the property, or property derived from it, becomes comprised in another settlement provision is made for the deceased person to be treated for TCGA purposes (except where the context otherwise requires) as having made that other settlement.

Where the deceased person is treated as having made a settlement – the deceased person is treated for TCGA purposes as having made the settlement in question immediately before his death. This will not apply in any case where the settlement in question arose on the death of the deceased person.

TCGA s 69

The Schedule amends TCGA s 69, which makes various provisions relating to trustees of settlements. The existing subsections (1) and (2) of s 69 are replaced – the amendments are to have effect from 6 April 2007 to the extent that they determine the residence status of the trustees of a settlement, and from 6 April 2006 to the extent that they have other purposes.

It provides for the trustees of a settlement to be treated as a single person (the deemed person) for TCGA purposes except where the context otherwise requires. The deemed person is to be treated as being resident and ordinarily resident in the UK for TCGA purposes whenever:

Condition 1 – All the trustees are resident in the UK, or

Condition 2 – At least one, but not all, of the trustees of the settlement is resident in the UK and that someone who was a settlor in relation to the settlement was resident, ordinarily resident or domiciled in the UK at a 'relevant time' (see below for definition of 'relevant time').

'Relevant time' can be defined as:

- if the settlement arose on the settlor's death – immediately before the death, or

- in any other case, any time at which the settlor made or is treated as having made a settlement.

If there is a transfer of property from one settlement to another, the relevant times for the second settlement in relation to that settlor will include all times which were relevant times in relation to him in respect of the first settlement.

In certain circumstances a trustee who is not resident in the UK will be treated as resident for the purposes of the two conditions set out above, for example, when he acts as trustee in the course of a business carried out in the UK if the business is carried on through a branch, agency or permanent establishment in the UK.

The deemed person will be treated as neither resident or ordinarily resident in the UK for the above purposes unless that person is treated as resident and ordinarily resident in the UK.

Interests in settlements

Paragraph 3 amends TCGA s 77 which applies in instances where a person who is a settlor in relation to a settlement and is resident or ordinarily resident in the UK has an interest in the settlement and the trustees of the settlement are resident and ordinarily resident in the UK.

For TCGA purposes a settlement will be regarded as settlor-interested if a dependent child of the settlor who is neither married nor in a civil partnership can, does or might benefit from the settlement or derived property. This will bring the TCGA treatment more closely into line with the income tax treatment.

A dependent child (including a stepchild) is one who is:

- aged under 18;

- unmarried; and

- does not have a civil partner.

Sub-fund settlements (TCGA Sch 4ZA)

(Paragraph 6 inserts s 69A into TCGA and Sch 4ZA to TCGA)

This Schedule provides for trustees of a settlement ('the principal 'settlement) to be elect that a fund or specified part of the settled property (the 'sub-fund') be treated for TCGA purposes as a separate settlement. The derived settlement is referred to as a 'sub-fund' settlement.

A sub-fund election must specify the date in which the division is to be treated as having taken effect. This must not be earlier than 6 April 2006, or later than the date the election is made.

If there is a deemed disposal of an asset by the trustees of the principal settlement which is triggered by the sub-fund election, the election is treated as having taken effect on that date but immediately after the deemed disposal.

A sub-fund election may be made only if the following conditions are met when the election is made and conditions 2–4 were satisfied throughout a specified period. The specified period begins when the election is treated as having taken effect and ends immediately before the election is made.

The conditions are set out below:

(1) The principal settlement must not itself be a sub-fund settlement.

(2) There must be some property comprised in the principal settlement which is not in the sub-fund.

(3) On the assumption that the sub-fund election had taken effect, there would not exist any asset in relation to which:

- an interest in the asset is held by the trustees of the sub-fund settlement,

- an interest in the asset is simultaneously held by the trustees of the principal settlement.

For these purposes the provisions of s 104(1) and s 109(2)(a) in respect of fungible assets do not apply.

A person has an interest in an asset if he is a co-owner of that asset.

(4) On the assumption that the sub-fund election had taken effect, there would be no person who was a beneficiary under both the principal settlement and the sub-fund settlement.

(a) A person is a beneficiary under a settlement for this purpose if any property which is or may at any time be, comprised in the settlement, or any 'derived property' (see (d) below) is or will or may become payable to him or applicable for his benefit.

(b) A person is also a beneficiary under a settlement for condition 4 if he enjoys a benefit deriving directly or indirectly from any of the settled property or any derived property.

(c) There are certain exceptions in that a person is not to be regarded as a beneficiary in the principal settlement and the sub-fund settlement if property comprised in the settlement in question or any derived property will or may become payable to him or applicable for his benefit by reason of a specific event such as:

  ● marriage or civil partnership with a beneficiary under the settlement in question;

  ● death of a beneficiary under that settlement;

  ● exercise by the trustees of a power of advancement which is subject to certain restrictions and;

  ● the failure or determination of a protective trust (Trustee Act 1925 s 33)

(d) 'Derived property' means

  (i) Income from that property,

  (ii) property directly or indirectly representing –

    (1) proceeds from that property, or

    (2) proceeds of income from that property, or

  (iii) income from property which is derived property by virtue of para (ii).

Sub-fund election procedure

The election must be made in the required form and by notice to an officer of HMRC.

An election may not be made after the second 31 January after the year of assessment in which the date on which the election is treated to have taken effect falls. So for example, an election to be treated as made in 2006/07 will need to be made before 31 January 2009.

A sub-fund election cannot be revoked once made.

Power to make enquiries

Notice must be given in writing to a person specified and must indicate a period (of at least 60 days) in which the information must be supplied.

The specified persons comprise any person who is or has been a trustee of, or beneficiary under, or settlor in relation to the principal or sub-fund settlement.

Consequences of a sub-fund election (paras 17–22)

The sub-fund settlement is to be treated for TCGA as having been created at the time when the sub-fund election takes effect.

Each trustee of the trusts on which the property comprised in the sub-fund settlement is held will be a trustee of the sub-fund settlement for these purposes.

A person who is a trustee of the sub-fund settlement will be treated from the time when the election is treated as having taken effect, as having ceased to be a trustee of the principal settlement unless he is also a trustee of trusts on which property comprised in the principal settlement is held.

A person who is a trustee of the principal settlement will not be treated as a trustee of the sub-fund settlement unless he is also a trustee of trusts on which property comprised in the sub-fund settlement is held.

The trustees of the sub-fund settlement will be treated for TCGA purposes as having become absolutely entitled to the property comprised in that settlement as against the trustees of the principal settlement. This happens at the time when the sub-fund election is treated as having taken effect.

The time at which any deemed disposal by the trustees of the principal settlement of an asset under s 71(1) or 80(2) of TCGA (being a disposal which is triggered by the sub-fund election) is made is the beginning of the day on which the sub-fund election is treated as having taken effect. Such a disposal under s 71(1) would occur by virtue of para 19 of Sch 4ZA. Such a disposal under s 80(2) would occur by virtue of para 18(2) of Sch 4ZA if that provision has effect to cause the deemed person/s who is/are the trustees of the principal settlement to cease to be resident and ordinarily resident in the United Kingdom.

The time the trustees of the sub-fund settlement are treated as acquiring any asset which is deemed to have been disposed of by the trustees of the principal settlement, is the time at which the sub-fund election is treated as having taken effect.

In any case where an asset is deemed to have been disposed of by the trustees of the principal settlement, it is not also treated as having been disposed of by the trustees under s 80(2) of TCGA by virtue of para 19 of Sch 4ZA.

The trustees of the sub-fund settlement are treated as having become absolutely entitled to money expressed in sterling (such property is not an asset for most TCGA purposes). The first effect is that, for TCGA purposes, the trustees of the principal settlement are treated as having disposed of the money at the beginning of the date on which the sub-fund election is treated as having taken effect.

The second effect of the provision is that, for TCGA purposes, the trustees of the sub-fund settlement are treated as having acquired the money at the time when the election is treated as having taken effect.

The trustees of the sub-fund settlement are treated as having become absolutely entitled to property as against the trustees of the principal settlement, and the property is treated as having been transferred by the trustees of the principal settlement to the trustees of the sub-fund settlement.

The rules are to have effect in relation to the year of assessment 2006-07 onwards, with the proviso that a sub-fund election may not be treated as having taken effect before 6 April 2006.

s 89 and Sch 13   **Settlements: amendments to ICTA and ITTOIA**

The section and Schedule amend ICTA and ITTOIA with regard to trustees and settlements.

The main amendments are:

- An increase in the standard rate band from £500 to £1,000;

- a definition of 'settlor';

- the treatment of sub-fund trusts;

- new rules for settlor interested trusts;

- a common charging system for certain receipts.

A new trustee residence test will apply from 6 April 2007.

Part 1 Principal amendments

Part 1 amends the meaning of 'settled property', 'settlement' and 'settlor' and the residence status of trustees so that these are the same for income tax and capital gains tax purposes.

ICTA s 685A (new section)

This provides a definition of 'settled property' as any property held in trust other than property held by one person as nominee for another, or as trustee for another who is absolutely entitled against the trustee (or would be if he were not an infant or otherwise under a disability). This definition follows the definition in s 68 of TCGA.

Further subsections ensure that references to property comprised in a settlement are references to settled property and clarifies the meaning of what is meant by being said to be absolutely entitled to property as against the trustee. This mirrors the effect of TCGA s 60 in relation to bare trustees and nominees.

Section 685B – Meaning of settlor

This section defines 'settlor'. A person is a settlor in relation to a settlement if the settlement was made (or is treated for the purposes of the Tax Acts as having been made) by that person.

There is also an interpretation provided in the subsection of 'settlor of property' used in some of the new provisions.

A person is treated as having made a settlement if he has made or entered into it, directly or indirectly, or if the settlement arose on his death and any of the settled property is, or is derived from, property of which he was competent to dispose immediately before his death.

In particular, a person is treated as having made a settlement if he has provided, or has undertaken to provide, property directly or indirectly for the purposes of the settlement.

Instances are considered where one person makes or enters into a settlement in accordance with reciprocal arrangements with another person and the provision determines who is to be treated as having made the settlement in those circumstances.

The section provides interpretation as to the property of which a deceased person was competent to dispose immediately before his death. It uses the words in TCGA s 62(10) relating to property of which a person was competent to dispose immediately before his death.

There is provision that a person who has been a settlor in relation to a settlement is treated as having ceased to be such if three conditions are met. These are:

(a) no property of which he is the settlor is comprised in the settlement,

(b)   he has not undertaken to provide property directly or indirectly for the purposes of the settlement in the future, and

(c)   he has not made reciprocal arrangements with another person for that other person to enter into the settlement in the future.

The section also provides interpretation for the references in ss 685B to 685D to property which is 'derived' from other property and defines the term 'arrangements' for the purposes of s 685B.

Section 685C – Transfer between settlements: identification of settlor

This section provides rules for identifying the settlor of property comprised in a settlement where property is transferred from one settlement to another for less than full consideration. The wording follows that of the new TCGA s 68B.

Section 685C applies in relation to 'transfers of property' between settlements which are made for no consideration or for consideration of an amount less than full consideration. In s 685C any references to 'Settlement 1' is the settlement from which the property is transferred, and 'Settlement 2' is the settlement to which it is transferred.

A 'transfer of property' is defined for the purposes of s 685C as a disposal of property by the trustees of Settlement 1 and the corresponding acquisition of property by the trustees of Settlement 2. Transferred property is property acquired on the disposal by the trustees of Settlement 2. What is acquired by the trustees of Settlement 2 could be property which is created by the disposal. This would happen if, for example, the trustees of Settlement 1 were to hold a freehold interest in land and grant a leasehold interest in it to the trustees of Settlement 2.

Any person who is a settlor of the property disposed of by the trustees of Settlement 1 is, from the time of the disposal, treated (except where the context otherwise requires) as having made Settlement 2. Any of the transferred property which was provided for the purposes of Settlement 1 (or which is derived from property that was so provided) is, from the time of the disposal, likewise treated as having been provided for the purposes of Settlement 2.

In any case where there is more than one settlor of the property disposed of by the trustees of Settlement 1, each person concerned is treated, in relation to Settlement 2, as the settlor of a proportionate part of the transferred property (except where the context otherwise requires).

The transferred property is treated for the purposes of the Tax Acts (except where the context otherwise requires) as having been provided for the purposes of Settlement 2 if and to the extent that the property disposed of by the trustees of Settlement 1 was provided for the purposes of Settlement 1, or is derived from property provided for that purpose.

Where transferred property is treated as having been provided for the purposes of Settlement 2 and the property disposed of by the trustees of Settlement 1 was provided by, or is derived from property provided by, one person for the purposes of Settlement 1, he is treated as having provided the transferred property for the purposes of Settlement 2. Where the property disposed of by the trustees of Settlement 1 was provided by, or is derived from property provided by, two or more persons for the purposes of Settlement 1, each of them is treated as having provided a proportionate part of the transferred property for the purposes of Settlement 2.

The conditions above will not to apply if:

- the transfer occurs only by reason of the assignment or assignation by a beneficiary of Settlement 1 of an interest in that settlement to the trustees of Settlement 2, or

- the transfer occurs only because of the exercise of a general power of appointment, or

- s 685D(6) applies.

There is an acquisition or disposal of property for the purposes of this section if there would be an acquisition or disposal of the property for TCGA purposes.

Section 685D – Variation of will or intestacy, and identification of settlor

This section applies where a disposition of property following a person's death is varied and the variation falls within the terms of s 62(6) TCGA.

The wording follows that of the new TCGA s 68C.

Section 685D applies where a disposition of property following a person's death is varied in circumstances where TCGA s 62(6) applies. The main conditions for s 62(6) to apply in respect of a variation are that the variation is made within two years after the deceased person's death, and the instrument of variation contains a statement that the provision is to apply.

The section is applicable in any case where property becomes settled property in consequence of the variation but would not otherwise have become settled property. In such circumstances, this subsection provides for a person listed below to be treated for the purposes of the Tax Acts (except where the context otherwise requires) as having made the settlement and as having provided the property for the purposes of the settlement.

There are four categories of persons:

- The first category comprises any person who, immediately before the variation, was entitled to the property (or to property from which it derives) absolutely as legatee. (The reference to derived property covers circumstances such as those where the person's entitlement, immediately before the variation, was to an interest in the property.)

- The second category comprises persons who would have become entitled to the property (or to property from which it derives) absolutely as legatee but for the variation.

- The other two categories comprise persons who would have fallen into either of the first two categories were they not to have been infants or other persons under a disability.

The section provides interpretation for the meaning of the references to a person being entitled to property absolutely as legatee, and mirrors the effect of TCGA s 64(2) and (3).

Section 685D is applicable in any case where property which is not settled property immediately before the variation would have become comprised in a settlement (whether it is a settlement which arose on the deceased person's death or a pre-existing settlement), but the effect of the variation is that the property, or property derived from it, becomes comprised in a different settlement. In such circumstances, the subsection provides for the deceased person to be treated (except where the context otherwise requires) as having made that other settlement.

The section applies in any case where, immediately before the variation, property is comprised in a settlement and is property of which the deceased person is a settlor, and the effect of the variation is that the property, or property derived from it, becomes comprised in another settlement. In such circumstances, this subsection provides for the deceased person to be treated for the purposes of the Tax Acts (except where the context otherwise requires) as having made that other settlement.

The effect of the above two provisions is that the deceased person is treated for the purposes of the Tax Acts as having made the settlement in question immediately before his death. This will not apply in any case where the settlement in question arose on the death of the deceased person.

Section 685E – Trustees of settlements

This section provides for trustees of a settlement to be treated as a single person for the purposes of the Tax Acts. It also provides the test used to determine the residence status of the trustees of a settlement.

The trustees of a settlement are treated as a single person except where the context requires otherwise. The deemed person is distinct from the persons who may from time to time be trustees of the settlement.

The deemed person is to be treated as being resident and ordinarily resident in the United Kingdom at any time when either of the following two conditions are satisfied:

Condition 1 – All the trustees of the settlement are resident in the United Kingdom.

Condition 2 – At least one, but not all, of the trustees of the settlement is resident in the United Kingdom and that a further requirement is satisfied. The further requirement is that someone who is a settlor in relation to the settlement was resident, ordinarily resident, or domiciled in the United Kingdom at a time which is a 'relevant time' in relation to him.

If the settlement arose on the settlor's death, then the time immediately before his death is the only time which is a relevant time in relation to him. In any other case, any time at which the settlor made, or is treated for the purposes of the Tax Acts as making, the settlement is a relevant time in relation to the settlor.

A further rule applies in any case where there is a transfer of property from one settlement ('Settlement 1') to another ('Settlement 2') in relation to which s 685C applies, and a person is treated as having made Settlement 2 by virtue of s 685C(3)(a) in consequence of the relevant disposal by the trustees of Settlement 1. The times which are relevant times in relation to that settlor as far as Settlement 2 is concerned include all times before the disposal which were relevant times in relation to him as far as Settlement 1 is concerned.

A trustee who is not resident in the United Kingdom will be treated as being resident there for the purposes of the conditions above when he acts as trustee in the course of a business he carries on in the United Kingdom. This applies only if the business is being carried on through a branch, agency or permanent establishment in the United Kingdom.

The deemed person referred to above is to be treated as being neither resident nor ordinarily resident in the United Kingdom unless that person is treated for those purposes as being resident and ordinarily resident in the United Kingdom.

Where part of the property comprised in a single settlement is vested in one trustee or set of trustees and part in another, those trustees are treated as constituting a single body of trustees. It mirrors the effect of TCGA s 69(3) for the purposes of the Income Tax Acts.

Where, for income tax purposes, a single settlement comes into existence as at 6 April 2006, and the only reason for that change is the introduction of ICTA 1988 new ss 685A and 685E, there will be deemed to be no cessation of a trade, nor the commencement of a new trade.

Section 685F – Application of ss 739 and 740

This section sets out the circumstances in which s 685E will not apply in relation to ICTA ss 739 and 740 (which relate to the transfer of assets abroad).

The section provides that, for the purposes of ICTA s 739, the new residence rules in ICTA s 685E do not apply in relation to income payable before 15 June 1989.

It also provides that, for the purposes of ICTA s 739(3), the residence rules in s 685E do not apply in relation to income that is or was payable on or after that date if the capital sum referred to in s 739(3) is received before 15 June 1989 and was either repaid (or the right to it was waived) before 1 October 1989.

Section 685F provides that, for the purposes of ICTA s 740, the new residence rules in ICTA s 685E do not apply in relation to benefits received before 15 June 1989. It also provides that, in relation to benefits received on or after that date, the references to 'relevant income' in ICTA s 740 will include income arising to the trustees of a settlement before 6 April 1989 notwithstanding that one or more of the trustees was not resident outside the UK, unless the trustees of the settlement have been charged to tax in respect of that income.

Section 685G – Sub-funds

This section sets out the income tax position where the trustees of a settlement have made a sub-fund election under TCGA new Sch 4ZA.

Where trustees have made a sub-fund election, the sub-fund settlement will be treated as a settlement made at the time the sub-fund election took effect. And from that time the trustees of the sub-fund settlement will be treated as trustees of that settlement and not the principal settlement, unless they are also a trustee of the principal settlement. Similarly, the trustees of the principal settlement will be treated as trustees of that settlement and not of the sub-fund settlement, unless they are also a trustee of the sub-fund settlement.

References to the time the sub-fund election took effect will be the time it is treated as taking effect in accordance with TCGA 1992 para 2 of Sch 4ZA.

Various terms used in this section are to have the same meaning as those given in TCGA 1992 Sch 4ZA.

The changes in ICTA ss 685A to 685C will come into force on 6 April 2006.

Changes in ICTA s 685D will have effect in relation to variations occurring on or after 6 April 2006 regardless of when the deceased person died.

The changes in ICTA 685E will have effect from 6 April 2007, for the purposes of determining the residence status of the trustees of a settlement whenever created, and from 6 April 2006 for any other purpose, for settlements whenever created.

Section 685F comes into force on 6 April 2006.

Section 685G takes effect for years of assessment beginning on or after 6 April 2006.

ICTA s 686, which provides for special rates of tax on income which may be accumulated or which is payable at the discretion of the trustees or any other person, is amended specifically to remove the exemption in s 686(2)(b) from the special trust rates for income arising to the trustees of a settlor-interested settlement. This means that trustees of settlor-interested trusts will be taxed at the special trust rates instead of at only up to the basic rate. This change takes effect from 6 April 2006.

ICTA has a new s 686A, in order to introduce a common charging mechanism for various types of capital receipt currently assessable to income tax in the trustees' hands under a variety of charging mechanisms.

Section 686A – Receipts to be treated as income to which section 686 applies

Where trustees, other than the trustees of a unit trust scheme, receive or are entitled to a payment, or are liable for tax in respect of a gain on a chargeable event, ICTA s 686 applies to that receipt in the same way as it applies to income arising to trustees of a settlement.

There are various types of payments and gains to which s 686 applies. These include:

- a payment made by a company on redemption, repayment or purchase of its own shares, or;

- on the purchase of rights to acquire its own shares;

- gains on contracts for life assurance etc;

- profits on disposal of deeply discounted securities;

- profits of property businesses in relation to lease premiums;

- the profit on the disposal of a future or option;

- profits on the disposal of deposit rights;

- proceeds of sale of a foreign dividend coupon;

- chargeable events in relation to employee share ownership trusts; offshore income gains; and

- gains on disposals of land.

The changes will have effect in respect of payments, or gains arising, to the trustees of a settlement on or after 6 April 2006.

There are amendments to ICTA s 686D relating to the standard rate band for trustees. The amendments increase the limit of the standard rate band from £500 to £1,000, make the standard rate band operate by reference to trustees of a settlement, and prevent multiple standard rate bands being obtained where a settlor has made more than one settlement.

ICTA s 686D(I) substitutes 'trustees of a settlement' for 'trustees of a trust'. It also provides for the increase in the standard rate band limit in ICTA s 686D(3) from £500 to £1,000.

Section 686E – Application of section 686D where settlor has made more than one settlement

ICTA s 686D will have effect with the modification following where a settlor has made more than one settlement.

The reference to £1,000 in s 686D(3) is to be replaced by £200, or by an amount obtained by dividing £1,000 by the number of settlements made by the same settlor, provided the amount is not less than £200.

The section sets out the position where there is more than one settlor of a settlement, and in such circumstances the amount is the amount obtained in relation to the largest class of settlements.

The provisions above came into force on 6 April 2006.

New ss 619(2) and (3) are substituted for ITTOIA ss 619(2) to 619(4), which provide for the treatment of income arising to the trustees of a settlor-interested settlement. These changes mean that, where ITTOIA s 619(I) applies, the income treated as arising to the settlor will be charged to income tax in the settlor's hands at the rates that would have applied had the income arisen directly to him.

ITTOIA new s 619 subsections (2) and (3) replace the existing subsections (2) to (4) inclusive.

The new s 619(2) provides that the income treated as arising to a settlor under a settlement (as defined in ITTOIA s 620(I)) will be chargeable to income tax in the same way as would have been the case had the income arisen directly to the settlor. Thus income from a trade will be charged in the settlor's hands as income under ITTOIA Part 2 at the rates set out in ICTA s 1(2), bank and building society interest will be assessable under ITTOIA Chapter 2 of Part 4 at the rates set out in ICTA s 1A(1A), income from property will chargeable under ITTOIA Part 3 at the rates set out in s 1(2), and so on. New s 619(3) ensures that it will not be possible for a settlor to get the benefit of any actual loss, from sources such as a trade, incurred by the trustees of the settlement.

The new sections come into effect in relation to income arising on or after 6 April 2006.

For income paid to a minor child of the settlor, where the child is unmarried and not in a civil partnership, the paragraph has effect in relation to such income to which s 631 ITTOIA 2005 applies (retained and accumulated income), irrespective of when the income arose.

A new s 685A is introduced into ITTOIA. This provision gives statutory effect to an existing practice of not taxing beneficiaries of settlor-interested settlements on discretionary income payments they receive from the trustees where the underlying income has already been taxed in the hands of the settlor.

Section 685A – Settlor-interested settlements

ITTOIA s 685A will apply where a person receives a discretionary income payment from the trustees of a settlement, and where the settlor is also chargeable to tax under ITTOIA s 619(I) on the income arising to the trustees of the settlement, whether income of the current year of assessment or of a previous year of assessment.

The section applies only to a proportion of the discretionary annual payment corresponding to the proportion of the trustees' income (of current and previous years of assessment) that has been charged to income tax under ITTOIA s 619 in the hands of the settlor. In such circumstances the recipient of the annual payment is treated as having paid income tax at the higher rate in respect of the annual payment.

The beneficiary who receives the discretionary annual payment is to be treated as receiving the sum with a higher rate tax credit, to the extent that the section applies to the income he receives.

The tax which the beneficiary is treated as having paid is not repayable, and prevents the tax that s 685A(3) treats as having been paid from being used to reduce a tax bill on other income. It also provides for the annual payment to be treated for the purposes of ICTA ss 348 and 349(I) as wholly payable out of profits or gains not brought into charge to income tax.

Where the recipient of the annual payment is the settlor then the annual payment is not a taxable receipt in the settlor's hands, and the rule that the beneficiary who receives the discretionary annual payment is to be treated as receiving the sum with a higher rate tax credit, to the extent that the section applies to the income he receives does not apply.

ICTA 1988 s 687 will not apply in relation to the payment, or to so much of the payment as falls within the terms of s 685A.

Section 685A has effect for payments in respect of income made on or after 6 April 2006.

s 156

Rates and rate bands for 2008/09 and 2009/10 – Summary

This section provides for stepped increases in the inheritance tax threshold to £312,000 in 2008-09 and £325,000 in 2009-10 and maintains the tax rate at 40% for each tax year on chargeable amounts in excess of these tax-free amounts.

The annual inheritance tax threshold increases automatically by reference to the rise in the RPI over the year to the previous September, unless Parliament decides otherwise. This section sets the threshold for the tax years 2008-09 and 2009-10 by stepped increases at £312,000 and £325,000 respectively.

The threshold levels of £285,000 for the tax year 2006-07 and £300,000 for the tax year 2007-08 were set in the Finance Act 2005.

s 157 and
Sch 20

Rules for trusts – Summary

This section and Schedule align the inheritance tax (IHT) rules for assets held in trust. So far as new trusts are concerned (created on or after 22 March 2006), it continues the current special treatment:

- for 'interest-in-possession' trusts created on intestacy and straightforward interest in possession trusts created by will and certain other circumstances (see below); and

- for 'accumulation and maintenance trusts' to trusts created on the death of a parent where beneficiaries will take the trust assets at age 18.

Detail

Trusts for 'disabled persons' will also continue to enjoy special treatment, as will existing regular premium life insurance policies written into trust. The IHT treatment for trusts which do not come within these rules will be aligned with the mainstream IHT rules for trusts. The section and Schedule provide transitional arrangements for existing trusts.

Inheritance Tax Act 1984 (IHTA) Part 3, Chapter 3 provides a specific regime for discretionary trusts (strictly, 'relevant property' trusts). It combines:

- an immediate 'entry' tax charge of 20% on lifetime transfers that exceed the inheritance tax (IHT) threshold into 'relevant property' trusts;

- a 'periodic' tax charge of 6% on the value of trust assets over the IHT threshold once every ten years; and

- an 'exit' charge proportionate to the periodic charge when funds are taken out of a trust between ten-year anniversaries.

However, there were special rules for 'interest in possession' (IIP) and accumulation and maintenance trusts. Lifetime transfers into these trusts were exempt from IHT if the settlor survived seven years, and the trusts were not subject to the periodic or exit charges.

These special rules will now be limited to trusts that are created:

- on death by a parent for a minor child who will be fully entitled to the assets in the trust at age 18; or

- on death for the benefit of one life tenant in order of time only (more than one such interest may be created on death as long as the trust capital vests absolutely when the life interest comes to an end); or

- either in the settlor's lifetime or on death for a disabled person;

- to direct self-settlements by vulnerable people and other situations affecting the disabled;

- to specify where property should go on breakdown of marriage.

The IHT treatment for trusts which do not come within these rules will be aligned with the mainstream IHT rules for 'relevant property' trusts. These changes take effect from 22 March 2006, but the section and Schedule provide transitional arrangements for existing trusts.

New and existing Accumulation and Maintenance Settlements

Broadly, where existing Accumulation and Maintenance trusts (A & M trusts) provide that the assets in trust will go to a beneficiary absolutely at 18 – or where the terms on which they are held are modified before 6 April 2008 to provide this – their current IHT treatment will continue.

For a new A & M trust if the capital is left on fully flexible trust with no set date for the beneficiary to become absolutely entitled, the trust will become subject to the 6% rule on the death of the parent and will remain so until the beneficiary is paid out.

For new and old A & M type arrangements – the trusts will not become subject to the 6% regime until the child reaches age 18 and will continue until they become absolutely entitled at age 25. There will be no 20% entry charge. However, for new arrangements (ie trust property settled after 21 March 2006), this applies only if one of the child's parents has died and the trust was established under the will of the parent or under the Criminal Injuries Compensation Scheme.

For existing A & M settlements where beneficiaries are under age 18 at the end of the transitional period on 6 April 2008, they will not be subject to the 6% charge until they reach age 18 provided the trust is modified before 6 April 2008.

Interest in possession settlements

The current rules for existing IIP trusts will run on until the interest in the trust property at 22 March 2006 comes to an end. Any new IIP that arises when an IIP created before 22 March 2006 comes to an end before 6 April 2008 – whether on death or otherwise – will be treated as an IIP that was in place on 22 March 2006. The current rules will also run on for existing regular premium life insurance policies written into trust before 22 March 2006, where payments continue to be made under pre-Budget arrangements. See below for the conditions for new settlements which will remain within the current rules for IIPs.

Capital gains tax implications

The new IHT rules for trusts have consequences for capital gains tax (CGT). Some of the necessary changes will happen automatically – for example, transfers into and out of trusts that will now come within the 'relevant property' rules will automatically be eligible for CGT hold-over relief. And the section and Schedule provide express amendments where they are needed to ensure that the IHT and CGT treatment remain in step.

The section and Schedule also provide that, where an individual is beneficially entitled to an interest in settled property, and continues to be treated for IHT purposes as owning the property, a termination of the interest in the individual's lifetime on or after 22 March 2006 will be treated as a gift for purposes of the IHT 'gift with reservation' rules. Therefore, if they retain the use of the settled property after their interest in it ends, it will remain chargeable in their hands in the same way as if they had formerly owned it outright.

Part 1 – Trusts for bereaved minors and Accumulation and Maintenance Trusts

A new provision is introduced for trusts for minor children at Inheritance Tax Act (IHTA) s 71.

(a) Property held on trust will be exempt from the mainstream IHT charges on trust property by virtue of new IHTA s 71A if it is held:

- on the statutory trusts applying to age 18 which arise for minor children on intestacy; or

- on trusts in similar terms established by a deceased parent's will or by the Criminal Injuries Compensation Scheme.

(b) New s 71B provides for a claw-back charge (parallel to the existing provision for 'accumulation and maintenance' trusts) where these rules cease to be satisfied otherwise than on maturity of the trust at age 18 or the death of a beneficiary before that age.

The existing provision for accumulation and maintenance trusts no longer applies, at IHTA s 71, as from 22 March 2006, with a saving for trusts already within s 71 at that date.

This transitional provision ends at 6 April 2008 unless the trusts in effect at that date provide for beneficiaries to become absolutely entitled to the trust property at age 18. If the beneficiary becomes absolutely entitled between age 18–25 – see above for how the 6% charge will be imposed.

Following lobbying by various representative bodies, new s 71D was introduced at a late stage in the passage of the Bill. It provides that A & M-type trusts (whenever created) can allow beneficiaries to delay receiving capital until they reach the age of 25. The cost of this measure is that between the beneficiary's 18th birthday and the day on which they receive the capital, the trust property becomes relevant property – attracting an exit charge of up to 4.2% (ie 6% x (25–18) years). However, for trust property settled after 21 March 2006, this concession is limited to trusts where at least one parent of the beneficiary has died and the trust was established under the will of the deceased parent or under the Criminal Injuries Compensation Scheme.

Part 2 – Interests in possession: when settled property is part of the beneficiary's estate

This part restricts IHTA s 49 (which treats property subject to an interest-in-possession as owned for IHT purposes by the person having the interest) to a specified class of cases where the interest arises on or after 22 March 2006, namely:

- an 'immediate post-death interest (49A)';

- a 'disabled person's interest (89A)'; or

- a 'transitional serial interest (49B–49E)'.

Immediate post-death interests

Part 2 introduces new material, starting with IHTA s 49A, which sets out the conditions to be satisfied by an 'immediate post-death interest' (IPDI), broadly: that the interest arises immediately on the death of the settlor; and will end with the trust property passing into absolute ownership, or on to trusts for a minor child, a disabled person or charity. This applies to interests created by a will or on intestacy.

Transitional serial interests

New tests are introduced, at new s 49B, for transitional protection as a 'transitional serial interest' (TSI). An interest in possession arising before 6 April 2008 will qualify if it arises on or after 22 March 2006, but follows a previous interest in possession in effect before that date (s 49C).

A TSI will also exist if one person had the beneficial interest in possession before 22 March 2006 and, on or after 6 April 2008, that interest ceases on that person's death and the person's spouse or civil partner becomes beneficially entitled to an interest in possession (s 49D).

Section 49E provides for TSIs to exist in respect of life insurance contracts.

Disabled persons' trusts

Trusts for 'disabled persons' (as defined in IHTA s 89) will continue to enjoy special treatment whether created before or after 22 March 2006. The meaning of 'disabled person' is extended for transfers of property on or after 22 March 2006 to cover a person who, when the property was transferred into the settlement, would have been in receipt of attendance allowance or disability living allowance if:

- one were to ignore the provision of certain accommodation, or

- the person was undergoing hospital treatment for renal failure.

Self-settlement for potential disabilities (s 89B)

A disabled person's trust will also cover trusts where:

- a person was beneficially entitled to property before settling it,

- that person has satisfied HMRC that, at the time, he or she had a condition which would reasonably expect that person to become (as a result):

  - incapable under the Mental Health Acts;

  - in receipt of attendance allowance, or

  - in receipt of disability living allowance by virtue of the care component at the highest or middle rate; and

- during that person's lifetime:

  - no interest in possession subsists; and

  - any application of the settled property is for the benefit of that person; and

  - any power to bring the trust to an end (if exercised) is exercised so that either:

    - a person will become absolutely entitled to it; or

    - on the trust coming to an end, a disabled person's interest will subsist in it.

Part 3 – Related amendments in IHTA

There are changes consequential on the new treatment of certain trusts provided for in Parts 1 and 2 and these are to have effect from 22 March 2006.

IHTA s 3(3) is amended so that omissions which increase the value of property subject to an interest-in-possession are only chargeable on that account where the property is treated as owned by the person owning the interest.

Potentially exempt transfers

Lifetime transfers into trust for a minor child (previously falling within IHTA s 71) are no longer potentially exempt transfers within IHTA s 3A. An interest in possession is not to be treated as part of a person's estate for IHT purposes where it is created on or after 22 March 2006, and is not an interest on trust for a bereaved child, a trust subject to a IPDI or a TSI or a disabled person's trust.

Property held on such trusts is instead charged to IHT by the mainstream IHT charges in trust property.

Charges and exemptions for new IIPs

The existing rules for disposals and terminations of interests in possession are adapted, at IHTA ss 51–54, so that for interests in possessions arising on or after 22 March 2006 they will be restricted to IPDIs and TSIs, and extend these rules to the case (covered by new s 51A) where an interest continues to be an interest-in-possession but ceases to satisfy the rules for an IPDI.

Equivalent changes are made to the exceptions from charge for certain interests-in-possession at IHTA s 53 and s 54; there are consequential charges to anti-avoidance rules at s 54A and the section adapts the relief at s 57A for 'heritage maintenance funds'.

IHT charges on trust property

Property held on trusts for a bereaved child is excluded from the scope of 'relevant property' for IHT purposes (ie, property subject to the mainstream periodic and exit charges on trust property).

The scope of 'relevant property' for IHT purposes is extended so that property held on interest in possession trusts created on or after 22 March 2006 will be relevant property, and subject to the mainstream trust charges, unless they are IPDIs, TSIs, trusts for disabled persons, an immediate self-settled interest, or a relationship breakdown settlement interest.

Trust property which is subject to a 'qualifying interest in possession' as defined in IHTA s 59 is excluded from these mainstream charges.

Part 3 modifies this definition to exclude new interests in possession which are not IPDIs, TSIs, interests under disabled trusts, an immediate self-settled interest or a relationship breakdown settlement interest. This in turn expands the potential application of the exemption at IHTA s 86 for property held on employee trusts or newspaper trusts.

The claw-back charge, at IHTA s 76, on property leaving a trust is amended for a bereaved child so that no IHT is charged when the property goes to charity (as none is currently charged when property leaves an accumulation and maintenance trust in this way).

An existing anti-avoidance provision is removed from IHTA s 80 which will no longer be relevant following the changes above to IHTA s 59. It is designed to prevent manipulation of the current clarifying rules for relevant 'property' trusts by providing for one initial period when the trust property is held on interest-in-possession trusts. Such trusts will no longer enjoy special treatment when created on or after 22 March 2006 so that the avoidance that s 80 seeks to prevent would no longer arise.

Protective trusts

Part 3 also modifies IHTA s 88, which treats an interest in possession as continuing for IHT purposes when it is subject to 'protective trusts': ie broadly, provisions which bring an interest in possession to an end in favour of discretionary trusts where the person with the interest tries to sell it. Where protective trusts are triggered on or after 22 March 2006 in relation to an interest in possession created before that date, they will continue to enjoy transitional protection, but special treatment for protective trusts will only be available for trusts created on or after 22 March 2006 where the underlying interest is entitled to special treatment as an IPDI or a TSI.

There is also consequential amendment to the provision at s 100 IHTA for the treatment of charges in the share capital of a close company, shares in which are subject to an interest in possession.

The treatment where a close company itself has an interest in possession is amended in Part 3.

There is an extension to the provision at s 144 which allows things done by the trustees of a trust established by the will of a deceased person to be treated for IHT purposes as done by the will itself, so long as they occur within two years of the death, and no-one has had an interest in possession in the trust property in the meantime. For the future, s 144 will be excluded in this way only where someone has had an interest-in-possession which is an IPDI or a disabled person's interest.

Part 4 – Amendments to TCGA

Part 4 introduces consequential amendments to the Taxation of Capital Gains Tax Act 1992 (TCGA).

There is an amendment to the current CGT treatment of trust property on the death of a person having an interest-in-possession so that for interests created on or after 22 March 2006 it applies only to IPDIs, TSIs or trusts for a bereaved child. The rule at TCGA s 72 is amended. This applies when a life interest comes to an end but the property continues to be held on trust; and there is a further amendment to the rule at TCGA s 73 which applies where the property ceases to be held on trust once the life interest comes to an end.

The current hold-over relief at TCGA s 260(2) for property leaving accumulation and maintenance trusts to property leaving the new trusts for a bereaved child is extended.

Gifts with reservation

Part 5 amends the rules charging IHT on 'property subject to a reservation' (at Finance Act 1986 s 102) to align the treatment of cases involving trust property formerly subject to an interest-in-possession (and treated at that time as owned for IHT purposes by the person owning the interest) with the treatment of similar facts where the property was formerly owned outright. In either case, there can be an IHT charge where the former owner or holder of the interest continues to enjoy the property after they have given it away or their interest has terminated.

(a)   New s 102ZA of Finance Act 1986 aligns the treatment of an interest-in-possession with outright ownership.

(b)   New para 4A of Sch 20 to Finance Act 1986 adapts the rules which allow for 'tracing' where the original property is replaced by other assets.

Purchase of interest in foreign trusts – Summary

Settled property situated outside the UK is excluded property and thus exempt from inheritance tax (IHT) unless the settlor was domiciled in the UK at the time the settlement was made. This treatment extends to holdings in authorised unit trusts and open ended investment companies.

The section provides that such property will no longer be excluded property where a person domiciled in the UK has acquired an 'interest in possession' in it as a result of a money transaction. The amendments apply to all transfers or other chargeable occasions on or after 5 December 2005 in relation to interests acquired on or after that date.

Background

IHTA s 48(3) provides that settled property situated outside the UK is excluded property unless the settlor was domiciled in the UK at the time the settlement was made. Section 48(3A) extends this treatment to holdings in authorised unit trusts and shares in open-ended investment companies (which are normally situated in the UK) where they are comprised in a settlement.

In particular, where someone has an 'interest in possession' (ie a right to the income from, or use of, the trust assets) in a settlement of this kind, there is no IHT charge when their interest ends, even if they are then domiciled in the UK. By purchasing interests in existing trusts originally settled by a person domiciled outside the UK, UK-domiciled individuals have increasingly exploited this exemption to convert their wealth into IHT-free form.

This section is aimed at blocking such avoidance by providing that property is not excluded property by virtue of IHTA s 48(3) or s 48(3A) if, at any time, a person domiciled in the UK has had an interest in possession in it, and their interest arose from a disposition for a consideration in money or money's worth. This applies whoever paid the money, and if the interest was acquired indirectly (for example, under a will or by intestacy) or has been passed on to someone else.

Details

IHTA s 48(3) and s 48(3A) are amended to make them subject to a new subsection (3B). IHTA new subsections (3B) and (3C) are inserted after s 48(3A).

(a) IHTA new subsection (3B) provides that property is not excluded property under s 48(3) or s 48(3A) if:

   - a person is, or has been, beneficially entitled to an interest in possession in the property at any time; and

   - the person is, or was, at that time domiciled in the United Kingdom; and

   - their entitlement arose directly or indirectly as a result of a disposition made on or after 5 December 2005 for a consideration in money or money's worth.

(b) New subsection (3C) provides that it is immaterial whether the consideration was given by the person with the interest in possession or by someone else, and that an entitlement that arose under a will or by intestacy is an example of an entitlement that arose indirectly.

Any IHT falling due as a result of the section before the Finance Bill is enacted (19 July 2006) will be treated as falling due at the end of 14 days following enactment (2 August 2006).

The section is deemed to have come into force on 5 December 2005.

Pension schemes and inheritance tax

This measure will affect the beneficiaries of members of registered pension schemes and clarifies how inheritance tax (IHT) will apply to choices made under the new pension scheme rules, which came into effect on 6 April 2006. It legislates an existing IHT concessionary practice for scheme members who die under the age of 75 and sets out how IHT is to be charged on death on or after age 75 where funds are held in an alternatively secured pension.

The operative date is effective on the death of a scheme member on and after 6 April 2006.

Death of scheme member before age 75

The present IHT rules will continue to apply to registered pension schemes in much the same way as they do currently. This measure will legislate the IHT concessionary practice dating from 1992 in relation to pension choices by scheme members. The practice was first published in Inland Revenue Tax Bulletin 2 (February 1992) and was subsequently updated in 1999 to take account of the introduction of income withdrawal under pension schemes.

An IHT charge can arise in a scheme member's lifetime under Inheritance Tax Act 1984 s 3(3) if they do not exercise their right to take pension benefits. The charge applies at the latest time when the right could be exercised ie immediately before death. For example, if a scheme member did not take their pension when their life expectancy was seriously impaired, and this resulted in an enhanced death benefit being paid to their beneficiaries, then IHT could apply.

Currently, by concession, IHT is not charged in respect of these enhanced death benefits where the beneficiary is a spouse, civil partner or person who is financially dependant on the scheme member. Nor is IHT applied where a scheme member chooses not to exercise a right at a time when this choice does not trigger a charge (for example, choosing not to take a pension when they are in good health) and does not subsequently vary that choice, even when a reduction in their life expectancy would in strictness trigger an IHT charge.

This concessionary treatment is legislated in the Finance Bill. In addition, payments arising in these circumstances which are made to charity will also be exempted from IHT.

Death of scheme member on or after age 75 – Alternatively Secured Pension

The pensions tax simplification rules provide that an individual must secure an income before they reach the age of 75. For most people an annuity or scheme pension is the best means by which they can do this. The new pensions tax regime introduces an additional option for securing their retirement income – an Alternatively Secured Pension (ASP).

Following a consultation by HMRC, legislation has been introduced to ensure that appropriate IHT charges will apply on left-over ASP funds.

The Government will apply an IHT charge on left-over ASP funds on death (or later) as follows:

any funds paid as a 'transfer lump sum death benefit' (ie where the funds remain within the scheme for the benefit of other scheme members) or refunded to an employer or used to provide benefits for a dependant in the pension scheme context who is not a spouse, civil partner or person who is financially dependent will be subject to an IHT charge on the death of the original scheme member as if the funds were part of the scheme member's own taxable estate on death;

any funds paid on the death of the scheme member to charity will be exempt from IHT, as will funds expended for the scheme member's spouse, civil partner or person who is financially dependent on the scheme member;

any left-over funds, once use by the spouse, civil partner or person who is financially dependent (the beneficiary) has come to an end, will be chargeable to IHT on the earlier of the cessation of those benefits and the death of the beneficiary. These remaining funds will be treated as if they were an addition to the original scheme member's estate. However, any left-over funds that are paid to charity will be exempt from IHT;

in certain circumstances, an IHT charge on ASP funds will fall on the estate of a dependant (rather than that of the original scheme member). This will apply where a dependant – within the meaning of the pension scheme rules – opts for an ASP derived from 'benefits' inherited from a scheme member who died before age 75. Here, any left-over funds on the dependant's death will be charged to IHT as if they were part of the dependant's taxable estate on death.

The IHT charge

IHT will be payable on the value of the taxable property at the time the charge arises, and calculated by reference to the tax-free threshold and rate of tax in place at that time. The pension scheme administrator will be responsible for accounting for and paying any IHT due on the ASP funds.

There are two instances where the tax charges on ASP funds overlap. One is where the funds are paid to an employer and the other is where on the death of a dependant under age 75 any remaining funds are paid out as a lump sum other than to a charity. The IHT charge takes priority over the pension scheme tax charge which is then applied to the net fund after deduction of IHT.

Personal representatives

Personal representatives of estates will be required to provide information in the estate account about the ASP. This will include an estimate of the value of the left-over ASP funds at the date of death together with details of the name and address of the scheme administrator (who will be liable for any IHT payable).

(i)   Outline the basic principles of inheritance tax.

(ii)   'Disposition', 'transfer of value', 'chargeable transfer' and 'potentially exempt transfer' are primary terms which need to be considered when determining whether an inheritance tax liability arises on a transaction. Explain the meaning of each term, demonstrating how the terms are linked together.

(iii)   Explain how inheritance tax can become payable at death in respect of transfers of value already made in lifetime.

(iv)   Outline the exemptions from inheritance tax.

(i)   **Basic principles of inheritance tax**

Introduction of inheritance tax

Inheritance tax was introduced by the Finance Act 1986 to apply from 18 March 1986.

It replaced capital transfer tax, most of the capital transfer tax legislation being retained, and the Capital Transfer Tax Act 1984 being renamed the Inheritance Tax Act 1984.

A husband and wife are separate chargeable persons for inheritance tax, each being able to take advantage of any available reliefs and exemptions.

Chargeable transfers and potentially exempt transfers

Lifetime transfers of value may be completely exempt from inheritance tax (see part (iv)). If they are not exempt, they are divided between *chargeable transfers* and *potentially exempt transfers* (see part (ii)), the essence of inheritance tax being that chargeable gifts are accumulated for seven years, the tax cost of gifts depending upon whether or not the sum of the accumulated gifts plus the present chargeable transfer exceeds the threshold at which tax becomes payable on the scale applicable at the time of the chargeable transfer. The present nil threshold is £285,000 (applicable to transfers on and after 6 April 2006), with tax being charged at 40% on the excess over that amount, or 20% for certain lifetime transfers (see below).

Position on death

On death the chargeable estate is added to the chargeable transfers made in the previous seven years to determine the tax liability. In addition, transfers made in that seven year period that were potentially exempt now become chargeable because of the death. In charging those potentially exempt transfers, chargeable transfers made within seven years before each particular gift are taken into account even though the scale of tax used is that applicable at the date of *death*. Tax will only be payable to the extent that the total transfers exceed the nil threshold in force at the date of death and a tapering relief is available as indicated in (iii) 3 below.

If a donor survives a *potentially exempt transfer* by seven years, it will not attract inheritance tax unless the donor retains an interest in or benefits from the gifted property, in which case the seven year survivorship period only starts to run from the time the interest or benefit ceases.

Where the donor has avoided a pre-owned asset income tax charge by making an election under FA 2004 Sch 15.21 or 15.22 then the asset is treated for inheritance tax as a gift with reservation and the seven year survivorship period starts from the time that the donor ceases to have any benefit or enjoyment from the property (see Example 23).

Chargeable lifetime transfers

Where a lifetime transfer (or deemed transfer) is *chargeable to inheritance tax when made*, the tax is calculated at one half of the then scale rates, the rate applicable to each transfer being arrived at by aggregating it with accumulated chargeable transfers in the previous seven years. If the donor should die within seven years after the chargeable transfer, tax is recalculated at the full rate, but using the scale of rates in force at the date of death, and a tapering relief is available as indicated in (iii) 3 below.

Calculation of tax

Because the inheritance tax threshold is increased annually (unless Parliament decides otherwise) and because tax rates may also change, it should be borne in mind that the correct starting point for calculating tax on a chargeable transfer is the cumulative chargeable transfers within the previous seven years. The tax on the transfer should then be calculated using a cumulative tax figure for the earlier transfers based on the *current* scale of rates (or the scale of rates at death, where tax or additional tax arises as a result of the donor's death within seven years). That cumulative tax figure will often not represent the tax that has actually been paid, but it is the simplest way to make the tax calculation (see the example in part (iii)).

Trusts

Where property is held in trust, the inheritance tax treatment depends on the type of trust. Where the trust is one in which there is an interest in possession (ie someone is entitled to the income), the person with that interest is treated as if the trust fund was part of his estate. Where the trust is a discretionary trust, in which no-one has a right to income, special rules apply to charge tax on transfers out of such trusts and also at ten-yearly intervals on the value of the trust fund. The detailed provisions relating to trusts are dealt with in Examples 42 to 65.

Until the Finance Act 2006 there were special rules for interest in possession (IIP) and Accumulation & Maintenance (A&M) trusts. Lifetime transfers into these trusts were exempt from IHT if the settlor survived seven years, and the trusts were not subject to the periodic or exit charges.

These special rules are limited from 22 March 2006 to trusts that are created:

1. on death by a parent for a minor child who will be fully entitled to the assets in the trust at age 18, or

2. on death for the benefit of one life tenant in order of time only (more than one such interest may be created on death as long as the trust capital vests absolutely when the life interest comes to an end), or

3. either in the settlor's lifetime or on death for a disabled person.

The IHT treatment for trusts which do not satisfy these rules follows the mainstream IHT rules for 'relevant property' trusts. These changes took effect from 22 March 2006, but the legislation provided transitional arrangements for existing trusts.

Broadly, where pre-22 March 2006 A & M trusts provide that the assets in trust will go to a beneficiary absolutely at 18 — or where the terms on which they are held are modified before 6 April 2008 to provide this — their current IHT treatment will continue.

A limited exception is given to trusts which allow the advance of capital to be delayed until the beneficiary is 25. It permits the relevant property rules to apply only when the beneficiary reaches the age of 18, so that the theoretical maximum exit charge will be 4.2% when the beneficiary turns 25. However, for trust property settled after 21 March 2006, this exception applies only where one of the beneficiary's parents has died and the funds come from the will of that parent or through a trust established under the Criminal Injuries Compensation Scheme.

IIP trusts commenced before 22 March 2006 will continue to be subject to the previous rules which provide that the capital is to be treated as part of the life tenant's taxable estate. Interests in possession which commenced after 21 March 2006 will be subject to these rules only if they relate to either:

(a) a bare trust; or

(b) an immediate past-death interest; or

(c) a disabled person's interest.

Otherwise, IIP trusts will now be subject to the 'relevant property' rules previously limited to discretionary trusts.

There is more detail on the changes in the summary of the Finance Act 2006 at 52.2 regarding new IIP trusts which will not fall within the 'relevant trust regime'.

(ii) **Dispositions, transfers of value, potentially exempt transfers and chargeable transfers**

Chargeable transfers and transfers of value

The Inheritance Tax Act 1984 Part I incorporates a number of sections in arriving at the definition of a *chargeable transfer of value*:

s 1 Inheritance tax shall be charged on the value transferred by a *chargeable transfer.*

s 2(1) A *chargeable transfer* is any transfer of value made by an individual other than an exempt transfer. (It is provided in s 2(3), however, that references to chargeable transfers include references to occasions on which tax is payable by discretionary trusts.)

s 3(1) A *transfer of value* is any disposition made by a person (the transferor) as a result of which the value of his estate immediately after the disposition is less than it would be but for the disposition and the amount by which it is less is the value transferred by the transfer. Unless otherwise provided, 'transfers of value' include events on which tax is chargeable (such as deemed transfers when someone with an interest in possession dies, or chargeable occasions in relation to discretionary trusts) (s 3(4)).

s 3(2) Any diminution in the value of the estate brought about by the disposal of 'excluded property' is ignored.

s 10 Furthermore any disposition which is not intended to confer any gratuitous benefit on any person and *either* was made at arm's length between unconnected persons *or* was such as might have been expected to be made in a transaction at arm's length between unconnected persons is *not* a transfer of value.

A *chargeable transfer of value* is therefore the difference between the value of the transferor's estate before and after the transfer less any exemptions and ignoring disposals of excluded property (as to which see Example 3).

A person's estate is defined by s 5(1) as the aggregate of all the property to which he is beneficially entitled, except that the estate of a person immediately before his death does not include excluded property. In addition, up to 21 March 2006 someone entitled to the *income* from a trust fund was always treated as beneficially entitled to the fund itself (s 49). 'Property' includes rights or interests of any description, but does not include 'settlement powers', ie powers over, or exercisable directly or indirectly in relation to, settled property or a settlement (s 272).

Dispositions

The term *disposition* is not defined but case law has determined that the word has no special or technical meaning (Ward v CIR (1956)). It therefore covers any act by which a person deliberately divests himself of the beneficial ownership of his property. The legislation extends its meaning where there are associated operations (ss 268 and 272), deliberate failure to exercise a right (s 3), and alterations of rights attaching to shares in a close company (s 98) (see Example 22). Certain dispositions are not transfers of value (see s 10 above and Example 2).

Potentially exempt transfers

The concept of a '*potentially exempt transfer*' is contained in s 3A, which was introduced by FA 1986 and extended by F(No 2)A 1987. Any lifetime transfer of value which:

1. is made by an individual on or after 18 March 1986, and

2. would but for this provision be a chargeable transfer, and

3. is an absolute gift to another individual, (or before 22 March 2006 a gift to an accumulation and maintenance trust, or to a disabled trust), or

4. is made on or after 17 March 1987 but before 22 March 2006 to a trust in which an individual at that point has an interest in possession, or from such a trust, including a transfer into another trust where an interest in possession is held by an individual, an accumulation and maintenance trust, or a disabled trust, or

5. arises because a life tenant with an interest in possession uses his own assets to buy a reversionary interest in the trust property,

is 'potentially exempt' from inheritance tax. It will therefore initially be treated as an *exempt transfer*. However if the transferor's death then occurs during the next *seven* years the transfer becomes a *chargeable transfer*. Any tax on the gift is paid by the transferee.

To come within the definition of a gift to an individual, the value transferred must be attributable to property that becomes part of the individual's estate, or as a result of which the individual's estate is increased.

Potentially exempt transfers which become chargeable transfers are charged to inheritance tax at their value at the time of the transfer, but using the rates applicable at the time of death. Where such transfers have occurred more than *three* years before death any tax due on that particular transfer is reduced by tapering relief, as in (iii) below. Even though the potentially exempt transfers have become chargeable transfers, no tax is payable (and tapering relief is not therefore relevant) if when added to the chargeable transfers in the previous seven years they do not exceed the nil threshold in force at the date of death. The nil band available in respect of the death estate is, however, correspondingly reduced.

The definition of potentially exempt transfer covers virtually all lifetime transfers except those into and out of discretionary trusts, but see (i) for changes to the rules for interest in possession, and accumulation and maintenance settlements from 22 March 2006 onwards.

(iii) **Tax chargeable on lifetime transfers following transferor's death**

Apart from tax becoming payable because a transfer which was potentially exempt becomes chargeable, additional tax may be due on chargeable lifetime transfers made within seven years before death, on which tax is recalculated by reference to the full rate at death.

Three points have to be taken into account in calculating such tax:

1.   If, because of a change in rate or for any other reason, the tax calculated at death is less than that calculated at the time of the gift, no repayment of tax is due.

2.   Lifetime gifts which are reckoned at death are brought in at their value at the time of the gift, but using the later rates applicable at the time of death (although if the value of the gift has fallen before death, the death value may sometimes be substituted).

3.   The tapering relief reduces the tax, not the value of the gift, for the purpose of calculating the tax payable by the following percentages:

Years between gift and death	% reduction in tax payable
0 to 3	0
3+ to 4	20
4+ to 5	40
5+ to 6	60
6+ to 7	80

(IHTA 1984 s 7).

Even though tax is only payable on most lifetime gifts if the donor does not survive them by *seven years*, it will still be necessary to keep records for inheritance tax purposes of lifetime transfers for up to 14 years.

Illustration

Edward, having used his available exemptions, makes a lifetime gift of £133,000 cash to a discretionary settlement on 31 May 1993. Although this is a chargeable transfer, no tax is payable since it is below the chargeable limit.

Edward makes a lifetime gift of £183,000 cash to Christopher on 30 April 2000. No tax is payable at that time since the first £6,000 of the gift is covered by two years' annual exemptions of £3,000 each, and the balance of £177,000 is a potentially exempt transfer.

Edward dies on 31 March 2007, leaving an estate at death of £223,000.

The tax arising at death is calculated as follows:

On £177,000 of the gift on 30.4.2000, which was within seven years before death

Having been a potentially exempt transfer, the gift of £177,000 is now chargeable by reference to the scale in force at 31.3.07:

	£	Tax on scale at time of death £
Gift within previous seven years (31.5.93)	133,000	–
Gift on 30.4.2000 (183,000 – 6,000 exempt, see part (iv))	177,000	10,000*
	310,000	10,000*

(* 310,000 – 285,000 = 25,000 @ 40%)

Tax on £177,000 potentially exempt transfer now chargeable	10,000
Less: tapering relief (80% for surviving 6 years but not 7)	8,000
Tax payable by donee, Christopher	2,000

On estate at death 31.3.07

	£	£
Gift within previous seven years (30.4.2000)	177,000	–
Estate at death	223,000	46,000*
	400,000	46,000*

(* 400,000 – 285,000 = 115,000 @ 40%)

Tax payable on estate at death	£ 46,000

The gift of £133,000 to the discretionary settlement was made more than seven years before death (almost 14 years in fact), but because of the seven year accumulation period it has to be taken into account in calculating the tax on the gift to Christopher on 30 April 2000, since that gift was made within seven years after the gift to the trust and within seven years before Edward's death. The tax chargeable on the gift to Christopher is therefore calculated at the rates applicable to transfers between £133,000 and £310,000. (Had the gift of £133,000 been *potentially exempt*, it would have become totally exempt on 31 May 2000, and would not have been taken into account in calculating the tax on the potentially exempt transfer of £177,000 that became chargeable because of Edward's death.)

The gift to the discretionary settlement is excluded from the accumulation seven years after it was made, that is at 31 May 2000, so that it does not enter into the cumulative total at death on 31 March 2007. The tax on the death estate is calculated at the rates applicable to transfers between £177,000 and £400,000. Note that in the death estate calculation, the tax on the gift of £177,000 is shown as nil, whereas the tax actually chargeable, before tapering relief, was £10,000. This is because the tax on the earlier cumulative transfers is a notional figure, based on the scale at death, in order to give the correct starting point for the calculation of tax on the death estate (see part (i)).

(iv)   **Inheritance tax exempt transfers**

Most transfers of value made by an individual are *potentially exempt*, only becoming chargeable if the donor dies within seven years after the gift (s 3A).

There are however some transfers which are *completely exempt*:

(a)   *Transfers between spouses and civil partners (s 18).*

This applies to all lifetime and death transfers between spouses including property to be held on trust for the transferee spouse except where the transferee spouse is foreign domiciled and the transferor spouse is UK domiciled, when transfers are only exempt to a cumulative total of £55,000.

The definition of spouse was amended from 5 December 2005 to include civil partners. This enables same sex couples who have performed a civil ceremony to have the same tax position as a married couple (FA 2005 s 103).

(b)   *Small gifts to same person* (s 20).

Any outright lifetime gifts to any one person in any one tax year are exempt up to the value of £250.

(c)   *Normal expenditure out of income* (s 21).

To obtain exemption the gift must be:

1.   Part of the donor's normal expenditure.

2.   Made out of income (taking one year with another).

3.   Such as will not reduce the donor's available net income (after all other similar transfers) below that required to maintain his usual standard of living.

An example would be payment of a life insurance or stakeholder pension premium for the benefit of another.

(d)   *Gifts in consideration of marriage* (ss 22 and 57).

A gift of up to £5,000 by a parent of a party to a marriage; of £2,500 by a lineal ancestor; of £2,500 by one party to the marriage to the other; or of £1,000 by any other person is exempt providing it is a lifetime gift made in consideration of the marriage. If it is a marriage settlement it must be primarily for the benefit of the parties to the marriage, their issue or the spouses of such issue. The limit applies to gifts by any one donor for any one marriage. For this exemption 'children' include step-children, adopted and illegitimate children.

From 5 December 2005 a civil partnership ceremony is deemed, for taxation, to be the equivalent of a marriage and therefore gifts in consideration of a civil ceremony, to the limits set out above, will be exempt transfers.

(e)   *All gifts to charities or registered community amateur sports clubs, either outright or held on trust for charitable purposes only or, in the case of a sports club, held for the purposes of the club or another registered club or an eligible sports governing body or a charity* (s 23 and FA 2002 Sch 18.9).

All such gifts are exempt whether in lifetime or on death.

(f)   *Gifts to political parties* (s 24).

Gifts to a qualifying political party, whether in lifetime or on death, are wholly exempt.

(g)   *Gifts for national purposes* (s 25 and Sch 3).

All such qualifying gifts are exempt whether in lifetime or on death.

(h)   *Maintenance funds for heritage property* (s 27 and Sch 4).

On a claim being made, transfers into a settlement established for the maintenance, repair or preservation of heritage property are exempt providing a Treasury direction is made in respect of the property under Sch 4. The exemption applies in lifetime or on death. A claim must be made within two years of the date of transfer or such longer period as HMRC may allow.

(i)   *Gifts to housing associations* (s 24A).

Gifts of land to a registered housing association are exempt whether in lifetime or on death.

(j)   *Employee trusts* (s 28).

Transfers by individuals of shares or securities in a company to a trust for the benefit of employees of the company are exempt, providing detailed conditions are satisfied.

HMRC concession F20 exempts certain compensation payments made to World War 2 survivors or their estates — see Example 3 part (a). As indicated in (ii) above, certain property that is not exempt is nonetheless left out of account because it is 'excluded property'. Details of excluded property are also in Example 3 part (a).

Where an exempt beneficiary settles a claim against a deceased's estate out of his own resources the exemption is abated. This could occur, for example, where a claim is made for financial provision against an estate by a non-exempt beneficiary (eg a child or mistress of the deceased). If, instead of the estate meeting the claim, an exempt beneficiary met the liability (eg spouse, charity etc) then tax would be avoided, since that part of the estate passing to the exempt beneficiary rather than to the non-exempt beneficiary would not have attracted tax. Section 29A provides that any such value transferred by the exempt beneficiary is treated as a chargeable part of the deceased's estate.

Annual exemption (s 19).

For those *lifetime transfers* which are not completely exempt there is an annual exemption.

The first £3,000 of transfers in any tax year are exempt provided they are completed in the lifetime of the individual. Any unused portion of the exemption may be carried forward for one year only for use in the following tax year after the exemption for that following year has been completely used.

The annual exemption is applied to lifetime transfers that are not completely exempt in strict chronological order. In the case of a lifetime transfer which does not give rise to an immediate charge, it is only the balance over and above any available exemptions, including any annual exemptions, which is a potentially exempt transfer, as illustrated in part (iii) above in relation to the gift by Edward.

Availability of exemptions to trusts

With the exception of (b), (c) and (j), the above exemptions are available to interest in possession trusts, subject in the case of the annual and marriage exemptions to certain conditions (s 57 — see Example 55 explanatory note 4).

The exemptions are not available on transfers out of discretionary trusts (except for certain transfers to employee trusts or charitable trusts — see Example 59 explanatory note 10).

Conditional exemption for heritage property (s 30).

On a claim being made within two years of the event, exemption is granted, subject to conditions, for the transfer of property that is designated by the Treasury as of pre-eminent national, scientific, historic, artistic or scenic interest (eg works of art and historic buildings). This applies to transfers on death and to lifetime transfers where the property has been owned for six years or more by the transferor and/or his spouse, or where it passed to the transferor on the death of another. Tax may be chargeable if the conditions are no longer satisfied — see explanatory note 4.

Explanatory Notes

Normal expenditure out of income

1.   'Normal expenditure out of income' was considered in the case of Bennett and Others v CIR (1994), where it was held that there was no fixed minimum period during which the expenditure must be incurred. All that was required was for the pattern of actual or intended payments to have been established, and for the pattern of payments to be intended to remain in place for a sufficient period to be regarded as a regular feature of the transferor's annual expenditure, and that the item in question conformed with that pattern.

Gifts in consideration of marriage or civil ceremony

2.   Whether a gift is in consideration of a marriage or civil ceremony is a question of fact. A gift made on the occasion of a marriage or civil ceremony or one made conditionally upon the marriage/civil

ceremony taking place, whilst usually qualifying, is not automatically in consideration of marriage/ civil ceremony. This is an involved legal point and reference to appropriate judicial decisions should be made if the point requires consideration in greater depth.

Gifts to political parties

3.   Exemption is not given for gifts to all political parties, but only to those where, at the last general election preceding the transfer:

   (a)   Two members of that party were elected to the House of Commons, or

   (b)   One member of that party was elected to the House of Commons and no fewer than 150,000 votes were given to candidates of that party (s 24(2)).

Heritage property

4.   The conditions under which exemption is available for heritage property and the circumstances in which inheritance tax becomes payable are dealt with in Example 29.

Gifts to housing associations

5.   Land is not defined for the purpose of the s 24A exemption on gifts to housing associations. It would appear therefore that buildings are included, since they are within the definition of land in the Interpretation Act 1978 Sch 1.

Annual exemption

6.   The treatment of the annual exemption outlined in part (iv) of the example appears to conflict with s 19(3A), which provides that if a potentially exempt transfer becomes a chargeable transfer because of the donor's death within seven years, any annual exemption which has not been used then becomes available, and is given against the earliest transfer if there is more than one. An annual exemption which has already been given on chargeable transfers in the same year is not to be disturbed, even if some or all of the potentially exempt transfers that have become chargeable were made before the transfers against which the annual exemption had been utilised. But potentially exempt transfers that become chargeable take priority over chargeable transfers in a *later* tax year, so that where an unused annual exemption had been carried forward and used in the following tax year, the exemption is to be given instead against the potentially exempt transfers, and the tax on the transfers which originally used it has to be recomputed.

The provisions of s 19(3A) are, however, redundant when considered in the light of the definition of 'potentially exempt transfer' in s 3A, namely that a potentially exempt transfer is a transfer that would be a chargeable transfer but for s 3A. Any part of a transfer covered by the annual exemption is an exempt transfer, and therefore would not be a chargeable transfer apart from s 3A. It follows that if a potentially exempt transfer becomes chargeable there cannot possibly be any available annual exemption to use against it. Despite the fact that a drafting error makes s 19(3A) meaningless, no action has been taken to correct it.

The capital gains tax gifts holdover relief provisions of TCGA 1992 s 260 are available against a slice of any lifetime gift, to the extent that it is covered by the inheritance tax annual exemption. Capital gains tax gifts relief is dealt with in the companion to this book, Tolley's Taxwise I 2006/07. See Example 25 part A (c) for the interaction between the annual exemption and business and agricultural property relief.

Voidable transfers

7.   A transfer which is set aside by enactment or rule of law (eg bankruptcy) is not counted as a transfer for inheritance tax purposes, and neither is the transfer back (s 150 — voidable transfers).

Dispositions that are not transfers of value

8.   This example deals with transfers of value that are wholly or partly exempt. Example 2 at part (a) illustrates that there are certain dispositions which are not treated as transfers of value at all.

Tapering relief

9.   It should be noted that even though transfers may immediately or subsequently be chargeable transfers, no tax is payable until the cumulative total exceeds the nil threshold. Any transfers within that nil rate slice do not attract any tax, later transfers above the threshold bearing the whole of the tax payable (subject to tapering relief if available). Since the transfers within the nil rate slice never attract any tax, the tapering relief that applies when a donor survives a gift by more than three years but less than seven is irrelevant on those transfers.

Illustration

A wealthy married couple who have made no previous gifts want to know how much cash they could give away on 4 April 2007 without any possibility of inheritance tax ever being payable on the gifts. (No specific exemptions are available.)

Each spouse could give £291,000, making a total of £582,000. £6,000 each would be covered by the current and previous years' annual exemptions, leaving potentially exempt transfers of £285,000 each. If they both then died the next day, the potentially exempt gifts would become chargeable, but they would be covered by the nil threshold. Tax at 40% would be payable on each of their chargeable estates at death, since the nil threshold would have been used up by the lifetime gifts.

If they survived for seven years, they could in the meantime each make annual gifts amounting to the £3,000 annual exemption plus any annual increase in the nil threshold and after the seven years they could then make further gifts equal to the then nil threshold each, because their initial potentially exempt gifts would become completely exempt at that point. Tapering relief would not be relevant no matter how long they survived, since all gifts would be either exempt or covered by the nil threshold. Again tax at the full rate would be paid on the whole of their chargeable death estates, since the nil threshold would have been fully used against lifetime gifts.

Failure to exercise a right

10.   As indicated in part (ii) of the example, the failure to exercise a right is a disposition for inheritance tax under s 3. Such a disposition is treated as made at the latest time that the right could have been exercised. On the other hand, s 10 provides that any disposition that is not intended to confer a gratuitous benefit is not a transfer of value.

Where an employee dies in service after the earliest age at which he could have retired, and a lump sum death benefit is held in trust for his dependants, the employee could be regarded as having failed to exercise his right to take the pension. HMRC have, however, stated that they will not take this point in genuine cases of deferred retirement, and will only do so where there is evidence that the intention of deferring benefits was to increase the estate of someone else.

Similar provisions apply in respect of Registered Pension Schemes from 6 April 2006. The new legislation is to be found in FA 2006, Sch 22. The present IHT rules will continue to apply to registered pension schemes in much the same way as they do currently. This measure will legislate the IHT concessionary practice dating from 1992 in relation to pension choices by scheme members.

An IHT charge can arise in a scheme member's lifetime under IHTA 1984 s 3(3), if they do not exercise their right to take pension benefits. The charge applies at the latest time when the right could be exercised ie immediately before death. For example, if a scheme member did not take their pension when their life expectancy was seriously impaired, and this resulted in an enhanced death benefit being paid to their beneficiaries, then IHT could apply.

Currently, by concession, IHT is not charged in respect of these enhanced death benefits where the beneficiary is a spouse, civil partner or person who is financially dependant on the scheme member. Nor is IHT applied where a scheme member chooses not to exercise a right at a time when this choice does not trigger a charge (for example, choosing not to take a pension when they are in good health) and does not subsequently vary that choice, even when a reduction in their life expectancy would in strictness trigger an IHT charge.

In addition, payments arising in these circumstances which are made to charity will also be exempted from IHT.

The Finance Act 2004 also introduced the Alternatively Secured Pension (ASP) for those over 75. The pensions tax simplification rules provide that an individual must secure an income before they reach the age of 75. For most people an annuity or scheme pension is the best means by which they can do this. The new pensions tax regime introduced an additional option for securing their retirement income — an Alternatively Secured Pension (ASP).

An IHT charge will be imposed on left-over ASP funds on death (or later) as follows:

(a)   Any funds paid as a 'transfer lump sum death benefit' (ie where the funds remain within the scheme for the benefit of other scheme members) or refunded to an employer or used to provide benefits for a dependant in the pension scheme context who is not a spouse, civil partner or person who is financially dependant will be subject to an IHT charge on the death of the original scheme member as if the funds were part of the scheme member's own taxable estate on death.

(b)   Any funds paid on the death of the scheme member to charity will be exempt from IHT, as will funds expended for the scheme member's spouse, civil partner or person who is financially dependant on the scheme member.

(c)   Any left-over funds, once use by the spouse, civil partner or person who is financially dependant (the beneficiary) has come to an end, will be chargeable to IHT on the earlier of the cessation of those benefits and the death of the beneficiary. These remaining funds will be treated as if they were an addition to the original scheme member's estate. However, any left-over funds that are paid to charity will be exempt from IHT.

(d)   In certain circumstances, an IHT charge on ASP funds will fall on the estate of a dependant (rather than that of the original scheme member). This will apply where a dependant — within the meaning of the pension scheme rules — opts for an ASP derived from 'benefits' inherited from a scheme member who died before age 75. Here, any left-over funds on the dependant's death will be charged to IHT as if they were part of the dependant's taxable estate on death.

IHT will be payable on the value of the taxable property at the time the charge arises, and calculated by reference to the tax-free threshold and rate of tax in place at that time. The pension scheme administrator will be responsible for accounting for and paying any IHT due on the ASP funds.

Personal representatives of estates will be required to provide information in the estate account about the ASP. This will include an estimate of the value of the left-over ASP funds at the date of death together with details of the name and address of the scheme administrator (who will be liable for any IHT payable).

Fall in value of gift before donor's death

11.   For detailed notes on the relief where the value of a gift has fallen before the donor's death see Example 12.

(a)   Consider whether the following are 'transfers of value':

     (i)   School fees paid for the education of the transferor's son.

     (ii)   School fees paid for the education of the transferor's grandson.

     (iii)   Sums paid to a sister of the transferor for her maintenance.

     (iv)   An entitlement to a bonus as sales director of a family company, and to a dividend on a holding of shares therein, both of which have been waived.

     (v)   Payment by a sole trader of £30,000 compensation for loss of office to a former employee.

     (vi)   A loan of £50,000 to a friend.

(b)   Charles, a widower, made the following gifts (after all exemptions other than the annual exemption):

(i)	10 July 1993	£66,000 to grandson
(ii)	20 May 1997	£223,000 to a discretionary settlement — on condition that the trustees paid the inheritance tax due
(iii)	12 June 1998	£37,000 to nephew
(iv)	20 October 1999	£193,000 to a discretionary settlement — on condition that the trustees paid the inheritance tax due
(v)	1 January 2003	£250,000 to an accumulation and maintenance settlement for his grandchildren

On 8 August 2006 Charles died leaving an estate of £400,000. By his will he left £200,000 to the Save the Children Fund and the balance to his daughter absolutely.

Calculate the inheritance tax payable on each of the gifts in lifetime and on death, and on the death estate.

(a)   **Dispositions that are not transfers of value**

Certain dispositions are not transfers of value:

1.   Dispositions which are not intended to confer any gratuitous benefit and made on arm's length terms (s 10).

2.   Expenditure on family maintenance (s 11). This covers dispositions:

   (a)   For the maintenance of the transferor's spouse, or former spouse if made on dissolution or annulment of the marriage (s 11(1) and (6)) (the same rules now apply to civil partnerships), or

   (b)   For the maintenance, education or training of a child for a period ending not later than the tax year in which the child becomes eighteen years of age or, after attaining that age, ceases to undergo full-time education or training.

   For this purpose 'child' includes:

   (i)   A child of the transferor by marriage or previous marriage (s 11(1) (6)).

   (ii)   An illegitimate child of the transferor (s 11(4)).

   (iii)   A child who is not in the care of a parent (but dispositions to such a child for a period ending after the year in which he reaches age eighteen will not be exempt unless the child was in the care of the transferor for substantial periods before he became eighteen) (s 11(2)).

   or

   (c)   Made for the reasonable care and maintenance of a dependent relative (s 11(3)). The term 'dependent relative' is defined in s 11(6).

3.   A waiver or repayment of remuneration (s 14), and a waiver of dividends made within twelve months before any right to the dividend has accrued (s 15).

4.   Expenditure which is allowable as a deduction in computing a person's profits or gains for income or corporation tax (s 12).

5.   Transfers to employee trusts by close companies (s 13).

6.   A grant of an agricultural tenancy for full consideration (s 16).

7.   Deeds of variation within s 142.

The position in the six situations given is therefore:

   (i)   *School fees for education of transferor's son*

   Leaving aside the possibility that the school fees were paid out of income and therefore may be exempt as annual expenditure out of income, school fees paid for the education of the transferor's son will not be a transfer of value providing the son is under eighteen or in full-time education or training.

   (ii)   *School fees for education of transferor's grandson*

   If the school fees for the grandson were not paid out of income then they will be a transfer of value unless the grandson is under eighteen and is not in the care of one of his parents; or the grandson is over eighteen and is not in the care of one of his parents *and* was in the care of his grandparent for substantial periods before reaching the age of eighteen.

   (iii)   *Gifts for maintenance of sister*

   Again leaving aside the question of non-chargeable payments out of income, gifts to the transferor's sister for her maintenance would be a transfer of value unless the sister was a dependent relative by reason of old age or infirmity *and* the amounts were reasonable for her care and maintenance, or unless she was not in the care of a parent and was either under eighteen years of age or if over eighteen, had been in the care of the transferor for substantial periods before reaching age eighteen and in that event was still in full time education or training.

(iv)   *Waiver of remuneration and dividends*

The waiver of remuneration is not a transfer of value, nor is the dividend waiver if waived within twelve months before any right to it has accrued.

(v)   *Compensation for loss of office*

So long as the compensation payment is allowed in computing profits, it will not be a transfer of value.

(vi)   *Loan to a friend*

If someone lends money or property for a prolonged period, or denies himself the opportunity to recall the money or property, the property is then worth less in the owner's hands than it was before. Thus if the £50,000 is lent free of interest for a fixed term of ten years and after making the loan the lender requires the cash, the only way to obtain it is to assign the debt to someone else. But for how much? Not £50,000, because the assignee will want a commercial return, which he will obtain by paying sufficiently below £50,000 to compensate for having to wait for the remainder of the ten years before the capital sum becomes repayable. A transfer of value will thus arise on the difference between the amount lent and the discounted present value of the future right to repayment.

If however the loan is at commercial rates of interest and repayable on demand or on reasonable notice, then there will be no diminution in its value, and a transfer of value will not arise.

If the various conditions stated above were not satisfied, the payments would be transfers of value, against which the current and previous years' annual exemptions could be used if available.

To the extent that the amounts in (iii) and (v) were not covered by the annual exemption, they would be potentially exempt transfers and therefore only brought into account if the donor died within the next seven years.

If the school fees under (i) and (ii) are not within the 'family maintenance' exemption and are not by way of settlement, it is possible that the transfers could be regarded as chargeable transfers of value (subject to any other available exemptions) rather than potentially exempt transfers because for a transfer to an individual to be potentially exempt, the transferee's estate must be increased by the transfer, which would not directly apply in these two instances. Similarly, any transfer of value arising out of the loan at (vi) would be a chargeable transfer rather than a potentially exempt transfer unless the estate of the borrower could be regarded as increased by the value of the right to have the loan on favourable terms.

(b)   **Charles — inheritance tax position on lifetime gifts and on estate at death**

				Gross £	*Tax* £
Tax payable in lifetime					
10 July 1993 —	gift to grandson			66,000	
	Less: Annual exemptions	1993/94	3,000		
		1992/93	3,000	6,000	
Potentially exempt transfer				60,000	
20 May 1997 —	gift to discretionary settlement			223,000	
	Less: Annual exemptions	1997/98	3,000		
		1996/97	3,000	6,000	
Lifetime chargeable transfer (one half rates)				217,000	400*

(* 217,000 – 1997/98 threshold 215,000 = 2,000 @ 20%)
Inheritance tax payable by trustees £400.

12 June 1998 —	gift to nephew			37,000	
	Less: Annual exemption	1998/99		3,000	
Potentially exempt transfer				34,000	

				Tax on 1999/2000 scale
			217,000	–
20 October 1998 —	gift to discretionary settlement		193,000	
	Less: Annual exemption 1999/2000		3,000	
Lifetime chargeable transfer (one half rates)			190,000	35,200*
			407,000	35,200*

(* 407,000 – 1999/2000 threshold 231,000 = 176,000 @ 20%)
Inheritance tax payable by trustees £35,200.

1 January 2003 —	gift to accumulation and maintenance settlement			250,000	
	Less: Annual exemptions	2002/03	3,000		
		2001/02	3,000	6,000	
Potentially exempt transfer				244,000	
20 May 2004 —	exclude transfer seven years earlier			(217,000)	
				190,000	

		Tax (using
On death of Charles — 8 August 2006	*Gross*	*2006/07 rates)*
	£	£

Transfers within seven years before death ie
  9 August 1999 to 8 August 2006:

20 October 1999 — gift to discretionary settlement
  Cumulative *chargeable* transfers within previous seven years

	Gross	Tax
(ie 21.10.92 – 20.10.99 — see explanatory note 3)	217,000	
Chargeable transfer (full rates)	190,000	48,800*
	407,000	48,800*

  (* 407,000 – 285,000 = 122,000 @ 40%)

1 January 2003 — gift to accumulation and maintenance settlement
  Cumulative *chargeable* transfers within previous seven years

	Gross	Tax
(ie 2.1.96 – 1.1.03)	407,000	48,800
Chargeable transfer	244,000	97,600
	651,000	146,400*

  (* 651,000 – 285,000 = 366,000 @ 40%)

8 August 2006 – date of death
  Cumulative chargeable transfers within previous seven years

		Gross	Tax
(190,000 + 244,000) (ie 9.8.99 – 8.8.06)		434,000	59,600*
Estate on death	400,000		
Less: Exempt – Legacy to charity	200,000	200,000	80,000
		634,000	139,600**

(* 434,000 – 285,000 = 149,000 @ 40%)
(** 634,000 – 285,000 = 349,000 @ 40%)

Inheritance tax payable — lifetime

	£
(i) grandson	nil
(ii) trustees of 1997 discretionary settlement	400
(iii) nephew	nil
(iv) trustees of 1999 discretionary settlement	35,200
(v) trustees of accumulation and maintenance settlement	nil

Inheritance tax payable — death

	£	£
By grandson, trustees of 1997 discretionary settlement and nephew (excluded as gifts were made more than seven years before death)		nil
By trustees of 1999 discretionary settlement		
Tax due on death scale	48,800	
Less: Tapering relief 80% (6–7 years)	39,040	
	9,760	
Less: Paid on lifetime transfer	35,200	nil

(No repayment will be made to the trustees)

	£	£
By trustees of accumulation and maintenance settlement		
Tax due on death	97,600	
Less: Tapering relief 20% (3–4 years)	19,520	78,080
By personal representatives		80,000
		158,080

Explanatory Notes

Dispositions for family maintenance

1. The distinction between school fees paid for the education of the transferor's son and his grandson illustrates how carefully the wording of a section has to be considered, particularly since the heading of a section is often widely descriptive, in this case being 'disposition for maintenance of family' (s 11). Broadly speaking, transfers for the maintenance of one's own children are not chargeable if the child is either under eighteen or in full time education. Transfers for the maintenance of other persons are chargeable (in the absence of other exemptions) unless the child is *not* in the care of a parent and if over eighteen, was in the care of the transferor for substantial periods before reaching age eighteen and is still in full time education or training.

Potentially exempt transfers to grandson and nephew

2. The gifts to grandson and nephew in part (b) are made after 17 March 1986 and are outright gifts by an individual to another individual, and are therefore potentially exempt transfers in so far as they exceed the available annual exemptions.

    Since the transferor did not die within seven years after the gifts, the potentially exempt transfers become exempt transfers, so there is no inheritance tax liability on them and they are not taken into account in the figure of cumulative chargeable transfers. For more detailed notes see Example 4 explanatory note 6.

Cumulation of transfers

3. When calculating the tax on a transfer, the tax on the brought forward figure is always recalculated on the current scale, and it may, or may not, represent the tax that was actually paid on the earlier transfers. This gives the correct starting point to calculate the tax on the current transfer. Now that there is only one rate of tax, this will only be relevant where the cumulative transfers are below the nil threshold applicable at the date of the current transfer, because later lifetime transfers will be at 20% and death transfers at 40%.

4. In the example the cumulative chargeable transfers within seven years before 20 October 1999 exclude the 10 July 1993 and 12 June 1998 transfers (as potentially exempt transfers that became exempt transfers after seven years), but include the 20 May 1997 transfer, whereas the total as at 1 January 2003 includes both the 20 May 1997 and 20 October 1999 transfers. On death the 20 October 1999 chargeable transfer and the 1 January 2003 potentially exempt, now chargeable, transfer are included.

In connection with inheritance tax:

(a)   Explain the meaning and inheritance tax treatment of excluded property.

(b)   Explain the 'grossing up' of a lifetime transfer.

(c)   Briefly describe the circumstances in which a charge to tax may arise on property comprised in a settlement.

(a)   **Excluded property**

'Excluded property' is defined in IHTA 1984 ss 6 and 48 as follows:

(i)   Foreign property owned by individuals domiciled outside the UK (s 6(1)).

(ii)   Government securities issued as being exempt from tax where they are in the beneficial ownership of persons of a description specified in the conditions of issue of the security concerned (s 6(2)). Securities issued before FA 1996 required a person to be neither domiciled nor ordinarily resident in the UK. Current issues of securities require the person to be not ordinarily resident in the UK but with no stipulation as to domicile.

(iii) National savings, premium savings bonds, and SAYE savings owned by persons domiciled in the Channel Islands or Isle of Man (s 6(3)).

(iv)   Emoluments and tangible movable property of visiting armed forces and certain allied headquarters staff (ss 6(4) and 155(1)).

(v)   Foreign property comprised in a settlement if the settlor was domiciled outside the UK when the property was settled (s 48(3)).

(vi)   Reversionary interests in settled property, subject to certain anti-avoidance provisions.

(vii) From 16 October 2002 UK authorised investment funds including unit trusts held by non-UK domiciled investors or by their trusts (ss 6(1A) and 48(3A)).

By HMRC concession F19, a decoration awarded for valour or gallant conduct is to be treated for inheritance tax as excluded property if it is shown never to have been transferred for consideration in money or money's worth.

By HMRC concession F20, ex gratia compensation payments of £10,000 made by the Government to British survivors of Japanese imprisonment or their spouses, and various other modest amounts paid by European bodies to slave labourers and other World War 2 victims or their spouses, or payments of such compensation made to the person's personal representatives, are left out of account in calculating the value of the person's estate for inheritance tax.

Excluded property is generally outside the scope of inheritance tax, because inheritance tax is not charged on the lifetime disposal of such property nor on such property passing at death (ss 3(2) and 5(1)). A charge to tax in respect of a lifetime transfer of non-excluded property can, however, be affected by excluded property, because excluded property is taken into account when measuring the value of the estate before and after the transfer of non-excluded property. If, for example, someone owned shares in a company in their own right, and had an interest in possession in shares in the company under a settlement made by a non-UK domiciled settlor, the two holdings together constituting a controlling interest, and a transfer was made of the shares held directly which reduced the combined holding to a minority holding, the loss to the donor's estate would reflect the fall in value of the combined holding.

Apart from the point made in the above paragraph, excluded property is treated in the same way as property that is exempt.

Certain other property, although not within the definition of 'excluded property', is also outside the scope of inheritance tax as follows:

Cash options under approved annuity schemes (s 152);

Overseas pensions, in valuing an estate at death (s 153);

Property passing as a result of death on active military service (s 154).

Foreign currency bank accounts, on the death of an individual not domiciled, resident or ordinarily resident in the UK (s 157).

Works of art, normally kept overseas, physically present in the UK on the death of a foreign owner are excluded if brought into the UK solely for public exhibition, cleaning or restoration (HMRC concession F7).

(b)   **'Grossing up' of a lifetime transfer**

'Grossing up' is a term that applies where the donor pays the inheritance tax arising on the making of a chargeable transfer. The donor is therefore effectively making two dispositions, one directly to the transferee and the second to HMRC in respect of a liability arising on the first disposition. The value of the donor's estate is reduced on each occasion and the inheritance tax is calculated by reference to the reduction in the value of the donor's estate.

Illustration

Mr Smith has already made chargeable transfers of £285,000 and has used up all his available exemptions. He makes a chargeable transfer of £8,000 to a discretionary settlement on 1 May 2006 and agrees to pay the inheritance tax. The rate of tax on lifetime gifts over £285,000 is one half of 40%, ie 20% so that the £8,000 received into the settlement must represent 80% of the gross gift, so the gross gift is 100/80ths of the net gift = £10,000.

The calculation is as follows:

	Gross £	Tax £	Net £
Cumulative chargeable transfers to date	285,000	–	285,000
1 May 2006 Gift to discretionary settlement			
Net			8,000
Grossed up			
$\frac{100}{80}$ x 8,000	10,000	2,000	
Cumulative chargeable transfers carried forward	295,000	2,000*	293,000

(* 295,000 – 285,000 = 10,000 @ 20%)

If Mr Smith's previous transfers had been £279,000 instead of £285,000, the position would have been:

	Gross £	Tax £	Net £
Cumulative chargeable transfers to date	279,000	–	279,000
1 May 2006 Gift to settlement within nil band	6,000	–	6,000
Remaining net gift			2,000
Grossed up			
$\frac{100}{80}$ x 2,000	2,500	500	
Cumulative chargeable transfers carried forward	287,500	500*	287,000

(* 287,500 – 285,000 = 2,500 @ 20%)

A potentially exempt transfer never has to be grossed up. This is because the transferor is never personally liable for the tax. If tax is payable it is because of the death of the transferor within the next seven years. In that event the donee is responsible for the tax.

(c)   **Charge to tax on property comprised in a settlement**

The charge to tax on property comprised in a settlement depends upon the type of settlement.

(i)   If the settlement has an *interest in possession*, broadly where one or more persons are entitled to the income, the property in the settlement is deemed to belong to the person who is entitled to that interest and any liability will arise when that person's interest in the property comes to an end, for example, if he makes a sale or gift of his interest, or his interest ceases by reason of a death or marriage or other reason. Like any other transfer in lifetime, however, the cessation of the life interest may be potentially exempt. This will apply where the trust property is transferred to an individual, or to another interest in possession settlement or to an accumulation and maintenance trust or a disabled trust. The transfer will only become a chargeable transfer if the life tenant who has given up his interest dies within the next seven years, the tax being computed by taking into account transfers within the seven years before the now chargeable transfer and calculating tax on the death scale.

(ii) If there is *no interest in possession* (eg the settlement is a discretionary settlement — broadly where the beneficiaries only have a hope as distinct from a right to receive the income arising) then a charge to tax will occur on the tenth anniversary of the creation of the trust and at ten yearly intervals thereafter. The tax is charged on the value of the 'relevant property' in the trust at 30% of the effective rate (called the 'principal charge').

The lifetime rate of tax is used to calculate the effective rate, and the maximum possible charge is 30% of 20%, ie 6%.

As it would be possible to avoid the forthcoming principal charge to tax on a discretionary settlement by distributing assets between ten-year anniversaries, an 'exit charge' arises when property ceases to be relevant property. The tax on the amount leaving the settlement is charged at the appropriate fraction of 30% of the effective rate, the appropriate fraction depending on the number of complete quarters that have elapsed since the creation of the trust or the last ten year anniversary as the case may be.

Explanatory Notes

Reversionary interest

1. 'Reversionary interest' is defined in s 47 as a future interest under a settlement, whether vested or contingent. Where, for example, property is settled on A for life, then to B absolutely, B (sometimes called the remainderman) has a reversionary interest in the settled property.

Deemed UK domicile

2. For heading (iii) of part (a) of the example (and also heading (ii) where the security concerned requires the holder to be non-UK domiciled), the provisions of s 267, which deem certain persons to be UK domiciled, do not apply.

For detailed notes on this and related points and on the treatment of foreign currency bank accounts see Example 27. Example 27 also illustrates excluded property held by a non-UK domiciled person. For the treatment of reversionary interests see Example 58.

Meaning of 'settlement'

3. For inheritance tax purposes a settlement is defined as any disposition or dispositions of property whereby the property is for the time being:

(a) held in trust for persons in succession, or for any person subject to a contingency (s 43(2)(a))

(b) held by trustees on trust to accumulate the whole or any part of any income of the property, or with power to make payments out of that income at the discretion of the trustees or some other person, with or without the power to accumulate surplus income (s 43(2)(b))

(c) charged or burdened (otherwise than for full consideration in money or money's worth) with the payment of any annuity or other periodical payment for a life or any other limited or terminable period (s 43(2)(c)).

Also treated as a settlement is a lease of property for the duration of a person's life or persons' lives, unless the lease was granted for full consideration in money or money's worth.

The words 'settlement' and 'trust' are usually regarded as being interchangeable, although as can be seen from the definition, 'settlement' has a wider coverage. Any reference in IHTA 1984 to a trustee, in relation to a settlement where there would otherwise be no trustees, is to any person in whom the settled property or its management is vested (s 45).

Classes of settlement

4.   For inheritance tax purposes settlements may be considered to fall into four main classes:

(a)   Interest in possession settlements.

(b)   Settlements in which there is no interest in possession (usually but not exclusively discretionary trusts).

(c)   Accumulation and maintenance trusts, which are a privileged form of discretionary trust.

(d)   Certain other special types of settlement, eg trusts for the benefit of employees, protective trusts, charitable trusts.

The distinction between settlements in which there is an interest in possession and settlements where there is no such interest is fundamental to an understanding of the inheritance tax legislation. The position is dealt with in detail in the section of this book dealing with settlements and trusts.

The inheritance tax settlement provisions do not apply to registered pension schemes which replaced tax approved pension schemes from 6 April 2006.

Adding property to a settlement

5.   With regard to heading (v) in part (a) of the example, HMRC take the view that a separate settlement is made when property is put into an existing settlement, so that even if a settlement of foreign property was made when the settlor was not UK domiciled, any further foreign property added to the settlement at a time when the settlor was UK domiciled would not be excluded property (Tax Bulletin February 1997).

Non-domiciled individuals holding residential property through an offshore company

6.   Care must be taken when structuring the affairs of a non-domiciled individual, as the introduction of a company into the structure can give rise to an income tax benefit in kind charge if the residential property held within the company is used by the individual or his family. This is because the individual will be considered to be a shadow director if the actual directors act in accordance with his directions or instructions (ITEPA 2003 s 67). This would apply even if the company was itself owned by an offshore trust and its actual directors were trustees of the offshore trust. The structure would be effective for inheritance tax but may not be appropriate for income tax, as a charge could arise on a benefit in kind under Chapter 5 of Part 3 of ITEPA 2003.

Mr C T Tax made the following lifetime gifts:

20 November 1999	£243,000 to a discretionary trust
11 January 2001	£48,000 to his sister, Ann
3 May 2003	£86,000 to his daughter, Joan
4 April 2004	£90,000 to his son, Ben.

Mr C T Tax died on 2 April 2007 leaving an estate of £608,000 equally to Ben and Joan.

(i)   Compute the tax payable by reason of the death of Mr C T Tax.

(ii)   Would the tax payable be different if Mr C T Tax had not made gifts to his children in 2003 and 2004 totalling £176,000 but had left an estate of £784,000 instead of £608,000?

(iii) Show the tax payable in lifetime and on death if the circumstances were as in (i) except that instead of giving £90,000 to Ben on 4 April 2004, Mr C T Tax transferred £90,000 to a discretionary trust (the trustees paying the tax) on:

(a)   4 March 2004

(b)   6 April 2005.

(i)   Inheritance tax position of Mr C T Tax

Tax payable in lifetime

			£	£
20 November 1999	gift to discretionary trust			243,000
	Less: Annual exemptions	1999/2000	3,000	
		1998/99	3,000	6,000
	Chargeable transfer			237,000
	Tax payable by trustees (on 1999/2000 scale) 237,000 – 231,000 = 6,000 @ 20%		£1,200	
11 January 2001	gift to Ann			48,000
	Less: Annual exemption	2000/01		3,000
	Potentially exempt transfer			45,000
3 May 2003	gift to Joan			86,000
	Less: Annual exemptions	2003/04	3,000	
		2002/03	3,000	6,000
	Potentially exempt transfer			80,000
4 April 2004	gift to Ben — potentially exempt transfer			90,000

On death of Mr C T Tax 2 April 2007

Potentially exempt transfers since 3 April 2000 now become chargeable transfers:

	Gross £	Tax (using rates at 2 April 2007) £
Cumulative transfers in seven years before gift to Ann		
20 November 1999 — discretionary trust	237,000	–
11 January 2001 — gift to Ann	45,000	–
	282,000	–
3 May 2003 — gift to Joan	80,000	30,800*
	362,000	30,800*
(* 362,000 – 285,000 = 77,000 @ 40%)		
4 April 2004 — gift to Ben	90,000	36,000
	452,000	66,800
20 November 2006 Deduct transfer made more than seven years previously (ie prior to 21.11.99)	237,000	
Cumulative transfers in seven years before death	215,000	–
Estate chargeable on death	608,000	215,200*
	823,000	215,200*
(* 823,000 – 285,000 = 538,000 @ 40%)		

		£
Inheritance tax payable:		
By Ann on gift made 11 January 2001:		nil
By Joan on gift made 3 May 2003:		
As gift is made more than 3 but not more than 4 years before death tax payable is 80% x £30,800 =		24,640
By Ben on gift made 4 April 2004:		
As gift is within 3 years of death there is no reduction in the tax payable		36,000
By Estate		215,200
Tax payable by reason of death of Mr C T Tax		275,840

(ii) **If no lifetime gifts made to children — position on death of Mr C T Tax 2 April 2007**

	Gross £	Tax £
Cumulative transfers in seven years before death (ie 3.4.2000 – 2.4.07)		
11 January 2001	45,000	–
Estate chargeable on death	784,000	217,600*
	829,000	217,600*

(* 829,000 – 285,000 = 544,000 @ 40%)

	Gross £	Tax £
Tax with gifts to children (part (i))		275,840
Tax without gifts to children — estate	217,600	
Tax on gift to Ann — as above	nil	217,600
Additional tax because of chargeable transfers made within seven years before lifetime gifts to children		£ 58,240

(iii) **Inheritance tax position of Mr C T Tax with gift to discretionary trust instead of to Ben**

(a) **Gift to discretionary trust on 4 March 2004**

Tax payable in lifetime		Gross £	Tax on 1999/2000 scale £
20 November 1999 —	chargeable transfer	237,000	1,200
11 January 2001 and 3 May 2003 —	potentially exempt transfers £45,000 and £80,000 as before		*Tax on 2003/04 scale £*
Cumulative transfers before gift to discretionary trust on 4 March 2004		237,000	–
4 March 2004 —	gift to discretionary trust	90,000	14,400*
		327,000	14,400*

(* 327,000 – 255,000 (using 2003/04 scale) = 72,000 @ 20%)
Tax payable by trustees £14,400

On death of Mr C T Tax 2 April 2007

	Gross £	Tax (using rates at 2 April 2007) £
Cumulative transfers in seven years prior to gift to Ann	237,000	–
11 January 2001 — gift to Ann	45,000	–
	282,000	–
3 May 2003 — gift to Joan	80,000	30,800*
	362,000	30,800*

(* 362,000 – 285,000 = 77,000 @ 40%)

	Gross £	Tax £
4 March 2004 — gift to discretionary trust	90,000	36,000
	452,000	66,800

		Tax £
Inheritance tax payable by Ann on gift made 11 January 2001		nil
Inheritance tax payable by Joan on gift made 3 May 2003 80% x £30,800 (tapering relief as before)		24,640

Additional inheritance tax payable by trustees — as gift is made more than 3 but not more than 4 years before death tax payable is:

	Gross £	Tax £
Tax on death scale	36,000	
Less 20% tapering relief	7,200	
	28,800	
Less paid in lifetime	14,400	14,400

Tax on estate:

	Gross £	
Cumulative transfers as above	452,000	
Deduct transfer made more than seven years previously	237,000	
	215,000	
Estate chargeable on death	608,000	
	823,000	

		Tax £
Tax payable (823,000 – 285,000 = 538,000 @ 40%)		215,200
		£ 254,240

(b)   **Gift to discretionary trust on 6 April 2005**

Tax payable in lifetime	Gross £	Tax on 1999/2000 scale £
20 November 1999 — chargeable transfer	237,000	1,200
11 January 2001 and 3 May 2003 — potentially exempt transfers £45,000 and £80,000 as before		
Cumulative transfers before gift to discretionary trust on 6 April 2005 (cf)	237,000	

		Gross £	Tax on 2005/06 scale £
Cumulative transfers before gift to discretionary trust on 6 April 2005 (bf)		237,000	–
6 April 2005 — gift to discretionary trust	90,000		
Less: Annual exemptions 2005/06	(3,000)		
2004/05	(3,000)	84,000	9,200*
		321,000	9,200*

(* 321,000 – 275,000 (using 2005/06 scale) = 46,000 @ 20%)

Tax payable by trustees £9,200

On death of Mr C T Tax 2 April 2007	Gross £	Tax (using rates at 2 April 2007) £
Cumulative transfers in seven years prior to gift to Ann (as above)	237,000	–
11 January 2001 — gift to Ann	45,000	–
	282,000	–
3 May 2003 — gift to Joan	80,000	30,800*
	362,000	30,800*

(* 362,000 – 285,000 = 77,000 @ 40%)

6 April 2005 — gift to discretionary settlement	84,000	33,600
	446,000	64,400
20 November 2006 Deduct transfer more than seven years previously (ie prior to 21.11.99)	237,000	
Cumulative transfers in seven years before death	209,000	–
Estate chargeable on death	608,000	212,800*
	817,000	212,800*

(* 817,000 – 285,000 = 532,000 @ 40%)

Inheritance tax payable by Ann on gift made 11 January 2001		nil
Inheritance tax payable by Joan on gift made 3 May 2003		
80% x £30,800 (tapering relief as before)		24,640

Additional inheritance tax payable by trustees on gift made 6 April 2005 (no tapering relief because within 3 years before death):

Tax on death scale	33,600	
Less paid in lifetime	9,200	24,400
Tax payable by estate		212,800
		£ 261,840

The total tax payable is £2,400 more than in (a):

	(a) £	(b) £
Ann	–	–
Joan	24,640	24,640
Trustees	28,800	33,600
Estate	215,200	212,800
Total tax payable	268,640	271,040
Paid in lifetime by trustees	14,400	9,200
Due on death	254,240	261,840

The increase in the tax payable arises as follows:

Loss of tapering relief on transfer to trust, since gift now less than three years before death (36,000 @ 20%)	7,200
Less: Reduction of trust transfer by 2005/06 and 2004/05 exemptions, saving 6,000 @ 40%	(2,400)
Consequential reduction in cumulative transfers at death, saving a further 6,000 @ 40%	(2,400)
	£ 2,400

The inheritance tax liability can therefore vary depending on the timing and amounts of lifetime gifts. C T Tax had the same value of assets in each of the above examples. The total tax payable by the first discretionary trust remains constant at £1,200, being a lifetime gift made more than seven years before death. The tax payable on death plus gifts made within seven years before death is:

(i)	(ii)	(iii)(a)	(iii)(b)
£275,840	£217,600	£268,640	£271,040

The reduction of £58,240 in (ii) is due to non-aggregation of the gift to the first discretionary trust with other lifetime gifts (see explanatory note 6). The reduction of £7,200 in (iii)(a) compared with (i) is because the chargeable gift to the trust of £90,000 on 4 March 2004 was more than three years before death, thus giving rise to taper relief of £7,200. The difference in tax payable in (iii)(a) and (iii)(b) is explained above.

Explanatory Notes

Potentially exempt transfers to sister and children

1. As the transfers to the sister and to the children are gifts by one individual to another they are potentially exempt, after deducting available annual exemptions from the earliest gift in any tax year. Accordingly no tax is payable at the time.

Inheritance tax liability arising on death

2. On the death of Mr C T Tax a liability arises both on his estate at death and also on transfers made within seven years before death.

    The additional charge on death is the tax due using the scale in force on the date of death less any tax paid on that gift during lifetime. If the tax already paid exceeds that now due no refund will arise. Any tax due is payable primarily by the donee (see Example 5).

Tapering relief on lifetime transfers

3. Transfers which were potentially exempt in lifetime become chargeable if the donor dies within seven years after the lifetime transfer. They are chargeable on their value when made, but at the full scale rate at the time of death. Where the period between the gift and death exceeds three years then the

tax calculated on the full scale rate is reduced as follows:

Years between transfer and death	Percentage reduction	Percentage of full rate tax due
3 to 4	20	80
4+ to 5	40	60
5+ to 6	60	40
6+ to 7	80	20

Thus, in part (i) of the example Ann's gift would attract an 80% reduction as the gift is made more than six but less than seven years before death. In fact no tax is payable on the gift and therefore the taper relief is lost. Joan can claim a 20% reduction as her gift was more than three but less than four years before death, but Ben cannot claim any reduction as his gift was within three years of death.

Calculating tax on potentially exempt transfers that become chargeable

4. When computing the tax on potentially exempt transfers which have become chargeable it is necessary to take into account other *chargeable* transfers made within *seven years before those transfers* even though those transfers themselves may not be subject to any uplift on death because they were made more than seven years before the date of death. Thus when computing any tax on the gifts in January 2001, May 2003 and April 2004 the cumulative chargeable transfers include the gift into settlement in November 1999. However when computing the tax due on the estate at death, the November 1999 chargeable transfer is excluded since it was made more than seven years prior to death. Even if it had exceeded the nil threshold at death, the November 1999 transfer could not have attracted additional tax, since Mr C T Tax survived it by seven years.

Interaction of annual exemption with chargeable/potentially exempt transfers

5. Part (iii) of the example illustrates the provisions relating to the annual exemption where there are both chargeable lifetime transfers and potentially exempt transfers within the same year. The detailed notes are in Example 1. The annual exemption is given against transfers in strict chronological order, thus the gift to Joan on 3 May 2003 (which is otherwise potentially exempt) receives the benefit of the annual exemptions, even though no tax would be payable if C T Tax survived for more than seven years. No exemptions are accordingly available to reduce the chargeable lifetime transfer on 4 March 2004 in part (iii) (a) and tax of £14,400 is immediately payable by the trustees. Note that if the gifts in (iii) (a) to Joan on 3 May 2003 and to the discretionary trust on 4 March 2004 had occurred in reverse order then the annual exemptions of £6,000 would reduce the chargeable transfer to the trust to £84,000 and the tax immediately payable to £12,600. This benefit would have been retained if C T Tax had lived for more than seven years. In fact death occurs within that period, so that the annual exemptions reduce the transfer on which Joan is chargeable and have not been wasted by being used against a potentially exempt transfer that never became chargeable.

Cumulation with earlier chargeable transfers

6. It is not always appreciated that making gifts within seven years before death rather than leaving a correspondingly greater amount at death can increase the overall tax liability. This occurs because of the need, in calculating the tax payable on a potentially exempt transfer which becomes chargeable, to include *chargeable* transfers made within the seven years before the gift. (Potentially exempt transfers are never taken into account unless the donor dies within seven years after making them, in which case they become chargeable transfers.) Thus a period of up to fourteen years might need to be taken into account to calculate the inheritance tax liability arising on a death. The earlier transfers (ie years 8–14 before death) are eliminated after seven years and are therefore not included in calculating the liability on the estate at the date of death. The additional charge is often mitigated by the tapering provisions set out at note 3 above and the amount chargeable is reduced by use of lifetime exemptions. However, as shown in parts (i) and (ii) of this example those provisions are insufficient to cover the additional charge arising through having to include the earlier gifts in calculating the tax payable on the potentially exempt transfers, the additional tax payable by reason of the lifetime transfers to the children being as follows:

	£

Savings:

Reduction in chargeable estate because of lifetime gift to Joan

Annual exemptions 2003/04 and 2002/03 (6,000 @ 40%)	2,400
Tapering relief on Joan's gift (30,800 – 24,640)	6,160
	8,560

Additional liability:

Gift of £237,000 20 November 1999 accumulated with gifts made
11 January 2001, 3 May 2003 and 4 April 2004 but not with estate,
causing lifetime gifts to Joan and Ben to exceed nil threshold (77,000 +
90,000) = £167,000 @ 40%   66,800

Net additional liability as in part (ii) of the example   £ 58,240

This problem only arises when transfers that were immediately chargeable in lifetime are taken into account in calculating the tax on potentially exempt transfers that become chargeable. If, for example, C T Tax's transfer on 20 November 1999 had been a potentially exempt transfer, the transfers to Ann, Joan and Ben would still have become chargeable transfers, but the potentially exempt transfer on 20 November 1999, more than seven years before C T Tax's death, would then be totally exempt and would not enter into the cumulative total.

Interaction with capital gains tax

7.   Where a gifted asset is a chargeable asset for capital gains tax, that tax needs to be considered in addition to inheritance tax. Capital gains tax is not payable on death, and there is normally an automatic uplift of base values to the probate value, unless the probate value of the asset has not been *ascertained* for inheritance tax (which would be the case, for example, if no inheritance tax was payable on the estate) (TCGA 1992 s 274). In that event the acquisition value for capital gains tax is the open market value at the date of death (TCGA 1992 s 272 — see Example 38 explanatory note 1). If an election has been made to avoid a pre-owned asset income tax charge then the asset is included within the estate at death for inheritance tax. However that election does not apply for capital gains tax and the value will remain at the capital gains tax value at the time of transfer (normally open market value at date of original gift) (TCGA 1992 s 18 see Example 23 explanatory note 13).

On gifts made in lifetime, capital gains tax may be payable unless the gain is deferred under the gifts holdover relief provisions — either the business gifts relief of TCGA 1992 s 165 or the relief under TCGA 1992 s 260 for gifts that are *immediately* liable to inheritance tax (such as gifts to discretionary trusts). Consequently, capital gains tax may be paid on a potentially exempt transfer, and if the donor dies within seven years the gift will also be liable to inheritance tax (unless covered by reliefs or exemptions). There is no direct relief against inheritance tax for the capital gains tax paid, although the chargeable estate at death will have been reduced by the capital gains tax paid or owing.

If the capital gains tax gifts holdover relief *is* available, and the potentially exempt transfer becomes liable to inheritance tax, any inheritance tax payable is deducted in computing the donee's gain when he eventually disposes of the asset (TCGA 1992 s 165(10)). The same applies in relation to the inheritance tax on a gift to which capital gains holdover relief under TCGA 1992 s 260 applied because the gift was immediately chargeable to inheritance tax (s 260(7)). The inheritance tax taken into account in each case to reduce the capital gain is the amount finally payable, after any adjustments following death.

For detailed coverage on capital gains tax see the companion to this book, Tolley's Taxwise I 2006/07.

(a)   When is inheritance tax due to be paid:

    (i)   on chargeable lifetime transfers?

    (ii)   when it arises because of death?

(b)   Who is accountable for the inheritance tax arising on:

    (i)   chargeable lifetime transfers?

    (ii)   potentially exempt transfers which become chargeable at death?

    (iii)   the estate at death?

    (iv)   settled property in which the deceased enjoyed a life interest?

(a)   **Due date of payment of inheritance tax**

Payment of inheritance tax may sometimes be made by instalments, but otherwise the due date is as follows (s 226):

(i)	Lifetime chargeable transfers between 6 April and 30 September	30 April in following year
	Lifetime chargeable transfers between 1 October and 5 April	6 months after end of month in which transfer was made
(ii)	Death, including tax on what were previously potentially exempt transfers and additional tax on chargeable lifetime transfers	6 months after end of month in which death occurred

The personal representatives must, however, pay any tax for which they are liable when they deliver their account in connection with their application for a grant of probate or administration, even if this is earlier than the due date shown above. This will be before they have access to the funds. However certain financial institutions may be prepared to release the funds of the deceased before probate is granted by way of an electronic transfer to HMRC against an inheritance tax reference (see explanatory note 10).

Interest on unpaid inheritance tax is charged at the rate of 3% from 6 September 2005 (see also explanatory note 1).

(b)   **Liability for payment of inheritance tax**

(i)   *Chargeable lifetime transfers*

On chargeable lifetime transfers of property not already comprised in a settlement, primary liability for payment of tax rests with the *donor* (except in the case of any extra tax payable on death which is primarily the responsibility of the *donee*. The personal representatives are only liable if the additional tax exceeds the value of the asset in the hands of the recipient, or if the tax is not paid by the recipient) (s 204).

The donor and donee may, however, agree between them who is to pay the tax, and if the donor is to pay the tax the transfer has to be grossed up, because the extent to which the donor's estate is depleted is the transfer to the donee plus the tax paid. If the donee pays the tax grossing up is not necessary.

Grossing up does not apply on a potentially exempt transfer since tax is not payable in the donor's lifetime.

A return for inheritance tax because of a chargeable transfer in lifetime has to indicate who is to pay the tax.

In the case of lifetime transfers of property comprised in a settlement, the primary liability is that of the trustees.

(ii)   *Potentially exempt transfers which become chargeable*

The liability on potentially exempt transfers which become chargeable at death is primarily that of the donees. The donee is also primarily responsible where property subject to reservation of an interest by the deceased becomes liable to tax on death.

(iii)   *Estate at death*

The personal representatives are liable to pay the tax on property which is not immediately before death included in a settlement, or owned jointly by the deceased and others as joint tenants (usually called the 'free estate').

They are also liable to pay the tax on UK land which is included in a settlement but which devolves on them in their capacity as personal representatives.

Property owned by the deceased and others as joint tenants is not dealt with by the personal representatives because it becomes the property of the other owner(s) and any tax attributable to the value of that property is payable by the person(s) in whom it is vested (s 200(1)(c)).

See explanatory note 8 as to who bears the tax.

(iv)   *Settled property in which deceased had life interest*

For settled property other than that in (iii) above, the liability rests with the trustees of the settlement.

Other persons liable for payment

In addition to the persons mentioned above, certain other people may be liable to pay inheritance tax, but usually only where tax remains unpaid after the due date.

This is because of s 199, which is headed 'Dispositions by transferor' and imposes a liability on:

1.   The transferor

2.   Any person whose estate is increased by the transfer

3.   In respect of tax attributable to the value of any property, any person in whom the property is vested, whether beneficially or otherwise, at any time after the transfer or who is beneficially entitled to an interest in possession in the property

4.   Where property has become settled property, any person for whose benefit any of the property or income from it is applied.

Where more than one person is liable for the same tax then each of them may be called upon for the whole amount (s 205).

Section 199 poses a problem for personal representatives, because the deceased's estate is liable for tax on potentially exempt transfers in the seven years before death (even though the liability would not arise if the tax was paid, as it ought to be, by the donee), and the personal representatives may not be able to trace all such transfers. HMRC have, however, stated that they would not usually pursue the personal representatives for any such unpaid tax if, after making full enquiries and doing all in their power to disclose all lifetime transfers to HMRC, the personal representatives had obtained a certificate of discharge and distributed the estate before a chargeable lifetime transfer came to light (Law Society's Gazette 13 March 1991).

Explanatory Notes

Rates of interest on unpaid and overpaid inheritance tax

1.   As stated in part (a) of the example, the current rate of interest on unpaid inheritance tax is 3%.

Previous interest rates from 6 February 2000 were:

6.2.2000 to 5.5.01	6.5.01 to 5.11.01	6.11.01 to 5.8.03	6.8.03 to 5.12.03	6.12.03 to 5.9.04	6.9.04 to 5.9.05
5%	4%	3%	2%	3%	4%

Where tax is overpaid, the overpayment carries interest in favour of the taxpayer from the date on which the payment was made at the same rate as overdue tax carries interest (s 235). In making interest calculations, IR Capital Taxes use a denominator of 366 for interest on overdue tax and 365 for interest on overpaid tax, whether or not a leap year is involved (March 1997 CTO Newsletter). In both cases this gives a slight advantage to the taxpayer.

Treatment of interest on overdue and overpaid tax

2.   Interest charged on overdue tax does not qualify for tax relief, nor is interest received on an overpayment taxable (ss 233(3) and 235). HMRC have issued a statement of practice (SP 6/95) indicating that they do not automatically initiate an assessment that would lead to a repayment of tax if the amount involved is £25 or less, although the repayment will be made if claimed.

Where payments are made before IR Capital Taxes notify the amount due, if their calculation shows a balance of tax due of less than £20 it will not be collected and if less than £10 is overpaid it will not be repaid unless claimed by the taxpayer (leaflet IHT 4). Payments in advance do not attract interest, which only runs from the date that tax is due for payment (see Example 28 for an illustration).

Conditionally exempt transfers

3.   Where tax has not been paid because a transfer was conditionally exempt (works of art and historic buildings etc), or because of the relief for woodlands, and it later becomes payable on those objects, buildings or woodlands, the due date is six months after the end of the month in which the event by reason of which it is chargeable occurs (s 226(4)), following which interest then runs (s 233).

Different payment dates re one transaction

4.   It should be noted that tax can be due at different times in respect of one transaction. If, for example, a chargeable transfer was made to a discretionary trust on 1 May 2006, the tax would be payable on the lifetime transfer on 30 April 2007. Any additional tax payable as a result of the subsequent death of the donor would be due six months after the end of the month in which the donor died. Therefore if the donor died on 21 May 2006 the additional tax would be payable on 30 November 2006, some five months before the date for payment of the original liability.

Payment by instalments

5.   Tax may be paid by equal yearly instalments over ten years on qualifying assets in respect of transfers on death; chargeable lifetime transfers if the donee pays the tax; and transfers of settled property where the property concerned continues to be comprised in the settlement (eg termination of an interest in possession without the property leaving the settlement; or ten yearly charges on trusts without an interest in possession) (s 227). The first instalment is due for payment on death transfers and on additional liabilities arising because of the death of the donor six months after the end of the month in which the death occurred. The first instalment on lifetime chargeable transfers is due on the normal due date as indicated in part (a)(i) of the example.

The instalment option applies to the following assets:

(a)   Land of any description, wherever situated.

(b)   Shares which gave the transferor control immediately prior to the transfer.

(c)   Unquoted shares and securities (unquoted being defined as not listed on a recognised stock exchange (ss 227(1AA) and 228(5)):

    (i)   where tax cannot be paid without undue hardship (s 228(1)(c)); or

    (ii)   for shares only, where they are valued in excess of £20,000 and either the nominal value of the shares is not less than 10% of the nominal value of all the shares of the company at that time or, if the shares are ordinary shares, their nominal value is not less than 10% of the nominal value of all ordinary shares in the company at that time (s 228(3)); or

    (iii)   where the tax payable on the shares or securities, together with the tax on the other instalment assets, amounts to 20% or more of the tax payable by the same person on the same transfer (s 228(2)). This applies only to transfers on death.

(d)   A business or an interest in a business.

(e)   Timber, when a chargeable transfer is made following its being left out of account on a previous death (s 229).

The facility to pay by instalments is only available on potentially exempt transfers which become chargeable transfers if the transferee still owns the qualifying property at the time of the transferor's death, (or, for transfers of property qualifying for business or agricultural relief, replacement property).

The instalment option on unquoted shares is not available for tax payable in consequence of the donor's death, unless the shares are still unquoted when the donor dies (or if earlier, when the donee dies) (s 228(3A)). This applies to both controlling and non-controlling holdings.

Unquoted shares include those dealt in on the Alternative Investment Market.

See Example 59 explanatory note 11, in relation to the instalment option and the ten yearly charge on a discretionary settlement.

6.   In the case of land, except land that forms part of a business (as distinct from land owned by partners or directors and occupied by their business) or land that qualifies for agricultural property relief, interest is charged on the *total* amount of tax for the time being remaining unpaid, the interest being added to each instalment as it falls due. Interest is also charged on any instalment that is paid late.

In the case of land that forms part of a business, land qualifying for agricultural property relief and all other assets in (b) to (e) of note 5 above (excluding shares in an investment company) interest is not charged unless an instalment is paid late, in which case the interest is charged only on the late instalment and not on the full amount of the deferred tax (s 234).

Sale of instalment property

7.   If instalment property is sold, the outstanding tax becomes payable immediately (s 227(4)). This explains why a lifetime transferor cannot pay tax on his chargeable transfer by instalments, because he cannot direct the actions of the transferee. If instalment property was comprised in a potentially exempt transfer and then disposed of by the donee, the instalment option would not be available to the donee if a charge to inheritance tax subsequently arose because of the donor's death within seven years.

Incidence of tax

8.   The question of who is liable to pay inheritance tax is complex and is dealt with in IHTA 1984 ss 199 to 214. HMRC have powers to collect tax from a wide range of persons, but in most cases tax would be paid by the persons indicated in part (b) of the example.

Where tax is unpaid there is normally a HMRC charge on the property concerned, however, this cannot take priority over an existing valid charge (s 237). No HMRC charge may be imposed on personal or movable property vested in personal representatives (other than settled property in which the deceased had a life interest). From 9 March 1999, the HMRC charge can also apply in relation to outstanding tax and interest on assets from which heritage reliefs have been withdrawn.

The person who is liable to pay inheritance tax because of death is not necessarily the person who ultimately bears the tax. Tax on death is borne as follows:

Tax relating to a life interest of the deceased in settled property is borne by the trust funds and thus reduces the value of the funds for the person who becomes entitled to them, or to an interest in them.

Tax relating to property nominated to others during the lifetime of the deceased or held jointly by the deceased and others as joint tenants is payable out of that property, and hence borne by the nominees or joint tenants.

In the absence of specific provisions in the will, tax on all other property, both real and personal, wherever situated in the UK, is a testamentary expense payable out of the residue of the estate and thus borne by the residuary legatees (s 211). This is most important in relation to the drafting of wills and if it is intended that any particular asset should bear its own tax, this should be expressly provided in the terms of the will.

The tax on property situated abroad is a charge on that property.

Income tax relief re loan to pay inheritance tax

9.   Income tax relief is available in respect of interest paid for a period of up to one year on a loan raised by personal representatives to pay inheritance tax on personalty (ie all property other than freehold land and buildings) in order to obtain probate. Any excess interest over income of the estate in the tax year of payment may be carried back against the income of the estate in the preceding tax year(s) and any remaining excess is carried forward against future income of the estate (TA 1988 s 364).

Electronic transfer of inheritance tax from participating financial institutions

10.   With effect from 31 March 2003 most banks and building societies are able to accept instructions from personal representatives to make a payment of inheritance tax, by electronic transfer, before probate is obtained.

If a personal representative wishes to use this facility they must contact HMRC at IR Capital Taxes, Ferrers House, PO Box 38, Castle Meadow Road, Nottingham NG2 1BB or telephone 0845 30 20 900 or fax 0115 974 2526.

HMRC will then allocate an IHT reference number to the estate. When the personal representative is ready to apply for probate (or letters of administration) they will send the form of authority (included with the probate pack) to the bank/building society. They in turn will transfer funds to HMRC electronically. HMRC will provide the personal representative with a receipt which must be presented to the Court Service to obtain the grant.

You have been asked by the chairman of your company for advice on the inheritance tax position on the death of his father.

The following information is available:

1.   The chairman's father died on 1 March 2007.

2.   His estate comprised:

   (a)   Freehold house and land valued for probate at £380,000. This property was owned jointly by the deceased and his wife (who survived him) as joint tenants.

   (b)   Stocks and shares:

      (i)   £50,000 6% bonds valued @ 92–96.
            Interest is payable half-yearly on 30 June and 31 December.

      (ii)   £20,000 5% stock valued @ 86–88 ex dividend.
            Interest is payable half-yearly on 31 March and 30 September.

   (c)   Bank deposit account   £24,305
         Accrued interest (net of 20% tax)   £1,000

   (d)   Proceeds of an insurance policy   £27,990

   (e)   Personal chattels   £20,000

3.   He was life tenant of a trust fund, the assets of which amounted to £201,000, including gross accrued non-savings income to 1 March 2007 of £1,000 (taxable at 22%). The trust funds are payable to the chairman on the death of his father.

4.   Debts and funeral expenses amounted to £2,675.

5.   By his will the deceased bequeathed legacies of £5,000 to each of two grandchildren, a legacy of £5,000 and the personal chattels to his widow and the residue to your chairman.

6.   There had been no lifetime transfers.

Prepare a statement showing the amount of inheritance tax payable, who is accountable for the payment, and upon whom the burden falls.

Estate of Chairman's Father   *Date of death 1 March 2007*

	£	£	£
Property jointly owned with spouse			
Freehold house — half share		190,000	
Less: devolving on widow by survivorship		190,000	–
Free estate			
£50,000 6% bonds @ 93		46,500	
£20,000 5% stock @ 86½% ex dividend	17,300		
Add: net interest 31 March 2007 (£1,000 less 20%)	800	18,100	
Bank deposit account, including accrued interest (net of income tax)		24,305	
Proceeds of insurance policy		27,990	
Personal chattels		20,000	
Accrued income from trust fund to 1 March 2007 (£1,000 less 22%)		780	
		137,675	
Less: debts and funeral expenses		2,675	
		135,000	
Less spouse exemption:			
legacy	15,000		
personal chattels	10,000	25,000	110,000
Settled property			
Trust fund		201,000	
Less: gross accrued income		1,000	200,000
			310,000

Inheritance tax due on death (2006/07 scale)

Inheritance tax payable on (310,000 – 285,000) = 25,000 @ 40%   £ 10,000

$$\text{Estate rate} = \frac{10,000}{310,000} \times 100 \qquad = 3.226\%$$

Payable by executors	110,000	@ 3.226%	3,548
Payable by trustees of trust fund	200,000	@ 3.226%	6,452
	£ 310,000		£ 10,000

The tax payable by the executors will fall on the residue of the estate, so that the two grandchildren will receive their £5,000 legacies in full, with the chairman receiving the balance of residue after legacies and inheritance tax.

The tax payable by the trustees will reduce the trust fund remaining for the chairman.

Explanatory Notes

Quoted securities — valuation, sale within twelve months of death

1.   Quoted securities are valued cum div at a price one-quarter up on the buying and selling quoted market prices. Thus the 6% bonds at 92–96 are valued at 92 + (¼ x (96 – 92)) = 93. If the midpoint between the highest and lowest recorded bargains gives a lower figure, then this is used instead (TCGA 1992 s 272(3)).

Where securities are quoted ex div then it is necessary to add the full amount of impending dividend or interest less lower rate tax to the above valuation.

Relief may be claimed if quoted securities are sold for less than the death valuation within twelve months after death. All securities sold have to be aggregated to determine whether there is any relief. In arriving at the aggregate sale proceeds the sale values are taken *before* deducting any expenses of sale. The relief is restricted if any purchase of quoted securities takes place in the period beginning at the date of death and ending two months after the date of the last sale within the twelve months period after death (ss 178–189). See Example 11 for a detailed illustration.

Life interest in settlement — accrued income

2.   Accrued income of a life interest in a trust fund forms part of the free estate of the deceased life tenant and not part of the settled property, the trustees having a liability to pay the accrued income less the appropriate rate of tax to the estate of the deceased life tenant (the appropriate rate being the rate of 10% on dividend income (covered by the tax credits), the lower rate on other savings income and the basic rate on non-savings income).

Joint tenancy and tenancy in common

3.   Assets held jointly by husband and wife (or civil partners) are deemed to be held on a joint tenancy unless this has been specifically rebutted.

The characteristic of a joint tenancy is that there are no separate shares which can be disposed of, so that on the death of a joint tenant his share automatically merges with that of the survivor. It therefore follows that the intestacy rules do not apply to the distribution of such assets.

There can be a joint tenancy between persons who are not husband and wife or civil partners, but this has to be specifically created (whereas with husband and wife and from 5 December 2005 civil partners it is implied).

If husband and wife (or civil partners) have specifically rebutted the joint tenancy and in other cases of joint ownership where a joint tenancy has not been specifically created, the ownership is on the basis of a tenancy in common. This means that there are separate shares which do not merge on death and which can therefore be independently dealt with by will or under an intestacy.

Had the chairman's father and mother owned the house in this example as tenants in common, his will would have covered the disposition of his share, and for it to have been exempt it would have had to be devised to his widow as distinct from accruing to her by survivorship in the circumstances of the joint tenancy indicated in the example.

4.   Had the house been owned by say the chairman's father and his uncle, the position would have been:

(a)   If held as tenants in common (which is presumed unless specifically rebutted) the will would cover the disposition of the share and it does not automatically go to the survivor.

The share would be exempt if devised/bequeathed to a spouse or a charity but otherwise would be chargeable.

(b)   If held under a specifically created joint tenancy the share of the deceased would automatically merge with the survivor's share. The share would accordingly be chargeable on the death of the chairman's father since clearly its devolution to the uncle would not be exempt.

In both cases, however, the value of the share in the property would be affected by the joint ownership in that the difficulty of dealing with the share would be taken into account in making the valuation.

5.   Where the property is held jointly by husband and wife or civil partners, whether as joint tenants or tenants in common, the related property provisions do not permit any such reduction in value, because the legislation provides that the whole is first valued and then divided pro rata between the part owners. For the detailed provisions see Example 10.

6.   As indicated in note 4 property held jointly may or may not be liable to inheritance tax.

Further, it may or may not form part of the estate for the purposes of applying for a grant of probate or administration and in administering the estate.

If it is held under joint tenancy with accrual to the survivor it does not technically form part of the estate (although it may be liable to tax, depending on who the other joint tenant is) and is not therefore comprised in the probate summary in the HMRC account.

This is one reason why the value of published estates often does not accord with what the public expects to see in that the value of assets held as a joint tenant will not be included in the total.

7.   In the administration of the estate all that is required in relation to assets held on a joint tenancy is the registration of the death, for example by a building society or bank in the case of joint accounts, or the placing of a death certificate with the title deeds in the case of properties, the share in the asset itself having accrued by survivorship.

A share of an asset held as a tenant in common does form part of the estate, will appear in the probate summary in the HMRC account and will require dealing with by the personal representative as distinct from accruing by survivorship.

Position of surviving spouse where private residence owned as tenants in common

8.   As indicated in note 3, where the home is held by husband and wife or civil partners as tenants in common, the will of the deceased will deal with that person's share, and in order to avoid wasting the inheritance tax nil band of the first to die, the share may be left other than to the survivor. In order to protect the survivor's right to remain in the home, however, it has been common for wills to provide for the surviving partner to be allowed to remain in the property free of charge, the share then passing, say, to the children. Such a provision has been held in CIR v Lloyd's Private Banking Ltd to create an interest in possession in favour of the survivor, so that the whole property is chargeable on the second death. Any such arrangement would need to be on the basis of an understanding between the parties, rather than by stipulation in the will. This could, of course, lead to other problems, for example if family relationships do not remain harmonious.

Position of co-habitees

9.   Care needs to be taken where unmarried couples share a house that was purchased in the name of only one of them. If it is intended that the ownership of the property is to be regarded as shared, the purchaser could make a written declaration that the property was held on trust for himself and the co-habitee as joint tenants in equal beneficial shares, and the treatment would then be as indicated in note 4 above, so that on the first death the survivor would acquire the deceased's share. Such a declaration would not represent a transfer of value by the purchaser to the extent that the other had contributed to the cost. Any amount not so covered would be a potentially exempt transfer.

In the absence of such a declaration the legal position is complex and HMRC may argue that, even if the co-habitee has made substantial direct or indirect contributions to the cost of the property (for example by sharing mortgage payments, cost of alterations and household bills generally), the whole property is chargeable on the death of the legal owner (see also Example 10 part A re valuing the share of a co-habitee).

Calculation of inheritance tax

10.   In the example, the legacy to the widow (cash and chattels) is exempt under s 18 and is therefore deducted from the free estate before the inheritance tax calculation is made.

11.   As no lifetime transfers had been made the scale rates apply to the taxable value of the estate without aggregation with any earlier transfers, giving an estate rate of 3.226%. The tax is then payable by the executors and by the trustees of the settled property on presentation of the probate papers. Interest is payable from 30 September 2006, being six months after the end of the month in which the death occurred (s 226(2) and s 233(1)).

12.   Had the trust funds in which the chairman's father had a life interest devolved on his death to his widow, either for her lifetime or absolutely, they would have been left out of the inheritance tax calculation because of the surviving spouse exemption. There would then have been no tax payable on the death, since the £110,000 free estate would have been below the £285,000 threshold.

Christopher died on 20 March 2007 at which date his assets were valued at:

Quoted investments	£156,000
Cash at bank	£5,312
Life policies on his own life, producing	£47,500

Outstanding liabilities at 20 March 2007 were £5,714 and the funeral expenses amounted to £1,748. The quoted investments were sold by the executors on 28 September 2007 for £150,000, less expenses of sale of £2,500 giving net proceeds of £147,500.

By his will Christopher gave the residue of his estate to his daughter absolutely.

Christopher had not made any chargeable transfers before 5 April 2001 but since then he had made the following cash gifts:

2001	26 April	Recognised charity	£110,000
2003	2 June	Discretionary trust	£273,000
	24 December	Daughter	£60,000
2004	20 February	Godson (on the occasion of his marriage)	£1,600
2005	24 December	Daughter	£90,000
2006	2 June	Discretionary trust	£55,000

Christopher had agreed to pay any tax due on the lifetime gifts.

Compute:

(a)   The original amounts of tax payable on the lifetime gifts, stating the due dates for payment.

(b)   The additional amount of tax payable on the gifts following Christopher's death, showing who is liable for the tax, and stating the due date for payment.

(c)   The amount of inheritance tax payable by the executors, stating the due date for payment.

Inheritance tax payable in Christopher's lifetime

	£	Gross £	Tax on 2003/04 scale £	Net £
26 April 2001				
Gift to charity	110,000			
Less: Exempt transfer (s 23)	110,000	–	–	–
2 June 2003 (explanatory note 1)				
Settlement on discretionary trust	273,000			
Less: Annual exemptions				
2003/04	3,000			
2002/03	3,000	6,000		
Net transfer, grossed up		267,000	270,000	3,000	267,000
24 December 2003				
Gift to daughter —				
Potentially exempt transfer	60,000			
20 February 2004				
Gift to godson	1,600			
Less: Marriage exemption (s 22)	1,000			
Potentially exempt transfer	600			
24 December 2005				
Gift to daughter	90,000			
Less: Annual exemptions 2005/06	3,000			
2004/05	3,000	6,000		
Potentially exempt transfer	84,000			

	£	Gross £	Tax on 2006/07 scale	Net £
2 June 2006 (explanatory note 1)				
Chargeable transfers within previous seven years		270,000	–	270,000
Settlement on discretionary trust	55,000			
Less: Annual exemption 2006/07	3,000			
	52,000			
Net transfer, grossed up				
(* 331,250 – 285,000 = 46,250 @ 20%)		61,250	9,250	52,000
		331,250	9,250	322,000

On Christopher's death – 20 March 2007

	Gross £	Tax on 2006/07 scale £
Gifts within seven years before death:		
Accumulation before first such gift	–	–
2 June 2003		
Settlement on discretionary trust	270,000	–
24 December 2003		
Gift to daughter	61,250	18,500*
(* 331,250 – 285,000 = 46,250 @ 40%)	cf 331,250	18,500

	Gross £	Tax on 2006/07 scale £
bf	331,250	18,500

20 February 2004
        Gift to godson

	600	240
	331,850	18,740

24 December 2005
        Gift to daughter

	84,000	33,600
	415,850	52,340

2 June 2006
        Settlement on discretionary trust

	61,250	24,500
Cumulative transfers in seven years prior to death	477,100	76,840

Estate of Christopher deceased

Date of death 20 March 2007

	£	£
Quoted investments		156,000
Cash at bank		5,312
Life policies		47,500
		208,812

Less:	Liabilities	5,714	
	Funeral expenses	1,748	
	Inheritance tax re settlement 2 June 2006	8,000	15,462
Value on death			193,350

Less:	Loss on sale of quoted securities		
	Probate value	156,000	
	Proceeds (before expenses)	150,000	6,000
Chargeable to inheritance tax on death			187,350

	£	£
Cumulative transfers in seven years before death	477,100	76,840
Chargeable estate and tax thereon	187,350	74,940
	664,450	151,780

Summary

(a)   The original amounts of inheritance tax payable on chargeable lifetime gifts were as follows:

Gift	Tax payable	Due date
2 June 2003	£3,000	30 April 2004
2 June 2006	£8,000	30 April 2007

(b)   The additional amounts of inheritance tax payable by reason of the death of Christopher are:

By discretionary trust

Amounts payable by trustees re transfers to discretionary trust made on:

2 June 2003 —	On death	–	
	Paid on original transfer	3,000	–
(No amount repayable)		cf	–

			bf	–
2 June 2006 —	On death	24,500		
	Payable on original transfer	9,250		15,250
			£	15,250

By daughter

24 December 2003 Gift		18,500	
Less: tapering relief as gift is made more than 3 but			
not more than 4 years before death – 20%		3,700	14,800
24 December 2005 Gift			33,600
		£	48,400

By godson

20 February 2004 Gift	240		
Less: tapering relief as above — 20%	48	£	192

The tax is payable in each case on 30 September 2007.

(c)   The amount of inheritance tax payable by the executors is £74,940. It is payable on 30 September 2007 (ie six months after the end of the month in which the death occurred), or if earlier, upon the application for a grant of probate.

Interest runs from 30 September 2007 (ie six months after the end of the month in which the death occurred).

If tax had been paid on the estate before relief was claimed for the shares sold at a loss (amounting to £6,000 @ 40% = £2,400), the amount paid would have been £77,340 and the £2,400 reduction due to the fall in value of the shares would be repaid with interest from 30 September 2007 (or the date of payment if later) once the claim for fall in value was made.

Explanatory Notes

Grossing up lifetime gifts to discretionary trust

1.   The gift to the discretionary trust on 2 June 2003 is a chargeable lifetime transfer liable to inheritance tax at one half of the full rate. As Christopher has agreed to pay the tax on the transfer the net chargeable gift must be grossed up using the 2003/04 lifetime table. The net transfer of £267,000 exceeds the nil band of £255,000 by £12,000, which is grossed up using the 20% lifetime rate. The calculation is therefore:

	Net £	Gross £
Nil band	255,000	255,000
Net amount within 20% rate band is	12,000	
Grossed up		
$12,000 \times \dfrac{100}{80}$		15,000
	267,000	270,000

The second transfer to the discretionary trust on 2 June 2006 must also be grossed up. Tax on the cumulative transfers brought forward is recomputed on the 2006/07 scale to give the starting point for later transfers. As the cumulative total of £270,000 does not exceed the 2006/07 nil threshold of £285,000, the second transfer to the discretionary trust of £52,000 falls within the 20% band to the extent of £37,000, the gross equivalent of which is:

	Net £	Gross £
Nil band	285,000	285,000
Net amount within 20% rate band	37,000	
Grossed up		
$37,000 \times \dfrac{100}{80}$		46,250
	322,000	331,250

The gross chargeable transfer is therefore (15,000 + 46,250 =) £61,250.

Potentially exempt transfers

2.   The other gifts are all potentially exempt transfers. They are reduced by the marriage exemption on the gift to the godson and the annual exemptions on the gift to the daughter on 24 December 2005 for the purposes of any future charge to inheritance tax.

Recomputation of tax following Christopher's death

3.   On the taxpayer's death, gifts within seven years before death must be reconsidered and the tax recomputed using the scale applicable at the date of death (s 7). If the original gift required grossing up, the originally calculated grossed up gift is used in the second calculation. The tax payable is the difference between that now calculated and the amount previously paid (Sch 2.2). If the amount paid exceeds the revised amount due on the new scale no refund of tax is made.

Quoted securities

4.   Quoted securities sold within the twelve months following death by the person liable to account for the inheritance tax thereon must be aggregated and if the resulting sale proceeds are lower than the probate value of those securities a claim may be made for the loss to be deducted from the probate value (ss 178-189). For this purpose proceeds means sale value *before* deducting any expenses of sale. For detailed notes see Example 8.

Due date of payment of tax

5.   Inheritance tax is payable on lifetime transfers six months after the end of the month in which the transfer was made, or at the end of April in the following tax year if this is later (s 226).

Inheritance tax on the estate at death (other than tax payable by instalments, as to which see Example 9) is payable on the delivery of the HMRC account. The account is submitted in conjunction with the application for a grant of probate or administration, which is usually made within twelve months after death. Interest runs from six months after the end of the month in which death occurred (s 226(2)(3)).

Inheritance tax on potentially exempt transfers that become chargeable and the additional inheritance tax on chargeable lifetime transfers made within seven years before death is payable by the transferee six months after the end of the month in which the death occurred (s 226).

(a)   On 31 May 2005 X died leaving a net estate included in the application for probate at £324,250. Application for probate was made on 2 March 2007 and inheritance tax of £15,700 was paid on that date. Interest of £117 was also paid.

(b)   The executors subsequently became aware that certain assets valued at £12,500 had been omitted from the Inland Revenue Account.

(c)   Before his death the deceased had contracted for certain alterations to be made to the house in which he resided. The work was completed on 10 June 2006 and the valuation for probate which was subsequently made had taken the improved condition of the house into account. The contractors were now requesting payment of their final account amounting to £9,500, which had not been deducted from the value of the estate for probate purposes, since it was not clear at that time whether all alterations had been paid for by progress payments.

(d)   Prior to his death the deceased had made an unsecured loan of £8,000 to the company XZ Ltd, which loan had been included in the value of the estate for probate at its face value. On 1 May 2006 the company had gone into liquidation and it was now clear that nothing would be available for the unsecured creditors.

(e)   In order to pay the cash legacies the executors had to sell all the deceased's quoted securities. They did this on 1 April 2007 as follows:

   (i)   2,000 £1 shares in CD plc, quoted at death at 219p–223p with recorded bargains of 219p, 220p and 222p, were sold at 190p.

   (ii)   4,000 £1 shares in DE plc, quoted at death at 109p–116p with recorded bargains of 109p, 109½p and 111p, were sold at 87½p.

   (iii)   12,000 6% preference shares in DE plc, quoted at death at 53p–61p with no recorded bargains, were sold at 60p.

Advise the executors how they should proceed, and calculate the inheritance tax and interest payable or repayable if the position were finalised on 2 September 2007, assuming the rate of interest on unpaid and overpaid inheritance tax in force since 6 September 2005 (3%) remains unchanged.

The executors should submit a corrective account which should include the omitted assets and other amendments (s 217).

Quoted securities (see explanatory note 1)

Where quoted securities are sold by the persons liable to account for the inheritance tax thereon within twelve months after death at an aggregate value that is lower than probate value, relief may be claimed for the loss. In arriving at the aggregate value the sale values taken into account are the gross proceeds *before* deducting selling expenses. In this case the position is:

	Death Value		*Realised Value*	
2,000 shares in CD plc	@ 220p	4,400	@ 190p	3,800
4,000 shares in DE plc	@ 110p	4,400	@ 87½p	3,500
12,000 6% preference shares in DE plc	@ 55p	6,600	@ 60p	7,200
		£ 15,400		£ 14,500

A reduction of £900 (£15,400 – £14,500) is available on a claim being made (ss 178–189).

Alterations to the house

The deceased had placed the contract for the work to be done and therefore he or his estate is liable for the cost, the value of his house having reflected the work done and that increased value being included in the net estate.

Unsecured loan to XZ Ltd

The loan must be valued at the price it would have realised on a sale on the open market at the time of death (s 160). The market value at the date of death in the circumstances outlined would be nil. Since the value included in the net estate was £8,000, a reduction of £8,000 will be made. The valuation is not affected by an event *after* death. Here the liquidation had commenced *before* death but the proper value *as at death* has been ascertained later.

After making the appropriate adjustments the revised inheritance tax will be:

Value per account submitted at the time of the application for probate		324,250
Omitted assets		12,500
		336,750
Less: Loss on quoted securities	900	
Additional debt	9,500	
Reduction in value of loan to XZ Ltd	8,000	18,400
Adjusted estate		£ 318,350
Inheritance tax on 2006/07 death scale		
(318,350 – 285,000 = 33,350 @ 40%)		13,340
Amount paid		15,700
Repayment due		£ 2,360
Interest overpaid 1 December 2006 to 1 March 2007		
91 days @ 3% x £2,360		£ 18
Inheritance tax overpaid		2,360
Interest overpaid		18
		2,378
Interest thereon (185 days @ 3% 2 March 2007 to 2 September 2007)		36
Total repayable		£ 2,414

Explanatory Notes

Valuation of quoted securities

1.   Quoted securities are valued at cum div prices at the lower of:

(a)   ¼ up from the lower of the closing prices

(b)   The midpoint of recorded bargains.

X's estate therefore included the following values:

				Lower
Value of CD plc shares				
(a) ¼ (223 – 219) = 1	+219	=	220)	220p
(b) ½ (219 + 222)		=	220.5)	
Value of DE plc shares				
(a) ¼ (116 – 109) = 1.75	+109	=	110.75)	110p
(b) ½ (109 + 111)		=	110)	
Value of DE plc preference shares				
(a) ¼ (61 – 53) = 2	+ 53	=		55p
(b) N/A				

Relief for a fall in value of quoted securities

2.   The relief for a fall in value of quoted securities sold in the twelve months following death is not available if the person who claimed the relief purchases further quoted securities of a value equal to or greater than the proceeds of sale within the period beginning with the date of death and ending two months after the date of the last sale in that twelve months. If the reinvestment does not amount to the whole of the sale proceeds the relief is withdrawn proportionately (s 180). For an illustration see Example 11.

3.   *All* sales of quoted securities, whether at a loss or at a profit, which take place in the period of twelve months following the death must be included in the computation for relief (s 179).

4.   The provisions giving relief where securities are sold at a loss within twelve months after death also apply to securities for which the quotation is suspended, or which are cancelled, within that period. For details see Example 11.

Interest on overpaid tax

5.   The repayment of inheritance tax, including the interest overpaid, carries interest against the Revenue from the due date (or the date of payment if later) to that of repayment, at the same rates at which tax (if outstanding) would have carried interest against the taxpayer (s 235) (see Example 5 explanatory note 1).

6.   The original tax and interest will have been calculated as follows:

Net estate per original grant application	£ 324,250
Tax on (324,250 – 285,000) = £39,250 @ 40%	£ 15,700
Interest at 3% pa from 1.12.06 to 1.3.07 (91 days)	£ 117

Provisional figures in HMRC Account

7.   Personal representatives need to take care when including provisional figures in the HMRC Account, because HMRC are taking a harsher attitude to penalties where asset values are understated — see Example 33 explanatory note 9.

Smith, who had been in partnership with his son for many years, died on 5 April 2007. He had made a lifetime gift on 12 November 2001 of £170,000. He had subsequently made gifts to use his annual exemptions but had made no other transfers of value.

The value of his estate at the date of his death was agreed as follows:

	£
Stocks and shares	10,000
Cash at bank	2,000
Furniture and effects	4,000
Interest as a partner in partnership of Smith & Son	200,000
His house, 5 Side Street	350,000
Let agricultural land (owned and let on same lease for 20 years)	173,000

His outstanding debts were:

General household bills	7,250
Income tax and capital gains tax	11,000

His funeral expenses amounted to £2,750.

Under his will his whole estate passed to his son absolutely.

Where possible the inheritance tax in connection with his death is being paid by instalments. The first instalment and the inheritance tax not payable by instalments was paid on 1 January 2008. The second instalment was paid on 1 January 2009.

Calculate the inheritance tax and interest payable on those two dates, assuming the rate of interest on unpaid inheritance tax in force since 6 September 2005 (3%) remains unchanged.

Estate of Smith deceased   *Date of death 5 April 2007*
                                                                                          £

Non-instalment option property

Stocks and shares			10,000
Cash at bank			2,000
Furniture and effects			4,000
			16,000
Less: Funeral expenses		2,750	
General household bills		7,250	
Income tax and capital gains tax		11,000	21,000
Amount to be deducted from instalment option personalty			(5,000)

Instalment option property

Freehold house			350,000
Let agricultural land		173,000	
Less: agricultural property relief 50%		86,500	86,500
Personalty – Interest as a partner			
in partnership of Smith & Son		200,000	
Less: balance of debts as above			
(see explanatory notes 3 and 4)		(5,000)	
		195,000	
Less: business property relief 100%		195,000	–
Chargeable to inheritance tax at death			436,500

				Tax on 2006/07 scale
			£	£
November 2001 — Gift		170,000		
Less: Annual exemptions 2001/02	3,000			
2000/01	3,000	6,000	164,000	
Chargeable estate			436,500	126,200*
			600,500	126,200*

(* 600,500 – 285,000 = 315,500 @ 40%)

Tax on estate at death is therefore:			£ 126,200
Part attributable to house	$\dfrac{350,000}{436,500}$	x 126,200	101,191
Part attributable to agricultural land	$\dfrac{86,500}{436,500}$	x 126,200	25,009
			£ 126,200

The tax may be paid by ten equal annual instalments in each case. Interest on the tax relating to the house is charged on the *total* amount for the time being remaining unpaid, the interest being added to each instalment as it falls due, and interest is also charged on the instalment if it is paid late. In respect of land qualifying for agricultural relief, interest is payable only on the amount of the instalment if it is paid late.

The amounts of tax and interest payable are therefore:

	£	£
On 1 January 2008		
Re agricultural land:		
Instalment due 31.10.07	2,501	
Interest thereon from 31.10.07 to 31.12.07		
£2,501 x 3% x 62/365	13	2,514
Re house:		
Instalment due 31.10.07	10,119	
Interest thereon from 31.10.07 to 31.12.07		
£10,119 x 3% x 62/365	52	10,171
Total tax and interest due		12,685
On 1 January 2009		
Re agricultural land:		
Instalment due 31.10.08	2,501	
Interest thereon from 31.10.08 to 31.12.08		
£2,501 x 3% x 62/365	13	2,514
Re house:		
Instalment due 31.10.07 (10,119 + 68)	10,187	
Interest thereon from 31.10.07 to 31.12.07		
£10,119 x 3% x 62/365	52	
Interest on unpaid tax of (£101,191 less 1st instalment of £10,119)		
£91,072 x 3% x 1 year	2,732	12,971
Total tax and interest due		15,485

Explanatory Notes

Recomputation of tax following donor's death

1. Where gifts are made within seven years before the donor's death, tax has to be recomputed on the death scale in force at the date of death and any additional tax arising is payable by the donee (but no tax is repayable should the tax on the current scale be less than the lifetime tax originally paid).

Payment by instalments

2. Tax may be paid by equal yearly instalments over ten years on certain assets where they are transferred on death. The instalment facility is also available for chargeable lifetime transfers where the donee pays the tax, and, so long as the assets are still owned by the donee, in respect of additional tax or tax on potentially exempt transfers that becomes payable on death. The detailed notes on the assets qualifying for this treatment are in Example 5. Smith's instalment assets are his freehold house and agricultural land. His partnership interest would also have qualified but as it attracts 100% business property relief no tax is payable in respect of that asset.

Debts payable out of estate

3. Debts payable out of a deceased's estate are payable primarily from personalty (ie property other than freehold land and buildings) unless charged against specific property, in which case the deduction is against that property (s 162(4)). It could be argued that the liabilities are to be deducted pro-rata against the non-instalment personalty (£16,000 in this example) and the instalment personalty (£200,000 in this example). Since the instalment personalty in the example qualifies for 100% business property relief, the effect would be to increase the chargeable estate by the proportion

of the debts set against that property. It is understood that in practice it is accepted that the debts reduce non-instalment option personalty before instalment option personalty.

Business property relief

4.   Business property relief is given at the rate of 100% or 50% on relevant business property (for detailed notes see Example 25). In the case of a business or an interest in a business the value is defined as the value of the assets used in the business (including goodwill) reduced by the liabilities incurred for the purpose of the business (s 110). Even if any of the taxation liabilities in this example relate to the business they were not incurred for the purpose of the business and do not affect the business property relief. Section 104 provides, however, that business property relief is given on such part of the value transferred as is attributable to relevant business property. In this example the excess of liabilities over non-instalment option personalty reduces the value transferred in respect of the partnership interest. The excess of £5,000 therefore reduces the amount on which 100% business property relief is given.

Agricultural property relief

5.   Agricultural property relief on agricultural property let before 1 September 1995 is at the rate of 50% (subject to special transitional provisions for certain property owned since before 10 March 1981 and let within a farming family). See Example 25 for details.

Interest on overdue tax

6.   Where tax is not paid on the due date, interest is payable thereon, currently at 3% (from 6 September 2005), in respect of transfers made on death and on the tax or additional tax payable on gifts within the seven previous years. The detailed provisions and the rates of interest prior to 6 September 2005 are in Example 5. HMRC use a denominator of 366 when calculating interest on overdue tax, as shown in the example (and a denominator of 365 when calculating interest on overpaid tax) — see Example 5 explanatory note 1.

7.   Although land is one of the assets qualifying for the instalment treatment as indicated in note 2 above, interest is charged not only on the amount of any instalment paid late but also on the *total* amount of tax remaining unpaid, the interest being added to each instalment as it falls due (s 227(3)). (This does not apply to land that forms part of a business or qualifies for agricultural property relief.) Thus in the example, interest arises re the freehold house on the balance of tax outstanding after deducting the first instalment, in addition to the interest that is due on the overdue instalment. The amount on which interest will be calculated at 31.10.09 is £80,953, being the previous balance of £91,072 less the second instalment of £10,119. Further interest will arise if the third instalment is paid late, and so on.

A. Inheritance tax is charged on the value transferred by a chargeable transfer.

How is property valued for this purpose, and how is the value affected if the property is 'related property'?

Comment upon the basis applicable to the following property:

(a) Unquoted securities

(b) Farm cottages and farmhouses

and the effect on that valuation of

(i) A special purchaser

(ii) Capital gains tax.

B. A testator who was a widower died in November 2006 leaving a freehold property, Blackacre. The value as at the date of his death is agreed by the executors with HMRC as being £400,000 and inheritance tax is paid on that basis.

What effect will there be, if any, on the inheritance tax payable in respect of Blackacre if eighteen months after his death the executors sell Blackacre for (i) £350,000 or (ii) £450,000?

A.   **Valuation of property**

The amount on which inheritance tax is charged on a chargeable transfer of value is the difference between the value of the transferor's estate before and after the transfer less any exemptions and ignoring disposals of excluded property (s 3).

The value of property is the price which it ought reasonably to be expected to fetch if sold on the open market at the time. The value is not, however, to be reduced on the ground that the whole property is to be placed on the market at one time (s 160).

With regard to open market value, it has been held by the Land Tribunal in the case of Walton (exor of Walton decd) v CIR (1994), that the interest of a partner in a non-assignable agricultural tenancy should be valued according to the extent to which the partnership profits were enhanced as a result of not paying a full market rent, rather than by reference to the vacant possession value compared with the tenanted value.

Valuation on death

The valuation of property on death is dealt with in ss 171–177. These sections provide that the value shall be that immediately prior to death, but taking into account changes in the value of the estate resulting from the death (other than changes relating to life interests or property passing by survivorship). However, allowances are to be made for reasonable funeral expenses (s 172) and for expenses incurred in administering or realising property situated outside the United Kingdom not exceeding five per cent of the value of that property, where the expense is incurred because of the situation of the property (s 173). Thus the deduction is limited to the additional cost of administering the property because it is situated outside the United Kingdom.

In some circumstances where the value of property has fallen between the date of a gift and the donor's death, the lower value may be taken into account to compute the tax or additional tax payable by the donee. The value in the accumulation for later transfers, including that on death, is not, however, altered.

Where a death estate includes quoted securities and they are sold, cancelled or the quotation is suspended within twelve months after the date of death, then a claim may be made for relief for the fall in value under ss 178–189. Similarly if the estate includes land which is sold within four years after death, ss 190–198 apply as detailed in part B below.

When valuing assets in a deceased's estate, care must be taken to ensure that all parts of an asset included in the estate are aggregated when considering its value, eg if the deceased owned a half share of a house personally and had a life interest in the other half then the value to be used will be that of the whole, allocated equally between the free estate and the settled property.

By comparison, if the deceased owned a half share of a house personally and the other half is owned by a co-habitee then the value of the deceased's share should be reduced by a discount, typically 15%, to reflect the fact that any purchaser would have to share the house with the co-habitee (Wright & Another v CIR (1982)). See Example 6 explanatory note 9 re establishing that co-habitees do actually share the ownership of the property.

Valuation of lifetime transfers

Similar valuation rules apply in relation to lifetime transfers, except where the property transferred is a life interest in a settlement. In that event s 52(1) provides that the value transferred is treated as being equal to the value of the property in which the life interest subsisted. Where a life tenant also owns property of a similar kind (eg shares in the same company) in his own right, the value of the life interest is valued independently. If therefore someone owned shares both directly and as a life tenant, and the combined holding gave a controlling interest, a gift of the shares owned directly that reduced the combined holding to a minority holding would be valued so as to reflect the loss of control, whereas a transfer of the life interest would be valued only in terms of the life interest shares, even though the life tenant's estate had fallen in value by a greater amount.

Related property

Special rules apply to calculate the value of an asset to which the related property rules apply (s 161). These rules do not apply if the asset is sold within three years after death and relief is claimed under s 176 (see explanatory note 4).

The related property rules provide that property is related to the property in a person's estate if it is:

(a)   Property belonging to his spouse.

(b)   Property which was the subject of an exempt transfer by the taxpayer or his spouse to a charity, political party, national heritage body or housing association after 15 April 1976 and which is owned by that body or has been owned by that body at any time in the previous five years.

If it produces a higher value than its unrelated value, the value of the property in the transferor's estate will be:

$$\frac{\text{Value of that property at unrelated value}}{\text{Value of that property and the related property at unrelated value}} \quad \text{x Related value of total}$$

In arriving at this proportion for shares or debentures etc of the same class, the respective unrelated values are deemed to be equivalent to the number of shares held (s 161).

For example, the shareholders of Related Ltd are Mr R 40%, Mrs R 25%, Discretionary trust created by Mr R in 1970 15%, Others 20%.

An 80% shareholding is valued at £80,000
A 65% shareholding is valued at £58,500
A 40% shareholding is valued at £24,000
A 25% shareholding is valued at £15,000
A 15% shareholding is valued at £ 4,500

The inheritance tax values of the shares held by Mr & Mrs R would be:

$$\text{Mr R} \quad \frac{40}{65} \quad \text{x £58,500 for a 65\% holding} = \text{£36,000}$$

$$\text{Mrs R} \quad \frac{25}{65} \quad \text{x £58,500 for a 65\% holding} = \text{£22,500}$$

since these are higher than £24,000 (for a 40% holding) and £15,000 (for a 25% holding) respectively.

Unquoted securities

Section 168 refers to *unquoted shares and securities* and states that the valuation is to be made on the basis that the prospective purchaser has available all the information which a prudent purchaser might reasonably require in an arm's length transaction.

Farm cottages and farmhouses

Section 169 deals with *farm cottages* occupied by agricultural employees. In valuing such agricultural property no account is to be taken of any value attributable to the fact that the cottages are suitable for residential purposes of any other persons. If the cottage is occupied by a retired employee or the retired employee's widow(er) it is deemed to be occupied by an employee provided it is occupied under a statutorily protected tenancy or under a lease granted to the employee (and surviving spouse) for life as part of his contract of employment.

In a Lands Tribunal decision in the Antrobus case it has been decided that only the agricultural value of a farmhouse qualifies for agricultural buildings allowance, not its full market value, which will often be much higher.

A special purchaser

A problem arises when the property to be valued could be the subject of a bid by a *special purchaser*. For example, a piece of land with a normal value of £100,000 might be worth more to an adjoining landowner for the value that it would add to his own holding. Although he might be prepared to bid up to, say £170,000, he would, in fact, only usually make the bid necessary to obtain the land. That might well be very little more than its normal market value. The value of such property will therefore be between its normal value and the highest price that a special purchaser would pay.

Capital gains tax

If the asset to be transferred will give rise to a liability to *capital gains tax* and the *donee* bears that tax, then the value transferred is reduced by the tax paid (s 165). Capital gains tax may be held over on the disposal of certain property otherwise than under a bargain at arm's length if a claim is made under the provisions of TCGA 1992 s 165 or s 260. In this event the inheritance tax value is not altered, and any inheritance tax payable, either immediately or as a result of the donor's death within seven years, is deducted in computing the chargeable gain arising when the donee eventually disposes of the asset (but not so as to create or increase a loss).

B. **Blackacre — sale after death above or below probate value of £400,000**

  (i) *Sale below probate value*

  If Blackacre is the only sale of land involved, then relief is available under s 191 for the reduction in value. This is given by comparing the value at death with the gross sale value of all land sold within three years after death, and with land sold at a loss within the fourth year after death.

  If the result of a disposal is a net adjustment which is less than £1,000 (or 5% of the value at death if lower) then no adjustment will be made for that disposal (s 191(2)).

  The relief can only be claimed if the land was sold to an unconnected person by the 'appropriate person', ie the person liable to pay the inheritance tax on the land at death (eg personal representative or trustee of settlement).

  In arriving at the *sale value* there are provisions to substitute for the *sale price*, the best consideration which could reasonably have been obtained at the time of sale.

  If a claim for relief is made, all sales within the *three* year period (except those covered by the de minimis rule above) must be taken into account, ie including sales at a profit. Sales at a profit in the *fourth* year are not taken into account.

  (ii) *Sale above probate value*

  If the property increases in value no additional inheritance tax is payable on the increase providing no claim for a reduction in value of other properties has been made (but capital gains tax at 40% *is* payable subject to any exemptions and reliefs available to the executors). Such a sale may, however, influence the agreement of a value on death. (See also explanatory note 7.)

Therefore if the executors sell Blackacre for £350,000 on the open market eighteen months after the date of death, and the estate does not sell any other land, a claim under s 191 should be made, reducing the value of the estate by £50,000. If the property were sold in similar circumstances for £450,000 the executors would be liable for capital gains tax on a gross gain of £50,000, reduced by the capital gains tax annual exemption. Capital gains taper relief is not available on a non-business asset unless it has been owned by the executors for at least three complete years.

Explanatory Notes

Open market value

1.   The 'open market value' rule is the general valuation rule applicable to both lifetime and death transfers. There are, however, a number of special rules relating to particular assets, some of which are dealt with in the example.

The special rules relating to valuation of quoted securities on death are dealt with in Examples 6, 8 and 11. The provisions for claiming relief for a fall in value of a gift before the donor's death are dealt with in Example 12. See also Example 38 explanatory note 1 for differences in valuation for capital gains tax and inheritance tax purposes.

Valuation of life policies

2.   The valuation of life insurance policies on the life of the transferor depends on whether it is a lifetime or death transfer. Market value applies to a lifetime transfer but the policy cannot normally be valued at less than the premiums paid (s 167). For death transfers the policy is valued as having matured.

Associated operations

3.   The valuation to be placed on a particular asset will be affected if it is disposed of as part of a series of associated transactions (see Example 22).

Related property

4.   Where property in a death estate has been valued under the related property rules, and the property is sold within three years after the death, a claim may be made under s 176 for the value of the property immediately before the death to be redetermined as if the related property rules did not apply. This does *not* mean substituting the *sale proceeds* for the probate value.

A claim may only be made if:

(a)   The property is sold either by the personal representatives or the person in whom the property is vested.

(b)   The sale is at arm's length for a freely negotiated price and not made in conjunction with a sale of any of the related property.

(c)   The vendor and purchaser are totally unconnected.

(d)   The vendor does not have a right to reacquire the property.

Valuation at death

5.   Although the value of property at death is deemed to be its value immediately prior to death, the valuation may anticipate the effect of the death, but not the effect of the sale of the assets. For example, the value of unquoted shares in a company would be affected by the death of the sole director who ran the business and this could be taken into account. But if someone had a large holding of shares, the availability of which affected the market and caused the price to drop, the drop in price could not be taken into account in arriving at the death valuation, since the drop would be attributable to the *sale* not to the *death*.

6.   Where an estate at death includes a building society account on which demutualisation profits in the form of a cash bonus and/or shares will arise, but the date when the benefits will be received is not determined at the date of death, the value of the rights in the demutualisation will be taken into account in the death valuation, but it will be discounted to reflect the degree of uncertainty or delay at the time of death.

Sale of land after death

7.   Valuation adjustments have to be made where the legal interest in land sold within four years after death is not the same as that held at death, and in connection with leases, exchanges and compulsory purchase (ss 192–198).

In order to qualify for relief under s 191, the sale of the land must actually take place. In the case of Jones v CIR (1997), contracts had been exchanged within the (then) three year period, but the sale did not take place and the intended purchaser forfeited his deposit. It was held that s 191 relief was not available.

HMRC Capital Taxes will not consider a claim under s 191 when there is not a chargeable transfer and as a consequence there is no appropriate person. This would arise where, for instance, 100% agricultural property relief would be due. This was confirmed in the case of Stonor & Mills (Dickinson's Executors) v CIR (SpC 288, 2001), where the executors sold land within three years of death at figures considerably in excess of the probate values. This did not increase the inheritance tax, because the value of the estate was covered by exemptions and the nil band, so no tax was payable. The executors' attempt to have the values revised under s 191 failed because the Special Commissioners upheld the Revenue's view that there was no 'appropriate person' who could make a claim.

Interaction of inheritance tax and capital gains tax gifts holdover relief

8.   If an asset is transferred in lifetime and a holdover election for capital gains tax is made under TCGA 1992 s 165 or s 260, any inheritance tax paid is allowed as a deduction in computing the chargeable gain when the donee disposes of the asset. This will also apply if the transfer is a potentially exempt transfer for inheritance tax purposes and a death occurs within seven years, causing inheritance tax then to be payable. But the inclusion of inheritance tax as an allowable cost cannot have the effect of creating an allowable loss. Where a potentially exempt transfer is made on which capital gains holdover relief is not available so that capital gains tax is payable, there is no set-off against inheritance tax should the potentially exempt transfer become chargeable on the donor's death. See Example 4 explanatory note 7 for further details (full details of when a chargeable capital gain may be held over under TCGA 1992 s 165 or s 260 are in companion book Tolley's Taxwise I 2006/07).

For notes on taper relief for capital gains tax see Example 50 part B.

When X, a widower, died on 7 April 2006 his own assets included a policy on his own life which produced £21,600. As soon as the proceeds of the policy were available his executors invested the whole sum in a new issue of 28,000 shares in AB plc, doing so in July 2006.

He owned at death:

  5,000 50p ords in AB plc quoted at 75–79 with bargains done at 75, 75½ and 78
  5,000 £1   ords in CD plc quoted at 121–129 with bargains done at 121 and 123
20,000 £1   ords in EF plc quoted at 240–242 but with no recorded bargains
15,000 £1   ords in GH plc quoted at 252–256 with a single bargain at 252
10,000 £1   ords in IJ plc quoted at 4–6 with no recorded bargains
  1,000 50p ords in KL plc quoted at 92–96 with bargains at 93 and 95

His executors made the following sales:

1 February 2007:	5,000	shares in CD plc sold for £7,500 gross
3 March 2007:	20,000	shares in EF plc sold for £40,550 gross
23 March 2007:	15,000	shares in GH plc sold to the residuary beneficiary Y for £37,000 gross
12 April 2007:	33,000	shares in AB plc sold for £26,400 gross

X had also received equally with his brother the income from a settled fund set up under the will of his father. The trust assets at the date of X's death were:

  8,000 50p ords in AB plc
12,000 £1   ords in EF plc
20,000 £1   ords in MN plc quoted at 251–256 with bargains done at 251, 251½ and 253

On 5 May 2006 the trustees sold half the shares in EF plc (6,000 shares) for £13,800 gross which they used to pay the inheritance tax in respect of half the trust fund in connection with X's death. They then retired and appointed new trustees. There was a dispute about the devolution of X's half share of the trust fund and the new trustees sold half the shares in AB plc on 24 February 2007 (4,000 shares) for £3,120 gross which they used to pay the cost of Counsel's Opinions etc. It is agreed that X's son S is entitled to X's half share of the trust fund absolutely and the new trustees accordingly transferred to him half of the shares in MN plc plus the remaining cash capital in hand. On 15 March 2007 S sold for £27,000 gross, the 10,000 shares in MN plc which were transferred to him.

In each sale or purchase, the expenses incidental to that sale or purchase may be taken to be equal to 1% of the gross sale or purchase price.

On 23 November 2006 IJ plc went into liquidation and the shares were subsequently cancelled without payment of dividend.

The Stock Exchange suspended the shares in KL plc on 5 March 2007, the market value of the 1,000 shares on 7 April 2007 being £400.

Appropriate claims for relief are made.

HMRC point out that at the time of the sale by the executors of the 15,000 shares in GH plc to the residuary beneficiary, such shares were quoted at 253–256, with a single recorded bargain at 253.

Calculate the original and revised values for taxation purposes placed on each holding of shares as at the date of death of X.

(1) **Valuation of X's own shares**

Date of death 7 April 2006

			£	£
5,000	50p	ord in AB plc @ 76	3,800	
5,000	£1	ord in CD plc @ 122	6,100	
20,000	£1	ord in EF plc @ 240½	48,100	
15,000	£1	ord in GH plc @ 252	37,800	
10,000	£1	ord in IJ plc @ 4½	450	
1,000	50p	ord in KL plc @ 93	930	97,180

Less relief for loss on shares sold, cancelled or suspended within one year after death:

AB plc —	Sold more than one year after death (12 April 2007)		–	
CD plc —	Sale price (1 February 2007)	7,500		
	Probate value	6,100	1,400	
EF plc —	Sale price (3 March 2007)	40,550		
	Probate value	48,100	(7,550)	
GH plc —	'Best price' (23 March 2007)	37,950		
	Probate value	37,800	150	
KL plc —	Suspended security — market value	400		
	Probate value	930	(530)	
Reduction in value			£ (6,530)	

		£
Acquisition of 'qualifying investments' —		
Shares in AB plc purchased by executors		21,600
Total value of disposals within year —		
(£7,500 + £40,550 + £37,950 + £400)		86,400

Reduction in value on death is therefore

restricted by $\dfrac{21,600}{86,400}$ ie ¼

Claim for reduction in probate value ¾ x 6,530	4,898
	92,282

The value of each holding on death then becomes:

Shares in	AB plc	3,800
	CD plc (£ 6,100 + ¾ of £1,400)	7,150
	EF plc (£48,100 – ¾ of £7,550)	42,438
	GH plc (£37,800 + ¾ of £150)	37,912
	IJ plc	450
	KL plc (£930 – ¾ of £530)	532
		£ 92,282

(2) **Valuation of Trust Fund** (in which X has a one half interest)

Date of death 7 April 2006

			£	£
8,000	50p	ord in AB plc @ 76	6,080	
12,000	£1	ord in EF plc @ 240½	28,860	
20,000	£1	ord in MN plc @ 252	50,400	£ 85,340

Relief for loss on shares sold within one year after death:

		£	£
EF plc	Sale price (5 May 2006)	13,800	
	Probate value		
	6,000 @ 240½	14,430	(630)
AB plc	Sale price (24 February 2007)	3,120	
	Probate value		
	4,000 @ 76	3,040	80
MN plc	Sale by beneficiary cannot affect position		–
Reduction in value			(550)

	£
Value of shares taxable on death of X	
½ of £85,340	42,670
Less: Reduction in value	
½ of £550	275
	£ 42,395

The value of each holding on death then becomes:

Shares in			£
	AB plc	½ of (£6,080 + £80)	3,080
	EF plc	½ of (£28,860 – £630)	14,115
	MN plc	½ of £50,400	25,200
			£ 42,395

Explanatory Notes

Quoted securities

1. The notes to Examples 6 and 8 relating to shares sold within twelve months after death apply also to this example, but the problems of partial reinvestment and a partial interest in trust property are also considered here.

2. Listed shares and securities are valued at the lower of:

   (a) The lower closing price plus one-quarter of the difference between the lower and higher closing prices; or

   (b) Half way between the highest and lowest recorded bargains for the day of valuation.

   The respective valuations are therefore:

Own Shares	Closing Prices	Bargains		Lower
AB plc	75 + 1/4 (79 – 75) = 76	$\frac{75 + 78}{2}$	= 76½	76
CD plc	121 + 1/4 (129 – 121) = 123	$\frac{121 + 123}{2}$	= 122	122
EF plc	240 + 1/4 (242 – 240) = 240½	None		240½
GH plc	252 + 1/4 (256 – 252) = 253	252		252
IJ plc	4 + 1/4 (6 – 4) = 4½	None		4½

KL plc	92 + 1/4 (96 – 92) = 93	$\dfrac{93 + 95}{2}$ = 94	93
Trust Shares			
MN plc	251 + 1/4 (256 – 251) = 252¼	$\dfrac{251 + 253}{2}$ = 252	252

Where a death occurs on a Sunday or other day for which no prices are available, the price of each individual item may be taken for either the first day before or after the death for which prices are available. Units in an approved unit trust are valued at the manager's buying price (ie the lower of the two prices quoted). If no price was published on the date of death the last published price before death should be used.

Sales within twelve months after death

3.   When qualifying securities are sold at an overall loss within twelve months after death, s 179 enables the 'appropriate person', ie the personal representatives or trustees accounting for the tax, to claim a reduction in the value of those securities at the time of death. 'Qualifying securities' means quoted securities or holdings in authorised unit trusts. 'Quoted securities' means securities listed on a recognised stock exchange (ss 178(1) & 272). Securities on the Alternative Investment Market (AIM) are unquoted.

To compute the reduction, if any, *all* qualifying securities sold within one year after death by the appropriate person are taken into account (s 179(1)(a)). The total sale proceeds, or if higher, the best consideration which could reasonably have been obtained for them at the time of sale, are substituted for probate value at death (s 179(1)(b)). No allowance is made for expenses (s 178(5)).

Thus the sale of shares in AB plc by the executors is ignored as it occurred more than twelve months after death.

Actual selling prices before expenses are substituted for probate value for the holdings by the deceased in CD plc and EF plc (subject to explanatory notes 5 and 6).

The shares in GH plc were sold to the residuary beneficiary for £37,000 but if they had been sold on the Stock Exchange they would probably have made 15,000 x 253 = £37,950.

HMRC would normally use the same valuation rules as for date of death ie the lower of

Closing Prices	*Bargains*	*Lower*
253 + ¼ (256 – 253) = 253¾	253	253

A claim cannot be restricted to disposals with losses; all disposals must be included in the computation.

Shares cancelled or in which dealings suspended

4.   If dealings in quoted shares are suspended as at the first anniversary of death, and the then market value is lower than the value at death, the security may be deemed to have been sold at its market value twelve months after death (s 186B). The shares in KL plc are therefore deemed to have given rise to a notional loss of £530. In practice it will be difficult to arrive at a market value of shares in which dealings are suspended. No guidance has been given as to how such a market value is to be arrived at.

Under s 186A, if a qualifying security is cancelled within twelve months after death, it may be treated as sold twelve months after death for £1. Shares are sometimes cancelled in company reorganisations, but the apparent intention of s 186A is to deal with company liquidations. Cancellation does not, however, take place when liquidation commences, but at the time the liquidation is completed. It would be rare for a company whose shares had a significant value on death to go into liquidation and for the liquidation to be completed within the required twelve month period. It appears, therefore, that s 186A does not meet its objective. One possible solution where shares have a significant value at death but then become worthless is to undertake a deed of variation to direct the shares to an exempt beneficiary, such as a charity. The value would not then be included in the chargeable estate.

It has been assumed that the liquidation of IJ plc in the example was not completed before 7 April 2007.

Sales followed by reinvestment

5. To prevent the appropriate person selling investments and reacquiring them shortly afterwards s 180 provides that, if any qualifying investments are acquired in the same capacity within a period beginning on the date of death and ending two months after the date of the last sale (or deemed sale), then the claim shall be reduced by the proportion which the purchase prices of all such qualifying purchases bears to the aggregate sale prices used in the claim.

    In this example the executors had invested £21,600 in quoted securities during the relevant period. The total relief is therefore reduced by the proportion which that investment bears to the sale values of securities disposed of or deemed to be disposed of within twelve months after death (ie CD plc + EF plc + GH plc + KL plc = £86,400) giving actual relief of

    $$£6,530 - (\frac{21,600}{86,400} \times 6,530) = £\ \underline{4,898}$$

    The purchase does not have to be made out of the proceeds of sale of the securities sold. Any purchase of qualifying shares made during the period commencing with the date of death and ending two months after the date of the last sale, whether before or after the sale, and irrespective of the source of the purchase money, reduces the amount of relief available.

6. The relevant proportion of gain or loss is then added to or subtracted from probate value at death of each security included in the claim for reduction in value to give the revised value for inheritance tax. That revised value is also deemed to be market value at date of death for capital gains tax (s 187).

    Thus the value of the shares in AB plc is unaltered because they are not sold within twelve months after death and therefore not included in the s 179 claim;

    The value of the shares in CD plc is increased by ¾ of the gain on sale, £1,400;

    The value of the shares in EF plc is reduced by ¾ of the loss on sale, £7,550;

    The value of the shares in GH plc is increased by ¾ of the notional gain of £150 on disposal, notwithstanding the fact that the actual proceeds showed a loss;

    The value of the shares in IJ plc remains unaltered because they were not cancelled within twelve months after death;

    The value of the shares in KL plc is reduced by ¾ of the notional loss on suspension, £530.

Shares forming trust property in which deceased had a part interest

7. As the trust assets have not been appropriated into separate funds for X and his brother, the entirety of the trust fund has to be calculated at the death of X (s 186) but only the one half proportion representing his life interest is included in the computation of tax due. This has the effect of treating a part of the securities disposed of as belonging to the non taxable part of the trust and therefore restricts the relief claimable. In this example one half of the trust fund is taxable and therefore only one half of the computed reduction in value is claimable.

8. The trustees of a settled fund are treated as a single and continuing body (s 178(4)) and therefore the computation includes the sales of shares by the old and new trustees.

    However the beneficiary is not the same person as the trustees and was not himself accountable for the tax on the death even though he ultimately bore the burden of its payment by receiving less funds from the trust and therefore the disposal by S as beneficiary of shares in MN plc transferred to him by the trustees is not included in the calculation of relief.

Investments not found until more than twelve months after death

9.   The relevant sale must take place within twelve months of the date of death for relief for loss to be available. In the case of Exors of CE Lee v IRC (SpC 349 2002) the documents relating to the investment were not found until more than twelve months after death. The shares had lost value. The value for inheritance tax was market value at date of death. Relief for loss in value was not available.

Pilling, who had been a widower since 1990, died on 3 May 2006. He was survived by one son and one daughter, who are twins born in 1952.

For many years up to 5 April 1999 he had made regular gifts, fully using the annual exemption for inheritance tax, but he had not made any chargeable transfers.

Pilling had made the following gifts after 5 April 1999:

15 June 2000	To nephew £176,400 in securities.
15 April 2001	10,000 £1 shares in Black plc, a listed company, to his niece. The shares were worth £13.00 each at the date of the gift. On 3 December 2000 Black plc was taken over by White plc and in exchange for her Black plc shares, Pilling's niece was given 15,000 White plc shares of 25p each, those shares being worth £7.00. At Pilling's death they were worth £2.80 each.
25 December 2001	Motor car worth £12,600 to his nephew. Two days before Pilling's death the car was totally destroyed by fire. The insurance compensation was £5,000.
4 July 2003	Cash gift of £63,000 to his grandson in consideration of his marriage, which took place on that date.

At the time of his death Pilling owned 3,200 ordinary shares in Briggs and Pilling Ltd; he had subscribed for these shares when the company was formed in 1957 and they were valued at £55 per share on his death. The company has an issued capital of 5,000 ordinary shares and is engaged in demolition contracting.

His other assets comprised quoted investments and personal chattels with a total value of £240,700. He had a bank overdraft of £33,100 and his funeral expenses were £1,100.

By his will, which was made immediately after the death of his wife in 1990, Pilling left his shares in Briggs and Pilling Ltd to his son, with the residue of his estate divided equally between his son and his daughter.

Pilling's son accepts that because he will receive the legacy of the shares in Briggs and Pilling Ltd, his sister or her family should have a larger share in the residue of the estate. In September 2006 they ask you for advice on dealing with their father's estate in the most efficient way in relation to inheritance tax. The son is married with two children whose ages are 13 and 10; the daughter is a widow whose only child is Pilling's grandson who was married in July 2003.

(a)   Calculate the inheritance tax payable as a result of Pilling's death, stating the due date of payment.

(b)   List the points that you would bring to the attention of Pilling's son and daughter in connection with altering the terms of Pilling's will.

(a) **Inheritance tax payable as a result of Pilling's death on 3 May 2006**
Lifetime transfers

			Gross	Tax on 2006/07 scale
Potentially exempt transfers now chargeable:		£	£	£
15.6.2000	Nephew — securities	176,400		
	Less: Annual exemptions 2000/01	(3,000)		
	1999/2000	(3,000)	170,400	–
15.4.01	Niece — shares	130,000		
	Less: Annual exemption 2001/02	(3,000)	127,000	4,960*
	(297,400 – 285,000 = 12,400 @ 40% = £4,960)		297,400	4,960
25.12.01	Nephew — car		12,600	5,040**
4.7.03	Grandson	63,000		
	Less: Marriage exemption	(2,500)		
	Annual exemptions 2003/04	(3,000)		
	2002/03	(3,000)	54,500	21,800
			364,500	

* On a claim by the niece, tax on her gift may be recomputed as follows:

Value of gift	130,000
Value on death (15,000 @ £2.80)	42,000
Reduce transfer by	£ 88,000

Giving chargeable transfer of (117,000 – 88,000) =   £29,000

When this is added to the chargeable transfers brought forward of £170,400, the total is £199,400, which is below the nil threshold, so that the inheritance tax payable by the niece is reduced to nil.

** Tapering relief of 40% will be available to the nephew on the gift on 25.12.2001, because it was made between 4 and 5 years before death. Inheritance tax payable will be 60% × £5,040 = £3,024.

		£	Due date
Tax payable on PETs which became chargeable because of Pilling's death within 7 years:			
15.6.2000	By nephew	nil	
15.4.01	By niece (after claim re fall in value)	nil	
25.12.02	By nephew (after tapering relief)	3,024	30.11.2006
4.7.03	By grandson	21,800	

Pilling's estate at death

	Date of death 3 May 2006	
	£	£
Shares in Briggs and Pilling Ltd 3,200 @ £55	176,000	
Less: 100% business property relief	176,000	–
Quoted investments and personal chattels		240,700
		240,700
Less: Debts and funeral expenses (33,100 + 1,100)		34,200
Chargeable estate at death		206,500

Since the lifetime transfers exceed the nil threshold, the tax payable by the personal representatives is £206,500 @ 40%, ie £82,600. The due date of payment is 30 November 2005, or when they deliver their account with their application for probate if earlier.

(b) **Points to be brought to attention of Pilling's son and daughter in connection with altering the terms of Pilling's will**

1. Pilling's son and daughter may vary the way in which the estate is distributed, providing they do so within two years after the date of his death. Both the son and daughter must sign the instrument of variation. The personal representatives will not be required to sign, since the variation will not result in any additional tax being payable by them. The variation will be treated for inheritance tax as if it had applied at the date of death (see explanatory note 7).

2. The variation is also effective for capital gains tax purposes (providing a statement to that effect is included within the deed — TCGA 1992 s 62(6) and (7)), so that the ultimate beneficiaries who receive any chargeable assets directly will be treated as having acquired them at market value at the date of Pilling's death.

3. For income tax purposes, any income arising on the assets before the variation is still treated as belonging to the original beneficiary and taxed at his/her tax rates. If that person is assessed to higher rate tax on the income, it may be thought appropriate for the tax to be paid by whoever receives the income.

4. If Pilling's son and daughter already have adequate income, they may wish to provide in the instrument of variation that some or all of Pilling's estate is transferred direct to their children. In the case of Pilling's son's infant children the funds would be held in trust until they reached age 18 or married before that time. If, however, Pilling's son gives up some or all of his entitlement in favour of his own infant children this would be treated as a parental settlement and the income arising from the assets would be treated as Pilling's son's income so long as his children were infant and unmarried, unless the funds were transferred by way of accumulation and maintenance settlement and the income was accumulated. There would be no problem in relation to Pilling's daughter, since her son is married, nor in relation to any transfer by Pilling's son to his nephew.

Explanatory Notes

Fall in value of gift before death

1. If the value of a gift has fallen between the date of gift and the date of death, a claim may be made for the tax to be computed as if the value transferred were reduced by the reduction in value of the asset. The recomputation does not affect the amount of the chargeable transfer taken into account in the figure of cumulative transfers for the purpose of computing the tax on any later chargeable transfers or on death. The relief does not apply to wasting chattels and hence the car value is not reduced in this example (s 131). If the asset is shares and there is a reorganisation or takeover prior to death, the original shares and the new holding are treated as the same property (s 135).

2. A claim for the relief must be made by the person liable to pay the tax. So, following a claim by Pilling's niece, the value of the shares given to her is reduced by £88,000 in computing the tax payable.

3. These provisions also apply where the asset has been sold prior to death by the transferee or his spouse, providing it was a bona fide sale at arm's length to an unconnected person (s 131(3)). In this case the relief applies to the difference between the value transferred and the sale proceeds.

4. If the property to which the claim for reduction of value relates qualified for business property relief (or agricultural property relief) then that relief is also reduced proportionately. This will only be relevant where the relief is less than 100%.

5.   If the original gift was a chargeable lifetime transfer on which the donor paid the tax, the *original* amount of tax would be added to the recomputed transfer.

EG   Cumulative transfers exceed nil threshold

	Gross £	Tax £	Net £
Net gift of 10,000 shares worth £4 each to discretionary trust			40,000
Grossed up (x $\frac{100}{80}$)	50,000	10,000	
		(½ rate)	
Shares worth £3 each on death within seven years			
Recomputed gift 10,000 @ £3	30,000		
Add tax on original gift	10,000	40,000	16,000
		(full rate)	

Additional tax payable because of death within seven years after the gift is £6,000 (£16,000 – £10,000), subject to any available taper relief.

Increase in value of gift before death

6.   If the value of a gift has *increased* between the date of gift and the date of death, the death scale is nonetheless only applied to the original chargeable transfer.

Deeds of variation

7.   The legislation on deeds of variation has been amended for variations made on or after 1 August 2002 (IHTA 1984 s 142). From that date deeds of variation do not have to be sent to HMRC Capital Taxes unless the variation results in additional tax becoming payable then the beneficiaries and personal representatives must send a copy of the variation to HMRC Capital Taxes within six months and notify them of the amount of additional tax payable (IHTA 1984 s 218A). See Example 34 for further details, in particular explanatory note 5.

Cross references

8.   For further notes on exemptions, see Example 1; business property relief, see Example 25; dates of payment, see Example 5 and the treatment of liabilities in relation to the instalment option and business property relief, see Example 9.

Hartford, who had never married, owned and operated a farm in Cheshire until his death on 14 September 2006.

Hartford had made two lifetime gifts as follows. On 14 October 1991 he gave £112,700 to his sister Providence. On 25 September 1998 he gave £148,500 to his cousin Lansing in consideration of Lansing's marriage, which took place on that date.

The assets owned by Hartford at the time of his death were valued for probate as follows:

	£
Freehold farm in Cheshire (agricultural value £640,000)	780,000
Quoted investments, personal possessions and bank balances	323,500

Debts due at death and funeral expenses (all allowable in calculating inheritance tax) totalled £7,280.

Hartford was also life tenant of a family trust in which his interest had commenced on the death of a brother on 25 November 2001, when the value of the trust fund was £83,800, out of which inheritance tax of £18,500 was paid as a result of the brother's death. On 14 September 2006 the trust fund consisted of quoted investments valued at £153,850 (including accrued income £2,410) and there was also undistributed income due to Hartford amounting to £3,730.

By his will, which was made in February 1998, Hartford made charitable bequests totalling £100,000 and also left £30,000 to a qualifying political party. The farm was left absolutely to his cousin Lansing and the residue was to be held in trust for the disabled infant children of his sister Augusta, who was born in 1994.

(a) State the points relating to taxation that should have been taken into consideration when drafting the terms of the trust created by Hartford's will for his sister's infant child.

(b) Calculate the inheritance tax payable as a result of Hartford's death, stating the persons responsible for payment of the tax and the amount payable by each.

(c) State what difference, if any, it would have made to the calculations in (b) if the gifts to Providence and Lansing had been made one year later, ie 14 October 1992 and 25 September 1999 respectively.

(a)   **Hartford — Tax points in relation to drafting trust for sister's children**

Until 2006, Part 3, Chapter 3 of IHTA set out the rules for discretionary trusts (strictly, *relevant property* trusts).These comprised:

   (i)   an immediate *entry* tax charge of 20% on lifetime transfers that exceed the inheritance tax (IHT) threshold into 'relevant property' trusts;

   (ii)   a *periodic* tax charge of 6% on the value of trust assets over the IHT threshold once every ten years; and

   (iii)   an *exit* charge proportionate to the periodic charge when funds are taken out of a trust between ten year anniversaries.

However, there were special rules for accumulation and maintenance (A&M) trusts.

Lifetime transfers into these trusts were exempt from IHT if the settlor survives seven years, and the trusts are not subject to the periodic or exit charges.

FA 2006 Sch 20 restricts the favourable rules to trusts that are created:

   (i)   on death by a parent for a minor child who will be fully entitled to the assets in the trust at age 18; or

   (ii)   on death for the benefit of one life tenant in order of time only (more than one such interest may be created on death as long as the trust capital vests absolutely when the life interest comes to an end); or

   (iii)   either in the settlor's lifetime or on death for a disabled person. Trusts for *disabled persons* will also continue to enjoy special treatment, as will existing regular premium life insurance policies written into trust.

The IHT treatment for trusts which do not come within these rules now fall within the IHT rules for 'relevant property' trusts. These changes took effect from 22 March 2006, but Sch 20 provides transitional arrangements for existing trusts.

Broadly, where pre-22 March 2006 A & M trusts provide that the assets in trust will go to a beneficiary absolutely at 18 — or where the terms on which they are held are modified before 6 April 2008 to provide this — the previous IHT treatment will continue.

A limited exception is given to trusts which allow the advance of capital to be delayed until the beneficiary is 25. It permits the relevant property rules to apply only once the beneficiary reaches the age of 18, so that the theoretical maximum exit charge will be 4.2% when the beneficiary turns 25. However, for trust property settled after 21 March 2006, this exception applies only if the beneficiary has lost one of his or her parents and the funds come from the will of that parent or through a trust established under the Criminal Injuries Compensation Scheme.

The new IHT rules for trusts have consequences for capital gains tax (CGT). Some of the necessary changes will happen automatically — for example, transfers into and out of trusts that will now come within the 'relevant property' rules will automatically be eligible for CGT hold-over relief. The new legislation will also make sure that the IHT and CGT treatment are parallel.

(b) **Inheritance tax payable as a result of Hartford's death on 14 September 2006**

£

Estate at death was as follows:

				£
Freehold farm in Cheshire				780,000
Less: agricultural property relief	100% x 640,000	640,000		
business property relief	100% x 140,000	140,000	780,000	–
Quoted investments, personal possessions and bank balances				323,500
Accrued income from trust fund*				2,410
Undistributed income due from trust fund*				3,730
(* Assumed to be net of income tax)				
				329,640
Less: debts and funeral expenses				7,280
				322,360
Less: charitable bequests			100,000	
qualifying political party bequest			30,000	130,000
				192,360
Settled property (153,850 – 2,410)				151,440
				343,800

The only lifetime transfers made by Hartford were the potentially exempt transfer to Providence on 14 October 1991, which became completely exempt on 14 October 1998, and the potentially exempt transfer to Lansing on 25 September 1998, which became completely exempt on 25 September 2005.

The tax payable on the death estate is therefore:

343,800 – 285,000 = 58,800 @ 40%   23,520

Less: quick succession relief 20% x 18,500 x $\dfrac{65,300}{83,800}$ 2,883   £ 20,637

Payable as to $\dfrac{192,360}{343,800}$ x 20,637 = £11,547 by Hartford's personal representatives

and as to $\dfrac{151,440}{343,800}$ x 20,637 = £9,090 by trustees of settled property.

(c) If the transfers to Providence and Lansing had been made a year later, the transfer to Providence would have been a potentially exempt transfer that became completely exempt on 14 October 1999. The transfer to Lansing would have been within seven years before Hartford's death and would thus become a chargeable transfer. The position would therefore be:

			Gross £	Tax £
Cumulative transfers at Hartford's death:				
25.9.99	Gift to Lansing	148,500		
	Less: Marriage exemption	(1,000)		
	Annual exemptions			
	1999/2000	(3,000)		
	1998/99	(3,000)		
	PET now chargeable		141,500	–
Estate at death			343,800	80,120
			485,300	80,120**

(** 485,300 – 285,000 = 200,300 @ 40%)

		Tax
Tax on estate at death		80,120
Less: quick succession relief 20% x 18,500 x $\dfrac{65,300}{83,800}$		2,883 £ 77,237

Payable as to $\dfrac{192,360}{343,800}$ x 77,237 = £43,215 by Hartford's personal representatives

and as to $\dfrac{151,440}{343,800}$ x 77,237 = £34,022 by trustees of settled property.

Thus the transfer to Lansing would not itself attract tax, since it was below the nil threshold, and the tapering relief of 80% for transfers within six and seven years before death would not therefore be relevant, but the transfer would take up £141,500 of the nil band otherwise available to the death estate. The tax on the death estate would accordingly increase by £141,500 @ 40% = £56,600 (ie 77,237 – 20,637).

Explanatory Notes

Will trusts

1.   When property is left by a will into a trust the normal rules for settlements apply (see Examples 52 to 63). Accordingly if the settlement had an interest in possession then the settlement would be deemed to be part of the estate of the person with that interest, as in the case of Hartford in this example. However, when the beneficiaries are minors it is usual to retain a degree of discretion over the income of the settlement and where that is done the rules relating to discretionary settlements apply (see Example 60).

Transfer to Providence

2.   Providence would have no liability as a result of Hartford's death whether her gift had been made on 14 October 1991 or 14 October 1992. As a potentially exempt transfer the gift becomes completely exempt after seven years. In computing the liability on the gift to Lansing if it had been made on 25 September 1999, only chargeable transfers in the previous seven years are taken to form the opening figures. The gift to Providence, being potentially exempt, and subsequently completely exempt, is not taken into account.

Cross references

3.   For notes on agricultural property relief and business property relief, see Example 25; for notes on exemptions, see Example 1; and quick succession relief, see Example 21.

Thomas died on 20 December 2006.

He left an estate valued at £400,000 after payment of all debts and funeral expenses.

By his will he gave a pecuniary legacy of £200,000 to his son Dick, with the residue of his estate to his wife.

He had on 31 December 2003 made a gift of £205,000 to Dick. This was the only gift made by Thomas since 1998.

Calculate the inheritance tax payable in consequence of Thomas's death.

Lifetime transfer

		£
31 December 2003		
Gift to Dick		205,000
Less: Annual exemptions 2003/04	3,000	
2002/03	3,000	6,000
Potentially exempt transfer		199,000

Inheritance tax payable on death of Thomas 20 December 2006

	Gross £	Tax on 2006/07 scale £
By Dick		
31 December 2003		
Gift — potentially exempt transfer now chargeable	199,000	–

By Estate
Tax is payable on the grossed up equivalent of the £200,000 legacy to Dick when added to an inheritance tax accumulation of £199,000 using the 2006/07 scale:

	Gross £	Tax £	Net £
Before death	199,000	–	199,000
Pecuniary legacy (see working note)	276,000	76,000	200,000
	475,000	76,000	399,000

Tax payable by estate		£ 76,000

The estate will accordingly be divided as follows:

	£	£
Gross estate		400,000
To HMRC — payment of inheritance tax		76,000
To Dick		200,000
To Wife (exempt transfer)		
(ie) £400,000 estate – £200,000 to Dick	200,000	
Less: Tax on Dick's legacy	76,000	124,000
		400,000

Working Note
As cumulative net transfers of £399,000 exceed £285,000 the 40% rate of tax applies to the excess of £114,000, giving a gross equivalent for that part of the legacy of:

$$\frac{100}{60} \times £114,000 = £190,000$$

with tax payable of £76,000.

Explanatory Notes

Potentially exempt transfer on 31 December 2003

1.   The gift made on 31 December 2003, in so far as it exceeded the available annual exemptions, was a potentially exempt transfer that became a chargeable transfer on the death of Thomas (s 19). It is then chargeable using the rates applicable at death. The lifetime gift attracts the nil rate band before the estate at death and accordingly no tax is due on that gift. If a liability had arisen it would be payable by the transferee.

Pecuniary legacies

2.   On death, the residue left to the wife is exempt (s 18) but it cannot be ascertained until the tax payable by the estate has been calculated. Tax is payable on the pecuniary legacy and since the legatee receives the actual amount of the legacy, the tax payable is found by grossing it up (ss 36–42).

3.   The amount received by the widow is much less than she at first sight appears entitled to:

Estate		400,000
Dick's legacy		200,000
Apparent entitlement		£ 200,000

but in fact she gets:

Estate		400,000
Dick's legacy	200,000	
after tax of	76,000	276,000
		£ 124,000

4.   Contrast the above with the position if the will had left a legacy of £200,000 to the widow and the residue (£200,000) to Dick. Then the taxable estate would be:

Value on death at 20 December 2006	400,000
Less: Exempt legacy — wife	200,000
Chargeable to inheritance tax on death	£ 200,000

Inheritance tax due on death

	£	2006/07 scale £
Chargeable transfers accumulation at death	199,000	–
Chargeable estate	200,000	45,600*
	399,000	45,600*

(* 399,000 – 285,000 = 114,000 @ 40%)

The estate would then be divided:

	£	£
Gross estate		400,000
To HMRC – payment of inheritance tax		45,600
To Wife		200,000
To Dick	200,000	
Less: Tax on residue	45,600	154,400
		400,000

The widow is better off by more than Dick is worse off, HMRC being the loser:

	Legacy to Dick Residue to widow	Legacy to widow Residue to Dick	Difference £
Dick	200,000	154,400	(45,600)
Widow	124,000	200,000	76,000
HMRC	76,000	45,600	(30,400)
	£ 400,000	£ 400,000	

There is nothing to prevent the widow making a personal gift to Dick from her own resources, covered in part by available exemptions and the amount reckonable being a potentially exempt transfer. If, however, a claim was made by Dick against the estate for an increased share of the estate and that claim was settled by Thomas's widow out of her own assets rather than out of assets from the estate, then s 29A would operate to treat that amount as being a payment out of the estate, reducing accordingly the exempt amount to the widow (claims under the Inheritance (Provision for Family and Dependants) Act 1975 that are settled out of the estate are already treated as if they were effected by the will (s 146)).

Samuel Smith died on 31 March 2007 leaving net estate valued as follows:

	£
His half share in the business of S and D Smith carried on in partnership for many years (his brother, David Smith, owning the other half share)	100,000
An office building occupied by S and D Smith	280,000
Bank and building society accounts	34,600
Quoted securities	82,300
Half share in the matrimonial home and contents, valued at £545,000, being held by himself and Mrs Smith (who survived him) as joint tenants	272,500
Life assurance policies on his own life — amount receivable	132,400
A house in France (there are no additional costs of administration because of the situation overseas)	140,800

He made bequests of £100 to each of three grandchildren and £5,000 to his daughter on her reaching the age of twenty-five or her earlier marriage.

He left £5,000 to charities and £100 to a political party.

He left his widow a legacy of £100,000.

The house in France was left to his daughter with the stipulation that she bore any inheritance tax applicable to it.

His share in the partnership business together with the office building occupied by the partnership was left to his son with the stipulation that he bore any tax thereon.

The residue of the estate was left equally to his son and daughter.

He had made no lifetime transfers.

(a)   Calculate the inheritance tax payable and show by whom it would be borne.

(b)   Explain the position regarding capital gains tax on the assets comprised in the estate.

(a)   **S Smith deceased**

		Date of death 31 March 2007	
	£	£	£
Share in matrimonial home and contents		272,500	
Less: Exempt because of devolution on widow		272,500	–
House in France (see explanatory notes 4 and 5)			140,800
Half share in S and D Smith		100,000	
Less: 100% business property relief		100,000	–
Office building occupied by S and D Smith		280,000	
Less: 50% business property relief		140,000	140,000
Residuary estate			
Bank and building society accounts		34,600	
Quoted securities		82,300	
Life assurance policy proceeds		132,400	
		249,300	
Less: Exempt legacies			
Gifts to charities	5,000		
Gift to political party	100		
Legacy to widow	100,000	105,100	144,200
Total estate on which inheritance tax is payable			425,000

Comprising:

Estate before reliefs and exemptions (*after* jointly owned assets which pass directly to widow)	770,100
Less: Business property relief	240,000
	530,100
Less: Exempt legacies	105,100
	£ 425,000

Tax payable on estate (425,000 – 285,000) = £140,000 @ 40%   £ 56,000

Which would be borne as follows:

	Tax	*Borne by*
Matrimonial home	–	
House in France $\dfrac{140,800}{425,000}$ x 56,000	18,552	Daughter
Office building $\dfrac{140,000}{425,000}$ x 56,000	18,447	Son
Residue $\dfrac{144,200}{425,000}$ x 56,000	19,001	Son and daughter out of residue
	£ 56,000	

The tax on the house in France and on the office building could be paid by instalments over ten years so long as the daughter and son retained the assets.

(b)   **Capital gains tax position on death**

There is no capital gains tax charge on death. The legatees or devisees who receive chargeable assets acquire them for capital gains tax purposes at the probate value, so that the increase in value during the ownership of the deceased escapes capital gains tax.

Explanatory Notes

Joint tenancies and tenancies in common

1.   For details of joint tenancies (and tenancies in common), see the explanatory notes to Example 6. Since Smith's matrimonial residence and contents are jointly owned with his wife as joint tenants, they automatically accrue to his widow who survived him, and are thus left out of the calculation of the estate for inheritance tax because of the spouse exemption.

Had the house been held under a tenancy in common, then husband and wife would each be entitled to a separate share, which would have formed part of the residue of the estate which devolved on the son and daughter, Smith's one half share of the value then being included in the calculation of the chargeable estate.

Life insurance

2.   The example illustrates that life insurance on one's own life swells the chargeable estate where the proceeds are payable to the estate. A preferable alternative is where the policy is taken out by the taxpayer on his own life but a trust is created in favour of his children, so that the proceeds of the policy eventually fall into the trust fund as distinct from the estate.

Any gifts will have occurred yearly as the taxpayer has maintained the policy by paying the premiums. They will usually be exempt as payments out of the donor's income. The proceeds in the form of the trust fund are received by the beneficiaries without any inheritance tax liability, since the beneficiaries have always had a right to the capital of the trust fund (which has now become cash instead of a life policy).

Alternatively the children of a taxpayer could themselves take out and maintain a policy on the life of their parent on a 'life of another' basis with the same inheritance tax advantages.

3.   Another advantage of life policies not belonging to the estate is that the beneficiaries have cash without waiting for the grant of probate. The policy monies do not belong to the deceased and their receipt does not depend upon the grant of probate. They are paid upon proof of death — the death certificate. This is often a useful way of putting the dependants in funds for family necessities, or to pay inheritance tax, as well as mitigating the inheritance tax charge.

Foreign property

4.   Property situated abroad does not escape inheritance tax unless the taxpayer is also domiciled abroad. Domicile has a specially extended meaning for inheritance tax. See Example 27 for further details.

5.   Where property is situated abroad, an allowance of up to a maximum of 5% of the value of the property may be claimed in respect of the additional expenses incurred in administering or realising that property because it is situated overseas (s 173).

Treatment of specific gifts and gifts of residue where there are exempt beneficiaries

6.   Detailed notes on business and agricultural property relief are in Example 25.

In this example the interests in the partnership business and related office building were left specifically to the son and thus did not attract any exemption from inheritance tax, as they would have done if left to a surviving spouse or to a charity. There are various ways in which a deceased may have dealt with business or agricultural property in his will, and the effect is as follows (s 39A):

(a) Business or agricultural property left specifically to a non-exempt beneficiary (as it was to the son in this example)

BPR/APR reduces the value of the business/agricultural property, reducing the tax accordingly, and it is not affected by any exempt legacies.

(b) Business or agricultural property left specifically to an exempt beneficiary, such as to a spouse (or as part of residue to an exempt beneficiary)

BPR/APR wasted, since no tax payable on the property in any event.

(c) Business or agricultural property left as part of residue that goes wholly to a non-exempt beneficiary, where there are no pecuniary or other specific gifts to exempt beneficiaries

BPR/APR reduces the value of the residue, reducing the tax accordingly.

(d) Business or agricultural property left as part of residue to a non-exempt beneficiary where there are pecuniary or other specific gifts to exempt beneficiaries, or where the residue is left partly to an exempt beneficiary (eg half to son, half to spouse)

BPR/APR is applied rateably to the exempt and non-exempt parts of the estate, and is thus wasted to the extent that it is attributed to exempt legacies or exempt residue.

For the technical way in which this is expressed in the legislation and the complications where part of the residue is exempt from tax and part is chargeable, see Example 17.

7. The exempt legacies in this example, which are pecuniary legacies rather than legacies of specific property, are paid out of assets not subject to business property relief and the business property relief is therefore fully available.

If the will had merely left the legacies as stated with the residue to the son and daughter, without specifically leaving the partnership share and office building to the son, then the relief for business property would be spread rateably between the exempt and non-exempt parts of the estate, that relating to the exempt part then being wasted as follows:

$$\text{Maximum business property relief } 240{,}000 \times \frac{\text{Exempt estate} \quad 105{,}100}{\text{Total estate} \quad 770{,}100} = £32{,}754$$

The full business property relief would still be deducted from the business property in ascertaining what tax relates to that property from an instalment option point of view (see note 10), the reduction in relief being regarded as reducing the exempt legacies. The estate liable to inheritance tax would become:

Estate before reliefs and exemptions as before			770,100
Less:	Business property relief		240,000
			530,100
Less:	Exempt legacies	105,100	
	Restricted by reference to business property relief	32,754	72,346
			£ 447,754
Comprising:			
	House in France		140,800
	Residue as before	249,300	
	Business property	380,000	
	Less: 100%/50% business property relief	240,000	140,000
			389,300
Less:	Exempt legacies	72,346	306,954
			£ 447,754

Tax payable would be (447,754 – 285,000) = £162,754 @ 40%   £ 65,102

Which would be borne as follows:

Daughter $\dfrac{140,800}{447,754}$ x 65,102   20,472

Residuary legatees $\dfrac{306,954}{447,754}$ x 65,102   44,630

                                                                                                    £ 65,102

8.   Similarly if the partnership share and office building formed part of the residue and the matrimonial home had not been held under a joint tenancy (and thus formed part of the estate), but £272,500 in respect thereof had been left as a specific gift to the widow, the position would be:

Estate before exemptions and reliefs as before	770,100
Add matrimonial home	272,500
	£ 1,042,600

Maximum business property relief is restricted by

$$240,000 \text{ x } \frac{\text{Exempt estate } (105,100 + 272,500)}{\text{Total estate}} = \frac{377,600}{1,042,600} = £86,921$$

The estate liable to inheritance tax becomes:

Estate				1,042,600
Less:	Business property relief			240,000
				802,600
Less:	Exempt legacies		377,600	
	Restricted by reference to business property relief		86,921	290,679
				£ 511,921

Comprising:

House in France				140,800
Matrimonial home			272,500	
Residue as before		249,300		
Business property	380,000			
Less: 100%/50% business property relief	240,000	140,000		
		389,300		
Less: Exempt legacies		290,679	98,621	371,121
			£	511,921

Tax payable would be (511,921 – 285,000) = £226,921 @ 40%   £ 90,768

Which would be borne as follows:

Daughter $\dfrac{140,800}{511,921}$ x 90,768   24,965

Residuary legatees $\dfrac{371,121}{511,921}$ x 90,768   65,803

                                                                                                    £ 90,768

9. The above shows that on S Smith's estate the increase in the inheritance tax payable if the business property is part of the residue is as follows:

	If exempt legacies were £105,100	*If exempt legacies were £377,600*
Tax payable	65,102	90,768
Compared with tax payable as per part (a) of example	56,000	56,000
	£ 9,102	£ 34,768

Although the exempt legacies are the *cause* of the higher tax, they do not themselves *bear* any of it. It is borne rateably by the residuary estate and by the specific legacies that bear their own tax under the terms of the will, as shown in notes 7 and 8.

10. In note 7, the tax of £44,630 borne by the residuary legatees would relate to the respective parts of residue as follows:

Business property
$$\frac{140,000}{389,300} \times 44,630 \qquad\qquad 16,050$$

Remainder of residue
$$\frac{249,300}{389,300} \times 44,630 \qquad\qquad 28,580$$

£ 44,630

In note 8, the tax of £65,803 borne by the residuary legatees would relate to the respective parts of residue as follows:

Business property
$$\frac{140,000}{389,300} \times 65,803 \qquad\qquad 23,664$$

Remainder of residue
$$\frac{249,300}{389,300} \times 65,803 \qquad\qquad 42,139$$

£ 65,803

The tax relating to the business property could be paid by instalments if the conditions were satisfied (see Example 5 explanatory note 5).

Mr Algernon died on 3 September 2006. His estate contained the following:

	Value at date of death £
Main residence	725,000
Proceeds from insurance policy	300,000
Quoted shares	775,000
Bank account	185,000
Other possessions	40,000
Mortgage on main residence	(25,000)

Mr Algernon's will which was executed in 2005 required that:

1.   his daughter receive £297,000 free of all taxes;

2.   his son John receive £400,000 bearing its own taxes;

3.   his wife receive one-half of the residue, the other half to pass into a trust for his grandchildren, and the division into equal shares to be made before deduction of inheritance tax thereon.

Mr Algernon had made no lifetime transfers.

Advise the trustees as to the amount of funds they can expect from Mr Algernon's estate.

Death of Mr Algernon 3 September 2006 — calculation of inheritance tax

His estate on death amounted to:	£	£
Main residence	725,000	
Less: Mortgage thereon	25,000	700,000
Insurance policy		300,000
Quoted shares		775,000
Bank account		185,000
Other possessions		40,000
Gross estate		2,000,000

Stage 1

Gross up specific gifts which do not bear their own tax as though they alone were chargeable to inheritance tax on death:

	£
Legacy to daughter (see explanatory note 5)	297,000
Tax thereon	8,000
Gross gift	305,000

Stage 2

Using gross gift as calculated in Stage 1, divide the estate between exempt and non-exempt parts:

	Exempt £	Non-Exempt £	£
Gross estate			2,000,000
Gross legacy to daughter		305,000	
Legacy to John bearing its own tax		400,000	
Residue (£1,295,000)			
Wife	647,500		
Trust		647,500	
	647,500	1,352,500	2,000,000

Stage 3

Calculate the inheritance tax on the non-exempt estate at Stage 2:

1,352,500 – 285,000 = £1,067,500 @ 40% = £427,000

Stage 4

Using the tax computed at Stage 3, recompute the grossing up of specific gifts not bearing their own tax:

Legacy to daughter $297,000 \times \dfrac{1,352,500}{1,352,500 - 427,000} = £434,028$

Stage 5

Using the revised gross gifts re-divide the estate between exempt and non-exempt parts:

16.3   PARTIALLY EXEMPT LEGACIES

	Exempt £	Non-Exempt £	£
Gross estate			2,000,000
Legacy to daughter as in Stage 4		434,028	
Legacy to John		400,000	
Residue (£1,165,972)			
Wife	582,986		
Trust		589,476	
	582,986	1,421,014	2,000,000

Stage 6

Calculate the inheritance tax on the revised non-exempt part of the estate and calculate the effective rate of tax:

1,421,014 – 285,000 = £1,136,014 @ 40% = £454,406

$$\frac{454,406}{1,421,014} \times 100 = 31.9775\% \text{ effective rate}$$

Stage 7

The residue of the estate is therefore as follows:	£	£	£
Gross estate			2,000,000
Less: Inheritance tax payable			454,406
			1,545,594
Less: Legacy to daughter		297,000	
Legacy to John	400,000		
Less IHT thereon at 31.9775%	127,910	272,090	569,090
Residue			976,504

However none of the charge to inheritance tax is to fall on the exempt part due to the spouse.

The estate is therefore distributed as follows:	£	£	£
Daughter			297,000
John			272,090
			569,090
Tax on legacies at 31.9775% (per Stage 6) at grossed up value (per Stage 4) 434,028 + 400,000 = £834,028 x 32.0%		266,702	
Residue before tax (2,000,000 – (569,090 + 266,702))	1,164,208		
Half to widow			582,104
Half to A & M Trust	582,104		
Less: Tax @ 31.9775% on £582,986 (per Stage 5)	186,425	186,425	
	395,679		395,679
Inheritance tax		453,127	453,127
Gross estate			2,000,000

The trustees may therefore expect to receive £395,679.

Explanatory Notes

Incidence of tax on deceased's estate

1. The calculation of the inheritance tax and the distribution of the estate is not straightforward where on a person's death part of the estate is the subject of an exempt transfer (for example, to the surviving spouse) and part is chargeable.

2. The incidence of tax on a deceased's estate is as follows:

    Tax relating to a life interest of the deceased in settled property is payable out of the trust funds.

    Tax relating to nominated and jointly held property of the deceased is payable out of that property.

    The tax on property situated abroad is a charge on that property.

    In the absence of specific provisions in the will, tax on all other property, both real and personal, wherever situated in the UK, is a testamentary expense payable out of the residue of the estate.

Partially exempt legacies

3. Thus, although the widow's share of the estate is exempt, the tax on specific legacies must come out of the residue (unless the will specifically provides that the legacy is to bear its own tax).

    If the residue then remaining is left partly to the widow and partly by way of chargeable transfer, the tax on the residue must be borne in accordance with the will. This is subject to s 41, which provides that notwithstanding the terms of the will, none of the tax on either a specific gift or a gift of residue is to fall on the gift if the gift is exempt.

    Re Benham

    In the case of Re Benham's Will Trusts (1995) it was held that the plain intention of the deceased's will was that each beneficiary should *receive* the *same amount* and that this was not inconsistent with s 41. Consequently the non-exempt shares of residue had to be grossed up so that the after tax amounts were equal. This had the effect of increasing both the tax charged on the estate and the shares of non-exempt residuary beneficiaries at the expense of exempt beneficiaries, which was contrary to the accepted practice and was not the view taken by the Capital Taxes Office. In the 1999 High Court case of Re Ratcliffe (deceased), the judge came to the opposite conclusion. He referred to the Benham approach as the 'net division' approach and the previously accepted approach as the 'gross division' approach, and held that the 'gross division' approach was correct. The case has not been taken to appeal, so it may be regarded as overriding the Benham decision. Even so, it would be sensible to review the wording of wills where there is partly exempt residue, to ensure that it is clear whether the division of residue is to take place before or after deducting the tax on the residue.

Stages in tax calculation

4. Unless the cumulative lifetime transfers exceed the nil threshold the method of calculation is complex (ss 36 to 42). The procedure is straightforward where lifetime transfers exceed the nil threshold, because all grossing calculations are at the same rate, ie 100/60 (see note 7).

    Where, as in this example, the lifetime transfers are less than the nil threshold, there are seven stages in the calculation, the first six of which are notional calculations used in order to ascertain the effective rate of inheritance tax on the estate.

    The stages are as follows:

    (1) Gross up specific gifts which do not bear their own tax as though they were the only chargeable transfers made at death (s 38(1) and (3)).

    (2) Using the grossed up gifts arrived at in (1) divide the estate between exempt and non-exempt parts.

    (3) Compute tax on the *notional* non-exempt part of the estate.

(4)   Once again gross up specific gifts which do not bear their own tax but using the tax arrived at in (3) (s 38(4) and (5)). This replaces Stage 1.

(5)   Using the revised gross gifts in (4) re-divide the estate between exempt and non-exempt parts.

(6)   Compute tax on the non-exempt part and calculate the effective rate of tax (s 38(1)).

(7)   Distribute the estate in such a way that the tax, if any, on the gifts in the will not bearing their own tax comes out of the whole of the residue, and the tax on the residue falls on the part of the residue that is not exempt (s 41).

5.   The grossing up calculation in Stage 1 of the example on the legacy to the daughter is as follows:

Cumulative net transfers of £297,000 exceed £285,000 by £12,000. This is grossed up using the 40% tax rate.

	Gross £	Tax £	Net £
	285,000	–	285,000
Gross equivalent $\frac{100}{60}$ x 12,000	20,000		12,000
and tax thereon		8,000	
	305,000	8,000	297,000

6.   The calculation of tax on the trustees' share of the residue is based upon their notional share of residue ie £582,986 per Stage 5 not their actual share of £582,104 at Stage 7. This method is used by HMRC Capital Taxes. Views have been expressed that the tax should be based upon the actual share of residue (ie £582,104 @ 31.9775% = £186,143 compared with £186,425 as computed). This does not appear to follow the requirement that none of the tax as computed is to fall on the spouse or other exempt transfers. Instead it recomputes the tax yet again.

Calculation if lifetime transfers exceed nil band

7.   If Mr Algernon had made cumulative lifetime transfers of £285,000, the seven stage calculation would not be necessary and the position would be as follows:

	Gross £	Tax £	Net £
Inheritance tax accumulation at death on 2006/07 scale	285,000	–	285,000
Legacy to daughter grossed up 297,000 x 100/60	495,000	198,000	297,000
Legacy to John	400,000	160,000	240,000
Leaving residue of 2,000,000 – (495,000 + 400,000) = £1,105,000, of which half, ie £552,500, is exempt, so that non-exempt residue is	552,500	221,000	331,500
	1,732,500	579,000	1,153,500

The estate would therefore be distributed as follows:

		Tax	Net
Daughter — legacy			297,000
John — legacy			240,000
Widow's share of residue			552,500
Trust's share of residue		552,500	
Less tax @ 40%		221,000	331,500

Inheritance tax:

On legacies — daughter	198,000	
John	160,000	
On Trust's share of residue	221,000	579,000
		£ 2,000,000

The same procedure would apply if the lifetime transfers had been any amount in excess of £285,000.

Further examples

8.   For further illustrations of the treatment of partially exempt legacies, including the provisions in relation to settled property, business and agricultural relief and intestacy, see Examples 17 and 18.

Grandchildren's trust

9.   If the will was executed in 2005, it is likely that the grandchildren's trust would have been an accumulation and maintenance settlement in accordance with IHTA 1984 s 71. This would have allowed the funds to have been accumulated without the trust fund becoming relevant property (and subject to the ten-yearly and exit charges regime).

However, since Mr Algernon died after 21 March 2006, any trust for his grandchildren would constitute relevant property unless it was an immediate post-death interest in possession under section 49A. That would require the grandchildren to have an interest in possession in the fund from the date of their grandfather's death and for this to arise under either the will or the law of intestacy. Consequently, it would not be possible for a post-death deed of variation to be entered into to allow the trust terms to be varied to allow it to qualify. (Such a variation would, in any event, require more than merely a change in the administrative powers to qualify for IHT purposes (s 142)).

17.1 PARTIALLY EXEMPT LEGACIES (AFFECTED BY TRUST FUNDS, BUSINESS AND AGRICULTURAL PROPERTY RELIEF)

On 1 January 2003 X, who had made no previous lifetime transfers, gave £111,000 to his daughter D and on 1 November 2003, £81,500 each to his daughter E and his son S.

On 1 June 2006 X died leaving an estate which, after payment of all debts and funeral expenses, was valued at £250,000, after deduction of business property relief of £150,000.

By his will he left business property valued at £120,000 (before business property relief of £60,000) equally to his daughter E and his wife W free of tax, £25,000 to a charity, a pecuniary legacy of £20,000 to his son S and the residue of his estate equally (before inheritance tax thereon) to W and three children D, S and E.

X was entitled for life to income of the residuary estate of his father (who died in 1973) with remainder to his son S. The assets of that settlement were valued at £100,000 on 1 June 2006.

Calculate the inheritance tax payable on X's death.

X — inheritance tax accumulation

1 January 2003		£
Gift to D		111,000
Less: Annual exemptions 2002/03	3,000	
2001/02	3,000	6,000
Potentially exempt transfer		105,000

1 November 2003		
Gift to E		81,500
Gift to S		81,500
		163,000
Less: Annual exemption 2003/04 (split equally)		3,000
Potentially exempt transfers		160,000

On death of X — 1 June 2006

	Gross £	Tax on 2006/07 scale £
PET to D — 1 January 2003	105,000	–
PETs to E and S — 1 November 2003	160,000	–
Inheritance tax accumulation at death	265,000	–

No tax payable on lifetime transfers since below nil threshold.

Estate on Death

Free estate	400,000	
Less: Business property relief	150,000	250,000
Settled property		100,000
		£ 350,000

Summary of specific gifts with business property relief

		£	£
To wife — W	½ of business property	60,000	
	Less: BPR of 50%	30,000	30,000
To daughter — E	½ of business property	60,000	
	Less: BPR of 50%	30,000	30,000
			60,000

Summary of specific gifts without business property relief

To charity — exempt	25,000
To son — S	20,000
	45,000

Division of estate to compute exempt transfers

(1) Allocate balance of business property relief pro-rata to specific and non-specific gifts after excluding specific gifts with such relief:

	Before BPR	*After BPR*
Estate	400,000	250,000
Less: Specific gifts of business property	120,000	60,000
	£ 280,000	£ 190,000

Specific gift to charity	$25,000 \times \dfrac{190,000}{280,000} =$		16,964
to son — S	$20,000 \times \dfrac{190,000}{280,000} =$		13,572
Residue	$235,000 \times \dfrac{190,000}{280,000} =$		159,464
	£ 280,000		£ 190,000

Gross up specific gifts that do not bear their own tax (as distinct from being exempt):

Half of business property (after BPR) to E	30,000
Legacy to S (after BPR)	13,572
	£ 43,572

	Gross £	Tax £	Net £
Inheritance tax accumulation at death	265,000	–	265,000
Specific gifts	59,287	15,715	43,572
	324,287	15,715	308,572[*]

* *Grossed up*
£308,572 exceeds £285,000 by £23,572

Net		Gross
285,000		285,000
23,572	x 100/60	39,287
£ 308,572		£ 324,287

(2) Divide estate after business property relief between exempt and non-exempt parts, using notional gross gifts per (1):

	Exempt £	Non-exempt £	Total £
Business property to wife	30,000		30,000
to E $\dfrac{30,000}{43,572} \times 59,287$		40,820	40,820
Legacy to S $\dfrac{13,572}{43,572} \times 59,287$		18,467	18,467
Charity $\dfrac{190,000}{280,000} \times 25,000$	16,964		16,964
	cf 46,964	59,287	106,251

	Exempt £	Non-exempt £	Total £
	bf 46,964	59,287	106,251
Residue — balance			143,749
Wife (¼)	35,937		
Children (¾)		107,812	
	82,901	167,099	250,000

(3) Inheritance tax payable on non-exempt estate:

	Gross £	Tax £
Accumulation at death	265,000	–
Non-exempt estate	167,099	58,840*
	432,099	58,840*

(* 432,099 – 285,000 = 147,099 @ 40%)

(4) Re-gross specific gifts:

$$£43,572 \times \frac{167,099}{(167,099 - 58,840)} = £67,254$$

(5) Re-divide estate

	Exempt £	Non-exempt £	Total £
Business property to wife	30,000		30,000
to E $\frac{30,000}{43,572}$ x 67,254		46,305	46,305
Legacy to S $\frac{13,572}{43,572}$ x 67,254		20,949	20,949
Charity — specific gift after BPR	16,964		16,964
			114,218
Residue			135,782
Wife (¼)	33,946		
Children (¾)		101,836	
	80,910	169,090	250,000

(6) Inheritance tax payable on non-exempt estate:

		Gross £	Tax £
Accumulation at death		265,000	–
Non-exempt estate	169,090		
Settled property	100,000	269,090	99,636*
		534,090	99,636*

(* 534,090 – 285,000 = 249,090 @ 40%)

Effective rate $\frac{99,636}{269,090}$ x 100 = 37.027%

Inheritance tax payable by

Personal representatives	169,090	x 37.027% =	62,609
Trustees of settled property	100,000	x 37.027% =	37,027
	£ 269,090		£ 99,636

(7)   Distribution of free estate:

Estate at death			400,000
Less:	Inheritance tax		62,609
			337,391
Less:	Exempt legacies		
	To wife	60,000	
	charity	25,000	85,000
			252,391
Legacies not bearing their own tax			
	To E	60,000	
	S	20,000	80,000
Net residue			£ 172,391

Distribution of net residue so that no inheritance tax relates to widow

Legacies to E and S (at grossed up value stages (4) and (5)) at final effective rate of 37.027%

Tax thereon = £67,254 x 37.027% = £ 24,902

Estate on death			400,000
Exempt legacies	— wife	60,000	
	— charity	25,000	
Legacies not bearing own tax			
	— E	60,000	
	— S	20,000	
	— tax thereon	24,902	189,902
Residue before tax			£ 210,098

Net residue as at stage (7) above		172,391
One quarter of residue before tax to widow ¼ x 210,098		52,525
Balance equally to children:		£ 119,866
	D	£ 39,956
	S	£ 39,955
	E	£ 39,955

Summary of division of estate and trust funds		£	£
To Son S from trustees of settled property		100,000	
Less: Inheritance tax thereon		37,027	62,973
To charity			25,000
To E	legacy	60,000	
	share of residue	39,955	99,955
To S	legacy	20,000	
	share of residue	39,955	59,955
To D	share of residue		39,956
To wife	legacy	60,000	
	share of residue	52,525	112,525
Inheritance tax (including that on settled property)			99,636
			£ 500,000

Explanatory Notes

Same day transfers

1. The first step is to compute the inheritance tax accumulation at death.

2. Where two or more transfers are made on the same day they are treated except in certain special circumstances as one transfer and the effective rate of tax on the total transfer is applied to the individual transfers (s 266(2)).

Interest in possession in settled property

3. Settled property in which the donor had an interest in possession is treated as belonging to the donor absolutely for inheritance tax purposes, although the tax relating to the settlement is payable by the trustees of the settlement (ss 49 and 200(1)(b)).

Partially exempt legacies and business and agricultural property relief

4. In order to compute the tax payable on death the rules for partially exempt transfers must be applied (ss 36–42). These are detailed in Example 16.

    Where an estate is entitled to business property or agricultural property relief and there are specific gifts then special rules apply in computing the inheritance tax payable, as follows:

    (a) Specific gifts of relevant business or agricultural property are taken at their value reduced by BPR or APR.

    (b) Specific gifts other than in (a) above are taken at the appropriate fraction of their value (s 39A), that is:

    $$\text{Specific gift} \times \frac{\text{Assets transferred (net of BPR/APR) less specific gifts of business/agricultural property (net of BPR/APR)}}{\text{Assets transferred (before BPR/APR) less specific gifts of business/agricultural property (before BPR/APR)}}$$

    A specific gift is any gift other than a gift of residue or of a share in residue (s 42). It therefore covers both specific legacies of particular property and general (ie pecuniary) legacies.

    Where specific gifts are tax-free then the grossing up rules are applied to the value so reduced, as shown on page 17.3.

Gifts out of different funds

5. Section 40 provides that where gifts take effect separately out of different funds (for example where a deceased has a free estate and a life interest in a settlement, and gifts are made out of the free estate), the partial exemption rules in ss 36–39A are to be applied separately to the gifts taking effect out of each of those funds. The rate of tax used to gross up the gifts is arrived at by looking at each fund separately and in isolation. In the example, therefore, the tax on the non-exempt estate at stage (3) that is used to re-gross the specific gifts is arrived at by taking into account only the free estate and not the settled property.

Pecuniary legacies

6. Where a will provides a pecuniary legacy (a gift of cash like the legacy of £20,000 to S), then the legatee receives the amount stated and any inheritance tax relating to that legacy is borne by the

residue of the estate unless the will provides that the legatee is to bear the tax (s 211). For further notes on this point see Example 5 explanatory note 8.

Re Benham and Re Ratcliffe

7.   Where a will provides that the residuary shares are computed on the residue after deduction of inheritance tax, there were conflicting views in Re Benham and Re Ratcliffe on how the shares of residue should be calculated. It may now be regarded as settled that the established approach in dealing with partly exempt estates is correct — see Example 16 explanatory note 3.

Jones died intestate on 10 June 2006 survived by his wife and two children.

He had made no chargeable lifetime transfers.

His estate according to the account accompanying the application for a grant of administration consisted of:

5,000 £1 shares in A plc quoted at 1088–1092 with recorded bargains at 1088, 1089, 1090 and 1091

10,000 £1 shares in B plc quoted at 295–297 with a sole recorded bargain at 295

8,000 50p shares in C plc quoted at 60–69 with bargains at 61, 61½, 62 and 63

10,000 shares in the Hong Kong Bank valued at £70,000

	£
Cash at bank	87,569
Policy on his life, insuring	135,000
Salary accrued due to date of death (net)	1,625
Rents from his father's will trust (net of basic rate income tax)	
accrued due	645
apportionment to date of death	621
Furniture and effects	10,500

His debts were shown as:

	£
Funeral expenses	1,650
General household bills (electricity, gas, etc)	220
Daughter, under a deed of covenant dated 1 January 1992	
binding his legal personal representatives to pay her on his death	5,000

Under the will of his father who had died in 1985 he also had a life interest in a house, No 12 High Street, valued at £158,000, which passed on his death to his children equally. The rent due to Jones at death is indicated above.

A grant of administration was obtained on 14 February 2007 when inheritance tax amounting to £3,400 and £16 interest was paid by the intended administrators on the basis of the above information.

The administrators subsequently discover:

(1) Jones is entitled to a pecuniary legacy of £10,000 free of tax under the will of his brother who died on 4 August 2005. Inheritance tax amounting to £13,000 had been paid on the brother's estate valued at £100,000.

(2) There was an outstanding income tax liability of £750.

(3) There were bonuses totalling £47,250 attaching to the life policy.

(4) The value of the shares in the Hong Kong Bank is agreed at £70,000, but death duties amounting to the sterling equivalent of £7,000 and £420 interest had to be paid locally because the shares were registered there. The additional cost of employing a local agent to make title to the shares, including agreeing the value with the local fiscal authorities, amounted to a sterling equivalent of £4,150.

(5) The remaining values were agreed with HMRC.

A corrective account is lodged and the final adjustment to the inheritance tax payable is made on 5 November 2007, the trustees also paying any tax and interest attributable to the trust funds on that day.

Given that the 'statutory legacy' payable to the spouse on an intestacy when the intestate leaves issue is £125,000 with the spouse also taking the personal chattels and a life interest in one half of the residue, whilst the other half of the residue devolves on the issue:

(a) Calculate the inheritance tax and interest paid by or repaid to the administrators on 5 November 2007.

(b)   Show the distribution of the free estate and trust funds upon Jones's death and the allocation of the tax payable.

Assume that the rate of interest on tax overpaid or repaid is 3% pa throughout.

(a)   **Estate of Jones** (after submission of corrective account)

	Date of Death 10 June 2006	
Free estate	£	£
Quoted shares:		
5,000 £1 shares in A plc @ 1089	54,450	
10,000 £1 shares in B plc @ 295	29,500	
8,000 50p shares in C plc @ 62	4,960	88,910
Cash at bank		87,569
Policy on life	135,000	
Bonuses thereon	47,250	182,250
Salary due		1,625
Rents accrued due to date of death		
(after basic rate income tax) (645 + 621)		1,266
Furniture and effects		10,500
Legacy due from unadministered estate of brother		10,000
Chattels abroad		
10,000 shares in the Hong Kong Bank	70,000	
Less: Costs of administration (maximum 5%)	3,500	66,500
		448,620
Less: Funeral expenses	1,650	
General household debts	220	
Income tax	750	
Covenanted debt — no deduction possible since		
no consideration was given	–	2,620
		446,000
Settled property		
Father's will trust		158,000
Inheritance tax payable on		604,000

The statutory legacy of £125,000 plus furniture and effects £10,500 and one half of the residue in trust for the widow are exempt transfers. To determine the amount deemed to be transferred to the trust for the widow it is necessary to apply the 'double grossing up' rules that apply to partially exempt residues.

Division of estate to compute exempt transfer

(1)   Gross up specific gifts not bearing own tax:

Covenanted gift to daughter D	£ 5,000
As there were no lifetime transfers and value is below £285,000, its grossed up value is	£ 5,000

(2)   Divide estate between exempt and non-exempt parts, using notional gross gifts:

		Exempt	Non-exempt	Total
Specific gift			5,000	5,000
To Wife	Statutory legacy	125,000		125,000
	Furniture etc	10,500		10,500
	½ of residue (life interest)	152,750		
To Children	½ of residue		152,750	305,500
		£ 288,250	£ 157,750	£ 446,000

(3)   Inheritance tax payable on non-exempt estate:

	Gross	Tax
Inheritance tax accumulation at death	–	–
Non-exempt estate	£ 157,750	£ –

As the value of the non-exempt estate is less than £285,000 (excluding settled property), it is not necessary to re-gross up the specific gift, or to re-divide the estate. The inheritance tax payable is therefore:

		Gross	Tax
Non-exempt estate	157,750		
Settled property	158,000	£ 315,750	£ 12,300*

(* 315,750 – 285,000 = 30,750 @ 40%)

	£
Inheritance tax on chargeable estate	12,300

Less: Quick succession relief

$$100\% \text{ of } \frac{10,000}{100,000} \times £13,000$$

	£
	1,300
	11,000

Less: Relief for overseas tax — re Hong Kong Bank shares. Amount paid £7,000 but restricted to inheritance tax attributable to that property

$$\frac{66,500}{604,000} \times 11,000 = 1,211$$

	£
	1,211
	9,789

Tax payable by administrators $\dfrac{157,750}{315,750} \times £11,000 = 5,496 - 1,211$ → 4,285

	£
Less already paid	3,400
Additional tax payable	885
Interest on £885 at 3% from 1.1.07 to 5.11.07 = 309 days	22
Total payable by the administrators 5.11.07	907

Tax payable by the trustees of father's will trust

$$\frac{158,000}{315,750} \times £11,000 =$$

	£
	5,504
Interest at 3% from 1.1.07 to 5.11.07 = 309 days	140
Total payable by the trustees 5.11.07	£ 5,644

(b)   **Distribution of funds and allocation of tax payable**

		£	£
Daughter	— specific gift		5,000
Widow	— Cash	125,000	
	Chattels	10,500	
	½ of residue as at (a) (2)	152,750	288,250
Children	— ½ of residue as at (a) (2)	152,750	
	Less inheritance tax payable	4,285	148,465
Inheritance tax payable by administrators			4,285
			446,000
Inheritance tax payable by trustees of father's will trust			5,644

The interest payable on overdue tax will be dealt with through the income accounts of the estate and the trust.

Explanatory Notes

Partially exempt legacies — intestacy

1. The notes to Examples 16 and 17 also apply to this example. The example highlights the fact that an intestacy will often create partially exempt residue. See in particular Example 17 note 5 regarding the treatment to be adopted where a partly exempt estate consists of free estate and an interest in settled property. The rules relating to distribution on intestacy are set out at explanatory note 6 below.

    For further details on:

Corrective and supplementary accounts	see Example 8
Administration of foreign assets	see Example 15
Quick succession relief	see Example 21
Double taxation relief	see Example 28

Valuation of quoted shares

2. Quoted shares are valued at the lower of

    (a) One quarter up on lower quoted closing price

    (b) Midpoint of bargain prices, thus:

	Closing Price	*Bargains*	*Lower*
Shares in A plc	$1088 + \frac{1}{4}(1092 - 1088) = 1089$	$\frac{1088 + 1091}{2} = 1089\frac{1}{2}$	1089
B plc	$295 + \frac{1}{4}(297 - 295) = 295\frac{1}{2}$	295	295
C plc	$60 + \frac{1}{4}(69 - 60) = 62\frac{1}{4}$	$\frac{61 + 63}{2} = 62$	62

Covenanted gift

3. The non-deductible covenanted sum is treated as a specific gift and thus does not bear its own tax (s 38(6)).

Double tax relief

4. Double tax relief is available where tax is charged both abroad and in the UK. For detailed notes see Example 28 explanatory note 6. The relief is given as a reduction of the tax on the relevant property (s 159). In this example therefore the relief reduces the tax on the non-settled part of the estate.

    The additional costs of administering or realising assets abroad may be deducted if shown to be attributable to the situation of the property, up to a maximum of 5% of the value of the property (s 173).

Intestacy rules for dividing estates

5. When a person dies without leaving a will, or leaves a will that does not fully dispose of his estate, then the rules of intestacy apply to the estate not disposed of by will. These rules determine to whom the estate is to be distributed. The inheritance tax rules then determine the amount of tax to be paid, with the amounts allocated to the spouse being exempt transfers. Section 211 provides that the tax payable is to be borne by the residue of the estate as a general testamentary expense. This is subject to s 41, which provides that none of the tax on residue is to fall on any part of the residue that is exempt. Thus, in this example, although the widow's share of the estate is exempt, the tax, if any, on specific legacies must come out of residue and the tax on the residue must be borne wholly by the chargeable part of the estate. The rules for calculating the tax are set out in ss 38 to 42.

6. The rules of intestacy for England and Wales provide that the estate is to be distributed as set out below. The rules applying to the distribution of an estate in Scotland are different and are not reproduced here.

Those surviving	*Those entitled to the estate*
Spouse/civil partner — no issue, parent, brother, sister or issue thereof	Spouse/civil partner absolutely
Spouse/civil partner and issue	Spouse/civil partner takes: (i) Personal chattels (ii) £125,000 (iii) Life interest in ½ of residue Issue share other ½ of residue (on statutory trust to 18) and take spouse's/civil partner's share on his (her) death.
Spouse/civil partner, no issue but parent(s)	Spouse/civil partner takes: (i) Personal chattels (ii) £200,000 (iii) ½ of residue absolutely Parent(s) share ½ of residue absolutely.
Spouse/civil partner, no issue or parents but brothers or sisters of the whole blood (or issue thereof)	Spouse/civil partner takes: (i) Personal chattels (ii) £200,000 (iii) ½ of residue absolutely Brothers and sisters (or their issue) share ½ of residue absolutely
No spouse/civil partner but issue	Issue take all absolutely (held on statutory trust if under 18)

No spouse/civil partner or issue but
    Parent(s)
    Brothers and sisters of the whole blood
    Brothers and sisters of the half blood
    Grandparents
    Uncles and aunts (whole blood)
    Uncles and aunts (half blood)
(Each category takes the whole estate to the exclusion of any later category.)
	
	Take absolutely
	Take absolutely
	Take absolutely
	Take absolutely
	Take absolutely
	Take absolutely

No relatives mentioned above	The Crown

'Issue' means children, grandchildren, great grandchildren etc. Where someone entitled to a share is deceased but has surviving children, the children will take the deceased's parent's share (and so on for grandchildren etc).

From 1 January 1996 a spouse (and since 5 December 2005, a civil partner) does not inherit under the intestacy rules unless he/she survives the deceased by at least 28 days.

I B Smart, aged 62 and in poor health, and his wife aged 55 and in excellent health, were worried about their potential inheritance tax liability on death. They had not made any chargeable transfers. They had two children, John aged 22 who is a director of the family trading company, Smart & Co Ltd, and Jill aged 24, who is married with one child aged 6 months.

Their estates consisted of:

	I B Smart	Mrs Smart
Shares in Smart & Co Ltd	49 shares	49 shares
Freehold offices rented at £10,600 pa to Smart & Co Ltd	£130,000	–
Villa in Spain valued at	£176,000	–

They also owned as joint tenants their private residence, valued at £292,000, and had joint accounts at building societies totalling £196,000.

Mr Smart had recently retired from the family company and was drawing a pension of £40,000 pa. This pension would increase by 3% pa and on his death a 2/3rds pension would be payable to Mrs Smart.

The estimated value of the shares in Smart & Co Ltd is:

100% holding	£1,230 per share
98% holding	£1,224 per share
51% holding	£1,200 per share
49% holding	£1,000 per share
2% holding	£100 per share

There are 100 shares in issue.

No dividends have been declared.

Mr and Mrs Smart wished to continue to live in their main residence but to spend four weeks per year in Spain. They believed that their personal expenditure would require the whole of the rent on the offices as well as the pension but were prepared to forgo the rent on the overseas property of £5,000 pa (rent £500 per week in season). They did not wish to give away any cash.

The wills of Mr and Mrs Smart each provide for the whole of their estates to be left to the surviving spouse for life and on the death of the survivor to be divided equally between the children.

After talking informally to an acquaintance who is a personal finance consultant they attempted to mitigate their liability by Mr Smart giving all of his shares in Smart & Co Ltd to John and the holiday home to Jill, reserving the right to use it rent free when they wished. Both gifts were made on the same day. They did not alter their wills.

Nine months after effecting the above Mr and Mrs Smart were involved in a boating accident in Spain. Mrs Smart died immediately and Mr Smart six weeks later.

Assuming that all values are unaltered and using the current legislation and 2006/07 rates throughout:

(a)   Set out the inheritance tax liabilities on the assumption that Mr Smart had not undertaken the above proposals.

(b)   Set out the inheritance tax liabilities which do arise following his actually having effected the proposals in May 2006.

(c)   Compute the tax liabilities on the assumptions that the following proposals had instead been adopted:

   (i)   Mr Smart to give the Spanish property to Jill.

   (ii)   Mrs Smart to give a 47% interest in Smart & Co Ltd to John.

   (iii)   The freehold office premises to be transferred to Mrs Smart.

(iv)   The building society accounts to be transferred into Mrs Smart's sole ownership.

(v)   Mr and Mrs Smart to pay open market rent of £500 per week when they visit the Spanish property.

(vi)   Each of their wills to provide that on death a discretionary trust should be created for the benefit of the surviving spouse, children and grandchildren, with specific bequests to the trustees of the business property, shares and residue of the estate (the house passing to the spouse by survivorship).

(d)   Compare the tax liabilities in the three situations had the deaths occurred nine years later rather than nine months, all values and tax rates remaining the same.

I B Smart — gifts with reservation

(a) **If proposals had not been implemented**

Death of Mrs Smart	£	£

Estate:
Shares in Smart & Co Ltd (explanatory note 3)

	£	£
49 x £1,224	59,976	
Less: 100% business property relief	59,976	–

½ share of jointly owned assets:

	£	£
Freehold house	146,000	
Building society accounts	98,000	244,000

		£
Not chargeable because of spouse/civil partner exemption – no inheritance tax payable		244,000

Death of Mr Smart

Estate:

	£	£
Freehold house	292,000	
Property in Spain	176,000	
Freehold offices	130,000	
Less: 50% business property relief	65,000	65,000	533,000

Shares in Smart & Co Ltd

	£	£
98 x £1,224 (one half owned by Mr Smart and one half life interest from Mrs Smart)	119,952	
Less: 100% business property relief	119,952	–

	£
Building society accounts	196,000
Estate chargeable to inheritance tax	729,000
Tax payable (at 2006/07 rates) (729,000 – 285,000 = 444,000 @ 40%)	177,600

(b) **If proposals were implemented in May 2006**

Death of Mrs Smart

Exempt as before — all to Mr Smart for life or absolutely as the surviving joint tenant.

Death of Mr Smart

(1) *Charging gift with reservation in death estate and ignoring the gift to Jill*

	£	£
Freehold house	292,000	
Property in Spain (gift with reservation)	176,000	
Freehold offices (no BPR as no control)	130,000	598,000

Shares in Smart & Co Ltd

	£	£
49 x £1,000 (life interest from Mrs Smart)	49,000	
Less: 100% business property relief	49,000	–
Building society accounts		196,000
		794,000

Tax on gifts made within seven years before death

Shares to John

	£
before transfer $\frac{49}{98}$ x (98 x £1,224) =	59,976
after transfer — no shares held	nil
	59,976
Less: 100% business property relief	59,976
	nil

As the shares still qualify for business property relief at 100% no amount is chargeable on death.

Inheritance tax payable on death	Gross £	Tax £
Cumulative transfers within seven years before death	–	–
Estate on death	794,000	203,600*
	794,000	203,600*

(* 794,000 – 285,000 = 509,000 @ 40%)

Tax payable on estate at death (which is the total tax payable as a result of Mr Smart's death, since no tax was payable on gifts within previous seven years) £ 203,600

(2) *Charging gift to Jill and ignoring the value of the gift in the death estate*

Death estate as above		794,000
Less property in Spain		176,000
		£ 618,000

Tax on gifts made within seven years before death

Shares to John as above		–
Property in Spain to Jill		176,000
		176,000
Less: Annual exemptions 2006/07	3,000	
2005/06	3,000	6,000
PETs now chargeable		£ 170,000

No tax payable since 2006/07 threshold is not exceeded.

Inheritance tax payable on death	Gross £	Tax £
Cumulative transfers within seven years before death	170,000	–
Estate on death	618,000	201,200*
	788,000	201,200*

(* 788,000 – 285,000 = 503,000 @ 40%)

Tax payable on estate at death		201,200
Add tax on gifts within previous seven years		–
Total tax payable as a result of Mr Smart's death		£ 201,200

As the first calculation is greater than the second, that is deemed to be the one that determines the tax liabilities. The effect is that the whole of the tax will be payable out of Mr Smart's estate, and borne equally between John and Jill.

(c) **If alternative proposals had been adopted**

Death of Mrs Smart

	£	£
Estate:		
Business property	130,000	
Less: 50% business property relief	65,000	65,000
Freehold house – ½	146,000	
Less: Exempt on devolution to spouse	146,000	–
Shares in Smart & Co Ltd		
2 x £1,200 (related property = 51%)	2,400	
Less: 100% business property relief	2,400	–
Building society accounts		196,000
Chargeable to inheritance tax		261,000

Gifts within seven years before death		Gross £	Tax £

Shares to John

$$\text{before transfer} \quad \frac{49}{98} \times (98 \times \pounds 1,224) = \quad 59,976$$

$$\text{after transfer} \quad \frac{2}{51} \times (51 \times \pounds 1,200) = \quad 2,400$$

	57,576
Less: 100% business property relief	57,576
	nil

	Gross £	Tax £
Cumulative transfers within seven years before death	–	
Estate on death	261,000	–
No tax payable since threshold is not exceeded	261,000	–

Death of Mr Smart

		£
Estate:		
Freehold house		292,000
Shares in Smart & Co Ltd		
49 shares @ £1,000	49,000	
Less: 100% business property relief	49,000	–
		292,000

Gifts within seven years before death			Gross £	Tax £
To Jill				
Spanish property		176,000		
Less: Annual exemptions 2006/07	3,000			
2005/06	3,000	6,000	170,000	–
Cumulative transfers within seven years before death			170,000	–
Estate on death			292,000	70,800*
			462,000	70,800*

(* 462,000 – 285,000 = 177,000 @ 40%)

Tax payable on estate at death   £ 70,800

(d)   **Comparative tax liabilities if deaths had occurred nine years later**

(a)   No change — as above   £ 177,600

(b)   *Original proposals*

If the donor survived the gifts (including the gift with reservation) by more than seven years, there would be no charge to tax on the gifts and therefore the double charges regulations would not apply. The Spanish property would, however, still be included in Mr Smart's estate, so the position would be:

	Gross £	Tax £
Cumulative transfers within previous seven years	–	–
Estate on death (including Spanish property)	794,000	203,600*

*(794,000 – 285,000 = 509,000 @ 40%)

(c)   *Revised proposals*

Mrs Smart

	Gross £	Tax £
Cumulative transfers within previous seven years	–	–
Estate on death	261,000	–

Mr Smart

	Gross £	Tax £
Cumulative transfers within previous seven years	–	–
Estate on death	292,000	2,800

(292,000 – 285,000 = 7,000 @ 40%)

Explanatory Notes

Effect of different scenarios on tax liabilities

1.   This example illustrates that it is possible to increase the liability to inheritance tax by making gifts without considering their tax implications.

The tax liability on the second death if none of the proposals were adopted would amount to £177,600 (nil liability on first death).

If the first proposals were adopted then following the earlier death of Mrs Smart the tax liability on the death of Mr Smart would be increased by £26,000 to £203,600.

Whereas if the second proposals had been adopted then on the first death (Mrs Smart) no tax would be payable and on the second death (Mr Smart) £70,800 would be payable. An overall reduction of £106,800 would arise.

If Mr Smart had predeceased his wife then the tax liabilities under the proposals at (c) would have become:

Mr Smart	£	£
Gifts within seven years before death		
— property to Jill (176,000 – 6,000 annual exemptions)		170,000
Estate on death:		
Shares in Smart & Co Ltd		
49 shares @ £1,200 (related property 51%)	58,800	
Less: 100% business property relief	58,800	–
Freehold house —	146,000	
Exempt since devolving on Mrs Smart	146,000	–
		170,000

No tax payable since threshold is not exceeded

	£	£
Mrs Smart		
Gifts within seven years before death (as before)		–
Estate on death:		
Freehold house	292,000	
Office premises	130,000	
Shares in Smart & Co Ltd		
2 x £100	200	
Less: 50% business property relief	100	100
Building society accounts	196,000	618,100
		618,100
Tax payable (618,100 – 285,000 = 333,100 @ 40%)		£ 133,240

Taking both deaths together the tax is £133,240.

Thus the reduction from £177,600 would be £44,360.

In considering how best to mitigate inheritance tax liabilities, one has to remember the continuing need for the income from the business property, and that the personal residence cannot be transferred (except to each other) whilst the Smarts remain in residence (such a transfer would be a gift with reservation and therefore ineffective). However the second proposals would mitigate the potential liabilities regardless of who died first. Furthermore after the earlier death of Mr Smart, Mrs Smart could possibly start to make use of the annual exemption by making gifts to her children or grandchildren if her capital was likely to increase by unspent income.

Transfers to discretionary trust

2.   The amounts transferred to the discretionary trust on the death of Mrs Smart would be potentially liable to further inheritance tax charges, as although she had made no transfers in the seven years before her death, the initial value of the property comprised in the settlement (being the values *before* business property relief) is above the inheritance tax threshold of £285,000, ie:

Business property	130,000
Shares in Smart & Co Ltd	2,400
Building society accounts	196,000
	£ 328,400

A liability will arise if there are any exits from the settlement within ten years. The initial rate applicable to such exits would be arrived at as follows:

(328,400 – 285,000) @ 20% = £8,680, which is an effective rate on £328,400 of 2.643%. The actual rate is 30% of the effective rate, ie 30% of 2.643% = 0.7929%.

The initial rate would be $0.7929\% \times \dfrac{x}{40}$

where x is the number of complete quarters since the creation of the settlement.

A liability at or after ten years would only occur if the assets increased in value to the extent that after business property relief their value exceeded the then threshold (which is usually increased annually by at least the rate of inflation). For detailed notes on discretionary trusts see Examples 59 to 63, particularly Example 62 explanatory note 5.

In the event that the property was appointed absolutely to the beneficiaries within two years after death (following the later death of Mr Smart) it will be deemed to have been transferred by Mrs Smart under her will (s 144) and no further tax would be payable. See Example 63 explanatory note 5.

Related property; valuations for capital gains tax

3.   The related property rules apply to the shares in Smart & Co Ltd and accordingly it is necessary to look at the appropriate proportion of the value of the combined holdings of Mr and Mrs Smart before and after the transfer. Furthermore the entitlement to business property relief depends on the total related shares held by Mr and Mrs Smart (but not the discretionary settlement). Business property relief is not available on the office premises if the combined holding drops below 51%. See Examples 10, 22 and 26 for the related property rules and Example 25 for the rules relating to business property relief.

The related property provisions are not relevant for capital gains tax. For capital gains tax purposes, the value of an asset in the hands of a beneficiary is its open market value at the date of death (TCGA 1992 s 62). It is, however, provided by TCGA 1992 s 274 that if the value of an asset has been *ascertained* for inheritance tax, the same value applies for capital gains tax. But if shares qualify for 100% business property relief, their value will not require to be ascertained for inheritance tax, so that the normal open market value rule will apply for capital gains tax. The beneficiary's acquisition value may thus be lower than the inheritance tax value, since it will be based on the number of shares held by the beneficiary in isolation. See Example 38 explanatory note 1 for further comments on this point.

Gifts with reservation

4.   FA 1986 s 102 and Sch 20 provide in respect of gifts on or after 18 March 1986 that if an asset is transferred and

(a)   possession and enjoyment of the property is not bona fide assumed by the donee at or before the beginning of the relevant period, (ie the period beginning seven years before the donor's death or on the date of the gift if later) or

(b)   at any time in the relevant period the property is not enjoyed to the entire exclusion, or virtually to the entire exclusion, of the donor and of any benefit to him by contract or otherwise,

then the gift is treated as property within the donor's estate as at the date of death.

The gifts with reservation provisions do not apply if or to the extent that the transfer is covered by one of the following inheritance tax exemptions (as to which see Example 1):

—   transfers between spouses/civil partners (s 18)

—   small gifts (s 20)

—   gifts in consideration of marriage or registration of a civil partnership (s 22)

—   gifts to charities (s 23)

—   gifts to political parties (s 24)

—   gifts to housing associations (s 24A)

—   gifts for national purposes etc (s 25)

—   maintenance funds for historic buildings (s 17)

—   employee trusts (s 28).

If it can be shown that the property ceased to be subject to a reservation prior to death then the donor is treated as making a potentially exempt transfer of the property at the time that the reservation ceased (FA 1986 s 102(4)). Such a transfer could not be reduced by annual exemptions.

The initial gift is still a transfer of value, although it may be potentially exempt (after deducting available annual exemptions). If it is potentially exempt then it will not be charged to tax if the donor survives seven years.

These provisions are illustrated in the example. The proposed gift of the Spanish property to Jill will not remove the property from Mr Smart's chargeable estate if Mr and Mrs Smart continue to use the property rent free. If, however, the gift was made nine years before Mr Smart's death as in part (d) of the example, the gift would escape tax, but the value of the property would be brought into his estate if the reservation was not released. If say he had released the reservation between three and four years before his death he would be treated as making a further potentially exempt transfer to Jill equal to the value of the property at that time (not reduced by any annual exemptions) and following his death tax would be charged, subject to tapering relief of 20%, but the value of the property would be excluded from his estate.

An exception to the gifts with reservation rules is made when either

(i) full consideration is given for any right of occupation or enjoyment retained or assumed by the donor and the property is land or chattels, or

(ii) in the case of land, the donor later occupies the property as a result of a change of circumstances that was unforeseen at the time of the original gift and the benefit provided by the donee to the donor only represents reasonable provision for the care and maintenance of an elderly or infirm relative.

Thus the occupation by Mr and Mrs Smart of the Spanish property at full rent would be sufficient to nullify the reservation of benefit, as would any occupation rent free by Mr Smart after the boating accident.

Continuing gifts made under the terms of a regular premium insurance policy effected before 18 March 1986 are not caught by the gifts with reservation rules, unless the policy is altered after that date.

There are special rules to provide for the benefits reserved to be followed through when the original property is substituted by replacement property, with appropriate adjustments if the donee provides consideration.

5. The gifts with reservation legislation was strengthened following the decision in Ingram v CIR (1999). The House of Lords held that the rules did not apply to Lady Ingram, who created a rent-free lease for herself of her freehold property and then gave away the freehold.

   Under FA 1986 ss 102A, 102B and 102C, gifts of interests in land or shares of interests in land made on or after 9 March 1999 will be treated as gifts with reservation if there is some significant interest, right or arrangement which enables or entitles the donor to occupy the land to a material degree without paying full consideration.

6. The provisions do not apply where the gift is covered by one of the inheritance tax exemptions listed in note 4, nor where exception (i) or (ii) in note 4 applies. Nor do they apply where, despite some negligible benefit retained, the donor is virtually excluded from any enjoyment of the land, or to gifts made more than seven years after the interest etc was created, or where the donor cannot occupy or enjoy the land until the interest given away expires (for example when a lease terminates).

7. Where there is a gift of an undivided share of an interest in land, the donor and donee may both occupy the land providing the donor receives no other benefit at the donee's expense in connection with the gift (ie the donee pays no more than his fair share of the outgoings) (s 102B(4), giving effect to existing Revenue practice as stated in their letter of 18 May 1987 to the Law Society Gazette following a ministerial statement in Standing Committee G on 10 June 1986).

8. For further comments on gifts with reservation relating to land see Example 23. For the interaction of the gifts with reservation provisions and business and agricultural property relief, see Example 25 explanatory note 9.

Pre-owned assets

9. With effect from 6 April 2005 where a potential inheritance tax liability does not arise under the gifts with reservation provisions a free-standing income tax charge will apply to the benefit of using an

asset that was formerly owned by the taxpayer. A similar charge will apply to the use of assets at low cost or to the use of assets purchased with funds provided by the taxpayer. The charge applies to tangible and intangible assets. For details see Example 23.

Relief for double charges

10. Making a gift with reservation as outlined in notes 4 and 5 is one of the occasions within the inheritance tax legislation where it is possible to get a double charge to tax. There are regulations to eliminate such double charges (SI 1987/1130). The operation of the regulations for gifts with reservation where the original gift was potentially exempt is illustrated in the example. See Example 20 for the other occasions when double charges arise and the detailed provisions of the regulations and Example 23 for interaction with the pre-owned assets provisions.

More than one double charge

11. Now that most lifetime transfers are potentially exempt, there will be few occasions in practice where the double charges regulations will come into effect. The regulations are very complex, and even so they do not cover the possibility of a single donor being affected by more than one occasion of double charge, such as for example if Mr Smart had made a cash gift to his daughter, in addition to the gift with reservation, and the daughter had then made a loan back to Mr Smart. No guidance has been given on the procedure to be followed in such a case.

Same day transfers

12. Where transfers that are or become chargeable transfers are made on the same day, the annual exemption is apportioned between them (s 19(3)(b)) even if one of the transfers was chargeable immediately and the other was potentially exempt. For detailed notes on this point, see Example 24 explanatory note 1.

Capital gains implication of gifts with reservation

13. Where there are gifts with reservation, not only is the inheritance tax chargeable on the higher of the two bases as indicated in the example, but for capital gains tax the tax-free uplift to market value on death does not apply. Instead the donee's capital gains tax cost will be the market value at the date of the gift plus taper relief from that date (subject to any available holdover relief claims).

(a)   Albert, a bachelor aged 70, sold his business for cash in the 1990s and subsequently carried out the following:

May 2000   Gave his younger sister Beryl cash of £142,000 (no previous gifts having been made)

June 2000   Created a discretionary trust with cash of £246,500, the trustees paying any tax due. The potential beneficiaries of the trust were his brothers and sisters and their children.

In June 2001 Beryl died. During her lifetime she had made an unsecured interest-free loan of £136,000 to her son's business. On her death she left to Albert the debt due from her son.

In July 2006 Albert died, leaving an estate of £317,000, including the £136,000 debt due from his nephew's business.

Calculate the tax payable as a result of Albert's death.

(b)   In July 2006 Andrew died, aged 87. He had been a widower for many years and had supported his only grandson Barry in his business ventures. In May 2002 Andrew had made a gift of £166,000 to Barry to help launch a new product in his business.

In June 2002 Andrew had created a discretionary trust with cash of £286,000, including as beneficiaries his only daughter Clarice, her children and Barry's children. The trustees paid any tax due.

In June 2003 Andrew was taken ill and had to move into a nursing home. He sold his house and received a loan from Barry of £100,000 to help fund the fees.

In July 2006 the value of Andrew's estate was £50,000, excluding the debt of £100,000 to Barry.

Calculate the tax payable as a result of Andrew's death.

Double charges regulations

(a) **Tax payable as a result of Albert's death**

Lifetime gifts		£	£
May 2000 Gift to Beryl			142,000
Less: Annual exemptions	2000/01	3,000	
	1999/2000	3,000	6,000
Potentially exempt transfer			136,000

		Gross £	Tax on 2000/01 scale £
June 2000 Gift to discretionary trust		246,500	2,500*

(* 246,500 – 234,000 = 12,500 @ 20%)

Tax payable by trustees	£ 2,500

On death of Albert — July 2006

(1) *Including loan inherited from Beryl in Albert's estate and ignoring gift to Beryl in May 2000*

		Gross £	Tax on 2006/07 scale £
June 2000	Gift to trust	246,500	–
July 2006	Estate on death	317,000	111,400*
		563,500	111,400*

(* 563,500 – 285,000 = 278,500 @ 40%)

Tax payable by trust	–
(No repayment of tax of £2,500 paid at time of gift)	
Tax payable by estate	111,400
Total tax payable	£ 111,400

(Note that if Albert had died earlier than June 2006, ie less than five years after Beryl's death, quick succession relief would have been available by reference to the tax paid in Beryl's estate on the £136,000 left to him by Beryl — see Example 21.)

(2) *Including gift to Beryl in May 2000 and ignoring value of gift back in Albert's estate*

		Gross £	Tax on 2006/07 scale £
May 2000	Gift to Beryl	136,000	–
June 2000	Gift to trust	246,500	39,000*
		382,500	
July 2006	Estate at death (excluding £136,000 loan)	181,000	72,400
		563,500	111,400

(* 382,500 – 285,000 = 97,500 @ 40%)

		Gross £	Tax on 2006/07 scale £
Tax payable by Beryl's estate on gift from Albert			–
Tax payable by trust		39,000	
Less tapering relief 80% (6 to 7 yrs)		31,200	
		7,800	
Less tax already paid at time of gift		2,500	5,300
Tax payable by Albert's estate			72,400
Total tax payable as a result of Albert's death			£ 77,700

As (1) shows the higher amount of tax payable, that calculation is used to calculate the tax liabilities (see explanatory note 4).

(b) **Tax payable as a result of Andrew's death**

Lifetime gifts		£	£
May 2002 — Gift to Barry			166,000
Less: Annual exemptions	2002/03	3,000	
	2001/02	3,000	6,000
Potentially exempt transfer			160,000

		Gross £	Tax on 2002/03 scale £
June 2002 Gift to discretionary trust		286,000	7,200*
(* 286,000 – 250,000 = 36,000 @ 20%)			
Tax payable by trustees			£ 7,200

On death of Andrew — July 2006

(1) *Excluding £100,000 of May 2002 gift and not deducting debt in Andrew's death estate*

		Gross £	Tax on 2006/07 scale £
May 2002	Gift to Barry	160,000	
Less amount subsequently lent back		100,000	
		60,000	
June 2002	Gift to trust	286,000	24,400*
		346,000	
July 2006	Estate at death	50,000	20,000
		384,000	44,400
(* 346,000 – 285,000 = 61,000 @ 40%)			
Tax payable by trust		24,400	
Less tapering relief 40% (4 to 5 yrs)		9,760	
		14,640	
Less tax already paid at time of gift		7,200	7,440
Tax payable by estate			20,000
Total tax payable as a result of Andrew's death			£ 27,440

(2)   *Charging full gift in May 2002 and allowing debt as a deduction in Andrew's death estate*

		Gross £	Tax on 2006/07 scale £
May 2002	Gift to Barry	160,000	–
June 2002	Gift to trust	286,000	64,400*
July 2006	Estate at death (50,000 – 100,000, see note 7)	–	–
		446,000	64,400

(* 446,000 – 285,000 = 161,000 @ 40%)

Tax payable by trust	64,400	
Less tapering relief 40% (4 to 5 yrs)	25,760	
	38,640	
Less tax already paid at time of gift	7,200	31,440
Total tax payable as a result of Andrew's death		31,440

The second calculation shows the higher amount of tax payable, therefore that is the calculation used to compute the tax liability.

Explanatory Notes

Relief for double charges

1.   There are several occasions within the inheritance tax legislation where it is possible to get a double charge to tax. Double charges occur where there are gifts with reservation, under the pre-owned asset rules, where there are 'mutual transfers' (ie where a gift is made and the donee makes a gift back), and where a gift is made and the donee then lends money to the donor. The debt is disallowed in the donor's estate at death.

A debt is only deductible from an estate if

(i)   it was incurred for full consideration and wholly for the benefit of the deceased, and

(ii)   it is not connected with any gifts received directly or indirectly by the lender from the deceased. (However this restriction does not apply if it can be shown that the loan was not made out of the property derived from the deceased and was not facilitated by the deceased's gifts.)

If a borrower repays a loan which would otherwise not be a deductible loan he is treated as making a potentially exempt transfer of the amount repaid at the time of repayment (FA 1986 s 103).

2.   Regulations have been made under the authority of FA 1986 s 104, by SI 1987/1130, to eliminate double charges. In each case two calculations are made, and the calculation that produces the higher amount of tax is the one used. If both produce the same amount of tax, the first calculation stipulated in the regulations is treated as producing the higher amount and is thus the calculation used to determine the liabilities. Whether or not the total amount of tax works out the same, the burden of the tax may fall on different people (see note 4 below).

Double charges relief for gifts with reservation

3.   A lifetime gift with reservation may be either potentially exempt, for example the gift of a house while reserving the right to live in it, or immediately chargeable, for example where a gift is made to a discretionary trust in which the donor is a beneficiary. The method laid down in the double charges regulations for gifts with reservation is firstly to charge the gift with reservation in the deceased's estate and ignore the lifetime transfer. The second calculation is to charge the lifetime transfer and leave the gift with reservation out of the deceased's estate. If the gift was a chargeable transfer on

which inheritance tax had been paid when it was made, and the first calculation produces the higher figure, the tax paid in lifetime is deducted from the tax payable on death (but not exceeding the part of the death tax payable that relates to that transfer).

The rules are illustrated in Examples 19, 24 and 32.

Double charges relief for pre-owned assets

4.   Where a taxpayer has a liability to income tax under the pre-owned assets rules (see Example 23 and Tolley's Taxwise I 2006/07) and elects to eliminate that charge by deeming the gifts with reservation provisions for inheritance tax to apply, then, a double charge to inheritance tax could arise. This would occur if the taxpayer died within seven years of the original gift. Tax would arise on the original potentially exempt transfer, and also on the property subject to the reservation. As in note 3 two calculations are made. The first is to charge the gift with reservation in the deceased estate and ignore the lifetime transfer. The second calculation charges the lifetime gift and excludes the value of the reservation. The higher tax liability applies.

These provisions only apply where both the lifetime gift and the reservation relate to the same individual. Therefore, where in certain schemes, such as "Eversden", one spouse or civil partner makes the lifetime gift, but the election under the pre-owned asset rules places the property in the estate of the other spouse or civil partner, no double charge relief is available.

Double charges relief for gift and gift back

5.   With regard to a gift and gift back where the first gift was initially potentially exempt but then becomes chargeable, the regulations provide for the first calculation to include the gift back in the estate of the original donor and ignore the potentially exempt gift, and the second calculation to charge the potentially exempt gift and ignore the value of the gift back in the hands of the original donor.

This is illustrated in part (a) of the example in relation to the gift by Albert to Beryl and her bequest to him of the debt owing from her son. The first calculation showed the higher amount of tax payable, so that calculation was used to calculate the tax liabilities.

Note how the incidence of tax may vary:

	Calculation 1	*Calculation 2*	*Saving/(Loss)*
	£	£	£
Payable by trust	–	5,300	5,300
Payable by estate	111,400	72,400	(39,000)

Double charges relief for gift and loan back

6.   Where a gift is made, followed by a loan to the donor by the donee, with the donor dying within seven years when the debt is still outstanding, the first calculation under the regulations is to ignore the debt and the part of the gift equal to the loan. The second is to charge the gift and also allow the debt. This is illustrated in part (b) of the example, where the second calculation (charging the full gift to Barry and allowing the debt to Barry as a deduction in Andrew's estate) showed the higher amount of tax payable and was thus used to calculate the tax liabilities. Where the first calculation shows the higher amount, credit may be due for all or part of any tax paid on the gift in lifetime.

7.   Normally Andrew's estate would be considered to be insolvent as the debt to Barry exceeds the available assets. This does not prevent a liability to inheritance tax arising on earlier gifts as that charge is made on the donees. The rules relating to gifts followed by subsequent loanbacks are designed to prevent avoidance of tax by the making of potentially exempt transfers at a time when death is very unlikely within seven years (and therefore term assurance is very cheap) followed by a loan of a similar amount thus removing assets from the tax computation whilst retaining effective control of both the capital and the income arising therefrom.

More than one double charge

8.   The double charges regulations do not cover the possibility of a single donor being affected by more than one double charge, and no guidance has been given as to the procedure to be followed.

Transfers to trusts

9.   Where transfers are made to most trusts (before 22 March 2006, only discretionary trusts), tax liabilities may arise within the trust if there are any exits from the trust within ten years. For details see Examples 59 to 63. There will be no such liabilities in this example, since the transfers in both parts (a) and (b) were of cash and were below the nil threshold at the death of the donor.

On 6 April 2002 Basil made gifts to his brothers Simon and Charles of £138,000 each.

Basil died on 26 November 2004 leaving an estate of £200,000.

By his will he provided for a legacy to Charles of £90,000 with the residue to Simon.

On 12 March 2005 Simon died. His estate was valued at £300,000 including the residuary legacy from Basil. He left the whole of his estate to his surviving brother Charles.

Charles died on 10 May 2007 when his estate was worth £457,000.

Compute the tax payable by the personal representatives of each of the brothers on the assumption that none of the brothers had made any lifetime transfers other than those stated.

Note that in 2007/08, inheritance tax will be payable on transfers of value in excess of £300,000.

Death of Basil — 26 November 2004

Tax on gifts made within seven years before death:

		Gross £	Tax on 2004/05 scale £
6 April 2002	Gift to Simon	138,000	
	Gift to Charles	138,000	
		276,000	

Less: Annual exemptions			
2002/03		3,000	
2001/02		3,000	6,000
PETs now chargeable			270,000	2,800*

(* 270,000 – 263,000 = 7,000 @ 40%)

The £2,800 is not reduced by tapering relief since the gifts are within three years before death.

		£
Tax payable —	Simon	1,400
	Charles	1,400
		2,800

Inheritance tax on Basil's Estate

	Gross £	Tax £
Cumulative transfers within seven years before death	270,000	2,800
Estate on death	200,000	80,000
	470,000	82,800

Division of Estate

	£
Pecuniary legacy to Charles	90,000
Inheritance tax	80,000
Balance to Simon	30,000
	200,000

Death of Simon — 12 March 2005

Inheritance tax on death

	Gross £	Tax on 2004/05 scale £
Cumulative transfers within seven years before death	–	–
Estate on death	300,000	14,800*

(* 300,000 – 263,000 = 37,000 @ 40%)

	£	£
Inheritance tax payable:		
Due on estate		14,800
Less: Quick succession relief		

Gift from Basil 6 April 2002

$$60\% \times \frac{133,600}{135,000} \times 1,400 \qquad 1,385$$

Legacy from Basil's estate 26 November 2004

$$100\% \times \frac{30,000}{50,000} \times 20,000 \qquad 12,000 \quad 13,385$$

Inheritance tax payable by personal representatives of Simon		1,415

	£
The estate passing to Charles is:	
Estate	300,000
Less: Inheritance tax	1,415
	298,585

Death of Charles — 10 May 2007

	Gross £	Tax on 2007/08 scale £
Inheritance tax on death		
Cumulative transfers within seven years before death	–	–
Estate on death	457,000	62,800*

(* 457,000 − 300,000 = 157,000 @ 40%)

	£	£
Inheritance tax payable:		
Due on estate		62,800
Less: Quick succession relief		

Gift from Basil 6 April 2002
  Over five years before Charles's death   –

Legacy from Basil's estate 26 November 2004

$$60\% \times \frac{90,000}{150,000} \times 60,000 \qquad 21,600$$

Legacy from Simon's estate 12 March 2005

$$60\% \times \frac{298,585}{300,000} \times 1,415 \qquad 845 \quad 22,445$$

Inheritance tax payable by personal representatives of Charles		40,355

Explanatory Notes

Quick succession relief

1. Where a person dies shortly after receiving a chargeable transfer, the transfer has increased the estate at death and therefore attracts tax in the deceased's estate, as well as having been taxed at the time of the transfer. Relief is provided where the *death occurs* within five years after the chargeable transfer, known as quick succession relief (s 141). There is no requirement to retain the asset obtained by that transfer.

2. The first step is to calculate the tax payable on the original transfer. A potentially exempt transfer becomes a chargeable transfer on the death of the donor within seven years. Although the tax is calculated using the rates applicable at the time of death, the date of transfer is relevant in calculating quick succession relief. The part of the transfer covered by the annual exemption does not bear tax and is therefore excluded from the QSR calculation. As the donee pays the tax on a PET, grossing up is not required.

3. The inheritance tax payable on the death of Basil is a charge on the residue (see Example 5 explanatory note 8). Thus the amount receivable by Simon is the net £30,000. The estate rate is 40% so that the figures to use in the calculation of quick succession relief are a gross legacy of £50,000 (£30,000 x 10/6) with tax paid of £20,000.

4. The total tax on the deceased's estate is reduced by the quick succession relief.

5. Where death occurs within one year of the transfer the relief is 100% of the *tax paid on the previous transfer*, reduced in the proportion of net value transferred to the deceased over the gross chargeable transfer.

    Where the period between transfer and death is over one year, the percentage becomes:

1+ to 2 years	80%
2+ to 3 years	60%
3+ to 4 years	40%
4+ to 5 years	20%

Donee dying before donor

6. If the donee dies before the donor then the original gift will continue to be a potentially exempt transfer at that time. Tax will be charged on the estate of the donee (including the gift) without relief. If the donor subsequently dies within seven years of the original gift then the original gift becomes a chargeable transfer, with the tax payable being a liability of the executors of the donee, and the inheritance tax due on the death of the donee recomputed. Furthermore quick succession relief may then be available. See Example 55 for an illustration of this point.

Quick succession relief on trust property

7. Quick succession relief is also available where there are successive charges within five years on trust property in which there is an interest in possession. The rates of relief are the same as those in note 5 above, with the percentage relief depending on the period between the successive charges (s 141). For a more complex example of quick succession relief, showing the treatment of settled property and giving further detailed notes, see Example 53.

Other double charges reliefs

8. Quick succession relief applies where as in this example successive transfers are charged in the estates of different donors. There are other occasions under the inheritance tax rules where property can be charged twice in the same estate. Regulations have been made by the Board of HMRC under the authority of FA 1986 s 104 to avoid double charges to tax (SI 1987/1130). This will normally be where there are gifts with reservation, pre-owned assets or liabilities are created which are non-deductible debts in calculating inheritance tax (see Example 19).

In order to reduce the potential liability to inheritance tax on his accumulated wealth, Henry, aged 80, proposes the following:

(a)   To sell one of a pair of antique objects to his daughter at its market value of £40,000, and then in a year's time to give her the other of equal value.

The value of the pair is £130,000.

(b)   To sell 2% of his holding of 51% of the shares of Henry Ltd, a property investment company, to John, an unconnected friend, for its market value, then to give the remaining 49% of the shares to his son, Simon, who already holds 35% of the shares.

The market value of the shares in Henry Ltd is:

51%	holding	£800,000
49%	holding	£500,000
15-20%	holding	£100,000
2%	holding	£5,000

(c)   If the scheme in (b) above is unsuitable, Henry proposes giving 2% of his shares to 'Help the Aged', a recognised charity, then to give the remaining 49% of the shares to Simon.

(d)   A further suggestion is that next winter while Henry is on a cruise around the world Henry Ltd should make a rights issue of four shares for every one share held. Henry will not be back until after the issue has been made and will not be able to take up his entitlement.

Henry has made cash gifts every year to use up his annual exemption.

Advise him of the inheritance tax effect of each of the above proposals.

(a) **Pair of antiques — sale followed by gift to daughter**

There are two problems in relation to Henry's proposed sale and gift of the two antique objects.

The first is whether the sale at full value to his daughter will itself escape being treated as a transfer of value at that time, since although she would be paying full price for the object, his estate would actually fall by £50,000 (£130,000 – cash received £40,000 and value of remaining object £40,000). A sale at full value is not a transfer of value if it was not intended to confer a gratuitous benefit on anyone and was either made at arm's length (which this transaction is not) or was such as might be expected to have been made at arm's length (s 10). Since the daughter would be paying the full market price, which is the same amount as a stranger would have paid, the transaction will probably not be treated as a transfer of value at that time.

But when Henry gives his daughter the other object the Revenue may use the associated operations rules of s 268 to treat the two events as one. There would then be a potentially exempt transfer on the second occasion of £90,000 (£130,000 – £40,000 cash received) which would become a chargeable transfer if Henry dies within seven years of the gift of the second object.

It would have been better for Henry to sell the pair of objects to his daughter for £40,000 in the first place, because the potentially exempt transfer of £90,000 would then be made one year earlier and the seven year survivorship period would start at that time.

(b) **Shares – sale followed by gift to son**

Again HMRC may use s 268 in determining the inheritance tax position on the gift of shares to Simon. The reason they might do so is that no inheritance tax implications would arise on the sale of shares to John, because in isolation this is a commercial transaction at arm's length and not a transfer of value and on the gift of shares to Simon inheritance tax would ordinarily be payable on death within seven years on a transfer of £500,000 (the value of a 49% holding), whereas but for the earlier sale the transfer would have been valued at the difference between a 51% holding (£800,000) and a 2% holding (£5,000), ie at £795,000.

If HMRC applied s 268 the value transferred to Simon would be as follows:

	£
Value of 51% before first of associated operations	800,000
Value of 0% after second of associated operations	–
	800,000
Less: Cash received (on the sale of the 2% holding)	5,000
Value transferred (potentially exempt transfer)	795,000

(c) **Shares — gift to charity followed by gift to son**

If Henry adopts the alternative of giving 2% of the shares to 'Help the Aged' the related property rules will be applied. These are contained in s 161. The rules provide (inter alia) that where property is transferred to a charity, political party etc by the taxpayer or his spouse/civil partner, such property is related to any other property of the taxpayer and his spouse/civil partner.

The property will continue to be related until five years after it is disposed of by the charity etc.

The value of appropriate parts of the related property is proportionate to the value of all related property, if this produces a higher value than the value of the appropriate part on its own.

Consequently the value transferred by Henry will be:

2% to charity — exempt transfer
49% to son — value before transfer

Own holding	49%	
Related holding	2%	
Value of 51% =		£ 800,000

Henry's 49% holding is therefore worth $\dfrac{49}{51}$ x £800,000 = 768,627

Value of Henry's holding after transfer	nil
Value of transfer (which is a potentially exempt transfer)	£ 768,627

The above computation would apply unless Henry deferred the gift of shares to Simon until five years after 'Help the Aged' had disposed of their shares. If the transfer took place after that time the potentially exempt transfer would be:

Value transferred (49% holding — assuming no change in values)	£ 500,000

(d) **Failure to take up rights shares**

Henry's proposal concerning the rights issue is covered by s 3(3), which provides that the deliberate omission to exercise a right is a transfer of value.

The issue of rights shares in the circumstances outlined would be caught by this subsection.

The value transferred would be:

				£
Value before transfer (51%)				800,000
Value after transfer:				
	Original Shares	*Rights Shares*	*Total*	
Henry	51	–	51	
Son	35	140	175	
Others	14	56	70	
	100	196	296	

Value of $\dfrac{51}{296}$ = 17.23% holding	100,000
Value transferred (potentially exempt transfer)	700,000

Because s 3(3) treats the deliberate omission as a disposition such an act would constitute an actual transfer of value and s 3A would apply treating the transfer as potentially exempt.

There would also be a CGT liability.

Explanatory Notes

Associated operations

1. The associated operations rules are contained in IHTA 1984 s 268. Certain associated operations are specifically covered by other legislation, viz:

   Related property — s 161 (see note 5)
   Omission to exercise a right — s 3(3) (see part (d) of the example)
   Alteration of capital — s 98 (see note 7)

2. One cannot be certain whether the Revenue will seek to use the associated operations rules in any particular case, but IHTA 1984 s 268 covers:

    (i) Two or more operations of any kind affecting the same property or property which represents whether directly or indirectly that property, or income arising from that property, or property representing accumulations of such income (s 268(1)(a)).

    (ii) Any two operations of which one is effected with reference to the other, or with a view to enabling the other to be effected, or facilitating its being effected and any further operation having a like relation to any of those two and so on (s 268(1)(b)).

    The operations might be effected by the same person or different persons and might or might not be simultaneous (s 268(1)).

    'Operation' includes an omission (s 268(1)).

3. Where a transfer of value is made by associated operations carried out at different times, it is treated as made at the time of the last of them (s 268(3)). But where one or more of the earlier operations also constitutes a transfer of value made by the same transferor, the value transferred by the earlier operations is treated as reducing the value transferred by all the operations taken together, except to the extent that the earlier operations were exempt because of the spouse transfer rules (s 18) but all operations taken together were not so exempt (s 268).

Series of settlements

4. The taxpayer was successful in the Court of Appeal, in the case of Rysaffe Trustee Co (CI) Ltd v IRC 2003 in contending that the associated operations provisions did not apply where five separate identical settlements were created on five separate dates within the same month (see Example 62 explanatory note 12).

Interaction of associated operations and related property provisions

5. HMRC Capital Taxes have indicated (in correspondence with Butterworths Tolley – see Taxation 15 February 1996) how the related property and associated operations provisions would interact where assets were transferred in stages, with some being routed via a spouse (or, now, a civil partner). The example illustrated is of a set of four antique chairs, of which two are given by husband to wife, and each then gives one to their son in successive years. The related property rules would value each of the first transfers to the son at half of the value of the set of four less half the value of a set of two, and the second transfers at half the value of a set of two, thus bringing into account the whole of the value of the set of four, half being a transfer by the husband and the other half a transfer by the wife.

    If the associated operations rules were invoked at the time the son became the owner of the set, the transfers by the wife would be treated as made by the husband (and so would not be taken into account in her own inheritance tax calculations). The overall effect would be the same in terms of the value transferred, but the whole of the transfer would affect the husband's estate.

    See Example 23 for other illustrations of associated operations.

Grant of a lease

6. The granting of a lease for full consideration in money or money's worth is not associated with any operation effected more than three years after the grant (s 268(2)).

    By granting a lease, even for full value, a property owner restricts his rights over that property. If he were then to make a gift of those rights (ie the right to receive the rent under the lease and the freehold reversion) the full value of both rights might be less than that of the unencumbered freehold. He might therefore first grant a lease followed by a gift, instead of giving the freehold out of which the donee could grant the lease.

    The associated operations rules will not apply if the gift is more than three years after the grant of the lease.

Alteration of rights re shares

7.   If, instead of a rights issue being made that is available equally to all shareholders, the unquoted share or loan capital of a close company is altered (or there is any alteration in the rights attaching to such shares or debentures) then s 98 applies. This provides that such a change is to be treated as a disposition made by the participators. Such a transfer cannot be a potentially exempt transfer (s 98(3)).

Where there are deferred shares, an alteration of rights within s 98(1)(b) takes place when the deferred shares come to rank equally, or become merged, with shares of another class.

Business property relief

8.   Business property relief is not available on the shares in Henry Ltd because it is a company that invests in land and buildings (s 105(3)).

Gifts with reservation etc

9.   In addition to the associated operations legislation donors must also be fully aware of the rules relating to gifts with reservation and the treatment of certain debts. These are illustrated in Examples 19, 20 and 23.

A. Lucton, a widower aged 80, lives with his unmarried and only daughter Frances at 1 Hayseech, a bungalow currently valued at £250,000.

His only other asset of significance is £300,000 invested in a building society account.

He has already made a transfer of £80,000 in the last but one tax year, £6,000 of which was covered by annual exemptions and the balance of £74,000 was a potentially exempt transfer.

He is conscious that the value of the bungalow is likely to increase, thus worsening the potential inheritance tax position upon his death, when the bungalow is to devolve upon Frances.

Three schemes have been suggested to him for the mitigation of inheritance tax:

(a) That the bungalow is given to Frances now, but that he continues to live in it with her, since at least this would ensure that whilst the gift less the annual exemption would be a chargeable transfer if he died within seven years, future growth would be in the hands of Frances and not his own.

(b) That the bungalow is sold to Frances for its current market value but that the purchase price would be left on loan to her. Lucton would then waive £3,000 of the loan each year, the waiver being covered by his annual exemption for inheritance tax.

(c) That the bungalow is retained by Lucton and instead £300,000 in cash is given to Frances. As Lucton would then have no liquid assets, Frances would each year lend £20,000 to Lucton to enable him to maintain his present lifestyle.

Discuss whether any of these schemes will be successful in mitigating inheritance tax.

B. A wealthy client, Mr Douglas, who is *not* a farmer, has been involved in the following transactions during the current tax year. All land has been owned by Mr Douglas for more than ten years.

(a) He divided his land at Ambridge into Upper and Lower Ambridge. He gave Lower Ambridge to his son Kirk and he and Kirk commenced to use the two properties in partnership. None of the land is partnership property.

(b) He granted a lease of Green Gables at a nominal rent to his wife and himself as tenants in common; he then gave the freehold reversion to his daughter Anne. Thereafter he occupied Green Gables with his wife.

(c) He granted a landlord's repairing lease of Blackacre at a commercial rent to his wife and himself. He then gave the freehold reversion to Anne.

Explain, with references to statute and case law as appropriate, whether any of these transactions are likely to constitute a gift with reservation for inheritance tax purposes.

C. Mrs Jones, a wealthy widow, wishes to reduce her estates' liability to inheritance tax. In order to do so she gives Catherine, her only daughter, £500,000 in cash in May 2004. Her daughter then buys a property in Cornwall in February 2005 for £700,000. Mrs Jones visits this property and in 2006 decides that she would like to live there each summer, taking up residence on 6th April 2007. For the remainder of the year Mrs Jones continues to live in her London residence. Although Mrs Jones is aged 72 she is in good health and would be expected to live for another 15+ years. She is a 40% income taxpayer. For 2007/08 the annual rental value of the Cornwall property would be £36,000 pa and its open market value on 6 April 2007 is £900,000. Mrs Jones has no legal obligation to contribute towards the costs of that property.

(a) Compute the income tax liability arising based upon the above facts.

(b) Set out any available election to mitigate that charge (assuming that inheritance tax rates and rules remain unchanged).

(c) Explain why the income tax charge arises and set out how long Mrs Jones could spend at the Cornwall property before a pre-owned assets charge arises.

A. **Lucton — proposals to mitigate inheritance tax**

(a) *Gift of property while continuing to live in it*

By continuing to live in the bungalow with Frances, Lucton will be retaining a benefit from the gift.

In order to make an effective transfer it is necessary to show that the subject matter of the gift is enjoyed to the entire or virtually the entire exclusion of the donor and of any benefit to him by contract or otherwise. The transfer of ownership to Frances, with Lucton continuing to live there, would not, therefore, be a viable way of mitigating the inheritance tax position, since in the case of land or a chattel the actual occupation or possession is only disregarded if it is made for full consideration.

In this case no consideration is proposed. If a full rent was paid by Lucton for his occupation of the bungalow this could give rise to a charge to income tax on Frances (subject to any 'rent a room' relief) and could also affect her capital gains exemption in respect of owner occupation of the bungalow.

Occupation of land is also disregarded where the occupation by the donor results from a change of circumstances arising since the time of the gift, being a change which was unforeseen at that time and was not brought about by the donor to save inheritance tax. Furthermore the occupation must occur at a time when the donor has become unable to maintain himself through old age or infirmity and must represent a reasonable provision by a donee who is a relative for the care and maintenance of the donor. Clearly Lucton would not qualify under this heading as he already occupies the bungalow and will continue to live there.

The original transfer to Frances, less the current and previous years' annual exemptions, will be a potentially exempt transfer, becoming chargeable if Lucton dies within seven years. As a gift with reservation the property will, however, continue to form part of Lucton's estate. The value of the property will only be taken out of Lucton's estate if it ceases to be property subject to a reservation. In that event Lucton would be deemed to make a potentially exempt transfer to Frances equal to the value of the property at that time, in addition to the potentially exempt transfer made when he gave her the property (and without the benefit of any annual exemptions). There are regulations to eliminate any double tax charge.

If Lucton made a gift of an *undivided share of the bungalow* to Frances and both she and Lucton continue to live at 1 Hayseech then the reservation of benefit rules will not apply provided the gift is unconditional and there is no collateral benefit to Lucton (see Example 19 explanatory note 7). The payment by Frances of Lucton's share of the running costs would be such a benefit.

(b) *Sale of property with purchase price left on loan*

If the bungalow were sold to Frances at its current market value, the purchase price being left on loan to her and then waived at £3,000 per annum, HMRC would probably argue that the associated operations rules should apply.

This means that the value at the time of the last waiver would have to be ascertained and any excess of that value over the value at the time of the actual transfer would be treated as a potentially exempt transfer at the time of the last of the waivers.

Thus, the mitigation of the potential inheritance tax liability by disposing of an appreciating asset for its present value in consideration for a non-appreciating loan debtor would be negated. The annual exemptions will, however, have been used against any waivers, avoiding them being wasted if there was no other facility for using them, and effectively limiting the potential chargeable transfer to the increase in value between the time of the last waiver and that of the actual transfer (the amount of the debt not waived at the time of death would itself form part of the estate). However in view of Lucton's age, it is probable that most of the value will fall to be charged to inheritance tax on death.

The fact that interest on the loan was or was not charged does not apparently affect HMRC's attitude.

(c)   *Cash gift followed by loans back*

The gift of £300,000 cash by Lucton to Frances less the current and previous years' annual exemptions totalling £6,000 would be a potentially exempt transfer provided possession and enjoyment is fully assumed by Frances. This means that there would be no immediate liability to tax. If Lucton died within seven years of his earlier potentially exempt transfer of £74,000, tax would be payable on the gift to Frances, unless the nil threshold had in the meantime increased above £368,000 (ie £294,000 + £74,000). Tapering relief would reduce any tax payable if Lucton survived the gift to Frances by three years, and after seven years the gift would cease to be potentially liable to tax.

However, if Lucton retains a benefit by way of contract or otherwise the gift is negated. If the amount repaid to Lucton is by way of loan then this will also affect the position, as any debt incurred after 17 March 1986 that arises from a disposition made by the borrower will not be a deductible debt on death. (But if, as is implied, Lucton uses the £20,000 cash each year to support his lifestyle, he will not have accumulated that money as savings upon which inheritance tax could be levied.) Furthermore any repayment of that debt by Lucton will be a further transfer, albeit potentially exempt.

If the amounts paid to him by Frances after his gift to her could be treated as a disposition made in favour of a dependent relative for his reasonable care and maintenance they would not be a transfer of value by Frances (s 11(3)), and may not be regarded by HMRC as a reservation of benefit to Lucton.

B.   **Douglas — land transactions**

(a)   *Gift of land subsequently used by partnership of donor and donee*

Unless the use of Lower Ambridge by Mr Douglas (through the partnership) is for full consideration then the transfer would appear to be a gift with reservation, as the property is not enjoyed to the entire (or virtually entire) exclusion of the donor (FA 1986 s 102). If, however, the two properties are of similar value and profit sharing and capital sharing ratios are equal, then full consideration would appear to be given and the gifts with reservation rules and pre-owned asset provisions would not apply (FA 1986 Sch 20.6).

All of the relevant circumstances would have to be taken into account to determine full consideration. These would include profit shares, values, actual input to the partnership and any actual rent paid.

(b)   *Division of asset followed by gift of part*

Where a donor splits an asset into parts and then makes a gift of the whole of a part without retaining an interest in that part then the gifts with reservation rules have previously been avoided. In this example Mr Douglas has divided Green Gables into a leasehold interest and a freehold reversion and then given the freehold reversion to his daughter Anne. Mr Douglas and his wife continue to occupy Green Gables under the leasehold interest.

Until FA 1999 this would have been outside the rules for gifts with reservation, although unless the grant of the lease and the subsequent gift of the freehold reversion were independent transactions, the Revenue might have sought to use the associated operations rules of s 268 to say that the grant of the lease and the gift of the freehold reversion were a single transaction occurring at the time of the gift of the freehold, so that the lease at a nominal rent would be a benefit retained by Mr Douglas. Under FA 1986 s 102A, from 9 March 1999 it is no longer possible to avoid the gifts with reservation rules by taking a leasehold interest and giving away the freehold (see explanatory note 6). Mr Douglas's gift of the freehold of Green Gables to Anne will therefore be treated as a gift with reservation.

(c) *Grant of lease followed by gift of freehold*

In giving away a freehold reversion Douglas must not reserve a benefit in that gift. In the case of Nichols v CIR 1975 it was held that where a gift was made of freehold land, subject to an obligation on the donee to grant an immediate lease back and to keep the property in full repair, this amounted to a gift with reservation. But in Mr Douglas's case he is paying a full commercial rent, so it is considered that the daughter's obligation to repair the property would be reflected in the rent and that no benefit would be regarded as having been reserved. The FA 1999 changes referred to in (b) above do not apply where the donor occupies the land to the exclusion of the donee for full consideration.

C. **Mrs Jones – pre-owned assets**

(a) *Income tax liability on pre-owned asset*

Mrs Jones has provided funds of £500,000 which have been used to buy the Cornwall property she now occupies. The appropriate rental value is:

$$£36,000 \times \frac{500,000}{900,000} = £20,000$$

which gives an income tax liability of:

£20,000 @ 40% = £8,000 per annum from 6 April 2007.

(See explanatory note 11)

(b) *Election to mitigate charge*

Mrs Jones could elect by 31 January 2009, by completing form IHT500, that the Cornwall property is not subject to an income tax charge, but instead, for so long as she continues to occupy the property, the relevant proportion of the property value will be treated as part of her estate. The proportion is as above, that is:

$$\frac{\text{Consideration provided by chargeable person (£500,000)}}{\text{Value of property at valuation date (£900,000)}}$$

Valuation date for this purpose is the first date of occupation.

If Mrs Jones ceases to occupy the Cornwall property then, as for a gift with reservation, the appropriate proportion of the value of the property at the date she ceases to occupy will be included in her estate for the following seven years.

(See explanatory note 13)

(c) *Attribution of gift towards property now occupied*

A charge to income tax arises because Mrs Jones has contributed towards a property she now occupies.

An absolute gift of cash is not normally subject to the inheritance tax gifts with reservation provisions. However under the pre-owned asset income tax rules a charge will apply where it is reasonable to attribute the gift as a contribution directly or indirectly, towards the acquisition of the property now occupied. This does not apply if the outright gift of money was made at least seven years before the taxpayer first occupied the premises. For Mrs Jones the period is only 2 years 2 months.

Occupation is a very wide term and could even include usage for storage or sole possession of the means of access linked with occasional use of the property. Incidental usage is not considered to be occupation. This could include:

- Stays not exceeding two weeks each year (one month if the owner is present and it is the owner's residence).

- Social visits that do not include overnight stays.

- Domestic visits eg babysitting the owner's children.

- Temporary stays eg for convalescence after medical treatment or to look after the owner whilst they are convalescing.

However if the property is a holiday home which is only used on an occasional basis by the owner then even occasional visits by the donor could be deemed to be occupational.

It would appear that Mrs Jones wishes to use the Cornwall property for a number of weeks each year. Unless she pays full market rent for that occupation (which would be liable to income tax in the hands of her daughter) she will be liable to a pre-owned asset income tax charge.

If her occupation was for less than one month per year no charge would arise provided her daughter lived in the property as her residence and was present, otherwise occupation could cause the charge to occur.

In practice it would be advisable to pay full market rent for limited occupation of holiday accommodation.

If Mrs Jones is unlikely to occupy the property for more than 2 or 3 years it would be beneficial to elect for inheritance tax to apply as there is a high probability that she would live more than seven years after vacating the property and therefore no tax charge would arise.

If Mrs Jones intends to remain in residence indefinitely it is possible that even 15+ years of charge to income tax would be less than the initial inheritance tax saving of £200,000 (£500,000 @ 40%). The actual inheritance tax payable would, of course, be higher if the value of the property increased over that period. For example if on the death of Mrs Jones the Cornwall property was worth £1,800,000 then the inheritance tax liability on her death in respect of her use of the pre-owned asset would be:

$$1,800,000 \times \frac{500,000}{900,000} = £1,000,000 @ 40\% = £400,000$$

Explanatory Notes

Associated operations

1.   Where a transfer of value is made by associated operations carried out at different times, it is treated as made at the time of the last of them (s 268). For the meaning of 'associated operations' see Example 22.

2.   Where any one or more of the earlier operations also constitutes a *transfer of value* made by the same transferor, the value transferred by the earlier operations is treated as reducing the value transferred by all the operations taken together (s 268).

3.   Thus, the annual waivers in part A (b) of the example, being themselves *transfers of value*, albeit potentially exempt, reduce the value transferred by taking all the operations together. The fact that the waivers are not chargeable does not alter the fact that they were transfers of value (as distinct from chargeable transfers), a chargeable transfer being a transfer of value other than an exempt transfer (s 2(1)).

Ensuring that gifts are properly made

4.   Care should always be taken to ensure that a gift is properly made. Whilst title to certain assets passes by delivery (eg a watch) there are legally proper ways of transferring title to other assets, such

as company shares by a properly constituted and stamped form of transfer and freehold and leasehold properties by deed (and registration where appropriate). An intended but incomplete gift will not therefore be sufficient for tax purposes, although in fact the donee might enjoy the benefit of the gift. If the donor has done all in his power to perfect a gift, an omission by the donee will not make it imperfect for tax purposes (eg if the donor has delivered a properly constituted and stamped share transfer but the donee has failed to have it registered or the company concerned has refused to register it). A cheque only constitutes a valid gift after it has been cleared by the donor's bank, so that if the donor dies before the cheque has been presented the gift is not complete.

In the 2004 case before the Special Commissioners of Sellars & Anor (SpC 401) it was held that where a building society account was changed to the name of a mother and two daughters, but mother was the only person who made transfers into the account and made withdrawals, that the whole of the balance remained in mother's estate even though one third of the interest had been declared for income tax on the returns of each of the daughters. This was held to be a gift with reservation, not an account held as tenants in common.

As far as loan waivers are concerned, HMRC Capital Taxes consider that they are not effective for inheritance tax unless the waiver was effected by deed.

Gifts with reservation

5.   FA 1986 ss 102 and 103 introduced anti-avoidance legislation relating to gifts with reservation and debts, applicable to events occurring on and after 18 March 1986. These rules apply where a donor reserves a benefit from a gift or subsequently enjoys the benefit of the gifted property (eg gift of a house that the donor continues to occupy, or a settlement into a discretionary trust where the settlor is also a beneficiary).

Under these rules a gift with reservation is treated in the same way as any other gift at the time it is made, but special rules apply on the death of the donor. If the reservation was released more than seven years before death then no charge arises on death. If the reservation was released within seven years before death then the gift is taxed as if it had been made at the time of release, on the basis of its value at that time (but without the benefit of any annual exemptions), even though the original gift will also be taxed if it was made within seven years before death. There are regulations to eliminate the double charge to tax. For details see Example 19.

Debts are not deductible from the estate of a deceased person unless they were incurred for full consideration for the deceased's own use or benefit and were not created out of property derived from the deceased as a transfer of value or part of an associated operation. Again there are regulations to prevent double charges to tax, which are dealt with in Example 20.

6.   In relation to gifts of land, the gifts with reservation rules are extended by FA 1986 ss 102A, 102B and 102C. The background to the legislation is the 1999 House of Lords' decision in Ingram v CIR and the effect of old estate duty law on the inheritance tax provisions.

Some of the estate duty cases drew very fine distinctions. In Chick v Commissioners of Stamp Duties of New South Wales 1958, a farmer had made a gift of grazing land to his son in 1934 and in 1935 the land was brought into a partnership in which the farmer was a partner. The farmer was deemed to have reserved a benefit in the land because of his partnership interest. The Chick case was followed by legislation under which no reservation was assumed if the later benefits were only available because of full consideration provided by the donor. In Munro v Commissioners of Stamp Duties of New South Wales 1934, a farmer gave away land but continued as a partner in the family partnership that farmed the land. He was considered not to have given the land itself, but his interest in the land subject to the rights of the partnership, so that no benefit had been retained. The difference between the two cases is that the Chick gift was initially unfettered but the farmer later enjoyed a benefit from the gifted property, whereas the Munro gift was subject to the partnership interest at the time it was made. It was stated by Lord Simonds in St Aubyn v AG 1952 that a donor does not bring himself within the provisions 'by retaining something which he has never given'.

This principle was considered in the case of Ingram v CIR, decided by the House of Lords in 1999. Lady Ingram conveyed the freehold of her property to a bare trustee, who then granted a lease to her and conveyed the freehold reversion to a trust for the family. The High Court held that there was no reservation of benefit, although it was also held that someone could not grant a lease to a nominee, since this would amount to contracting with himself. The Court of Appeal held that the lease was a nullity as the interposing of a mere nominee did not alter the fact that Lady Ingram was effectively both landlord and tenant of the property (Rye v Rye 1962). It was also noted that a nominee cannot effectively contract with his principal (following the Scottish case of Kildrummy (Jersey) Ltd v CIR 1990). This was overruled by the House of Lords, where it was held that 'if the benefits which the donor continues to enjoy are by virtue of property which was never comprised in the gift, he has not reserved any benefit out of the property of which he disposed'. The House of Lords unanimously declined to follow Kildrummy, stating that 'a trustee in English law is not an agent for his beneficiary'.

This decision has led to the changes in the law referred to above where a gift is made of an interest in land (for details see Example 19 explanatory notes 5 to 7).

Pre-owned assets

7.   With effect from 6 April 2005 a free-standing income tax charge applies to the benefit of using an asset that was formerly owned by the taxpayer. A similar charge will apply to the use of assets at low cost or to the use of assets purchased with funds provided by the taxpayer. The charge applies to tangible and intangible assets.

8.   The income tax charge does not apply:

(i)   To property given away before 18 March 1986 (FA 2004 Sch 15.3(2); 15.6(2) and 15.8(2)).

(ii)   If the property was transferred to a spouse/civil partner (or to a former spouse/civil partner under a Court Order) (Sch 15.10(1)(c)). This also applied where the property is held in trust and the spouse/civil partner or former spouse/civil partner has an interest in possession (Sch 15.10(1)(d)).

(iii)   If the property remains within the estate of the former owner under the 'Gift with Reservation' rules (Sch 15.11).

(iv)   If the property was sold by the taxpayer at an arm's length price (Sch 15.10(1)(a)).

(v)   Where the assets of an estate have been redirected by a deed of variation (ss 142–147) then the deed of variation applies to the asset from date of death for the pre-owned asset rules (Schs 15-16).

(vi)   To property transferred into an interest in possession trust for the benefit of the former owner. This is excluded from the income tax charge because the property remains in the estate of the donor for inheritance tax purposes (Sch 15.10). However the exemption ceases when the interest in possession comes to an end (Sch 15.10(2)).

(vii)   Where the gift is of property and the former owner has given part of their interest to someone with whom they share occupation or the former owner needs to move back into the gifted property following changes in circumstances (Sch 15.11(1)). These rules are the same as gift with reservation rules for inheritance tax.

(viii)   The disposal was an outright gift covered by annual exemption, small gifts or was for the maintenance of the family (Sch 15.10(1)(d), (e)).

(ix)   An outright gift of money made more than seven years before the first date of enjoyment of property/chattels acquired with the funds will not be deemed to be consideration (Sch 15.10(2)(c)).

(x)   Use of a commercial equity release scheme.

9. The pre-owned asset charge does not apply in any fiscal year:

    (a) Where the former owner is not resident in the UK, or

    (b) Where the former owner is resident in the UK but domiciled elsewhere for inheritance tax purposes and the property is not UK property, or

    (c) Where the former owner was previously domiciled outside the UK for inheritance tax purposes the charge does not apply to property disposed of before becoming domiciled in the UK (Sch 15.12).

10. The income tax charge applies to the use of land or enjoyment of land, chattels and intangible assets.

    For the charge to apply to land the taxpayer must:

    •   occupy the land (wholly or with others) and either

    •   the disposal condition, or

    •   the contribution condition must apply (Sch 15.3(1)).

    The disposal condition is that after 17 March 1986 the taxpayer owned the relevant property or property the disposal of which has directly or indirectly funded the relevant property and has disposed of all or part of that interest otherwise than by an excluded transaction (see note 8 above).

    The contribution condition is that the taxpayer has since 17 March 1986 contributed directly or indirectly to the purchase of the relevant property otherwise than by an excluded transaction (see note 8 above).

11. The charge for land is calculated by taking the appropriate rental value less any amount that the chargeable person is legally obliged to pay the owner of the relevant land in the period in respect of its occupation. The appropriate rental value is:

$$R \times \frac{DV}{V}$$

where:

R is the rent that might reasonably be expected to be obtained on a year to year letting where tenant pays all rates, charges and council taxes and the landlord bears the cost of repairs, maintenance and insurance.

DV is the contribution by the former owner that can reasonably be attributed to the cost of the relevant property.

If the property, or a property that this property replaced, was previously owned by the taxpayer, it is its value on valuation date. If the taxpayer only owned, or disposed of, a part of the land, it is the relevant proportion of its value.

V is the value of the relevant land at the valuation date.

For example, John gave a property worth £100,000 to his son Peter in 1994. Peter sold the property for £350,000 in 1999 buying a further property for £400,000. John moves into the relevant property in 2006 when it is worth £1,000,000. The contribution that could reasonably be attributed to the gifted property would be:

$$\frac{350,000}{400,000}$$

(being the proportion of the cost of the relevant property funded by John's gift)

That proportion is then applied to the value of the property as at the valuation date of £1,000,000.

$$\frac{350,000}{400,000} \times 1,000,000 = 875,000$$

Contrast this with the example at C where cash was given. In the example the gift of cash is compared with the current value of the property, whereas it would appear that if property is given then the DV value is increased by the increase in value of the property between gift and commencement of enjoyment. Although the legislation is unclear in the case of a cash gift it is difficult to see how any increase in the value attributed to the investment decision of the recipient can be said to be reasonably attributed to the donor of the cash.

Valuation date is set out in SI 2005/724 para 2 being 6 April in the relevant year, or if later the first day in the year on which enjoyment of the asset occurs.

The first valuation date occurs when use commences, and thereafter the valuation date is the first valuation date for a further four years and then the valuation on the previous fifth anniversary.

The income tax payable is calculated by adding the appropriate rental value to the taxable income of the donor.

In the case of chattels the charge is based upon 5% pa of the value of the chattel at valuation day with similar rules to land applying to replacement chattels and cash.

For intangibles a charge only arises where they are held within a settlement and the settler retains an interest. Again the liability is based upon 5% pa of the value at valuation date.

Where the asset is only enjoyed for part of a year the charge is reduced accordingly. There is no charge if open market rent is paid for use of the asset, and the charge is reduced by payments made under a legal obligation for the use of the asset.

12.   If the aggregate notional values before contribution do not exceed £5,000 then this is *de minimus* and there is no charge (Sch 15.13).

There are provisions preventing a double charge to income tax under both the benefit in kind rules and the pre-owned asset rules (Sch. 15.18).

13.   Where a taxpayer is potentially chargeable to income tax by reference to their enjoyment of any land, or chattels, or intangible property for the first time, then they may make an election. The effect of which is that the asset is deemed to be in their estate for inheritance tax and therefore no income tax charge arises. This is a deeming provision, the asset does not actually form part of their estate and therefore there is no uplift in value for capital gains tax when death occurs.

If the taxpayer permanently ceases to have occupation or use and enjoyment of the asset then the gifts with reservation rules apply so that a potentially exempt transfer is deemed to have occurred at the cessation of use. If more than seven years have elapsed since last enjoyment of the asset then no charge arises.

The election is required by 31 January following the end of the fiscal year of first use. If use first commenced in 2005/06 or earlier the election is required by 31 January 2007 (Sch 15.21–23).

Where the whole of the asset would not be attributed to the donor then a similar restriction will apply to the chargeable amount; ie:

Chargeable proportion of Asset Value is:

$$\text{Value} \times \frac{DV}{V}$$

where DV and V have the meaning set out in note 11 above.

Value is at death (if use continues) or at cessation of use if within seven years of death.

14. The charge is intended to penalise users of inheritance tax avoidance schemes, such as the double trust home loan scheme (the intention of which is to remove the value of the principal private residence from the donors' estate but to enable continued use of the property), or, where the full consideration for the use of the asset is negligible as compared with the open market value of the asset.

15. However, the charge will also apply to situations where a taxpayer would not expect a charge to arise. For example where a donor gives away assets (eg cash) and then in the future uses property acquired with those assets without paying a full commercial consideration, and does not fall within any of the exceptions for inheritance tax set out at note 4 (i) or pre-owned asset exceptions at note 8. Previously if the gift was at least seven years before the death of the donor there were no tax consequences. Now an income tax charge will arise.

Example

John gave £300,000 in cash to his daughter, Wendy, on the occasion of her marriage in 2001. She used £200,000 to buy a picture. In May 2006 Wendy moves to Australia on a temporary contract for three years. She leaves the picture with John who hangs it in his hall. The open market value as at May 2006 is £500,000. Wendy returns in May 2009 reclaiming possession of the picture. John is still alive in 2017. Assume an Official Rate of 5% throughout, and that John pays tax at 40%.

The valuation date is May 2006. The charge for 2006/07 is:

$$11/12 \times 5\% \times 500,000 \times \frac{200,000 \text{ (DV)}}{500,000 \text{ (V)}} = 9.166 @ 40\% = £3,666$$

For 2007/08 and 2008/09 a full year's charge of £10,000 @ 40% = £4,000 applies

For 2009/10 the charge is:

$$1/12 \times 5\% \times 500,000 \times \frac{200,000 \text{ (DV)}}{500,000 \text{ (V)}} = 834$$

Tax charged is NIL.

(Amounts below £5,000 are not charged)

The cash/picture cannot be included in John's estate because Wendy took full bona fide possession and enjoyment of the cash in 2001. Because the picture is not included in the estate of John for inheritance tax it is not excluded from the pre-owned asset charge. An income tax charge arises because John has the use of property purchased with funds provided by him within the last seven years.

The income tax charge would be avoided if John elected by 31 January 2008 for gifts with reservation rules for inheritance tax to apply. As he is alive in 2017 no charge would ever arise.

Alternatively John could pay full rental value for the use of the picture. If he is responsible for insurance this could be very low.

16. See also the companion book, Tolley's Taxwise I 2006/07, for calculation of the rate of income tax payable by a donor.

Agnes Brown was a wealthy widow who doted on her nephew Simon. Having not made any gifts previously, she decided in 1999 to begin passing on some of her wealth to Simon and on 17 October 1999 she made a gift to him of a number of investments as follows:

1. 3,000 shares out of her holding of 16,500 shares in Brown Retailing Ltd, a trading company with an issued share capital of 30,000 shares. The other 13,500 shares are already held by Simon.

2. 15,000 shares in Landy plc, which were quoted at 180-188p with marked bargains at 180 and 182p.

On 11 November 2001, following the birth of Simon's first child, Agnes settled her remaining shares in Brown Retailing Ltd on discretionary trust, including herself, Simon and his child amongst the class of beneficiaries.

Feeling that perhaps she had favoured Simon to an unfair extent, she gave £100,000 to her niece Pauline on 21 December 2001.

On 10 March 2002 upon the advice of her professional adviser, she excluded herself from all benefit under the discretionary trust dated 11 November 2001.

An offer of £1 million for the whole of the issued share capital of Brown Retailing Ltd was received on 14 November 2004. This was accepted by all shareholders. The discretionary trust reinvested its proceeds into quoted shares which were all held on 26 September 2007.

Agnes died on 30 September 2006, leaving an estate valued at £700,000 including the following assets:

(i) a 30% holding valued at £50,000 in Blue Ltd, an unquoted investment company;

(ii) a 5% holding valued at £60,000 in Pink plc, a trading company on the Alternative Investment Market;

(iii) a 60% holding valued at £100,000 in Green Ltd, an unquoted investment company; and

(iv) a 40% holding valued at £200,000 in Black Ltd, an unquoted trading company.

Under the terms of her will Agnes added a further £100,000 cash to the discretionary trust. The rest of her estate was divided equally between Simon and Pauline.

On 26 September 2007 the trustees of the discretionary trust appointed £50,000 from the cash received from the executors to Simon on the basis that he was to pay any tax due.

The value of an ordinary share in Brown Retailing Ltd at the relevant times was as follows:

	17.10.99	11.11.01	10.3.02
	£	£	£
75–100%	25	42	40
50–74%	20	31	30
25–49%	15	24	23
0–24%	10	16	15

There are no other relevant transfers of shares in Brown Retailing Ltd.

Calculate the inheritance tax payable in respect of the above events.

Agnes Brown — inheritance tax position in lifetime

	£
17 October 1999	
Gifts to Simon:	
3,000 shares in Brown Retailing Ltd	
16,500 shares at £20 (55% holding)	330,000
13,500 shares at £15 (45% holding)	202,500
Loss to estate	127,500
Less: Business property relief 100%	
(see explanatory note 1)	127,500
Transfer of value	–
15,000 shares in Landy plc @ ½ (180 + 182) = 181p,	
giving transfer of value of	27,150
Less: Annual exemptions 1999/2000 and 1998/99	6,000
Potentially exempt transfer	21,150
11 November 2001	
Settlement on discretionary trust	
13,500 shares in Brown Retailing Ltd	
at £24 per share (45% holding)	324,000
Less: Business property relief 100%	
(see explanatory note 2)	324,000
Transfer of value	–
21 December 2001	
Gift to Pauline	100,000
Less: Annual exemptions 2001/02 and 2000/01	6,000
Potentially exempt transfer	94,000
10 March 2002	
Release of reservation —	
13,500 shares in Brown Retailing Ltd at	
£23 per share (45% holding) – potentially	
exempt transfer (see explanatory note 4)	310,500

On death of Agnes Brown — 30 September 2006

	Gross £	Tax on 2006/07 scale £
Transfers within seven years before death:		
Accumulation in seven years before gift on 17 October 1999*	–	–

17 October 1999
  Gifts to Simon (see explanatory note 1):

		Gross £	Tax on 2006/07 scale £
Shares in Brown Retailing Ltd	122,553		
Shares in Landy plc	26,097		
		148,650	–

Accumulation in seven years before transfer to trust on 11 November 2001 (to calculate additional tax only, cumulative transfers not affected — see explanatory note 2):

		Gross £	Tax on 2006/07 scale £
17 October 1999			
Gift previously potentially exempt		148,650	–
11 November 2001			
Settlement on discretionary trust as above	–		
Add business property relief no longer available (see explanatory note 2)	324,000		
	324,000		
Less: Annual exemptions 2001/02 and 2000/01	6,000	318,000	72,660*
		466,650	72,660

(* 466,650 – 285,000 = 181,650 @ 40%)

As death takes place between 4 and 5 years after the transfer, the tax payable is reduced by 40% to £72,660 x 60% = £ 43,596.

Accumulation in seven years before gift to Pauline on 21 December 2001:

	Gross £	Tax on 2006/07 scale £
17 October 1999	148,650	–
11 November 2001 (see above)	–	–
21 December 2001		
Gift to Pauline (annual exemptions reallocated to trust as above — see explanatory note 2)	100,000	– *
	248,650	– *

(* 248,650 – 285,000 = Nil)

10 March 2002
  Release of reservation — total inheritance tax
  payable will be the higher of:
  (i) Disregarding the original gift and charging the
       potentially exempt transfer on release, or
  (ii) Charging original gift and disregarding
       subsequent potentially exempt transfer.

	Gross £	Tax on 2006/07 scale £
The first calculation would be:		
Accumulation in seven years before gift on 17 October 1999	–	–
17 October 1999 Gift to Simon — as above	148,650	–
11 November 2001 Settlement on discretionary trust — ignored	–	–
21 December 2001 Gift to Pauline — as above	100,000	–
10 March 2002 Release of reservation Potentially exempt transfer now chargeable (13,500 shares @ £23 per share)	310,500	109,660*
	559,150	109,660

(* 559,150 – 285,000 = 274,150 @ 40%)

As death takes place between 4 and 5 years after release of reservation, tax payable is 60% x £109,660 = £65,796

The second calculation is as already calculated above, ie cumulative transfers of £466,650 and tax payable of £43,596

The tax due on death must then be taken into account in both calculations. In the first case, however, the lifetime transfers exceeded the nil threshold at death, so the tax payable on the death estate would be:

	£	£
30 September 2006 — death of Agnes Brown		
Estate on death		700,000
Less: Business property relief		
100% x £60,000 (shares in Pink plc)	60,000	
100% x £200,000 (shares in Black Ltd)	200,000	260,000
		440,000
Tax @ 40%		176,000

In the second case the tax would be:

	Gross £	Tax on 2006/07 scale £
30 September 2006 — death of Agnes Brown — accumulation in seven years before death		
17 October 1999	148,650	–
11 November 2001 (see above)	–	–
21 December 2001	100,000	–
	248,650	–
Estate on death (less business property relief)	440,000	161,460*
	688,650	161,460

(* 688,650 – 285,000 = 403,650 @ 40%)

Total tax payable on lifetime gifts and death is:

First calculation	(65,796 + 176,000)	£241,796
Second calculation	(43,596 + 161,460)	£205,056

The first calculation therefore shows the higher total tax liability, and inheritance tax is therefore payable as follows:

	£
By Agnes Brown on creation of discretionary trust	–
By Simon	–
By Pauline	–
By trustees of discretionary trust	65,796
By personal representatives	176,000
On appointment by discretionary trust to Simon on 26 September 2007	–

(being within two years of death — s 144 — see explanatory note 5)

Explanatory Notes

Same day transfers

1. Where two or more transfers of value are made on the same day, the annual exemption is apportioned between them (s 19(3)(b)). Business property relief is deducted in arriving at the amount of a transfer of value. The treatment of the annual exemption in relation to potentially exempt transfers outlined in Example 1 makes the calculation of the potentially exempt transfers by Agnes Brown in this example particularly difficult. The gift of the shares in Brown Retailing Ltd on 17 October 1999 qualifies for 100% business property relief (see Example 25 part A(c) for rates of business property relief) so that the transfer of value is reduced to nil as shown. On the same day as the gift of the Brown Retailing Ltd shares, Agnes made the gift of the shares in Landy plc, the transfer of value being £27,150, which is not eligible for business property relief. Annual exemptions for 1999/2000 and 1998/99 are therefore allocated to the gift of shares in Landy plc.

   When Agnes Brown died on 30 September 2006, the shares in Brown Retailing Ltd no longer qualified for business property relief. It is understood to be the view of HMRC that the annual exemption should then be reallocated between the gifts as follows:

Brown Retailing Ltd shares	$\dfrac{127,500}{154,650}$ x 6,000	£4,947
Landy plc shares	$\dfrac{27,150}{154,650}$ x 6,000	£1,053

   The revised potentially exempt transfers would then be:

Brown Retailing Ltd shares	127,500	– 4,947	122,553
Landy plc shares	27,150	– 1,053	26,097
			£ 148,650

   Alternatively it could be argued that the original allocation of the annual exemption stands despite the withdrawal of business property relief. The gifts to Simon would then be £127,500 in respect of the shares in Brown Retailing Ltd and £21,150 in respect of the shares in Landy plc. In this instance the tax position is the same in any event, as both gifts were made to Simon and there is no inheritance tax liability. However, if a tax liability arose payable by different persons, this point may be taken. The total gifts to Simon would still amount to £148,650 and this amount is included in subsequent calculations.

Business property relief

2.   For detailed notes on business property relief see Example 25. The relief is not available when calculating the tax on a potentially exempt transfer that becomes chargeable as a result of the donor's death within seven years if the relevant conditions are no longer satisfied (s 113A(1)). Similarly, where business property relief has been given against a transfer that was a chargeable transfer in lifetime, the relief is not available when calculating any additional tax payable as a result of the death of the transferor within seven years unless the conditions for the relief are satisfied at that time (s 113A(2)) (see Example 25 part A(c)). Note that the withdrawal of business property relief on a transfer that was a chargeable transfer in lifetime only affects the calculation of any additional tax payable on that transfer. The original chargeable transfer is taken into account in the accumulation for the purpose of working out the position on later transfers and on the death estate. In this example the original chargeable transfer to the discretionary trust on 11 November 2001 qualified for 100% relief so it did not increase the cumulative total at that time. The cumulative total taken into account in calculating the tax on the later gift to Pauline on page 24.3 therefore shows the 11 November transfer at nil. For a further illustration see the example at page 25.4.

The wording of the legislation supports the view that business property relief is effective immediately to the extent that the original transfer is covered by the annual exemption and that only the balance can be affected by the withdrawal of business property relief if the donor dies within seven years. For transfers on or after 28 November 1995, subsection (7A) was introduced into s 113A, which provides that when applying the rules for withdrawing business property relief on transfers within seven years before death, the relief is disregarded in establishing whether there is a potentially exempt or chargeable transfer. The reason for the change is that it had been contended that a transfer that initially qualified for 100% business property relief became a transfer of nil, and was therefore wholly within the £3,000 annual exempt limit, so no chargeable or potentially exempt transfer remained to be reconsidered if the donor died within seven years and no withdrawal of relief could therefore take place. The Revenue did not agree with this view, and the FA 1996 change was made 'for the removal of any doubt'. A similar change was made to s 124A (in subsection 7A) in relation to agricultural property relief.

The change is intended only to establish that a transfer exists, and does not seek to quantify the amount of the transfer. It is considered, therefore, that it does not affect the view stated above that if a slice of the original transfer is covered by the annual exemption, the business property relief on that slice cannot later be withdrawn. This is not relevant where the original transfer qualified for 100% relief, because the annual exemption would not be used against a nil transfer.

Care needs to be taken in relation to the treatment of the annual exemption when business property relief is withdrawn. Note 1 deals with the situation where the 100% relief is withdrawn from a transfer that was originally potentially exempt, ie the gift to Simon of shares in Brown Retailing Ltd, with the additional complication that another transfer was made on the same day. The example also illustrates the 100% relief being withdrawn from a transfer that would otherwise have been a chargeable transfer, ie the transfer to the discretionary trust on 11 November 2001. The annual exemptions of 2001/02 and 2000/01 were originally given against the 2001/02 gift to Pauline. When the business property relief is withdrawn at Agnes's death, the annual exemptions will be reallocated to the transfer to the discretionary trust, since the trust transfer occurred earlier in the tax year than the transfer to Pauline.

3.   No business property relief is available on Agnes Brown's holdings in:

Blue Ltd — an *investment* company

Green Ltd — an *investment* company.

Business property relief of 100% is available on the holding in Pink plc as it is a trading company on the Alternative Investment Market (AIM), and on the investment in Black Ltd, an unquoted trading company.

Double charges relief

4. The situations when a double charge to tax occurs and the reliefs under the Inheritance Tax (Double Charges Relief) Regulations 1987 (SI 1987/1130) are dealt with in Examples 19 and 20. The regulations apply to the release of reservation on 10 March 2002 in this example, when Agnes Brown excludes herself from benefit under the discretionary trust. The release is specifically treated as a potentially exempt transfer by FA 1986 s 102(4), despite the fact that someone else's estate has not been increased, nor has an interest in possession in the trust been created.

    In this example no tax was payable by the trustees of the discretionary settlement in the settlor's lifetime. If any lifetime tax had been payable on such a transfer, then where, as in this example, the first calculation produced the higher figure, the lifetime tax (up to but not exceeding the part of the death tax payable relating to the transfer) would be deducted from the tax payable by the trustees following Agnes Brown's death (see Example 20 explanatory note 3).

Post-death variations of a will

5. The assets of the discretionary trust following Agnes Brown's death consist of shares acquired on the takeover of Brown Retailing Ltd in November 2004 and £100,000 added in cash under the terms of Agnes Brown's will. The appointment of £50,000 to Simon on 26 September 2007 is in cash, the shares being retained in full. Accordingly it is a variation of the property settled by will within two years of the date of death and is treated as a disposition at death for inheritance tax and not as a distribution out of the discretionary trust (s 144). (Section 144 applies where a distribution is made out of property settled by will within two years after the death and before any interest in possession has subsisted in the property. The distribution is treated as if it had been made under the terms of the will.) See Example 60 explanatory note 9 for a problem where such a distribution is made within the first three months after death.

6. For detailed notes on post-death variations of a will see Example 34.

A.   Relief from inheritance tax is available on 'relevant business property'.

   (a)   What is relevant business property?

   (b)   What types of business do not qualify for this relief?

   (c)   What is the nature of the relief and at what rates is it given?

B.   Relief from inheritance tax is also available for 'agricultural property'.

   (a)   Under what circumstances is a transferor entitled to inheritance tax relief when transferring agricultural property and what is the nature of the relief?

   (b)   Is the relief available to a transferor of shares or debentures in a farming company?

   (c)   Whiteacre is a farm of 200 acres which for the last ten years has been owned and farmed by Arthur personally with assistance from his son.

   It has been proposed that Arthur should form a partnership with his son because of his advancing age, failing health and the necessity of providing for his wife when he dies.

   Arthur would then grant a lease of the land at full rent to that partnership so that on his death the land will be valued at tenanted value.

   The current agricultural value of the land is £2,000 per acre vacant possession; £1,400 per acre tenanted.

   Advise Arthur as to the viability of the above proposal, quantifying the value chargeable to inheritance tax on Whiteacre on his subsequent death.

   (d)   X owned 800 acres of freehold farmland known as Greenacre let to and farmed by the partnership of X himself, Mrs X and their son Y. The tenancy was granted in 1973.

   In July 2006 X died leaving his interest in Greenacre to his son Y (subject to Y paying the inheritance tax thereon). It was valued (tenanted) at £455,000. X left the residue of his estate (including his interest in the partnership) to his wife. He had not made any previous lifetime gifts.

   After an accident on the farm Y, who was unmarried, died in September 2006.

   Y's estate consisted of:

	£
Greenacre Farm (let to the farming partnership of himself and his mother)	455,000
Interest in the farming partnership	60,000
Other assets	76,000

   Compute the inheritance tax payable

   (i)   on the death of X

   (ii)   on the death of Y assuming he had not made any lifetime transfers and that he left the whole of his estate to his mother.

A.   **Business property relief**

(a)   *Relevant business property*

Relevant business property means (s 105):

(i)   A sole trader's business, or a partnership share, including professions and vocations.

(ii)   Unquoted *securities* of a company which, together with any unquoted *shares* of the company (including related property in both instances), give the transferor control immediately before the transfer.

(iii)   *Any* unquoted *shares* in a company.

(iv)   Quoted shares and/or securities of a company which, together with any related property, give the transferor control immediately before the transfer.

(v)   Land, buildings, plant or machinery which immediately before the transfer were used wholly or mainly for the purposes of a business carried on by a company of which the transferor then had control, or by a partnership of which he was then a partner.

(vi)   Any land or buildings, machinery or plant which, immediately before the transfer, were used wholly or mainly for the purposes of a business carried on by the transferor and were settled property in which he was then beneficially entitled to an interest in possession.

Quoted shares and securities are defined as shares and securities listed on a recognised stock exchange (ss 105(1ZA), 113A(3B)). Shares or securities on the Alternative Investment Market (AIM) are treated as unlisted and therefore qualify as unquoted under (ii) and (iii) above.

In the case of CIR v Mallender and others (exors of Drury-Lowe decd) (2001), it was held that an asset (which in this case was land) used as security for a guarantee was not itself used in the business and was not therefore part of the relevant business property.

The relevant business property concerned must have been owned by the transferor throughout the two years preceding the transfer (s 106) or be property replacing relevant business property where the combined period of ownership of the original and replacement property is at least two years out of the last five years (but relief is then granted only on the lower of the value of the original or replacement property) (s 107). Property acquired as a result of death is deemed to have been owned from the date of death, or for property acquired by a spouse, from the date the deceased spouse acquired it (s 108). The two year rule does not apply where the property was eligible for business property relief on an earlier transfer and either the earlier transfer or the subsequent transfer was made on the death of the transferor (s 109). Where a person starts up a new business, however, (rather than inherits it) and then dies within two years, business property relief is not available.

(b)   *Non-qualifying businesses*

A business, or an interest in a business, or shares in or securities of a company, are not relevant business property if the business, or as the case may be, the business of the company, consists wholly or mainly of:

(i)   Dealing in securities, stocks or shares (except for market makers and discount houses)

(ii)   Dealing in land or buildings

(iii)   Making or holding investments (see explanatory note 21 re land which is let).

George & Anor (Exors of Stedman dec'd) v IRC concerned a claim for business property relief by the executors where the deceased owned 85% of the shares in a company carrying on the business of running a caravan park. The Inland Revenue contended the business of the company was making or holding investments. The Court of Appeal allowed the executors' claim on the ground that making or holding investments was only one (and not the main) component of a composite business.

A. (c) *Nature and amount of relief*

The relief applies to transfers of value in lifetime or on death or to the 10 yearly charge on discretionary trusts, the value attributable to relevant business property being reduced by 100% in respect of (a) (i) to (iii) above and 50% in respect of (a) (iv) to (vi) (s 104).

Before 6 April 1996, unquoted shares qualified for relief at only 50% unless, together with related property, they gave the transferor control of *more* than 25% of the votes of the company (and the 25% control had to have been held *throughout* the two years before the transfer, or shorter period under the successions rules in (a) above — s 109A). For chargeable events occurring on or after 6 April 1996 (lifetime transfers, tax uplift on death, etc), 100% relief is available on qualifying unquoted shares regardless of the size of the holding.

The relief is applied automatically without the need for a claim and is given before applying any other relief (eg annual exemptions, as indicated below).

Meaning of control

Control means control of voting on all questions affecting the company as a whole. In considering which shares give control care must be taken with shares that only have votes in special circumstances (eg preference shares entitled to votes when the preference dividends are in arrears). When voting rights relate only to the question of winding-up, or to questions primarily affecting shares of a particular class, then such rights are ignored (s 269(4)). Otherwise the rights are included in determining control. For example, say an unquoted company had a total issued share capital of £100, consisting of 25 ordinary shares of £1 held by A, and 75 preference shares of £1 held by B, the preference shares having votes when the preference dividends were in arrear and on reduction of capital. Neither A nor B *control*s the votes on *all* questions affecting the company as a whole, so neither would qualify for business property relief on any land etc owned personally and used by the company. If the voting rights on the preference shares related only to winding-up, A would then control the company and would be entitled to the 50% relief on land etc owned personally. B's position would be unchanged.

Death of donor within seven years

For lifetime gifts made after 17 March 1986, whether chargeable at the time or potentially exempt, where the death of the donor occurs within seven years, business property relief is only available when calculating the tax/additional tax arising as a result of the death providing that:

1. the original property (or qualifying replacement property — see below) was owned by the transferee throughout the period beginning with the date of the chargeable transfer and ending with the death of the transferor, and

2. immediately before the death of the donor the original property (or qualifying replacement property) is relevant business property in the hands of the transferee (ignoring the two year period of ownership rule), except that where property qualified as a transfer out of a controlling holding, it is only necessary for the transferee to retain what he was given (which may not give control). In order for unquoted shares to be relevant business property they must still be unquoted when the donor dies (s 113A(3A)).

If the transferee dies before the donor then the property must qualify at the date of his death rather than the date of the donor's death.

Proportionate relief is available where only part of the property is owned at the date of death (s 113A).

To the extent that the original transfer was covered by annual exemptions, whether the balance was chargeable at the time or potentially exempt, it is considered that the business property relief relating to that part of the transfer is not affected by the death of the donor within seven years. See Example 24 explanatory note 2, and the illustration in that example.

It should be noted that if business property relief is not available in calculating additional tax on a *chargeable* lifetime transfer resulting from the donor's death within seven years, it is only that tax calculation that is affected. The donor's total of cumulative transfers is not altered.

Example

A donor who had made no other transfers settled a building worth £312,000 and used for business purposes into a discretionary trust in July 2006. If it qualified for 50% business property relief, £12,000 of the transfer, reduced to £6,000 after 50% business property relief, would be covered by annual exemptions and the balance of £300,000 would, after 50% business property relief, be a chargeable transfer of £150,000. No tax would be payable because the transfer was below the then nil threshold of £285,000. If the donor died within seven years and the trustees had in the meantime disposed of the property, they would pay tax on £300,000 less the nil threshold at the date of the donor's death, but the donor's lifetime transfers to be aggregated with any subsequent transfers and with his estate would remain at £150,000.

By comparison, if the donor had instead gifted the same building to his son in July 2006 it would be a potentially exempt transfer. On the donor's subsequent death within seven years (son having sold the property), the son would similarly be liable to tax on £300,000 less the nil threshold at the date of the donor's death, but the lifetime transfer to be aggregated with subsequent transfers and with the donor's estate would be £300,000, the business property relief available at the time of the gift not being available to compute the *chargeable transfer* resulting from the donor's death.

Qualifying replacement property

Provision is made for property that replaces all or part of the original property to satisfy the continuing ownership test up to the donor's (or donee's) death providing the replacement property also qualifies as business property, and providing the whole of the proceeds of the original property are used in the purchase of the replacement property within three years after the disposal of the original property, or such longer period as HMRC may allow (s 113B).

If unquoted shares in trading companies (for example on AIM) are sold and replaced with other such shares, then it is understood that the new shares will be treated as replacement property under s 107(1). Replacement shares or property must not be acquired in advance of the disposal of the original property.

Excepted assets

For the purpose of calculating the relief the value of the relevant business property excludes *excepted assets*, ie assets which were neither used wholly or mainly for the purposes of the business throughout the two years preceding the transfer, nor required at the time of the transfer for future use for those purposes.

See the Special Commissioners' case of Barclays Bank Trust Co Ltd (SpC 158) for the denial of relief to the extent that there were substantial cash balances held within a company. Note also the Special Commissioners' case of Farmer & Giles (Farmer's Executors) v CIR 1999 (SpC 216), which held that in determining whether assets were relevant business property the whole business should be considered 'in the round'. This includes turnover, profits and assets used in the business and investment sides of the business. It could also include time spent by the owners, employees and others on the respective parts of the business. It would appear that if a single set of accounts is prepared for the whole business, there is unified management and the majority of the above tests point to business, then there is a single business for inheritance tax, and let property within the balance sheet is not therefore treated as an excepted asset but as an integral part of the qualifying business.

B.   **Agricultural property relief**

(a)   *Availability of agricultural property relief*

Agricultural property relief is available on the transfer of agricultural property (that is, agricultural land or pasture; also woodland and any building used in the intensive rearing of livestock or fish if the occupation of the woodland or building is ancillary to that of the agricultural land or pasture; and also such cottages, farm buildings and farmhouses occupied with the agricultural land as are of a character appropriate to the property) (s 115).

The cultivation of short rotation coppice (ie the harvesting of trees planted at high density at intervals of less than ten years) is regarded as agriculture, therefore the land used for this purpose is agricultural land and ancillary buildings are farm buildings (FA 1995 s 154).

Agricultural property relief is also available on land taken out of farming and dedicated to wildlife habitats under the Government Habitat Schemes, together with buildings used for the management of the land (s 124C).

The provisions for agricultural property relief are very similar to the rules for business property relief, in that the agricultural value is reduced by (s 116):

(i)   Where the transferor had the right to vacant possession immediately before the transfer or the right to obtain such possession within the next twelve months, extended to twenty four months by HMRC Concession F17; or (also by Concession F17) the property is valued at an amount broadly equivalent to the vacant possession value   100%

(ii)   Where the agricultural property transferred is let on a tenancy granted on or after 1 September 1995 (including successions to tenancies following the death of the previous tenant on or after that date – see explanatory note 14)   100%

(iii)   Where the transferor has been beneficially entitled to his interest in the property since before 10 March 1981 and satisfies certain conditions (see explanatory note 10)   100%

(iv)   Otherwise.   50%

For transfers before 10 March 1992 the rates of relief were 50% for the first and third categories and 30% otherwise.

The percentage deduction only applies to the agricultural value of the property transferred, ie its value on the assumption that the property was subject to a perpetual covenant prohibiting its use otherwise than as agricultural property. In arriving at the agricultural value any loan secured on the agricultural property must be deducted.

Meaning of agricultural land or pasture

The term 'agricultural land or pasture' is given the narrow meaning of bare land. Therefore to obtain relief for any farmhouse etc, it is necessary to show that its occupation is ancillary to that of agricultural land (Starke (Brown's Exors) v CIR 1994). Furthermore in Exor of Higginson v IRC 2002 it was held that the farmhouse must be of a character and size appropriate to the property and the requirements of the farming activities conducted on the agricultural land. A further recent case on the interaction of farmhouses and agricultural property relief is Lloyds TSB (personal representatives of Antrobus dec'd) v IRC 2002 (SpC 336). This case set out five principles which had been established for deciding whether a farmhouse is of a character appropriate to the property. The requirement that the buildings are occupied for agricultural purposes is satisfied if they are tenanted by a person employed solely for agricultural purposes, or by retired farm workers or their widow(er)s, and such occupation is a statutorily protected tenancy or the lease was granted to the employee for life as part of his/her terms of employment.

In the case of Rosser v IRC (2003) SpC 368 the Inland Revenue refused a claim to agricultural property relief on a house and barn owned by the deceased on the basis that they were not agricultural land. The case was subsequently referred to the Special Commissioners who allowed the appeal in part — the barn was of a character appropriate to the property and was owned and occupied for the relevant period. Relief was granted on the barn but not the house.

Qualifying conditions

The agricultural property must at the time of the transfer have been either:

(i)   occupied by the transferor for the purposes of agriculture throughout the period of two years ending with the date of the transfer or have replaced other agricultural property which, together with the replacement property, was occupied for agricultural purposes for at least two years out of the last five years ending with the date of transfer, or

(ii) owned by the transferor throughout the period of *seven years* ending with the date of transfer and occupied for the purposes of agriculture by him or another throughout that period. In the case of replacement property this condition is satisfied if the other property and the replacement property were owned by him and occupied for the purposes of agriculture by himself or another for at least seven years out of the period of ten years ending with the date of transfer.

The two year rule in (i) or seven year rule in (ii) does not apply where: the property was eligible for agricultural property relief on an earlier transfer; either the earlier transfer or the subsequent transfer was made on the death of the transferor; and the property is occupied by the second transferor for agricultural purposes at the date of the subsequent transfer.

Where the transferor had acquired the agricultural property on the death of his spouse/civil partner, their respective periods of occupation and/or ownership are aggregated to determine whether the transferor meets the occupation/ownership requirements (ss 117 to 121).

For lifetime gifts, whether chargeable at the time or potentially exempt, where the death of the donor occurs within seven years, agricultural property relief is only available when calculating the tax/additional tax arising as a result of the death providing that:

(a)   the original property (or qualifying replacement property) was owned by the transferee throughout the period beginning with the date of the chargeable transfer and ending with the death of the transferor, and

(b)   immediately before the death of the donor the original property (or qualifying replacement property) is relevant agricultural property in the hands of the transferee (ignoring the two year or seven year period of ownership rule).

If the transferee dies before the donor then the property must qualify at the date of his death rather than the date of the donor's death.

Proportionate relief is available where only part of the property is owned at the date of death (s 124A).

Annual exemptions and effect of donor's death

The same provisions apply as for business property relief in relation to annual exemptions, and also for calculating the additional tax payable on a chargeable lifetime transfer as a result of the donor's death within seven years, where the agricultural property is no longer owned by the donee (see part A(c)).

Provision is made for property that replaces all or part of the original property to satisfy the continuing ownership test providing the replacement property also qualifies as agricultural property, and providing the whole of the proceeds of the original property are used in the purchase of the replacement property within three years after the disposal of the original property, or such longer period as HMRC may allow (s 124B).

Business property relief on non-agricultural value

Where agricultural property satisfies the conditions for business property relief, business property relief is available in respect of any part of the value transferred that does not qualify for agricultural property relief (s 114). Since agricultural property relief is given only on the agricultural value of the land then business property relief where applicable will be given on any excess over that value.

Where agricultural property is replaced by business property, then providing the agricultural property is qualifying property for business property relief, the period of ownership of the agricultural property will be taken into account in deciding whether the conditions for business property relief are satisfied.

(b)   *Transfer of shares or debentures in farming company*

Agricultural property relief is available on the transfer of shares or debentures in a farming company, providing the holding gave the transferor control of the company immediately before the transfer and the agricultural property forms part of the company's assets (s 119). Relief is given only on that part of the value of the holding that reflects the agricultural value of the underlying property. The rate of relief is 100% where the company occupies the property or where the property is let on a tenancy granted on or after 1 September 1995, and 50% for property let before that date, and the two year/seven year rules in (i) and (ii) in part (a) above apply as if the company were the transferor. (For this purpose the company is treated as having occupied the property at any time when it was occupied by a person who subsequently controls the company.) Furthermore the shares or securities must have been owned by the transferor throughout the two year or seven year period.

Business property relief is available on the non-agricultural value of a holding where the relevant conditions are satisfied at 100% on holdings in unquoted farming companies and at 50% on quoted controlling holdings.

Both agricultural property relief and business property relief are given automatically without the need for a claim.

(c)   *Mitigation of inheritance tax through lease of land*

The immediately perceived advantage of the proposal is that the value of the agricultural land would be reduced from £400,000 (200 x £2,000) to £280,000 (200 x £1,400) on the granting of the tenancy. This act by itself would not have any inheritance tax consequences providing the grant is for full consideration in money or money's worth (s 16).

Furthermore, the rate of agricultural property relief on tenanted property for tenancies granted on or after 1 September 1995 was increased from 50% to 100%, so that unless there are adverse changes in the agricultural property relief provisions, there will be no disadvantage in terms of the rate of relief available. Unless the conditions for agricultural relief were no longer satisfied at the time of Arthur's death, there would therefore be no charge to inheritance tax at that time. If the conditions were not satisfied, then providing the property remained tenanted, the proposal would achieve the objective of reducing the value of the property in the death estate.

(d)   (i)   *Inheritance tax payable on the death of X in July 2006*

	Gross £	Tax £
Inheritance tax accumulation prior to death	–	–
Estate on death		
Freehold property – Greenacre		
Agricultural value (tenanted)	455,000	
Less: 100% agricultural property relief (note 13)	455,000	– –
Residue of estate to spouse — exempt	–	–
	–	–

Inheritance tax payable nil.

(ii)   *Inheritance tax payable on the death of Y in September 2006*

	£	£
Estate on death		
Greenacre (tenanted since 1973)	455,000	
Less: 50% agricultural property relief (note 13)	227,500	227,500
Interest in farming partnership	60,000	
Less: 100% business property relief	60,000	–
Other assets		76,000
		303,500
Tax thereon (no lifetime transfers)		
(303,500 – 285,000 = 18,500 @ 40%)		£ 7,400

Explanatory Notes

Business property and agricultural property relief legislation

1.   The provisions relating to business property relief are contained in ss 103–114B and those for agricultural property relief in ss 115–124C.

2.   The main provisions are dealt with in the example, other points of importance being covered in the following notes.

Meaning of control

3.   Control of a company means the control of voting on all questions affecting the company as a whole, subject to what is said in part A(c) of the example (s 269).

Shares or securities which are related property under s 161 are taken into account in determining whether a person controls a company (s 269(2)), except where related property is left out of account under s 176 because of a sale after death (ss 105(2), 122(2)) (see Example 10 for the related property rules, explanatory note 4 of that example dealing with s 176).

The voting powers attaching to shares or securities comprised in a settlement are deemed to be exercisable by the person beneficially entitled in possession to the shares or securities (broadly the person entitled to the income for the time being) (s 269(3)).

Business property relief and agricultural property relief are also available on the occasion of a ten yearly charge on a settlement without an interest in possession. For this purpose the trustees are deemed to be a transferor (ss 66, 103(1)(b), 115(1)(b)).

Agricultural value

4.   Agricultural value is that which would be the value of the property if it were subject to a perpetual covenant prohibiting its use otherwise than as agricultural property (s 115(3)). The relief does not therefore extend to any value in excess of the agricultural value as defined. For example, if the value was £100,000 because it was hoped that permission would shortly be forthcoming for a caravan site, but the value on the basis that it must be used perpetually for agriculture was £10,000, the agricultural relief would only be available on the lower £10,000.

Occupation by company

5.   Occupation of agricultural property by a company controlled by the transferor is treated as occupation by the transferor for the purpose of the minimum two year period of occupation or seven year period of ownership (s 119(1)).

      Hence agricultural property owned by a controlling shareholder and occupied by his farming company qualifies for relief.

Parcels of shares acquired over a period of time — matching provisions

6.   As indicated in the example, an asset is not relevant business property unless it has been owned by the transferor throughout the two years before the transfer (or it is qualifying replacement property). As far as shares are concerned, they may have been acquired in separate parcels over a period of time and some of the acquisitions may have been within the last two years.

      Unlike the capital gains position, there are no matching rules in the inheritance tax legislation, so that there is uncertainty over which shares are contained in a transfer. In practice this may be overcome either by the separate parcels of shares having been originally registered in the names of different nominees or by the share certificates that are cancelled as a result of the gift being those acquired more than two years previously.

Binding contract for sale

7.   Property that is subject to a binding contract for sale at the time of the transfer is not relevant business or agricultural property unless:

      (a)   the sale is to a company that is to carry on the business, the consideration being wholly or mainly shares or securities in the company (which, in the case of agricultural property relief, will give the transferor control of the company), or

      (b)   the property is shares or securities of a company and the sale is made for the purpose of reconstruction or amalgamation (ss 113 and 124).

      Where partners or company directors have entered into 'buy and sell' agreements whereby on their death the personal representatives are *obliged* to sell and the survivors *obliged* to buy the deceased's interest (funds often being provided by life assurance policies), such an agreement in HMRC's view constitutes a binding contract for sale and business property relief or agricultural relief is not available (Statement of Practice 12/80). If, however, a double option agreement is entered into under which the surviving partners or shareholders have an option to buy and the deceased's personal representatives an option to sell, such options to be exercised within a stated period after the partner's death, this does not cause business or agricultural relief to be lost.

Other reliefs and exemptions

8.   Business and agricultural property relief are given before any exemptions since they apply to transfers of value (ss 104(1) and 115(1)), such transfers being calculated before reliefs and exemptions (s 3(1)). In relation to potentially exempt transfers that become chargeable transfers, neither relief is available unless the relevant conditions are satisfied at the time of death, as indicated in the example (ss 113A(1) and 124A(1)).

Gifts subject to a reservation

9. Where a gift of business or agricultural property is subject to a reservation, and a transfer of value is treated as made by the donor on his death (or on the donee's death, if earlier), then in considering the availability of business or agricultural relief the donor's transfer is treated as made by the donee (otherwise the donor would not usually be able to satisfy the ownership/occupation requirements) (FA 1986 Sch 20.8). Where the requirements for 100% relief are satisfied, the fact that a gift of qualifying property was subject to a reservation will not result in any extra tax charge on death.

As far as the donee's entitlement to relief is concerned, there are provisions to enable him to satisfy the occupation/ownership requirements by reference to the occupation/ownership of the donor (FA 1986 Sch 20.8).

For the gifts with reservation provisions see Example 19.

Pre 10 March 1981 transfers of agricultural property and transitional relief

10. For transfers prior to 10 March 1981, agricultural property relief was 50% of the agricultural value of the agricultural property after reduction for exempt transfers. The relief had to be claimed within two years of the transfer and was limited to relief on £250,000 or on 1,000 acres, whichever was the greater (counting rough grazing land as one-sixth of its actual area).

In order to be eligible to claim relief the transferor had broadly to be a working farmer, although relief could still be claimed after the farmer retired, providing the property had been occupied for agricultural purposes by his family throughout the period between his retirement and the date of the transfer, either under a lease or under some informal arrangements.

Relief was not available on let agricultural land except where it was let to a member of the family (as above) or where it was let to a farming partnership of which the transferor was a member or to a farming company controlled by the transferor.

As a transitional measure, where the transferor has been beneficially entitled to his interest in the property since before 10 March 1981, he is entitled to 100% agricultural property relief providing the following conditions are satisfied:

(a) He would have been entitled to claim the (then) 50% agricultural property relief had he disposed of his interest before that date, and

(b) His interest did not at any time between 10 March 1981 and the date of transfer carry a right to vacant possession and did not fail to carry such a right through any act or deliberate omission of his.

Where the former relief would have been limited by reference to value or acreage, the 100% relief is available up to the limit and any excess agricultural value attracts relief at 50%.

Where a transferor has acquired agricultural property on the death of his spouse/civil partner on or after 10 March 1981, the transitional 100% relief is available where the spouse/civil partner satisfied condition (a) above and both spouses/civil partners satisfy condition (b) above.

These transitional provisions thus enable relief to be claimed on the first subsequent transfer at the 100% rather than the 50% rate by retired farmers whose families have continued to work the farm and by partners or controlling directors who let land to the partnership or company.

The transitional relief will not be relevant where a tenancy commences on or after 1 September 1995, because relief is now available on such tenanted property at the 100% rate in any event. Had Arthur in part B(c) of the example not been entitled to the 100% relief under the normal provisions, he would not have been able to claim the transitional relief because he had the right to vacant possession after 9 March 1981 and before the transfer (on his death) on which relief is to be claimed.

Formation of partnership

11. The formation of a partnership between Arthur and his son would not give rise to any current or potential liability to inheritance tax provided that any reduction in the value of the estate of either

resulted from an agreement that was not intended to confer any gratuitous benefit and was such as would have occurred in an agreement made at arm's length between unconnected persons (s 10).

Grant of agricultural tenancy

12. The grant of the tenancy of Whiteacre by Arthur in part B(c) of the example will not give rise to any liability to inheritance tax because of the exemption provided by s 16 for agricultural tenancies if the grant is made for full consideration. It should be noted, however, that the rent receivable by Arthur will be investment income whereas previously the income was earned income, being embraced in the profits of a farming business carried on by Arthur personally. This will reduce the Class 4 national insurance contributions payable, but will affect the future earnings on which Arthur can claim income tax relief for personal pension premiums (but note that a personal pension premium of up to £3,600 a year may be paid with basic rate tax relief at source by someone who has no earnings). If the tenancy was not granted for full rent, a charge to inheritance tax could arise on the reduction in the value of Arthur's estate and the 'gift' could be 'with reservation' as Arthur would still have a benefit in the land and accordingly could be valued at vacant possession value at the date of Arthur's death.

    See Example 10 part A regarding the valuation of tenanted agricultural property.

13. On the death of X in part B(d) of the example Greenacre qualifies for 100% relief because the tenancy was granted before 10 March 1981 and all of the conditions mentioned in explanatory note 10 are satisfied.

    On the death of Y Greenacre qualifies for relief even though Y only owned it for three months because the minimum occupation/ownership rules do not apply on a succession where all of the following conditions are satisfied:

    (i) The value transferred by the earlier transfer qualified for relief

    (ii) The property became that of the later transferor as a result of such an earlier transfer and at the time of the subsequent transfer was *occupied* by the later transferor or the personal representative of the earlier transferor for the purposes of agriculture

    (iii) The property would have qualified for relief if the normal minimum ownership and occupation conditions had been met

    (iv) Either the earlier or later transfer was a transfer on death.

    Alternatively Y would still have qualified under the two year occupation test as Y occupied the land as a tenant farmer in the farming partnership for two years even though his ownership did not commence until the death of his father.

    The rate of relief on Y's death is only 50%, because the tenancy was granted before 1 September 1995 and Y does not satisfy the conditions for the transitional relief, having not become the owner of Greenacre until his father's death.

    Although Y's death is within twelve months of X's death, quick succession relief is not relevant because no tax was payable on X's estate.

14. The availability of 100% agricultural relief in relation to tenanted property was extended by FA 1996. Where a tenant dies on or after 1 September 1995 and someone else succeeds to the tenancy, the new tenancy is deemed to commence on the date of the first tenant's death. Accordingly, if the landlord dies after the death of the first tenant, but before the succession by the second tenant, 100% agricultural property relief is available on the landlord's death. 100% relief is similarly available where a succession to a tenancy is triggered by a notice of retirement given by the retiring tenant to the landlord, and the succession takes effect after the landlord's death (on or after 1 September 1995) and within 30 months of the notice (s 116(5A), (5B) and (5D)).

Deed of variation

15. The tax on the death of Y in part B(d) of the example (£7,400) could be avoided by a deed of variation under which the executors of X and of Y agreed to vary the terms of X's will so that the freehold property devolved to X's widow instead of to Y. This would save the whole of the tax on the death of Y since his estate would then only amount to £76,000 (£227,500 for the farm property no longer being in his estate) which is below the taxable threshold.

    The respective executors should have no reservations about this variation, since the estate of Y has in any event been left to his mother, who would simply take the farm property on the death of her husband rather than of her son. See Example 34 for details of deeds of variation.

    Furthermore the income tax 'pre-owned' asset rules will not impose an income tax charge on Y as FA 2004 Sch 15.16 provides that a party to a deed of variation is not taxed as a former owner simply because of having an interest which they have now signed away (Y's Executor signing on behalf of Y).

Exempt and partially exempt estates

16. Where business or agricultural property forms part of an estate at death, the benefit of the business or agricultural property relief will be lost if the property is left to an exempt beneficiary. Even if it is not left to an exempt beneficiary, part of the relief will be wasted where there are exempt legacies and the business or agricultural property forms part of the residue of the estate, rather than being left as a specific gift, because the relief is then regarded as applying to the whole estate, including the exempt part of it, so that again relief is wasted to the extent that it is allocated to the exempt legacies. For further notes on this point see Example 15 explanatory notes 6 to 9.

Gifts out of and into trusts

17. Business and agricultural property relief is available on transfers of trust property providing the conditions are satisfied. For life interest trusts, the person with the interest in possession is treated as the beneficial owner of the property (s 49) and when the interest comes to an end, he is treated as having made a transfer at that time (s 52). For discretionary trusts, the relief is available when relevant property is transferred out of the trust and on the occasion of the ten yearly charge, the trustees being treated as the transferor (ss 103, 113) (see Example 62 explanatory note 5).

    Detailed notes on the inheritance tax treatment of trusts are contained in Examples 52 to 65. See Examples 60 and 62 in particular for the treatment of business and agricultural property.

    Various points need to be borne in mind when placing business or agricultural property into a trust, and the possible effects for the different types of trust need to be carefully considered.

18. Before 22 March 2006, if property was placed into a life interest trust, the transfer was potentially exempt and will only become chargeable if the donor dies within seven years after the transfer. If the property is business or agricultural property, the relief would be taken into account in arriving at the amount of the potentially exempt transfer. The trustees need to hold the property for two years before any transfer by them would qualify for relief.

    If the donor dies within seven years after transferring the property to the trust, so that the potentially exempt transfer becomes a chargeable transfer, the trustees still need to hold the property at that time in order for the relief to be available. (If the donor died within two years this would not prevent the relief being available providing the property was still held in the trust.) If the trust does not satisfy the conditions at the donor's death, the relief is not available against the now chargeable transfer, and the donor's 'clock' of cumulative transfers will include that chargeable transfer.

19. Since 22 March 2006, the transfer of property into most types of trust is now an immediately chargeable transfer (at half of the rates of tax payable on death) after being reduced by business or agricultural property relief where available. The trustees need to retain the property for two years before being entitled to relief on any appointments of the property out of the trust. Furthermore, if there are any appointments of the property after that time but within ten years after the trust's

creation, then although the relief is available on the transfer the *rate of tax* is based on the full value of the property when settled (see Example 62 explanatory note 5). This would not be a problem, however, if the property qualified for 100% relief because the amount chargeable would be nil.

If the donor dies within seven years after the transfer, the tax on the lifetime transfer is recalculated on the death scale, additional tax being payable accordingly. As with life interest trusts, the trustees still need to hold the property when the donor dies in order for the relief to remain available on the donor's transfer (and they would be entitled to the relief even if the donor died within two years providing the property was still held in the trust). If the trust does not satisfy the conditions for relief when the donor dies, the relief is not taken into account in calculating the additional tax on the lifetime transfer, but the amount of the donor's cumulative transfers would not be affected (see the example on page 25.4). Relief will not be available against the lifetime transfer to the trust because the trustees have disposed of the property between the time of the gift and the time of death.

Let property, including holiday lettings

20.   Holiday lettings are not agricultural property. HMRC take the view that a property letting business will not usually qualify for business property relief, because it will be regarded as a business of making or holding investments (s 105(3)). This is supported by the Special Commissioners' decisions in Exors of Moore decd and Exor of Burkinyoung decd (1995). In both cases business property relief was denied, even though the taxpayers (or in the Burkinyoung case, the managing agents) carried out considerable work as part of the lettings, eg repairs, decoration and maintenance.

Hotels, bed and breakfast and residential homes will usually qualify for relief because of the level of services provided. In the case of *short-term* holiday lettings (eg weekly or fortnightly), where the property owner or his agent is substantially involved with the holidaymakers during the holiday, business property relief will normally be available even if the lettings were for part of the year only (HMRC's Inheritance Tax Manual INTM25278). Most furnished holiday lettings should satisfy these tests.

In a decision of the Special Commissioners (Furness v CIR 1999), it was held that a caravan park business qualified for business property relief. Although there were both static and touring caravans, the larger part of the profits came other than from renting out caravan pitches, and the activities of the owner and his staff were greatly in excess of what one would expect in a business concerned wholly or mainly with investments.

The opposite decision was reached in Weston (exor of Weston decd) v CIR 2000, where the Court confirmed the Special Commissioner's decision that the greater part of a caravan park's profits came from pitch fees and bank interest rather than caravan sales, so that the business was mainly one of making or holding investments. The same conclusion was reached in IRC v George & Anor (Exors of Stedman dec'd) 2002 where the main activities were the letting of sites for 167 residential mobile homes; storage of touring caravans; letting of a shop and warehouse and fields let on grazing licences. This outweighed the ancillary activities of a country club and an insurance agency, so the business was mainly one of making or holding investments. However, that decision was subsequently overturned by the Court of Appeal which reinstated the Special Commissioner's finding that the company was mainly trading.

The comments in the Farmer & Giles case mentioned in part A(c) of the example provide a good basis on which to judge whether a business consists mainly of making or holding investments. Once the hurdle of qualifying for business property relief is crossed then, as the example indicates, the assets used for the investment side of the business will probably not be regarded as 'excepted assets' and will not therefore be excluded from relief.

On 19 July 2001 Stanley (who has never made a lifetime gift before) gave Elizabeth (his granddaughter) the whole of his shares in Printers Ltd, a trading company, together with the freehold of the land and buildings occupied by the company, but which he owned personally.

On the same day Peter (who has made chargeable transfers within the previous seven years amounting to £180,000 and has fully utilised his exemptions for 2001/02 and 2000/01) gave Elizabeth (his daughter) his shareholding in Printers Ltd.

Prior to the above transfers the shareholdings in Printers Ltd (which had remained unchanged for many years) were:

		Shares
Stanley		4,000
Phyllis	(Stanley's wife)	4,000
Peter	(Stanley's son)	1,000
Barbara	(Peter's sister)	900
Elizabeth	(Peter's daughter)	100
		10,000

and the agreed values for inheritance tax purposes were:

100% holding	£1,600,000	51% holding	£900,000
80% holding	£1,400,000	40% holding	£300,000
60% holding	£1,000,000	10% holding	£40,000

The value of the land and buildings transferred by Stanley was agreed at £750,000.

On 13 November 2006 Stanley died. Elizabeth still owned the property and shares at that date.

(a) Compute the inheritance tax payable by Elizabeth;

(b) Assuming that the instalment option will be used, state the date on which the first instalment is due, and the amount payable on that day;

(c) Explain under what circumstances interest will be payable on the instalments (without calculating the amount of any interest).

(a)   **Inheritance tax payable by Elizabeth as donee of lifetime transfers:**

On death of Stanley 13 November 2006

Potentially exempt transfers 19 July 2001, now chargeable transfers (see explanatory notes 2 and 3):

	Gross £	Tax £
Shares in Printers Ltd	–	–
Land and buildings (see note 2)	369,000	33,600*

(* 369,000 – 285,000 = 84,000 @ 40%)

Tax payable (after 60% tapering relief) is 40% of £33,600 = £13,440, which is payable over 10 annual instalments.

Peter — inheritance tax accumulation

	Gross £	Tax £
Previous transfers	180,000	–

19 July 2001 — potentially exempt transfer £40,000 less 100% business property relief £40,000 = nil. (No tax payable even if Peter dies within seven years and business property relief is not then available, since cumulative transfers total of £180,000 plus £40,000 is within nil rate band. See explanatory note 4.)

(b)   The first instalment of the tax of £13,440 in respect of the land and buildings, amounting to £1,344, is payable on 31 May 2007.

(c)   Interest is payable on the tax in respect of land and buildings from 31 May 2007 to the date of the instalment, calculated on the full amount of tax for the time being unpaid. In addition interest is paid on the instalment from its due date to the actual date of payment of the instalment.

Explanatory Notes

Business property relief

1.   A transfer of a business or an interest in a business qualifies for business property relief of 100% where the business is carried on for gain (ss 103(3), 104 and 105(1)(a)). Transfers out of a holding of unquoted shares also qualify for business property relief of 100% (ss 104(1)(a) and 105(1)(bb)).

Controlling holdings of quoted shares qualify for business property relief of 50% (ss 104(1)(b) and 105(1)(cc)).

Business property relief of 50% is available on the transfer of land and buildings used for the business of a company of which the transferor has control.

Related property

2.   Using the related property rules (s 161) (see Example 10), Stanley's gift of shares on 19 July 2001 must be valued as a proportion of an 80% holding (ie his own plus his wife's holding), of which one-half relates to him. The related holding determines the size of the holding for the purposes of the rate of business property relief (s 269(2)). The rate of business property relief at 19 July 2001 was 100% on the shares and 50% on the land and buildings, so the original calculation would be:

		£
Value of shares (80%) 1,400,000 x $\dfrac{4{,}000 \text{ shares}}{8{,}000 \text{ shares}}$ =		700,000
Less: Business property relief (100%)		700,000
Transfer of value		–

The transfer of value on the same day in respect of the land and buildings was:

		£
Value of property		750,000
Less: Business property relief (50%)		375,000
		375,000
Less: Annual exemptions 2001/02	3,000	
2000/01	3,000	6,000
Chargeable transfer		369,000

For the position where business or agricultural property relief is withdrawn at death because the conditions are no longer satisfied see Example 24 explanatory note 2.

Availability of business property relief

3.   To get the 100% business property relief on the *shares*, Elizabeth merely needs to retain the shares that were transferred to her out of Stanley's holding (s 113A).

To get the 50% relief on the *land and buildings*, Elizabeth needs to *control* Printers Ltd when Stanley dies (s 113A(3)).

The shares owned by Elizabeth following the gifts on 19 July 2001 and still held by her at 13 November 2006 were:

Original shareholding	100
Gift from Stanley	4,000
Gift from Peter	1,000
Total shares held	5,100

so she has control of Printers Ltd and is therefore entitled to business property relief on the land and buildings.

Because Stanley died more than five but less than six years after the date of gift, tapering relief of 60% applies to the tax payable.

4.   Peter's gift of his Printers Ltd shareholding to Elizabeth on 19 July 2001 qualified for 100% business property relief. The whole of the gift is a potentially exempt transfer. If he should die before 19 July 2008, the potentially exempt transfer will become chargeable, and the business property relief will only then be available if Elizabeth satisfies the qualifying conditions at that time. In fact no tax will be payable on Peter's gift in any event, since the cumulative transfers are within the nil rate band, but if 100% business property relief was not available the gift would be taken into account in the cumulative total for a death within seven years.

5.   Detailed notes on business property relief are given in Example 25.

Instalment option

6.   Inheritance tax payable on certain assets on death (or on lifetime chargeable transfers where the transferee pays the inheritance tax) may be paid by ten annual instalments (ss 227 and 228). See Examples 5 and 9.

The instalment option is available on potentially exempt transfers that become chargeable because of the donor's death within seven years providing the donee still owns the gifted property (or, for transfers of property qualifying for business or agricultural relief, replacement property) at the time of the donor's death.

Unquoted shares and securities (including shares which do not qualify for business property relief, eg shares in property investment companies) that do not represent a controlling holding only qualify as instalment assets if:

(a)   the inheritance tax cannot be paid in one sum without undue hardship, or

(b)   (for shares only) they are valued at more than £20,000 and their nominal value is at least 10% of the nominal value of all the company's shares (or if they are ordinary shares, 10% of the nominal value of the company's ordinary shares), or

(c)   in the case of a transfer on death, the tax payable on the shares or securities, together with the tax on other instalment assets, amounts to 20% or more of the tax payable by the same person on the same transfer.

Furthermore the instalment option on unquoted shares is not available for tax payable in consequence of the donor's death unless the shares are still unquoted when the donor dies (or if earlier, when the donee dies).

The gift of 10% of the shares in Printers Ltd by Peter to Elizabeth would not satisfy any of the conditions listed above so that had tax become chargeable the instalment option would not have been available.

The instalment option is available as indicated in respect of Stanley's gift to Elizabeth of the land and buildings.

A. To what extent is domicile relevant for inheritance tax purposes?

Explain the extended meaning given to domicile for the purposes of inheritance tax.

B. Leonardo, who was born in, and whose home country is, Italy, has lived in the UK since 1991, but plans to return to Italy following his retirement.

On 31 January 2007 he made a chargeable transfer of £293,000 before deducting exemptions, paying the inheritance tax due himself on the due date, having made no earlier transfers.

His remaining assets, at current values, comprise:

(a) 10,000 £1 shares in Exodus plc quoted on the Stock Exchange at 134p–140p with recorded bargains at 134, 135 and 136.

(b) 10,000 no par value bearer shares in Canadian Timber Limited. The company register is in Ontario, Canada, and the shares are quoted on the Ontario Stock Exchange at the sterling equivalent of 90–92.

(c) A half share in a painting in the UK which Leonardo and his brother, Vincento, had bought in 1976, each providing one half of the purchase money. Its value is £48,000 but a half share is worth £22,000.

(d) A house in Pisa, Italy, valued at €200,000.

(e) Three insurance policies with a UK insurance company on his life:

(i) taken out in 1978; the proceeds of £50,000 will be left to his wife, who will receive nothing else,

(ii) taken out in 1984 on which he had paid the premiums and under which £15,000 will become payable to his executor,

(iii) taken out in 1988 for the benefit of his grand-daughter under which £30,000 becomes payable on his death. Leonardo had paid each annual premium of £600 himself.

(f) Debts owing to him of:

(i) £1,500 by Michael living in the UK, and,

(ii) €1,000 by Manolo living in Italy.

(g) Cash held in bank accounts:

(i) in the UK £4,250,

(ii) in Italy €3,000.

(h) His gold watch valued at £800 and gold ring valued at £1,450, both held in the UK.

(i) His private dwelling-house in London valued at £370,000 plus furniture valued at £20,000.

(j) His UK trading business which he has run as a sole trader since his arrival in the UK, valued at £160,000.

Assume the current rate of exchange to be €1.50 = £1.

All share certificates and house deeds are held by Leonardo's solicitor at his office in Italy.

Leonardo is considering making further gifts during his lifetime as follows:

(i) his Canadian Timber Ltd shares to his niece living in Canada,

(ii) his half share in the painting to his brother, Angelo, living in London,

(iii) his house in Pisa, Italy, to his daughter living in London,

(iv) his gold ring to his grandson, living in London, in consideration of his forthcoming marriage,

(v)   his business in the UK to his son, living in London.

1.   Compute the inheritance tax payable by Leonardo following the January 2007 transfer, stating the date it falls due, and the inheritance tax which would be payable if Leonardo were to die unexpectedly within the week following the transfer, not having made any further gifts, his estate (after the 1978 insurance policy proceeds to his wife) being left to his grandchildren.

In the case of tax payable on death, identify the amounts which can be paid in instalments, the period over which instalments are payable, and the extent to which relief from interest is given on tax so payable.

2.   State whether any amounts would become chargeable to inheritance tax if Leonardo, not having died in February 2007, had made the further gifts in (i) to (v) above in March 2007 and whether any additional tax would arise if Leonardo were then to die at any time in the eight years following the making of those gifts (assuming the inheritance tax legislation remains unaltered).

A.   **Relevance of domicile for inheritance tax**

Domicile is relevant for inheritance tax purposes because, whilst the tax is charged on gratuitous transfers of UK assets regardless of the domicile of the transferor, it is also charged on gratuitous transfers of assets by persons of UK domicile regardless of where the property is situated.

Therefore it is necessary to know the domicile of the transferor when the transfer involves assets situated outside the UK.

Until the Domicile and Matrimonial Proceedings Act 1973 s 1 a married woman acquired the domicile of her husband. However, that ceased to apply with respect to marriages after 31 December 1973. Accordingly in the case of transfers between spouses/civil partners it is necessary to know the domicile of both parties because if the transferor is domiciled in the UK but the transferee is domiciled abroad then the spouse/civil partner exemption is limited to £55,000 (s 18(2)).

A person's country of domicile is usually the country that he regards as his natural home, and a change of domicile requires a high standard of proof. A domicile of origin is acquired at birth. This may be abandoned and a domicile of choice acquired. To do so requires positive action, eg changing residence, making a new will in the country of choice, obtaining citizenship etc, and abandoning the previous country. However, retaining electoral voting rights will not be taken into account (FA 1996 s 200). If the domicile of choice is lost without a new domicile being established then the domicile of origin is revived. (It is considered that Leonardo would have retained his domicile of origin in this example, as he was born in Italy and intends to return there on retirement. He also retains a house and a bank account in Italy and keeps his documents with his Italian solicitor.)

For inheritance tax purposes domicile has an extended meaning and the following persons are treated as domiciled in the UK (s 267):

(i)   Persons who on or after 10 December 1974 were domiciled in the UK and were so domiciled within the three years preceding the transfer.

(ii) Persons who were resident in the UK on or after 10 December 1974 and in not less than seventeen out of the twenty income tax years ending with the tax year of transfer.

B.   **Leonardo — inheritance tax payable**

1.   *Inheritance tax payable re January 2007 transfer*

Leonardo is domiciled in Italy, therefore property located outside the UK is excluded property. (If he was still in the UK in the year ending 5 April 2008 he would have been UK resident for 17 years and would be deemed to be UK domiciled, as indicated in A above.) The inheritance tax position on the transfer on 31 January 2007 is as follows:

			Gross	Tax (2006/07 scale)	Net
			£	£	£
31 January 2007					
Gifts within previous seven years			–	–	–
Chargeable lifetime transfer		293,000			
Less: Annual exemptions 2006/07	3,000				
2005/06	3,000	6,000			
Net transfer grossed up*			287,500	500	287,000
			287,500	500	287,000

* Net		Gross
285,000		285,000
2,000	x 100	2,500
287,000	80	287,500

Inheritance tax payable by Leonardo on 31 July 2007 = £500.

If Leonardo died in February 2007	Gross	Tax (2006/07 scale)
	£	£
Gifts within seven years before death:		
31 January 2007		
Chargeable transfer	287,500	1,000*
Cumulative transfers in seven years prior to death	287,500	1,000

(* 287,500 – 285,000 = 2,500 @ 40%)

Inheritance tax payable by donee on 31 January 2007 transfer:

On death	1,000
Less: due on lifetime transfer	500
Due from donee 31 August 2007	£ 500

Estate on death would be

		£
Shares in Exodus plc (UK listed company) 10,000 £1 shares @ 135 (midpoint between 134 and 136, being less than 134 + (¼ x (140 – 134) = 135½))		13,500
Canadian Timber Limited shares — excluded property		–
Painting held in UK — one half share		22,000
House in Italy — excluded property		–
Insurance policies — 1978		50,000
— 1984		15,000
Loans — Michael		1,500
— Manolo — excluded property		–
Cash at bank — UK		4,250
— Italy — excluded property		–
Possessions — gold watch		800
— gold ring		1,450
UK house		370,000
Furniture		20,000
Business	160,000	
Less: 100% business property relief	160,000	–
		498,500
Less: Debts — inheritance tax due on chargeable gift made 31.1.07		500
		498,000
Less: Exempt legacy — widow (1978 insurance policy)		50,000
		448,000

Note The 1988 life policy for the benefit of Leonardo's grand-daughter does not form part of the estate, the annual premiums having been exempt as gifts out of income.

As business property is left as part of residue to non-exempt beneficiaries and there is a specific gift to an exempt beneficiary (widow), business property relief will be reduced rateably (s 39A):

		£
Estate before reliefs and exemptions (448,000 + 160,000 + 50,000)		658,000
Less: Business property relief		(160,000)
		498,000
Less: Exempt legacy to widow	50,000	
Restricted by reference to business property relief		

$$160,000 \times \dfrac{\text{Exempt estate} \quad 50,000}{\text{Total estate} \quad 658,000}$$

	12,158	(37,842)
Estate chargeable to inheritance tax		460,158
Tax thereon @ 40% (lifetime transfers being above nil threshold)		£ 184,063

Amount payable by instalments

$$\text{UK house} \qquad \dfrac{370,000}{498,000} \times 184{,}063 = £136{,}754$$

Payable by ten equal yearly instalments of £13,675 from 1 September 2007 plus interest on the full outstanding balance.

2.   *Inheritance tax position if gifts in (i) to (v) were made in March 2007 and Leonardo died within following eight years*

(i)   As the Canadian Timber Ltd shares are situated outside the UK, they are excluded property and not chargeable to UK inheritance tax on transfer.

(ii)   The transfer of the half-share of the painting to Angelo would be a potentially exempt transfer of £22,000 (no annual exemptions being available since they are already fully used). No inheritance tax would be due providing Leonardo lived for seven years, otherwise the gift would be added to the transfers of £287,500 made within seven years before the date of the gift and inheritance tax would be due based upon the scale and rate of tax applicable at the date of death.

(iii)   The transfer of the house in Pisa to Leonardo's daughter would be excluded as Leonardo is not domiciled in the UK.

(iv)   The gift of the ring valued at £1,450 to Leonardo's grandson, whilst not excluded property, would be exempt as a gift of not more than £2,500 made by a grandparent in consideration of the grandson's marriage.

(v)   The transfer of the business to Leonardo's son would attract 100% business property relief, so that the potentially exempt transfer would be nil. The transfer would not be liable to inheritance tax unless Leonardo died within seven years after making the transfer. If death occurred within the seven year period, the entitlement to business property relief would have to be reconsidered at that time. The relief would only continue to be available providing the son continued to satisfy the qualifying conditions up to the date of Leonardo's death.

If Leonardo died more than three but less than seven years after giving away the painting or business, any tax payable upon the potentially exempt transfers becoming chargeable would be reduced as follows:

Death more than	3 years but less than	4 years after gift	— 20%
	4 years	5 years	— 40%
	5 years	6 years	— 60%
	6 years	7 years	— 80%

After seven years no liability would arise on death in respect of these gifts.

Explanatory Notes

Situation of property

1. The normal rules of English law apply to determine where property is situated.

    (a) Land is in the country where it is physically situated (but mortgages of land are treated as debts).

    (b) Debts are in the country where the debtor resides.

    (c) Shares are located where the share register is kept.

    (d) Life insurance policies are situated where the proceeds are payable (unless under seal, in which case they are situated where the policy is).

    (e) Business property is situated where the business is carried on.

    (f) Tangible property (including currency) is wherever it is physically situated.

    (g) Bank accounts are situated at the branch at which the deposits are payable (subject to what is said in note 4 re foreign currency accounts).

Excluded property

2. Foreign property in foreign ownership is excluded property for inheritance tax purposes. The property must be situated outside the UK and the person beneficially entitled to it must be non-UK domiciled (s 6(1)).

3. The following is also excluded property:

    (a) National Savings etc owned by persons domiciled in the Channel Islands or Isle of Man (s 6(3)).

    (b) Certain government securities issued as being exempt from tax where they are owned by persons of a description specified in the conditions of issue of the security concerned (s 6(2)) (see Example 3 part (a)(ii)). The specified conditions prior to FA 1996 required the holder to be neither domiciled nor ordinarily resident in the UK, but the reference to domicile is excluded in current issues.

    In these two cases domicile has its ordinary meaning and not the extended inheritance tax meaning.

    For further notes on the meaning and treatment of excluded property see Example 3.

Foreign currency bank accounts

4. Where a person who is *neither resident, ordinarily resident nor domiciled* in the UK dies, any foreign currency bank accounts with the Bank of England, the Post Office, or an institution authorised under the Banking Act 1987 are left out of account in valuing the estate immediately prior to death. This also applies to such accounts held by trustees of settled property in which the deceased held a beneficial interest in possession unless the settlor was domiciled in the UK at the date of the settlement or the trustees are UK domiciled, resident and ordinarily resident at the time of the beneficiary's death (s 157) (the provision in FA 1989 s 110 deeming trustees of whom one or more is UK resident all to be UK resident regardless of how many foreign resident trustees there are applies only for income tax). The individual's residence status will be determined using the normal income tax rules.

Works of art

5. Where a work of art is normally kept overseas, but becomes liable to inheritance tax on the owner's death solely because it is physically situated in the UK, that liability will be waived by Concession F7. This relief is only available if the work of art was brought into the UK solely for public exhibition, cleaning or restoration. The liability will similarly be waived if a work of art which would otherwise have left the UK to be kept overseas is retained in the UK solely for those purposes.

Business property relief

6.   For further examples and notes on the interaction of exempt legacies and business property relief see Examples 15 and 17. For details of business property relief, see Example 25.

David, domiciled in England, who had worked a small agricultural holding for many years, died on 1 May 2006 leaving the following estate in England:

Freehold agricultural land extending to 30 acres and buildings together valued at £123,500 of which the agricultural value was £92,000.

Farming machinery and stores valued at £24,884.

Timber (growing on separate freehold land) valued at £123,000, being operated on a commercial basis. The land itself was valued at £150,000 but was subject to a mortgage of the same amount, for which the lender held no security other than the land.

Leasehold house valued at £157,500.

Household chattels and car valued at £22,850.

A quoted shareholding valued at £80,822 (being a 20% holding that David had owned for many years).

Bank balance £2,303.

English debts and funeral expenses (all allowable) totalled £7,233.

In addition David owned the following property in Afaria:

Freehold house valued at 74,500 fars.

Furniture valued at 28,750 fars.

Bank balance 9,580 fars.

His gardener was owed wages of 830 fars.

He also owned the following property in Nyria:

Leasehold house valued at 22,450 nyrs.

Furniture valued at 12,250 nyrs.

Bank balance of 3,750 nyrs.

There were no outstanding liabilities in Nyria.

Death duties abroad, with no interest if paid within six months of death, are calculated on total assets less liabilities at the following flat rates:

Afaria 10%; Nyria 8%.

The UK and Afaria (but not Nyria) have a double taxation agreement.

On 1 May 2006 exchange rates were:

Afaria 1 far = 100/120p; Nyria £1 = 0.48/0.50 nyrs.

On 1 July 2006 the executor obtained probate by presenting a provisional account in which, after appropriate reliefs, realty was included at £75,000, instalment option personalty at £200,000 and non-instalment option personalty at £171,000.

Inheritance tax was not paid on realty or the instalment option personalty.

The timber was sold standing for £127,500, which was received on 1 August 2006, no election having been made for the value at death to be left out of account under ss 125 to 130.

On 20 June 2004 David had made a potentially exempt transfer (after exemptions) of £107,000 to his sister, which was his only lifetime transfer.

By his will he left £30,000 to his brother, with the residue to his sister.

On 30 November 2006 the executor presented a corrective account.

Prepare statements showing:

(a)   Death duty payable in Afaria and Nyria.*

(b)   Any balance of inheritance tax and interest payable in England on 30 November 2006 on the assumption that the minimum amount of inheritance tax was paid at that time, the balance being deferred.

(c)   The amount of tax that can be deferred.

* Assuming the rates of exchange when the duty was paid were unchanged from 1 May 2006.

(a)   **Death duty payable overseas**

		Fars		£
Afaria —	House	74,500		74,500
	Furniture	28,750		28,750
	Bank balance	9,580		9,580
		112,830		112,830
	Less: Debts	830		830
		112,000	@ 1 far = 100p	112,000
	Death duty in Afaria @ 10%	11,200	@ 1 far = 120p	£ 13,440

		Nyrs		£
Nyria —	Leasehold house	22,450		44,900
	Furniture	12,250		24,500
	Bank balance	3,750		7,500
		38,450	@ £1 = 0.5 nyrs	76,900
	Death duty in Nyria @ 8%	3,076	@ £1 = 0.48 nyrs	£ 6,408

(b)   **Computation of inheritance tax due on 30 November 2006 (Death 1 May 2006)**

Inheritance tax paid on account 1 July 2006 on non-instalment option personalty of £171,000:

		Gross £	*Tax* £
Potentially exempt transfers within seven years before death, now chargeable:			
20 June 2004		107,000	–
Estate on death per provisional account:			
Realty after reliefs	75,000		
Instalment option personalty after reliefs	200,000		
Non-instalment option personalty after reliefs	171,000	446,000	107,200*
		553,000	107,200*

(* 553,000 – 285,000 = 268,000 @ 40%)

Tax paid 1 July 2006 on £171,000 non-instalment option personalty:

$$\frac{171,000}{446,000} \text{ x £107,200} = £\,41,101$$

Chargeable estate on death   *Date of death 1 May 2006*

		£	£	£
Realty				
Freehold agricultural land and buildings			123,500	
Less: Agricultural property relief	100% x £92,000	92,000		
Business property relief	100% x £31,500	31,500	123,500	
			–	
Freehold land less mortgage thereon (£150,000 – £150,000)			–	
Freehold house in Afaria			74,500	74,500
		carried forward		74,500

	£	£	£
		brought forward	74,500
Personalty — with instalment option			
Farm machinery and stores	24,884		
Less: Business property relief — 100%	24,884	–	
Leasehold house in England		157,500	
Leasehold house in Nyria		44,900	202,400
Personalty — without instalment option			
Timber (sold)	123,000		
Less: Business property relief — 100%	123,000	–	
Quoted shares (20% holding)		80,822	
Chattels		22,850	
Bank balance		2,303	
In Afaria — chattels	28,750		
bank balance	9,580	38,330	
In Nyria — chattels	24,500		
bank balance	7,500	32,000	
		176,305	
Less: Debts and funeral expenses — UK	7,233		
Debts in Afaria	830	8,063	168,242
Chargeable estate			445,142

	Gross £	Tax £
Inheritance tax accumulation in seven years before death	107,000	–
Estate chargeable on death and tax thereon	445,142	106,857*
	552,142	106,857*

(* 552,142 – 285,000 = 267,142 @ 40%)

Estate rate is $\dfrac{106,857}{445,142} \times 100 = 24.005\%$

Since this average rate clearly exceeds the rates paid overseas, the double taxation relief will be the duty paid overseas.

	£	£	£
Liability on estate		106,857	
Less: Double tax relief —			
Afaria	13,440		
Nyria	6,408	19,848	
		87,009	
Less: Paid on account (see page 28.3)		41,101	45,908
Less: Tax deferred (at estate rate of 24.005%)			
Realty			
House in Afaria £74,500	17,884		
Less: Double tax relief:			
$\dfrac{74,500}{112,000}$ x £13,440	8,940	8,944	
Instalment option personalty £202,400	48,586		
Less: Double tax relief on house in Nyria:			
$\dfrac{44,900}{76,900}$ x £6,408	3,741	44,845	53,789
Tax repayable to personal representative on non-instalment property			(7,881)
Being: Tax on non-deferred personalty of £168,242 at estate rate of 24.005%		40,387	
Less: Double tax relief:			
Afaria $\dfrac{37,500}{112,000}$ x £13,440	4,500		
Nyria $\dfrac{32,000}{76,900}$ x £6,408	2,667		
		7,167	
		33,220	
Less: Paid on account (see page 28.3)		41,101	
		£ (7,881)	
Tax payable by personal representative on deferred property			
$\dfrac{1}{10}$ x 53,789			5,379
Total amount repayable 30 November 2006 (no interest due)			(2,502)
(c) Tax deferred			53,789
Less: First instalment			(5,379)
Amount deferred as at 30 November 2006			£ 48,410

Explanatory Notes

Converting values of foreign assets and foreign tax

1.   Foreign assets are valued by using the lower value of the exchange rate quoted, ie the more advantageous to the taxpayer. Where foreign tax is paid it is converted to sterling by using the higher value of the exchange rate on the date of payment (restricted to the amount paid if in sterling).

Agricultural and business property relief

2.   (a)   Agricultural property relief at 100% is available under s 116 on the agricultural value of the farm land and buildings. Business property relief at 100% is available under s 104 on the excess over the agricultural value and on the farming machinery and stores.

      (b)   Business property relief is also available at 100% on the growing timber. An election could have been made under s 125 for the timber (but not the land on which it stands) to be left out of account on David's death, but with business property relief at 100% there is no point in doing so. Had it been left out it would have had to be brought in later at its sale value, and only 50% business property relief would have been available on the subsequent sale (s 127(2)) (see Example 31 explanatory note 10).

             Business property relief is also available on the land on which the timber stands but it is only given on the value of business assets less liabilities so that the land does not attract the relief in this case because its value is wholly eliminated by the mortgage.

             Where the only security for the mortgage is the business land, it is not possible to reduce the business property by business property relief and then deduct the mortgage from other assets.

      (c)   For detailed notes on agricultural and business property relief and growing timber see Examples 25 and 31.

Instalment option

3.   The option for tax to be paid by ten yearly instalments is available on the following assets in this example:

      Land in the UK and abroad (including leaseholds)
      Business and agricultural property

      The first instalment is due six months after the end of the month in which the death occurred, ie on 30 November 2006 (s 227(3)).

Payment of tax and interest on underpaid/overpaid tax

4.   Inheritance tax on death is payable on presentation of the HMRC Account (s 226(2)), ie on 1 July 2006 in this example, the tax then accounted for being on the provisional amount of £171,000 non-instalment option personalty. The inheritance tax, however, is not due until six months after the end of the month in which the death occurred, ie by 30 November 2006, so the corrective account showing the revised amount payable was submitted in time to stop any interest arising on unpaid tax. In fact the provisional amount paid exceeded the actual liability, so that a refund of £2,502 is due and the question of interest on unpaid tax does not arise.

      The amount overpaid on the presentation of the account on 1 July 2006 does not attract an interest supplement. This is not overpaid tax but tax paid in advance of the due date. The amount of £2,502 found to be overpaid at 30 November 2006, on the other hand, will attract interest from that date until it is repaid.

      Interest on unpaid tax on instalment assets is charged only from the date the instalment is payable, except for land which, unless the land is agricultural property or part of an interest in a business, attracts interest on the whole of the tax unpaid.

      The first instalment due on 30 November 2006 was paid on time and accordingly no interest was payable thereon.

      Interest will therefore arise from 1 December 2006 to the date of payment on the remainder of the tax on the freehold house in Afaria, the English leasehold and the leasehold house in Nyria, whether or not the instalments are paid on time.

      In this example the inheritance tax payable on the estate is less than the amount payable on the provisional account that the personal representatives had submitted. Personal representatives need to be aware that HMRC are taking a harsher attitude to penalties where a provisional account understates the values of the assets — see Example 33 explanatory note 9.

Overseas liabilities

5. Overseas liabilities are allowable as a deduction from the deceased's estate providing such debts would be allowable if UK debts. Normally the liabilities are deducted primarily from the value of overseas assets with any surplus deductible from UK assets (s 162(5)). If the liability is secured on UK property or is payable in the UK then the debt is deductible from UK property.

Double tax relief

6. (a) Double tax relief is available where the same property is charged to tax both in the UK and overseas. Relief is given under s 158 where the UK has a double tax agreement with the country concerned and otherwise unilaterally under s 159. Where there is a double tax agreement it will usually give greater relief than that available under s 159, but if it does not, the taxpayer is given the benefit of the unilateral relief of s 159.

    (b) Section 159 enables the overseas duty paid to be deducted provided that this does not exceed the UK tax on the same property. In determining whether the UK tax is greater than the overseas tax, the average rate of UK tax is taken. This differs from double taxation relief for income tax where the UK tax applicable to overseas income can be taken as the highest rate of UK tax which applies to that taxpayer in that year of assessment.

    The UK tax on the overseas property in this example is clearly greater than the overseas tax on the same property, the UK average rate being 24.005% compared with 10% in Afaria and 8% in Nyria.

    (c) Section 159 also gives relief where both the UK and another country impose tax on property situated in a third country, or where property is situated in the UK under UK law and in another country under that country's law. Relief is calculated by the formula:

$$\frac{A}{A + B} \times C$$

    where A is the inheritance tax, B is the overseas tax and C is whichever of A and B is smaller.

A has made cumulative chargeable transfers amounting to £189,000, all in the year ending 5 April 2001.

In May 2001 he gave a fine painting that he had owned for the last ten years to his son S. The picture was worth £95,000 in the open market at the time of the gift.

In November 2001 he gave a similar picture, then worth £100,000 in the open market, to his daughter D.

In both cases any liability for capital gains tax was held over.

On 20 March 2003 S gave his picture, then valued at £117,500, to his wife W, who is an American citizen but domiciled and resident in the UK. She immediately took it to New York to hang in the family gallery.

A died in December 2005 leaving an estate valued at £400,000 equally to his son S and daughter D.

An undertaking was given by the daughter that she would keep the picture in the UK; that she would take reasonable steps for its preservation; and that she would allow reasonable access to the public to view it.

On 3 April 2007 D sold her painting at an international auction room for £150,000, out of which the auctioneers took £15,000 in fees, and capital gains tax on the sale amounted to £8,800.

Both pictures were designated by the Treasury as being of national, scientific, historic or artistic interest. Appropriate claims for relief are made in connection with all transfers.

Calculate the inheritance tax payable as a result of these events.

A

Inheritance tax

May 2001	Picture to S	95,000
	Less: Annual exemption 2001/02	3,000
	Potentially exempt transfer	92,000

| November 2001 | Picture to D — potentially exempt transfer | 100,000 |

On death of A – December 2005

		Gross	Tax on 2005/06 scale
		£	£
Gifts in lifetime:			
Cumulative transfers (year ended 5.4.2001)		189,000	–
May 2001			
Gift of picture to S (potentially exempt transfer now chargeable)		92,000	2,400*
		281,000	2,400*

(* 281,000 – 275,000 = 6,000 @ 40%)

		Gross	Tax on 2005/06 scale
November 2001			
Potentially exempt transfer of picture to D, now a chargeable transfer	100,000		
Less: Conditional exemption	100,000	–	
Inheritance tax accumulation at death		281,000	2,400
Estate on death		400,000	160,000
		681,000	162,400

| Tax payable by S (with interest on unpaid tax from 1 July 2006) after 40% tapering relief | | |
| 60% x £2,400 | £ | 1,440 |

| Tax payable by personal representatives (with interest on unpaid tax from 1 July 2006) | £ 160,000 |

Breach of conditional exemption — sale of picture by D 3 April 2007

			Gross	Tax at half rate (2006/07 scale)
			£	£
A's inheritance tax accumulation			681,000	78,800*
(* 681,000 – 285,000 = 394,000 @ 20%)				
Value of picture (sale proceeds)		150,000		
Less: Fees	15,000			
Capital gains tax	8,800	23,800	126,200	25,240
			807,200	104,040
Tax payable by D (with interest on unpaid tax from 1 November 2007)				£ 25,240

Explanatory Notes

Conditional exemption for works of art etc

1. Conditional exemption from inheritance tax for works of art etc is provided in ss 30 to 35A. Eligible assets are:

    Works of art and other objects or collections or groups of objects that are pre-eminent for their national, scientific, historic or artistic interest

    Land of outstanding scenic, historic or scientific interest

    Buildings of outstanding historic or architectural interest together with their amenity land and objects historically associated with them.

2. Transfers are conditionally exempt if designated by the Treasury *following a claim* made within two years of the event (for example following death), providing an appropriate undertaking is given by such person as the Treasury consider appropriate (usually the transferee).

3. The undertaking depends upon the category, but generally requires reasonable public access, preservation and in the case of objects, retention in the UK, until death or further disposition (s 31). Public access cannot be by prior appointment only, and the owner may be required to publicise information about the conditionally exempt asset.

4. The conditional exemption is not available if the transfer would be exempt anyway by reason of transfers to charities or one's spouse/civil partner (s 30). But on a transfer to a spouse/civil partner of property that is the subject of an earlier conditional exemption, the spouse/civil partner would have to renew the undertaking to retain the conditional exemption (s 32).

Availability of conditional exemption

5. Conditional exemption is available upon:

    (i)   Death.

    (ii)   Lifetime transfers where transferor and spouse/civil partner have between them been beneficially entitled to the subject matter throughout the preceding six years.

    (iii) Lifetime gifts not qualifying under (ii) where the transferor acquired the subject matter on an inheritance tax/capital transfer tax conditionally exempt death transfer (s 30(3)).

Potentially exempt transfers

6. When a potentially exempt transfer of heritage property is made, no claim for conditional exemption may be made until the transferor dies, and a claim will not then be relevant if the transferor has survived the gift by seven years. If he dies within seven years, s 26A provides that the potentially exempt transfer will nonetheless be exempt if the property has in the meantime been sold by private treaty to an approved body (Sch 3) or surrendered to HMRC in satisfaction of tax (s 230). If the property has been sold other than to an approved body, no claim for conditional exemption may be made. The circumstances at the transferor's death will determine whether conditional exemption is available, and if an undertaking is already in force for capital gains tax or for maintenance fund purposes it will be treated as an undertaking under s 30.

    In this example both gifts in 2000 are potentially exempt (after deducting the annual exemption from the earlier gift), so claims for conditional exemption for inheritance tax would not be made at the time of the gifts. In order to avoid capital gains tax arising on the gifts, however, it would have been necessary to make conditional claims to treat the gifts as being on a no loss no gain basis under the provisions of TCGA 1992 s 258, the appropriate undertaking as indicated in note 3 being required (see explanatory note 13).

    The removal of the picture to America by W in 2003 does not affect a potentially exempt transfer.

On the death of A the potentially exempt transfers become chargeable. S cannot claim conditional exemption (because the conditions are not satisfied at the time of A's death) and tax is payable. (The transfer from S to W was an exempt transfer and therefore did not affect the inheritance tax accumulation of S.) D can claim conditional exemption, thus saving inheritance tax of 40% x £100,000 = £40,000 less tapering relief of 40% = £24,000 at that time.

Chargeable events

7.   Inheritance tax is payable following a conditionally exempt transfer when a chargeable event occurs.

A 'chargeable event' is:

(i)   Material breach of undertaking.

(ii) Death (when a new conditionally exempt transfer might occur).

(iii) Disposal by sale, gift (when a new conditionally exempt transfer might again occur) or otherwise.

In cases (ii) and (iii), that is death or disposal, a surrender to the Board of HMRC to pay inheritance tax, or a sale by private treaty to an approved body (eg museum) is not a chargeable event (s 32). A private treaty sale to an approved body would be below market value, but above the after tax sum that would arise on an open market sale, thus dividing the benefit of the tax saving between the vendor and the approved body.

8.   Inheritance tax is chargeable on the value of the subject matter at the time of the chargeable event. The value is the sale proceeds or market value as appropriate. An unconnected sale will usually fix the value at the sale proceeds (s 33(1)(a) and (3)).

9.   The tax is calculated according to the inheritance tax accumulation of the 'relevant person' at the date of the chargeable event. The relevant person is the person who made the conditionally exempt transfer of the property. If there have been two or more such transfers, but only one within the last thirty years ending with the event then the relevant person is that last person. Otherwise HMRC may select the accumulation of any transferor out of those making appropriate claims in the last thirty years (s 33(5)).

If the relevant person is alive at the time of the chargeable event (which cannot apply in the case of a potentially exempt transfer, because such a transfer only becomes chargeable, and therefore eligible for conditional exemption, on the donor's death), half the scale rate is used, and the rate is not increased to the full rate even if the donor then dies within seven years of the date of the conditionally exempt transfer. If the relevant person is dead at the time of the chargeable event, the full scale rate is charged if the transfer was made on death, and the half scale rate if it was made in lifetime (s 33(1)(b) and (2)).

10. When D sold her picture, this was a chargeable event giving rise to a charge under s 32, with inheritance tax payable by her on the net proceeds of sale (s 33(3)). The half rate applies as the conditional exemption was given on a lifetime potentially exempt transfer that became chargeable because of the death of A within seven years after the gift. The tax has therefore been calculated by adding the proceeds to A's lifetime and death transfers, but using half the scale rates in force at the date of A's death. If, however, the rates of tax have reduced between death and the date of the chargeable event, the rates at the time the asset ceases to qualify for exemption apply (Sch 2.5). There appears to be an anomaly here in that the half scale rate can never apply in normal circumstances to a potentially exempt transfer. It appears therefore that tax could be avoided by claiming conditional exemption on death, if the undertakings were breached soon afterwards. It may be that such conduct would be attacked by HMRC as a composite transaction under the Ramsay doctrine, thus treating the chargeable event as occurring on the death and attracting tax at the full rate.

Variation of undertakings

11. Once given, an undertaking may be varied by agreement between HMRC and the person bound by the undertaking (s 35A). If that person does not agree with a variation proposed by HMRC within

six months, and the Special Commissioners consider it to be just and reasonable, they may direct that it should be made, with effect from a date not less than 60 days after the date of the direction.

Due date of payment of tax

12. Where tax becomes payable as a result of the occurrence of a chargeable event, such as the breach of an undertaking as in this example, the due date is six months after the end of the month in which the event by reason of which it is chargeable occurs (s 226(4)). Interest on overdue tax runs from that due date (s 233(1)(c)).

Capital gains tax

13. As far as capital gains tax is concerned, a gift of heritage property in lifetime that is potentially exempt from inheritance tax does not qualify for the gifts holdover relief of TCGA 1992 s 260. The gain may, however, escape tax conditionally under TCGA 1992 s 258 if the appropriate undertaking described in IHTA 1984 s 31 is given as indicated in note 6. The effect for capital gains tax purposes is that the person making the disposal by way of gift and the person acquiring it are treated as if the asset was acquired from the one making the disposal for a consideration of such an amount as would secure that on the disposal neither a gain nor a loss would accrue to the one making the disposal (TCGA 1992 s 258(4)).

On sale (other than to an approved body) or material breach the asset is treated as sold for its market value and capital gains tax arises (TCGA 1992 s 258(5)), taper relief for capital gains tax being given according to the period of ownership of the donee. If inheritance tax is chargeable on the same occasion, any capital gains tax payable reduces the value to be included as a chargeable transfer for inheritance tax (TCGA 1992 s 258(8)).

In the example, claims for conditional no gain no loss treatment for capital gains would have needed to be made by S and D to avoid an immediate capital gains tax charge on the 2001 gifts. When S gave his picture to his wife W, the gift would be a breach of the undertaking unless the undertaking was renewed by W. If it was not, S would be deemed to have sold and reacquired the asset at market value. If W made the undertaking, it would be breached when she took the asset out of the UK and the deemed disposal and reacquisition would be made by her. Although S also becomes liable to inheritance tax on the 2001 gift of the painting because of his father's death within seven years, he cannot deduct the capital gains tax paid by him (if any) from the inheritance tax value, because the occasion of the inheritance tax charge is the 2001 gift from the father, not the 2003 breach of the undertaking by S.

As far as D is concerned, she still held the painting at her father's death and the conditional exemption for inheritance tax will therefore apply, the capital gains tax undertaking being treated as an undertaking under s 30 (see note 6). When she breached the undertaking by selling the painting, both inheritance tax and capital gains tax are charged on that occasion, so the capital gains tax may be deducted from the value of the inheritance tax, as shown in the example.

Mackenzie Ltd is a property holding and investment company.

The following is a summary of its balance sheet at 31 December 2006:

	£		£	£
Issued Capital: shares of £1 each	10,000	Freehold Properties (Market value £3,000,000)		1,720,000
Reserves	1,420,000			
		Quoted Investments (Market value £1,250,000)		1,200,000
Loan Accounts;				
Robert Mackenzie 1,200,000				
James Mackenzie 200,000		Bank Deposit Account	200,000	
Duncan Mackenzie 300,000	1,700,000			
		Bank Current Account	10,000	210,000
	3,130,000			3,130,000

The issued capital had since December 1982 been held by:

Robert Mackenzie		4,000
James Mackenzie	) Robert's sons	3,500
Duncan Mackenzie	)	2,500
		10,000

On 11 January 2007 Mrs Newman, Robert Mackenzie's daughter, and her three children returned to this country from overseas. To provide for them, Robert withdrew £400,000 from his loan account with the company, which enabled him on 15 January 2007 to give £437,500 to Mrs Newman. Some of the company's investments were sold to produce sufficient cash to pay the £400,000 to Robert.

A meeting of the members was held on 18 January 2007 at which it was resolved that one of the freehold properties owned by the company and valued at £900,000 should be conveyed to Miss Diana Crawley, a very close friend of Robert's. The house was conveyed to her on 20 January 2007 without payment.

Assuming that Robert had made previous chargeable transfers totalling £290,000 in 2002/03, that James had made a gift of £81,000 to his son on 31 December 2006 and that Duncan had made no gifts other than £200,000 to his wife in December 2003, calculate the inheritance tax payable in connection with the above.

Mackenzie Ltd — apportionment of transfer of value on 20 January 2007

Transfer of value by close company on 20 January 2007 apportioned amongst participators:

Robert Mackenzie	0.40 x	900,000	=	360,000
James Mackenzie	0.35 x	900,000	=	315,000
Duncan Mackenzie	0.25 x	900,000	=	225,000
				£ 900,000

Inheritance tax payable:

Robert Mackenzie

Inheritance tax accumulation

	Gross	Tax on 2006/07 scale	Net
	£	£	£
Previous transfers within seven years	290,000	1,000*	289,000

(* 290,000 − 285,000 = 5,000 @ 20%)

15 January 2006					
Gift to daughter		437,500			
Less: Annual exemptions 2006/07	3,000				
2005/06	3,000	6,000			
Potentially exempt transfer		431,500			

		Gross	Tax	Net
20 January 2007				
Apportioned from Mackenzie Ltd (net amount)				360,000
Grossed up		450,000(*)	90,000	
		740,000	91,000	649,000

(*) £360,000 is wholly within the tax band of 20% for lifetime gifts.

The gross transfer is therefore: $360,000 \times \dfrac{100}{80} = £450,000$.

James Mackenzie

Inheritance tax accumulation

	Gross	Tax on 2006/07 scale	Net
	£	£	£

Gift to son on 31 December 2006 is a potentially exempt transfer of:			
Gift		81,000	
Less: Annual exemptions 2006/07	3,000		
2005/06	3,000	6,000	
		75,000	

	Gross	Tax	Net
20 January 2007			
Apportioned from Mackenzie Ltd (net amount)			315,000
Grossed up	322,500(*)	7,500	
	322,500	7,500	315,000

(*) £315,000 − £285,000 = £30,000 is within tax band of 20% for lifetime gifts.

The gross transfer is therefore:

30,000	x	$\dfrac{100}{80}$	=	37,500
285,000	@	nil rate		285,000
315,000				£ 322,500

Duncan Mackenzie

Inheritance tax accumulation			Gross	Tax on 2006/07 scale	Net
			£	£	£
Previous transfer to wife — exempt			–	–	–
20 January 2007					
Apportioned from Mackenzie Ltd (net amount)		225,000			
Less: Annual exemptions 2006/07	3,000				
2005/06	3,000	6,000	219,000(*)	0	219,000
Net gift grossed up			219,000	0	219,000

(*) £219,000 – £285,000 = nil within 20% tax band for lifetime gifts. The transfer is wholly within the nil rate band.

Inheritance tax payable

	£
On conveyance by company	
Robert Mackenzie	90,000
James Mackenzie	7,500
Duncan Mackenzie	0
Payable by Mackenzie Ltd	97,500
By Robert Mackenzie on gift to his daughter (£6,000 of transfer covered by annual exemptions, balance of £431,500 potentially exempt transfer)	£ nil

Explanatory Notes

Apportionment of close company transfers of value

1. Where a close company makes a transfer of value, the transfer is apportioned amongst the participators and each participator is deemed to have made a net transfer of the amount apportioned to him (s 94(1)). HMRC take the view that only actual transfers (as distinct from those apportioned to participators from a close company) can be potentially exempt transfers, so that the apportioned amounts in this example are immediately reckoned for inheritance tax.

    If, however, the estate of a participator increases in consequence of the transfer, that increase is deducted from the amount chargeable on him, because his personal wealth has only decreased by his share of the close company transfer less the consequential increase in his wealth.

2. The exempt transfer reliefs for small gifts, normal expenditure out of income and marriage gifts are not available, but the annual exemption is (s 94(5)).

3. The surrender of losses under the corporation tax group relief provisions (TA 1988 s 402) does not constitute a transfer of value (s 94(3)).

4. Where an asset is transferred between group companies on a no loss no gain basis under the provisions of TCGA 1992 s 171, the rights of minority participators are not taken into account for the purpose of apportioning transfers of value under s 94 providing the transfer has only a small effect on the value of the minority participators' rights (s 97). The provisions of s 97 have been extended by FA 2001 s 106 to cover *deemed* intra-group no loss no gain transfers on or after 1 April 2000 under the provisions of TCGA 1992 s 171A. For detailed provisions relating to the tax treatment of groups of companies see the companion book Tolley's Taxwise I 2006/07.

Transfers liable to income tax or corporation tax

5.   The apportionment rules do not apply to any part of the transfer that is liable to income tax or corporation tax in the recipient's hands (s 94(2)(a)). This will eliminate transfers of assets to participators who are employees earning £8,500 or more and to directors, which would be charged to income tax as employment income under the benefits code (ITEPA 2003 s 206) and also transfers to other participators, because they would be charged as distributions (TA 1988 s 418). A transfer by a close company to an Employee Benefit Trust may give rise to a transfer of value.

      In the circumstances of this example, HMRC would arguably seek to treat the value of the property as a benefit chargeable to income tax as employment income on the directors, in that an asset has been transferred out of the company at their direction without payment. If this were the case then the inheritance tax apportionment provisions would not apply.

Alterations of capital etc

6.   Changes in the rights or number of unquoted shares of a close company are treated as if made by a disposal at that time by the participator and are chargeable accordingly (s 98). Such transfers cannot be potentially exempt (s 98(3)).

Effect of apportionment on participators

7.   The apportioned amounts are included in the inheritance tax accumulations of the participators, unless an individual has not more than 5% of the transfer apportioned to him, in which case although the tax is computed by reference to his inheritance tax accumulation at that time, the transfer is not added to his cumulative total (s 94(4)).

Liability for payment of tax

8.   The liability to pay the inheritance tax is primarily that of the company, but if the company does not pay by the due date, liability extends to the participators and to the person who received the property transferred, except that a participator to whom not more than 5% of the transfer has been apportioned has no liability (s 202).

Capital gains tax

9.   Transfers at an undervalue by a close company also have a capital gains tax effect, in that the difference between the price paid (if any) and the market value is apportioned amongst the shareholders and regarded as reducing the capital gains tax base cost of their shares (TCGA 1992 s 125).

10.   The realisation of investments by the company has nothing to do with the inheritance tax position of any of the shareholders. It is just exchanging one asset for another (but it might trigger a charge to corporation tax on a capital gain).

11.   The gift of the property to Miss Crawley by the company is a disposal for capital gains purposes. Since the disposal is not at arm's length the company has a chargeable gain of the difference between the market value of the property and its cost plus indexation allowance to date (TCGA 1992 s 17).

      The 'loss to the donor', ie the company, in respect of the gift comprises the net of tax proceeds that the property would have realised if sold plus the tax the company has to pay on the gain, which together amount to the sum of £900,000 that is treated as a transfer of value.

Withdrawals from loan account

12.   The withdrawal by Robert of £400,000 from his loan account with the company does not comprise a transfer of value by him. He has simply put himself in cash funds by exchanging one asset for another.

The conveyance of the property to Miss Crawley would have been better arranged as a withdrawal of Robert's loan account. The personal capital gains effect at note 9 would have been avoided, and the gift of the property *by him* to Miss Crawley would have been a potentially exempt transfer. An immediate tax cost of £97,500 would have been avoided and the inheritance tax accumulations of all three shareholders not affected.

In 1986 Mr and Mrs John Webb acquired shares in Pirling Ltd, a small private investment company, of which they have since been directors.

The shares in the company are held as follows:

	Shares held	% of issued share capital
Mr Webb	1,201	26.69
Mrs Webb	1,199	26.64
	2,400	53.33
Others (not related persons)	2,100	46.67
	4,500	100.00

Mr and Mrs Webb are each considering transferring out of their respective holdings 350 shares to their adult son David by way of gift. In the event that they proceed, the transfers will be effected on the same day in January 2007, but Mrs Webb will execute her transfer first.

It is expected that HMRC Shares Valuation Division will agree valuations as follows:

53.33% holding	£500 per share
45.55% holding	£315 per share
37.77% holding	£250 per share

Mr Webb's father died in 2001 when his estate comprised an investment in standing timber valued at £120,000, which he left to John, and other assets of £391,000. An election was made to leave the timber out of account and inheritance tax was paid on the £391,000 at the death scale applicable at that time.

Mr Webb now proposes to sell the timber for £220,000 during 2006/07.

He estimates that felling expenses will amount to £24,000 and that the subsequent cost of restoring roads and fences will be £16,000.

The potentially exempt transfers (after exemptions) made up to 5 April 2006 by Mr and Mrs Webb were £318,000 and £133,000 respectively, all made between 6 April 2004 and 5 April 2005.

Assuming the legislation remains unchanged for future years, calculate:

(i)   The potential liability to inheritance tax of Mr and Mrs Webb resulting from their proposals if they die during 2008/09.

(ii) The inheritance tax liability in respect of the disposal of the timber.

(i) **Mr and Mrs Webb — Potential liability to inheritance tax on death in 2008/09 following gifts of shares**

Mr Webb

		Gross £	Tax on 2008/09 scale £
Potentially exempt transfers at 5.4.06 now chargeable		318,000	2,400*

(* 318,000 – 312,000 = 6,000 @ 40%)

January 2007			
Gift of shares in Pirling Ltd to son (working note (b))	165,565		
Less annual exemptions 2006/07 and 2005/06	6,000		
Potentially exempt transfer now chargeable		159,565	63,826
		477,565	66,226

Inheritance tax payable:

By donees of potentially exempt gifts made in 2004/05 (ie more than three years before Mr Webb's death)

Tapering relief of either 20% or 40% would be available depending on the dates of the gifts and the date of Mr Webb's death. If he died less than four years after making the gifts the amount payable would be 80% x £2,400

£ 1,920

By David on gift of shares (within three years before death therefore no tapering relief)

£ 63,826

Mrs Webb

		Gross £	Tax on 2008/09 scale £
Potentially exempt transfers at 5.4.06 now chargeable		133,000	–

January 2007			
Gift of shares in Pirling Ltd to son (working note (a))	332,065		
Less annual exemptions 2006/07 and 2005/06	6,000		
Potentially exempt transfer now chargeable		326,065	58,826*
		459,065	58,826*

(* 459,065 – 312,000 = 147,065 @ 40%)

Inheritance tax payable:

No tax is due from the donees of the gifts made in 2004/05 because the amount chargeable is below the nil threshold.

By David on gift of shares (within three years before death therefore no tapering relief)

£ 58,826

(ii) **Liability to inheritance tax on sale of timber in 2006/07**

			Gross £	Tax on 2006/07 scale £
Father's estate at death (excluding timber) (391,000 – 285,000 = 106,000 @ 40%)			391,000	42,400
Sale of timber		220,000		
Less: Expenses				
Felling	24,000			
Restoration*	16,000	40,000	180,000	72,000**
			571,000	114,400

The person who is entitled to the sale proceeds, ie Mr Webb, is liable to pay the tax, although the tax is calculated by reference to the father's estate.

Inheritance tax payable by Mr Webb is therefore £72,000.

*   Allowable expenses are expenses of disposal and of replanting. It is considered that the restoration of the roads and fences would form part of the disposal expenses.

**   If the timber constituted 'relevant business property', 50% relief would be available, which would halve the tax payable (see explanatory note 10).

Working Notes

Computation of gifts

(a)   *Mrs Webb* (using related property rules)

	£
Value of shares before transfer (53.33% holding)	
$\dfrac{1,199}{2,400}$ x (2,400 @ £500) =	599,500
Value of shares after transfer (45.55% holding)	
$\dfrac{849}{2,050}$ x (2,050 @ £315) =	267,435
Reduction in estate	332,065

(b)   *Mr Webb* (using related property rules)

	£
Value of shares before transfer (45.55% holding)	
$\dfrac{1,201}{2,050}$ x (2,050 @ £315) =	378,315
Value of shares after transfer (37.77% holding)	
$\dfrac{851}{1,700}$ x (1,700 @ £250) =	212,750
Reduction in estate	165,565

Explanatory Notes

Business property relief on shares

1. Business property relief is not available in respect of the transfer of shares by Mr and Mrs Webb because they are shares in an investment company. See Example 25 for detailed notes on business property relief.

Consecutive transfers

2. Care must be taken to calculate the transfers in the correct order. The example states that Mrs Webb makes her transfer first, thus her accumulation must be used to record the loss in value attributable to the loss of control. Note that although the shares held by Mr Webb also lose value that loss is not due to a transfer of value made by Mr Webb and is therefore not chargeable. HMRC could use the associated operations provisions to counter the loss to the Exchequer but do not normally do so unless the transactions are actually linked or form part of an avoidance package.

    For notes on associated operations, see Examples 22 and 23.

    Even though the associated operations provisions may not apply, the related property provisions will apply. See notes to Example 10 for further details.

3. If Mr Webb were to make his transfer of shares first then the potential liabilities (using related property rules) would become:

Mr Webb	£
Value of shares before transfer (53.33% holding)	
$\frac{1,201}{2,400}$ x (2,400 @ £500) =	600,500
Value of shares after transfer (45.55% holding)	
$\frac{851}{2,050}$ x (2,050 @ £315) =	268,065
Reduction in estate	332,435

Inheritance tax payable on death in 2008/09

		Gross £	Tax on 2008/09 scale £
Cumulative chargeable transfers (as before)		318,000	2,400
January 2007			
Gift of shares in Pirling Ltd to son	332,435		
Less annual exemptions 2006/07 and 2005/06	6,000		
Potentially exempt transfer now chargeable		326,435	130,574
		632,435	132,974

Mrs Webb	£
Value of shares before transfer (45.55% holding)	
$\frac{1,199}{2,050}$ x (2,050 @ £315)	377,685
Value of shares after transfer (37.77% holding)	
$\frac{849}{1,700}$ x (1,700 @ £250)	212,250
Reduction in estate	165,435

Inheritance tax payable on death in 2008/09

	Gross £	Tax on 2008/09 scale £
Cumulative chargeable transfers (as before)	133,000	–
January 2007		
Gift of shares in Pirling Ltd to son	165,435	
Less annual exemptions 2006/07 and 2005/06	6,000	
Potentially exempt transfer now chargeable	159,435	–
	280,435	–

(* 280,435 – 312,000 = nil)

A comparison of the potential inheritance tax liabilities is:

	Mrs Webb makes first transfer £	Mr Webb makes first transfer £
On death in 2008/09 of		
Mr Webb	63,826	130,574
Mrs Webb	58,826	–
	122,652	130,574

This illustrates that the order in which transfers are made may alter not only the potential total liabilities, but also where the burden of the tax falls and the future accumulation for inheritance tax. This will be particularly important not only where there are different beneficiaries but also in the context of future gifts.

Growing timber

4. Where an estate *on death* includes growing timber, an election may be made under s 125 to leave the timber (but not the land on which it stands) out of account in valuing the estate at death. The election must be made within two years of the date of death and is only available if the deceased either had been beneficially entitled to the land throughout the previous five years, or had become entitled to it without consideration (for example, by gift or inheritance).

5. The election may not be made if the woodland is occupied with agricultural land and the occupation is ancillary to that of the agricultural land. In those circumstances, however, agricultural relief would be given if the necessary conditions were fulfilled.

   For details of agricultural relief, see Example 25.

6. Following an election, the subsequent disposal by sale or gift of the timber gives rise to a charge to inheritance tax under s 126 on the sale price less allowable expenses, or if the disposal is for less than full consideration, the market value (s 127(1)). Allowable expenses are the costs of sale and expenses of replanting within three years of disposal, or such longer time as the Board allows (s 130(2)).

7. The disposal proceeds are treated as value transferred at the date of *death*, forming the top slice of the property passing on death and thus attracting the highest rates of tax (s 128). But where there have been reductions in the rates of tax, the death scale current at the time of *disposal* is used (Sch 2.4). The tax is due six months after the end of the month in which the disposal takes place, with interest payable from that date. Section 208 provides that the person entitled to the proceeds of sale (or the person who would be entitled if the disposal were a sale) is liable for the tax.

Instalment option

8. If the disposal of the timber was itself a chargeable transfer, or a potentially exempt transfer that becomes chargeable because of the donor's death within seven years, the value transferred thereby is

reduced by the tax charged under explanatory note 7 in arriving at the chargeable transfer (s 129). Section 229 provides that a claim may be made for the tax chargeable on such a transfer to be paid by ten equal annual instalments, commencing six months after the end of the month in which the transfer is made. Although this would be possible for a chargeable lifetime transfer, such as to a discretionary trust, it could not apply to a potentially exempt transfer, nor to any additional tax on a chargeable lifetime transfer, because the liability would not exist until after the donor's death. It appears, therefore, that this provision should have been amended to take account of the current treatment of potentially exempt transfers and additional liabilities on chargeable lifetime transfers. It is considered that the instalment option would in practice be available, with the first instalment being due six months after the end of the month in which the donor died. If any instalment is paid late, interest is payable only on the late instalment and not on the full amount outstanding (s 234).

Death before disposal

9.   If the person who inherits woodlands on which an election has been made dies before the timber is disposed of, no inheritance tax charge can arise in respect of the earlier death (s 126(1)).

Furthermore, a new election may then be made on the second death.

Business property relief for growing timber

10.   Where woodlands constitute 'relevant business property', ie where they are operated on a commercial basis, they qualify for 100% business property relief. But if an election is made to leave such timber out of account on a death, the net sale proceeds on subsequent sale are reduced by only 50% (s 127(2)). Elections should not therefore be made where the 100% relief is available (although part of the 100% relief may not be effective because of the way the estate devolves — see Examples 15 and 17). Where an election has already been made, as in this example, and the timber is subsequently sold, the relief can only be given at the 50% rate.

For notes on business property relief see Example 25.

Transitional estate duty provisions

11.   Under the transitional provisions that were introduced when estate duty was replaced by capital transfer tax (now inheritance tax), a liability to estate duty will arise on the sale of timber that was left out of account on a pre 13 March 1975 death. But if an inheritance tax transfer of value (other than to a spouse) intervenes (for example, the death of the person beneficially entitled) estate duty will not be chargeable at all and the transfer will be dealt with under the inheritance tax provisions (Sch 7.2). Such a transfer cannot be a potentially exempt transfer and will therefore be a chargeable transfer unless covered by exemptions (FA 1986 Sch 19.46). This provision strictly applies to the whole of any property of which any part, however small, is subject to the deferred estate duty charge. By HMRC Concession F15, any part of the property that is not subject to the deferred charge will not be prevented from being a potentially exempt transfer.

Mr Rosewell, a UK domiciled individual, owned a set of four Rennie Mackintosh chairs which he wanted to give to his son. Rather than gift them as a set, he gifted them individually to his son in August 2002, 2003, 2004 and 2005 so as to lower the gifted value.

The relevant values were:

Number of chairs	2002 £	2003 £	2004 £	2005 £
Four	40,000	44,000	48,000	52,500
Three	30,000	33,000	36,500	40,000
Two	17,500	19,250	21,000	23,500
One	6,250	6,875	7,500	8,250

In September 2005 Mr Rosewell gifted £285,500 cash into a discretionary trust of which he is a beneficiary. The trustees agreed to pay any tax due.

Mr Rosewell's father (a widower) had died in May 1998. In his will he left woodlands including standing timber with a then value of £125,000 to Mr Rosewell. The father's estate was worth £575,000 excluding the timber and the executors elected to exclude the timber from the chargeable estate. In February 2006 Mr Rosewell gifted the woodland to his son, who agreed to pay any tax due. The land was then worth £350,000 and the timber £150,000. The woodland was not run as a business.

After the transactions detailed above Mr Rosewell's estate was worth £200,000. Under his will he left half of the estate to his wife and the balance equally between his son and daughter.

Mr Rosewell is concerned about the inheritance tax exposures were he to die, for example, in December 2007. His health has significantly deteriorated in the last few months. He has made no other gifts or transfers apart from those stated above.

Explain the inheritance tax implications of the above transactions if Mr Rosewell were to die on 30 December 2007 (assuming all assets retain their current values and that the legislation remain unchanged).

Inheritance tax implications of transactions by Mr Rosewell in the event of his death on 30 December 2007

Position on gifts in lifetime

Gifts of Rennie Mackintosh chairs to son (using associated operations rules for second and subsequent gifts)

		£	£
August 2002	Value of set of four chairs	40,000	
	Value of three chairs	30,000	
	Transfer of value	10,000	
	2002/03 annual exemption	3,000	
	2001/02 annual exemption	3,000	6,000
	Potentially exempt transfer		4,000
August 2003	Value of four chairs	44,000	
	Value of two chairs	19,250	
	Loss to donor	24,750	
	Less: earlier transfer	10,000	
	Transfer of value	14,750	
	2003/04 annual exemption	3,000	
	Potenitally exempt transfer		11,750
August 2004	Value of four chairs	48,000	
	Value of one chair	7,500	
	Loss to donor	40,500	
	Less: earlier transfers (10,000 + 14,750)	24,750	
	Transfer of value	15,750	
	2004/05 annual exemption	3,000	
	Potentially exempt transfer		12,750
August 2005	Value of four chairs	52,500	
	Less: earlier transfers		
	(10,000 + 14,750 + 15,750)	40,500	
	Transfer of value	12,000	
	2005/06 annual exemption	3,000	
	Potentially exempt transfer		9,000

Gift with reservation to discretionary trust

		Gross £	Tax (2005/06 scale) £
Sept 2005	Settlement on trust	285,500	2,100

(* 285,500 – 275,000 = 10,500 @ 20%)

Tax payable by trustees £2,100

Gift of woodlands to son

The gift of the woodlands to Mr Rosewell's son would trigger a charge to inheritance tax in respect of the timber in Mr Rosewell's father's estate, based on the value at the date of disposal. Since the estate was well in excess of the inheritance tax threshold the tax charge would be £150,000 @ 40% = £60,000, payable by Mr Rosewell six months after the end of the month of disposal, ie by 31 August 2006. The tax would reduce the value of the transfer to the son, as follows:

		£	£
February 2006	Market value of woodlands (350,000 + timber 150,000)	500,000	
	Less: Tax payable re father's estate	60,000	
	Potentially exempt transfer		440,000

On Mr Rosewell's death – 30 December 2007

Since Mr Rosewell made a gift with reservation to the discretionary trust, the double charges regulations must be used when computing the tax following his death. The first calculation is to charge the gift in the death estate and ignore the transfer to the trust, and the second to charge the gift to the trust and exclude it from the death estate.

First calculation (ignoring gift to trust)

			Gross £	Tax (on 2007/08 scale) £
Gifts within seven years before death:				
August 2002	PET re gift of chairs		4,000	–
August 2003	PET re gift of chairs		11,750	–
August 2004	PET re gift of chairs		12,750	–
August 2005	PET re gift of chairs		9,000	–
Sept 2005	Gift to trust — ignored		–	–
Feb 2006	Gift of woodlands		440,000	71,000*
			477,500	71,000*

(* 477,500 – 300,000 = 177,500 @ 40%)

Value of estate on death:				
Free estate	200,000			
Less: Spouse exemption	100,000	100,000		
Settled property		283,400**	383,400	153,360
			860,900	
Total tax payable				224,360

** Initial value of trust £285,500 less tax of £2,100 paid by trustees out of the amount settled.

Second calculation (excluding value of trust from death estate)

		Gross £	Tax (on 2007/08 scale) £
Gifts within seven years before death:			
August 2002	PET re gift of chairs	4,000	–
August 2003	PET re gift of chairs	11,750	–
August 2004	PET re gift of chairs	12,750	–
August 2005	PET re gift of chairs	9,000	–
Sept 2005	Chargeable transfer to discretionary trust	285,500	9,200*
(* 323,000 – 300,000 = 23,000 @ 40%)		323,000	9,200*
Feb 2006	Gift of woodlands	440,000	176,000

	£	Gross £	Tax £
Value of estate on death	200,000		
Less: Spouse exemption	100,000	100,000	40,000
		863,000	
			225,200
Less tax paid in lifetime			2,100
Total tax payable			223,100

Since the first calculation shows the higher tax figure, that calculation applies. The tax of £2,100 paid by the trustees in lifetime is, however, allowed as a credit against the tax payable in respect of the trust property at death, reducing the total payable to £222,260 (see explanatory note 5). Inheritance tax is therefore payable as follows:

	£	£
By son re woodlands		71,000
By trustees of discretionary trust 283,400 @ 40%	113,360	
Less paid in lifetime	2,100	111,260
By personal representatives		40,000
		222,260

Explanatory Notes

Associated operations

1. The attempt by Mr Rosewell to reduce the value of the gift of the chairs by giving them in different tax years is blocked by the associated operations provisions of s 268 (for details see Examples 22 and 23). Spreading the gifts does, however, enable the annual exemptions to be used.

Growing timber

2. The provisions enabling growing timber to be left out of a deceased's estate are dealt with in Example 31. Where the disposal of the timber is a chargeable transfer or, as in this example, a potentially exempt transfer that becomes a chargeable transfer, the tax charged in respect of the original estate as a result of the disposal of the timber reduces the value transferred, as illustrated for Mr Rosewell (s 129). See Example 31 explanatory note 8 re paying tax by instalments.

Gifts with reservation and double charges regulations

3. By including himself as a beneficiary of the discretionary trust, Mr Rosewell has made a gift with reservation. The effect is that the gift to the trust is chargeable when made, but the value of the trust is still included in his estate for inheritance tax purposes so long as he is included as a beneficiary. See Example 24 for an illustration of the release of such a reservation in lifetime.

4.   The effect of the gifts with reservation rules is to charge tax twice, and the double charges regulations (SI 1987/1130) give relief for the double charge by providing for tax to be charged at the higher of two calculations, the first being to charge the gift in the death estate and ignore it in lifetime and the second to charge the gift in lifetime and exclude it from the death estate. For the detailed provisions and further illustrations see Examples 19, 20 and 24.

5.   When making the first calculation, in which the gift to the trust in lifetime is ignored and is included in the death estate at its then value, the tax paid on the gift in lifetime is not taken into account. If, however, the first calculation proves to give the higher figure of tax payable, the tax paid in lifetime is credited against the tax attributable to the gift. Note, however, that this credit is taken into account *after* deciding which of the two calculations shows the higher figure (SI 1987/1130 reg 5(4)). In this example, had the lifetime tax been deducted before making the comparison, the second calculation would have shown the higher tax figure (£223,100 compared with £222,260).

        When giving credit for the tax paid in lifetime in the second calculation, that figure will be restricted to the tax payable on death shown in the earlier part of the calculation. That restriction does not apply in this example.

Capital gains tax implications of gift of chairs

6.   Mr Rosewell's gifts of the chairs to his son also have implications for capital gains tax. There are two separate provisions affecting the capital gains calculations. The first is the connected persons provisions of TCGA 1992 ss 19 and 20. Where assets are disposed of within a period of six years to one or more connected persons (such as Mr Rosewell's son in this example) and their value taken together is higher than their separate values, the disposal value is taken to be a proportionate part of the aggregate value, and the legislation provides that earlier tax charges should be adjusted appropriately. The second is the chattels exemption of TCGA 1992 s 262, which provides that chattels such as antiques are exempt if sold for £6,000 or less, with marginal relief for proceeds above £6,000. If articles that constitute a set are sold on different occasions to the same person (or connected persons) the transactions are treated as a single transaction for the purpose of the exemption, earlier tax charges similarly being required to be adjusted appropriately. See the companion to this book, Tolley's Taxwise I 2006/07, for full details of the capital gains tax provisions.

(a)   In relation to inheritance tax there is a statutory duty laid on solicitors, accountants and others (except barristers) to make a return to the Board of HMRC when they have been acting in a professional capacity on behalf of a settlor in certain given circumstances.

When does that statutory duty arise and what are its limitations?

(b)   A client who has undertaken to discharge any inheritance tax payable informs you that he has received a Notice of Determination from HMRC in which it is specified that the value of a holding of 2,500 shares in T Ltd (25% of the equity) which he had transferred to a discretionary settlement, has been determined at £20 per share.

If your client considers that the value of the shares is not more than £5 each, what advice would you offer?

(c)   When and in what circumstances is it possible to obtain a grant of representation to a deceased person without first delivering an HMRC Account?

How is the legal personal representative protected against any subsequent claim from the Revenue for inheritance tax in connection with the death when a grant has been issued in this way, and in what circumstances is such protection lost?

Can he still be called on to complete an HMRC Account?

(d)   When and in what circumstances is it necessary to render an account of transfers of value made during the lifetime of the transferor?

(a)   **Duty to make return to Revenue re settlements**

Section 218 provides that where any person, other than a barrister, has in the course of his trade or profession been concerned with the making of a settlement where the settlor is domiciled in the UK and the trustees are not or will not be resident in the UK, he must within three months of the making of the settlement make a return to the Board of HMRC. The return must state the names and addresses of the settlor and of the trustees.

For this purpose the trustees are regarded as non-resident unless the general administration of the settlement is carried on in the UK and the trustees or a majority of them are also resident in the UK (s 218(3)).

A return is not required where the settlement was created by a will or where such a return has already been made by another person, for example the trustees (s 218(2)).

(b)   **Notice of Determination relating to value of shares**

The client should be advised to appeal in writing against the determination of the value of the shares specified in the notice. The appeal must be made within thirty days of service of the notice and must state the client's grounds of appeal, ie that the true value of the shares is not more than £5 each (s 222(1)).

The appeal will normally be made to the Special Commissioners, but it may be made to the High Court if either:

(i)   it is agreed between the client and HMRC that the appeal will be to the High Court, or

(ii)   following an application by the client, the High Court is satisfied that the matters to be decided are substantially questions of law (s 222(2) and (3)).

If the client makes the appeal outside the thirty day limit it will be allowed to proceed providing there is a reasonable excuse for the delay (s 223).

(c)   **Grant of representation to deceased's estate, exempt and excepted estates**

Personal representatives are not required to produce an account to the probate registry to obtain a grant of representation; instead they provide a form P26A. The HMRC account must be sent to HMRC Capital Taxes and the inheritance tax on the non-instalment property must be paid before the grant is issued. Form P26A is incorporated within the HMRC account form IHT200.

Excepted estates

To apply for a grant of representation for an excepted estate the personal representative completes form IHT 205 (C5 in Scotland) or IHT 207 for those domiciled abroad. The form is given to the Probate Registry.

There is an excepted estate where the conditions set out below are satisfied.

There are three types of excepted estate set out in SI 2004/2543 applicable from 1 November 2004 with respect to deaths on or after 6 April 2004.

A.   Under paragraph 4(2) the conditions are:

(i)   The deceased was domiciled in the UK at the date of death;

(ii)   the estate consists only of property passing under the deceased's will or intestacy or under a trust, nominated property, or joint property passing by survivorship;

(iii)   where any trust assets were held in a single trust in which the deceased had an interest in possession with a value not exceeding £100,000;

(iv)   not more than £75,000 represents the value of property situated outside the UK;

(v) the deceased died without having made any chargeable transfer in the seven years before his death except cash, quoted shares or quoted securities, or land and buildings (and contents), with a total gross value not exceeding £100,000. For this purpose paragraph 4(7) indicates that business property relief and agricultural property relief shall not apply.

(vi) the gross value of the estate plus transfer within seven years of death plus exempt transfers to spouse/civil partner, charities etc within seven years of death do not exceed the nil rate band at death.

B. Under paragraph 4(3) the conditions are:

(i) The deceased was domiciled in the UK at the date of death;

(ii) the conditions set out in A above at (ii) to (v) apply;

(iii) The gross value of chargeable assets of the estate (before deducting liabilities, reliefs or exemptions), when added to the cumulative chargeable gifts made in the seven years before death, does not exceed £1,000,000 and the net chargeable estate after deduction of spouse/civil partner and charity exemptions only does not exceed the nil rate band.

C. Under paragraph 4(5) the estate is exempt if the deceased was never domiciled (or deemed domicile) in the UK, the estate consists only of cash or quoted shares and the gross value does not exceed £100,000.

The requirement for an HMRC account to be submitted is relaxed by regulations issued under the provisions of s 256. The regulations enable a grant of representation to be issued without the completion of an HMRC account in the case of excepted estates. The procedures are explained in HMRC leaflet IHT12.

An estate is not an excepted estate if the deceased had made a gift with reservation of benefit which either continued until death or ceased within seven years before death.

Protection from liability to inheritance tax:

After thirty-five days (the 'prescribed period') from the issue of the grant all persons potentially liable for inheritance tax in respect of the excepted estate are automatically discharged from liability and any charge for such tax on any property comprised in the estate is removed.

The protection is lost:

1. in the case of fraud or failure to disclose material facts or

2. if it subsequently comes to light that there is further property which causes the excepted estate conditions not to be satisfied (eg the gross value exceeds £1,000,000, or other property exceeds the stipulated limits) or

3. if within the 'prescribed period' a notice in writing is issued by HMRC to the personal representatives requiring delivery of an HMRC account.

If it is discovered at any time that the estate is not an excepted estate then the personal representative must deliver a Corrective Account (C4) to the Revenue within six months of the discovery.

If an estate ceases to be an excepted estate because of a deed of variation then again a C4 is required within six months of the date of variation. HMRC say it will help them process accounts more quickly if copies of the signed IHT 205/C5 or if appropriate the instrument of variation are attached to the C4.

The Revenue have agreed to adopt this procedure instead of insisting on a full form IHT 200 being delivered (see HMRC IHT Newsletter Aug 2004).

(d) **Rendering an account of chargeable transfers**

Under section 216 persons liable to inheritance tax are required to submit an account in respect of *chargeable transfers* made in lifetime before the end of twelve months from the end of the month in which the transfer is made unless the transfer is an excepted transfer or excepted termination (in relation to life interest trusts) or, in the case of discretionary trusts, the settlement is an excepted settlement. There were previously no provisions excepting trustees of discretionary trusts from making returns of chargeable transfers (ie ten yearly charges or exit charges), even though the trust funds were too small to give rise to any tax liability. New provisions for 'excepted settlements' have been introduced for chargeable events on or after 6 April 2002 (SI 2002/1733).

An account is also required in the case of alternatively secured pension funds following the death of a member of the scheme or a relevant dependant of the member. The account is required from the scheme administrator of a registered pension scheme within 12 months of the end of the month in which the individual died.

Whilst a potentially exempt transfer is a transfer of value it is not a chargeable transfer unless the transferor dies within seven years. Accordingly there is no requirement to notify HMRC Capital Taxes on the making of such a transfer. On the death of the transferor the transferee is primarily liable for any inheritance tax on the potentially exempt transfer and is obliged to submit an account within twelve months from the end of the month in which the transferor died (s 216(6)). The personal representatives of the transferor have a secondary liability for any inheritance tax arising, and they are required under s 216 to give details of all chargeable transfers made by the deceased with the seven years before his death. If they cannot establish the exact value of any property, the account may contain a provisional figure, but they must undertake to deliver a further account as soon as the exact amount is ascertained.

Where a person holds property subject to a reservation (or within seven years after the release of a reservation) then on the death of the donor that person must deliver to the Board an account of such property within twelve months from the end of the month in which the donor died (s 216(6)(ab)).

An 'excepted termination' is the termination of a life interest in a trust where the life tenant has given notice to the trustees of the availability of annual or marriage exemptions and the value transferred is covered by the exemptions.

An 'excepted settlement' is a discretionary trust in relation to which there are no related settlements (ie settlements created by the settlor on the same day) and in respect of which:

(i) the assets have always comprised only cash (and the settlor has not added any capital to the trust after its creation)

(ii) the trustees have been UK resident throughout the trust's existence

(iii) the total value of the assets at the time of the chargeable event is less than £1,000.

If someone who has submitted an account discovers that it is materially incorrect, he must submit an amended account within six months after the discovery of the defect (s 217).

Under s 219A HMRC may require anyone liable to deliver an account under s 216 or 217 to produce relevant documents and accounts. The person receiving the notice may appeal against it within thirty days from the date on which the notice was given (s 219B).

Explanatory Notes

Accounts, returns and provision of other information

1. An *Account* is a document completed by a transferor (or other taxable person) providing details of a transaction to which a liability to inheritance tax may apply.

A *Return* is a document submitted by a person about transactions affecting others.

2. In addition to the returns dealt with in part (a) of the example, the Board has power to require a person to provide information as specified in a notice under s 219. This does not extend to information in respect of which a lawyer could maintain a claim of professional privilege, except that solicitors may be obliged to disclose the names and addresses of clients. There is no right of appeal against a s 219 notice.

A notice under this paragraph may be combined with one relating to income tax.

The s 219 requirement to provide information is extended by FA 1990 s 125 to require someone to provide information in respect of tax liabilities outside the UK that are of a similar nature to inheritance tax if this is provided for in a double tax agreement, and the s 219 requirements also apply from 28 July 2000 where a tax information exchange agreement has been made by the UK with the country concerned (s 220A).

Both double taxation and information exchange agreements may provide that information may not only be exchanged with, but also obtained for, the relevant overseas country.

Notice of Determination

3. The notice of determination by the Board under s 221 dealt with in part (b) of the example may be issued to the transferor, or to any person liable for any of the tax chargeable on the value transferred, or to anyone making a claim in respect of the value transferred.

The notice may specify all or any of the following:

(a) Date of transfer

(b) Value transferred and value of any property to which the value transferred is wholly or partly attributable

(c) Transferor

(d) Tax chargeable and persons liable

(e) Tax overpaid and date from which interest will be added on overpayment (and rate of interest)

(f) Any other relevant matter (s 221(1) and (2)).

4. The determination of any fact relating to a transfer is to be in accordance with the account or return submitted if the Board is satisfied that it is correct but otherwise is to be made by the Board to the best of their judgment (s 221(3)).

Appeals against Notices of Determination

5. Appeals are to the Special Commissioners or High Court unless the notice is in connection with the value of land, when the appeal is to the Lands Tribunal (s 222(4)). The Special Commissioners may refer any question as to the value of land directly to the Lands Tribunal, rather than the taxpayer being required to make a fresh appeal.

6. An appeal on the determination of the Special Commissioners may be made on a point of law by requesting a 'case stated' for the opinion of the High Court (s 225).

The procedure is the same as that relating to income tax appeals on a point of law.

Excepted estates

7. Where an estate is an excepted estate the personal representatives will swear a revised form of oath stating that the gross value of the estate does not exceed the appropriate amount.

Persons required to deliver an account

8.   The provisions requiring those liable to inheritance tax in lifetime to render an account are dealt with in part (d) of the example.

The personal representatives of a deceased person must deliver an account of all property which formed part of the estate at death unless the estate is an excepted estate. Where there are no personal representatives then:

(a)   every person in whom property of the estate vests, or who is beneficially entitled to an interest in possession on or after the deceased's death, and

(b)   where property passes to a settlement without an interest in possession, every person for whose benefit any of that property, or income from it, is applied

must deliver an account to the Board specifying the property in which he has an interest.

The account is submitted on HMRC account form IHT200. This is accompanied by a worksheet (IHT(WS)). HMRC produce a booklet IHT210 (How to fill in form IHT200), individual guidance notes for each of the supplementary pages and booklet IHT213 (How to fill in form IHT(WS)). A practitioner's guide booklet IHT215 collects all the guidance together in a single volume.

Penalties

9.   The legislation imposes various penalties in relation to inheritance tax as follows (ss 245, 245A, 247):

(a)   Under s 247, someone liable for tax on a chargeable transfer who fraudulently or negligently provides any incorrect account, information or document, is liable to a penalty not exceeding £3,000 (unless no additional inheritance tax is payable as a result of the misinformation).

Where the person who provided the incorrect information is not liable for the tax, a penalty is payable of up to £3,000 for fraud or negligence.

(b)   The penalties for negligence apply equally to someone who discovers that information has been supplied that is incorrect in a material respect (regarded by HMRC as involving a tax error of £1,000 or more) and fails to notify HMRC without unreasonable delay (considered by HMRC to be within 30 days), whether that person is the person who supplied the information or the person who is liable for the tax (s 248). HMRC have, however, stated that if incorrect accounts result from an innocent error they will not seek a penalty if they are notified within six months after the error is discovered.

(c)   Anyone who assists in or induces the delivery of information known to be incorrect is liable to a penalty of up to £3,000 (s 247(4)).

(d)   Under s 245, a penalty of £100 (restricted to tax due) applies if someone fails to deliver an account under s 216 or s 217 unless there is a reasonable excuse.

A further penalty of up to £60 a day may be charged if the failure continues after it has been declared by a court or by the Special Commissioners. If daily penalties have not been sought, and the account is more than six months late, a further penalty of £100 may be charged.

(e)   Under s 245A, a person who fails to make a return under s 218 relating to a trust with non-resident trustees (as to which see part (a) of the example), or to comply with a notice requiring information under s 219 (see explanatory note 2), is liable to a penalty of up to £300 plus a further penalty of up to £60 a day if the failure is declared by a court or by the Special Commissioners. A penalty of up to £3,000 will apply where the failure continues one year after the due date. The section also provides for a penalty of up to £50 plus a daily penalty of up to £30 for failing to comply with a notice under s 219A (see part (d) of the example).

For deeds of variation made on or after 1 August 2002, s 245A has been amended by FA 2002 s 120 to include a penalty where personal representatives fail to send the Revenue a copy of the variation and notify the amount of additional tax payable (see Example 34 explanatory note 5). The penalty is an amount of £100 plus a further penalty of up to £60 a day if the failure is declared by a court or by the Special Commissioners.

The penalties under (d) above cannot exceed the tax chargeable, and penalties will not be charged under (d) or (e) if there is a reasonable excuse for the delay. The daily penalties are not imposed if the fault is remedied before proceedings have started.

HMRC's stated practice is to mitigate penalties according to the degree of disclosure, the cooperation given and the gravity of the offence. Further details are in the penalties leaflet IHT13 issued by HMRC Capital Taxes.

Personal representatives should be aware that HMRC are taking a harsher attitude to the question of penalties where they consider that an HMRC Account containing estimated valuations has been submitted without the personal representatives having made 'the fullest enquiries that are reasonably practicable in the circumstances' as required by s 216(3A). In a case before the Special Commissioners (Robertson v CIR, SpC 309, 2002), they sought to impose a penalty of £10,000 on an executor who had submitted an account within six weeks after the testator's death containing estimated figures which were later found to be substantially understated, even though corrective accounts had been submitted less than six months after the death. The Special Commissioners found in favour of the executor, commenting that the Revenue had wholly failed to show that the executor was guilty of negligence. He had acted in accordance with accepted practice in submitting estimated figures and making prompt arrangements for professional valuations. The Revenue were held to have acted wholly unreasonably and the executors were entitled to costs in connection with the hearing. Despite the executor's success in this case, it would be advisable for personal representatives to ensure that they have made all enquiries that are *reasonably practicable* before including estimated figures in HMRC Accounts.

Dr and Mrs Slowe made their wills without professional advice, each leaving the whole of his/her estate to the surviving spouse with the proviso that should the spouse predecease him/her the estate should be divided between their children.

On 31 December 2006 they were involved in a road accident in which Dr Slowe (aged fifty) died instantly. Mrs Slowe (aged fifty-one) was seriously injured and died seven days later. They had two children, John (aged twenty-five) and Jill (aged eighteen).

At death Dr Slowe's interest in the group practice in which he was a partner was valued at £76,000. He also owned assets valued at £33,000, and the family home, valued at £310,000, was in his sole ownership. He had no interest in any settlements nor had he made any lifetime gifts.

Mrs Slowe had assets of her own valued at £23,000 and was the life tenant of the estate of her late father, who died on 20 February 1985, the reversionary interest passing to her children equally. The settlement was valued at £200,000 on 7 January 2007. During her lifetime Mrs Slowe had made chargeable transfers amounting to £85,000 (all less than three years before death).

(a)   Compute the inheritance tax payable by reason of the deaths of Dr and Mrs Slowe.

(b)   Consider whether it would be possible to mitigate that liability.

(c)   Comment on what the tax position would have been if they had died simultaneously.

(d)   Assuming professional advice had been obtained before death so that the wills had included an appropriately worded survivorship clause, recompute the inheritance tax payable consequent upon their deaths.

(e)   Prepare a table comparing the tax payable at (a) and (d), and comment on the difference in tax payable at (d) with what would have been payable under (b) and (c).

(a) **Inheritance tax payable on death of Dr Slowe — 31 December 2006**

Nil, since all property passes to Mrs Slowe which is an exempt transfer.

Inheritance tax payable on death of Mrs Slowe — 7 January 2007

		£	£
Free estate			
Family home			310,000
Other assets —	Own	23,000	
	Husband's estate:		
	Assets from partnership	76,000	
	Other assets	33,000	132,000
			442,000
Settled property			
Life interest in estate of late father			200,000
Amount subject to inheritance tax			642,000

Inheritance tax accumulation	Gross £	Tax £
Cumulative transfers prior to death	85,000	–
Amount liable on death	642,000	176,800*
	727,000	176,800*

(* 727,000 – 285,000 = 442,000 @ 40%)

Estate rate $\dfrac{176,800}{642,000} \times 100 = 27.5389\%$

Inheritance tax payable:		
By personal representatives	442,000 @ 27.5389%	121,722
By trustees of settled property	200,000 @ 27.5389%	55,078
		£ 176,800

(b) **Mitigating Mrs Slowe's inheritance tax liability**

The personal representatives of Mrs Slowe could, within two years after Dr Slowe's death, make a written disclaimer of the gift to her under his will (s 142). This would result in an intestacy, and under the intestacy rules a 28 day survivorship period applies to the spouse entitlement, so the effect of such a disclaimer would be that Dr Slowe's estate would pass to the children. The same effect would be obtained if, again within two years of Dr Slowe's death, Mrs Slowe's personal representatives entered into a written variation under s 142 to redirect the assets to the children.

If a deed of variation or disclaimer is executed, it will not be a transfer of value and inheritance tax will be calculated as though the deed displaced the provisions of the will (ie computed as in part (d) of the example) *providing* in the case of a variation (not a disclaimer) that the instrument of variation contains a statement that the variation is intended to have that effect.

Since additional tax would be payable on Dr Slowe's estate, then within six months after the date of such a variation Dr Slowe's personal representatives, together with Mrs Slowe's personal representatives, would have to notify HMRC Capital Taxes of the amount of extra tax and send a copy of the variation. See explanatory note 5 for further details.

(c) **Simultaneous deaths (commorientes)**

Where two or more persons die at the same time or in circumstances where it cannot be known which survived the other(s), it is assumed under the rule of commorientes that the elder died first and accordingly that the younger is deemed to have survived the elder (Law of Property Act 1925 s 184). However, for inheritance tax purposes s 4(2) provides that they shall be assumed to have died at the same instant.

Any bequest from one to the other will accordingly be ignored for inheritance tax purposes since neither survived the other. Therefore if Dr and Mrs Slowe had both died at the same time (or if it could not be determined who died first) then for the purposes of general law (ie the actual devolution of the assets) Mrs Slowe (being the elder) would be deemed to have died first, and her estate would pass under her will to her husband. On the death of Dr Slowe his estate (now including his wife's estate) would pass under his will to the children.

For inheritance tax purposes, however, Dr Slowe would be deemed to have died at the same time as Mrs Slowe and his estate for inheritance tax would not include his wife's assets.

Even so, when computing the inheritance tax liability on the estate of Mrs Slowe the assets other than the settled property would in fact pass to Dr Slowe's estate and therefore would be exempt (s 18), whereas the settled property would revert under the terms of the settlement to the children and a liability would arise as follows:

Inheritance tax payable on simultaneous deaths

	£	£
Mrs Slowe (elder)		
Free estate	23,000	
Less: Exempt transfer to Dr Slowe	23,000	nil
Settled property		
Life interest in estate of late father		200,000
Amount subject to inheritance tax		200,000

Inheritance tax accumulation	Gross £	Tax £
Cumulative transfers prior to death	85,000	–
Amount liable on death	200,000	0*
	285,000	0*

(* 285,000 – 285,000 = 0 @ 40%)

	£
Inheritance tax payable:	
By personal representatives	nil
By trustees of settled property	0

	£	£
Dr Slowe (younger)		
Family home		310,000
Interest in practice	76,000	
Less: 100% business property relief	76,000	–
Other assets (excluding Mrs Slowe's assets of £23,000)		33,000
Amount subject to inheritance tax		343,000

Inheritance tax accumulation	Gross £	Tax £
Cumulative transfers prior to death	–	–
Amount liable on death	343,000	23,200*
Inheritance tax payable by personal representatives		23,200*

(* 343,000 – 285,000 = 58,000 @ 40%)

(d) **Survivorship clauses**

To prevent devolution and taxation problems relating to deaths at or near the same time, it is common to include a survivorship clause in a will. For example, the bequest to the spouse is made conditional upon that person surviving for a specified period such as thirty days after the first death. Such clauses are effective for inheritance tax purposes providing the specified period does not exceed six months (s 92) and tax is computed as if the dispositions which take effect at the end of the period (or on the earlier death of the contingent legatee) had taken place at the first death. If survivorship clauses had been included in the wills of Dr and Mrs Slowe (or if Mrs Slowe's personal representatives had disclaimed the inheritance or entered into a variation as indicated in part (b) above) the tax position on their deaths would have been as follows:

Inheritance tax payable on death of Dr Slowe — 31 December 2006

		£
Family home		310,000
Interest in practice	76,000	
Less: 100% business property relief	76,000	–
Other assets		33,000
Estate on death for inheritance tax		343,000

Inheritance tax accumulation	Gross £	Tax £
Cumulative transfers prior to death	–	–
Estate on death	343,000	23,200
Inheritance tax payable by personal representatives (as in (c))		23,200

Inheritance tax payable on death of Mrs Slowe — 7 January 2007

	£
Free estate	
Assets	23,000
Settled property	
Life interest in estate of late father	200,000
Estate on death	223,000

Inheritance tax accumulation	Gross £	Tax £
Cumulative transfers prior to death	85,000	–
Estate on death	223,000	9,200*
	308,000	9,200*

(* 308,000 – 285,000 = 23,000 @ 40%)

Estate rate $\dfrac{9,200}{223,000}$ x 100 = 4.126%

Inheritance tax payable:		£
By personal representatives	£23,000 @ 4.126%	948
By trustees of settled property	£200,000 @ 4.126%	8,252
		9,200

(e)   **Comparison of tax payable**

	Under (a) above (without variation) £	With survivorship clause £
By personal representatives of Dr Slowe	–	23,200
By personal representatives of Mrs Slowe	121,722	948
	121,722	24,148
By trustees of settled property	55,078	8,252
	176,800	32,400

Tax of £36,400 would also be payable if a disclaimer or variation as at (b) were executed.

The tax payable in the event of simultaneous deaths (c) is £23,000 (£4,000 + £23,200). The difference of £9,200 compared with the tax payable had the survivorship clause or a family deed operated is because Mrs Slowe's own assets of £23,000 are in the event of simultaneous deaths exempt from inheritance tax since they none the less pass under her will to her husband (but are not reckoned in his estate for inheritance tax purposes); whereas they are chargeable in her estate if they pass directly to her children as they would under the survivorship clause or family deed, and attract tax at 40% = £9,200.

Explanatory Notes

Inheritance tax on estates of Dr and Mrs Slowe

1.   Because Dr Slowe predeceased his wife the whole of his estate passed to her under the will. This is an exempt transfer and no inheritance tax is payable (s 18). Accordingly when Mrs Slowe died there was no quick succession relief because her estate had not been increased by a chargeable transfer (s 141).

2.   Mrs Slowe's estate includes the value of her husband's share in the professional partnership. As she is not a partner this does not qualify for business property relief. For notes on business property relief see Example 25.

3.   The wording of the wills resulted in the second estate being increased in value and attracting a large amount of tax, whilst the first estate failed to utilise its nil rate band. The benefit from the deed of variation would be very substantial because the total inheritance tax payable would be reduced from £176,800 to £32,400, giving an overall saving of £144,400. Such a deed would not have been necessary if the wills had contained a survivorship clause.

Deeds of variation

4.   In this example the use of the provisions in s 142 (alteration of dispositions taking effect on death) would be fairly straightforward and could be used to rewrite the provisions of Dr Slowe's will to advantage. In practice complications can occur if the family cannot agree on a revised disposition of the estate, or if one or more of the original beneficiaries is an infant and therefore does not have the legal capacity to agree to a variation. Court consent would be needed to reduce an infant beneficiary's entitlement.

5.   As indicated in part (b) of the example, a variation of the way in which a deceased's estate is distributed, either under a will or under an intestacy, is effective for inheritance tax providing the instrument of variation includes a statement that it is intended to have that effect, made by those making the variation, and by the personal representatives of the deceased whose estate is subject to the variation if additional tax is payable (s 142(2), (2A)). The personal representatives can only refuse to make the statement if they hold insufficient assets to discharge the additional tax liability (s 142(2A)). If a beneficiary has died before the date of the variation, his personal representatives can act in his stead.

Where the effect of a variation is that additional tax is payable, the beneficiaries and the personal representatives of the deceased whose estate is subject to the variation must notify IR Capital Taxes of the amount of extra tax and send a copy of the variation within six months after the date it is made (s 218A). Penalties apply for failure to comply (s 245A(1A).

Instruments of variation are also effective for capital gains purposes providing the instrument contains a statement by those making it that it is intended to have that effect (TCGA 1992 s 62(7)).

6.   The property which may be subject to variation or disclaimer under s 142 includes 'excluded property' (as to which see Example 3) but not property in which the deceased had retained a benefit (see Example 19) or settled property in which the deceased at the time of his death had a life interest (s 142(5)) (someone who *becomes entitled* to an interest in settled property may disclaim, but not vary, his entitlement under s 93). Where an asset is held jointly as joint tenants, and one of the joint tenants dies, then even though the survivor acquires the deceased's share automatically, he may use a deed of variation to redirect his entitlement to someone else (see Revenue's Tax Bulletin October 1995). Section 142 can also be used in cases of intestacy. The provisions do not, however, apply to any disclaimer or variation which is made for consideration in money or money's worth (s 142(3)) (the same applies to a disclaimer under s 93). Where a variation results in property being held in trust for not more than two years from the date of death, the disposition at the end of the trust is treated as made by the deceased at the date of death (s 142(4)). This provision prevents a variation being used to obtain the benefit of the surviving spouse exemption by redirecting property left as part of the chargeable estate to the spouse, who then, within the two year period, disposes of it by potentially exempt transfer. A disposal outside the two year period would not be caught.

7.   The survivorship clause and a deed of variation affect the devolution of the property itself. The treatment for inheritance tax purposes where there are deaths at the same instant does not, however, affect the provisions of the will, commorientes applying where relevant and thus making a survivorship clause valuable from the devolution point of view, quite apart from for tax purposes.

Commorientes

8.   The deeming provisions of s 4(2) apply when it is not known which of two or more persons have died first (see part (c) of the example). They do not, however, apply where there is evidence that one died before the other(s) when, in the absence of a survivorship clause or a family deed, the best one can hope for in terms of tax relief is quick succession relief. The insertion of a survivorship clause in a will is therefore most important since as indicated earlier a deed of variation is not always practicable.

For notes on quick succession relief see Example 21.

Deeds of variation — effect on other taxes etc

9.   It should be noted that a deed of variation is effective both for inheritance tax and capital gains tax (providing the variation includes a statement to that effect) and does not give rise to a charge to stamp duty. The inheritance tax effect is valid for all purposes of inheritance tax (s 142). In the case of Marshall v Kerr (HL 1994), it was held that the capital gains tax effect was restricted to eliminating a capital gains charge by not treating the redirection of the assets as a disposal by the original beneficiaries, and that it did not affect other capital gains tax provisions (so that if, for example, the variation consisted of creating a trust in which the original beneficiary had an interest, the beneficiary would be regarded as a settlor for TCGA 1992 s 77 and would be charged on the trust's gains — see Example 50 part C).

It is possible to make a deed of variation effective for capital gains tax and not inheritance tax, or vice versa. If the variation was not effective for inheritance tax, the redirected assets would be treated as being transferred under the normal inheritance tax rules, so that the transfers would be potentially exempt unless they were to a discretionary trust. Where a discretionary trust is created through a deed of variation, the settlement is regarded as commencing at the date of death, so that the ten year anniversaries date from that time.

The deed of variation does not affect the income tax position. Any income arising before variation is charged to tax on the original beneficiary. Furthermore, if a parent varies in favour of his/her infant child, this constitutes a settlement within the terms of ITTOIA 2005 ss 620, 648 (formerly TA 1988 s 660G) and any subsequent income arising before the child becomes 18 or marries under that age is chargeable as income of the parent under ITTOIA 2005 ss 629, 631, 632 (formerly TA 1988 s 660B).

A new section 68C to TCGA 1992 (and TA 1988 s 685D) affects variations of wills or intestacies etc occurring on or after 6 April 2006, irrespective of the date of death of the deceased person in question.

Section 68C applies where a transfer of property following a death is varied in circumstances where TCGA 1992 s 62(6) applies. The main conditions for section 62(6) to apply in respect of a variation are that the variation is made within two years after the deceased person's death, and the instrument of variation contains a statement that the provision is to apply.

The section also applies in any case where property becomes settled property in consequence of the variation but would not otherwise have become settled property. In such circumstances, a person listed below will be treated for TCGA purposes (except where the context otherwise requires) as having made the settlement and as having provided the property for the purposes of the settlement.

Four categories of person are identified in this context:

1. The first category comprises anyone who, immediately before the variation, was entitled to the property (or to property from which it derives) absolutely as legatee.

2. The second category relates to a person who would have become entitled to the property (or to property from which it derives) absolutely as legatee but for the variation.

3. The other two categories relate to individuals who would have fallen into either of the first two categories were they not to have been infants or other persons under a disability.

The legislation applies in any case where property which is not settled property immediately before the variation would have become comprised in a settlement (whether it is a settlement which arose on the deceased person's death or a pre-existing settlement), but the effect of the variation is that the property, or property derived from it, becomes comprised in a different settlement. In such circumstances, the deceased person will be treated for TCGA purposes (except where the context otherwise requires) as having made that other settlement.

Where, immediately before the variation, property is comprised in a settlement and is property of which the deceased person is a settlor, and the effect of the variation is that the property, or property derived from it, becomes comprised in another settlement the deceased person is to be treated for TCGA purposes as having made that other settlement.

Where the deceased person is treated as having made a settlement, he or she is treated for TCGA purposes as having made the settlement in question immediately before their death. This will not apply in any case where the settlement in question arose on the death of the deceased person.

Edward (aged 65 and just retired) is considering settling property worth £300,000 on his wife for life with remainder to their only son, Brian, completely excluding himself from any interest in the settlement.

The settlement may either be made now or included in Edward's will to take effect after his death.

Indicate the taxation implications of Edward's proposals, and explain the general principles governing the taxation of such settlements.

The taxation implications of Edward's proposals are as follows:

Inheritance Tax

Settlement on spouse

Transfers in favour of one's spouse are exempt from inheritance tax so long as the spouse is domiciled in the UK (the exemption being limited to £55,000 if the transferee spouse is domiciled abroad). This is so whether the transfer is made in lifetime or upon death, and if it takes the form of an absolute gift or a transfer into settlement. There will not, therefore, be any inheritance tax charge upon Edward settling £300,000 worth of property upon his wife during his lifetime or upon death (s 18).

Upon the death of Edward's wife, the then capital value of the settlement will be liable to inheritance tax (s 49) by aggregation with the other property liable to inheritance tax upon her death, the rate applicable to all chargeable assets at death depending not only upon the value of the assets liable at death, but also the cumulative chargeable transfers made within seven years before death.

The inheritance tax applicable to the trust property will be payable by the trustees out of the trust property, so that Brian will receive a correspondingly lesser capital sum upon the death of his mother.

For example, if the position at the death of Edward's wife were (say):		*Gross*	*Tax*
Lifetime transfers within seven years before death		60,000	–
Her free estate at death	100,000		
Value of husband's settlement at death of wife	325,000	425,000	80,000*
		£ 485,000	£ 80,000*

(* 485,000 – 285,000 = 200,000 @ 40%)

the inheritance tax payable by the trustees out of the fund would be:

$$£80,000 \times \frac{325,000}{425,000} = £61,177$$

and Brian would receive: the fund assets	325,000
less inheritance tax	61,177
	£ 263,823

Release of life interest

If, prior to her death, Edward's wife relinquished her life interest in the settlement in favour of Brian, this would be a transfer of value, against which her annual exemptions for the year of release and previous year would be available unless otherwise used (s 57) and the balance would be a potentially exempt transfer and therefore not chargeable to tax if she survived the transfer by seven years. If she died within seven years, any tax payable would still come out of the trust fund, the trustees retaining sufficient funds to deal with that contingency, and Brian receiving a correspondingly lesser amount in that event. Tapering relief would be given if the death occurred more than three years after the life interest was relinquished.

Release to settlor

However this is not the case where the release takes the form of a transfer to spouse (who was the original settlor).

The law relating to settlements on spouses has been amended to block the loophole which is deemed to exist following the decision of the Court of Appeal to find in favour of the taxpayer in the case of IRC v Eversden [2003] EWCA Civ 668 and [2003] STC 822.

An amendment was made to FA 1986 s 102 by FA 2003 s 185. This section introduced changes to the IHT tax provisions for lifetime gifts within FA 1986 s 102 where the donor reserves or receives any material benefits in relation to the gifted asset — a gift with reservation.

The previous provision was amended so that the normal 'gift with reservation' charge applies to gifts made on or after 20 June 2003 where:

- the gift is made into trust and the donor's spouse enjoys an interest in possession;

- the interest in possession comes to an end (whether on the donee's death or otherwise); and

- the subsequent use of the gift is such that it would count as a 'gift with reservation' if the gift had been made at the time the interest in possession comes to an end.

The rules are further amended in FA 2006 Sch 200. The rules charging IHT on *property subject to a reservation* (at section 102 of the Finance Act 1986) are amended by insertion of a new section 102ZA of the Finance Act 1986. This is intended to bring into line the treatment of cases involving trust property formerly subject to an interest-in-possession (and treated at that time as owned for IHT purposes by the person owning the interest) with the treatment where the property was formerly owned outright. In either case, there can be an IHT charge where the former owner or holder of the interest continues to enjoy the property after they have given it away or their interest has terminated.

These rules would therefore apply if the wife relinquished her life interest in the settlement to Brian.

Capital Gains Tax

Settlement by will

If Edward waits until his death to make the transfer into the settlement for his wife, there will be no capital gains tax payable because death is not a chargeable occasion for capital gains tax, although the deceased's assets are regarded as acquired at probate value by those on whom they devolve (ie legatees, trustees, or personal representatives as the case may be) (TCGA 1992 s 62). The trustees would therefore be deemed to acquire the trust property at probate value.

Lifetime settlement

If Edward makes the transfer into the settlement for his wife during his lifetime, then the capital gains tax exemption for absolute transfers between spouses does not apply. FA 2004 s 116 and Sch 21 introduce provisions into TCGA 1992 preventing gift relief under s 165 or s 260 of that Act being available in respect of disposals of assets to the trustees of a trust in which the settlor has an interest where the disposal is made on or after 10 December 2003. Section 169F provides that any interest of the spouse is to be treated as the interest of the settlor.

These provisions also claw back or prevent any gifts relief in relation to disposals made after 10 December 2003 to trusts which become settlor-interested settlements within a certain time period. This period begins immediately after the disposal and ends immediately before the sixth anniversary of the start of the tax year next following that in which the disposal is made.

As Edward's wife will have a life interest in the new settlement, Edward will be deemed to have an interest in the settlement and the new provisions will apply so that holdover relief will not be available.

Death of life tenant

When a life tenant dies, the trust property is treated as having been disposed of and immediately reacquired at probate value, but as with the death of someone owning assets absolutely, there is no capital gains tax charge on the trust assets. (If the settlement had been made in lifetime, however, and any gains had been deferred under the holdover provisions of s 165 or s 260 prior to 10 December 2003, the deferred gains would become chargeable on the life tenant's death, any available taper relief being given by reference to the period of ownership by the trust. If any of the property is qualifying property for holdover relief under s 165, the deferred gains on that property could be the subject of a further claim for holdover relief. Taper relief would then not reduce the gain to be deferred but would depend on the period of ownership by the person acquiring the assets, or, if there was a successive life tenancy, by the trust until the death of the next life tenant.)

When Edward's wife dies, therefore, neither the trustees nor Brian will be liable to capital gains tax in respect of the assets in the settlement. Those assets which devolve upon Brian (some may have to be sold in order to pay inheritance tax unless Brian wishes to retain all the assets and fund the tax by other means — perhaps by instalments if the property is instalment option property) will do so for capital gains purposes at their market value at the date of his mother's death, and those retained by the trustees in order to sell them to raise cash for the payment of inheritance tax will also have a base value equivalent to their market value at that time (TCGA 1992 s 73).

Release of life interest

If Edward's widow relinquishes her entitlement during her lifetime, Brian then becoming absolutely entitled to the trust property, the trustees will be deemed to make a disposal at that time at the then market value, any gains held over if the settlement was created in lifetime becoming chargeable, and capital gains tax will be payable accordingly (less any taper relief and annual exemption available to the trustees and subject to any available holdover relief) (TCGA 1992 s 71).

Trustees' own gains

If, during the continuation of the trust, the trustees themselves realise capital gains on the disposal of trust assets, for example on the switching of investments, then if this occurs during Edward's lifetime, the gains are treated as Edward's gains, on which he is liable to pay the tax (TCGA 1992 s 77). He is entitled, however, to recover the tax from the trustees (TCGA 1992 s 78). The gains would be reduced by any taper relief that would have been available to the trustees. If gains are realised after Edward's death, the trustees are liable to tax on the gains at 40%, subject to availability of the annual exemption (TCGA 1992 Sch 1.2(1)). The annual exemption for an interest in possession trust is half that available to individuals (£4,400 for 2006/07), providing it is the only settlement created by the settlor since 6 June 1978 (see Example 50 part C).

Enterprise investment scheme relief

Providing the beneficiaries of the trust are confined to individuals and charities, then the gains may be deferred to the extent that they are reinvested in cash by subscribing for ordinary shares in a qualifying unquoted trading company under the enterprise investment scheme, the money raised being used within twelve months for a qualifying business activity (TCGA 1992 Sch 5B).

For further notes on the capital gains tax position of trusts see Example 50.

Income Tax

Lifetime settlement

If the settlement is made by Edward in his lifetime, then since his wife is entitled to the income it will be treated as a settlement in which he retains an interest, and all income arising, whether distributed by the trustees or retained by them, will be liable to income tax as part of Edward's statutory total income during his lifetime (ITTOIA 2005 s 624 (formerly TA 1988 s 660A)). The settlement is not sufficient to transfer income from Edward to his wife for income tax purposes because he is giving his wife only a right to income and not outright ownership of the assets. Following Edward's death, the income whether distributed or not will be treated as Edward's widow's income. This will also apply if the settlement is made on Edward's death.

Tax liability of trustees

The trustees in each case will have a basic rate liability (or lower rate or dividend ordinary rate liability if the income is savings income) unless the income is mandated direct to Edward's wife in order to save administrative cost and inconvenience, any liability at the higher rate (or dividend upper rate) being assessed on Edward or his widow as the case may be. Edward would be entitled to recover any tax paid by him from the trustees or from his wife (ITTOIA 2005 s 646 (formerly TA 1988 s 660D)).

Charge on Edward and on wife after his death

Where income is treated as Edward's income, the amount on which he is charged to tax cannot be reduced by any trust expenses, since he is only permitted to deduct amounts that would have been deductible if he had received the income directly (ITTOIA 2005 ss 619, 621, 623 (formerly TA 1988 s 660C)). Furthermore, for income other than dividends, the income is taxed as miscellaneous income, so it cannot be taxed at the savings rate of 20% whether or not Edward is liable at higher rates. Dividend income is, however, charged at the dividend ordinary rate of 10% or upper rate of 32½% (ITTOIA 2005 ss 619, 621, 623 (formerly TA 1988 s 660C)).

After Edward's death, his widow is taxed as the beneficiary of an interest in possession trust. Unless the income has been mandated direct to her, the trust expenses will be paid out of the taxed income of the trust, and the balance remaining will be paid to her, the trustees giving her a certificate indicating the amounts of tax deducted at the basic, lower or dividend ordinary rate of tax as the case may be. The tax deducted will count towards the tax payable by her or will be repayable if it exceeds her liability. This does not apply to dividend tax credits, which are not repayable.

Your client, Charles, a wealthy widower, is a director and majority shareholder in an unquoted trading company that was established many years ago.

His wife died suddenly six months ago, leaving her estate comprising shares in quoted companies, life insurance policies, cash, jewellery and personal possessions, valued in total at £335,000, to Charles.

Charles is aged sixty-two and is considering retiring within the next year or so. He is also considering disposing of some of his assets, either by sale or possibly by gift, but is undecided whether to dispose of them during his lifetime or by will on his death.

Taxation will be a major factor influencing his decision regarding the disposition of his assets, and he has stated that he wishes to minimise any tax liability arising.

He has estimated his total estate to have a value of approximately £940,000, including the £335,000 left to him by his deceased wife, broadly comprised as follows:

His 70% shareholding in the unquoted family trading company, valued at £140,000

His 18% shareholding in an unquoted company which supplies the family company, valued at £60,000, (the other shares being held by his brothers and sister)

Quoted shares valued at £108,000

His private residence valued at £295,000

A plot of land on which he and his wife had planned to build a bungalow for their retirement valued at £40,000

A life insurance policy on his life with a market value of £40,000 and a surrender value of £36,000

Furniture, jewellery and other chattels with a total value of £25,000, the highest value item being valued at £2,500

Cash at bank, building society and at home — total value £232,000

Private motor car valued at £9,000

All assets have been acquired since 5 April 1965.

He has one daughter and two grandsons, one of whom joined him last year in the family company. He has also developed a considerable interest in Heartbeat (UK) — a registered charity.

(a)   In relation to both capital gains tax and inheritance tax, summarise:

   (i)   the events giving rise to a charge

   (ii)   the amount chargeable

  (iii)   the rates of tax

  (iv)   some common exemptions and reliefs

   (v)   whether phasing of disposals is advantageous

  (vi)   the advantages/disadvantages of lifetime disposals as compared to a transfer on death

 (vii)   the benefits, if any, of Charles emigrating.

(b)   Suggest action that Charles might take and disposals he might make which would result in a nil or small tax liability, and which would reduce the tax payable on his eventual death.

(a) **Capital gains tax summary**

(i) *Chargeable disposals*

The capital gains tax provisions apply to the disposal of chargeable assets during lifetime. No charge is made on death. 'Disposal' includes sales, gifts and loss or destruction of assets; chargeable assets are all assets other than those that are specifically exempt. Options, debts, currency other than sterling, and rights are included, but not bettings winnings or damages for personal or professional injuries.

(ii) *Calculation of gain or loss*

The chargeable gain (or allowable loss) is calculated by comparing the value on disposal with the sum of the cost price, costs of acquisition, costs of sale and indexation allowance to April 1998. For assets owned on 31 March 1982, an election may have been made to regard the assets as having been acquired on 31 March 1982 for their market value on that date. This election is irrevocable. If the election has not been made, two computations are required. The result using the acquisition costs is compared with the result using market value on 31 March 1982. If both computations show a gain (or loss) the smaller is taken. If one shows a gain and the other a loss then the transaction is treated as giving neither gain nor loss.

Indexation allowance

Indexation allowance is based on the increase in the retail prices index and applies from the month of acquisition (or from March 1982 if later) to the month of disposal or April 1998 if earlier. For assets acquired after 31 March 1982 it is based on cost. For assets owned on that date it is based on the value at that date if the irrevocable election referred to above has been made. If not, the indexation allowance is based either on cost or 31 March 1982 value, whichever is higher. Indexation allowance cannot be used to create or increase an allowable loss. For periods after April 1998 it is available only to companies.

Treatment of losses

Chargeable gains are reduced by losses of the same year. In addition, they are reduced by losses brought forward (or carried back from the year of death), but not so as to waste the annual exemption of the year of disposal.

Taper relief

The gain after loss relief is subject to taper relief, which depends on the period of ownership and whether the asset is a business or non-business asset.

Taper relief is calculated according to complete years of ownership from 6 April 1998. A wider definition of business assets was introduced in FA 2000 s 67, and the definition was further amended by FA 2001 s 78 and Sch 26 and by FA 2002 s 47 and Sch 10. This has significantly improved the amount of relief available. Section 160 of the FA 2003 relaxed further the conditions determining whether assets other than company shares or securities qualify as business assets. The main effect of this change is that assets used wholly or partly for trades carried on by individuals, personal representatives and trustees will qualify as business assets irrespective of whether the owner of the asset is involved in carrying on the trade involved. The new provisions came into effect for periods of ownership from 6 April 2004.

If a non-business asset was acquired before 17 March 1998, an extra year is added to the ownership period. Non-business assets attract no relief unless they are held for three complete years, relief being given at 5% for each complete year from three to ten years' ownership to a maximum 40%.

The maximum taper relief on business assets is 75%.

For disposals on and after 6 April 2002, the maximum 75% relief is given after two complete years of ownership, the relief for one complete year being 50% (TCGA 1992 s 2A(5)).

From 6 April 2000 business assets as far as individuals are concerned comprise the following. Any reference to 'shares' includes securities.

– Assets used wholly or partly for a trade carried on by the individual, or a partnership of which an individual was at that time a member.

– Assets owned personally but used for the purposes of a trade carried on by a trading company that is within the definition of the individual's qualifying company (or by a subsidiary of such a company) or from 6 April 2004 by a partnership whose members at that time include such a company.

– Assets held for use in his office or employment by an individual working for a person carrying on a trade.

– Shares in the individual's qualifying company.

An individual's qualifying company is:

(1) A trading company or the holding company of a trading group where either

    (i) the company is unlisted*, or

    (ii) the individual is an officer or employee of the company or another group company, or

    (iii) at least 5% of the voting rights are exercisable by the individual.

(2) A non-trading company or holding company of a non-trading group in which the individual is an officer or employee, where the individual does not have a material interest in the company or a company controlling it.**

Where an individual acquires an asset as legatee, it counts as a business asset for any period during which it was a qualifying business asset in the hands of the personal representatives (see below). In addition, from 6 April 2004, any asset an individual acquires as legatee includes one used wholly or partly for the purposes of a trade carried on by a trading company within the definition of the personal representatives' qualifying company (or a subsidiary of such company) or a partnership whose members at that time included such a company.

As far as personal representatives are concerned, assets are business assets if they are shares in a company that is a qualifying company by reference to the personal representatives, or are other assets used for a trade carried on by the personal representatives or by a company which is a qualifying company by reference to the personal representatives (or a subsidiary of such a qualifying company). A qualifying company is a trading company or holding company of a trading group that either is unlisted* or is a company in which the personal representatives hold not less than 5% of the voting rights (the definition of qualifying company for personal representatives was not extended by FA 2001). From 6 April 2004 assets are treated as business assets if they are being used either wholly or partly for a trade carried on by a partnership whose members at that time include a qualifying company. In addition assets will qualify as business assets if they are used wholly or partly for a trade carried on by a partnership that includes the personal representatives of the deceased person or any one or more of the individuals who at that time are personal representatives of the deceased.

For trustees, shares are business assets if the company is a qualifying company by reference to the trustees, and other assets are business assets if they are used for a trade carried on by the trustees (or a partnership in which one or more trustees is a partner acting in his capacity of trustee or from 6 April 2004 any one or more persons who were at that time trustees of the settlement so far as acting in their capacity as trustees) or by an eligible beneficiary***, or by a company that is a qualifying company by reference to the trustees or the beneficiary (or is a subsidiary of such a qualifying company), or are used for an office or employment held by an eligible beneficiary*** with a person carrying on a trade.

From 5 April 2004 assets are treated as business assets if they are being used either wholly or partly for a trade carried on by a partnership whose members at that time included a qualifying company. A qualifying company as far as trustees are concerned is:

(1)   A trading company or holding company of a trading group that either is unlisted* or is a company in which an eligible beneficiary*** is an officer or employee, or in which the trustees hold not less than 5% of the voting rights.

(2)   A non-trading company or holding company of a non-trading group in which an eligible beneficiary*** is an officer or employee, where the trustees do not have a material interest in the company or a company controlling it.**

*   Unlisted companies include companies on the Alternative Investment Market (AIM).

**   Individuals or trustees have a material interest in a company if they and/or one or more people connected with them control more than 10% of the company's issued shares or voting rights, or would be entitled to more than 10% of the company's income if the whole income were distributed, or more than 10% of the assets if the company were wound up.

***   An eligible beneficiary is one who has an interest in possession in the trust.

Changes were made to the definition of trading company and trading group from 17 April 2002 (TCGA 1992 Sch A1.22A and 22B). The intention was to clarify the definitions without altering their substance. A trading company is 'a company carrying on trading activities whose activities do not include to a substantial extent activities other than trading activities'. Trading activities include activities for the purpose of preparing to carry on a trade, or with a view to acquiring a significant interest in the share capital of a trading company/group. The definition of trading group has been amended along similar lines, a trading group being one whose activities, taken as a whole, do not include to a substantial extent non-trading activities (there are severe anti-avoidance provisions for close companies, which previously included denying taper relief for any period before a 'relevant change of activity'. For disposals on or after 17 April 2002 this provision has been replaced by provisions excluding from the period qualifying for taper relief any period after 5 April 1998 during which the close company was not active. Companies are regarded as active when they are carrying on or preparing to carry on a business or the business is being wound up).

Since *any* unlisted trading company is a qualifying company, the business assets rate of taper relief is available on property owned by a landlord if his tenant is an unlisted trading company. From 6 April 2004 the business assets rate applies if the tenant is carrying on a trade not just a qualifying company.

On a disposal of assets that have not been business assets throughout the period of ownership (including assets that became business assets with effect from 6 April 2000), the taper relief available is apportioned over the period from the date of acquisition (or 6 April 1998 if later) to the date of disposal, or if shorter, over the last ten years of ownership, and the proportion relating to the non-business period will qualify only for the non-business assets rate of relief. Although these proportions take into account only the period from 6 April 1998, the period to determine the rate of relief for the non-business assets proportion still includes the extra year for non-business assets acquired before 17 March 1998 where relevant (see Example 40 part (a) for an illustration).

(iii)   *Rates of tax*

An individual has an annual exempt amount (£8,800 for 2006/07). The remaining chargeable gains are taxed as though they formed the highest part of taxable non-dividend savings income. The charging rates on gains above £8,800 are therefore 10%, 20% and 40% depending on the taxable income.

See page (vii) for the rates applying to personal representatives and trustees.

(iv)   *Exemptions and reliefs*

Exempt assets include:

Principal private residence (subject to certain conditions)

Private motor cars

Tangible movable assets (chattels) that are wasting assets, including racehorses, but excluding chattels used in a business on which capital allowances have been or could have been claimed

Other chattels (including business chattels) if sold for less than £6,000

Gifts of assets to charities.

Reliefs include:

Rollover relief or holdover relief enabling gains to be deferred when qualifying business assets are sold and replaced. Where gains are rolled over to reduce the cost of the replacement asset, taper relief (see (ii) above) is available when the replacement asset is disposed of, based upon the period of ownership of the *new* asset. Where gains are held over against the acquisition of depreciating assets, the taper relief when the replacement asset is disposed of is based on the period of ownership of the *original* asset.

Deferral relief when a gain is reinvested by a cash subscription either for unquoted shares in a qualifying trading company under the enterprise investment scheme or for shares in a venture capital trust. The gain is deferred until the qualifying shares are sold or replaced, taper relief being based on the period of ownership of the *original* asset. Where, however, there are successive investments in enterprise investment scheme shares (but not venture capital trust shares) issued on or after 6 April 1998 and disposed of on or after 6 April 1999, capital gains tax taper relief in relation to deferred gains on each such investment is based on the period from acquisition of the investment to the date of final disposal without the proceeds being reinvested in another EIS investment. This only applies to reinvested gains on the enterprise investment scheme shares, and not to the original gain that was invested in the first enterprise investment scheme shares. The taper relief on that gain is still based on the ownership of the original asset.

Gifts holdover relief enabling gains to be regarded as reducing the donee's acquisition cost for capital gains tax, in respect of gifts of business assets, agricultural land, shares giving 5% voting control in an unquoted trading company, or gifts subject to an immediate charge to inheritance tax. Taper relief is based on the period of ownership of the *donee*.

(v)   *Advantages of phasing disposals*

By disposing of assets over a period of years a number of annual exemptions may be used. Furthermore by restricting the amount of gain chargeable, tax may be payable at a lower rate. Note that unused annual exemption cannot be carried forward, and unused losses cannot be carried back (except losses of the year of death, which may be carried back against gains in excess of the annual exemption in the three previous years, latest first). But this does not apply to disposals of items to the same person if they form part of a set.

(vi)   *Disposals in lifetime or on death*

On death there is no charge to capital gains tax and there is an automatic uplift to market value at that time for those entitled to the assets, whereas a disposal in lifetime may give rise to a charge. If a gain has been rolled over or held over against the cost of qualifying replacement business assets, the death of the taxpayer means that the gain never gets charged to tax. By contrast, where holdover relief has been claimed on a gift of an asset, the donee's capital gains tax cost is reduced as indicated in (iv), thus resulting in a higher gain when the donee disposes of the asset. The donee's acquisition cost is not affected by the subsequent death of the donor.

(vii) *Effect of emigration*

Capital gains tax is chargeable on worldwide assets of taxpayers who are resident or ordinarily resident in the UK.

If a taxpayer ceases to be both resident and ordinarily resident then he will not be liable to UK capital gains tax unless the assets are situated in the UK and are used in a trade carried on in the UK. A charge can also occur on accrued gains on the export of a UK company or trust.

Charles can therefore avoid UK capital gains tax by emigration if gains are realised after he has become neither resident nor ordinarily resident, except in relation to any assets used in the UK for the purposes of a trade. If, however, he returned to the UK and became resident or ordinarily resident within five complete tax years of the date of departure, gains on assets held on emigration that were realised while he was non-resident would be chargeable in the tax year of return. Any such gains realised in the tax year of departure would be taxed as gains of that tax year. Finance (No 2) Act 2005 provisions prevent the exploitation of double tax agreements during the period of absence. If a gain has been charged to tax in another country, and is also charged in the UK on the taxpayer's return within five years then the tax paid overseas is deductible from the UK liability. If a taxpayer is resident or ordinarily resident in the UK, but under a double tax treaty would be treated as non-resident (such that a gain would be taxed at a low or nil rate) then UK capital gains tax will be payable overriding the DTA provisions (F(No 2)A 2005 s 32 amending TCGA 1992 s 10A). Similar provisions are introduced for trustees (F(No2)A 2005 s 33 introducing TCGA 1992 s 83A).

Inheritance tax summary

(i) *Chargeable transfers*

Inheritance tax is chargeable on certain lifetime gifts, on wealth at death and on certain transfers into and out of trust. If a taxpayer makes a lifetime gift to an individual, or to an accumulation and maintenance trust, or to a trust for the disabled, or to an interest in possession trust, then provided the donor survives the gift by seven years or more, it is not liable to inheritance tax. This is known as a potentially exempt transfer, and it covers virtually all lifetime gifts that an individual might make, except to a discretionary trust, which are chargeable at the time they are made. Certain gifts are totally exempt from tax (see (iv) below).

(ii) *Chargeable amount*

Where a lifetime gift is immediately chargeable, the chargeable amount is the difference between the value of the donor's estate before the transfer and its value after the transfer. If the donor bears the inheritance tax then that tax will reduce the value of the estate after the transfer, increasing the chargeable transfer. This is known as grossing up the gift.

(iii) *Rates of tax*

Any *chargeable* transfers of the last seven years are added together. To that total is added the value of the current chargeable transfer, which is charged to tax as the highest part of the total. For 2006/07 there is no inheritance tax on the first £285,000 of cumulative transfers. Lifetime chargeable transfers in excess of £285,000 are taxed at 20%, which is half of the full rate.

The nil rate band for 2007/08 has been set at £300,000, at £312,000 for 2008/09 and at £325,000 for 2009/10.

Potentially exempt gifts made within seven years before death become chargeable transfers on death, any chargeable transfers within the seven years before the gift being taken into account in calculating the tax payable. The value taken into account is that at the time of the gift, but the rate of tax used is the full rate (not the half rate) applicable at the date of death (currently 40%). If the gift was made more than three years before death then any tax payable on the gift is reduced by a tapering relief.

Where a transfer was chargeable in lifetime, and the donor dies within seven years, tax is recalculated at the full rate on the scale in force at the date of death, tapering relief being available as for potentially exempt transfers, and the tax payable, if any, being reduced by the tax paid in lifetime, but no repayment being available if the lifetime tax exceeds the tax due at death.

Tax on the death estate is calculated by adding the estate to chargeable transfers within the seven years before the death.

(iv) *Exemptions and reliefs*

Exemptions include:

Transfers between spouses and civil partners (unless transferee is not UK domiciled, when exempt limit is £55,000)

Annual exemption for lifetime gifts	— £3,000 pa
Small lifetime gifts to same person	— not exceeding £250 pa

Normal expenditure out of income
Gifts in consideration of marriage
or registration of a civil partnership   — £5,000 by a parent
                                        — £2,500 by a grandparent or a party to the marriage/civil partnership
                                        — £1,000 by any other person

Gifts to charities, political parties, housing associations, or for national purposes
Conditional exemption for heritage property
Gifts made more than seven years before death (see (i) above).

Reliefs include:

Business property relief (relief being at 100% on an interest in a business or unquoted shareholdings; controlling holdings in quoted companies qualify for 50% relief)

Agricultural property relief (at 100% for owner-occupied property and property let on leases granted on or after 1 September 1995 and 50% for other let property)

Quick succession relief, reducing the tax payable where a donee dies within five years after receiving a chargeable transfer.

It is also possible to use a deed of variation within two years after death to alter the way a deceased person's estate is distributed (see Example 34).

(v) *Advantages of phasing disposals*

Regular gifts could be covered by the exemption for normal expenditure out of income providing they are habitual (eg by payments of regular premiums under an insurance policy), and leave the taxpayer with sufficient income to live in his normal style.

Other lifetime gifts would be potentially exempt in so far as they are not covered by the annual exemption of £3,000. If the previous year's annual exemption was not used, that would also be available to reduce the transfer. The earlier year's annual exemption is only available after the later year has been used in full. Any of the previous year's exemption not then utilised will be lost. Potentially exempt transfers only become chargeable transfers if the donor dies within seven years. Transfers that are not potentially exempt are taxed at one-half of the full rate once the nil threshold is exceeded.

Even though a gift is not covered by a specific exemption, no tax is payable in lifetime or on death to the extent that the gift is covered by the nil threshold (taking into account gifts made within the previous seven years).

(vi) *Disposals in lifetime or on death*

Although gifts made more than three but less than seven years before death attract tapering relief, that is irrelevant unless the cumulative total at the time of the lifetime gift exceeds the nil threshold applicable at the date of death, since no tax will be payable to which any tapering relief can apply.

Because lifetime gifts are accumulated with earlier chargeable transfers (made within seven years before the date of the gift) it is possible for gifts made within seven years before death to increase the overall burden of inheritance tax.

Subject to the above, potentially exempt lifetime gifts are normally advantageous as they are completely exempt after seven years, are not chargeable in any event if covered by the nil threshold, and if chargeable, possibly attract tapering relief. Any part of the nil threshold used to cover such transfers would, however, reduce the amount available on the death estate.

In the case of assets attracting 100% business property relief it may not be advantageous to make a lifetime transfer. This is because a liability to capital gains tax can arise on the gift. The gain may be held over for capital gains purposes (see point (iv) under capital gains tax summary above), but it will reduce the base value to the donee (point (vi) of the capital gains tax summary above), whereas on death there is an automatic uplift to market value for capital gains tax purposes without any capital gains tax being payable. There would, however, be no liability to inheritance tax at the time of a lifetime gift because of the 100% relief, nor if the donor died within seven years, providing the gifted business assets were still held and still qualified.

(vii) *Effect of emigration*

Inheritance tax is chargeable on worldwide assets of a person domiciled in the UK. To emigrate without changing domicile has no effect.

Even if Charles changes his domicile he will still be deemed UK domiciled for three years, and thereafter will be liable to inheritance tax on UK based property no matter where his domicile is.

(b) **Suggested course of action for Charles**

Although the transfer to Charles on his wife's death was exempt because of the spouse exemption, her nil rate band has been wasted (unless she had made chargeable or potentially exempt gifts in the seven years before her death). The following points should be considered in order to improve the present and potential future tax position.

(i) Charles should consider a deed of variation to redirect some of the assets left to him by his wife. This could go directly to his daughter, or to the grandchildren, thus utilising the nil rate threshold of his wife at her death and avoiding the value of the appropriate assets becoming part of his estate. Alternatively he could direct his wife's estate to a discretionary trust, for which he is a trustee, so that he can still exercise some control over the assets.

The deed would also be effective for capital gains tax (providing the deed contains a statement that it is intended to have that effect), avoiding any tax if the assets have increased in value since the wife's death (although if the variation included a trust in which Charles had an interest, he would be regarded as the settlor and would be charged on the trust's gains).

(ii) Charles could make transfers of his shareholding in the family trading company in 2006/07, covering any capital gains tax liability with gifts holdover relief. The gifts would initially be potentially exempt transfers covered by 100% business property relief for inheritance tax. If Charles died within seven years, then providing the donees had retained the shares given to them, business property relief of 100% would still be available so long as the company's activities still qualified. If Charles does not wish to give all of the shares directly to his family, trusts could be used.

(iii) Further gifts could be made in so far as no liability to capital gains tax is crystallised (eg cash gifts; chattels worth less than £6,000; possibly the land owned if it has a high base value); or on which gifts holdover relief would be available (eg shares in supplier company or gifts to a discretionary trust; although the latter would be chargeable transfers for inheritance tax, the gifts could be restricted so that they were covered by available reliefs and the nil threshold).

(iv) Thereafter annual gifts could be made utilising the capital gains tax annual exemption, currently £8,800. For inheritance tax, such gifts would be reduced by the £3,000 annual exemption. Gifts could include quoted shares and/or the unquoted shares in the supplier company. The latter would attract 100% business property relief for inheritance tax.

(v) Care must be taken not to allow the taxation advantages of a gift to outweigh the personal requirements of the taxpayer.

(vi) Either in lifetime or on death Charles could make gifts to charity. These would reduce the estate without giving rise to a liability either to capital gains tax or inheritance tax, and he can make gift aid payments of any amount to charity and save higher rate tax on the gross equivalent, providing he makes an appropriate gift aid declaration. From 6 April 2000 he can also obtain higher rate relief for gifts to charities of quoted stocks and shares, and also shares on the Alternative Investment Market (AIM), and from 6 April 2002 this also applies to gifts of UK land and buildings. All such gifts are valued at their open market value plus any incidental costs of making them.

Supplementary Note

For further notes on liability to inheritance tax see Examples 1 to 4; business property relief see Example 25; deeds of variation see Example 34; and domicile see Example 27. Capital gains tax is dealt with in detail in the companion book Tolley's Taxwise I 2006/07.

Mr Gregory is a 68 year old widower for whom you act as tax adviser. He came to see you on 31 May 2006 and told you that he had just been informed by his doctor that he had only three months left to live. He intends that all his wealth should pass to his only son Neil (who will be his sole executor). He has heard that in some circumstances it might be advantageous either to transfer some of his assets immediately to Neil as a gift or alternatively to sell some of his assets and then to transfer the sale proceeds to Neil as a gift.

Mr Gregory is not currently in a position to make cash gifts as he has just drawn out the last of his savings from his bank account. He provides you with the following information concerning his assets:

(i) He owns 2,000 shares in Bingo plc, a quoted company, currently valued at £480. He had acquired the shares for £14,350 in December 1989 (indexation allowance was 36.9% from December 1989 to April 1998).

(ii) He had acquired 20,000 £1 shares at par out of an issued share capital of 200,000 shares in Peck Limited, a retail company, in February 2004. His shares have been valued recently at £1.20 each. The investment qualified for income tax relief at 20% under the enterprise investment scheme.

(iii) He had acquired 10,000 £1 shares out of an issued share capital of 10,000,000 shares in Zingo plc, a quoted land dealing company, for £7.13 each in November 1992. The shares are currently worth £20 per share (indexation allowance from November 1992 to April 1998 was 16.4%).

(iv) All tax liabilities have been agreed and paid on the due date up to 5 April 2006. Mr Gregory does not expect to have any income tax liabilities outstanding on his death, as his income should be just enough to cover his outgoings up to that time. It is estimated that the income tax computation up to the date of his death will show a repayment due of £1,250.

Other relevant information is as follows:

(v) He had taxable capital gains in the previous four years of assessment as follows:

	2002/03	2003/04	2004/05	2005/06
	£	£	£	£
Net gains	11,900	10,900	–	11,225
Less: Annual exemption	(7,700)	(7,900)	–	(8,500)
Taxable gains	4,200	3,000	nil	2,725

(Mr Gregory's rate of capital gains tax was 40% throughout. Only non-business assets were disposed of in 2002/03, 2003/04 and 2004/05, the rate of taper relief on the disposals in 2003/04 being 5% and 2005/06 being 10%.)

(vi) In January 2005 he had made an outright gift of his principal private residence to his son Neil who now resides there. Mr Gregory went to live with his brother. The value of the residence at that time was £250,000 but it has since risen to £300,000. Neil has now suggested that Mr Gregory should come to live with him rent-free. Mr Gregory has refused to go to live with Neil partly on personal grounds, but also because he believes that if he does, problems might arise in connection with inheritance tax. The gift of his residence is the only gift which Mr Gregory has made so far.

(vii) His son Neil, who is due to get married shortly, has recently started up in business and has indicated that he will need to convert any assets which he receives from his father into cash by 31 December 2006 at the latest, in order to invest in the business.

(a) Indicate the optimum tax strategy for Mr Gregory regarding lifetime gifts.

(b) Assuming that Mr Gregory had in fact gone to live with Neil in his former private residence, state the inheritance tax consequences which would have arisen.

(c) Assuming that Mr Gregory adopts the strategy suggested under (a) above, calculate the inheritance tax liability arising on the basis that he died on 30 September 2006.

(a) **Tax strategy re lifetime gifts**

Disposals of assets in lifetime may attract capital gains tax on their growth in value. Furthermore, if the disposal is a gift, it may be reckonable for inheritance tax.

Mr Gregory is almost certain to die within seven years, and therefore even if a gift was initially a potentially exempt transfer for inheritance tax, it would become chargeable on his death. The tapering relief for inheritance tax applicable after three years will almost certainly not be available.

By comparison, assets retained until death obtain a capital gains tax free uplift to probate value, thus avoiding a liability to capital gains tax. A gift in lifetime may therefore attract a liability to both capital gains tax and inheritance tax, whereas the same asset given on death would only be liable to inheritance tax.

Against that double charge, a gift in lifetime attracts any unused inheritance tax annual exemptions or marriage exemption and the value subsequently chargeable on death because the seven year period has not been survived is the value at the date of the gift. Mr Gregory gave his house to his son in January 2005. The value at that date of £250,000 will be reduced by the annual exemptions for 2004/05 and 2003/04 and will be included in calculating the inheritance tax on Mr Gregory's death at £250,000 – £6,000 = £244,000, not at its current value of £300,000.

As Mr Gregory does not have long to live, the increase in value up to the date of death of any asset given away now is likely to be minimal, but the inheritance tax annual exemptions of 2005/06 and 2006/07 are available. In ordinary circumstances an exemption is available for gifts that are normal expenditure out of income. Although there is no fixed minimum period during which regular gifts have to have been made to constitute 'normal expenditure', it is necessary that a pattern of actual or intended payments has been established (Bennett & Others v CIR (1994)). Thus a 'death bed' resolution to make periodic payments for life does not create an exemption for such payments under the normal expenditure out of income provisions.

To create a liability to capital gains tax would not be advisable. If, however, the disposals realised net capital losses, any losses in the tax year of death may be carried back against the capital gains liabilities of the three preceding years, latest first, tax being repayable accordingly. The loss carryback relief is not wasted against gains already covered by the annual exemption. Losses must, however, be set off before taper relief, so as 10% taper relief was given in arriving at the gains of £11,225 in 2005/06, those gains will absorb losses of (11,225 x 100/90 =) £12,472. In the same way 5% taper was given against 2003/04 loss of (10,900 x 100/95 =) £11,474. As Mr Gregory is likely to die before 5 April 2007, immediate crystallisation of losses would be useful. Care must be taken not to give loss-producing assets to connected persons such as Neil, as a loss on a disposal to such a person can only be utilised against future gains on disposals to the same person, which are very unlikely if death is imminent.

The recommended stategy would be to:

(i) Sell the shares in Bingo plc, realising a capital loss as follows:

	£
Cost of shares December 1989	14,350
(Indexation allowance December 1989 to April 1998 36.9% but restricted to chargeable gain, therefore nil)	
Sale proceeds in say July 2006	480
Loss on Bingo plc shares	13,870

(ii) Relieve the loss on the Bingo plc shares against gains of the three years preceding death (assuming death in 2006/07):

	2005/06 £	2004/05 £	2003/04 £	£
Gains	12,472*	–	11,474*	
Loss re Bingo plc shares	(3,972)		(3,574)	7,546
	8,500		7,900	
Less: Annual exemption	(8,500)		(7,900)	
	–		–	
Available loss (as above)				13,870
Unused losses				6,324

* Before taper relief

The tax saving from carrying back the loss to 2005/06 is £2,725 @ 40% = £1,090 (3,972 – 2,725 = £1,247 of the loss offset representing taper relief no longer available). The due date of payment for the 2005/06 tax is 31 January 2007, so if Mr Gregory died before that date the capital gains tax originally due would not be paid. Otherwise it would be repaid. The repayment due as a result of carrying back the loss to 2003/04 is £3,000 @ 40% = £1,200.

As far as repayment supplement is concerned, although the *tax saving* is calculated by reference to the tax position of the earlier year, the claim relates to the later year, and repayment supplement is payable only if the repayment is made after 31 January following that later year. Where losses are carried back from the year of death, the deduction is made automatically without the need for a claim (TCGA 1992 s 62(2)). TMA 1970 Sch 1B.2(7) provides, however, that for supplement purposes the carryback is treated in the same way as if a claim was required. In this example, supplement would only be payable if the tax was repaid after 31 January 2008. The tax will almost certainly have been repaid by that date, but if it has not been, repayment supplement will be payable from that date at 3% per annum (based on the current rate).

(iii)   Make a gift during 2006/07 to Neil of the appropriate number of shares in Zingo plc.

	£	£
The gain on each Zingo plc share would be:		
Market value		20.00
Less: Cost	7.13	
Indexation allowance 16.4%	1.17	8.30
Gain per share		11.70
Less: Taper relief @ 35%		4.10
		7.60

The available capital loss in 2006/07 after carry back against 2005/06 and 2003/04 is £6,324 as indicated in (ii) above, which covers a gift of 540 shares (@ £11.70 gain per share, losses being set against gains before taper relief as indicated above). The available exemptions for inheritance tax are:

	£
Annual 2006/07	3,000
2005/06	3,000
Marriage (on gift to Neil)	5,000
	11,000

This covers a gift of 550 shares (@ £20 each). Mr Gregory should therefore give Neil 550 shares in Zingo plc.

(Note that the sale or gift of shares in Peck Limited would give rise to a clawback of enterprise investment scheme relief at 20%, since they will not have been held for three years until February 2007.)

By gifting 550 shares instead of 540 (see above re maximum gift for CGT purposes) the loss to be set back is restricted by £117 (10 x £11.70). This however is better than paying inheritance tax on £200 (10 shares @ £20).

If larger gains than £6,324 were made, the losses available to carry back would be reduced to below £7,546 and the capital gains tax repayment for earlier years would be reduced accordingly. As a result Mr Gregory's annual capital gains tax exemption and any available taper relief cannot be used in 2006/07, because to use the annual exemption, gains would need to exceed the losses of £13,870, and no losses would be left to carry back. The executors are unlikely to make losses when they convert assets to cash for Neil because they take the assets at probate value, and even if they did, those losses are not available to carry back against Mr Gregory's gains.

(b)   **Inheritance tax consequences of Mr Gregory going to live with Neil**

It is reasonable to assume that Mr Gregory's illness is such that he is unable to maintain himself. Provided such an eventuality was not foreseeable in January 2005 (at the time of the original gift of the property), then Mr Gregory could return to his former residence without breaching the gifts with reservation rules or the use of pre-owned asset provisions.

FA 1986 Sch 20.6(1)(b) provides such an exemption in relation to gifts of an interest in land when the donor's circumstances change in a way that was unforeseen at the time of the original gift and the benefit provided by the donee to the donor represents reasonable provision for the care and maintenance of an elderly or infirm relative. This provision also applies to prevent a pre-owned asset charge (FA 2004 Sch 15.11(5)(d)).

Without such exemption Mr Gregory's return to his former residence would nullify the original gift and would return the value of the house to his estate. In addition the original gift, which was a potentially exempt transfer, would still be included in the lifetime chargeable gifts if death occurred within seven years after the original gift. However, relief is given to prevent double charging (FA 1986 s 104 and SI 1987/1130).

(c) **Inheritance tax as a result of Mr Gregory's death on 30 September 2006**

	£	Gross £	Tax (2006/07 scale) £
Gifts in lifetime:			
January 2005			
Gift to Neil — house		250,000	
Less: Annual exemptions 2004/05	3,000		
2003/04	3,000	6,000	
Potentially exempt transfer now chargeable		244,000	–
July 2006			
Gift to Neil			
550 shares in Zingo plc @ £20 per share		11,000	
Less: Marriage exemption	5,000		
Annual exemptions 2006/07	3,000		
2005/06	3,000	11,000	–	–
		244,000	–
Mr Gregory's estate at death — 30 September 2006			
Proceeds of sale of Bingo plc shares	480		
Income tax repayment	1,250		
Capital gains tax repayment**	1,153		
Shares in Zingo plc			
10,000 – 550 = 9,450 @ £20	189,000		
Shares in Peck Limited			
20,000 @ £1.20	24,000		
Less: Business property relief 100%	24,000	–	191,883	60,353*
		435,883	60,353*

Inheritance tax liability on death of Mr Gregory — £ 60,360

(* 435,883 – 285,000 = £150,882 @ 40%)

** Assuming that the 2005/06 tax of £1,090 was discharged, the repayment will consist of 2003/04 gains of £3,000 less loss used in 2006/07 of £117 = £2,883 @ 40% = £1,153

Supplementary note

The general principles of inheritance tax are dealt with in earlier examples. In particular normal expenditure out of income is dealt with in Example 1, gifts with reservation in Example 19 and pre-owned assets in Example 23. The capital gains tax provisions are outlined in Example 36. Capital gains tax is dealt with in detail in the companion to this book, Tolley's Taxwise I 2006/07.

Thomas and Maria have been married for many years. Their daughter, Julia, was born in February 1968 and their son, Edmund, in October 1969. Thomas, who was born in 1934, started in business on his own account in 1958 as a manufacturer of domestic hardware. Their relevant financial history is as follows:

March 1965 — The family home is bought by Maria for £6,000.

May 1979 — Thomas buys 100,000 ordinary shares in Huntingdon Ltd, a trading company that has since become listed on the Stock Exchange, for 34p per share (value 31 March 1982 25p per share).

September 1988 — Thomas buys 25,000 ordinary shares in Portsmouth plc for £45,000.

31 March 1989 — Thomas transfers all his business assets (except plant of £30,000 which he retains personally) to a new company, Thomas Ltd, in consideration for ordinary shares valued at £300,000 (Maria holding one share as nominee). Business assets immediately before the transfers were:

	£
Goodwill	110,000
Plant, at cost less depreciation	55,000
Vehicles, at cost less depreciation	30,000
Stock, at cost or lower market value	65,000
Debtors	90,000
Cash	40,000
Creditors	(60,000)
	330,000

Thomas Ltd continues the trade without a break.

November 1999 — Maria gives the family home (then valued at £80,000) in equal shares to Julia and her husband Henry. Maria and Thomas then move to their second home (which cost £62,000 in 1988, at which time an election had been made for capital gains tax that the original home remained the principal private residence).

June 2002 — Maria places £32,500 cash into trust for Edmund for life, with remainder to Julia or her children (Julia has a son and a daughter). The trustees invest the money in a building society account which pays interest monthly.

Thomas gives 70% of the shares in Thomas Ltd to Edmund.

Company assets, at historical cost, are:

	£
Goodwill on acquisition from Thomas	110,000
Freehold factory bought July 1989	225,000
Shares in 100% subsidiary, allotted May 1992	100,000
Other non-chargeable assets	368,000
	803,000

In June 2002 goodwill is valued at £400,000. The factory is used for the trade (which is to continue) and is worth £600,000. The subsidiary's only assets are a portfolio of investment properties worth £230,000. (Ignore deferred tax.)

October 2002 — Thomas places his shares in Huntingdon plc (then valued at £130,000) into a discretionary trust. The beneficiaries are Julia, Edmund and all their descendants. Thomas's holding was less than 5% and he did not work for the company. The trustees decide to accumulate all the income arising.

May 2006   — Edmund dies intestate. He is unmarried and without children. In addition to his shares in Thomas Ltd (which have not changed in value since June 2002) he leaves a house worth £165,000 and other investments of £70,000. Under the rules of intestacy his estate will pass to Thomas and Maria.

No person elects to rebase all their chargeable assets to 31 March 1982 values.

Shares in Thomas Ltd at June 2002 are to be valued:

(i)   as to a 100% holding, on an assets basis;

(ii)   as to a 70% holding, on an assets basis discounted by 20%;

(iii)   as to a 30% holding, £225,000 for the holding.

Any inheritance tax on lifetime transfers is paid by the donor.

The Retail Prices Index at the relevant dates was as follows:

March 1982	79.44
September 1988	108.4
March 1989	112.3
April 1998	162.6

The capital gains tax annual exemption was as follows:

1999/2000	£7,100
2000/01	£7,200
2001/02	£7,500
2002/03	£7,700
2003/04	£7,900
2004/05	£8,200
2005/06	£8,500

(a)   Using all available reliefs, compute all chargeable gains/losses arising from 6 April 1999 onwards, stating which events will trigger an immediate liability to capital gains tax and which will not.

(b)   Identify and quantify all chargeable and potentially exempt transfers, advising how much inheritance tax is payable on chargeable transfers, when it is payable, and any other factors that may be relevant.

(c)   Advise the beneficiaries under Edmund's intestacy of the main planning points that arise on his death.

(a) **Capital gains tax liabilities 6 April 1999 onwards**

November 1999 — Gift of family home by Maria — covered by principal private residence exemption — no chargeable gain.

June 2002 — Cash into trust by Maria — no chargeable disposal.

Gift by Thomas to Edmund of 70% of shares in Thomas Ltd:

Valuation of Thomas Ltd — assets basis		£
Factory		600,000
Subsidiary		230,000
Non-chargeable assets		368,000
Goodwill		400,000
		1,598,000
Valuation of gift: 70% x (1,598,000 x 80%)		894,880
Cost — March 1989 (70% x 300,000)	210,000	
Indexation allowance to April 1998		
$(\frac{162.6 - 112.3}{112.3} =)$ .448	94,080	
		304,080
Gain		590,800

Retirement relief will be available, restricted to the fraction:

$$\frac{\text{Chargeable business assets}}{\text{Total chargeable assets}} \quad \text{ie} \quad \frac{600,000 + 400,000}{600,000 + 400,000 + 230,000}$$

Available for relief $\frac{1,000,000}{1,230,000}$ x 590,800		£ 480,325
Retirement relief on the disposal in June 2002 will be:		
100% x 50,000 =		50,000
50% x (200,000 – 50,000) =		75,000
		125,000

Holdover relief will be available for any remaining gain relating to the chargeable business assets, ie:

	£
Gain which could be held over (as for retirement relief)	480,325
Less: Retirement relief (50,000 + 75,000)	125,000
Heldover gain	355,325
Gain chargeable on Thomas (590,800 – 480,325)	£ 110,475

Capital gains tax position of Thomas for 2002/03 is:

	£
Gain on Thomas Ltd shares*	110,475
Less: Taper relief 15% non-business asset owned 17 March 1998	16,571
	93,904
Less: Annual exemption	7,700
Chargeable @ 2002/03 rates	86,204

* It is considered that the shares do not qualify for business assets taper relief — see explanatory note 3.

October 2002 — Gift by Thomas of shares in Huntingdon plc to discretionary trust

	£	£	£	£
Value of gift		130,000		130,000
Less: Cost May 1979/31.3.82 value	34,000		25,000	
Indexation allowance to April 1998				
$34,000 \times (\dfrac{162.6 - 79.44}{79.44} =) 1.047$	35,598		35,598	
		69,598		60,598
		60,402		69,402

Lower gain of £60,402 (ie based on original cost) applies and can be held over under TCGA 1992 s 260, as disposition is immediately liable to inheritance tax.

Note Base cost of shares in Huntingdon plc to trustees is 130,000 – 60,402 = £69,598. Taper relief will depend on the period of ownership of the trustees. It would have been 15% in 2002/03, since the shares are non-business assets (see explanatory note 2).

May 2006 — No liability to capital gains tax on death of Edmund.

(b) **Inheritance tax**

Inheritance tax position of Maria

		£	£
November 1999			
—	Gift of house		80,000
	Less: Annual exemptions 1999/2000	3,000	
	1998/99	3,000	6,000
	Potentially exempt transfer		74,000

The transfer will only become chargeable if Maria dies before November 2006, but no tax will be payable in any event, since the transfer is below the nil threshold (although the nil threshold available against Maria's estate at death would be correspondingly reduced).

		£	£
June 2002	— Gift of cash into interest in possession trust		32,500
	Less: Annual exemptions 2002/03	3,000	
	2001/02	3,000	6,000
	Potentially exempt transfer		26,500

Again the transfer will only become chargeable on the death of Maria, this time before June 2009, but again the cumulative transfers are in any event covered by the nil threshold.

Inheritance tax position of Thomas

June 2002 — Gift of 70% of shares in Thomas Ltd to Edmund.

		£
Valuation of gift:		
Holding before gift — 100% of 1,598,000		1,598,000
Holding after gift — 30% minority		225,000
Loss to estate		1,373,000
Less business property relief		
100% x 1,373,000	1,368,000*	
x	‾‾‾‾‾‾‾‾‾	1,175,384
	1,598,000	
		197,616

(* The investment holding subsidiary is an excepted asset for business property relief)

Less: Annual exemptions 2002/03	3,000	
2001/02	3,000	6,000
Potentially exempt transfer		191,616

Note The shares that were returned to Thomas following the death of Edmund would also form part of Thomas's estate. However should he die within seven years, ie before June 2009, relief will be given to prevent double charging. No liability will arise on the potentially exempt transfer itself, since it is below the nil threshold.

October 2002 — Gift of shares in Huntingdon plc to discretionary trust

Value of gift	£ 130,000

No inheritance tax is payable at the time of the gift as the cumulative total of gifts immediately liable to inheritance tax is below the 2002/03 threshold of £250,000. If Thomas should die before June 2009, the gift would be aggregated with the June 2002 potentially exempt transfer that then became chargeable and inheritance tax would be payable to the extent that the aggregate amount exceeded the nil threshold at the time of death. If he should die after June 2009 but before October 2009 no tax would be payable on the gift to the discretionary trust, but it would be aggregated with later gifts and the death estate, thus increasing the inheritance tax payable.

Inheritance tax position re death of Edmund in May 2006

	£	£

Value of free estate:

Shares in Thomas Ltd (70% holding) (1,598,000 x 70%, less 20%) — 894,880

Less: Business property relief (100% available
as second transfer was on death even though
not owned for two years)

$$100\% \times 894{,}880 \times \frac{1{,}368{,}000^*}{1{,}598{,}000}$$ 766,080 — 128,800

(* The investment holding subsidiary is an excepted asset)

House — 165,000

Other investments — 70,000

363,800

Settled property — trust of Maria — 32,500

396,300

Inheritance tax payable (396,300 – 285,000) @ 40% = £44,520

£

Payable by:

Personal representatives $\dfrac{363{,}800}{396{,}300}$ x 44,520 = 40,869

Trustees $\dfrac{32{,}500}{396{,}300}$ x 44,520 = 3,651

44,520

Of the total liability, the tax relating to the Thomas Ltd shares can be paid by instalments without interest to the due date and that relating to the house by instalments with interest from 1 December 2006; therefore the amount actually due from the personal representatives on application for probate will be:

Shares $\dfrac{128{,}800}{363{,}800}$ x 40,869 x $\dfrac{1}{10}$ = 1,447 (with interest on balance only if paid late)

House $\dfrac{165{,}000}{363{,}800}$ x 40,869 x $\dfrac{1}{10}$ = 1,854 (with interest on balance from 1 December 2006)

Other investments $\dfrac{70{,}000}{363{,}800}$ x 40,869 = 7,864

£ 11,165

(c) **Advice to Thomas and Maria as beneficiaries of the estate of Edmund**

The value in Edmund's estate is reverting to yourselves. As the oldest generation, you are likely to die before other members of the family. It may be preferable for Edmund's estate to go to your daughter Julia or to your grandchildren. If this course of action is decided on then it could be achieved by use of a deed of variation. Such a deed would not save inheritance tax on Edmund's death but might significantly reduce the potential liability on your own deaths. The deed must be executed within two years of Edmund's death.

It should be noted that if an instalment option asset (ie either the Thomas Ltd shares or Edmund's house) is sold, the outstanding instalments of inheritance tax become payable immediately.

The funding of the inheritance tax could be achieved by Thomas Ltd purchasing its own shares from the estate. This would qualify for special treatment and HMRC clearance should be obtained for the purchase not to be treated as a distribution by Thomas Ltd.

If no deed of variation occurs then should either of you die within five years after Edmund's death (ie before May 2011) quick succession relief would be available in your estates in respect of the assets inherited from him. In the same way, should the devolution of Edmund's estate be varied in favour of Julia and she were to die or make a chargeable transfer of her interest in the settled property devolving on her following Edmund's death, before May 2011, quick succession relief would be available by reference to the tax payable on Edmund's death.

Explanatory Notes

Valuation of assets for capital gains tax and inheritance tax

1. This example shows the way in which both capital gains tax and inheritance tax may be relevant when gifts are made, and the different rules that apply when dealing with each tax. Note particularly that in valuing a shareholding, the open market value of the holding is taken for capital gains tax (TCGA 1992 s 272), hence the gift of 70% of Thomas's 100% holding in Thomas Ltd to Edmund in June 2002 is discounted by the 20% reduction for a 70% holding, whereas for inheritance tax the 'loss to the donor' principle applies, the shares therefore being taken into account for inheritance tax as a 100% holding, reduced to a minority holding. (See Revenue's Tax Bulletin August 1996 concerning when two or more separate assets may be treated as a single unit of property for valuation purposes.) The value of the gift is therefore different for capital gains tax and inheritance tax, ie:

Capital gains tax	£894,880
Inheritance tax	£1,373,000

When considering the capital gains tax acquisition value for those who inherit a deceased's assets, on the other hand, TCGA 1992 s 274 provides that where the value of an asset has been *ascertained* (whether in any proceedings or otherwise) for the purposes of inheritance tax, that value is taken to be the market value of the asset at the date of death for capital gains tax (overriding the normal 'open market value' provisions in TCGA 1992 s 62). This enables the higher 'loss to the donor' amount to be used in those circumstances, including any value attributable to related property.

Where, however, no tax is due because of reliefs or exemptions, the value of assets will not be *ascertained* for inheritance tax, so their capital gains acquisition value would be the open market value. This would apply, for example, where 100% business property relief is available on family company shares, or where a transfer of such shares is covered by the nil threshold. It has been suggested that where this would give lower acquisition values, the problem could be overcome by having a minimal amount of 'excepted assets', not qualifying for business property relief, within the company (see note 2), so that a valuation would then be necessary. The Revenue have, however, stated that if very little or no tax was at stake, it was unlikely that an ascertained value would be negotiated by Shares Valuation Division (Tax Bulletin April 1995).

In the case of Stonor & Mills (Dickinson's Executors) v CIR (SpC 288, 2001), no inheritance tax was payable on the estate because of the nil rate band and the charities exemption. The executors sold freehold properties from the estate for significantly more than the probate value, resulting in large capital gains. They tried to get the Revenue to accept the sale values as amended probate values, but the Revenue refused on the grounds that an investigation into values was not necessary since charity relief had been claimed. The executors then made a claim under IHTA 1984 s 191 (land sold within three years after death – see Example 10 part B) to substitute the sale proceeds for the probate value, thus increasing the capital gains tax base cost and eliminating the gains. It was held that since no one was liable to pay any tax on the estate no one was entitled to make a s 191 claim.

Capital gains tax taper relief

2.   Detailed notes on taper relief for capital gains tax are in Example 36 part (a)(ii). See note 3 below re Thomas's gift of shares in Thomas Ltd to Edmund in June 2002. Huntingdon plc is not a qualifying company as far as Thomas is concerned, since it is a listed company in which he does not work and owns less than 5% of the voting power, so the shares are non-business assets.

Investment assets

3.   Both for capital gains tax taper relief and for inheritance tax business property relief, the amount of the relief is affected where a company holds assets as investments rather than for use in the business. Although capital gains tax retirement relief looks at the group's assets where there is a parent/subsidiary structure, Thomas Ltd's subsidiary company's assets consist wholly of investment properties. Similarly, capital gains tax business assets taper relief was not available prior to 5 April 2002 where a group's activities include to any substantial extent activities carried on otherwise than in the course of trade (see Example 36 part (a)(ii)), so the shares in Thomas Ltd given to Edmund in 2002/03 do not qualify because of the non-trading subsidiary. But they do qualify for non-business assets taper relief because they have been held for four years from 6 April 1998, plus the bonus year because they were owned on 17 March 1998.

      Capital gains tax holdover relief on gifts under TCGA 1992 s 165 is also available only on business assets and not on assets held as investments (other than farming land owned by an agricultural landlord, which can qualify for s 165 relief). Gifts relief under TCGA 1992 s 260 is available on any asset, providing the gift is immediately liable to inheritance tax, hence the relief on the October 2002 gift by Thomas to the discretionary trust.

Transfer of business to company

4.   Thomas will not have been able to hold over the chargeable gains on the transfer of his personal business to Thomas Ltd in 1989, since not all of the assets were transferred in consideration for shares. Hence the value of the shares received, £300,000, is not reduced by holdover relief.

Cross references

5.   See Example 4 explanatory note 7 for the position when both capital gains tax and inheritance tax are payable on the same transfer. For detailed notes on business property relief see Example 25, on quick succession relief see Example 21, on the instalment option see Example 5 and on deeds of variation in relation to a deceased's estate see Example 34. Note in this example that a variation would not result in additional tax payable on Edmund's estate, since there are no exempt beneficiaries. Had additional tax been payable, the amount would have had to be notified to HMRC Capital Taxes and a copy of the variation sent, within six months after the deed was effected. Capital gains tax is dealt with comprehensively in the companion to this book Tolley's Taxwise I 2006/07.

Y died on 5 April 2005 leaving small bequests to each of three friends and the residue to his son X, for life. The administration of the estate was completed by the personal representatives on 5 April 2007.

Details of the estate income (which is wholly interest) are as follows:

	Expenses borne £	Leaving residuary income		Payments to X £	made on
		Net £	Gross equivalent £		
2005/06	1,130	1,760	2,200	1,600	3 March 2006
2006/07	1,150	2,880	3,600	3,040	20 June 2007

(a) Indicate the tax liability of the personal representatives in relation to the estate income and state what their responsibilities for reporting the income are under self-assessment.

(b) Calculate for 2005/06 and 2006/07 the amounts of estate income to be included in X's taxable income.

(c) State whether the estate income that would have been included in X's taxable income would have been different had he been absolutely entitled to the residue (as compared with his limited (life) interest).

(a) **Personal representatives — income tax liability and self-assessment**

Income tax liability

The personal representatives are liable to income tax on the income arising during the administration period. Since all the income is interest, the rate of tax payable is the lower rate of 20%, the tax being covered by the amount deducted at source. Had the income been dividends, the rate would have been the dividend ordinary rate of 10%. If there had been any non-savings income, tax would have been payable thereon at the basic rate of 22% (see explanatory note 5).

Self-assessment

The personal representatives are required to submit a tax return form SA 900 not later than 31 January following the relevant tax year, eg by 31 January 2007 for 2005/06. Where, however, as in this case, all the income is taxed income, no amounts have to be entered on the return and only the information section needs to be completed (see explanatory note 1).

(b) **Estate income to be included in taxable income of life tenant, X**

Where a person has a life interest in a will settlement, the amounts to be included in his statutory income during the period of administration are the grossed up equivalents of the net income payments actually made to him in the tax year (ITTOIA 2005 ss 649–662 (formerly TA 1988 s 695(2)(4))). The amount of the grossing addition depends on the rate of tax on the underlying income, ie for 2005/06 and 2006/07, 10% for dividend income, 20% for other savings income and the basic rate of 22% for non-savings income (see explanatory note 5).

Thus the amount to be included in the statutory income of X in 2005/06 is £1,600 x 100/80 = £2,000.

Upon the completion of the administration, any amounts due to the life tenant which remain unpaid are deemed to be paid as income of the tax year in which the administration is *completed* (ITTOIA 2005 ss 649–662 (formerly TA 1988 s 695(3))).

Since the administration is completed in 2006/07, X will be deemed to have received the balance due to him in that tax year, ie £3,040 x 100/80 = £3,800.

(c) **Effect on X's estate income if he had had an absolute interest in residue**

Where a person has an absolute interest in the residue of an estate, the amounts to be included in his statutory income during the period of administration are the same as for a life tenant, ie the net income payments actually made to him, grossed up at the appropriate rate. However, the maximum amount that can be included is the 'aggregated income entitlement' to date, that is the total amount taxable in any year cannot exceed the aggregate amount of the residuary income to which the person is entitled, less amounts paid in previous tax years (ITTOIA 2005 s 668 (formerly TA 1988 s 696)).

Upon the completion of the administration, any amounts not paid, up to the aggregated income entitlement, are deemed to be paid to the beneficiary immediately before completion.

The amounts taxable on X would therefore be the same as in (b) above, ie a gross amount of £2,000 in 2005/06 and a gross amount of £3,800 in 2006/07.

Explanatory Notes

Self-assessment position of personal representatives

1. Under self-assessment, personal representatives complete the same tax return as trusts (form SA 900) and are subject to the same requirements, ie the return must be submitted by 30 September following the tax year if HMRC are to calculate the tax and otherwise by 31 January following the tax year, returns may be amended by the personal representatives within twelve months, HMRC may make corrections within nine months or enquire into the return within twelve months, and records must be retained for the appropriate period (TMA 1970 ss 8, 9A, 12B).

If, however, all the estate income is taxed income and there are no capital gains, then in most cases no amounts have to be entered on the return and only the information section needs to be completed (see Example 41 re Mrs Daley). In that event there would be no requirement to submit the return until the 31 January date.

The personal representatives supply beneficiaries with form R185 (estate income) showing income payments split according to whether the underlying income was taxed at the basic, lower or dividend ordinary rate of tax and whether the tax is repayable or non-repayable (see note 7).

Income of beneficiaries

2. All payments made to a beneficiary with a limited interest (usually a life interest) will be income. For a beneficiary with an absolute interest, payments must be treated as being liable to income tax in the hands of the beneficiary, up to the gross equivalent of the amount of income received by the estate. In the legislation references to amounts paid include assets transferred to beneficiaries, or debts set off or released, the amount for such items being their value at the relevant date (ITTOIA 2005 s 681 (formerly TA 1988 s 701(12))).

    Where assets have been transferred to absolute beneficiaries during the administration period, therefore, the gross equivalent of their value must be taken into account as a distribution of estate income even though the distribution was of capital, so particular care must be taken in calculating the amount to be shown on forms R185 (estate income). See Example 40 for the capital gains implications of transferring assets to a beneficiary during the administration period.

Beneficiaries with an absolute interest

3. For someone with an absolute interest in the estate, if the amounts to be deducted from the income of the estate exceed the income in any year, the excess is carried forward and deducted from future income in computing the aggregated income entitlement (ITTOIA 2005 s 666(2), (6) (formerly TA 1988 s 697(1A))).

4. If, when the administration is completed, it is found that the total residuary income of the estate is less than the amounts paid to someone with an absolute interest (for example, because large bills are paid in the later stages of the administration), then the amount included in the statutory income of the person concerned is reduced to the actual net income. This is done by reducing the income of the tax year in which the administration is completed, then, if necessary, the previous year, and so on (ITTOIA 2005 s 668 (formerly TA 1988 s 697(2))).

Identification of income received by beneficiaries

5. As indicated in the example, amounts paid to beneficiaries by personal representatives are regarded as net of 10% tax to the extent that they represent dividend income, 20% tax to the extent that they represent other savings income and the basic rate (currently 22%) if they represent non-savings income. The rate of tax for the different categories of income is known as the 'applicable rate' (ITTOIA 2005 ss 663, 670, 679 (formerly TA 1988 s 701)).

    'Just and reasonable' apportionments of income bearing tax at different rates are to be made between beneficiaries with interests in residue. After making any such apportionments, payments to beneficiaries are regarded as being out of brought forward and current income charged at the basic rate in priority to other income, and as being out of brought forward and current savings income charged at the lower rate (which will include pre 6 April 1999 dividends) in priority to dividends charged at the ordinary rate of 10% (ITTOIA 2005 ss 670, 679 (formerly TA 1988 s 701(3A))).

Changes in the applicable rate

6. As indicated in the example, amounts payable on completion of the administration are deemed to be income of the tax year in which the administration is completed, and they are therefore regarded as having been taxed at the applicable rate in force for that year, even if the rate of tax actually deducted from the income was different. This treatment applies only where the *applicable rate* changes. Where income was previously treated as being subject to a *different* applicable rate, any brought forward

amounts are still regarded as having been taxed at the applicable rate that was relevant when they were received. For dividends received before 6 April 1999, the applicable rate was the *lower* rate of 20%, and that rate has remained unchanged. If any pre 6 April 1999 dividends were undistributed and were therefore brought forward to 1999/2000 or a later year, they would be regarded as distributed (along with any other savings income) in priority to post 5 April 1999 dividends and the applicable rate would be 20%.

Forms R185

7. Personal representatives supply beneficiaries with an income certificate form R185 (estate income) showing the amounts paid as income and tax deducted (or treated as deducted), split between savings income (with tax at the lower or dividend ordinary rate) and other income (with tax at the basic rate). The beneficiaries include the information from the R185 in the trusts etc pages in their personal returns.

    The tax on some of the income may be shown as non-repayable (ITTOIA 2005 s 680 (formerly TA 1988 s 699A)). Non-repayable tax at the lower rate arises on life policy gains (basic rate before 6 April 2004). Before 6 April 1999, non-repayable tax at the lower rate arose where the income was a scrip dividend or foreign income dividend, where a close company loan written off was treated as income and where there were non-qualifying distributions within ITTOIA 2005 ss 399, 400 (formerly TA 1988 s 233(1)) (mainly bonus issues of redeemable shares or securities). From 6 April 1999, ITTOIA 2005 s 680 (formerly TA 1988 s 699A) was amended to provide that non-repayable tax also includes tax credits on dividends, and the applicable rate for all non-repayable tax except that on life policy gains is the dividend ordinary rate of 10%. References to foreign income dividends have been deleted, since they are no longer payable from that date.

    For beneficiaries with only a limited interest in residue, non-repayable tax did not arise before 6 April 1999 except in relation to foreign income dividends, because the other items on which non-repayable tax arose were treated as part of the estate capital. From 6 April 1999 it will arise in relation to dividend income.

Completion of administration

8. When the administration of the estate is complete, the personal representatives will have assigned the interest in the assets to the trustees of the life interest settlement, who take those assets for capital gains tax purposes at their value at the date of death. This will normally be the probate value, but where a probate value was not *ascertained* for inheritance tax (because no inheritance tax was payable) the capital gains 'open market value' rule applies (see Example 38 explanatory note 1). Once the interest in the assets has been assigned to the trustees, the trustees are responsible for making the relevant income tax self-assessment returns, using forms R185 (trust income) and paying any tax due. The beneficiary is then liable to tax on the amount shown on the R185. See the examples in the book relating to trusts and Example 43 in respect of the income tax position of a life interest will trust.

Enterprise investment scheme and venture capital trusts

9. Where someone has invested under the enterprise investment scheme or venture capital trust scheme, their death does not trigger the withdrawal of the income tax relief on the shares nor will it cause deferred gains to become chargeable. The personal representatives would be liable to capital gains tax on sale of the shares, the acquisition cost being the market value at the date of death.

John Bird died on 26 February 2006. By his will he left one half of his estate to his wife (aged 65) and one half to his son (aged 42). His executors, Mrs Bird and her son Rupert, obtained probate on 8 June 2006. There was no inheritance tax payable. The estate, which was valued at £500,000 (gross), included the following assets:

Asset	Probate value £
950 shares of £1 each in Bird Enterprises Ltd, a trading company (the other 50 shares being owned by Mrs Bird, who was a director working part-time and had subscribed for the shares at par in February 1989)	235,000
10,000 shares in Computer Games plc, a quoted company	17,500
3,600 shares in Midwest Bank plc held in a single company PEP following the flotation of the former building society	10,200

Mrs Bird and her son decided to sell Bird Enterprises Ltd because without its founder, Mr Bird, they were too dependent on the skills of individual employees. Although a number of outside offers were made, on 5 July 2006 they accepted a bid of £332,500 from the management for the whole of the company.

The Midwest Bank received a takeover offer of £2.50 per share from a High Street bank in September 2006 which Mrs Bird and her son accepted.

On 18 November 2006 Micro plc made a cash offer of £3.30 per share or 4% Redeemable Loan Stock to the same value in any proportions for each share in Computer Games plc (the loan stock is within the definition of qualifying corporate bonds (QCB)).

The administration of the estate was completed in December 2006.

Neither Mrs Bird nor her son will have any further capital disposals in 2006/07. Mrs Bird is a 40% taxpayer. Her son still has £10,000 of his basic rate band available for capital gains.

(a)   State the capital gains tax payable for 2006/07 if all of the above transactions are undertaken by Mrs Bird and her son as executors (and they accept cash for the Computer Games shares).

(b)   Set out alternative suggestions which would have mitigated the tax payable.

(a) **Capital gains tax payable for 2006/07**

	£	£	£
Estate of John Bird deceased			
Bird Enterprises Ltd — sale proceeds 950 shares July 2006		332,500	
Probate value February 2006	235,000		
Costs of title 0.75%	1,763	236,763	95,737
Midwest Bank plc —			
Sale proceeds September 2006 3,600 shares @ £2.50		9,000	
Probate value	10,200		
Costs of title 0.75%	77	10,277	(1,277)
Computer Games plc —			
Sale proceeds November 2006 10,000 shares @ £3.30		33,000	
Probate value	17,500		
Costs of title 0.75%	132	17,632	15,368
			109,828
Annual exemption			(8,800)
Chargeable gains for the year			101,028
Capital gains tax payable by executors @ 40%			£ 40,411

No taper relief is available to the executors since they have held the assets for less than a year.

Mrs Bird

	£	£	£
Bird Enterprises Ltd —			
Sale proceeds 50 shares July 2006		17,500	
Cost February 1989	50		
Indexation allowance to April 1998 45.4%	23	73	
		17,427	
Taper relief *		10,909	6,518
Annual exemption			(8,800)
Chargeable gains for the year			Nil
Capital gains tax payable by Mrs Bird @ 40%			£ Nil
Total capital gains tax payable by executors and Mrs Bird			£ 40,411

* Mrs Bird's holding of Bird Enterprises Ltd shares becomes a business asset from 6 April 2000, since it is an unlisted company. To determine the taper relief available, therefore, the period from 6 April 1998 to 5 July 2006 is apportioned between non-business/business periods as follows (the length of the qualifying period to determine the *rate* of relief remaining at nine years, including the extra year for pre 17 March 1998 ownership, for the non-business proportion and eight years for the business proportion (see Example 36)):

Non-business assets taper relief
(6.4.98 – 5.4.2000)   24/99 x 35% =   8.48%
Business assets taper relief
(6.4.2000 – 5.7.06)   75/99 x 75% = 56.8%
Taper relief available   65.3% x 17,427 = £11,380

(b)   **Ways of mitigating tax payable**

The overall tax payable could be mitigated as follows:

Transferring shares in Bird Enterprises Ltd to beneficiaries before sale

If Mrs Bird and her son as executors had transferred the shares to themselves as individuals prior to the sale, the transfer would be deemed to occur at the date of death (TCGA 1992 s 62(4)). Their revised personal capital gains tax position for 2006/07 (subject to any losses arising to them as individuals) would be:

	£	£	£
Mrs Bird			
Bird Enterprises Ltd —			
Sale proceeds 525 shares July 2006 (166,250 + 17,500)		183,750	
Indexed cost of 50 shares February 1989 as in (a)	73		
Probate value of 475 shares February 2006	117,500	117,573	
		66,177	
Taper relief on 50 shares as above		11,380	54,797
Annual exemption			(8,800)
Chargeable gains for the year			45,997
Capital gains tax payable by Mrs Bird @ 40%			£ 18,399

	£	£	£
Rupert Bird			
Bird Enterprises Ltd —			
Sale proceeds 475 shares July 2006		166,250	
Probate value February 2006 (no taper relief available)		117,500	48,750
Annual exemption			(8,800)
Chargeable gains for the year			39,950
Capital gains tax payable by Rupert:			
10,000 @ 20%		2,000	
29,950 @ 40%		11,980	£ 13,980

Such a transfer would, however, be taken to be a distribution of income, giving rise to taxable income in the hands of the beneficiaries to the extent that undistributed income had arisen in the estate, and would therefore trigger a charge to higher rate tax. Since the administration was completed within the same tax year as the transfer, however, this is irrelevant, since the income would already have been distributed.

Shares in Computer Games plc

The executors could transfer the whole of the shares to themselves as beneficiaries, enabling the beneficiaries to take loan stock, or they could take loan stock themselves as executors and pass it on to themselves as beneficiaries, thus deferring the capital gain. In September 2006, however, they had incurred a loss on the disposal of the Midwest Bank plc shares. To use that loss and also their annual exemption, the executors could take the cash offer on 6,557 Computer Games plc shares and loan stock in respect of 3,443 shares, giving the estate a capital gains liability of:

	£	£
Sale proceeds 6,557 shares @ £3.30	21,638	
Proportion of probate value:		
$\dfrac{6,557}{10,000}$ x 17,632	11,561	10,077
Loss on Midwest Bank plc shares as in (a) above		(1,277)
		8,800
Annual exemption		(8,800)
Chargeable gains		–

This enables both the executor's annual exemption and the loss on the Midwest Bank shares to be fully utilised. (Losses incurred by executors can only be offset against a gain accruing to them as executors in the same or a future year and cannot be transferred to beneficiaries. A similar tax saving could have been achieved if the Midwest Bank shares had been transferred to the beneficiaries before the Bank was taken over, so that the loss would arise to Mrs Bird and Rupert. The Computer Games plc shares on which the cash offer was taken could then be reduced so as to realise gains of approximately £8,800 as before.)

Effect of above suggestions

As a result of the above, the capital gains tax payable for 2006/07 would be reduced from £40,411 to (18,399 + 13,980) £32,379, ie by £8,032. Mrs Bird and Rupert would, however, each have redeemable loan stock in Micro plc with accrued gains of:

	£
1,721 shares @ £3.30	5,679
Proportion of probate value $\dfrac{1,721}{10,000}$ x 17,500*	(3,012)
Accrued gain	2,667

* See explanatory note 4.

Even so, if the loan stock was redeemed in a year in which the beneficiary had no other gains, the accrued gain would be covered by the annual exemption of the year of disposal. (Taper relief will not be available, since it would be taken into account in calculating the accrued gains on the shares at the time of the takeover, at which time the shares had been held for less than twelve months since the date of Mr Bird's death.)

Explanatory Notes

Treatment of personal representatives

1. On death the deceased's assets are acquired by the personal representatives at market value, but there is no deemed disposal by the deceased and no capital gains tax is payable as a result of the death.

2. The personal representatives — the executors in this example — are treated as a separate single and continuing body of persons. All their dealings as personal representatives are completely separate from their dealings as individuals. Capital gains and losses are accordingly computed and assessed on them as personal representatives. Under self-assessment any tax due on capital gains is payable on 31 January following the end of the tax year. The rate of tax on personal representatives' gains is 40% (TCGA 1992 s 4).

3. The personal representatives are entitled to an annual exemption of the same amount as an individual for the tax year of death and the following two tax years. If the administration of the estate has not been completed in that time there is no annual exemption for later years and any gains arising are chargeable at the 40% rate.

Probate valuation costs

4. When computing the gain or loss on sales of assets by the personal representatives, the cost of acquiring the assets can be increased by the costs incurred in valuing them for probate (CIR v Richards' Executors 1971). HMRC have agreed a scale for the costs of establishing title for estates with a gross value not exceeding £750,000, which can be claimed instead of the actual expenditure. This is set out in SP 8/94 as follows:

Gross value of estate	*Allowable expenditure*
Up to £40,000	1.75% of the probate value
Between £40,001 and £70,000	£700 to be divided between all assets in proportion to probate value
Between £70,001 and £300,000	1% of the probate value
Between £300,001 and £400,000	£3,000 divided as above
Between £400,001 and £750,000	0.75% of the probate value

    Allowable expenditure on gross estates exceeding £750,000 is negotiated according to the facts of the particular case.

    Although the matter is far from clear, it is the view of HMRC that a deduction for probate valuation costs only applies where the sale is by the personal representatives and not where the sale is by the beneficiaries themselves. It should be noted that the actual costs, if any, of the *beneficiary* relating to the acquisition of the asset are deductible (TCGA 1992 s 64(1)(a)), and also any costs of the personal representatives *in transferring* assets to them (s 64(1)(b)). As Mrs Bird and Rupert have undertaken the transactions themselves it is unlikely there are any such costs.

    Where the estate is administered by a corporate trustee, HMRC will allow £20 per holding (plus any exceptional expenditure for *unquoted* shares) as costs of transfer from personal representatives to beneficiaries (SP 8/94) otherwise the amount claimable is the actual costs incurred by the personal representatives *in transferring* the asset to the beneficiary (TCGA 1992 s 64(1)(b)) rather than the costs of acquiring the asset or valuing it for probate.

Valuation for capital gains tax where no inheritance tax payable

5. Where no inheritance tax is payable on death, the values included in the application for probate will not be binding on HMRC for capital gains tax unless specifically agreed with them (see Example 38 explanatory note 1). The personal representatives may therefore wish to file form CG34 after the sale of shares in Bird Enterprises Ltd to agree the acquisition cost and gain prior to the submission of the self-assessment return.

Shares held in a PEP

6. Although the shares in Midwest Bank plc were held in a single company PEP and were not therefore liable to capital gains tax, that treatment ceases on death. The shares are held by personal representatives as a normal chargeable asset. Therefore the loss between death and disposal is available for relief (a gain would have similarly been a chargeable gain).

Taper relief for capital gains tax

7. Capital gains tax taper relief applies where appropriate to disposals on or after 6 April 1998 other than by companies (TCGA 1992 s 2A and Sch A1) (see Example 36 part (a)(ii)). The minimum qualifying period is one complete year for business assets and three complete years for non-business

assets. Where non-business assets were held on 17 March 1998 and also on 6 April 1998, an extra year is added to the qualifying period. The definition of business asset changed from 6 April 2000. Full details are in Example 36.

John Bird's shares in Bird Enterprises Ltd would have qualified for business assets taper relief both before and after 6 April 2000 if he had disposed of them himself, and would have qualified in the hands of the executors if they had held the shares for more than one year before they were sold. Mrs Bird owns only 5% of the shares and is a part-time director, so the non-business assets rates applied up to 5 April 2000 and the business assets rates thereafter, as indicated in the example.

Considerations to be taken into account on deciding appropriate course of action

8.   The executors must carefully consider the taxation implications of selling assets themselves or transferring them to the beneficiaries. These include:

Sale by executors

Capital gains tax rate is 40%
Annual exemption is available in year of death and two following years only
Base costs of assets include costs of the estate (SP 8/94)
Losses are only available against gains of the estate

Sale by beneficiaries

Capital gains tax rate is highest marginal rate (ie up to 40%)
Each beneficiary has own annual exemption
Acquisition value is probate value (subject to what is said in Example 38 explanatory note 1)
Acquisition date is date of death
Personal losses may be offset against gains on assets acquired; losses on assets acquired may be offset against personal gains

The distribution of a capital asset triggers an income tax charge in the hands of the beneficiary to the value of any undistributed income arising in the estate (see Example 39 explanatory note 2).

Furthermore, the tax may be borne by different beneficiaries. In this example the cash to be distributed following a sale by the executors in respect of the three shareholdings held in the estate would be:

		£
Sale proceeds:	Bird Enterprises Ltd	332,500
	Computer Games plc	33,000
	Midwest Bank plc	9,000
		374,500
Less: Capital gains tax		40,411
Divided equally		334,089

Thus Mrs Bird has suffered capital gains tax of half of £40,411 = £20,205. Rupert's share of the tax is £20,206.

If the proposals in (b) had taken place the tax would have been:

	Mrs Bird £	Rupert £
Re Bird Enterprises Ltd	18,399	13,980
Re estate	–	–
	18,399	13,980
Tax saved	1,867	6,226

Thus Rupert would have had a large saving compared with Mrs Bird.

Because Mrs Bird would not otherwise use all of her annual exemptions, and Rupert has not used his annual exemption for 2006/07 it would be better for the beneficiaries to make the disposals than the executors.

Private residence exemption

9. Where following a death, the private residence is to be sold by the personal representatives, a chargeable gain may arise between death and sale. Under TCGA 1992 s 225A, the private residence exemption is available if the property has both before and after the death been used as the main residence of individuals who are entitled to 75% or more of the sale proceeds either absolutely or for life. If the exemption does not apply, the personal representatives could, if appropriate, assent to a transfer of the property to the beneficiaries, so that the gain would be charged at their personal tax rates rather than the 40% rate applicable to the personal representatives on gains above the annual exemption. This would not be appropriate if the beneficiaries were chargeable at 40%, as with Mrs Bird in this example.

Gifts holdover relief

10. Personal representatives do not qualify for gifts holdover relief under TCGA 1992 s 165 or s 260, but trustees do. Where the residue of the estate is left on trust, the personal representatives should ensure that assets on which gifts holdover relief is to be claimed have been formally appropriated to the trustees before being gifted. The trustees are then treated as acquiring the assets at the date of death.

The Finance Act 2006 changes to IHT for trust also impinge on the CGT holdover provisions in so far that:

- transfers into and out of trusts that will now come within the 'relevant property' rules will automatically be eligible for hold-over relief under section 260(2)(a) of TCGA 1992;

- hold-over relief under TCGA 1992 s 260(2)(d) will be restricted to trusts that meet the new IHT rules for trusts for minor children;

- the special rules in TCGA 1992 ss 72, 73 relating to the death of a person entitled to an IIP will be restricted to assets that are subject to an IIP which meets the new IHT rules.

See the summary of new legislation starting on page ix for more details of the changes.

Mr and Mrs Daley were killed in a road accident on 18 August 2006. Under their wills each appointed their son Arthur as executor. They had each left their entire estate to the other, subject to a 30 day survivorship clause. As default beneficiaries, Mr Daley left his used car business to his son together with one half of residue, the other half being divided between various charities. Mrs Daley, who only had building society investments worth £50,000, named her son as the only beneficiary in default of her husband.

Mr Daley's estate is expected to be valued for probate at:

	£	£
Used car business		900,000
Private residence		240,000
Quoted securities		8,900
PEPs with English Life Unit Trust		41,600
ISA at Midnorth Building Society		10,100
Government securities (interest paid gross)		26,800
Life policies		82,500
Pension policies		104,200
Bank accounts		1,400
Premium bonds		20,000
		1,435,500
Less: Mortgage	125,000	
Other debts, funeral expenses	10,500	135,500
		1,300,000

Because of business property relief and exemption for charities, no inheritance tax will be payable. Arthur, as executor, will convert all his father's assets (including the business) to cash, and pay the liabilities and legacies. He will use a current account with his bank, and will invest surplus funds on the money market. A premium bond prize of £100,000 was received after his father's death. Arthur anticipates completing the administration of the estate by the end of 2007.

Arthur will also obtain probate on his mother's estate, and will cash the investments and pay all debts and legacies by March 2007.

Arthur has contacted your firm for advice as to his obligations as executor under self-assessment. Set out the taxation points to be considered from death to the completion of the administration of the estate for both Mr and Mrs Daley.

Tax liabilities of Mr Daley deceased — executor's obligations

Arthur should notify HMRC as soon as possible after his father's death. They will send form R27 asking if probate is to be applied for. Arthur will return the form marked accordingly and in due course he will forward probate, together with a copy of the will, to HMRC.

Cessation of used car business

The death of Mr Daley will denote a cessation of the business for income tax purposes. Ideally accounts should be drawn up to the date of death and submitted with the final self-assessment return, otherwise the accounts covering the date of death must be apportioned.

2005/06 tax return

If the 2005/06 tax return of Mr Daley had not been filed before his death, Arthur as executor is responsible for filing it by 31 January 2007. He is also responsible for paying the outstanding tax for 2005/06 by that date. Interest will be charged on tax paid late, although by Concession A17, interest on tax falling due after death will not start to run until thirty days after the grant of probate.

If the tax is not paid by 28 February 2007 (ie 28 days after the due date), a surcharge of 5% is payable. This increases to 10% if the tax is still unpaid by 31 July. Interest is also payable on any surcharge not paid within thirty days. If there was a reasonable excuse for non-payment throughout the period of default, HMRC (or Commissioners) may set aside the surcharge. Inability to pay is not in itself a reasonable excuse.

HMRC can open an enquiry into the affairs of the business, for any reason, up to one year from the filing date, ie by 31 January 2008 or later if the return is filed after 31 January 2007. If fraudulent or negligent conduct is discovered, HMRC can issue an assessment for years ending not earlier than six years before death (ie for 2000/01 onwards) and such assessments must be issued not later than three years after 31 January following the end of the tax year in which the death occurred, ie three years after 31 January 2008 (TMA 1970 s 40). Normally penalties may be charged where there is fraudulent or negligent conduct. Under the Human Rights legislation, however, it is probably not possible to impose tax geared penalties on personal representatives in respect of tax evasion by the deceased.

However, it appears that consequent to guidance given to HMRC, penalties will still be sought from personal representatives in these situations by way of addition to the settlement offer. Upon request HMRC will issue a letter stating that if in the future there is an adverse decision on the matter in the courts, the penalty will be repaid with interest.

2006/07 tax return

Following Mr Daley's death in August 2006, HMRC will, on request, issue a tax return for 2006/07 before the end of that tax year (and also before the end of the tax year in which the administration of the estate will be completed). When returns have been submitted HMRC will give early confirmation if they do not intend to enquire into the return.

Because of Mr Daley's death it will be appropriate for Arthur to apply to HMRC to reduce the payment on account due on 31 January 2007 in respect of 2006/07. The application should be made on the return, or on form SA 303.

Any tax due for the year of death (or earlier years) will be a liability of the estate.

Tax position on investments

The ISA and PEP investments retain their tax exemption until death. Thereafter the normal income and capital gains tax rules apply. An ISA insurance policy will pay out on death and consequently the personal representatives will need to claim the death benefit. Before the claim is accepted by the insurer there are no income tax or capital gains tax implications but any interest paid as a result of late settlement of the claim will be taxable and paid net of tax.

The premium bond continues to be tax-exempt, including the prize received. The amount received will add to the residue of the estate and be distributed accordingly as capital.

The accrued income scheme does not apply to securities vested in personal representatives following the holder's death (TA 1988 s 710(5)). No adjustments are therefore required in respect of the government securities. Similarly, if Arthur had transferred the securities to a beneficiary in satisfaction of the beneficiary's entitlement under the will, no accrued income calculation is required (TA 1988 s 721).

Interest on investments and dividends on shares are taxable when received. They are *not* apportioned for income tax over the period to which they relate. For probate and inheritance tax purposes, however, dividends receivable after death on ex dividend shares (exclusive of the tax credits) and amounts of interest accrued to the date of death on securities (less lower rate tax) are included in the value of the estate (see Example 43). Relief is given where an absolute beneficiary is liable to higher rate tax and the estate paid inheritance tax on net accrued income (see Example 43 explanatory note 4 on page 43.5).

Tax liabilities of Arthur as executor of Mr Daley's estate

Arthur will receive a trust and estate self-assessment return (form SA 900) for the period 19 August 2006 to 5 April 2007, and in due course for the period 6 April 2007 to the date of completion of the administration of the estate. The returns must be filed by 31 January following the end of the relevant tax year, or by 30 September following the tax year if HMRC are to compute the tax liabilities.

Personal representatives are not entitled to personal allowances and are charged tax on the estate income at the basic rate if it is non-savings income, the lower rate if it is savings income other than dividends, and the dividend ordinary rate on dividends. Any capital gains arising on the disposal of assets in excess of probate values are liable to tax at 40%, after deducting an annual exemption (£8,800 for 2006/07) in the tax year of death and the next two tax years.

Used car business

Because the period of trading by the estate will be less than two years the actual basis of assessment will apply, ie:

2006/07	19 August 2006 to 5 April 2007
2007/08	6 April 2007 to date of sale

Supplementary pages will be required to be completed. If only one set of accounts is prepared details will be shown on the first return, with the profits for the period after 5 April 2007 deducted. On the second return the box indicating that all details have been shown on the previous return will be ticked. The profits (after capital allowances) will be shown with the exclusion of the amount assessed in the earlier year. There is no liability for Class 4 national insurance contributions.

Investment income

Investment income received gross must be declared and tax paid at the savings rate. This will include interest on government securities, on investments for a fixed term over £50,000, and on overseas investments. Interest is also paid gross on all quoted eurobonds, now defined as interest-bearing securities issued by a company (or building society) and listed on a recognised stock exchange (TA 1988 s 349). Other interest will have had tax deducted at source. This is also shown on the self-assessment return.

Any charge arising under the accrued income scheme on a sale by the executor will be taxed at 20%. Where there is any accrued income relief, the relief is given by deducting it from the gross income received, thus reducing the amount chargeable at 20%.

Payment of tax

If the net income tax payable for 2006/07 exceeds £500, or 20% of the total income tax liability for the year (including tax deducted at source), then payments on account will be required for 2007/08. Capital gains tax is not included in calculating payments on account. The 2006/07 income tax and capital gains tax will be due on 31 January 2008. As the administration of the estate is likely to be almost complete at that time it should be possible accurately to determine the actual liability for 2007/08. Unless covered by the de minimis limits, one half of that liability (excluding capital gains tax), or one half of the 2006/07 net tax liability if less, will be due on 31 January 2008. The second instalment will be due on 31 July 2008 and the balance, together with any capital gains tax, on 31 January 2009.

Arthur as executor may prefer to pay the whole amount at an early date in order to complete the administration of the estate.

The same provisions as to interest on overdue tax and surcharges apply as stated above in relation to the tax position of Mr Daley deceased.

Tax liabilities in relation to Mrs Daley

Tax position of Mrs Daley deceased

Arthur has similar obligations as stated above in respect of his mother's estate. Since her only assets are building society accounts, however, it may be that it will only be necessary to submit a tax repayment return to the date of her death. Even that will not be necessary if Mrs Daley had elected to receive interest gross.

Tax position in relation to Mrs Daley's estate

Following a taxpayer's death, any election to receive interest gross ceases to have effect and all subsequent payments are made net of tax at the savings rate. Since Mrs Daley's only asset is building society interest, Arthur will be able to tick the second box in Step 1 on the trust and estate tax return confirming that he is the personal representative of a deceased person and that all the following points apply:

All the income arose in the UK
He does not wish to claim reliefs
No annual payments have been made out of capital
All income has had tax deducted before it was received (or is UK dividends with tax credit)
There are no chargeable disposals
There are no accrued income charges or reliefs, no income from relevant discounted securities, offshore income gains or gains on life insurance policies etc.

Arthur can then go straight to Question 19 in the return to give his, or his agent's, telephone number and sign the declaration at Question 22. When the administration of the estate is complete the date of completion is shown at Question 21.2. It is likely that this will occur in 2006/07, so that only one return will be required in relation to Mrs Daley's estate.

Supplementary Notes

1. Where HMRC enquire into a return, they will issue a closure notice stating their conclusions and showing the revisions to the self-assessment and the additional tax due (TMA 1970 s 28A). The personal representatives then have thirty days in which to appeal in writing against conclusions stated or amendments made by the closure notice, giving the grounds of appeal (TMA 1970 ss 31, 31A).

2. The personal representatives may give HMRC notice of an amendment to the self-assessment return (within the permitted twelve months after the filing date for the return) whilst an enquiry is in progress. The amendment will not restrict the scope of the enquiry but may be taken into account in the enquiry. If it affects the tax payable, it will not take effect unless and until it is incorporated into the s 28A closure notice (see note 2 above) (TMA 1970 s 9B).

3. Questions relating to the subject matter of an enquiry may be referred to the Special Commissioners for their determination while the enquiry is in progress on a joint written application by the personal representatives and HMRC. Either party may withdraw from the referral process providing they give notice before the first hearing of the matter by the Special Commissioners. The determination will be binding on both parties as if it were a decision on a preliminary issue under appeal (TMA 1970 ss 28ZA–28ZE (and ss 31A–31D for companies)).

4. For detailed notes on the self-assessment provisions see the companion to this book, Tolley's Taxwise I 2006/07.

Outline the provisions determining the rates of tax applicable to trust income and the way in which the tax payable is accounted for.

Rates of tax on trust income

Certain trust income is taxed as income of the settlor. Certain other trust income is charged at the 'rate applicable to trusts' of 40%, or in the case of dividend income, the dividend trust rate of 32.5%.

Originally introduced under FA 2005 s 14 and amended under TA s 686D, the first £1,000 (£500 for 2005/06) of relevant income will not be charged at the special trust tax rates, but will instead be charged at the income tax rate appropriate to the type of income, known as standard rate band. Therefore, if payments are received net of tax (for example, building society interest) up to the limit of the standard rate band, then the trustees will have no further tax to pay.

For more detailed information see page 47.4.

Otherwise trustees are liable to tax at the dividend ordinary rate of 10% on tax credit inclusive dividend income, the lower rate of 20% on other savings income and the basic rate of 22% on non-savings income. The trust income is determined using the principles applicable to each type of income.

Trustees in their capacity as such are not entitled to personal allowances, nor are they liable to pay income tax at the higher rate.

Treatment of expenses

Any expenses applicable to the particular income are deducted in arriving at the assessable income, but there is no relief for the general trust expenses. Such expenses are regarded as paid first out of dividend income, then out of other savings income, then out of non-savings income (TA 1988 s 689B — see Example 43 at page 43.4 note 10 for details of relief for expenses when the rate applicable to trusts or the dividend trust rate applies).

HMRC have confirmed that the standard rate band set out in FA 2005 s 14 will apply to trust income *net* of trust management expenses so potentially it will apply to other charges as well.

Although the management expenses are deducted from the trust income taxed at the lowest rate first, the standard rate band will apply in the order — basic rate income at 22% first, followed by lower rate 20% income and finally dividends at 10%.

Income certificates to beneficiaries (forms R185)

At the end of each tax year the trustees give income beneficiaries a certificate of their entitlement to trust income (form R185), and of income tax paid thereon by the trustees, and that income will be included in the statutory income of the beneficiary, whose unused personal allowances and starting rate band, if any, will be available to give an income tax repayment, and upon whom any higher rate or dividend upper rate tax will be charged. The trustee's certificate will show the rates at which tax has been paid. For trusts liable to the rate applicable to trusts, the tax rate shown will be 40%. For other trusts the rates will be 22% on non-savings income, 20% on non-dividend savings income and 10% on dividends, distributions on which tax is treated as paid (ie dividends on which a non-resident is not entitled to a tax credit (ITTOIA 2005 s 399 (formerly TA 1998 s 233(1A))), bonus issues of redeemable securities (ITTOIA 2005 s 400(4), (5) (formerly TA 1988 s 233(1B))), scrip dividends (ITTOIA 2005 s 411 (formerly TA 1988 s 249)), close company loans written off or released (ITTOIA 2005 s 416 (formerly TA 1988 s 421)), and dividends from abroad. The 10% tax credits will be shown as non-repayable.

Rate applicable to trusts and dividend trust rate

TA 1988 s 686 provides that distribution income received by trusts is chargeable at the 'dividend trust rate' of 32.5% and at the 'rate applicable to trusts' of 40% otherwise. These rates are not fixed annually and will remain in force unless changed in a subsequent Finance Act. The latest change was reflected in the Finance Act 2004 s 29. The rates previously in force comprised a 'rate applicable to trusts' of 34% and a Schedule F trust rate of 25%.

Trustees are liable at the s 686 rates where they have a power to accumulate income or where they have a discretion as to whether or not the income is made available to income beneficiaries.

TA 1988 s 686 is amended specifically by FA 2006 Sch 13 to remove the exemption in s 686(2)(b) from the special trust rates for income arising to the trustees of a settlor-interested settlement. This means that trustees of settlor-interested trusts will be taxed at the special trust rates instead of at only up to basic rate. This change takes effect from 6 April 2006.

The dividend trust rate applies to distribution type income, ie UK dividends, dividends from abroad taxed as miscellaneous income, qualifying distributions arising to non-UK resident trustees, non-qualifying distributions (ie bonus issues of redeemable securities — ITTOIA 2005 s 400(4), (5) (formerly TA 1988 s 233(1B)), scrip dividends (ITTOIA 2005 s 411 (formerly TA 1998 s 249) — but see Example 49 part B(a)), close company loans written off or released (ITTOIA 2005 s 416 (formerly TA 1988 s 421)), and amounts taxable under s 686A (purchase by company of own shares etc — see below). In each case there is an actual or notional tax credit to reduce the tax payable by the trustees (except for dividends from abroad).

The additional tax of 22.5% payable by trustees on distributions in respect of the balance of the dividend trust rate of 32.5% represents 25% of the cash dividend. For example a dividend of £90 carries a tax credit of £10 and the trustees have to pay a further 22.5% of (90 + 10), or 25% of 90, = £22.50, leaving a net amount of £67.50. If the trustees make discretionary payments to beneficiaries, however, they must make the payments net of 40% tax and they cannot treat the dividend credit as tax already paid in calculating how much of the tax at 40% has already been paid by them. This significantly increases the tax burden on such payments. For the detailed provisions see Example 48.

Purchase by company of own shares etc

Where a company redeems, repays or purchases its own shares from trustees of a settlement, TA 1988 s 219 (purchase by unquoted trading company of own shares to be treated as a capital payment rather than a distribution) does not apply and the payment is treated as income of the trustees liable at the dividend trust rate of 32.5% on the grossed up equivalent, as indicated above. This treatment applies to life interest trusts as well as accumulation/discretionary trusts, but not to unit trusts, charitable trusts, pension funds or where the income is treated as belonging to the settlor (TA 1988 s 686A).

Income not liable to s 686 rates

Where someone has a life interest in a trust fund, or part thereof, or is entitled to an annuity from the fund, that person cannot avoid liability at the higher rate of tax simply because the trustees do not pay out all of the trust income to which that person is entitled, since the income is in any event included in his statutory income, by reference to the statement of trust income and form R185 (trust income), and he will be a creditor of the trust for any balance of income due to him. Liability at the s 686 rates does not therefore apply to income to which someone is absolutely entitled as against the trustees.

Nor do the s 686 rates apply to income treated for tax purposes as that of the settlor *before* it is distributed (eg where the settlor has settled funds and he and/or his wife are discretionary income beneficiaries — in that event all income is assessable on the settlor under ITTOIA 2005 ss 625–629 (formerly TA 1988 s 660A)). The s 686 rates *do* apply to income paid to infant, unmarried children of the settlor, even though such income is treated as the settlor's under ITTOIA 2005 ss 629–632 (formerly TA 1988 s 660B) (see below).

The rate applicable to trusts does not apply to capital receipts such as lease premiums, even though they are partly charged to income tax (see Example 48 for an illustration).

Income of charitable trusts and income from property held for certain occupational and personal pension funds is also excluded from s 686 (see Example 48 explanatory note 6).

Income taxed as income of settlor

Income taxed as the settlor's income under ITTOIA 2005 ss 629–632 (formerly TA 1988 s 660A) or ITTOIA 2005 ss 625–629 (formerly TA 1988 s 660B) (see above under *Income not liable to s 686 rates*) is treated as the highest part of the settlor's income (other than employment income lump sum compensation payments under ITEPA 2003 s 403 and life policy gains under ITTOIA 2005 s 465 (formerly TA 1988 s 547)). The settlor can recover any tax paid by him from the trustees or from the person who received the income (ITTOIA 2005 s 646 (formerly TA 1988 s 660D)).

Where the settlor has retained an interest in the trust, and income is therefore taxed as his income before distribution, the charge under ITTOIA 2005 ss 619, 621, 623 (formerly TA 1988 s 660C) on dividend income is at the dividend ordinary rate of 10% or upper rate of 32½% as the case may be. Any other income is charged as miscellaneous income at 22% or 40%.

By comparison, if income is treated as the settlor's income under ITTOIA 2005 ss 629–632 (formerly TA 1988 s 660B), ie because it is paid to his infant, unmarried child, it will have been liable to tax in the hands of the trustees when it arose at either 40% for non-dividend income or 32.5% for dividend income. When any distribution is made, however, it will come out of the general pool of trust income and it will not be dividend income. The distribution will be made net of 40% tax, but the trustees will not be able to include the 10% dividend tax credit in accounting for that tax. This will therefore result in a higher tax charge where a dividend is paid to an infant child via a discretionary trust compared with a direct settlement by the parent on the child. Using the example above of a net dividend of £90 paid to a discretionary trust with a tax credit of £10, the net distribution to the child would be 60% of £90 = £54 (tax £36). If the settlor had made a direct settlement on the child the additional tax payable would be only £22.50, ie:

Gross income (90 dividend + tax credit 10)	100.00
Tax @ 32½% (£22.50 payable after tax credit)	32.50
Net receipt	£ 67.50

This principle applies even where the first £500 of income is taxed at the standard rates as only the tax paid is included within the tax pool to frank distributions to beneficiaries.

Payment of tax

Self-assessment applies to trusts as for individuals. The trustees are required to file their tax return together with a self-assessment by 31 January following the end of the tax year, or file the return by 30 September following the end of the tax year if they require HMRC to prepare the self-assessment. All sources of income, and also any capital gains, are dealt with in the self-assessment, and trustees make payments on account of income tax (not capital gains tax) in the same way as individuals.

The tax payment dates are:

31 January in the tax year	1st payment on account, being one half of the total tax payable for the previous tax year (including the tax at the rate applicable to trusts or dividend trust rate where appropriate but excluding capital gains tax), as reduced by any tax deducted at source
31 July after end of tax year	2nd payment on account (same amount as 1st payment)
31 January after end of tax year	Full liability for year (including capital gains tax) less payments on account and tax deducted at source

For a detailed illustration see Example 47.

T, a widower, who had been in business as a sole trader for many years, died on 6 April 2006.

By his will S, his accountant, was appointed executor and trustee and the whole estate was left in trust to his son, U, for life, with remainder to V, his grandchild, absolutely.

The will did not bar the application of the Apportionment Act 1870, and empowered S to continue T's business so that it could be sold as a going concern.

By the will, S is allowed a fixed annual sum of £1,500 for his services as executor and trustee.

T's income-producing assets apart from the business consisted of:

£20,000 listed 10% loan stock in X plc — interest receivable 31 July and 31 January. Interest was received on the due dates and S apportioned it between capital and income under the Apportionment Act 1870.

Building society deposit — net interest receivable 30 June and 31 December. Interest of £160 was received in June and £64 in December 2006. S apportioned the June interest between capital and income under the Apportionment Act 1870.

Property let unfurnished producing rental income during 2006/07 of £1,130 with allowable expenses of £430. At 5 April 2006, there were unutilised losses arising from this property of £100.

The business accounts were made up to 5 April each year. Accounts were produced for the two years to 5 April 2006 and 2007 showing tax adjusted profits of £17,200 and £16,420 respectively.

The deceased had a mortgage of £16,000 on his home, provided by a relative. The interest paid by S for the period from 6 April 2006 until December 2006, when the property was sold, was £900.

T, until his death, had been the life tenant of a settled fund, the sole asset of which was an investment of £40,000 listed 8% debenture stock in Z plc. The due dates for receipt of the interest were 6 April and 6 October. The trustees normally paid the income to T shortly after it was received, and paid to S the income due until T's death, on 31 July 2006.

A loan was taken out by S to enable inheritance tax to be paid on the estate personalty. The loan interest charged for 2006/07 was £500.

Certain administration expenses were paid on 31 March 2007. These were allocated as to £500 for capital and £1,195 for income. On that date S was paid the annual sum of £1,500 due to him.

(a)   Prepare a statement showing the trust income for 2006/07 together with supporting notes explaining your treatment of each of the items mentioned above, and

(b)   Show the entries on the R185 (trust income) to be given to U for 2006/07.

(a)   **Statement of trust income 2006/07**

Refer to note		£	£	Tax £
1	Trading profit	16,420		
2	Unfurnished lettings	700	17,120	
	Savings income			
3	£20,000 10% loan stock, X plc	2,000		
4	Life tenancy (debenture interest)	1,600		
5	Building society interest ((160 + 64) × 100/80)	280	3,880	56
			21,000	56
	Less charges on income:			
6	Executor's remuneration (annuity)	1,500		
7	Loan interest re payment of IHT	500	2,000	
	Total income of trust		19,000	56

Tax thereon:

			£	£
Non-savings income	15,120 @ 22%	3,326		
Savings income (non-dividend)	3,880 @ 20%	776		
	19,000	4,102	4,102	

Refer to note		£		Tax £
6	*Add:* Tax deducted from executor's remuneration (1,500 @ 22%)	330		
	Total tax due	4,432		4,432
	of which tax payable by self-assessment is (see explanatory note 7)			4,376
			14,898	
	Less trust expenses:			
8	Mortgage interest	900		
9	Administration expenses	1,195	2,095	
	Net income of trust		12,803	
	Less apportioned to capital per (b)		1,652	
	Net income available for beneficiary		11,151	

Comprising:

Refer to note		£	£
	Non-dividend savings income (3,880 – 776)	3,104	
	Less apportioned to capital	1,652	
		1,452	
10	Used to pay trust expenses (part)	1,452	–
	Non-savings income (15,120 – 3,326)	11,794	
10	Used to pay trust expenses (balance)	643	11,151
	Gross equivalent is 11,148 x 100/78 =		14,296

(b) **Computation of income treated as capital**

<table>
<tr><td>Refer to
note</td><td></td><td></td><td style="text-align:right">£</td></tr>
<tr><td>3</td><td>£20,000 10% loan stock X plc
1 February 2006 to 6 April 2006   65/181 x £1,000</td><td></td><td style="text-align:right">359</td></tr>
<tr><td>4</td><td>Life tenancy
7 October 2005 to 6 April 2006</td><td></td><td style="text-align:right">1,600</td></tr>
<tr><td>5</td><td>Building society interest received
1 January 2006 to 6 April 2006   96/181 x (£160 x $\frac{100}{80}$)</td><td></td><td style="text-align:right">106</td></tr>
<tr><td></td><td></td><td></td><td style="text-align:right">2,065</td></tr>
<tr><td></td><td>Income tax @ 20%</td><td></td><td style="text-align:right">413</td></tr>
<tr><td></td><td>Net income apportioned to capital</td><td></td><td style="text-align:right">1,652</td></tr>
</table>

Form R185 (trust income) to be given to U for 2006/07

11		*Gross*	*Tax*	*Net*
	Savings income	–	–	–
	Non-savings income	£14,296	£3,145	£11,151

Notes relating to statement of trust income

1. The death of T constitutes a cessation of the sole trade for tax purposes. The trustees are regarded as commencing the business from that date

   The first year of charge is 2006/07. Tax will be charged on the profit from 7 April 2006 to 5 April 2007. (Trustees are not liable to Class 4 national insurance contributions – Social Security Contributions and Benefits Act 1992 Sch 2.5.)

2. The income from lettings is:

Rent income in 2006/07	1,130
Allowable expenses	430
	£ 700

   The unutilised losses of T personally are not available for carry forward against the income of the will trust.

3. Despite the income from the 10% loan stock having to be allocated to the capital of the estate in so far as the proportion up to the date of death of T is concerned (Apportionment Act 1870), the entire income *received* after death has to be included for *income tax purposes* as that of the will trust. From 1 April 2001 tax is no longer deducted at source from interest on loan stock such as that of X plc (see explanatory note 7).

4. The settlement income is *received* after death, and despite the allocation to estate capital under the Apportionment Act, is for *income tax purposes* regarded as income of the will trust. From 1 April 2001 tax is no longer deducted at source from such debenture stock interest (see explanatory note 7).

5. Building society interest will partly have to be allocated to capital of the estate under the Apportionment Act, but since it is *received* after death it is for *income tax purposes* regarded wholly as income of the will trust.

   The interest is paid after deduction of lower rate tax, except where the recipient is unlikely to be a taxpayer and has provided an appropriate certificate to the building society. As a trust is not entitled to personal allowances it cannot give such a certificate.

6. The £1,500 pa payable to S as executor is regarded as an annuity, from which income tax at the basic rate must be deducted when making the payment (TA 1988 ss 4, 348). See explanatory note 6 for the way in which the tax is accounted for.

    Had the will contained a professional executor's charging clause, the amount paid to S would be an administration expense, payable out of the net income.

7. The interest paid on the loan to pay inheritance tax is allowable in calculating the trust income (TA 1988 ss 353(1B) and 364).

8. The mortgage interest paid is a trust expense payable out of taxed income.

9. Administration expenses have to be paid out of taxed income.

10. Trust expenses are the expenses of administration and as such are regarded as paid out of income which has already suffered tax. They must be distinguished from expenses relating to a particular source, like those of the trade and of the lettings in this case which are allowable in computing the income from that particular source.

    Trust expenses are treated as being set against income in the following order (TA 1988 s 689B):

    (i)   Income carrying non-repayable credits (ie dividends, dividends on which a non-resident is not entitled to a tax credit (ITTOIA 2005 s 399 (formerly TA 1988 s 233(1A))), bonus issues of redeemable securities (ITTOIA 2005 s 400(4), (5) (formerly TA 1988 s 233(1B))), scrip dividends (ITTOIA 2005 s 411 (formerly TA 1988 s 249)), and close company loans written off or released (ITTOIA 2005 s 416 (formerly TA 1988 s 421))

    (ii) Taxed dividends from abroad

    (iii) Savings income other than that in (i) and (ii)

    (iv) Non-savings income.

    The set-off order is in fact the most beneficial, in that it maximises the amount of tax paid by the trust that may be passed on to beneficiaries.

11. Although for income tax purposes, any income received after death is treated as income of the estate and charged on the trustees, as stated in notes 3, 4 and 5, any part of that income that has been apportioned to trust capital is not available to the life tenant and is excluded from his income. The form R185 therefore excludes the net amount of £1,652 apportioned to capital.

Note   In this example U only has a limited (life) interest in the residue of the estate. If his interest had been an absolute interest then in so far as income was included both in the estate (for calculation of inheritance tax) and as residuary income (for calculation of income tax) relief would be available for higher rate tax (ITTOIA 2005 s 669 (formerly TA 1988 s 699)) – see explanatory note 4.

Explanatory Notes

Apportionment of income

1. The Apportionment Act 1870 requires income accrued up to the date of death to be taken into the estate. This is compulsory for inheritance tax, but for succession purposes the Act may be excluded, so that, for example, all income received after death goes to the life tenant, rather than some being treated as part of estate capital. For income tax purposes, any income received after the date of death is regarded as income of the estate. Note that the date of death is counted as one of the days prior to the date of death.

    This may lead to double taxation, ie for inheritance tax in the estate and for income tax.

    Most modern and competently drafted wills or trust deeds will specifically exclude the application of all apportionments.

Where the deceased was life tenant of a trust fund, any income accrued to the date of death (net of tax) is part of his estate for inheritance tax, the settled fund being reduced accordingly. Again this may result in double taxation.

Where double taxation occurs, some relief is available to an *absolute* beneficiary (not a beneficiary with a life interest) in respect of higher rate tax — see explanatory note 4.

2. Where income is received prior to death it is not apportioned even if all or part of it relates to a period after death. Where income received after death is to be accrued up to the date of death as indicated in note 1 above, the amount to be included in the estate for inheritance tax is as follows:

Shares

Where the shares are cum dividend, no apportionment is necessary. Where they are ex dividend, the forthcoming dividend (exclusive of the tax credit) is taken into the estate.

Other securities

The price must include the accrued interest (less tax at the lower rate) as at the date of death.

Rents

Where the amount received after death relates wholly or partly to a period before death it must be apportioned on the basis that the income accrues evenly from day to day.

Salaries, pensions, annuities

These are again accrued on a day to day basis and the amount receivable (net of tax) must be apportioned to the periods before and after death.

Income of life tenant during administration of estate

3. Where a person has a life interest in the residue of an estate, the amounts to be included in his statutory income during the period of administration are the grossed up equivalents of the actual income payments made to him (see Example 39 for further details). Where part of the income has been apportioned to trust capital under the provisions of the Apportionment Act 1870, the amounts actually paid to the life tenant will be less than the net income of the trust, as shown in part (b) of the example.

Income of beneficiary with absolute interest during administration of estate

4. Where a person has an absolute interest in the residue of an estate (ie a right to capital as well as to income) again the amounts included in total income during the administration period will be the grossed up equivalent of the actual income payments made to him (see Example 39).

If interest is paid on overdue inheritance tax, it is not an allowable deduction for someone with an absolute interest (IHTA 1984 s 233(3)). (For someone with a life interest, his income is the gross equivalent of the amounts actually paid to him, so that interest on overdue tax is effectively allowed for higher rate purposes.)

Where, owing to the apportionment rules, income is included in the estate and charged to inheritance tax, and is also charged as income after death, an absolute beneficiary may claim to reduce his income for *higher rate* or *upper rate* purposes (not for starting, basic or lower rate tax or dividend ordinary rate tax) by the inheritance tax charged on the grossed-up amount of the accrued income (ITTOIA 2005 s 669 (formerly TA 1988 s 699)).

Nature of payments from estate to beneficiaries

5. Payments from the estate to beneficiaries are treated as made first from income taxed at the basic rate, then savings income (excluding dividends) taxed at the lower rate, then dividend income taxed at 10% (ITTOIA 2005 s 679 (formerly TA 1988 s 701(3A))).

The different types of income (net of expenses) and the tax deducted therefrom are shown separately on forms R185, with tax relating to the income in note 10(i) of the example shown as being non-repayable.

Executor's remuneration

6. The executor's remuneration of £1,500 represents an annuity, which is a charge on income and reduces the trust's income for tax purposes. Tax relief has, however, already been retained out of the payment at 22%. In order to ensure that the tax retained is balanced by an equivalent amount of tax payable (so that the trust suffers no tax on that slice of its income), the trust's income is first reduced by the annuity, and tax is calculated on the resulting trust income at the appropriate rates. The tax payable is then increased by basic rate tax on the amount of the annuity. For an illustration of the treatment where charges exceed the trust income see Example 44 part B.

Self-assessment

7. The self-assessment provisions apply to trustees and personal representatives in the same way as for individuals. Payments on account are due on 31 January in the tax year and 31 July following, each equal to half of the total income tax payable (net of tax deducted at source) for the previous tax year (unless it was below the de minimis thresholds). A balancing payment is then due on the following 31 January (which will include any capital gains tax payable). At the same time the first payment on account for the next year is due.

    Payments on account will not be made for the tax year in which a trust commences, since no tax was payable for the previous year. In this example therefore all the tax payable by self-assessment, amounting to £4,376, will be due for payment on 31 January 2007. Note that this tax figure is made up of the tax of £3,326 on the non-savings income plus the tax of £720 on the savings income of £3,600 not taxed at source plus the tax of £330 deducted at source from the executor's remuneration.

    The first payment on account for 2007/08 is also due on 31 January 2008. Since there is no capital gains tax in the tax figure of £4,376, the first payment on account for 2007/08 will be half of that figure, ie £2,188. The total amount payable by the trustees on 31 January 2008 is therefore £6,564.

    TA 1988 s 349 now provides that tax is not deducted from payments of interest on quoted eurobonds, which are defined as interest-bearing securities issued by a company and listed on a recognised stock exchange.

    For further notes on self-assessment see Examples 41, 46, 47 and 48.

Will trusts

8. Often it will be necessary for the executors to administer the estate of a deceased person and then to transfer their responsibilities to the trustees of the life interest settlement in respect of the residue of the estate. In this example the trustees and personal representatives are the same. Furthermore the whole of the estate is left in trust to the son. In practice in these circumstances, it is usual to treat all of the income as belonging to the trustees from the date of death and to allow the expenses of administration etc against that income. More correctly the executor should issue a form R185 (estate income) and complete a self-assessment return for the period of administration of the estate and then do the same as trustee, ie issue form R185 (trust income) and complete a further self-assessment return for the remaining part of the same tax year.

A.   Herbie Fritter is the life tenant of a trust fund set up by his grandfather.

The trust income in 2006/07 consisted of taxed interest on £80,000 3% Treasury Stock which had been held for a number of years.

Trust expenses amounted to £320.

Herbie is a widower aged seventy, whose only other income in 2006/07 is a state retirement pension of £7,250.

(a)   Prepare a statement showing the trust income and show the details to be stated on the income certificate given to Herbie.

(b)   Compute Herbie's income tax repayment for 2006/07.

B.   Assume the same facts as above except that Herbie is an annuitant entitled to an annuity from the trust amounting to £3,200 per annum gross.

The trustees paid the full annuity in 2006/07, being authorised to use capital to make up the deficiency.

(a)   Show the position of the trustees and the figures on the certificate to be given to Herbie.

(b)   Compute Herbie's income tax repayment for 2006/07.

A. **Herbie Fritter — Trust Income**

(a) *Statement of trust income 2006/07*

	Net £	Tax £	Gross £
3% Treasury Stock interest	1,920	480	2,400
Trust expenses paid therefrom	320		
Regarded as net amount with tax deduction of		80	
and a gross equivalent of			400
Net amount, tax thereon and gross equivalent remaining	1,600	400	2,000

Certificate by trustees to Herbie (R185 (non-discretionary trusts))

Gross	Tax	Net
£2,000	£400	£1,600

(b) *Herbie's income tax repayment claim 2006/07*

	£	Tax £
Retirement pension	7,250	
Trust income	2,000	400
	9,250	
Age allowance	7,280	
Taxable income	1,970	
Tax payable @ 10%		197
Repayment due		203

B. **Tax payable by trustees under TA 1988 s 350**

(a) *Statement of trust income 2006/07*

The trustees in this example are taxed at only 20% on their Treasury Stock interest of £2,000 (after expenses), but must account for tax at 22% (since they have deducted tax at that rate when paying the income to Herbie as part of his annuity). They must therefore pay a further 2%, amounting to £40. The result is that the total tax accounted for on the interest is balanced by the tax deducted from the annuity. In addition, basic rate tax has to be accounted for under s 350 on the payment of £1,200 out of trust capital, amounting to £264. The position is therefore:

	Net £	Tax £	Gross £
Trust income after expenses as before	1,600	400	2,000
Annuity to Herbie	2,496	704	3,200
Further tax to be paid by trustees		304	

The annuity is income in Herbie's hands, even though part of it was paid out of capital. Having accounted for tax at 22% on the full amount of the payment, the trustees will give Herbie the appropriate certificate on form R185 as follows:

Gross	Tax	Net
£3,200	£704	£2,496

B.   (b)   *Herbie's income tax repayment claim 2006/07*

	£	*Tax* £
Retirement pension	7,250	
Annuity	3,200	704
	10,450	
Age allowance	7,280	
Taxable income	3,170	
Tax payable @ 10% on £2,150	215	
@ 22% on £1,020	224	439
Repayment due		265

Explanatory Notes

Paying expenses out of capital

1.   Had the trustees been empowered to pay the expenses from capital, their income of £2,400 would have been intact. In part A of the example, Herbie would have received £1,920 net, the gross equivalent of which would have been the full £2,400 received by the trustees.

   If Herbie had been liable to tax at 40%, his higher rate liability would be increased if the trust expenses were paid out of the trust capital.

Payment of annuities

2.   Annuities reduce the payer's income for tax purposes (the payer being the trust in part B of the example). It is, however, provided by TA 1988 ss 348 and 349 (and s 3) that tax must be deducted from annuities at the basic rate. The tax relief is therefore normally given by allowing the payer to retain the tax deducted, but an equivalent amount of the payer's income must be taxed at the *basic rate* (TA 1988 s 3). The net result is that no tax is suffered on that part of the payer's income. If there is insufficient income to cover the annuity, tax must be accounted for at the basic rate on the excess under TA 1988 s 350, and no tax relief is available on the payment, since it is made out of trust capital.

   Note that the effect of Herbie being entitled to an annuity rather than having a life interest in the trust income is to cause tax to be charged on the Treasury Stock interest at 22% rather than the lower rate of 20% that normally applies to savings income. For further comments see Example 45 explanatory note 1.

Assessments under TA 1988 s 350

3.   Where tax is payable under TA 1988 s 350 as indicated in note 2 above, HMRC issue assessments outside the self-assessment system for the amount due. Interest on such assessments runs from 31 January after the tax year to which the assessment relates, regardless of when the assessment is issued.

Interest on government stocks

4.   From 6 April 1998, interest on all government stocks is paid gross where the stocks are acquired on or after that date, unless the holders apply to receive the interest net (TA 1988 s 50). Those like Herbie's trustees who already hold such stocks are treated as having *opted* for net payment, but they may apply for the gross payment rules to apply. If such an application has been made, the interest received would normally be taken into account in calculating the half-yearly payments on account, but in this example it would be covered by the de minimis limit of £500 so that half-yearly payments would not be required.

Self-assessment

5.   See Example 47 for detailed notes on the treatment of trusts under self-assessment.

A and his wife died in a car crash on 6 April 2005, being survived by their four children C, D, E and F.

The children's dates of birth are:

C   20 January 1985
D   6 October 1988
E   11 November 1990
F   23 May 1992

By his will, in addition to bequests to more distant relatives and friends, A created the following separate trusts for his children:

For C, an annuity of £1,500 to be paid out of the income from 20,000 £1 shares in X plc. It is stipulated that if the income of any year is insufficient to meet the annuity in full, capital is to be used to make good the deficiency. Because of falling profits, X plc was only able to pay a 4% dividend during 2006/07.

For D, 10,000 shares in Y plc if he attains 25 years of age. By Trustee Act 1925 s 31, the income may, at the discretion of the trustees, be applied for D's maintenance. When D attains 18 years of age the income has to be paid to him. The dividends received from Y plc shares in 2006/07 (exclusive of tax credits) totalled £1,600, of which £800 was in the period to 6 October 2006. Maintenance paid to D until 5 October was £240. £500 was paid to D between 6 October and the end of the tax year.

For E, a vested interest in 10,000 8% preference shares of £1 each in Z plc. The capital cannot be paid to E until the child's 18th birthday, but power is given for payments to be made for E's maintenance out of income. Any income not distributed will be accumulated until E becomes 18. £700 was paid to E during 2006/07.

For F — Rannoch House — if he attains 18 years of age. The house is currently let at an annual rent of £7,500 from 6 April 2006 but was empty in the period from 1 May 2003 until 5 April 2006 for major renovation work so no rents were received in this period. Consequently no election for the special income tax treatment for trust with vulnerable beneficiary was made for 2005/06 but an election has been made for 2006/07 before the deadline of 31 January 2008.

No maintenance was paid to F during 2006/07 as he has a part time job from which he earns £2,500 a year with no tax deducted. He has no other income.

By 5 April 2006 the estate had been administered and the funds to satisfy the bequests to C, D and E had been set aside.

(a)   Calculate the income tax payable by the trustees of each of the above funds for 2006/07.

(b)   State the amounts which will be treated as taxable income of each beneficiary for 2006/07.

(a)   **Income tax payable by trustees for 2006/07**

C Trust:

	Gross £	Tax £
Dividends (20,000 x 4% = 800 + 89 (tax credit of 1/9))	889	89
Less charges: Annuity (part)	889	
	–	
Tax on trust income	–	
Tax on charges 889 @ 22%	196	196
Tax payable by trustees under self-assessment (due 31 January 2007)		107
Tax payable by trustees under s 350 assessment re annual payment made out of capital (see explanatory note 1):		
Balance of annuity of (1,500 – 889) 611 @ 22%		134

Form R185 to the annuitant will show:

	Gross £	Tax £	Net £
Annuity	1,500	330	1,170

D Trust:

Trustees are liable to tax in respect of dividend income at the dividend trust rate of 32.5% on the tax credit inclusive amount until the beneficiary has an absolute interest in income (6 October 2006). From that date the trust becomes an interest in possession trust until D reaches age 25. The tax payable on the dividends is then covered by the tax credits, so the trustees are not liable to pay any tax thereon. The position is therefore as follows.

Dividend income (6.4.06 to 5.10.06)	800		
Tax credits £800 x 1/9	89		
	£ 889		
Tax payable at dividend ordinary rate	500	@ 10% =	50
dividend trust rate	389	@ 32.5% =	126
			176
Less: Tax credits			89
Tax payable by trustees under self-assessment (due 31 January 2008)			£ 87
Tax Pool			
Tax added	87		
Tax on distribution	160		
Further tax due under s 687	73		

No election can be made to treat the trust as one with a vulnerable beneficiary since D does not become entitled to the settled property until he is 25. To qualify as a trust for a vulnerable person, D would need to become entitled to all the trust assets on reaching the age of 18.

Until Finance Act 2006, there were special rules for accumulation and maintenance (A&M) trusts. Lifetime transfers into these trusts were exempt from IHT if the settlor survives seven years, and the trusts are not subject to the periodic or exit charges.

FA 2006 Schedule 20 restricted the favourable rules to trusts that are created:

- on death by a parent for a minor child who will be fully entitled to the assets in the trust between the age of 18 of 25; or

- on death for the benefit of one life tenant in order of time only (more than one such interest may be created on death as long as the trust capital vests absolutely when the life interest comes to an end); or

- either in the settlor's lifetime or on death for a disabled person. Trusts for *disabled persons* will also continue to enjoy special treatment, as will existing regular premium life insurance policies written into trust.

The IHT treatment for trusts which do not come within these rules will in future fall within the IHT rules for 'relevant property' trusts.

These changes took effect from 22 March 2006, but Schedule 20 provides transitional arrangements for existing trusts.

Broadly, where existing A&M trusts provide that the assets in trust will go to a beneficiary absolutely at 18 — or where the terms on which they are held are modified before 6 April 2008 to provide this — their current IHT treatment will continue.

For a new A&M trust if the capital is left on fully flexible trust with no set date for the beneficiary to become absolutely entitled, the trust will become subject to the 6% rule on the death of the parent and will remain so until the beneficiary is paid out.

For new and old A& M type arrangements, the trusts will not become subject to the 6% regime until the child reaches age 18 and this will continue until they become absolutely entitled at age 25. There will be no 20% entry charge. However, for new arrangements (ie trust property settled after 21 March 2006), this applies only if one of the child's parents has died and the trust was established under the will of the parent or under the Crimial Injuries Compensation Scheme.

For existing A&M settlements where beneficiaries are under age 18 at the end of the transitional period on 6 April 2008, they will not be subject to the 6% charge until they reach age 18 provided the trust is modified before 6 April 2008.

Therefore, the trustees of the D settlement must arrange that the trust deed is modified so that the assets devolve absolutely in D as soon as he has reached his 18th birthday or by 6 April 2008 at the latest to avoid the new interest in possession settlement being treated as a relevant property trust.

E Trust:

Income received

10,000 x £1 x 8% = £800 + tax credit £89 = £889.

Tax at the dividend trust rate does not apply as E has an absolute right to the income.

The tax liability on the dividend income is at 10%, covered by the tax credit. Although the trustees will have to send in a tax return form SA 900, they will not need to make any income entries since the tax on the income was covered by tax credits. The due date for submitting the return is 31 January 2008.

F Trust:

Because F is absolutely entitled to all of the trust assets on reaching 18 an election can be made for special income tax treatment (FA 2005 Chapter 4). The tax liability is then calculated by reducing the normal trust tax payable (referred to in FA 2005 s 27 as TQTI) by the excess of that figure over the extra amount of tax the vulnerable beneficiary would pay (FA 2005 s 28 VQTI) on the assumption that the trust income is the highest part of his or her income and disregarding any relief given by way of a reduction of income tax (eg married couple's allowance).

The calculation of the trustees tax liability, as set out in FA 2005 ss 26–28 is:

2006/07
Steps

TLV2	Compute F's liability to income and capital gains tax on the basis that any income distributed to him by the trustees is disregarded and that any reliefs given by way of an income tax deduction (for example – married couple's allowance) are also ignored for this purpose.
TLV1	This is the tax due computed by assuming that the trust income relating to the vulnerable beneficiary was in fact charged on F as the highest part of his income.
VQTI	VQTI = TLV1 – TLV2
TQTI	This is the tax due on the trustees without reference to the vulnerable person rules.
The relief	The trustees' income tax liability is reduced by TQTI – VQTI. This gives the answer of VQTI as trustees reduced liability.

F's Trust calculation of relief

TLV2   F's income ignoring the trust income is £2,500 which is within his personal allowance – no tax is payable on this.

	£
Earnings	2,500
Personal allowance (restricted)	2,500
	0

TLV1

	£
Earnings	2,500
Trust income	7,500
	10,000

	£
Income including trust (TLV1)	10,000
Personal allowance	5,035
Taxable income	£ 4,965

Tax payable thereon

£		£
2,150	@ 10%	215
2,815	@ 22%	619
4,965		£ 834

VQTI   TLV1 minus TLV2 equals VQTI (834 – 0 = 834)
So VQTI is £834

TQTI   Tax on trustees (assumes no management expenses for purpose of this example)

£		£
500	@ 22%	110
7,000	@ 40%	2,800
7,500		2,910

The relief   Trustees' income tax liability reduced by TQTI – VQTI

	£
TQTI	2,910
The relief (2,910 – 834)	2,076
Revised liability	834

(b)   **Amounts treated as taxable income of the beneficiaries for 2006/07**

C	Annuity	£1,500	Tax deducted		£330

D   Maintenance to 5.10.06

$$£240 \times \frac{100}{60} = \qquad 400 \quad \text{Tax deducted} \qquad £160$$

Income of trust from 6.10.06 — Dividends

$$£800 \times \frac{100}{90} \qquad \underline{889} \quad \text{Tax credit (non-repayable)} \qquad £89$$

$$\underline{£1,289}$$

E   Income vested (that is, an absolute entitlement to it whether or not distributed)   £889   Tax credit (non-repayable)   £89

F   Nil.

In all cases the beneficiary's income is below the level of the single personal allowance. Dividend tax credits are, however, not repayable. Unless their personal allowances are covered by other income, C will be able to reclaim the whole of the tax deducted of £330 and D will be able to reclaim the tax of £160 deducted from his maintenance. Neither D nor E will be able to reclaim the tax credits of £89.

The tax paid by the trustees of F trust will equal the liability on trust income.

Explanatory Notes

Payment of annuities

1.   Where an annuity is payable, tax must be deducted at the basic rate, and tax must be accounted for at that rate on an equivalent amount of income. The effect is to cause tax to be charged on the dividend income of the C trust at 22% rather than the dividend rate of 10%. TA 1988 s 350 provides that tax also has to be paid at the basic rate on the part of the annuity paid out of the capital of the trust. HMRC issue assessments outside the self-assessment system in respect of such tax. Although the tax on such an assessment is payable thirty days after it is issued (unless an appeal and postponement application is made) (TMA 1970 s 59B(6)), interest on unpaid tax runs from 31 January after the tax year to which the assessment relates (see Example 44 explanatory note 3).

     Now that dividend credits are not repayable, the fact that the trust's dividend income is effectively taxed at 22% will not disadvantage C.

     For a further illustration of the treatment of an annuity see Example 44 part B.

Contingent interest

2.   At present D only acquires shares in Y plc provided he attains the age of 25 but see 45.2(a). Until age 18 the trustees have the power to accumulate income and therefore the dividend income received by the trust before D's 18th birthday on 6 October 2006 is chargeable to tax at the dividend trust rate (currently 32.5%). As and when payments are made to D during that time, they are net of tax at 40%, and the tax may be reclaimed by D if appropriate, as indicated in the example. The trustees must, however, account for the 40% tax deducted from the payments and they cannot treat the dividend credit relating to the amount distributed as tax paid by them when calculating how much tax they must pay. They could not, therefore, have paid a distribution of more than £800 gross (£480 net), to D before 6 October 2006, ie:

	£	Available income £
Trust income		
Dividend 800 x (100/90)	889	800
Tax due (per 45.2 at D)	176	
Less tax credit	89	
Tax payable	87	(87)
If £800 gross distributed		
Tax at 40% on £800	320	
Already paid	87	
Further tax payable	233	(233)
		480

For a more detailed illustration of these provisions see Example 48.

From his 18th birthday D is entitled to the income whether it is actually distributed or not. The amount of £500 paid to him after his 18th birthday in the tax year is irrelevant, since he is entitled to and will eventually receive the rest.

Vested interest

3. Although E is under 18, he has a vested interest in the preference shares in Z plc. Whilst the capital cannot be distributed, the income can. As the settlors (E's parents) are dead, ITTOIA 2005 s 629 (which treats income from a parental settlement on an infant child as belonging to the parent) cannot apply and therefore this income is taxed on E personally.

Contrast the interest of E (vested) with that of D (contingent). Although E cannot personally have the shares in Z plc until he is 18, or even the income for his personal unrestricted use, the shares belong to him. If he dies the asset will form part of his estate. The income from the shares forms part of his statutory income. By comparison D's interest in the shares of Y plc is conditional upon his living to age 25. If he dies then the asset will revert to the will trust. D has no right to the income until he is 18 (other than at the discretion of the trustees). Thereafter he has an absolute right to income which is taxed in his name. Only after the contingency has been eliminated (ie on attaining age 25) will the shares vest in D. There is a considerable body of case law on the question of whether an interest under a will is vested or contingent, and it involves a detailed knowledge of the general law of trusts, which is outside the scope of this book.

Trust with vulnerable beneficiary

4. The rate applicable to trusts (40%) and the dividend trust rate (32.5%) were raised in FA 2004 with effect for the tax year 2004–05 as a tax avoidance deterrent. To prevent these changes having an adverse effect on trusts with vulnerable beneficiaries, particularly trusts for disabled people and for children with a deceased parent — FA 2005 Chapter 4 (ss 23–45) brings in provisions to protect such individuals.

Income tax

FA 2005 ss 25–29 sets out the special tax treatment rules. The mechanics of working out the reduction in the trustees tax liability are set out in detail for the F trust in (a) but basically the trustees will be able to take account of the vulnerable beneficiary's personal allowances and starting and basic rate income tax bands to reduce the amount of income tax paid.

For income tax purposes, the trustees therefore include in their return the tax that would normally be due by them and then calculate what the tax would be if the income had been given directly to F, taking into account his other income, gains and allowances. The difference is claimed as a deduction — see the calculations for F on 45.3–45.4.

Capital gains

If a trust has any capital gains, and the trustees and the vulnerable beneficiary are UK resident then an election for special tax treatment by the trustees would mean that the gain would be treated as arising to a settlor in a settlor-interested trust (s 31). The trustees are not chargeable to capital gains tax — instead the gain is charged on the vulnerable person who should return it in their tax return. Clearly this may pose a problem for some vulnerable beneficiaries who have not been required to submit a self-assessment return previously and suddenly find themselves confronted with the need to work out their capital gain.

This provision does not apply in the tax year of the death of the vulnerable beneficiary (s 30).

Non-UK resident beneficiaries and trustees

Where the beneficiary is non-UK resident for the tax year for the purposes of Chapter 4, the trustees' tax liability in respect of the gains will be whatever the vulnerable beneficiary's tax liability in respect of the gains would have been had the gains arisen to him or her directly.

The special capital gains tax regime does not apply in any case where, in the tax year in question, the trustees are not, for TCGA 1992 purposes, resident in the UK during part of the year, or ordinarily resident in the UK during the year (ss 32, 33 and Sch 1).

Election for special tax treatment

The trustees of relevant trusts will be able to make an irrevocable joint election with a vulnerable beneficiary which will have effect, for any tax year for which the election is in force, to allow the trustees to make a claim for the special tax treatment provided by FA 2005 Chapter 4 to apply for that year.

The election must state the date from which it is to be valid and must be made no later than 12 months after 31 January following the tax year in which that date falls.

If the election becomes invalid, the trustees have 90 days from the time of the change in circumstances to notify HMRC (s 37).

Disabled person

A disabled person is defined in FA 2005 s 38 as a person with a mental disability who is incapable of administering his property or managing his affairs, or, a person in receipt of attendance allowance or disability living allowance at the middle or highest rates (or who would be so entitled to such an allowance if they were UK resident).

Relevant minor

A child is a relevant minor if aged under 18 *and* at least one of their parents has died (s 39).

Qualifying trust — disabled persons

To be a qualifying trust for a vulnerable disabled person that person must be entitled to all of the income arising from the trust fund, or, no income of the trust may be applied for the benefit of any other person. Any capital distribution must be for the benefit of the disabled person (s 34).

Qualifying trust — relevant minor

A trust is a qualifying trust for a relevant minor if it is:

–   a statutory trust for a minor on an intestacy, or

–   a trust established under the will of the deceased parent of the relevant minor, or

–   a trust established under the Criminal Injuries Compensation Scheme.

To qualify the trust must provide that the relevant minor will be absolutely entitled to income and capital including accumulations at age 18. Before that age any distribution must be applied for the benefit of the relevant minor and no income may be applied for the benefit of any other person (s 35).

It must therefore be noted that any trusts established by parents, by will or intestacy, for their minor children, where the children do not become entitled to the settled property until age 25 (eg accumulation and maintenance settlements) will not qualify. Hence the D settlement does not qualify but that for F does.

Part qualification

References to qualifying trusts include trusts where only part of the property qualifies provided that part and any income arising from that asset can be identified (s 36). In such cases only the relevant proportion of management expenses will be allowed against the income of each part. The proportion being the amount of qualifying income as a proportion of total income allowed against qualifying income (s 27(2)).

Part years

Where the trust only qualifies for part of a tax year then income and expenses are related to the qualifying and non-qualifying periods based upon when income arises (s 29).

Self-assessment

5.   See Example 47 for further details on the way in which income is shown in the self-assessment tax return of the individual.

Garth, a bachelor aged forty-five, was injured in a road accident some years ago and the Court awarded the sum of £50,000 compensation to be paid to him.

Garth created a settlement of this sum under which he was himself to receive the income for life, the capital upon his death being divisible amongst certain relatives.

The trust income for the year ended 5 April 2007 comprised:

		£
Building society interest (amounts received)		1,280
Taxed interest from government stocks (gross amounts)		660
National Savings Bank interest (investment account)		76
Rents receivable		1,570
Repairs and maintenance of rented property	329	
Insurance	205	(534)
Dividends from UK companies (amount received)		1,800

Trust expenses amounted to £450. There was a loss brought forward of £205 on the rented property.

In 2006/07 Garth's only personal income, other than non-taxable social security allowances, consisted of National Savings Bank interest (Easy Access Account) of £20.

(a)   Prepare a statement showing the trust income for 2006/07.

(b)   Compute Garth's personal tax position for 2006/07.

Garth — Trust Income

(a)   *Garth's Trustees — Statement of Trust Income 2006/07*

	£	Gross £	Tax £
Rent receivable	1,570		
Less: Expenses	(534)		
Loss brought forward	(205)	831	
Savings income			
Building society interest			
(1,280 x 100/80)	1,600		320
Government stocks interest	660		132
NSB interest	76	2,336	
Dividends (1,800 + 200)		2,000	200
Total income of trust		5,167	652
Tax thereon:			
Non-savings income 831 @ 22%	183		
Non-dividend savings income 2,336 @ 20%	467		
Dividend income 2,000 @ 10%	200	850	850
	5,167		
of which tax payable by self-assessment is			198
Net income of trust treated as Garth's income		4,317	

(b)   *Garth — Income tax liability 2006/07*

	£	Tax £
NSB interest	20	–
Trust income (both savings and non-savings)	5,167	850
	5,187	850
Personal allowance	5,035	
	152	
Tax payable thereon @ 10%		15
		835
Non-repayable dividend tax credits (200 – 29)		171
Repayment due		664

Explanatory Notes

Settlement in which settlor retains an interest

1. For income tax purposes, income from a settlement is treated as the settlor's income if he or his wife has retained an interest in the settlement (ITTOIA 2005 s 625 (formerly TA 1988 s 660A)).

    Garth is therefore assessable on the trust income whether he receives it or not, since he was the settlor, and no relief is available for the trust expenses of £450. Furthermore, income other than dividend income is treated as miscellaneous income, so the savings rate of 20% does not apply to the non-dividend savings income. This makes no difference in Garth's case, since dividend income is treated as the top slice of taxable income and the income remaining chargeable after deducting his personal allowance is part of his dividend income of £2,000, so it is taxed at 10% in any event. For further notes on settlements in which the settlor retains an interest, see Example 35.

ITTOIA 2005 ss 622–627 (formerly TA 1988 s 660A) is part of the anti-avoidance legislation in ITTOIA 2005 Part 5 Chapter 5, which also provides, in ITTOIA 2005 ss 629, 631 (formerly TA 1988 s 660B), that payments to unmarried minor children of the settlor are treated as the settlor's income (see Example 42).

2. Where a settlor retains an interest in a discretionary settlement, the income is not liable to the rate applicable to trusts or the dividend trust rate — see Example 42 under the headings *Income not liable to s 686 rates* and *Income taxed as income of the settlor.*

3. Special provisions apply for capital gains tax where a settlor retains an interest in a non-resident settlement — see Example 51 for details.

4. FA 2004 introduced new rules for private residence relief and gift relief for disposals of assets on or after 10 December 2003 by trustees of settlements in which the settlor retains an interest. For more detailed information see page 50.6–50.7.

5. A new section 685A is introduced into ITTOIA 2005. This gives statutory effect to an existing practice of not taxing beneficiaries of settlor-interested settlements on discretionary income payments they receive from the trustees where the underlying income has already been taxed in the hands of the settlor.

    ITTOIA 2005 s 685A will apply where a person receives a discretionary income payment from the trustees of a settlement, and where the settlor is also chargeable to tax under ITTOIA 2005 s 619(1) on the income arising to the trustees of the settlement, whether income of the current year of assessment or of a previous year of assessment.

    The section applies only to a proportion of the discretionary annual payment corresponding to the proportion of the trustees' income (of current and previous years of assessment) that has been charged to income tax under ITTOIA 2005 s 619 in the hands of the settlor. In such circumstances the recipient of the annual payment is treated as having paid income tax at the higher rate in respect of the annual payment.

    The beneficiary who receives the discretionary annual payment is to be treated as receiving the sum with a higher rate tax credit, to the extent that the section applies to the income he receives.

    The tax which the beneficiary is treated as having paid is not repayable, and prevents the tax that s 685A(3) treats as having been paid from being used to reduce a tax bill on other income. It also provides for the annual payment to be treated for the purposes of TA 1988 ss 348 and 349(1) as wholly payable out of profits or gains not brought into charge to income tax.

    Where the recipient of the annual payment is the settlor then the annual payment is not a taxable receipt in the settlor's hands, and the rule that the beneficiary who receives the discretionary annual payment is to be treated as receiving the sum with a higher rate tax credit, to the extent that the section applies to the income he receives does not apply.

    ICTA 1988 s 687 will not apply in relation to the payment, or to so much of the payment as falls within the terms of s 685A.

    Section 685A has effect for payments in respect of income made on or after 6 April 2006.

Gifts to charity

6. Where a UK resident trust that is caught by the anti-avoidance legislation of ITTOIA 2005 Part 5 Chapter 5 (see note 1) gives money to a charity, the amount taxable on the settlor is reduced by the amount (plus tax) given to the charity (ITTOIA 2005 ss 628, 630 (formerly FA 2000 s 44)).

    This means that the income given to the charity will be net of tax at the relevant rate applicable to the trustees, ie 40% for discretionary trusts and the basic, lower or dividend ordinary rate for interest in possession trusts. Where the trust's income exceeds the amount given to the charity, the amount given to the charity is treated as made rateably out of the trust's different sources of income (unless the trust stipulates that the charity should receive certain sources of income). Trust management expenses are similarly allocated between income that goes to the charity and the remainder of the trust income.

The rate of tax recoverable by the charity depends on the tax payable by the trust. Say a trust gives a charity bank interest of £500. If the trust is a discretionary trust with income (after management expenses) of £10,000, the interest would be net of 40% tax, so that the tax thereon would be (500 x 40/60 =) £333. The charity would receive £500 plus a tax refund of £333, making £833 in all. If the trust is an interest in possession trust, the tax on the gift of £500 would be (500 x 20/80 =) £125. The charity would receive £500 plus a tax refund of £125, making a total of £625.

7. For the purpose of the anti-avoidance provisions mentioned in note 1, an interest free or low interest rate loan is an 'arrangement' that is within the definition of settlement, so that income from the investment of such a loan is treated as the settlor's income. It is provided by ITTOIA 2005 ss 628, 630 (formerly FA 2000 s 45) that this does not apply where the loan is made to a charity.

Self-assessment

8. See Example 47 explanatory note 7 for the entries on self-assessment returns in relation to trusts in which the settlor retains an interest. HMRC Helpsheet IR 270 contains detailed information on how to decide whether an interest has been retained and also relating to parental settlements on minor children (as to which see Example 64). Where gifts or loans are made to charity as outlined in notes 5 and 6 above, the income does not have to be included in the settlor's self-assessment return.

Settlements on oneself

9. A settlement may be made by a settlor on himself for a number of reasons. In this example Garth may well have made the settlement so that trustees can administer his assets on his behalf whilst he is suffering from a mental or physical disability. Other reasons for such settlements would include:

    (a) A couple with no children, but each having relatives, wishing to ensure that each set of relatives obtained the appropriate share of their respective estates (rather than the whole devolving upon the relatives of the spouse/civil partner who died last as could occur in intestacy).

    (b) To provide certainty for the next generation(s) by creating a settlement under which each of husband and wife would receive the income during their lifetime, their children having the knowledge that the destination of the capital could not be altered by such events as the remarriage of a widow/widower.

    (c) A couple with children from different relationships who wish to ensure that their own offspring obtain the appropriate share of their respective estates (removing the possibility that the destination of the capital could be altered after their own deaths, whilst providing income for their co-habitee in the meantime).

Interest on government stocks

10. Garth's trustees could make an election to receive interest on the government stocks gross (see Example 44 explanatory note 4 for details). If this was done in relation to interest receivable from 2006/07, tax would not be payable on the 2006/07 interest until 31 January 2008, but the tax would be included in payments on account for later years, unless covered by the de minimis limits.

The Colenso Trust was created in 1985 by a settlor who had already created five other trusts since 6 June 1978. Under the terms of the trust deed the trustees have discretionary power to pay income to any of the named beneficiaries and to accumulate any income that is not so applied.

The income and expenses of the trustees for the year ended 5 April 2007 were as follows:

Income	£
Dividends from UK companies (amount received)	2,520
Rent of property let unfurnished	2,850
Interest on National Savings investment account	465

Expenses	
Property expenses — ground rent	34
— repairs	646
Accountancy fees	588

The income tax liability of the trust for 2005/06 amounted to £1,696, of which tax credits covered £546. In addition the trustees had made payments on account of £486 on each of 31 January 2006 and 31 July 2006.

The trustees had a tax pool brought forward at 6 April 2006 of £326. During the year the trustees had net capital gains of £3,290, after indexation and taper relief but before deduction of the annual exemption.

One of the beneficiaries of the trust is Clery, a widower who was born in 1924.

The trustees paid £4,200 to Clery out of the trust income in 2006/07.

His other income for that year was a state pension of £4,372 and income from purchased life annuities totalling £20,000, of which the capital content was £16,000.

(a)   Prepare a statement of income and gains for the Colenso Trust for 2006/07.

(b)   Compute the tax pool to carry forward to 2007/08 or s 687 tax payable.

(c)   Show the tax payable by the trustees under self-assessment.

(d)   Calculate Clery's repayment of income tax for 2006/07.

The Colenso Trust

(a)   *Statement of trust income and gains 2006/07*

			Gross	Tax
Trust income:		£	£	£
Rent receivable		2,850		
Less: expenses		680	2,170	
Savings income				
NSB interest			465	
Dividends (2,520 + 280)			2,800	280
Total income of trust			5,435	280

Tax thereon:
On amount equal to grossed up trust expenses
(paid out of dividend income and not chargeable
at dividend trust rate)

(588 x 100/90) =	653 @ 10%	65		
On balance of dividends at dividend trust rate				
(2,800 – 653)	2,147 @ 32.5%	698		
On £1,000 @ standard rate (see Explanatory note 1)	1,000 @ 22%	220		
On remaining income at rate applicable to trusts	1,635 @ 40%	654		
	5,435	1,637		1,637
Of which tax payable by self-assessment is				1,357
Used to pay trust expenses		588	2,225	
Net income of trust			3,210	

Capital gains:

	£
Net gains for 2006/07	3,290
Less: Annual exemption (see explanatory note 13)	880
Chargeable gains	2,410
Capital gains tax thereon @ 40%	964

(b)   *Tax pool and position under TA 1988 s 687*

		£
Unutilised tax brought forward at 6 April 2006		326
Tax already accounted for by trustees at:		
Standard rate	220	
Rate applicable to trusts	654	
Dividend trust rate, net of tax credits (2,147 @ 22.5%)	483	
		1,357
		1,683
Tax on payments made out of income to Clery:		
$4,200 \times \dfrac{40}{60}$		2,800
Tax payable under s 687		1,117

(c)   *Tax payable by trustees under self-assessment (POA — payment on account)*

		£	£	Tax payable £	Re 2006/07 £
31.1.06	1st POA 2005/06			486	
31.7.06	2nd POA 2005/06			486	
31.1.07	Balancing payment 2005/06:				
	Tax due (1,696 – tax credits 546)	1,150			
	Less POAs	972	178		
	1st POA 2006/07 (½ x 1,150)		575	753	575
31.7.07	2nd POA 2006/07			575	575
31.1.08	Balancing payment 2006/07:				
	Income tax as in (a)	1,637			
	S 687 liability as in (b)	1,117			
	Capital gains tax as in (a)	964			
	Total liability	3,718			
	Less tax credits	280			
	Tax due	3,438			
	Less POAs	1,150	2,288		2,288
	1st POA 2007/08 ½ x (3,438 – CGT 964)		1,237	3,526	
	Total tax paid directly for 2006/07				3,438
31.7.07	2nd POA 2007/08			1,237	

(d)   *Clery's income tax repayment claim 2005/06*

		£	Tax £
Trust income £4,200 x $\dfrac{100}{60}$		7,000	2,800
State pension		4,372	
Savings income:			
Purchased life annuities (income element)		4,000	800
		15,372	3,600
Age allowance (over 75)		7,420	
		7,952	
Tax payable thereon:			
On non-savings income	2,150 @ 10%	215	
	1,802 @ 22%	396	
On savings income	4,000 @ 20%	800	1,411
Repayment due			2,189

Explanatory Notes

Rates applicable to trusts

1.   For 2006/07 the income of accumulation and discretionary trusts is liable to tax at the dividend trust rate of 32.5% if it is distribution income (see Example 42 for details) and otherwise at the rate applicable to trusts of 40% (TA 1988 s 686).

But see the new rules introduced in FA 2005 s 14 as set out on page (vii) in the Summary of Provisions of Finance Act 2005.

Originally introduced under FA 2005 s 14 and amended by TA 1988 s 686D, the first £1,000 (£500 for 2005/06) of relevant income will not be charged at the rate applicable to trusts, but will instead be charged at the income tax rate appropriate to the type of income. Therefore, if payments are received net of tax (for example, building society interest) up to the limit of the standard rate band, then the trustees will have no further tax to pay.

As previously mentioned there are amendments to TA 1988 s 686D relating to the standard rate band for trustees. The amendments increase the limit of the standard rate band from £500 to £1,000.

TA 1988 s 686D(1) substitutes 'trustees of a settlement' for 'trustees of a trust'. It also provides for the increase in the standard rate band limit in s 686D(3) from £500 to £1,000.

Section 686E applies s 686D where a settlor has made more than one settlement. The reference to £1,000 in s 686D(3) is replaced by £200, or by an amount obtained by dividing £1,000 by the number of settlements made by the same settlor, provided that amount is not less than £200.

The section sets out the position where there is more than one settlor of a settlement, and in such circumstances the amount is the amount obtained in relation to the largest class of settlements.

The provisions above come into force on 6 April 2006.

HMRC have confirmed that the new standard rate band will apply to trust income *net* of trust management expenses so potentially it will apply to other charges as well.

Although the management expenses are deducted from the trust income taxed at the lowest rate first, the standard rate band will apply in the order — basic rate income at 22% first, followed by lower rate 20% income and finally dividends at 10%.

Trustees are liable to tax at the rate applicable to trusts or dividend trust rate on income as the case may be if:

(a)   the income is to be accumulated or payable at the discretion of the trustees, and

(b)   it exceeds the trust expenses paid out of income, grossed up at the appropriate rate of tax. The expenses are treated as coming first out of dividends and other income carrying a non-repayable tax credit, then out of dividends from abroad, then out of non-dividend savings income, then out of non-savings income (see Example 43 note 10 at page 43.4). The grossing up rate for the expenses is 10% for dividend income, 20% for non-dividend savings income and 22% for non-savings income. The expenses are not allowable deductions for basic or lower rate tax or for dividend ordinary rate tax, so tax is charged on an equivalent amount of income at the appropriate rate (10% in this example).

2.   See Example 48 for an illustration of a trust liable at the rate applicable to trusts where there is a non-UK resident beneficiary.

3.   In this example, it may be possible to agree that some of the accountancy fees relate to the property income, rather than treating them as general trust expenses, thereby reducing the assessable income and the overall tax liability of the trust.

Self-assessment returns

4.   The HMRC Trusts, Settlements and Estates Manual — Section TSEM 1405 states that a new trust that does not have any income or gains does not have to notify them of the existence of the trust. Existing trusts who do not have any income or gains may ask HMRC to close the trust's record. The trustees are, of course, obliged to notify HMRC by 5 October following the relevant tax year in the same way as individuals if they do have income and/or gains chargeable to tax (TMA 1970 s 7).

5.   Where a self-assessment return is required, all types of trusts and estates complete the same return (SA 900). The requirement for trustees to complete a return is in TMA 1970 s 8A and the same rules

apply as for individuals for amending returns within twelve months, for HMRC to make corrections within nine months and to enquire into the return within twelve months, and for records to be maintained for the appropriate period (TMA 1970 ss 9A, 12B). Various changes to the self-assessment procedure were made by FA 2001 s 88 and Sch 29, with the intention of clarifying and simplifying the provisions. They are outlined in relation to personal representatives in Example 41, supplementary notes 1 to 3. The same provisions apply for trustees.

Interest in possession trusts are not required to show any *taxed* income in the return, except where accrued income relief is due on the income. (Accrued income *charges* are untaxed income and must be shown.) The trustees will still, however, need to know the overall tax position in order to be able to ascertain the income payable to the life tenant to be shown on form R185 (trust income) (see note 8). The returns for discretionary trusts show both taxed and untaxed income and the amount of the unused tax pool (if any) brought forward from the previous year. For both types of trust, supplementary pages have to be completed where income arises from a trade, partnership, land and property or from abroad, or where there are capital gains, or where the trust is non-resident or dual resident. From April 2003 returns will include supplementary Land and Property pages and/or Capital Gains pages if such pages were submitted with the previous year's return.

The return must be submitted by 30 September following the tax year if the trustees want the Revenue to calculate the tax, or by 31 January following the tax year if they are making their own tax calculation.

6.   To minimise administration burdens, HMRC have a scheme under which trustees responsible for at least 50 trusts dealt with in a single tax office may receive a single notice calling for trust returns and may make a single declaration when submitting a batch of returns. Trustees wishing to operate the scheme must make a written application. More information can be found in the HMRC Trusts, Settlements and Estates Manual at TSEM 3052.

Trusts in which settlor retains an interest

7.   Where the settlor retains an interest in the trust, all income (other than certain income derived from charitable gifts and loans — see Example 46 explanatory notes 5 and 6), *before* deducting expenses, is taxable on the settlor. The amount included on the trust pages of the settlor's personal tax return depends on whether the settlor also has an absolute entitlement to income.

Where the settlor does have an absolute entitlement, the amounts of income will be entered on the trust pages of the settlor's return net of management expenses. The management expenses must, however, also be treated as his income, so they have to be entered as 'other income' under Question 13 in the main part of the return, grossed up by the appropriate tax rate (dividend rate, lower rate or basic rate according to the income used to meet the expenses). Exceptionally, tax may not have been deducted from the income at all, for example if the trustees are non-resident. Even if the expenses are grossed up at the dividend or lower rate, the rate of tax payable by the settlor will be the non-savings rate.

If the settlor is not absolutely entitled to income, then the amounts entered in the trust pages of the return will be the whole of the trust income *before* management expenses.

See HMRC Help Sheet IR 270 for further details.

Forms R185 and beneficiaries' own tax returns

8.   It is advisable for trustees to compute the overall tax position of the trust as quickly as possible after 5 April each year to comply with their responsibilities under self-assessment.

Where the beneficiary is absolutely entitled to the income it will be essential to do so, in order that the R185 may be completed and forwarded to the beneficiary in plenty of time for him to complete his own self-assessment return or to claim a repayment as the case may be. For such beneficiaries, if all the income is taxed at source and there are no expenses, it is usual to mandate the income directly to the beneficiary and to include the income in the beneficiary's return as if it was his own income. In the case of a bare trust, ie where the beneficiary has an absolute right to both income and capital, all of the trust income is deemed to be that of the beneficiary and entered as such on the beneficiary's tax return. Trustees of bare trusts are not required to send trust returns but may, if they wish, send a trust return of the trust income, but not capital gains. This does not affect the beneficiary's liability to make his own returns.

Income paid out to discretionary beneficiaries

9. Under TA 1988 s 687, trustees are required to account for tax at the 40% rate applicable to trusts on income paid out in exercise of their discretion to beneficiaries, and the beneficiaries will be given form R185 showing the income as non-savings income with tax deducted at 40%. The tax suffered is available for repayment, as illustrated in the example.

Tax does not have to be accounted for under s 687 on capital payments, nor on payments of accumulated income that have become part of capital. If, however, the payment is advanced in such a way that it becomes income in the hands of the beneficiary, s 687 applies. For example where trustees are empowered to make payments to bring a beneficiary's income up to a certain level, such payments will be income whether paid out of current or accumulated income or capital.

From 6 April 1999 the trustees can reduce the tax to be accounted for under s 687 by the following (excluding any tax on income that has been used to cover trust expenses (see note 1(b)):

(i)   Tax paid on income liable to the rate applicable to trusts, including tax deducted at source

(ii)   The excess of the tax paid at the dividend trust rate on distributions and dividend type income over the dividend ordinary rate

(iii) The whole of the tax paid at the dividend trust rate on dividends from abroad

(iv)   Any pool of unused tax brought forward at 5 April 1999 (see note 11)

(v)   From 6 April 2006 tax at the basic or lower rate on the first £1,000 of trust income (£500 for 2005/06).

10. If a beneficiary of a discretionary trust has not received a form R185, he should gross up the income received for tax deducted at 40%. If there is any doubt that part of the payment received is not income, the amount should be shown on his personal return as a provisional figure with a tick in box 23.2 and the reason for the figure being provisional should be shown in the additional information box at 23.5. The beneficiary should not delay submitting his return because of the failure of the trustees to provide a form R185.

S 687 tax pool

11. In many instances, the pool of tax under s 687 will exceed the amount that is due, so no amount will be payable. Furthermore tax could be paid on income that is used to cover non-deductible expenses (see Example 48). From 6 April 1999, however, none of the tax credits on dividends are included in the tax pool, whereas the payments out of income will still have repayable tax of 40% (34% prior to 5 April 2004) deducted. Except to the extent that there is an unused pool of tax brought forward, this will restrict the maximum payment out of dividend income to 60% of the net dividend, giving a s 687 liability of 40% of the net dividend (see Example 45 explanatory note 2 for an illustration). Although any excess of tax paid over tax on distributions can be carried forward to a later year, no credit is given for s 687 tax paid if the tax paid at the rate applicable to trusts exceeds the tax on distributions in later years. That surplus is carried forward as unutilised tax in the pool.

Note that the unused pool brought forward at 6 April 1999 will include tax credits on any pre 6 April 1999 dividends that have not been paid out to beneficiaries, and those credits are available to cover s 687 tax on discretionary payments after 5 April 1999.

12. The s 687 tax payable is added to the tax due under self-assessment and is accounted for in the balancing payment. It also counts, however, in the calculation of the payments on account for the following year. Thus it can increase the tax payable on 31 January following the end of the tax year by 150% of the s 687 liability.

The trustees may not intend to make distributions to beneficiaries in the following tax year and may be tempted to apply to reduce the payments on account by the amount of the s 687 tax. Payments on account are, however, compared with the actual tax due for the subsequent year, and if the reduced payment is below the actual liability for that year, interest is payable on the difference (restricted to the amount of the reduction). It does not matter that the claim to reduce the payments on account was in respect of s 687 tax and the additional liability arises because of an increase in tax because of increased income, tax rate increases, reduced expenses or for any other reason.

Capital gains tax

13. A trust is liable to capital gains tax at 40% from 6 April 2004 on the gains less the annual exemption. The exemption for a trust is one half of that applicable to individuals (half of £8,800 for 2006/07 = £4,400), but it is further reduced where the settlor has created more than one settlement after 6 June 1978 (see Example 50 part C). The limit is divided between the settlements, with a minimum exemption of one tenth of the amount available to individuals, ie £880 for 2006/07. In this example, the £880 limit applies since it is higher than one sixth of £4,400 = £733.

    The tax applies to the gains less losses of the year, as reduced by losses brought forward (but not so as to lose the annual exemption) and any available taper relief.

    The amount due is payable on 31 January following the tax year, but is not included in the calculation of payments on account for the following year, nor is it available for inclusion in the tax pool for s 687 liability.

A trust was established on 6 April 1991. The trust deed stipulates that after paying an annuity of £6,500 per annum to the settlor's sister, the remaining income of each year is to be distributed or accumulated as the trustees deem fit.

The assets placed into the trust consisted of certain properties let unfurnished on landlord's repairing short leases, and cash. The latter was placed on bank deposit and used to fund investments in government securities and quoted shares.

At 6 April 2005 the pool of unutilised tax brought forward under TA 1988 s 687 was £3,750.

The receipts and payments of the trust for 2005/06 and 2006/07 were as follows:

	2005/06 £	2006/07 £
Receipts		
Rents receivable	11,300	11,300
Premium received on granting of 21 year lease	–	10,000
Interest on £10,000 9% Government Stock (gross amount)	900	900
Bank interest received (see below)	1,400	1,500
Dividends from quoted UK companies (including tax credits)	3,200	2,762
Payments		
Trustees' expenses properly chargeable to income	405	450
Trustees' expenses re investment advice	–	100
Loan interest (see below)	350	550
Repairs to the let properties	200	400
Annuity to settlor's sister (gross amount)	6,500	6,500
Discretionary payments of cash from the trust income:		
to A, who is resident in the UK	3,366	–
to B, who is neither resident nor ordinarily resident in the UK	–	3,700

The amounts stated in respect of bank interest received are the gross amounts. The interest was received net of tax. The loan was obtained to finance an extension to one of the let properties. Interest on the 9% Government Stock, which is received net of 20% tax, is exempt from tax in the hands of a non-resident. The trustees' expenses for investment advice have been charged to income by authority of the trust deed.

For 2004/05, the amount of income tax paid on account equalled the liability for the year of £3,478.

Calculate:

(1) The income of the trust for 2005/06 and 2006/07, showing any liability in respect of income chargeable at the rate applicable to trusts under TA 1988 s 686, and the due dates of payment of tax.

(2) The income available for distribution to discretionary beneficiaries for 2005/06 and 2006/07.

(3) The trust's position under TA 1988 s 687 at the end of 2006/07.

(4) Any income tax that may be reclaimable by the non-UK resident beneficiary in respect of the discretionary payment made to him.

Note: Ignore capital gains tax.

(1)   **Statement of trust income**

2005/06		Gross	Tax deducted or credited
		£	£
Property income (see explanatory note 6)		10,750	
Savings income			
Interest on Government Stock		900	180
Bank interest		1,400	280
Dividends		3,200	320
		16,250	780
Less: Charges (annuity)		6,500	
Net total income of trust		9,750	
Tax thereon:			
On amount equal to grossed up trust expenses, excluding those for investment advice (450 x 100/90) =	500 @ 10%	50	
On lease premium (see explanatory note 6)	6,000 @ 22%	1,320	
On £500 of income at standard rate under FA 2005 s 14 (22% on property income)	500 @ 22%	110	
On dividend income at dividend trust rate (2,762 – 500)	2,262 @ 32.5%	735	
On balance at rate applicable to trusts	488 @ 40%	195	
	9,750		
Tax deducted from annuity	6,500 @ 22%	1,430	
Total income tax due		3,840	3,840
Of which tax payable by self-assessment is			3,060

Amounts of income tax payable by trustees direct to HMRC under self-assessment for 2005/06 and payments on account for 2006/07 are as follows:

		£	£
31 January 2006:			
½ x 4,208			2,104
31 July 2006:			
½ x 4,208			2,104
31 January 2007:			
Total income tax payable for 2005/06		3,060	
Less: Payments on account	4,208		
Tax/tax credits at source	780	4,988	
		(1,928)	(1,928)
			2,280
First payment on account for 2006/07 (½ x 3,060)		1,530	
Total amount re-payable		(398)	
31 July 2007:			
Second payment on account for 2006/07 (see explanatory note 6)		1,530	

2006/07		Gross	Tax deducted or credited
		£	£
Property income (see explanatory note 6)		16,350	
Savings income			
Interest on Government Stock		900	180
Bank interest		1,400	300
Dividends		2,762	276
		21,512	756
Less: Charges (annuity)		6,500	
Net total income of trust		15,012	

Tax thereon:			
On amount equal to grossed up trust expenses, excluding those for investment advice (450 x 100/90) =	500 @ 10%	50	
On lease premium (see explanatory note 6)	6,000 @ 22%	1,320	
On £500 of income at standard rate under FA 2005 s 14 (22% on property income)	1,000 @ 22%	220	
On dividend income at dividend trust rate (2,762 – 500)	2,262 @ 32.5%	735	
On balance at rate applicable to trusts	5,250 @ 40%	2,100	
	15,012		
Tax deducted from annuity	6,500 @ 22%	1,430	
Total income tax due		5,855	5,855
Of which tax payable by self-assessment is			5,099

Amounts of income tax payable by trustees direct to HMRC under self-assessment for 2006/07 and payments on account for 2007/08 are as follows:

		£	£
31 January 2007:			
As above ½ x 3,060			1,530
31 July 2007:			
½ x 3,060			1,530
31 January 2008:			
Total income tax payable for 2006/07		5,855	
Less: Payments on account	3,060		
Tax/tax credits at source	756	3,816	
		2,039	2,039
			5,099
First payment on account for 2007/08 (½ x 5,099)		2,549	
Total amount re-payable		4,588	
31 July 2008:			
Second payment on account for 2007/08 (see explanatory note 6)		2,550	

(2) **Income available for distribution to discretionary beneficiaries**

		2005/06 £		2006/07 £
Trust income (excluding lease premium) after annuity and expenses		9,300*		8,512**
Less: Tax at Standard Rate (22%) under FA 2005 s 14	110		220	
Tax at rate applicable to trusts per part (1)	195		2,100	
Tax at dividend trust rate per part (1)	735		735	
Trustees' expenses for investment advice (see explanatory note 7)	100	1,140	–	3,055
Available for beneficiaries		8,160†		5,457†
Amount actually distributed was		£ 3,366		£ 3,700
Leaving undistributed income of		£ 4,794†		£ 1,757†

* £9,750 net total income as at part (1) less expenses £450

** £15,012 net total income as at part (1) less lease premium £6,000 and expenses £500.

† Note that in so far as the amount shown as available to the beneficiaries includes dividend income, it cannot all be distributed without the trustees incurring a further tax liability, except to the extent that there is unutilised tax brought forward (see explanatory note 9).

(3) **Trust's position under TA 1988 s 687 at end of 2006/07**

		2005/06 £		2006/07 £
Tax at 40% on amounts paid at trustees' discretion to beneficiaries: $£3,366 \times \dfrac{40}{60}$		2,244		
Tax at 40% on amounts paid at trustees' discretion to beneficiaries: $£3,700 \times \dfrac{40}{60}$				2,467
Less: Tax already accounted for by trustees: on trust income charged at standard rate under FA 2005 s 14	110		220	
on trust income chargeable under TA 1988 s 686 – at rate applicable to trusts, ie 40%	195		2,100	
at dividend trust rate excluding non-repayable tax credits (2,262 @ 22.5%)	509			
(2,262 @ 22.5%)			509	
Unutilised tax bf	3,750		2,320	
	4,564		5,149	
Utilised	2,244	2,244	2,467	2,467
Unutilised tax cf	2,320		2,682*	
Amount due from trustees under TA 1988 s 687		–		–

* The amount of £2,682 carried forward represents tax paid at the rate applicable to trusts plus the excess of the dividend trust rate over the dividend ordinary rate, and it can be used to cover tax at 40% on the gross equivalent of future income distributions.

(4) **Tax reclaimable by non-resident beneficiary** (see explanatory note 10)

2005/06   No distribution to B – no repayment.

2006/07   Distribution of £3,700 to B (who is neither resident nor ordinarily resident in UK) comes from trust income that includes £900 from Government Stock that is exempt from tax in B's hands.

The part of the total tax paid on the discretionary payment of trust income in 2006/07, ie £2,467, that represents the interest on the Government Stock is therefore repayable, thus:

$$£2,467 \text{ x } \frac{900}{15,512^*} \text{ = } £ \underline{143}$$

* Being taxable income of £21,512 before charges, less lease premium of £6,000 which is a capital receipt.

Explanatory Notes

Trusts liable to the rate applicable to trusts and dividend trust rate (special trust rates)

1.   A trust that can accumulate income, or pay income to the beneficiaries at the discretion of the trustees, is liable to tax on non-dividend income at the rate applicable to trusts, currently 40%, and at the dividend trust rate of 32.5% on 'distribution income', ie UK dividend income and certain other income carrying non-repayable tax credits, and foreign dividends (TA 1988 s 686). In the case of UK dividends and other income carrying a non-repayable tax credit of 10%, the trustees have to pay the balance of 22.5% for 2005/06 and 2006/07 of the tax credit inclusive amount. In the case of dividends from abroad, the trustees have to pay the full 32.5% for 2005/06 and 2006/07 (subject to a claim for double tax relief where foreign tax has been paid). From 6 April 2001, where foreign dividends are paid through a UK paying or collecting agent, agents no longer deduct UK tax from foreign dividends or interest. See Example 42 for details of income carrying non-repayable tax credits and for details of amounts that are not chargeable at the rate applicable to trusts.

In this example, the amounts excluded from the charge under s 686 are the lease premium (see note 6) and the annuity to the settlor's sister. The trustees have to account for tax on such amounts at the basic rate. Under self-assessment, tax is not charged separately for each source of income, and the tax under s 686 is accounted for as part of the overall figure.

Amount on which special trust rates are charged

2.   The liability under s 686 applies to the *income* of the trust after deducting any excluded amounts per note 1 and allowing for the trustees' expenses of managing the trust. Trust expenses are regarded as being met first from income taxed at the dividend trust rate, then other savings income, then non-savings income, grossed up appropriately. See Example 43 note 10 at page 43.4 for further details.

Non-resident discretionary trusts and non-resident life tenants

3.   Where a discretionary trust has income not chargeable to UK income tax, because it is not resident in the UK, or deemed to be not resident under a double tax treaty, the management expenses must be apportioned between the taxable and non-taxable income of that year, and only the proportion applicable to taxable income is allowable in computing the tax under s 686 (TA 1988 s 686(2A)). (Income which is strictly taxable income may not be charged to tax on non-residents because of FA 1995 s 128, which broadly limits the charge to the tax, if any, deducted at source. Any such income from which tax is *not* deducted is treated by s 686(2B) as non-taxable income for the purposes of s 686(2A).)

Similar provisions disallow a proportion of trust expenses in computing the income of a non-resident beneficiary with a life interest (TA 1988 s 689A).

Interest on government stocks

4. If the trustees had so elected, the interest on the Government Stock in the example would have been paid gross. There is a cash flow advantage of receiving gross interest, because payments on account are made half-yearly on 31 January in the tax year and 31 July following, with a later balancing payment (or repayment), on the next following 31 January. See Example 44 explanatory note 4 for the rules for paying gross interest on *all* government stocks from 6 April 1998.

Bank and building society interest

5. Tax is deducted from both building society interest and bank interest paid to trustees of discretionary trusts, providing in the case of bank interest on deposits made before 6 April 1995 that the trustees or HMRC have notified the bank since that date that the income is income of a discretionary trust (TA 1988 s 481(5B)).

Lease premiums

6. In relation to the let property, although the lease premium is a capital amount, it is chargeable in part to income tax under ITTOIA 2005 s 277 (formerly TA 1988 s 34) thus reducing the amount of the credit to capital.

Therefore the taxable property income is:

		2005/06 £		2006/07 £
Rents receivable		11,300		11,300
Premium			10,000	
Less: Treated as part disposal for capital gains tax 2% for (21 − 1) yrs = 40%			4,000	6,000
		11,300		17,300
Less: Expenses – Repairs	200		400	
– Loan interest	350	550	550	950
		10,750		16,350

As a capital receipt, however, the lease premium is not subject to the rate applicable to trusts, and is therefore deducted in calculating the tax payable under TA 1988 s 686 (see note 1).

Since the lease premium is a non-recurring item, the trustees might think it appropriate to apply to reduce the payments on account for 2007/08. If, however, the final liability proves to be higher than the payments on account actually made (up to the total of the payments due without a claim, ie £5,099), interest would be charged on the shortfall from the half-yearly payment dates, the rate of interest at the time of writing being 6.5% per annum (from 6 September 2005).

If the payments on account had exceeded the liability for 2006/07, interest at the appropriate rate (2.25% per annum from 6 September 2005) would be paid on the overpayment from the respective dates that the half-yearly instalments were paid to the date the repayment order was issued. There should therefore be a non-taxable credit to income in the trust accounts, equal to the interest that would have been received, the credit to capital for the lease premium being reduced accordingly (in addition to being reduced by the income tax on the premium plus capital gains tax, if any).

Investment advice

7. The cost of investment advice is of a capital nature and is not allowable for additional rate tax notwithstanding the authority of the trust deed to charge it to income (Carver v Duncan and Bosanquet v Allen 1985). Nonetheless, the trust deed authorises the expenses to be charged to income, so that the amount available for distribution to income beneficiaries is reduced accordingly.

Income payments to discretionary beneficiaries

8. Any income payments made to beneficiaries of discretionary trusts are treated for income tax as being amounts paid net of 34% tax for 1996/97 to 2003/04 or 40% for 2004/05 onwards.

Under TA 1988 s 687 trustees are required to account for tax at the rate applicable to trusts on income paid out in exercise of their discretion to beneficiaries. In arriving at the amount payable, they may deduct the tax that has been accounted for already on the trust non-dividend income that is liable to the rate applicable to trusts and on the trust dividend income at the excess of the tax at the dividend trust rate of 32.5% over non-repayable tax credits (see Example 47 explanatory note 11 for further details). Note that the amount of tax deductible will not always cover the full amount of tax paid by the trustees, because the trustees' expenses have to come out of the taxed income of the trust. This is not relevant, however, where, as in the example, the expenses have come out of dividend income, so that the dividend credits are used to cover the tax, because the dividend credits, being non-repayable, are not taken into account under s 687 in any event.

In many instances the 'pool' of tax under s 687 will exceed the amount that is due, so that no amount will be payable, as shown in part (3) of the example. In this example there is the further point that the cost of investment advice was not allowable in calculating the tax due at the rate applicable to trusts, but nevertheless reduced the income available for distribution.

9.   From 6 April 1999 the fact that dividend credits are not repayable means that unless there is an unused pool of tax brought forward, the maximum distribution that can be made out of dividend income is 66% of the tax credit exclusive amount until 2003/04 and 60% for 2004/05 onwards.

The effect on the amount available for beneficiaries in part (2) of the example is as follows:

	2005/06 £	2006/07 £
Tax credit inclusive dividend income (net of trust expenses)		
(3,200 – 450)	2,750	
(2,762 – 500)		2,262
Less: Tax credits 10%	275	226
Tax credit exclusive amounts	2,475	2,036
60% thereof	1,485	1,222
Amount shown as available for beneficiaries per part (2)	8,160	5,457
Dividend income included therein as above	2,750	2,262
Less: Tax at dividend trust rate of 32.5%	893	735
	1,857	1,527
Actual amount available as above	1,485	1,222
Further reduction required	372	305
Reducing amount available for distribution to	7,788	5,152

As stated above, higher distributions could be made to the extent that the tax was covered by the pool of unutilised tax brought forward.

Tax credits on pre 6 April 1999 dividends *were* repayable and were thus included in the s 687 pool. If those dividends had not been distributed before 6 April 1999, therefore, the credits will be available to cover tax on a post 5 April 1999 distribution.

FOTRA securities

10.   Government securities held by someone who is neither resident nor ordinarily resident in the UK are free of UK tax, such securities being referred to as FOTRA securities (ITTOIA 2005 ss 713–716 (formerly FA 1996 s 154) and ITTOIA 2005 ss 153, 713 (formerly FA 1998 s 161)). If a discretionary trust holds such securities and makes distributions to beneficiaries who are both not resident and not ordinarily resident in the UK, then under Concession B18, a repayment claim may be made based upon the proportion of exempt income over total income (before charges) of tax credits attributed to distributions. Under the concession, the distribution is treated as made rateably out of income on a

last in first out basis. Relief is available for payments out of income arising not earlier than 6 years before the end of the tax year of payment, providing the trustees have filed tax returns and paid all tax, interest, surcharges and penalties due. Claims must be made within five years from 31 January following the relevant tax year.

The claim by B re the distribution of £3,700 to him in 2006/07 will be regarded as relating wholly to the 2006/07 trust income, since that income exceeds the amount of the distribution.

The tax accounted for by the trustees for 2006/07 on the distribution of £3,700 is £2,467 per part (3) of the example. The repayment available to B is the proportion of that amount that the £900 interest on the Government Stock bears to the 2006/07 total income before charges of (21,512 − 6,000 =) £15,512 (the lease premium not being taken into account since it is a capital receipt). This amounts to £143 as shown in part (4) of the example.

Income paid to settlor's children

11.   Where income is paid to an unmarried minor child of the settlor, it is treated as income of the settlor in the year of distribution (ITTOIA 2005 ss 629, 631 (formerly TA 1988 s 660B)) and taxed as the highest part of that income (ITTOIA 2005 ss 619, 621, 623 (formerly TA 1988 s 660C) – see Example 42 for details). Provided the trust is UK resident, full credit is given to the settlor for the tax paid by the trustees at the rate applicable to trusts (TA 1988 s 687).

By Revenue concession A93 this treatment is extended to tax paid by non-resident trusts to the extent that the distribution to the child is made out of income that arose not earlier than 6 years before the end of the year of distribution (on a last in first out basis). Credit will be given to the extent that the distribution is made from income chargeable to UK tax and the trustees have complied with their UK obligations, ie filed tax returns and paid all tax, interest, surcharges and penalties due. No credit will be given for non-repayable tax, eg on dividends. Such tax will not, however, be taken into account in calculating the gross income taxable on the settlor under the concession. Claims under the concession must be made within five years from 31 January following the tax year in which the beneficiary received the payment from the trust.

Anti-avoidance provisions re payments made by discretionary trusts to companies

12.   Before F(No2)A 1997, companies with surplus franked investment income who had made trading losses could obtain repayment of the tax credits in the franked investment income. This is not possible for periods from 2 July 1997. To prevent companies circumventing the rules by routing dividends through discretionary trusts, thus receiving the income not in the form of dividends but as annual payments from which income tax had been deducted, TA 1988 s 687A provides that payments made to a *company* by a discretionary trust are not liable to corporation tax in the receiving company's hands, but the income tax deducted from the payments by the trustees is not repayable. This does not apply if the recipient company is a charity, heritage body etc, and it only applies to a non-resident company if the payments would otherwise be chargeable to corporation tax as income of a UK branch or agency. It is not common for companies to receive payments from discretionary trusts, but these provisions are aimed at preventing possible abuse.

A. Mrs Spencer, who was born on 3 April 1937, has a life interest in income under a will trust established by her late husband who died on 30 May 2005.

The trust fund consists of loan stocks and similar securities having a nominal value of £50,000, the interest on which is received gross. In addition a small building society deposit account is held on which interest is received net of income tax.

During the year to 5 April 2007 the trustees had the following transactions:

(i) On 16 December 2006 contracted to purchase £69,780 nominal of 7% Treasury Stock for settlement on 17 December 2006. The interest payment dates of this stock are 22 May and 22 November.

(ii) On 5 May 2006 contracted to sell £2,059 nominal National Midland 9% Unsecured Loan Stock for settlement on 6 May 2006. The interest payment dates of this stock are 30 June and 31 December.

During the year to 5 April 2007 the trustees received the following income (no expenses being incurred):

	£
Building society interest received (net)	400
Gross income from securities	5,000

Mrs Spencer's only other income comes from state and occupational pensions totalling £15,500 gross less tax deducted of £2,000 for 2006/07.

(a) Compute the accrued income relief or charge on the will trust and state how this will be dealt with.

(b) Compute the income tax payable by or repayable to Mrs Spencer for 2006/07.

B. Outline the tax problems for trusts in relation to:

(a) Scrip dividends

(b) Demergers.

A.   **Mrs Spencer – accrued income scheme**

(a)   *Accrued income relief or charge on will trust*

Purchase of Treasury Stock:

| Interest accrued to date of settlement | 23.11.06 to 17.12.06 | = | 25 days |

Accrued 7% x £69,780 = £4,885 x $\dfrac{25}{365}$ =   £ 334

Trustees are entitled to accrued income relief on this amount.

Sale of National Midland Stock:

| Interest accrued to date of settlement | 1.1.06 to 6.5.06 | = | 126 days |

Accrued 9% x £2,059 = £185 x $\dfrac{126}{365}$ =   £ 64

Trustees are liable to an accrued income charge on this amount.

Taxation treatment:

Accrued income charges and reliefs are taken into account in the tax year in which the next interest payment date falls after the settlement date. Accrued income charges are taxed at the rate applicable to trusts (see note 1). Accrued income relief is given by reducing the assessable interest. Charges and reliefs are not netted off unless they relate to the same kind of stock with the same interest payment dates.

The first receipt of interest on the 7% Treasury Stock will be in May 2007. From that income accrued income relief of £334 will be deducted, the balance being taxable as trust income of 2007/08. If the stock is sold before May 2007 then the accrued income relief will be deducted from the accrued income charge on sale.

The next interest payment date on the National Midland Stock was June 2006, so the £64 is taxed in 2006/07 and is liable to tax at the rate applicable to trusts of 40%. By TA 1988 s 686D(8) (introduced by FA 2005 s 14) accrued income is to be treated as income chargeable at the lower rate for the standard rate band charge. Accordingly the liability will be £64 @ 20%. The accrued income will not be assessed on Mrs Spencer, because although it is taxed as income it actually represents an accretion to capital (which is why it is taxed at the rate applicable to trusts).

As both stocks are exempt from capital gains tax no related adjustments for that tax are required.

(b)   *Income tax payable by or repayable to Mrs Spencer for 2006/07*

		£	*Tax paid* £
Pension income		15,500	2,000
Will trust (savings income):			
Securities	5,000		
Building society interest	500	5,500	100
Total income		21,000	2,100
Age allowance 7,280 less half of (21,000 – 20,100)		6,830	
		14,170	

Tax thereon:	2,150 @ 10%	215	
	6,520 @ 22%	1,434	
	5,500 @ 20% (savings income)	1,100	2,749
	14,170		
Tax payable			649

B.   (a)   **Scrip dividends**

Where a UK resident company offers scrip shares as an alternative to a cash dividend, certain shareholders taking the scrip option are treated as having income equal to the 'appropriate amount in cash' (ITTOIA 2005 s 411 (formerly TA 1988 s 249)). This means the amount of the cash option, unless it differs by more than 15% from the market value of the shares (ITTOIA 2005 ss 410–413 (formerly TA 1988 s 251)), in which case the deemed income is the market value of the shares on the first day of dealing. The notional income is deemed to be net of the dividend ordinary rate of tax of 10% and is grossed up accordingly. The grossing addition represents a notional tax credit, which is not repayable to non-taxpayers.

This treatment applies where an *individual* is beneficially entitled to the *shares*, or where the shares are received by personal representatives or by trustees for whom a cash dividend would be liable at the 'dividend trust rate' under TA 1988 s 686.

Where the shares are treated as income, the 'appropriate amount in cash', before grossing up, is treated as the capital gains cost of the scrip shares. From 6 April 1998, such scrip dividend shares are treated as a separate free-standing acquisition and are not added pro-rata to existing holdings (TCGA 1992 s 142).

As far as life interest trusts are concerned, the trustees must decide whether, in the light of trust and general law and the terms of the particular trust, the shares are received as capital or income.

HMRC's Statement of Practice (SP 4/94) gives their view of the position. They will not seek to challenge the view taken by the trustees (providing the facts support that view) if they have treated the scrip shares either as belonging to the life tenant, or as belonging to trust capital, or as being part of trust capital, but with the life tenant being compensated for the loss of the cash dividend he would have had.

If life tenant is treated as beneficially entitled to the shares

If the life tenant is treated as beneficially entitled to the shares, the trustees would be regarded as holding the shares as bare trustees (except in Scotland, where different rules apply). Any transfer to the beneficiary would therefore be disregarded. For income tax purposes the life tenant would have notional income equal to the appropriate amount in cash. For capital gains tax, the shares would not form part of the trust holding and the life tenant would be regarded as having purchased the shares separately for the 'appropriate amount in cash'. Any sale of the shares by the trustees would be regarded as a sale by the life tenant, so if the shares were sold at the time of issue under the terms of a cash offer from a broker, the last in first out identification rule would apply (see below), there would be no taper relief and there would in fact be an allowable loss because the amount paid by the broker would be less than the issue price of the shares.

If shares are treated as belonging to trust capital

If the trustees treat the shares as belonging to trust capital, there are no income tax implications and the shares are treated as normal scrip shares for capital gains tax and added to the trust's existing holding at a *nil cost*, so that the whole of their value will represent a capital gain on disposal. The trust's position when the shares are disposed of will depend on whether they have exemptions etc available to cover the potential gain. The tax liability (at present tax rates) could be nil or 40%.

If shares are treated as belonging to trust capital with cash payment to life tenant

If the trustees treat the shares as capital, but make a cash payment to the life tenant to compensate him for not getting the dividend, the treatment of the shares is the same as in the previous paragraph. The cash payment to the life tenant is not, however, an income dividend but a payment out of trust capital, so that income tax must be deducted at 22%. There may still be a problem with how much cash to pay, because if the life tenant is a basic rate taxpayer, the effective tax rate on actual dividends is only 10%. The trustees must account for the tax on the payment under TA 1988 s 350 (see Example 44 part B), and will show the payment separately on the form R185 issued to the life tenant.

If shares are treated as belonging to capital and immediately sold

If the shares are treated as an addition to capital and the trustees sell them immediately under the terms of the offer, the shares are first added to the trust's holding at a nil cost (and if the holding includes both pre 1982 and post 1982 pools each pool will attract the appropriate number of scrip shares). For sales on and after 6 April 1998, the sale is identified with acquisitions in accordance with TCGA 1992 s 106A, ie in the following order:

- acquisitions on the same day as the disposal

- acquisitions within 30 days after the disposal

- acquisitions after 5 April 1998 on a last in first out basis

- the post 1982 pool

- the pre 1982 pool.

Discretionary and accumulation trusts

The treatment of scrip dividends received by discretionary and accumulation trusts is not clear. As indicated in the second paragraph of this section, such trusts are treated as having notional income under ITTOIA 2005 ss 409–414 (formerly TA 1988 s 249(6)) if a cash dividend would have been income to which TA 1988 s 686 applies, the notional income being regarded as accompanied by a notional tax credit at 10% of the tax credit inclusive amount. If, however, the scrip dividend is required under the terms of the trust to be treated as trust capital, there is an argument that it cannot be charged to the dividend trust rate under s 686 (but that even so, since the scrip shares are within s 249, they would be treated as a free-standing acquisition for capital gains tax with a base cost equal to the 'appropriate amount in cash'). The Revenue do not share this view, and consider that the trustees are liable to tax at the excess of the dividend trust rate of 32.5% over the grossed up amount of the scrip dividend, so that a further 22.5% tax is payable. Only the tax actually paid is taken into account when calculating how much tax is payable by the trustees under s 687 on distributions to beneficiaries (see Example 42 for further details). The shares have a base cost for capital gains tax equal to the appropriate amount in cash and are treated as a free-standing acquisition, disposals being matched with acquisitions according to the rules of TCGA 1992 s 106A outlined above.

In the case of Red Discretionary Trustees v HMIT (2003) Sp C 397, IHT, the discretionary trust received a stock dividend. The settlement trustees elected to receive dividends consisting of further shares in the relevant company. The market value of the stock dividends represented taxable income — the Trust return was submitted on the basis that the stock dividend was taxable at the ordinary trust rate but the Inland Revenue amended the return to increase income tax payable to the dividend trust rate. The Special Commissioners dismissed the trustee's appeal and confirmed that the dividends were taxable at the higher dividend trust rate. This decision was confirmed by the Court of Appeal in Howell v Trippier (2004).

(b) **Demergers**

Demergers treated as exempt distributions

There is specific legislation in relation to demergers in TA 1988 ss 213–218. The legislation prevents some of the tax problems that a demerger would otherwise cause. Providing the relevant conditions are satisfied, a demerger may be classed as an 'exempt distribution', and in that event the distribution is not treated as income in the hands of the shareholders. For capital gains tax it is treated either as a reorganisation under TCGA 1992 ss 126–131 (by s 192) or a reconstruction under TCGA 1992 ss 136 and 139, depending on the type of demerger, and there is therefore neither chargeable gain nor allowable loss.

Direct demergers and indirect demergers

Demergers may either be direct demergers, where a company distributes shares in one or more 75% subsidiaries direct to its shareholders, or indirect demergers, where a company transfers either a trade or shares in its 75% subsidiaries to another company and that other company makes an issue of shares to the transferor company's shareholders.

Where there is a direct distribution in the form of shares, the shares are regarded as income in the hands of trustees (although exempt from tax as indicated above). It was, however, held in the case of Sinclair v Lee (1993) that this did not apply to an indirect demerger. The case related to ICI/Zeneca, where ICI transferred shares in its wholly owned subsidiary Zeneca Ltd to Zeneca Group plc (which was not ICI's subsidiary), and Zeneca Group plc issued shares to ICI shareholders. On the facts, this was held to be a capital distribution, the ICI holding being split for capital gains purposes into separate ICI/Zeneca holdings according to the market value of the shares on the first day after the demerger (for unquoted shares the relevant date would be the date of disposal).

This does not, however, determine the treatment of trust holdings for all demergers and it is necessary to look at the particular circumstances, and also the provisions of the particular trust. The Revenue made a detailed statement of their views in the October 1994 issue of the Tax Bulletin, a summary of which follows.

Where there is a direct demerger, the shares are regarded as *income* of the trust, because under company law they are a dividend paid out of accumulated profits. If, exceptionally, they were treated as capital, the capital gains tax treatment for the trustees would be as for individuals.

In an indirect demerger, the Revenue view is that the shares would normally be an addition to capital (following Sinclair v Lee), the capital gains treatment of the trustees being the same as for individuals, but this is not necessarily true of all indirect demergers.

Discretionary trusts

The trustees are treated in the same way as individuals, ie they are not liable to income tax or capital gains tax. If shares are then distributed to beneficiaries, they are treated for capital gains tax as a disposal of a proportionate part of the holding at market value, the cost plus the available indexation allowance for that part of the holding being allowed against the deemed proceeds.

If the trustees exercise a power to accumulate the 'income' as part of the trust fund, and later distribute the shares as capital, no income tax arises. If the shares are distributed as income rather than accumulated, the distribution is treated as being net of 40% tax (the value of the distribution being the lower of the value at the date of the demerger and the value when distributed). Since income tax will not have been paid on the demerged shares under TA 1988 s 686, the trustees may have to pay tax under s 687 (unless there is a sufficient fund of tax already accounted for). (See Example 48 for details of ss 686 and 687.)

Life interest trusts

The following relates to the treatment of English life interest trusts. (Different rules apply in Scotland.)

In a direct demerger, the shares would belong to the life tenant directly, so they would not form part of the trust's holding, the capital gains tax cost of which is unaffected. The life tenant would be treated for capital gains as acquiring the shares at market value at the date of the demerger (the distribution being other than at arm's length – TCGA 1992 s 17(1)), even though there would have been no reduction of the trustees' allowable cost. (If the trustees retained the shares, there would be a disposal of them by the life tenant to the trustees, and unless he was paid their cash value, he would be the settlor of shares into the trust.)

In an indirect demerger, the shares would usually be treated as capital as indicated above, so that they would not affect the life tenant. If *exceptionally* they were treated as income, the capital gains tax position would be the same as for a direct demerger, except that s 17(1) would not apply (because there would be no disposal by the transferor company *directly* to the share-holder), and the beneficiary's capital gains tax cost would be nil.

For direct demergers, there would be no income tax on the life tenants (because of s 213) nor on the trustees under TA 1988 ss 686, 687, since the shares are treated as belonging to the life tenant. The same would apply where, exceptionally, shares are treated as income in an indirect demerger. If the shares are treated as capital, the trustees would have no income tax liability. If, however, they then distributed the shares under provisions in the trust deed, such that the shares were income in the hands of the life tenant, the trustees would have to deduct tax and pay it over to the Revenue under s 350.

Explanatory Notes

Accrued income scheme

1.   The accrued income scheme provisions are in TA 1988 ss 710–728. A consultation document proposing amendments to the scheme was issued in conjunction with Budget 2004. The consultation period has now ended but no legislation has yet been forthcoming although it was intended for incorporation in the 2006 Finance Bill.

The accrued income scheme causes particular difficulties in relation to trusts. The scheme treats amounts that are capital sums under the general (and trust) law as being income for tax purposes and tax is charged (or refunded) accordingly.

The fact that the sums are to be accumulated as part of capital, rather than being income of a beneficiary, is, however, recognised by s 720(5), which provides that the trustees are taxed in respect of accrued income charges at the rate applicable to trusts, ie 40%. However s 686D(8)(a) provides that for the standard rate such deemed income is chargeable at the lower rate. Mrs Spencer's trust is only liable to tax at special trust rates on accrued income of £64, as this is less than £500. The whole is chargeable at the lower rate (ie 20%).

These rules can lead to an anomaly. The trustees could receive a reduction for accrued income relief at lower rate but be liable at special rate on an amount in excess of £500 and have to pay tax at 40% on the excess. Individuals are charged at the savings rate on accrued interest, but this does not apply to trustees.

Because the accrued income charges represent capital sums, they do not form part of a beneficiary's income and are not shown on form R185.

The trustees then have the problem of how to deal with accrued income charges and accrued income reliefs in the trust accounts. The Accounting Recommendations of the Institute of Chartered Accountants state that where a life tenant may be interested in such accruals, consideration should be given to accounting for the interest and the associated tax on an accruals basis when the securities are purchased and sold. The alternative view, which the authors prefer, is that the accruals treatment should not apply to accrued income charges, and that the tax on accrued income charges should be debited to the capital account of the trust as it would have been if it had been capital gains tax.

There is also doubt as to the treatment of accrued income relief. The relief reduces the trustees' income for tax purposes as shown in part A (a) above, and the beneficiary's income for tax purposes is similarly reduced, so that in 2007/08 Mrs Spencer's interest from the 7% Treasury Stock shown on form R185 will be the gross interest of (7% x £69,780 =) £4,885, reduced by £334, giving taxable income of £4,551. Tax thereon amounts to £910 compared with tax on £4,885 of £977. The reduction of £334 at 20% = £67 in the tax payable will have been reflected in the amount payable by the trustees under self-assessment. If tax had been deducted at source from the interest, the trustees would have a tax refund of £67. The question then is how much should the trustees actually pay to Mrs Spencer. HMRC have stated that this is a matter for the trustees in accordance with the general law, and whatever is paid will not affect the tax treatment. There are several possibilities:

(a)   Taxable income £4,551 less tax £910 = £3,641.

(b)   Actual gross income £4,885 less tax thereon £977 = £3,908.

(c)   As (b) plus tax reduction of £67 = £3,975.

The trustees have actually received net income of £3,908 and have had a tax reduction of £67, and some people therefore favour paying the beneficiary £3,975 as in (c). Before the introduction of the accrued income scheme, however, the part of the purchase price representing accrued interest, ie £334, would have been part of the capital cost of the security. The authors take the view that the logical approach is to regard the £67 as a reduction in the cost and to pay to the beneficiary what would previously have been paid, ie £3,908. Thus both accrued income charges and accrued income reliefs would be dealt with through the trust capital account.

Scope of accrued income provisions

2.   The accrued income provisions apply to 'transfers'. This means 'transfer by way of sale, exchange, gift or otherwise' (s 710(5)), and would include a settlement of securities by an individual, and a transfer of securities to beneficiaries on termination of a trust, as well as the trustees buying and selling the trust securities. The provisions do not apply where securities are vested in an individual's personal representatives on his death (s 710(5)). Nor do they apply if the personal representatives transfer the securities to legatees or to those entitled on an intestacy in the interest period in which the individual died (s 721). There is no exemption for a transfer in a later interest period.

Scrip dividends and demergers

3.   The problems of trustees who receive scrip dividends or shares on a demerger are outlined in part B of the example. The Revenue have given detailed comments on their views, but there are many grey areas which it would be difficult to resolve, even with amended legislation, because of the mismatch between trust law and tax law.

       As far as scrip dividends are concerned, where the shares are worth the same as the cash dividend, the simple way to avoid problems is to take the cash. The enhanced scrip dividends which were offered by listed companies a few years ago were worth half as much again as the cash dividend, and there was the option of obtaining the extra cash by selling immediately, thus giving rise to the particular problems mentioned in the example. Such offers have not been made recently, although enhanced scrip offers may arise in other circumstances.

Purchase by company of own shares etc

4.   Where a company redeems, repays or purchases its own shares from the trustees of a settlement, the excess of the amount paid over the original issue price is treated as if it were an income distribution with a notional tax credit attached, and the trustees are liable to tax at the excess of the dividend trust rate of 32.5% over the tax credit rate of 10%, so that a further 22.5% is payable (TA 1988 s 686A). This does not apply where the trust income is treated as belonging to the settlor, or where the trust is a unit trust, charitable trust, or pension trust (or presumably where the trust is a bare trust — see Example 64 explanatory note 8), but it applies to all other trusts, including interest in possession trusts.

       If the purchase is by an unquoted trading company in order to benefit its trade, and specified conditions are satisfied, the purchase is treated as a chargeable disposal for capital gains tax rather than as an income distribution (TA 1988 ss 219 to 229).

Cross references

5.   See Example 44 explanatory note 4 for the provisions that apply from 6 April 1998 for receiving interest gross on government stocks, Example 43 explanatory note 7 for the provisions that apply for receiving interest gross on listed company securities and Example 47 for the self-assessment provisions in relation to trusts.

A.   The termination of a life interest in settled property can occur in various circumstances, including:

(a)   where, on the death of the life tenant, the settlement (or a part) comes to an end,

(b)   where, on the life tenant's death, there is a successive life tenancy,

(c)   where the life tenant dies and the property passes to the original settlor, and

(d)   where the interest ceases otherwise than on the death of the life tenant.

State the capital gains tax situation in each of the events (a) to (d) above, giving appropriate statutory references.

B.   Outline the capital gains tax taper relief introduced by FA 1998, with particular reference to its effect on trusts.

C.   Where capital gains tax is payable by trustees, state the position regarding the capital gains tax rate and the annual exemption, and indicate the position if the settlor has retained an interest in the settlement.

A. **Termination of life interests in settled property — capital gains tax treatment**

(a) *Where the settlement or part thereof comes to an end on the death of the life tenant*

The settled property to which someone becomes entitled is deemed to be disposed of at market value and immediately reacquired by the trustees, but no chargeable gain (or allowable loss) arises on the disposal except as indicated below (TCGA 1992 ss 71–73). In other words there is an adjustment to the base cost of the settled property and the trustees then hold that property as bare trustees for the person entitled thereto.

Where the asset disposed of, or part thereof, was the subject of a claim for gifts holdover relief under TCGA 1992 s 165 or s 260 (or FA 1980 s 79 for holdover claims before 14 March 1989) when the trustees acquired it, then a chargeable gain will arise, restricted to the amount of the heldover gain less any available taper relief according to the period of ownership of the trustees (TCGA 1992 s 74). A further holdover relief claim may, however, be made if the property is qualifying property, as in (d) below, in which case it is the untapered gain that is held over and taper relief will depend on the period of ownership of the person acquiring the asset). (Taper relief is dealt with in detail in part B.)

If the trustees' acquisition was after 31 March 1982 and before 6 April 1988, and the heldover gain under FA 1980 s 79 was attributable directly or indirectly, in whole or in part, to the disposal of an asset acquired before 31 March 1982, it appears that where the deemed disposal of the trust assets occurs on or after 6 April 1988, the deferred charges provisions of TCGA 1992 Sch 4 will apply to reduce the chargeable gain to one half of the heldover gain. Where the trustees' acquisition was after 5 April 1981 (when gifts relief was introduced for gifts to trustees) and before 31 March 1982 and the asset is disposed of on or after 6 April 1988, it is understood that the Revenue will accept that the heldover gain escapes tax even though the legislation does not strictly cover this situation.

Where the life interest did not extend to the whole of the settled property to which someone became entitled on the life tenant's death, then there is no exemption from the capital gains charge on the deemed disposal, but any gain arising is reduced by a proportion representing the life tenant's interest (TCGA 1992 s 73).

A further instance where a chargeable gain arises is where deferral relief has been claimed in respect of a subscription for enterprise investment scheme shares (see explanatory note 7).

(b) *Where, on the life tenant's death, there is a successive life tenancy*

The consequences are similar to those in (a) above. The settled property is deemed to be disposed of at market value and immediately reacquired by the trustees, but no chargeable gain arises on the disposal (TCGA 1992 s 72), other than any gain held over under the gifts holdover provisions (TCGA 1992 s 74) or enterprise investment scheme deferral relief provisions (see explanatory note 7). The provisions in (a) concerning the halving of the chargeable gain where it relates to an asset acquired before 31 March 1982 and exempting a gain arising before 31 March 1982, and the possibility of a further holdover relief claim (and taper relief consequences), would also apply in these circumstances.

(c) *Where the life tenant dies and the property passes to the original settlor*

There is a deemed disposal and reacquisition of the settled property as in (a) above, but the consideration is deemed to be such that no gain or loss accrues to the trustees, after taking any available indexation allowance into account (TCGA 1992 ss 73 and 56). The indexation allowance incorporated into the acquisition cost cannot, however, create or increase a loss on a subsequent disposal, so that it is necessary to have a separate record of the cost and the indexation. Taper relief would not be taken into account until the settlor disposed of the property, and would then be based on the period of ownership of the settlor from the time he reacquired it.

If the trustees first acquired the property before 6 April 1965 the disposal and reacquisition are deemed to be at that earlier date (except as regards taper relief, for which the actual date of transfer applies). This means that the settlor effectively reacquires the asset at the value it had when originally settled by him, but he retains his right to use time apportionment if appropriate in calculating any gain when he disposes of the asset.

Where the property reverts to the settlor after 31 March 1982 then the original settlor is also deemed to have held the assets on 31 March 1982 (providing the settlement actually owned the assets on that date). Therefore on a subsequent disposal by the original settlor it is possible to treat the assets as acquired at market value as at 31 March 1982 even though the assets were actually owned by the settlement on that date.

(d)   *Where the life interest ceases otherwise than on the death of the life tenant*

Such a termination has no capital gains tax effect if the property remains in trust, and the capital gains tax base value of the property remains the same. If, however, a beneficiary becomes absolutely entitled to any property against the trustees at that time, there is a deemed disposal and reacquisition at market value as bare trustees, and the trustees are chargeable to capital gains tax accordingly (TCGA 1992 s 71) (subject to any halving of gains held over between 31 March 1982 and 5 April 1988 as indicated in part (a) and subject to any available indexation allowance and taper relief). A claim may, however, be made by the trustees and beneficiary jointly for any gain to be held over under the provisions of TCGA 1992 s 165 and Sch 7 if the property consists of any of the following:

Assets used in a business by the trustees or the life tenant
Unquoted shares in a trading company
Shares in a trading company in which the trustees hold 25% or more of the voting rights
Property that would qualify for agricultural property relief (Sch 7.1–7.3).

Taper relief will then not apply at the time of the deferral and will depend on the subsequent period of ownership of the beneficiary.

Before FA 1999, if losses arose on the property transferred to the beneficiary, or if and to the extent that brought forward losses related to an asset previously sold at a loss that was represented by property transferred (for example if cash from such disposals was transferred to the beneficiary), they were first set against any gains the trustees had made earlier in the tax year on other property, then any excess losses were transferred to the beneficiary (TCGA 1992 s 71(2)).

Where a beneficiary becomes absolutely entitled on or after 16 June 1999, s 71(2) is amended by FA 1999 s 75 to provide that:

(i)   Losses on actual disposals by the trustees before the beneficiary becomes absolutely entitled cannot be transferred to the beneficiary. Such losses will remain losses of the trustees, for which relief may be obtained within the trust according to the normal rules.

(ii)   Losses arising on the deemed market value transfer to the beneficiary that the trustees cannot use against gains arising at the time of the transfer of the property or earlier in the same tax year will be treated as made by the beneficiary who has become absolutely entitled to the asset, but the beneficiary will be able to use the loss only to reduce a gain on the disposal of the asset, or in the case of land, an asset derived from the land.

These changes were made to prevent abuse of the rules by artificial schemes enabling people unconnected with a trust to purchase the trust losses, including schemes set up specifically to manufacture losses within trusts to be used in this way.

See explanatory note 3 re the connected persons rules.

If someone with an interest in a settlement (either a life interest or a reversionary interest) sells his interest, the disposal is not subject to capital gains tax (unless the interest was acquired for money or money's worth) (TCGA 1992 s 76(1)). The exemption does not, however, apply to disposals on or after 6 March 1998 of an interest in a trust whose trustees have at any time been not resident or not ordinarily resident in the UK (s 76(1A), (1B)). If a reversionary interest was purchased, then when the purchaser becomes absolutely entitled to the assets of the settlement, he is deemed to have disposed of his interest for the then market value of the assets (TCGA 1992 s 76(2)). This charge is in addition to any charge on the trustees under TCGA 1992 s 71 (as above). The assets to which the purchaser becomes entitled then have a base value equal to that market value.

If the disposal takes place at a time when the trustees are neither resident nor ordinarily resident in the UK, then the exemption in s 76(1) does not apply, even if the interest in the settlement was not acquired for money or money's worth (TCGA 1992 s 85). Some relief is, however, available in certain circumstances where the trust became non-resident after 18 March 1991 (s 85(2)–(9)).

The treatment of the disposal for a consideration of an interest in settled property was changed for certain disposals on or after 21 March 2000 by TCGA 1992 s 76A and Schedule 4A. The revised provisions apply where the trust is UK resident or ordinarily resident in the tax year of disposal, the settlor is or has been resident or ordinarily resident in the UK in the current year or in any of the previous five tax years (excluding years before 1999/2000), and the settlor has an interest in the trust (or has had an interest at any time in the period commencing two years before the start of the tax year of disposal and ending with the date of disposal, excluding any period before 6 April 1999). Where a beneficiary sells an interest in such a trust, the trustees are deemed to dispose of and reacquire all the trust assets at market value, and the settlor is charged on the resulting gains (unless the disposal is of an interest in a specific fund, in which case the deemed disposal relates to the assets in that fund, or the disposal is an interest in a specific fraction of the income or capital, in which case the deemed disposal is of that fraction of the underlying assets). The settlor will not be able to claim gifts holdover relief in respect of the gains. He may, however, recover from the trustees the tax suffered (TCGA 1992 s 78), and they in turn may recover the tax from the beneficiary who sold the interest (Sch 4A.11).

B.   **Capital gains tax taper relief**

Introduction of taper relief

FA 1998 froze indexation allowance for non-corporate taxpayers at April 1998 and introduced a taper relief instead (TCGA 1992 s 2A and Sch A1). Taper relief is given for complete years of ownership from 6 April 1998 and the rate of relief depends on whether the asset is a business or non-business asset, being up to 75% for business assets and up to 40% for non-business assets. The relief in each case is given for complete years of ownership from the date of acquisition of the asset (or 6 April 1998 if later) and the maximum relief is reached after ten years. An extra year is added to the qualifying period if the asset was acquired before 17 March 1998. Following FA 2000 s 67 the definition of business asset was significantly widened, and s 160 of the FA 2003 relaxed further the conditions determining whether assets other than company shares or securities qualify as business assets. The main effect of this change is that assets used wholly or partly for trades carried on by individuals, personal representatives and trustees will qualify as business assets irrespective of whether the owner of the asset is involved in carrying on the trade involved. The new provisions came into effect for periods of ownership from 6 April 2004.

The maximum rate of relief on business assets applies after two years for disposals on or after 6 April 2002 (FA 2002 s 46). From 6 April 2000, however, business assets no longer qualify for the extra year for pre 17 March 1998 ownership. Non-business assets do not qualify for relief until after three complete years of ownership, but they still qualify for the extra year if they were acquired before

17 March 1998. For the definition of business assets, including changes to the definitions of trading company and trading group made by FA 2002 Sch 10.9 and 10.10, see part (ii) of the capital gains tax summary in Example 36 part (a).

Where an asset has not been a business asset throughout the period of ownership, the gain is split on a time apportionment basis according to the usage over the last ten years (or since 6 April 1998 if shorter) and the gains are regarded as arising on separate business and non-business assets. The period after 5 April 1998 for which the asset is regarded as held is not, however, affected. These provisions have to be applied where a non-business asset has become a business asset under the new definition from 6 April 2000. See Example 40 part (a) for an illustration. Where there is mixed use of an asset, the appropriate fraction of the gain is deemed to relate to a business/non-business asset.

Taper relief is subject to various anti-avoidance provisions.

Business and non-business assets in relation to trusts

For detailed notes on this see Example 36 part (a)(ii) on page 36.2.

Position on gifts holdover relief

Where gifts holdover relief is claimed either under TCGA 1992 s 165 or s 260, the amount held over is the untapered gain. Taper relief is then given by reference to the holding period of the transferee. This is dealt with in part A of the example.

Gains attributed to settlors and to beneficiaries of non-resident settlements

Where trustees' gains are attributed to settlors of resident trusts as indicated in part C, or to settlors or beneficiaries of non-resident settlements as indicated in Example 51, the attributed gains will not be reduced by taper relief, any taper relief available to the trustees already having been taken into account in arriving at the attributed gains (TCGA 1992 ss 77, 86 and 87). (But see below for the position for 2003/04 onwards.)

Any personal losses of the settlors or beneficiaries cannot be used to reduce the gains. The settlor's or beneficiary's annual exemption is, however, first used against any trust gains charged on him before applying the rules relating to brought forward losses, so that his brought forward losses reduce his own untapered gains only to the extent that such gains remain after setting off any balance of his annual exemption not used against the trust gains (TCGA 1992 s 2). (But see below for 2003/04 onwards.)

The treatment of gains taxed on settlors changed for 2003/04 and later years (TCGA 1992 ss 2, 77, 86, 86A, 87). Under the revised provisions, subject to the exception mentioned below where a settlor has been temporarily non-resident, trust gains that are treated as gains of the settlor will be calculated without being reduced by taper relief. Any personal losses of the settlor that cannot be set against his personal gains will be set against the trust gains, and taper relief will apply to the gains remaining. The rate of taper relief on the trust gains will be the same as that which would have applied to the trustees.

The above provisions will not apply where gains are taxed on a settlor under the temporary non-residence rules after being reduced by gains already taxed on beneficiaries (see Example 51 explanatory note 12). The above FA 2002 rules will still apply to such gains, so that the amount on which the settlor will be charged will be the tapered amount, and he will not be able to reduce such gains by his personal losses.

Similarly FA 2003 s 163 and Sch 29 introduce a change to ensure that where the beneficiary is chargeable under TCGA 1992 Sch 4C and the amount charged is reduced by any amount already charged on a settlor (by virtue of TCGA 1992 s 86) the amount by which it is reduced is the tapered rather than the untapered amount.

How taper relief is given and interaction with annual exemption

Subject to what is said above in connection with gains attributed to settlors, taper relief is applied to the chargeable gains net of allowable losses in the same year and also net of losses brought forward from earlier years. Losses are set against gains so as to give the lowest tax charge, which means setting them first against any gains on which no taper relief is available, then against gains with less taper relief before other gains.

The annual exemption reduces chargeable gains after taking into account taper relief, so that all or part of the exemption may be wasted. Before FA 1998 it was provided that brought forward losses were not set against gains covered by the annual exemption. This still applies from 6 April 1998, but if the gains exceed the annual exemption, any brought forward losses that are used against gains must be set off *before* taper relief as indicated above, so the annual exemption may still be effectively wasted.

C. **Capital gains tax rate etc**

Charging gains to tax

Subject to what follows, and what is said below regarding trusts in which the settlor retains an interest, trustees are chargeable to tax on their chargeable gains less allowable losses as for individuals. There are anti-avoidance provisions in TCGA 1992 s 79A that prevent losses arising on trustees' disposals being set against gains they make on or after 21 March 2000 on assets that had been transferred to the trust if the transferor or someone connected with him had bought an interest in the trust and had claimed gifts holdover relief on the transferred assets.

The capital gains tax rate for all trusts other than bare trusts is 40%, except where gains are taxed on a settlor as indicated below (TCGA 1992 s 4). The 40% rate also applies to personal representatives of a deceased's estate.

Trusts in which settlor retains an interest

Where both the settlor and the trustees are resident or ordinarily resident in the UK and the settlor or spouse has or may have a present or future interest in the income or property of the settlement, or enjoys a benefit from the settlement (eg free use of property or an interest-free loan) then the chargeable gains of the settlement are treated as belonging to the settlor and therefore chargeable at his marginal rate(s) of tax (TCGA 1992 ss 77–79 — see part B above). (This is subject to an exception in respect of income from assets given or interest free or low interest rate loans made to charity – see Example 46 notes 5 and 6. See also Example 51 explanatory note 16 re anti-avoidance provisions to prevent the settlor avoiding the charge to tax.) Any tax due on such gains may be recovered by the settlor from the trustees. For this purpose the settlor may require HMRC to issue him with a certificate of the tax paid (s 78) and under s 79 HMRC may require the settlor, trustees or beneficiary to provide relevant information in relation to ss 77 and 78. There is no provision for the settlor to obtain payment from the trustees before he has paid the tax, even though the disposal proceeds relating to the gains will be in the trust.

For gains attributed between 6 April 1998 and 5 April 2003 (or earlier if the settlor so elects), the settlor cannot reduce the trust gains by his own losses. See part B above for the interaction of this provision with the provisions relating to the annual exemption and the revised treatment of losses from 2003/04 (or earlier if the settlor so elects).

Gains in the tax year in which the settlor dies are not attributed to the settlor under the above provisions. In addition if the interest or benefit relates to the spouse (and not the settlor) the provisions do not apply to gains made in the tax year in which the spouse dies or the settlor and spouse divorce.

FA 2004 s 116 and Sch 21 introduce a restriction of gift relief into the provisions of TCGA 1992 s 165 or s 260 in respect of the disposal of assets preventing gift relief being available in respect of disposals of assets to the trustees of a trust in which the settlor has an interest where the disposal is made on or after 10 December 2003.

These provisions will also claw back or prevent any gifts relief in relation to disposals made after 10 December 2003 to trusts which become settlor-interested settlements within a certain time period.

This period begins immediately after the disposal and ends immediately before the sixth anniversary of the start of the tax year next following that in which the disposal is made.

There are exclusions from the provisions in disposals to settlements benefiting disabled persons or which provide maintenance income for historic buildings.

FA 2004 s 117 and Sch 22 are intended to complement and extend s 116 and Sch 21.

The effect is to prevent private residence relief (PPR) being available in certain circumstances where the trustees of a settlement make a disposal on or after 10 December 2003.

The circumstances arise where the computation of the amount of any gains arising on the disposal has to take account of gift relief obtained in respect of an earlier disposal.

This is subject to a transitional provision restricting the amount of relief available in respect of the disposal if there has been no earlier disposal on or after 10 December 2003.

These provisions do not apply where the gain arising on the disposal in not in any way affected by a gifts relief claim under TCGA 1992 s 260.

Capital gains tax annual exemption

Where tax is chargeable in the name of the trustees on a heldover gain, or under the provisions in part A (d) above, or on disposals of trust assets by the trustees, the trustees can claim an annual exemption equal to half the amount exempt for an individual, ie £4,400 for 2006/07.

If, however, the same person is the settlor in relation to more than one trust created after 6 June 1978 (excluding charitable trusts), the exemption of £4,400 is divided between those trusts, with a minimum exempt slice for each trust of £880 (TCGA 1992 Sch 1.2(3)). This rule applies to settlements arising under a will or intestacy as well as those created in lifetime.

If the trust is a trust for the disabled, the full annual exemption of £8,800 is available, reduced pro rata if there is more than one disabled trust established by the same settlor after 9 March 1981, with a minimum slice for each trust of £880 (TCGA 1992 Sch 1.1).

No trust annual exemption is available if the settlor has retained an interest in the trust, as indicated above.

Explanatory Notes

Types of trust and amendments to IHT and CGT treatment in Finance Act 2006

1. The main types of trust are bare trusts, trusts with an interest in possession, discretionary trusts and accumulation and maintenance trusts.

   Where someone is a bare trustee this means that the beneficiary is absolutely entitled to the trust property as against the trustee. The capital gains treatment is therefore to look through the trust and to deem the trustee's acts as being those of the beneficiary (TCGA 1992 s 60). For further details, and also for the treatment of accumulation and maintenance trusts, see Example 64.

   Most interest in possession trusts are life interest trusts, but sometimes an interest may cease earlier, for example if a widow remarries. The treatment of life interest trusts in part A of the example applies to *all* interest in possession trusts and also on the death of an annuitant (TCGA 1992 ss 72, 73).

   Inheritance Tax Act 1984 (TA) sets out the rules for discretionary trusts (strictly, 'relevant property' trusts). These include:

   - an immediate 'entry' tax charge of 20% on lifetime transfers that exceed the inheritance tax (IHT) threshold into 'relevant property' trusts;

- a 'periodic' tax charge of 6% on the value of trust assets over the IHT threshold once every ten years; and

- an 'exit' charge proportionate to the periodic charge when funds are taken out of a trust between ten year anniversaries.

However, there are special rules for 'interest in possession' (IIP) accumulation & maintenance (A&M) trusts, which are now of limited application. Lifetime transfers into these trusts are exempt from IHT if the settlor survives seven years, and the trusts are not subject to the periodic or exit charges.

FA 2006, Sch 20 provides that these special rules will in future be limited to trusts that are created:

(a) on death by a parent for a minor child who will be fully entitled to the assets in the trust at age 18, or

(b) on death for the benefit of one life tenant in order of time only (more than one such interest may be created on death as long as the trust capital vests absolutely when the life interest comes to an end), or

(c) either in the settlor's lifetime or on death for a disabled person.

The IHT treatment for trusts which do not come within these rules have been brought into line with the mainstream IHT rules for 'relevant property' trusts. These changes took effect from 22 March 2006, subject to transitional arrangements for some pre-existing trusts.

The previous rules for existing IIP trusts will run on until the interest in the trust property at 22 March 2006 comes to an end. Any new IIP that arises when an IIP created before 22 March 2006 comes to an end before 6 April 2008 — whether on death or otherwise — will be treated as an IIP that was in place before 22 March 2006.

TA 1988 s 49 (which treats property subject to an interest-in-possession as owned for IHT purposes by the person having the interest) is restricted to a specified class of trusts where the interest arises on or after 22 March 2006, namely:

(i)   an 'immediate post-death interest (49A)',

(ii) a 'disabled person's interest (89A)', or

(iii) a 'transitional serial interest (49B-49E)'.

TA 1988 s 49A, which sets out the conditions to be satisfied by an 'immediate post-death interest' (IPDI) is expanded: broadly, so that the interest arises immediately on the death of the settlor. This applies to interests created by a will or on intestacy.

New tests are introduced, at new s 49C, for transitional protection as a 'transitional serial interest' (TSI). An interest in possession arising before 6 April 2008 will qualify if it arises on or after 22 March 2006 but follows a previous interest in possession in effect before that date. Alternatively, s 49D covers transitional serial interests where the new interest arises on or after 6 April 2008. This is, however, limited to cases where the second interest is held by the widow or surviving civil partner and acquired on the death of the previous life tenant.

Broadly, where existing A&M trusts provide that the assets in trust will go to a beneficiary absolutely at 18 — or where the terms on which they are held are modified before 6 April 2008 to provide this — their current IHT treatment will continue.

For a new A&M trust if the capital is left on fully flexible trust with no set date for the beneficiary to become absolutely entitled, the trust will become subject to the 6% rule on the death of the parent and will remain so until the beneficiary is paid out.

For new and old A&M type arrangements, the trusts will not become subject to the 6% regime until the child reaches age 18 and this will continue until they become absolutely entitled at age 25. There will be no 20% entry charge. However, for new arrangements (ie trust property settled after 21 March 2006), this applies only if one of the child's parents has died and the trust was established under the will of the parent or under the Criminal Injuries Compensation Scheme.

For existing A&M settlements where beneficiaries are under age 18 at the end of the transitional period on 6 April 2008, they will not be subject to the 6% charge until they reach age 18 provided the trust is modified before 6 April 2008.

The new IHT rules for trusts have consequences for capital gains tax (CGT). Some of the necessary changes will happen automatically — for example, transfers into and out of trusts that will now come within the 'relevant property' rules will automatically be eligible for CGT hold-over relief.

There is an amendment to the current CGT treatment of trust property on the death of a person having an interest-in-possession so that for interests created on or after 22 March 2006 it applies only to the above categories of IIP. The rule at TCGA 1992 s 72 is amended. This applies when a life interest comes to an end but the property continues to be held on trust; and there is a further amendment to the rule at s 73 which applies where the property ceases to be held on trust once the life interest comes to an end.

2.   Trustees are treated as a continuing body of persons distinct from those who may from time to time occupy the position of trustee, and gains arising on the disposal of trust assets are assessable on the trustees (other than bare trustees, as indicated in note 1 above, or trusts in which the settlor retains an interest) (TCGA 1992 s 69).

Creation of settlement

3.   When a settlement is created the settlor is deemed to have disposed of the entire property in the settlement at its market value, even if he retains an interest as beneficiary or is a trustee under the settlement, and he is therefore chargeable to capital gains tax accordingly (subject to any available reliefs and exemptions).

If the assets transferred are business assets (as defined by TCGA 1992 s 165) or the transfer is *immediately* chargeable to inheritance tax (whether or not there is any actual inheritance tax payable (TCGA 1992 s 260)) then the settlor can avoid paying tax on the gain by making an election to hold it over so that it reduces the trustees' base acquisition cost, and unlike other gifts relief elections the donees do not have to join in the election. For gifts into settlement on or after 10 December 2003 this facility is not available if the settlor retains an interest or the trust becomes settlor related within six years. Where the trust is a life interest trust or an accumulation and maintenance trust, gifts holdover relief is not available under s 260 (because the transfers are *potentially exempt* from inheritance tax), so gains on chargeable assets may only be held over if the assets are qualifying business assets under s 165. (For disposals between 6 April 1981 and 13 March 1989 inclusive, there was a general gifts relief available under FA 1980 s 79, under which there was no restriction in the assets in respect of which the relief could be claimed.)

In a life interest trust, the heldover gains crystallise when the life tenant dies, as indicated in part A of the example (subject to any halving of gains that were held over between 31 March 1982 and 5 April 1988 and any further holdover relief claim). In a discretionary trust, the heldover gains are similarly triggered when assets are transferred to beneficiaries (see note 5).

Where holdover relief is claimed, the amount held over is the untapered gain, taper relief being given by reference to the period of ownership of the transferee, as indicated in parts A and B of the example.

If the settlor's disposal gives rise to losses rather than gains, then under the 'connected persons' rules, the losses can only be set against gains on other disposals to the trustees. The trustees are, however, no longer connected with the settlor's spouse and relatives after the settlor's death. If the trustees and beneficiaries *are* connected, this does not prevent the trustees' losses arising from the disposal to the beneficiaries being transferred to the beneficiaries under TCGA 1992 s 71(2), as indicated in part A (d) of the example.

Emigration of trustees

4.   Before 19 March 1991 a gain held over when the funds were settled crystallised if the donee trustees emigrated. From 19 March 1991 emigrating trustees are charged not only on gains held over at the time the funds were settled but on the whole of any increase in value of the trust assets up to the time of emigration (TCGA 1992 s 80). For detailed notes on non-resident trusts see Example 51.

Persons becoming absolutely entitled to trust property

5.   TCGA 1992 s 71 applies not only when a beneficiary under an interest in possession trust becomes absolutely entitled as against the trustees, as outlined in part A (d) of the example, but also where a beneficiary of a discretionary trust becomes so entitled. The trustees are deemed to have disposed of the assets to the beneficiary at market value at that time and are chargeable to capital gains tax accordingly (subject to any halving of deferred gains as indicated in part A of the example).

The gifts holdover relief provisions of ss 165 and 260 outlined in note 3 are, however, available if the conditions are satisfied. The distribution from the discretionary trust will be a chargeable event for inheritance tax, triggering an exit charge under IHTA 1984 s 65 and thus satisfying the s 260 requirement, unless it takes place within three months after the creation of the settlement or within three months after a ten-year anniversary. There is, however, a problem in some circumstances where the settlement is an accumulation and maintenance settlement (see Example 64 explanatory note 3).

Where a discretionary trust is created by will, distributions to beneficiaries within the two years after the death (but not within the first three months) are treated as if made under the will for inheritance tax purposes (IHTA 1984 s 144 – see Example 60 explanatory note 9). For capital gains tax purposes, however, if such a distribution was of chargeable assets that had grown in value since the date of death, the trustees would be liable to tax on the gain arising under TCGA 1992 s 71 (subject to any available annual exemption), unless the business gifts holdover relief of s 165 was available. Relief under s 260 would not be available because the distribution would not be a chargeable event for inheritance tax. One way of avoiding a capital gains tax charge in these circumstances would be for the trustees to appoint assets to a beneficiary *before* the assets were appropriated to the trustees by the personal representatives. The trustees would then be bare trustees (as to which see explanatory note 1), and as and when the assets were appropriated to them by the personal representatives, the beneficiary's deemed acquisition cost would be the market value at the date of death.

Creation of life interest out of discretionary trust

6.   If property is held under a discretionary trust, and a life interest is created in the property, it has to be established whether a separate settlement has been created or whether the original settlement continues (Roome v Edwards 1981 and Bond v Pickford 1983). If the original settlement is treated as continuing, there would be no capital gains consequences on the creation of the life interest.

If the creation of the life interest was held to constitute a separate settlement, this would be an occasion of charge under TCGA 1992 s 71, since another 'person', ie the trustees of the new settlement, would become entitled to the trust property as against the trustees of the original settlement. The creation of the life interest would, however, usually result in an exit charge for inheritance tax on the discretionary trust under IHTA 1984 s 65 as indicated in note 5 above, and therefore the capital gain could be held over under TCGA 1992 s 260 and treated as reducing the acquisition cost of the property for the new trustees.

Enterprise investment scheme deferral relief

7.   If trustees reinvest gains by making a cash subscription for enterprise investment scheme (EIS) shares, they may claim deferral relief under the provisions of TCGA 1992 Sch 5B (but not EIS income tax relief or capital gains exemption) (Sch 5B.17). This applies to interest in possession trusts in which any of the beneficiaries is an individual or a charity and to discretionary trusts in which all beneficiaries are individuals or charities. Where, however, a life tenant dies and EIS shares pass to a

succeeding life tenant or remainderman, the deemed disposal under TCGA 1992 s 71(1) or s 72(1) (see part A(a) of the example) triggers the deferred gain, even though no gain arises on the shares themselves.

Anti-avoidance provisions — apportionment of gains of non-resident companies

8.   There are provisions in TCGA 1992 s 13 to attribute gains in a non-resident company to UK resident participators if the company would have been a close company if UK resident. For gains realised after 20 March 2000, where the UK participators are trustees, the gains cannot be prevented from being so attributed by reason of the provisions of a double tax agreement (TCGA 1992 s 79B). For further details of the provisions of TCGA 1992 s 13 see Example 51 explanatory note 18.

A.   In May 1988 Stephen Jones set up a discretionary trust for the benefit of his cousins. The trust paid inheritance tax of £44,000 on a chargeable transfer of £330,000. Stephen acted as trustee, together with his solicitor and a close friend. Capital gains of £110,000 were held over. Stephen had not set up any other trusts.

In February 1989 Stephen emigrated (permanently) and the administration of the trust was transferred to new trustees all of whom were and are resident outside the UK. Had the trust's assets been disposed of at that time capital gains of £155,000 would have arisen (including the gain held over).

The beneficiaries, Matthew, Mark, Mary and Matilda were all minors, resident and ordinarily resident in the UK. However, although all the children were born in the UK, Matthew's father was born in the USA and had retained his American domicile.

The trustees subsequently undertook the following transactions:

June 1997	Disposal of a freehold office property for £360,980 (net of costs). The property was part of the original trust fund. It had cost Stephen Jones £50,000 in March 1982 and was worth £100,000 in May 1988.
September 1997	Disposal of quoted shares in Jonah plc for £25,000. These shares had been acquired by the trustees in March 1990 for £9,650.
May 1998	Purchase of warehouse property in England for £150,000.
June 1998	Sale of UK residential property for £200,000. This property had been bought by the trustees in December 1988 for £62,034 including costs.
June 2006	Sale of chargeable non-business assets for £244,652 which had originally been settled by Stephen. The gain after indexation allowance but before taper relief was £111,401. There was no heldover gain in respect of these assets.

In addition to distributing all income, the trustees made capital distributions out of the settlement as follows:

	Matthew £	Mark £	Mary £	Matilda £
May 1996	–	–	60,000	20,000
December 1997	90,000	60,000	–	70,000
May 1999	6,000	6,000	6,000	–
July 2006	10,000	10,000	10,000	15,000

The re-referenced retail prices index for the dates given was:

March 1982	79.44
May 1988	106.2
December 1988	110.3
February 1989	111.82
March 1990	121.4
June 1997	157.5
September 1997	159.3
April 1998	162.6

Calculate the capital gains chargeable on the trustees and the beneficiaries in respect of the above transactions, stating if any supplementary charge will apply.

The capital gains tax annual exemption was as follows:

1997/98	£6,500
1998/99	£6,800
1999/2000	£7,100
2000/01	£7,200
2001/02	£7,500
2002/03	£7,700
2003/04	£7,900
2004/05	£8,200
2005/06	£8,500
2006/07	£8,800

The annual exemption for discretionary trusts is half the above amounts (except where several trusts have been made by the same settlor). The rate of capital gains tax payable by such trusts was 34% for 1997/98 to 2003/04 and has been 40% thereafter.

B. Set out the capital gains that would have been chargeable on the trustees and beneficiaries in respect of the settlement in A if, although Stephen Jones had emigrated in 1989, the trustees had remained UK resident.

C. Set out the capital gains that would have been chargeable on the trustees and settlor on the assumption that the settlement was on Stephen Jones for life and then to his four cousins absolutely. Assume also that he did not emigrate in 1989, but the administration of the trust was transferred to non-resident trustees in February 1989 (no inheritance tax being payable as the transfer would be a potentially exempt transfer), that the capital payments up to May 1998 were all made to Stephen Jones, that on 1 December 1998 Stephen Jones excluded himself from any further benefit from the trust by releasing his life interest in favour of his cousins and that the capital payments in May 1999 and July 2006 were made to the cousins.

D. Explain briefly how the rules relating to the residence status of trustees has changed under Finance Act 2006.

A. **Overseas trusts — capital gains tax treatment — pre 1991 trust**

Capital gains on creation of settlement

When a settlement is created, the settlor is deemed to have disposed of the entire property in the settlement at its market value, even if he retains an interest as beneficiary or is a trustee of the settlement, and he is therefore chargeable to capital gains tax accordingly (subject to available reliefs and exemptions).

When the assets transferred are business assets (TCGA 1992 s 165) or the transfer is immediately chargeable to inheritance tax (TCGA 1992 s 260), then providing the settlement is a UK resident settlement (see TCGA 1992 s 166), the settlor can avoid paying tax on the gains by making an election to hold them over so that they reduce the trustees' base acquisition costs. For disposals prior to 19 March 1989 the holdover relief was under FA 1980 s 79 and covered all assets, although no relief was then available on a subsequent disposal for inheritance tax paid.

Since Stephen Jones had created a UK resident discretionary trust, the transfer of assets to the trust would be chargeable to inheritance tax. (If he had retained an interest in the trust, the trust income would be chargeable on him, as would any capital gains remitted as long as he was resident in the UK — see part C.)

The gain arising on the creation of the settlement was held over under FA 1980 s 79.

Capital gain on emigration of Stephen Jones

The emigration of Stephen Jones in February 1989 does not create a liability for capital gains tax on any gains held over, or on any increase in value to the date of emigration.

Export of trust prior to 19 March 1991

When the trust was taken over by non-resident trustees in February 1989, the gains of £110,000 held over on the creation of the trust became chargeable but the accrued gains of £45,000 on the trust's assets were not chargeable as they were not realised (TCGA 1992 s 168) (see explanatory note 8 for emigration of a trust on or after 19 March 1991). The liability for the capital gains tax on the heldover gains was that of the trustees, although if the amount was not paid within twelve months from the due date then the Revenue could recover the tax from Stephen Jones.

Subsequent disposals

Although the trustees, as non-residents, are not chargeable to UK capital gains tax, the capital gains on disposals by the trustees must still be calculated as though they were still resident in the UK. The gains are then apportioned to beneficiaries in proportion to any capital sums they have received from the trust in that or any earlier year, except to the extent that those capital sums have already been allocated to earlier capital gains. The apportioned amounts cannot exceed the actual capital sums received, and are chargeable on the beneficiaries in the year of apportionment. Only beneficiaries who are resident or ordinarily resident in the UK *and* domiciled in the UK are assessed to capital gains tax on gains apportioned to them (TCGA 1992 s 87). The normal annual exemption for capital gains tax is available to the UK domiciled beneficiaries on the apportioned amounts, and is applied against the gains attributed to them in priority to their own gains. The apportioned gains do not, however, attract taper relief, since the gains will have been reduced by any available taper relief when they arose in the trust. From 6 April 1998 it is no longer possible to offset a beneficiary's own capital losses against apportioned gains other than to gains attributed to the settlor (see Example 50 part B). See explanatory notes 5, 9 and 10 in respect of the attribution of gains to resident settlors and also explanatory notes 16 and 17 re anti-avoidance provisions applicable from 21 March 2000.

The position in respect of the non-resident trust is as follows:

Gains		£	£
1997/98			
Sale proceeds freehold office property June 1997			360,980
Market value May 1988		100,000	
Indexation allowance ($\dfrac{157.5 - 106.2}{106.2}$) = .484		48,400	
			148,400
Gain			212,580
Sale proceeds Jonah plc shares September 1997			25,000
Cost March 1990		9,650	
Indexation allowance ($\dfrac{159.3 - 121.4}{121.4}$) = .313		3,020	
			12,670
Gain			12,330
Total gains for 1997/98 (212,580 + 12,330) =			£ 224,910

1998/99		£	£
Sale proceeds UK property June 1998			200,000
Cost December 1988		62,034	
Indexation allowance to April 1998 ($\dfrac{162.6 - 110.3}{110.3}$) = .475		29,466	
			91,500
Total gains for 1998/99			108,500

2006/07	£
Gain on disposal of non-business assets June 2006	111,401
Less taper relief 35%	38,990
Total gains for 2006/07	72,411

Apportionment of gains

		Matthew £	Mark £	Mary £	Matilda £	Total £
1997/98						
Capital payments to date		–	–	60,000	20,000	80,000
Capital payments in year		90,000	60,000	–	70,000	220,000
		90,000	60,000	60,000	90,000	300,000
Apportioned gain (90:60:60:90)		67,473	44,982	44,982	67,473	224,910
Excess capital payments to date	cf	22,527	15,018	15,018	22,527	75,090

		Matthew £	Mark £	Mary £	Matilda £	Total £
	bf	22,527	15,018	15,018	22,527	75,090
1998/99						
Apportioned gain (restricted to actual payments to date)		22,527	15,018	15,018	22,527	75,090
Actual gain						108,500
Apportioned above						75,090
Unallocated gain of 1998/99 cf						33,410
1999/2000						
Capital payments in year		6,000	6,000	6,000	–	18,000
Apportioned gain (restricted to actual payments)		6,000	6,000	6,000	–	18,000
Unallocated gain bf						33,410
Apportioned in 1999/2000						18,000
Unallocated gain of 1998/99 cf						15,410
2006/07						
Capital payments in year		10,000	10,000	10,000	15,000	45,000
Apportionment of unallocated gain bf (10:10:10:15)		3,424	3,424	3,425	5,137	15,410
Apportionment of gain of year (restricted to actual payments)		6,576	6,576	6,575	9,863	29,590
Actual gain						77,981
Apportioned above						29,590
Unallocated gain of 2006/07						48,391

The apportioned gains will be chargeable on the beneficiaries (except Matthew, who is not UK domiciled) in the year of apportionment, eg Mark will be chargeable on £44,982 in 1997/98, £15,018 in 1998/99, £6,000 in 1999/2000, and £10,000 in 2006/07, less his annual exemption in each case unless otherwise used.

In 2006/07 the capital gains tax payable by the beneficiaries other than Matthew on their shares of the apportioned gain of £15,410 is increased by a supplementary charge, as the gain arose in 1998/99, and was not distributed in that year, or the following year (1999/2000). The charge runs from 1 December in the tax year following that in which the gain was made to 30 November in the tax year following that in which the capital payment was made (although the period cannot start earlier than six years before that 30 November date). The charge therefore runs from 1 December 2000 to 30 November 2006 = 6 years (maximum period) @ 10% per annum, so the capital gains tax payable by each beneficiary other than Matthew is increased by 60% (see note 13). The apportioned gain may, however, be treated as the lowest part of the chargeable gains of the year. For example:

Assume Matilda is liable to capital gains tax at 40% in 2006/07 but has no gains in her own right in that year. Her liability will be:

Total apportioned gains	15,000		
Less Annual exemption	8,800		
Capital gains tax @ 40% on	6,200	=	£ 2,480
Of which proportion relating to 1998/99 is 5,137/15,000		=	£ 849
Supplementary charge re 1998/99	£849 @ 60%	=	£ 509

(to be shown in box 8.9 on the capital gains supplementary sheets of the self-assessment tax return)

By comparison, if in 2006/07 Mary had capital gains of £6,100 in her own right, but had only used £26,300 of her lower and basic rate band, her liability would be:

Total apportioned gains	10,000		
Less annual exemption	8,800		
	1,200		
Own gains	6,100		
	7,300		
Capital gains tax (33,300 – 26,300)	7,000 @ 20%		1,400
	300 @ 40%		120
			£ 1,520
Tax relating to apportioned gains	£1,200 @ 20%		£ 240
Of which proportion relating to 1998/99 is 3,425/10,000		=	£ 82
Supplementary charge re 1998/99	£82 @ 60%	=	£ 49

B. **Position if trust had remained UK resident after Stephen Jones emigrated**

If the trustees had remained UK resident, the gain held over when the trust was created would not be chargeable until the underlying assets were disposed of. The revised capital gains on the trustees' disposals would be chargeable on them in the tax year in which the disposal took place. The trust would have an annual exemption of one half of the exemption for individuals and tax would be payable on the remaining gains at the rate applicable to trusts (currently 40%). There would be no relief by reference to the non-resident beneficiary, Matthew. The position would therefore be:

		£	£
1997/98			
Sale proceeds freehold office property June 1997			360,980
Market value May 1988		100,000	
Less heldover gain:			
Cost March 1982	50,000		
Indexation allowance ($\frac{106.2 - 79.44}{79.44}$) = .337	16,850		
	66,850		
Market value on transfer to trust	100,000		
Gain held over	33,150		
		66,850	
Indexation allowance .484 as in A		32,355	99,205
Gain (cf)			261,775

	£	£
1997/98		
Gain (bf)		261,775
Gain on Jonah plc shares acquired by trustees in March 1990 (as in A)		12,330
Total gains		274,105
Less annual exemption (½ x 6,500)		3,250
Gains chargeable at 34%		270,855

Note No capital gains relief for inheritance tax paid is given for gains held over before 19 March 1989.

1998/99		
Gain on sale of UK property bought by trustees in December 1998 (as in A)		108,500
Less annual exemption (½ x 6,800)		3,400
Gains chargeable at 34%		105,100
2006/07		
Gain on sale of non-business chargeable assets June 2006 as in A		111,401
Less taper relief 35%		38,990
		72,411
Less annual exemption (½ x 8,800)		4,400
Gains chargeable at 40%		68,011

C. **Position if Stephen Jones had been life tenant and had remained UK resident but the trust had emigrated**

The creation of a life interest settlement on Stephen Jones in May 1988 would give rise to chargeable gains which could be held over under FA 1980 s 79 as before. The heldover gain would then be chargeable on Stephen Jones on the export of the trust in February 1989 as in A above.

The subsequent disposals by the trust would be treated as in A, ie there would be a capital gains tax computation as though the trustees were still resident in the UK. Since the trust emigrated before 19 March 1991, the provisions of TCGA 1992 s 86 charging a settlor who retains an interest in a trust on gains as they arise would not apply before 1999/2000, in respect of gains arising on or after 17 March 1998 (see below). Gains arising before 17 March 1998 would be chargeable on Stephen Jones when remitted, with a supplementary charge if not remitted in the tax year in which the gain arose or the following tax year (as in A above).

By FA 1998 s 132 any gain arising on or after 17 March 1998 on a pre 19 March 1991 settlement will be chargeable on the settlor if he or his immediate family (or companies they control) can benefit from the settlement. Gains arising between 17 March 1998 and 5 April 1999 were deferred until 6 April 1999 to allow settlors to reorganise their affairs. Stephen Jones did this in December 1998 by releasing his life interest in favour of his cousins. The release would be a potentially exempt transfer for inheritance tax (see Example 55).

The gains attributable to Stephen Jones would be as follows (before his personal annual exemption or any personal losses prior to 6 April 1998):

	£
1997/98	
Capital payments to date	80,000
Capital payments in year	220,000
	300,000
Gains chargeable on Stephen Jones (actual)	224,910
Excess capital payments to date	75,090
1998/99	
Actual gains	108,500
Gains chargeable on Stephen Jones — excess capital payments to date	75,090
Unremitted gain of 1998/99 cf	33,410

As Stephen Jones excluded himself from benefit on 1 December 1998, the unremitted 1998/99 gain of £33,410 carried forward would not be chargeable on him, but would be apportioned among the four cousins along with subsequent gains and taxed as and when capital payments were made to them. The first capital payment was made in 1999/2000 and would be treated as in part A of the example.

D.   Until the introduction of FA 2006, there were different rules determining the residence status of trustees for income and capital gains tax. These have been harmonised so that trustees are treated as resident and ordinarily resident in the UK if either:

(a)   all the trustees are resident in the UK; or

(b)   (i)   at least one trustee is resident in the UK, and

     (ii)   a settlor in relation to the settlement was resident, ordinarily resident or domiciled in the UK when the settlement is made. (ICTA 1988 s 685E).

To allow existing trusts to rearrange their affairs, the new rules do not come into effect until 6 April 2007.

Explanatory Notes

Legislation relating to offshore trusts

1.   The capital gains tax charges relating to offshore trusts contain many points of difficulty. On 21 May 1992 the Revenue issued a lengthy Statement of Practice (5/92) and also concession D40 dealing with the approach they will take in applying certain areas of the rules. The Revenue gave additional guidance in their Tax Bulletin of April 1995. The changes made by FA 1998 have, however, introduced many more areas of complexity and anomaly. Significant further changes were introduced by FA 2000, which are dealt with briefly below.

Effect of emigration of trust on trustees

2.   If an election to hold over a settlor's gains had been made under TCGA 1992 s 165 or s 260 (or previously under FA 1980 s 79), the heldover gain crystallised if donee trustees emigrated before 19 March 1991. The amount chargeable was the gain originally held over (TCGA 1992 s 168).

For trusts emigrating on or after 19 March 1991, the emigrating trustees are charged not only on gains held over at the time the funds were settled but on the whole of any increase in value of the trust assets up to the time of emigration (see note 8). Since 19 March 1991 TCGA 1992 s 168 has accordingly no longer applied where a trust becomes non-resident and now relates only to the emigration of donees who are individuals.

3.   Where a heldover gain has been charged under TCGA 1992 s 168 as a result of the emigration of the donee, the base cost at which the donee is deemed to have acquired the asset is its full value at the time of the gift, so that the trustees are treated as having acquired the assets at their value on the

creation of the settlement. Where that was before 31 March 1982, HMRC apparently take the view that a general 31 March 1982 rebasing election can only be made by the trustees, even though any charge to capital gains tax will be made on the beneficiaries.

4.   Where a heldover gain is triggered on or after 6 April 1988 and is wholly or partly attributable to a disposal before 6 April 1988 of an asset acquired before 31 March 1982, only half of the heldover gain is charged to tax (TCGA 1992 Sch 4.4).

Attribution of gains of offshore trusts to beneficiaries or settlor

5.   TCGA 1992 s 87 charges beneficiaries to tax on gains made by a non-resident trust to the extent that they receive capital payments from the trust. Before FA 1998 this applied where the trustees were neither resident nor ordinarily resident at any time in the tax year, if at any time in that year or at the time when he made the settlement the settlor was domiciled and either resident or ordinarily resident in the UK. In respect of gains realised and capital payments made on or after 17 March 1998, the conditions relating to the settlor's residence and domicile no longer apply (FA 1998 s 130). Both before and after 17 March 1998, however, a beneficiary is not charged unless he is resident or ordinarily resident in the UK and was domiciled in the UK at some time in the year in which the gains were apportioned to him (TCGA 1992 ss 2(1), 87(7)). Note that where the income tax provisions of TA 1988 ss 739, 740 apply (transfer of assets abroad – liability of non-transferors on benefits received), any remittances are treated as being made first from accumulated income before being treated as capital payments under TCGA 1992 s 87. In this example all income has been remitted in addition to the capital payments made.

If the settlor retains an interest in the trust, gains are charged on him as and when they arise under the provisions of TCGA 1992 s 86 if the settlement becomes non-resident on or after 19 March 1991, or if funds are added or the beneficiaries are varied on or after that date, and in any event from 6 April 1999 in respect of gains arising on or after 17 March 1998 (see explanatory notes 9 and 10). Gains taxed on the settlor are not charged on the beneficiaries (s 87(3)).

As and when chargeable gains are made that are not taxed on the settlor, they are apportioned to the beneficiaries and charged to tax, but only to the extent that capital payments of an equivalent amount have been paid to the beneficiaries, either in the year in which the gains are made or in an earlier year. (See notes 16 and 17 for anti-avoidance provisions to counter schemes to avoid the charge on the beneficiaries.) Any gains that have not been distributed in this way are carried forward and apportioned as and when capital payments are made, as in 1999/2000 and 2006/07 in part A of the example. The capital payments carried forward at the end of 1997/98 represented amounts that the beneficiaries had already received in respect of which no chargeable gains had arisen. When chargeable gains next arose in 1998/99 they were apportioned to the beneficiaries because of the excess capital payments at 5 April 1998.

6.   It should be noted that the chargeable gains can exceed the capital payments received in a year because of amounts received in prior years (but not before 10 March 1981) (TCGA 1992 s 87(4), (5), (10)). Therefore Mary, who does not receive any capital payments in 1997/98, has a liability in that year on gains of £44,982, since she had received capital payments in excess of that amount in earlier years. On the other hand, a charge to tax may occur in a year in which no gains are made, because capital payments are made when there are unallocated gains brought forward. In 1999/2000 there are no gains but Mark and Mary are charged on brought forward gains because of the capital amounts received. Furthermore, if those unallocated gains brought forward were realised in an earlier year than the immediately previous year, a supplementary charge is payable, as shown (see note 13).

7.   Matthew is not chargeable on the gains apportioned to him as, although he is resident and ordinarily resident in the UK, he is not UK domiciled.

Emigration of trust on or after 19 March 1991

8.   In part A of the example the trust became non-resident in February 1989 and the gains held over on creation of the settlement became chargeable at that time, but not accrued gains on the trust's assets, as they had not been realised. If trustees of a settlement become non-resident on or after 19 March

1991, then they are deemed to have disposed of and immediately reacquired the settled property at market value on the day they become non-resident, so that not only any heldover gains but also accrued gains become chargeable at that time (TCGA 1992 s 80). TCGA 1992 s 168 imposing a separate charge on heldover gains, as illustrated in part A, therefore no longer applies where trustees become non-resident on or after 19 March 1991.

The deemed disposal under TCGA 1992 s 80(2) does not apply to trading assets of a branch or agency which remain chargeable to UK capital gains tax under TCGA 1992 s 10. Rollover relief on replacement of business assets under TCGA 1992 ss 152-156 cannot be claimed if the new assets are acquired after the trust becomes non-resident and are outside the UK tax charge. These provisions also apply to dual resident trusts that are exempt from UK tax on gains because of a double tax treaty.

On the emigration of a trust, beneficiaries would normally be treated as having acquired their interest in the trust at the market value at the date of the trust's emigration. Where a trust becomes non-resident on or after 21 March 2000, this uplift to market value does not apply where the trust has a stockpile of gains at the date of emigration that have not been attributed to beneficiaries (TCGA 1992 s 85).

Trusts in which the settlor retains an interest

9. Where a settlement with non-resident trustees is made on or after 19 March 1991, or becomes non-resident on or after that date, and the settlor is resident or ordinarily resident and domiciled in the UK, and the settlor or his spouse/civil partner, children, children's spouses/civil partners, a company controlled by one or more of those persons, or an associated company, can benefit from the settlement, then the gains of the settlement are attributed to the settlor (TCGA 1992 s 86). For settlements with non-resident trustees made on or after 17 March 1998, grandchildren and their spouses (and, since 5 December 2005, their civil partners) are added to the list of defined persons for s 86 (FA 1998 s 131). This also applies to pre 17 March 1998 trusts if they become non-resident or if funds are added or grandchildren become beneficiaries on or after that date (or a grandchild who was already a beneficiary enjoys a benefit for the first time on or after that date that he would not have been able to enjoy under the terms of the settlement as it stood at that date) (FA 1998 Sch 22). See note 16 for anti-avoidance provisions to counter schemes to avoid the charge on the settlor.

Before FA 2002 a trust's gains were reduced by taper relief before being attributed to a settlor and the settlor could not use his personal losses to reduce the gains (see Example 50 part B). With one exception, this will no longer apply for gains attributed to the settlor from *2003/04*, or by election for any one or more of the years 2000/01, 2001/02 and 2002/03 (FA 2002 s 51 and Sch 11). (If such an election would have the effect of increasing the tax the settlor could recover from the settlement for the relevant years – see below – the trustees would have to join in the election.) The settlor's losses will first be set against his own gains, then against any trust gains attributed to him *before* taper relief. If there is more than one attributed gain the loss will be set off against the gain with the lowest taper entitlement. If the loss is insufficient to cover all attributed gains and there are two or more settlements attributing gains, then a pro rata proportion of the available losses will be deducted from each of the attributed gains with taper relief at the same rate. Any remaining gains will attract taper relief at the rate that would have applied to the trust. The exception to the revised provisions is where a settlor resumes UK residence after being temporarily non-resident and gains have in the meantime been charged on UK resident beneficiaries (see explanatory note 12).

The settlor can recover the tax he has paid from the trustees without that amount being treated as a capital payment by the settlement. For this purpose he may require the Revenue to issue him with a certificate of the tax paid (TCGA 1992 Sch 5.6). There is no provision for the settlor to obtain payment from the trustees before he has paid the tax, even though the disposal proceeds relating to the gains will be in the trust. If the settlor fails to recover the tax, then that amount will be considered to be an addition to the settlement unless the trust is unable to remit the amount because of local restrictions.

The provisions of s 86 do not apply in a tax year in which the settlor dies, nor in which all those individuals who cause him to have an interest die, or, where the interest is that of a spouse/civil partner, they cease to be married/the civil partnership is dissolved.

The gains of resident settlements are attributed to the settlor in similar circumstances under TCGA 1992 ss 77-79 (see Example 50 part B). The provisions for non-resident settlements in TCGA 1992 s 86 are, however, wider than those for resident settlements.

10. Before FA 1998 a non-resident trust made before 19 March 1991 was only subject to the provisions of TCGA 1992 s 86 outlined in note 9 if funds were added or the beneficiaries were varied to include any of the defined persons.

With effect from 6 April 1999, gains of pre 19 March 1991 non-resident trusts are no longer excluded from the provisions of TCGA 1992 s 86 (TCGA 1992 Sch 5). Unremitted gains of the period 17 March 1998 to 5 April 1999 were deemed to arise on 6 April 1999, thus bringing them within the provisions. The charge was delayed to enable trusts to reorganise their affairs, for example by excluding the range of defined persons as beneficiaries, or by becoming resident or by winding up the trust. There are, however, anti-avoidance provisions in Sch 23 to prevent exploitation of the transitional period.

The revised provisions do not apply to 'protected settlements', ie where the beneficiaries are confined to:

(i)   Children of the settlor or his spouse/civil partner who are under 18

(ii)   Unborn children of the settlor or his spouse/civil partner

(iii) Future spouses/civil partners of the settlor or his children

(iv)   Persons outside the defined categories (eg cousins, as in part A of the example).

This protection ceases, however, when the child reaches age 18. Furthermore, distributions to grandchildren are caught as a result of FA 1998 s 131 (see note 9). The Revenue have, however, stated that the existence of grandchildren (of whatever age) as beneficiaries of a pre 19 March 1991 settlement at 6 April 1999 will not cause the settlement to fall outside the 'protected' category (Tax Bulletin December 1998).

11. Where capital payments are made on or after 6 April 1999 to beneficiaries of pre 19 March 1991 trusts in which the settlor has an interest, they will be matched with any unallocated gains that arose before 17 March 1998, earliest first (attracting the supplementary charge if appropriate – see note 13), and only when all such unallocated gains have been matched with capital payments will capital payments to beneficiaries be regarded as having been already charged on the settlor.

Settlor who is temporarily non-resident

12. To be liable to UK capital gains tax the settlor must be UK resident or ordinarily resident in the tax year that gains arise. Under TCGA 1992 ss 10A and 86A, however, a UK domiciled settlor can also be liable if after becoming non-resident he returns to the UK having been away for fewer than five complete tax years. The charge is made in the tax year of return to the UK, but it is reduced by any gains that have been charged on UK resident beneficiaries during his period of non-residence.

From 2003/04 (or earlier by election), gains will not normally be reduced by a trust's taper relief *before* being attributed to a settlor (FA 2002 s 51 and Sch 11) (see explanatory note 9). This does not, however, apply where the gains on which a returning settlor is charged have been reduced by gains already attributed to UK resident beneficiaries during the settlor's absence. The gains in such circumstances will continue to be reduced by the trust's taper relief before they are attributed to the settlor and will not be able to be reduced by the settlor's losses (TCGA 1992 s 86A as amended by FA 2002 Sch 11.5).

Supplementary charge

13.   Before FA 1991 it was possible to defer payment of capital gains tax on gains realised by offshore trusts by not remitting the gains. Where such gains are assessable on beneficiaries for 1992/93 onwards, the tax payable is increased by a supplementary charge (TCGA 1992 ss 91-97). The charge runs from 1 December in the tax year following that in which the trustees' gains arose to 30 November in the tax year after that in which the gain is apportioned to the beneficiary as a result of a capital payment (any capital payments being regarded as applying to the earliest unallocated gains first). If the period would otherwise exceed six years, however, it starts on 1 December six years before the 30 November charging date (TCGA 1992 s 92(4)(5)). The supplementary charge does not apply where gains are matched by capital payments in the same or following tax year. Gains made before 6 April 1990 were treated as made in 1990/91. Trustees could distribute such gains before 6 April 1992 without any supplementary charge on the beneficiary. Later gains may be distributed in the same or the following tax year without the supplementary charge becoming payable, subject to the 6 April 1990 fund of undistributed gains being matched with payments first. The charge is at an annual rate of 10% of the tax on the capital payment, giving an overall maximum possible rate of 60% of 40% = 24%, in addition to the capital gains tax of up to 40% already payable.

In part A of the example, the 1997/98 capital gain is more than matched by capital payments made in or before that year, so that the whole gain is apportioned to beneficiaries in that year. The 1998/99 gain of £108,500 is distributed as to £75,090 in that year and £18,000 in 1999/2000, but £15,410 remains unallocated until 2006/07, so that the supplementary charge arises on the 2006/07 assessable gains.

14.   In some cases, careful planning of capital payments may reduce the overall amount of supplementary charge payable. Say, for example, an overseas trust has two beneficiaries, one liable to capital gains tax at 20% and the other at 40%, and the trustees are to make a capital payment which will partly relate to gains of a year to which the supplementary charge will apply and partly to a later year for which the supplementary charge is not relevant. If a capital payment is made to the lower taxed beneficiary first, this will relate to earlier gains before later gains, so that any part of the payment that attracts the supplementary charge will suffer the additional charge on a 20% tax bill. A subsequent payment can then be made to the higher taxed beneficiary out of gains not liable to the supplementary charge. Similar planning points will apply where there is a non-UK domiciled beneficiary, like Matthew in this example, or where, although UK domiciled, a beneficiary is not resident or ordinarily resident in the UK.

Treatment of interest-free loans

15.   Many non-resident trustees have regarded payments to beneficiaries to be by way of loan (often interest-free), rather than capital payments to which gains would be apportioned. Such a loan was considered in a criminal case in relation to a confiscation of property order (R v Harvey 1998). The loan was secured by way of a charge on the offender's property. The loan was disregarded, because it was stated to be in reality a gift and that the charge was unlikely to be enforced. The Revenue have taken a similar view for tax purposes in relation to offshore trusts, and succeeded in the cases of Billingham v Cooper and Edwards v Fisher, heard by the Court of Appeal in 2001. In both cases overseas trustees had made interest-free loans, repayable on demand, to UK resident (settlor) beneficiaries of pre March 1991 trusts. Although the Revenue conceded that such loans had little initial benefit, they contended that the continuation of the loans meant that the benefit was provided on a continuing basis. The Court of Appeal agreed, stating that in giving effect to the purpose of TCGA 1992 ss 87 and 97, it needed to be considered what benefit a beneficiary actually received, so that the 'loan' payments to beneficiaries were within the capital payments and supplementary charges rules.

Anti-avoidance provisions re 'flip flop' schemes

16.   Anti-avoidance provisions were introduced in FA 2000 s 92 and Schs 25 and 26 to counter avoidance of capital gains tax by means of a device known as the 'flip flop'. This applied mainly in two situations.

The first enabled a UK settlor who had retained an interest in a UK or offshore trust to avoid being charged on the trustees' gains. This was achieved by the trustees borrowing money on the security of the trust's assets and lending it to a second trust in which the settlor was also interested. The settlor then severed his interest in the first trust. In the next tax year the trustees of the first trust sold the trust assets and repaid the debt, and the settlor received his money from the second trust. Since the settlor no longer had an interest in the first trust, tax on any gains in the case of a UK trust was charged on the trustees at their tax rate of 34% rather than on the settlor at his rate of 40%. There was no tax charge at all in the case of a non-resident trust.

The second situation involved non-resident trusts in which the beneficiaries were liable to tax on capital payments, as indicated in note 5. As in the first situation, trustees of one trust borrowed money to lend to a second trust, with the gains then being realised in the first trust. This enabled UK beneficiaries to receive tax-free capital payments from the second trust.

Both variants of the flip flop scheme were countered from 21 March 2000 by new provisions in TCGA 1992. Under new s 76B and Sch 4B, where the trustees of any trust except a UK trust in which the settlor does not have an interest borrow money and advance it to another trust, the trustees are deemed to dispose of the trust assets and reacquire them at market value, thus crystallising the chargeable gains in the first trust. If the trust is a UK or non-resident trust in which the settlor has an interest, the tax will be charged on the settlor. Gifts holdover relief cannot be claimed on the deemed disposal. The provisions do not apply if the proceeds from the trust borrowing have been used wholly for normal trust purposes.

17.   Where the trust is a non-resident trust in which a UK resident settlor does not have an interest, so that a charge cannot be made on the settlor, then under TCGA 1992 new s 85A and Sch 4C, tax will be charged on UK resident beneficiaries who receive capital payments in respect of gains arising under Sch 4B.

A further countering of flip flop schemes has been introduced by FA 2003 s 163 and Sch 29 and F(No2)A 2005.

A new version of the flip flop scheme triggers the FA 2000 legislation with a view to stranding already realised gains in one settlement and potentially permitting capital payments to be made to beneficiaries of another settlement without incurring a capital gains charge. See Trennery v West (HMIT) [2005] UKHL5.

To counter the scheme the gains pool created by Sch 4C is extended so that where there is a transfer under Sch 4B, unattributed gains already realised by trustees of the transferor settlement go into it as well as any gains arising from the Sch 4B deemed disposal of any chargeable assets that are not charged on the settlor.

Furthermore, from 9 April 2003 a new rule that applies only to Sch 4C pools (and not to s 87 or s 89 pools) was introduced. The newly extended Sch 4C pool is computed differently, so that only payments to UK resident and domiciled beneficiaries will reduce that pool.

An additional small change has been introduced to ensure that where a beneficiary is chargeable under Sch 4C, and the amount charged is reduced by any amount already charged on a settlor (by virtue of TCGA 1992 s 86) the amount by which it is reduced is the tapered rather than the untapered amount.

Apportionment of gains of non-resident companies

18.   A chargeable gain that arises in a non-resident company which would be a close company if resident in the UK is apportioned between its participators. In so far as a participator has at least 10% (5% prior to 7 March 2001) of the gain apportioned to him, and is UK resident or ordinarily resident (and, if an individual, domiciled) in the UK, he is chargeable to capital gains tax on the apportioned amount. These provisions apply to UK resident trustees as well as to individuals (see Example 50 explanatory note 8 for special anti-avoidance provisions for trustees). Although chargeable to capital

gains tax, the gain is computed using corporation tax rules, with indexation allowance but not taper relief applying (see Tolley's Taxwise I 2006/07 Example 70 for details) (TCGA 1992 s 13).

Such gains may also be apportioned to non-resident trustees (s 13(10)), and may in turn be chargeable on the settlor or beneficiaries under the provisions in note 5 above.

These provisions do not apply to gains on the disposal of an asset used for the purposes of a trade carried on by the non-resident company wholly outside the UK, or to trading currency.

If the gain is distributed within four years of the date the gain is realised or, if earlier, three years after the end of the accounting period in which the gain is realised (within two years after the gain was realised for gains realised before 7 March 2001), then the capital gains tax on the apportioned amount can be offset against the income tax on the distribution (or capital gains tax if a capital distribution). If not so relieved the tax is treated as an expense for capital gains tax in computing any subsequent gain on the disposal of the participator's interest in the company (TCGA 1992 s 13).

For settlements made before 22 March 2006 inheritance tax treatment of a settlement is dependent upon whether or not an 'interest in possession' subsists in it.

Explain, with appropriate reference to both statute and case law, in what circumstances an interest in possession will exist in a settlement, commenting specifically on the impact that powers granted to the trustees may have on the position.

Summarise the changes made by Finance Act 2006 to the inheritance tax regime for trusts.

Meaning of 'interest in possession'

The term 'interest in possession' is not defined clearly in the legislation.

The definition put forward by the Revenue is that 'an interest in possession in settled property exists where the person having the interest has an immediate entitlement............ to any income produced by that property as the income arises; but that a discretion or power, in whatever form, which can be exercised after income arises so as to withhold it from that person negatives the existence of an interest in possession. For this purpose a power to accumulate income is regarded as a power to withhold it, unless any accumulations must be held solely for the person having the interest or his personal representatives.'

The Revenue's view was upheld by the House of Lords in Pearson and Others v CIR 1980 in which it was stated that it is the present right of present enjoyment that constitutes an interest in possession.

Inheritance tax treatment of settlements with an interest in possession

The term 'interest in possession' is crucial to the taxation treatment of settlements for inheritance tax.

Where an interest in possession exists in respect of a settlement made before 22 March 2006, then the person beneficially entitled to that interest is treated for inheritance tax purposes as being beneficially entitled to the underlying property in which the interest subsists (s 49).

Thus the value of the settled property in which a person has an interest in possession is deemed to be part of the estate of that person and any transfer of that interest will appear on his inheritance tax accumulation if chargeable.

Although the actual tax may well be paid by the trustees, the effect of this treatment is to increase the rate of tax on any subsequent chargeable transfer by the person in possession or, in the case of a liability on death, to increase the estate rate and therefore the tax payable on the free estate at death by reason of the aggregation of the free estate and the interest in possession.

Inheritance tax treatment of discretionary settlements

If, however, a settlement made before 22 March 2006 does not have an interest in possession then:

(a)   The trust has its own inheritance tax accumulation, the method of calculating the rate of tax on a transfer of trust funds depending upon the date the settlement was created.

   The tax scale used is one half of the normal scale applicable at the date of charge.

(b)   On the tenth anniversary of the creation of the settlement it is subject to a ten-year charge (s 64).

   The charge is 30% of the tax that would be payable on the relevant property in the trust if the whole of the trust property were distributed on that day.

   A further charge will occur every ten years thereafter.

(c)   There is also an exit charge when property in such a settlement ceases to be relevant property (either because the property leaves the settlement or for any other reason, for example the property becoming subject to an interest in possession) (s 65).

Inheritance tax treatment of trusts post 22 March 2006

Settlements made on or after 22 March 2006 are now generally subject to the rules which previously applied only to discretionary trusts. Therefore, the assets held by the trustees of an interest in possession settlement will not usually form part of the estate of the life tenant provided that the settlement was made after 21 March 2006.

This, however, has its drawbacks. In particular, the creation of the settlement will represent a chargeable event (previously, lifetime transfers into interest in possession settlements constituted PETs). Furthermore, the settlement will be subject to the ten-year charge and exit charge rules described above.

The Government originally proposed a limited number of exceptions to these new rules. Following intense lobbying a modest number of amendments were made during the passage of the Finance Bill through Parliament. Consequently, the following trusts will remain outside the rules previously limited to discretionary trusts:

(a)   Bare trusts (where the beneficiary continues to be treated as entitled to the assets held under the bare trust)

(b)   Interest in possession trusts where the interest in possession is:

    (i)   an immediate post-death interest; (see below)

    (ii)   a disabled person's interest (broadly an interest in possession for a person incapable of looking after their affairs because of mental disorder, or a person in receipt of an attendance allowance or a disability living allowance); or

    (iii)   a transitional serial interest (see below) (IHTA 1984 s 49(1A)).

An immediate post-death interest is one:

–   created on an individual's death under the deceased's will or under the law of intestacy

–   which gave the life tenant the beneficial entitlement to the trust fund on the individual's death, and

–   which is not and has not been a disabled person's interest or an interest of a bereaved minor (IHTA 1984 s 49A).

To be a transitional serial interest in a settlement:

    (i)   the settlement must have been set up before 22 March 2006; and

    (ii)   immediately before 22 March 2006, there must have been an individual with a beneficial interest in possession in the settlement; and

    (iii)   that person's interest must have come to an end after 21 March 2006 but before 6 April 2008; and

    (iv)   the person with the current interest in the settlement became beneficially entitled to that interest at that time; and

    (v)   the interest is not a disabled person's interest or an interest of a bereaved minor (IHTA 1984 s 49B).

The rules for bereaved minors are found in IHTA 1984 s 71A. They apply only for settlements which:

(a)   are set up by:

    (i)   a parent of the beneficiary in their will, or

    (ii)   the Criminal Injuries Compensation Scheme

(b)   give the minor the capital and income of the trust absolutely when the minor reaches the age of 18.

Explanatory Notes

Effect of having an interest in possession in a settlement in a pre-22 March 2006 settlement

1.   Inheritance tax cannot be avoided on a capital sum simply because the person presently entitled to the income has no recourse to the capital.

    The supporting capital is deemed to be part of his wealth for inheritance tax (s 49(1)).

2.   There are two consequences:

    First, a cessation of the interest in possession attracts an inheritance tax charge by reference to the accumulated transfers of the taxpayer who ceases to have possession.

Second, an advance of capital to a person presently entitled to the income does not attract an inheritance tax charge. The supporting capital was previously part of the taxpayer's estate in the form of trust property and is now part of his estate in the form of free estate.

Since 22 March 2006, such a transfer is a PET only if made to

– another individual,

– a disabled trust, or

– a bereaved minor's trust on the coming to an end of an immediate post-death interest (IHTA 1984 s 3A(1A)).

so that if the potentially exempt transfer becomes chargeable because of the taxpayer's death within seven years, it increases his cumulative transfers for the purpose of calculating tax on later transfers.

3.   Thus, contrast the position where trustees use their powers to pay a capital sum to:

(a)   The person presently enjoying the income — no inheritance tax charge.

(b)   The person eventually entitled to the capital (ie when the interest in possession comes to an end) — there is a potential inheritance tax charge.

Creation of interest in possession settlement

4.   It was thus possible for a transferor to make an immediate transfer into a trust fund and thereby fix the value of the transfer at that time. Such a transfer would have been a potentially exempt transfer for inheritance tax (after deducting annual exemptions if available), providing another individual was beneficially entitled to the interest in possession. Accordingly inheritance tax would have been payable only if the settlor died in the next seven years. If the period between settlement and death is more than three years the tax charge, if any, on the transfer would have been reduced by tapering relief. There would have been no inheritance tax charge upon the funds leaving the trust so long as their destination was the person presently entitled to the interest in possession. This was particularly useful if one wished to transfer appreciating assets (ie to trustees) without the intended beneficiary being able to have absolute personal control of them. Further transfers into the trust, and the termination of the life interest during the lifetime of the person entitled to the interest, followed either by another life interest or by someone becoming absolutely entitled to the trust property, would all have been potentially exempt transfers (again subject to any available annual exemptions).

There would, however, have been a chargeable event for capital gains tax on the termination of the interest in possession (TCGA 1992 s 71) unless occasioned by the death of the life tenant (TCGA 1992 s 73), or where the property remained in trust (TCGA 1992 s 72), subject to the trustees and the transferee being able to make a claim under TCGA 1992 s 165 or s 260 for the gain to be held over in appropriate circumstances (for detailed notes see Example 50).

Interest in possession and residential property

5.   The capital gains tax exemption for only or main residence is extended by TCGA 1992 s 225 to a beneficiary who is entitled to occupy a property owned by a trust. The view of the Revenue is that non-exclusive occupation of a property would not constitute an interest in possession (Statement of Practice 10/79), but a lease for life for less than full consideration will create an interest in possession. Thus obtaining the capital gains tax exemption means that a charge to inheritance tax can arise as set out above.

Where substantially the whole of the assets of a married couple consist of the matrimonial home, it is often difficult to utilise both nil rate bands. A possible solution is for the home to be held by the couple as tenants in common, and for the half share to be left on the first death to a discretionary trust, the surviving spouse then buying the trust's half share at full price with the consideration left outstanding. On the second death full capital gains tax exemption applies, but there is a deduction in the inheritance tax computation for the outstanding loan. If the property had remained in the trust it would appear that only one half of the value of the property should be included in the inheritance tax computation, as the surviving spouse had occupied the property with the permission of the trustees and this may not equate to an interest in possession of the whole (Woodhall v CIR, SpC, 2000).

Discretionary trusts

6. Detailed notes on the tax treatment of discretionary trusts are given in Examples 59 to 63.

Interests in possession post 22 March 2006

7. Settlements made on or after 22 March 2006 are now generally subject to the rules which previously applied only to discretionary trusts. Therefore, the assets held by the trustees of an interest in possession settlement will not usually form part of the estate of the life tenant.

Following intense lobbying a modest number of amendments were made during the passage of the Finance Bill through Parliament. Consequently, only the following interests in trusts will form part of the estate of the life tenant:

(a) bare trusts (where the beneficiary continues to be treated as entitled to the assets held under the bare trust);

(b) interests in possession which commenced before 22 March 2006;

(c) later interests in possession trusts where the interest in possession is:

   (i) an immediate post-death interest (see below)

   (ii) a disabled person's interest (broadly an interest in possession for a person incapable of looking after their affairs because of mental disorder, or a person in receipt of an attendance allowance or a disability living allowance) or

   (iii) a transitional serial interest (see below) (IHTA 1984 s 49(1A)).

As has been seen, an immediate post-death interest (IPDI) is one:

(a) created on an individual's death under the deceased's will or under the law of intestacy

(b) which gave the life tenant the beneficial entitlement to the trust fund on the individual's death, and

(c) which is not and has not been a disabled person's interest or an interest of a bereaved minor (IHTA 1984 s 49A).

This wording means that it will not be possible for an IPDI to be created using a deed of variation. It might be arguable that a disclaimer (where appropriate) would not prevent an IPDI from being set up. However, to be an IPDI it appears that one has to ignore the fact that no life tenant will have beneficial entitlement to a trust fund until the deceased's assets are properly administered.

Most notably, lifetime transfers into interest in possession settlements will constitute chargeable transfers but the life tenant will not be treated as beneficially entitled to the trust fund. This can lead to multiple taxation. See Example.

Example

Hardy settles £500,000 for himself for life, the remainder for his wife. The transfer is a chargeable lifetime settlement and so inheritance tax will be payable at the lifetime rates. The settlement will be subject to ten-year and exit charges as appropriate. However, because Hardy still has the use of these funds, the transfer will be treated as a gift with the reservation of benefit. Consequently, the £500,000 will form part of Hardy's estate when he dies. The problem would have been worse had Hardy settled assets which gave rise to a chargeable gain. The transfer would have given rise to a capital gains tax liability with no scope for any holdover relief (because the donee trust was settlor-interested).

Robin died on 30 June 2002 and the inheritance tax on his estate was payable out of residue, at an estate rate of 25%.

His will provided for the following:

(1)   A bequest to his married daughter Merle of 25,000 shares of £1 each in Fieldfare plc, quoted on the Stock Exchange at 398-406p.

(2)   The creation of a settlement, the assets of which amounted to £30,000, under which the income was payable to Merle for life, then to Merle's daughter Jenny for life, with remainder to Merle's son Martin.

On 1 September 2005 Merle gave Jenny 12,500 of the shares in Fieldfare plc that she had inherited from her father. The shares were quoted on that day at 272-276p. She had made previous potentially exempt transfers amounting to £259,000 (after exemptions), all on 30 September 2000.

Merle and Jenny were involved in an accident and as a result Merle died on 30 September 2006, leaving her free estate to her son Martin. Jenny died on 31 October 2006, having made no lifetime transfers, and leaving her estate to her brother Martin.

Their respective estates were valued for probate as follows:

	Merle 30.9.06 £	Jenny 31.10.06 £
12,500 shares each in Fieldfare plc	36,750	38,000
Other assets (net of liabilities)	24,025	236,250
Settled fund (net of liabilities)	32,000	22,750

Compute the inheritance tax payable:

(a)   on the death of Merle

(b)   on the death of Jenny.

Jenny's date of birth is 15 January 1980.

(a)   **Inheritance tax payable on death of Merle (30 September 2006)**

			Gross £	Tax on 2006/07 scale £
Gifts within seven years before death:				
During 2000/01			259,000	–
1 September 2005				
Gift to Jenny 12,500 shares @ 273		34,125		
Less: Annual exemptions 2005/06	3,000			
2004/05	3,000	6,000		
Potentially exempt transfer now chargeable			28,125	850*
Cumulative transfers in seven years prior to death			287,125	850*

(* 287,125 – 285,000 = 2,125 @ 40%)

Estate of Merle deceased

	Date of death 30 September 2006 £
Free estate:	
12,500 shares in Fieldfare plc	36,750
Other assets (net of liabilities)	24,025
	60,775
Settled property (Robin's will trust) (net of liabilities)	32,000
Chargeable to inheritance tax on death	92,775

	Gross	Tax on 2006/07 scale £
Cumulative transfers in seven years prior to death	287,125	850
Chargeable estate on death	92,775	37,110*
	379,900	37,960

(* £92,775 @ 40% = £37,110)

Inheritance tax payable:

On gifts within seven years before death		
Payable by transferees of gifts in 2000/01 (previously potentially exempt transfers)		nil
Payable by Jenny (or her executors) re gift of shares on 1 September 2005, previously potentially exempt		£ 850
On estate at death as computed		37,110
Less: Quick succession relief re gift of shares from Robin (see explanatory note 6)		
20% of ($\frac{100,000}{133,333}$x 33,333)	5,000	
Quick succession relief re settled property (see explanatory note 7)		
20% of ($\frac{30,000}{40,000}$x 10,000)	1,500	6,500
Inheritance tax payable on Merle's estate		£ 30,610

Payable by executors:

$$\frac{60,775}{92,775} \times £30,610 \qquad\qquad £ 20,052$$

Payable by trustees of settled property:

$$\frac{32,000}{92,775} \times £30,610 \qquad\qquad £ 10,558$$

(b)   **Inheritance tax payable on death of Jenny (31 October 2006)**

Estate of Jenny deceased	*Date of death* *31 October 2006*
Free estate:	
12,500 shares in Fieldfare plc	38,000
Other assets (net of liabilities)	236,250
	274,250
Settled property (Robin's will trust) (net of liabilities)	22,750
	£ 297,000

Inheritance tax payable:

		£
On £297,000 (297,000 – 285,000 = 12,000 @ 40%)		4,800

Less: Quick succession relief re gift of shares
from Merle (see explanatory note 9)

$$80\% \text{ of } \left(\frac{27,275}{28,125} \times £850\right) \qquad\qquad 659$$

Quick succession relief re settled property
(see explanatory note 10)

$$100\% \text{ of } \left(\frac{21,442}{32,000} \times £10,558\right) \qquad\qquad 7,075$$

Total quick succession relief available	£ 7,734	
But relief restricted to total tax chargeable		4,800
		–

Accordingly no inheritance tax is payable on Jenny's death.

Explanatory Notes

Quick succession relief

1.   Under the provisions of s 141, quick succession relief applies where the value of a person's chargeable estate for inheritance tax purposes was increased by a chargeable transfer made not more than five years before

      (a)   his death

or   (b)   a lifetime charge on settled property in which the deemed transferor had an interest in possession (where the earlier transfer was or included the making of the settlement or was made after the making of the settlement).

The rates of quick succession relief are as follows:

Period between transfer and death	Percentage relief
1 year or less	100%
1+ to 2 years	80%
2+ to 3 years	60%
3+ to 4 years	40%
4+ to 5 years	20%

The percentage relief is calculated on the part of the tax paid on the previous transfer that the net value then transferred bears to the gross chargeable transfer at that time.

Where the later transfer is made on death, whether it relates to free estate or settled property, the quick succession relief reduces the total tax chargeable because of the death, as shown in the example, so that the apportionment of the tax payable between free estate and settled property is of the tax as reduced by quick succession relief.

Successive transfers

2.   Where an individual who has a life interest in possession in settled property transfers parts of his interest therein at different times and more than one later transfer occurs within five years of his acquisition of the life interest, then quick succession relief is available on the second and subsequent transfers within the five years, but only to the extent of any tax not used up on the earlier transfers. In this connection a transfer uses up the full amount of tax paid on the earlier transfer of which the tax relievable on the later transfer is a percentage (s 141(4)(5)).

For example:

A grants a life interest to B by will trust. Within two years B releases part of his interest to a discretionary trust (C), then in the fifth year after A's death B releases the remainder of his interest to a second discretionary trust (D).

Proportion of tax on A's transfer relevant to the increase in B's estate is say £25,000. Transfer of part interest within two years to C trust attracts tax of say £8,000 and transfer of remainder to D trust within five years tax of say £7,000.

The quick succession relief available on the transfer to C trust is 80% x £25,000 so the amount of £8,000 is fully covered by quick succession relief, representing £10,000 of the original £25,000 (£8,000 = 80% x £10,000) leaving £15,000 still available. The transfer to D trust attracts quick succession relief of 20% of £15,000 = £3,000 to set against the tax payable of £7,000.

Valuation of quoted securities

3.   Quoted securities are valued one quarter up from the lower of the two quoted prices. Thus on Robin's death a quotation of 398-406p per share becomes 400p.

Gift by Merle to Jenny of inherited shares

4.   Quick succession relief was not available on the Fieldfare plc shares given by Merle to Jenny despite Merle having acquired the shares by a chargeable transfer less than five years earlier, because it only applies where the *later transfer* is on death or termination of an interest in possession in settled property.

Position on death of Merle

5.   As Merle's death occurred more than four years but within five years after Robin's death, quick succession relief is available at 20%. The quick succession relief applies both on the shares transferred to her and on the life interest in the settled fund that passes to Jenny on Merle's death.

6. The value of the shares transferred to Merle on Robin's death was:

25,000 shares in Fieldfare plc @ 400p (see explanatory note 3)	100,000
Tax thereon (25% of gross = 25/75 of net)	33,333
Gross transfer	£ 133,333

7. The value of the assets transferred to the settled fund on Robin's death was:

Assets	30,000
Tax thereon (25% of gross = 25/75 of net)	10,000
Gross transfer	£ 40,000

Position on death of Jenny

8. The liabilities in Jenny's estate will have included the inheritance tax on the gift from Merle and the value of the settled property will have been reduced by the inheritance tax payable by the trustees because of the death of Merle.

9. Jenny's death occurred within two years after the gift of shares from Merle, so 80% quick succession relief is available thereon.

    The value of the shares transferred was:

Chargeable transfer – gross	28,125
Less: Inheritance tax on death of Merle	850
Net chargeable transfer	£ 27,275

10. Jenny's death occurred within one year of Merle's death, so the rate of quick succession relief on the assets in the settlement is 100%.

    The net value transferred on Merle's death was:

Settled fund	32,000
Inheritance tax payable thereon	10,558
	£ 21,442

    The value of £22,750 at Jenny's death reflects the movement in the value of the fund for reasons other than the liability for tax.

11. Jenny is not a minor and therefore the interest she acquired in her mother's estate is not subject to the rules in section 71A.

    However, the interest in Robin's will trust is a transitional serial interest because:

    (i)   the settlement was set up before 22 March 2006 (on Robin's death); and

    (ii)   immediately before 22 March 2006, there was an individual (Merle) with a beneficial interest in possession in the settlement; and

    (iii)   that person's interest must have come to an end after 21 March 2006 but before 6 April 2008 (on 30 September 2006 on Merle's death); and

    (iv)   Jenny became beneficially entitled to that interest at that time; and

    (v)   the interest is not a disabled person's interest or an interest of a bereaved minor.

    Consequently, Jenny is treated as beneficially entitled to the assets in the fund at her death.

Mr Maxford died on 7 January 2007. He was UK domiciled. The following information is held:

(1)   He had previously owned a 14% shareholding (70,000 shares) in Maxford plc, an unquoted trading company, for many years.

(2)   In February 1997 he gifted 30,000 of the Maxford plc shares to trustees of a discretionary trust for his children.

(3)   In May 2001 he gifted 20,000 of the Maxford plc shares to a trust in which his daughter has a life interest. (He was excluded from benefit under both trusts and the trustees retained the shares.)

(4)   The agreed share values at the time of both gifts were:

Shareholding	Per share value
	£
11% to 15%	10.00
5% to 10%	5.00
Below 5%	3.00

In February 2003 Maxford plc was listed on the Alternative Investment Market. All donees had retained their shares.

(5)   In 1991 he had inherited a 51% shareholding in Minota plc, a company whose shares are listed on the London Stock Exchange. In July 2003 he gifted a 10% shareholding then worth £600,000 to his daughter and she held them at his death when they were worth £200,000.

(6)   No other transfers had been made. Donees agreed to pay any tax due in respect of transfers to them.

His estate at death comprised:

(i)   His house worth £800,000.

(ii)   A life interest in his uncle's estate. The uncle had died in June 2002 with an estate worth £235,000 on which inheritance tax of £27,500 was suffered. On Mr Maxford's death his daughter became entitled to the capital, which was then worth £300,000.

(iii)   20,000 shares in Maxford plc valued at £10 per share.

(iv)   Holdings of quoted shares as follows:

Number/%	Company	Value at death
		£
7,000	Green plc	107,000
3,500	Blue plc	42,000
6,000	Red plc	8,000
41%	Minota plc	850,000

In the six months following death the following share sales occurred:

Shares sold	Company	Gross proceeds
		£
6,000	Green plc	84,000
2,000	Blue plc	35,000
600	Red plc	950

In his will, Mr Maxford left his Maxford plc shares to his daughter. His house was left equally to his widow and daughter, subject to his widow having full use and enjoyment of the house for her lifetime or for so long as she wished. The balance of his estate went to his son.

(a)   Calculate the inheritance tax payable as a result of the death of Mr Maxford.

(b)   Calculate the allocation of any tax due between the free estate and settled property.

(a) **Inheritance tax payable as a result of death of Mr Maxford**

Position on gifts in lifetime

		Gross £	Tax on 1995/96 scale £
February 1997	Gift of 30,000 Maxford plc shares to discretionary trust –		
	Value of 70,000 shares @ £10	700,000	
	Value of 40,000 shares @ £5	200,000	
	Loss to estate	500,000	
	Less: business property relief	500,000	
	Transfer of value	–	
May 2001	Gift of 20,000 Maxford plc shares to life interest trust –		
	Value of 40,000 shares @ £5	200,000	
	Value of 20,000 shares @ £3	60,000	
	Loss to estate	140,000	
	Less: 100% business property relief	140,000	
		–	
July 2003	Gift of 10% holding of Minota plc shares to daughter	600,000	
	Less: 50% business property relief	300,000	
		300,000	
	Less: Annual exemptions 2003/04 and 2002/03	6,000	
	Potentially exempt transfer	294,000	

On Mr Maxford's death 7 January 2007

Lifetime transfers in seven years before death

No additional tax is payable on the February 1997 gift, since this was more than seven years before Mr Maxford's death. (It is, however, included in the inheritance tax accumulation until February 2004, affecting the July 2003 gift accordingly.)

Business property relief remains available on the other gifts providing the transferees have retained what they were given and the property still qualifies as relevant business property. A listing on the Alternative Investment Market does not affect the status of unquoted shares, so that the May 2001 gift to the life interest trust will still retain entitlement to the 100% relief. The position on the July 2003 gift of Minota plc shares to the daughter is as follows:

	Gross £	Tax on 2006/07 scale £
Cumulative transfers in previous seven years	–	–
July 2003 PET now chargeable	294,000	3,600*
	294,000	3,600*

(* 294,000 – 285,000 = 9,000 @ 40%)

As the Minota plc shares have fallen in value at the date of death, the daughter may claim to have the tax on her gift recomputed as follows:

Value of gift as above		294,000
Value on death	200,000	
Less: 50% business property relief	(100,000)	
Annual exemptions	(6,000)	94,000
Reduce transfer by		200,000

This reduces the tax figure to nil. The amount included in the inheritance tax accumulation, however, remains at £294,000.

Estate at death

	£	£
House	800,000	
Less: Spouse exemption (see explanatory note 4)	800,000	–
20,000 shares in Maxford plc @ £10	200,000	
Less: 100% business property relief	200,000	–
Quoted shares**:		
Green plc 7,000 shares	107,000	
Blue plc 3,500 shares	42,000	
Red plc 6,000 shares	8,000	
Minota plc 41%	850,000	1,007,000
Free estate		1,007,000
Settled property – life interest in uncle's estate		300,000
		1,307,000

** See explanatory note 5.

Inheritance tax thereon:

	£	£
Cumulative transfers in previous seven years	294,000	–
Estate at death	1,307,000	526,400*
	1,601,000	526,400

(* 1,601,000 – 285,000 = 1,316,000 @ 40%)

Tax on estate	526,400
Less: Quick succession relief re uncle's estate (4 to 5 years)	
$20\% \times \dfrac{207,500}{235,000} \times 27,500$	4,856
	521,544

(b)   **Allocation of tax between free estate and settled property**

	£
Tax on estate as above	521,544

Estate rate = $\dfrac{521,544}{1,307,000}$ x 100 = 39.904%

	£
Tax on free estate 1,007,000 @ 39.904%	401,832
(payable by personal representatives)	
Tax on settled property 300,000 @ 39.904%	119,712
(payable by trustees, reducing daughter's entitlement accordingly)	
	521,544

Explanatory Notes

Business property relief

1.   Business property relief increased to 100% on 6 April 1996.

     Thus the Maxford plc shares retained by Mr Maxford until his death qualify for 100% business property relief in the death estate. Since they were left as a specific gift to his daughter, there is no restriction of the exempt legacy of the house to the spouse by reference to the business property relief (see Example 15 for further details).

2.   From 10 March 1992 quoted shares qualify for business property relief of 50% if they give the transferor control immediately before the transfer, hence the relief in respect of the gift of the Minota plc shares to the daughter. There is no relief in the death estate on the Minota plc shares retained by Mr Maxford, since he no longer had a controlling holding.

Fall in value of gift

3.   The claim for tax to be computed on the value of a gift at death where that is lower than the value at the time of the gift does not affect the cumulative transfers figure for the purpose of later transfers, so the amount included in lifetime transfers remains at £294,000. For detailed notes on such claims see Example 12.

Legacy of house to spouse and daughter

4.   The stipulation in Mr Maxford's will that his spouse was entitled to full use of the property created a life interest in the daughter's share of the property (CIR v Lloyds Private Banking 1998). Mrs Maxford therefore owns half the property outright and has a life interest in the other half. In both cases the spouse exemption applies. For detailed notes on interests in possession and property see Example 52.

Sale of quoted shares at a loss within twelve months after death

5.   Although 6,000 of the Green plc shares were sold at a loss within twelve months after death, no relief may be claimed, since the overall result of the sales was a profit as follows:

			Death Value	Realised Value
			£	
Green plc	6,000 shares	6,000/7,000 x 107,000	91,714	84,000
Blue plc	2,000 shares	2,000/3,500 x 42,000	24,000	35,000
Red plc	600 shares	600/6,000 x 8,000	800	950
			116,514	119,950

     For detailed notes on claims for a loss on quoted shares see Example 8.

A. (a) Brian is the life tenant of a settlement valued at £159,000 and on 31 December 2003 he released his life tenancy for the benefit of the succeeding life tenant, Carol.

Brian made a previous transfer in the form of a gift to his brother on 26 March 2002 of £161,000.

After relinquishing his interest in the settlement he made a gift of £60,000 to a friend on 8 June 2004.

On 2 April 2007 Brian died leaving free estate of £120,000.

Calculate the inheritance tax payable.

(b) Carol, who succeeded to the life tenancy from Brian in (a) above, died on 1 February 2005, having made no previous transfers.

The settlement was then valued at £182,000. On the death of Carol the property passed to David, the remainderman, absolutely.

Carol left free estate of £104,000.

Calculate

(i) the inheritance tax position on her death, and

(ii) the effect of the subsequent death of Brian.

B. Antony and Benjamin each have a life interest in trust funds, with remainder to Denis, the assets of each fund consisting entirely of a loan of £60,000 to a close company, repayable at seven days' notice.

On 30 June 2005 Antony sold his interest to Clive for its full market value of £20,000.

Before Antony sold his interest to Clive he had made chargeable transfers of £254,000 in August 1998, but had not made any later transfers of value.

Antony died on 30 September 2006 leaving an estate of £398,000.

Clive, before his acquisition of Antony's interest, had made a potentially exempt transfer (after exemptions) of £200,000 in February 2001 and made no further gifts.

Benjamin died on 30 December 2006. Before his death he had made potentially exempt transfers (after exemptions) in the previous seven years amounting to £186,000 and his estate was valued at £100,000, excluding his interest in the trust.

Sufficient of the loans was repaid for the trustees of each fund to meet their inheritance tax liabilities on each occasion.

Compute the inheritance tax payable by the trustees of each fund by reference to the above events.

Where relevant, proper notice was given to the trustees of availability of exemptions within the appropriate time limit for both part A and part B of the example.

A.   (a)   **Brian**

Inheritance tax accumulation

26 March 2002		
Gift to brother		161,000
Less: Annual exemptions 2001/02	3,000	
2000/01	3,000	6,000
Potentially exempt transfer		£ 155,000
31 December 2003		
Release of life tenancy		159,000
Less: Annual exemptions 2003/04	3,000	
2002/03	3,000	6,000
Potentially exempt transfer		£ 153,000
8 June 2004		
Gift to friend		60,000
Less: Annual exemption 2004/05		3,000
Potentially exempt transfer		£ 57,000

Death of Brian — 2 April 2007

Inheritance tax payable on gifts within seven years before death

	Gross £	Tax (on 2006/07 scale) £
26 March 2002		
Gift to brother	155,000	–
31 December 2003		
Release of life tenancy	153,000	9,200*
	308,000	9,200*
(* 308,000 – 285,000 = 23,000 @ 40%)		
8 June 2004		
Gift to friend	57,000	22,800
Cumulative chargeable transfers at death	365,000	32,000
Free estate on death	120,000	48,000
	485,000	80,000

Inheritance tax payable	£	£	By
Re 26 March 2002 gift		nil	
Re 31 December 2003 release of life interest (3–4 years before death)	9,200		
Less: Tapering relief 20%	1,840	7,360	trustees of settlement
Re 8 June 2004 gift (less than 3 years before death)		22,800	friend
On free estate		48,000	personal representatives

A. (b) (i) **Estate of Carol — Inheritance tax position as at date of death 1 February 2005**

		£
Free estate		104,000
Settled property		182,000
		286,000

		£	
Inheritance tax on 2004/05 death scale (no previous transfers)		£	9,200*

(* 286,000 – 263,000 = 23,000 @ 40%)

Payable by:

Personal representatives $\dfrac{104,000}{286,000}$ x £9,200 =   3,345

Trustees of settlement $\dfrac{182,000}{286,000}$ x £9,200 =   5,855**

          £   9,200

(ii) **Estate of Carol — Revision of inheritance tax position following death of Brian**

	£	£
Free estate		104,000
Settled property	182,000	
Less: Inheritance tax payable by reference to now chargeable transfer dated 31.12.03	7,360	174,640
		278,640*

Inheritance tax payable (* 278,640 – 263,000 = 15,640 @ 40%)   6,256*

Quick succession relief by reference to
earlier chargeable transfer on 31.12.03:

$80\% \times \dfrac{145,640}{153,000}$ x £7,360   5,605

Tax payable   £   651

Payable by:

Personal representatives $\dfrac{104,000}{278,640}$ x 651 = 243

Trustees of settlement $\dfrac{174,640}{278,640}$ x 651 = 408

Repayable to: Personal representatives	(3,345 – 243)	3,102
Trustees of settlement	(5,855 – 408)	5,447**
		£ 8,549

** See also explanatory note 11.

B. **Antony**

Inheritance Tax Accumulation

Cumulative transfers to date			254,000
30 June 2005			
Sale of life interest in trust			
Value transferred		60,000	
Less: Proceeds of sale		20,000	
		40,000	
Less: Annual exemptions 2005/06	3,000		
2004/05	3,000	6,000	
Potentially exempt transfer		£ 34,000	

30 September 2006 — Death of Antony

	Gross £	Tax (on 2006/07 scale) £
Tax payable by trustees on potentially exempt transfer 30 June 2005:		
Cumulative transfers within seven years before 30 June 2005 –		
Chargeable transfers in August 1998	254,000	–
Potentially exempt transfer 30 June 2005	34,000	1,200*
	288,000	1,200*

(* 288,000 – 285,000 = 3,000 @ 40%)

Tax payable by personal representatives on estate at death:

	Gross £	Tax (on 2006/07 scale) £
Cumulative transfers within seven years before 30 September 2006	34,000	–
Estate on death	408,000	62,800*
	442,000	62,800*

(* 442,000 – 285,000 = 157,000 @ 40%)

Inheritance tax payable:
 By trustees (no tapering relief since death occurs within three years) .... £ 1,200
 By personal representatives .... £ 62,800

Clive

Inheritance Tax Accumulation

Potentially exempt transfer February 2001		£ 200,000	
30 September 2006			
Transfer of life interest because of death of Antony		60,000	
Less: Annual exemptions 2006/07	3,000		
2005/06	3,000	6,000	
Potentially exempt transfer		£ 54,000	

Benjamin — Date of death 30 December 2006

Inheritance Tax Accumulation		Gross £	Tax (on 2006/07 scale) £
Potentially exempt transfers within seven years before death, now chargeable		186,000	–
Value chargeable on death:			
Free estate	100,000		
Settled property	60,000	160,000	24,400*
		346,000	24,400*

(* 346,000 – 285,000 = 61,000 @ 40%)

Tax payable:

By personal representatives

$$\frac{100,000}{160,000} \times £24,400 = \qquad 15,250$$

By trustees

$$\frac{60,000}{160,000} \times £24,400 = \qquad 9,150$$

£ 24,400

Summary of Inheritance Tax payable by Trustees	£
By trustees of Antony's trust fund	
On sale of Antony's life interest to Clive 30 June 2005	nil
On Antony's death 30 September 2006:	
Re potentially exempt transfer 30 June 2005	1,200
Re termination of life interest (by reference to inheritance tax accumulation of Clive who is in possession, providing Clive lives until after 30 September 2013)	nil
By trustees of Benjamin's trust fund	
On Benjamin's death 30 December 2006	9,150

Explanatory Notes

Disclaiming interest in a settlement

1. A person who becomes entitled to an interest under a settlement (any type of interest, not just a life interest) may disclaim his entitlement and providing this is not done for money or money's worth, he is treated as never having become entitled to the interest (s 93). This only applies where an interest is disclaimed *before* any benefit is accepted, and the disclaimer must be of the whole interest and not just part of it. Once benefits have been accepted the normal tax consequences follow.

Termination of interest in possession

2. Where a person, before 22 March 2006, had an interest in possession in the whole or any part of a settlement, the appropriate part of the trust fund is treated for inheritance tax purposes as belonging to that person absolutely (s 49(1)). (An interest in possession broadly means an entitlement as of right to *income* from a settlement. For further notes on this point see Example 52.)

Clive acquired his interest before 22 March 2006 and, therefore, is treated as beneficially entitled to the assets in the fund until Antony's death.

Had Clive acquired his interest in the fund after 21 March 2006, it would not have been treated as part of his taxable estate as the limited exceptions discussed in Example 52 do not apply.

Therefore, for pre-22 March 2006 interests, if the person with the interest dies (s 4(1)) or terminates that interest by releasing or selling it (s 52) there will be a potential charge to inheritance tax. It would be unfair for the person in possession of the interest to have to pay any inheritance tax arising as that person has no control over the assets of the settlement. The tax is therefore payable by the trustees (s 201(1)). If the transfer is or becomes a chargeable transfer, however, it is added to the inheritance tax accumulation of the person with the interest in possession (s 52) and the tax is calculated as though the transfer had been made by that person.

3. The termination of an interest in possession during the lifetime of the person beneficially entitled to that interest is treated under s 52(1) as a transfer of value equal to the value of the property in which the interest in possession subsisted. The estate of the transferor immediately before the transfer is deemed to include the whole of the property in which he had an interest in possession and therefore the reduction in value of the estate as a result of the assignment is the full value of the property in which he had an interest in possession less any amount received as consideration for the assignment (s 52(2)). Where consideration is received, exemption cannot be claimed as a commercial transaction because s 52(1) and (2) expressly provide for tax to be payable. The easiest way to look at it is that whilst the life tenant's reservoir of assets has been depleted by the underlying value of the trust fund which it is deemed to contain, the free estate included in the reservoir has increased by the proceeds received, so that the transfer of value is the difference between the two.

Availability of exemptions

4. For events after 21 March 2006, if the termination occurs during the person's lifetime and the property devolves upon

   (i)   a gift to another individual,

   (ii) a gift into a disabled trust, or

   (iii) a gift into a bereaved minor's trust on the coming to an end of an immediate post-death interest

then the transfer is a potentially exempt transfer and will only become a chargeable transfer should the former life tenant die within seven years. The transfer is, however, a *deemed* transfer of value and accordingly the small gifts exemption and exemption for normal expenditure out of income do not apply (ss 20(3), 21(5)). The annual and marriage gifts exemptions are, however, available providing the transferor gives the trustees of the settlement a notice informing them of the availability of the exemptions, within six months after the date of *termination*, in a form prescribed by HMRC (s 57). Notice is required within that period even though the transfer is a potentially exempt transfer. Both the annual and marriage exemptions would be taken into account in arriving at the potentially exempt transfer (ss 51(2), 57). Other exemptions are also available (see explanatory note 6).

After the transfer the interest in possession does not concern the transferor, but instead forms part of the inheritance tax reservoir of assets of the transferee. If, however, the transferor dies within seven years after the date of transfer the potentially exempt transfer rules apply in the normal way and tax on the potentially exempt transfer is chargeable on the normal scale, any tax arising being payable by the trustees (or the transferee if the trust came to an end as a result of the transfer).

5. Even though any tax that may arise on the termination of the life interest is payable by the trustees and not by the transferor, his accumulation is increased by the amount of the transfer if it becomes a chargeable transfer, thus increasing his tax liability on any later transfers. Brian in part A and Antony

and Clive in part B of the example would therefore surrender their annual exemptions to the trustees for use against the transfers if they had made no other transfers against which the exemptions could be utilised.

6. If the termination of the life interest occurs on the life tenant's death, the value of the assets in the settlement is added to the free estate and tax calculated on the aggregate. The trustees are then liable to pay a proportionate part of the total inheritance tax payable.

For both lifetime and death terminations the exemptions for transfers to spouse/civil partner, charities or political parties are available.

For most interests in possession created on or after 22 March 2006, the death of the life tenant will not give rise to any inheritance tax consequence as the trust fund would not be deemed to form part of the life tenant's estate.

Release of Brian's life interest

7. On the release of Brian's life interest in part A of the example there is a transfer of value based on the underlying assets in the settlement. Since Brian is entitled to the whole of the income of the trust, the whole capital value of the fund is deemed to be transferred. Because the release is to another interest in possession settlement in which an individual, Carol, is beneficially entitled, the transfer is at that point potentially exempt (after deducting annual exemptions, following notice by Brian to the trustees of their availability).

On the death of Brian his accumulation is recomputed for the seven years prior to death, with the potentially exempt transfers now being treated as chargeable transfers. The rates used for the recomputation are those applicable on 2 April 2007. In the case of transfers occurring more than three years before death, tapering relief reduces the tax on those particular transfers without affecting the overall computation.

Death of Carol

8. In part A (b) Carol has not made any previous transfers and her free estate of £104,000 is below the threshold for inheritance tax on her death. But the estate for inheritance tax purposes includes both free and settled property. The possession of the life interest therefore causes tax to be payable on the free estate, as well as giving rise to a liability in the settlement. A tax liability of £3,345 therefore arises on the free estate at the time of Carol's death. This liability is, however, reduced to £243 through a combination of less tax being payable because of the tax debt which has to be deducted from the settled property and quick succession relief when the position is recomputed on the subsequent death of Brian (see note 10).

Quick succession relief etc

9. If, on death, a person's estate has been increased by a chargeable transfer within the previous five years then quick succession relief is available. The total tax chargeable on death is reduced by a percentage of that part of the tax charged on the previous transfer that the net value then transferred bore to the gross chargeable transfer at that time. The percentage is as follows:

Time between transfer and death	*Percentage relief*
1 year or less	100%
1+ to 2 years	80%
2+ to 3 years	60%
3+ to 4 years	40%
4+ to 5 years	20%

The release of the life interest by Brian in part A of the example on 31 December 2003 was potentially exempt so that no quick succession relief was due on Carol's death on 1 February 2005. However, when Brian dies on 2 April 2007 his release of his life interest which was previously potentially exempt becomes chargeable (s 3A(4)) with tax payable of £7,360.

Quick succession relief is then available by reference to the death of Carol on 1 February 2005, giving a repayment of inheritance tax to the trustees and her personal representatives.

The time between the two chargeable transfers is just over one year, and the percentage is therefore 80% (s 141).

The tax of £7,360 charged on the earlier transfer reduces the gross chargeable transfer of £153,000 so that the increase in the estate of Carol resulting from that chargeable transfer is only £145,640.

For further notes on quick succession relief see Example 53.

10. On the subsequent death of Brian the inheritance tax liability of the trust fund on the original transfer is £7,360. Whilst this liability does not arise until the death of Brian on 2 April 2007, it nonetheless affects the value of the trust property on Carol's earlier death on 1 February 2005 since it derives from the now chargeable transfer by Brian on 31 December 2003.

The inheritance tax liability on the death of Carol is therefore not only recomputed by quick succession relief, but also by the inclusion of a different figure for the value of the trust property itself.

Retaining funds to meet potential liabilities

11. This example illustrates that trustees of settlements will have a potential tax liability for seven years after a release of a life interest although this will become less relevant now that most post-22 March 2006 settlements are no longer treated as part of the life tenant's estate. Accordingly funds must be retained for that period to meet those liabilities. Thus on the death of Carol the trustees should not distribute to the remainderman, David, all of the assets remaining after the tax of £5,855 on her death since by doing so they would find themselves with a personal liability for tax on the subsequent death of Brian should they be unable to recover from David the tax due of £1,893 (£7,360 – £5,467) by reference to Brian's death.

12. In part B of the example, when Antony dies, Clive's reservoir of assets is reduced as the property passes to the remainderman, Denis. This is a potentially exempt transfer after deduction of annual exemptions for 2006/07 and 2005/06 and provided Clive lives for at least a further seven years, it will not give rise to a charge. If, however, Clive died within that time the transfer would become chargeable by reference to his accumulation. The tax would be payable out of the trust funds, and in transferring the trust assets to the remainderman Denis, the trustees should provide for this contingent liability.

On the death of Benjamin his interest in possession is chargeable in the normal way, that is by aggregation with the free estate and the tax on the total is apportioned rateably to the various parts of his estate.

Reversion to settlor or spouse/civil partner

13. If an interest in possession comes to an end during the settlor's lifetime, and the settled property reverts to the settlor, tax is not chargeable (s 53(3)). Furthermore tax is not chargeable if the settlor's spouse/civil partner (or widow/widower or surviving civil partner if settlor had died less than two years earlier) becomes beneficially entitled to the property and is domiciled in the UK (s 53(4)).

Tax is chargeable if the settlor or spouse/civil partner acquired the reversionary interest for a consideration in money or money's worth (s 53(5)).

Anti-avoidance provisions

14. When property is transferred to a discretionary trust, the transfer cannot be potentially exempt. And since 22 March 2006 it is no longer possible for a settlor, whilst alive, to make a potentially exempt transfer into an interest in possession trust, on which no tax would be payable if he survived seven years.

(a) Fred, an annuitant under a settled fund, died on 31 August 2006. The amount of the annuity was £5,000. The value of the fund as a whole on that date was £500,000 and it produces an average annual income yield of 10%. Assume the current yield shown in the FT Actuaries Share Index was 4.17% for British Government Stocks (Irredeemables).

Calculate the value of the annuity fund for inheritance tax purposes on the death of Fred.

(b) Jim, the life tenant of a settled fund, died on 31 August 2006. His life tenancy was subject to an annuity of £5,000. The value of the fund as a whole was £500,000 on that date and the annual income yield was 6%. Assume the current actual dividend yield of the FT Actuaries All Share Index was 3%.

Calculate the value of the life tenancy for inheritance tax purposes on the death of Jim. Assume Jim acquired his interest in the fund before 22 March 2006.

(a)   **Fred deceased — 31 August 2006**

Value of Annuity Fund   £

Without s 50(3)

Annuity £5,000
Income of fund (£500,000 x 10%) £50,000
Share of capital attributable to Fred

$$\frac{5,000}{50,000} \ \text{x} \ 500,000$$ 50,000
                                                                                    ———

With s 50(3)

Annuity £5,000
Notional income of fund (£500,000 x 4.17%) £20,850
Minimum share of capital attributable to Fred

$$\frac{5,000}{20,850} \ \text{x} \ 500,000$$ 119,904
                                                                                    ———

Value for inheritance tax of Fred's annuity fund   £ 119,904

(b)   **Jim deceased — 31 August 2006**

Value of part remaining after an annuity   £

Without s 50(3)

Annuity £5,000
Income of fund (£500,000 x 6%) £30,000
Share of capital attributable to Jim
(ie after annuity of £5,000)

$$(\frac{30,000 - 5,000}{30,000}) \ \text{x} \ 500,000$$ 416,667
                                                                                    ———

With s 50(3)

Annuity £5,000
Notional income of fund (£500,000 x 3%) £15,000

Value of fund   500,000
Less: Maximum value of annuity fund

$$\frac{5,000}{15,000} \ \text{x} \ 500,000$$ 166,667
                                                                                    ———

Minimum value of part remaining   333,333

Value for inheritance tax of Jim's life tenancy   £ 416,667

Explanatory Notes

1.   A person who has a life interest in settled property is treated for the purposes of inheritance tax as owning it absolutely provided the interest was acquired before 22 March 2006 (s 49(1)).

Where one beneficiary of a settlement is entitled to a fixed amount of income and another to the remainder of the income, then to arrive at their respective shares of the trust fund the fund is divided in proportion to their shares of income (s 50(1)). The income arising over the previous twelve months is usually used for this purpose.

2. However, if only one of the interests in the settlement is to be valued for the purpose of calculating a chargeable transfer, s 50(3) contains anti-avoidance provisions to prevent loss of tax to HMRC where the yield of the fund may have been arranged to reduce the taxable amount.

    The anti-avoidance provisions *do not apply* where chargeable transfers of *both* of the interests are made *at the same time*, since the whole of the supporting capital will in those circumstances be caught in any event.

3. The value of the annuity fund becomes:

    (a) In the case of a transfer of the annuity — not *less* than its capital value using the current yield on the FT Actuaries Index for British Government Stocks (Irredeemables).

    (b) In the case of a transfer of the remainder — not *more* than its capital value using the current actual yield on the FT Actuaries All Share Index.

    The use of these particular indices is prescribed by SI 2000/174, effective from 18 February 2000. The figures are obtainable from the Financial Times.

4. The value of Fred's annuity fund included in his estate is therefore the higher of £50,000 (arrived at using the actual income yield of the fund) and £119,904 (arrived at using the notional income yield of 4.17% being the yield on British Government Irredeemable Stocks).

    In arriving at the value of Jim's life tenancy, the value of the annuity fund using the actual income yield is 1/6th of £500,000 = £83,333. Since this is less than the maximum permitted value of £166,667 using the All-Share Index, the anti-avoidance provision in s 50(3) does not apply in valuing Jim's interest for inheritance tax purposes on his death.

5. For interests created on or after 22 March 2006 the rules apply only to

    – interest in possession trusts where the interest in possession is:

        – an immediate post-death interest (see below)

        – a disabled person's interest (broadly an interest in possession for a person incapable of looking after their affairs because of mental disorder, or a person in receipt of an attendance allowance or a disability living allowance) or

        – a transitional serial interest (see below) (IHTA 1984 s 49(1A)).

    An immediate post-death interest is one:

    (a) created on an individual's death under the deceased's will or under the law of intestacy,

    (b) which gave the life tenant the beneficial entitlement to the trust fund on the individual's death, and

    (c) which is not and has not been a disabled person's interest or an interest of a bereaved minor (IHTA 1984 s 49A).

    To be a transitional serial interest in a settlement:

    (a) the settlement must have been set up before 22 March 2006; and

    (b) immediately before 22 March 2006, there must have been an individual with a beneficial interest in possession in the settlement; and

    (c) that person's interest must have come to an end after 21 March 2006 but before 6 April 2008; and

    (d) the person with the current interest in the settlement became beneficially entitled to that interest at that time; and

    (e) the interest is not a disabled person's interest or an interest of a bereaved minor (IHTA 1984 s 49B).

The rules for bereaved minors are found in IHTA 1984 s 71A. They apply only for settlements which:

(a)   are set up by:

    (i)   a parent of the beneficiary in their will or

    (ii)   the Criminal Injuries Compensation Scheme

(b)   give the minor the capital and income of the trust absolutely when the minor reaches the age of 18.

Amelia Dobbin, a widow, died on 15 July 2006.

Her first husband, George Sedley, who died in 1971, had by his will left the residue of his estate to her absolutely. In 1973 she made a settlement of this absolute interest under which she took a life interest with remainder to her son.

At her death the settled fund consisted of investments valued at £249,000.

Her second husband, William Dobbin, who died in July 1974, settled the residue of his estate on her for life with the remainder to Rebecca, his daughter by a previous marriage.

This settled fund on Amelia Dobbin's death was valued at £300,000.

Amelia had made two transfers of value prior to her death.

On 1 January 1997 she transferred assets to Rebecca's husband, the value of the transfer being £70,900. On 10 June 2004 she gave £132,000 to her son.

For many years up to the date of her death Amelia had owned and farmed 200 acres of agricultural land, the open market value of which is £400,000 and the agricultural value £300,000. The farm's business assets are valued at £96,000.

Amelia's free estate at death, apart from the farm land and business assets, consisted of £40,000 Crawley Corporation 6% Stock 2004, quoted at 92-94 ex div (interest paid 15 February and 15 August), furniture and effects valued at £13,500, income due to her from the settlements £4,320 and a bank balance of £8,590.

Her liabilities and funeral expenses amounted to £4,370.

By her will she left £50,000 to a registered charity, £2,000 to a major British political party, and the residue to a close friend.

(a)   Prepare a statement of the amount on which inheritance tax is chargeable on Amelia's death.

(b)   Compute the inheritance tax payable, stating by whom it will be borne.

Amelia Dobbin deceased

(a) **Calculation of amount on which inheritance tax is chargeable on death — 15 July 2006**

				£
Free estate				
Agricultural property:				
Agricultural value		300,000		
Less: Agricultural property relief 100%		300,000	–	
Business property:				
Non-agricultural value (£400,000 – £300,000)		100,000		
Farm business assets		96,000		
		196,000		
Less: Business property relief 100%		196,000	–	
£40,000 Crawley Corporation 6% stock @ 92½% ex div		37,000		
Interest due (half year)	1,200			
Less: Income tax @ 20%	240	960	37,960	
Furniture and effects			13,500	
Income due from settlements			4,320	
Bank balance			8,590	
			64,370	
Less: Funeral expenses and liabilities			4,370	60,000
Settled property				
1973 Settlement by Amelia on herself for life				
Investments				249,000
1974 Surviving spouse settlement				
Transitional exemption (see explanatory note 4)				–
				309,000
Less: Exempt legacies				
Charity			50,000	
Political party			2,000	
			£ 52,000	
Giving a deduction after agricultural and business property relief attributable thereto of				
$£52,000 \times \dfrac{60,000 \text{ (free estate } after \text{ APR/BPR)}}{556,000 \text{ (free estate } before \text{ APR/BPR)}}$				5,612
Chargeable to inheritance tax on Amelia's death				303,388

(b)   **Inheritance tax payable at death — 15 July 2006**

On potentially exempt transfers within seven years before death (ie 16 July 1999 to 15 July 2006):

			Gross £	Tax £
10 June 2004				
Gift to son		132,000		
Less: Annual exemptions 2004/05	3,000			
2003/04	3,000	6,000		
Potentially exempt transfer now chargeable			126,000	–
			126,000	–

On estate at death:

	Gross £	Tax £
Inheritance tax accumulation within seven years before death as above	126,000	–
Chargeable assets at death and tax thereon	303,388	57,755*
	429,388	57,755*

(* 429,388 – 285,000 = 144,388 @ 40%)

The inheritance tax of £57,755 is borne as follows:

By personal representatives

Value of free estate (as reduced by APR and BPR)	60,000	
Less: Exempt transfers (as reduced by APR and BPR)	5,612	
	£ 54,388	

$$£57,755 \ \times \ \frac{54,388}{303,388} \ = \qquad\qquad 10,354$$

By trustees of 1973 settlement

Value of settled property	£ 249,000	

$$£57,755 \ \times \ \frac{249,000}{303,388} \ = \qquad\qquad 47,401$$

£ 57,755

Explanatory Notes

Valuation of quoted securities

1.   Quoted securities are valued at a quarter up from the lower of the quoted prices (or halfway between the highest and lowest bargains marked if less), any accrued income therefore being included in the quotation. If quoted ex interest, the whole of the forthcoming income (net of lower rate income tax) must be added to the resultant valuation, since the whole of that income would have been forthcoming had a sale been made at the point of death, not just the part accrued on a day to day basis up to the death.

Agricultural and business property relief

2.   For detailed notes on agricultural property and business property relief see Example 25.

3.   The free estate is reduced by the exempt legacies to the charity and political party. Such legacies are completely exempt (ss 23, 24). However unless agricultural and business property is left as a specific legacy rather than as part of the residue of the estate, the benefit of agricultural property and business property relief is allocated over the exempt and chargeable free estate, thus effectively reducing the value of those reliefs where there are exempt legacies (see Examples 15 and 17).

     For detailed notes on the charity and political party exemptions see Example 1.

Estate duty — surviving spouse exemption

4.   Where one party to a marriage died before 13 November 1974 and the other dies after 12 March 1975 (the date on which estate duty was abolished and capital transfer tax/inheritance tax commenced to be chargeable on death) any property which would have been exempt from estate duty under the 'surviving spouse' exemption of FA 1894 s 5(2) is left out of account for inheritance tax (Sch 6.2).

     The estate duty exemption applied only to property in which the spouse had a limited interest (eg for life or widowhood) and of which she/he was at no time competent to dispose, and not to property that passed absolutely. The property comprised in the settlement established by Amelia's second husband on his death in July 1974 is therefore left out of account for inheritance tax under this transitional provision.

5.   Although Amelia at her death only had a life interest in the 1973 settlement comprising the assets from her first husband's estate, she did at one time (between 1971 and 1973) have an absolute interest in those assets, having herself created the settlement in her own favour. The transitional relief at note 4 does not therefore apply. A settlement upon oneself with remainder to specified persons is a useful way of determining in one's lifetime the destination of specified property upon death. For further notes on this point see Example 46 explanatory note 8.

     The assets comprised in the settlement itself remain in the reservoir of assets of the settlor through the interest in possession rules, so there is not even a potentially exempt transfer when the settlement is made, no transfer of value having taken place.

     The settled fund remains chargeable to inheritance tax on the death of the settlor, so no tax is avoided, but the lifetime settlement has determined the devolution on death, thus safeguarding against any possible family problems arising, say, from remarriage or other doubts within a family.

Potentially exempt transfers

6.   Amelia made potentially exempt transfers on 1 January 1997 and 10 June 2004. The earlier transfer became completely exempt on 1 January 2004. The second transfer became a chargeable transfer by reason of her death on 15 July 2006, but since it is below the nil threshold no tax is payable (and tapering relief is not therefore relevant). It does, however, reduce the nil band available against the death estate.

Richard died in 1993 and left his estate consisting of marketable securities in trust for his brother Alan for life and thereafter absolutely to Alan's son, Lawrie.

Lawrie died on 1 June 2006. His estate, including his interest in expectancy on the death of Alan, was left to his only daughter Gladys for life and thereafter to his nephew John absolutely.

Lawrie's estate comprised:

Personal assets £295,000
Interest expectant on the death of Alan valued at £32,000.

His funeral expenses amounted to £1,700 and his debts, including £100 owed to his turf accountant, amounted to £3,400. He had made no lifetime transfers.

Alan died on 31 December 2006, the value of the settled property on that date amounting to £55,000. Alan's personal estate was valued at £221,000. He had made one previous transfer on 6 October 2003, being a gift of quoted shares then valued at £115,000.

Calculate the inheritance tax payable on the above events.

Inheritance tax computation on death of Lawrie (1 June 2006)

			£
Value of estate for inheritance tax			
Free estate			295,000
Reversionary interest:			
Interest in expectancy on death of Alan – excluded property, therefore			nil
			295,000
Less: Funeral expenses		1,700	
Debts	3,400		
Less: Turf accountant	100	3,300	5,000
Chargeable to inheritance tax			290,000
Inheritance tax on 2006/07 scale (290,000 – 285,000 = 5,000 @ 40%)		£	2,000

Inheritance tax computation on death of Alan (31 December 2006)

Inheritance tax accumulation			Gross £	Tax £
6 October 2003				
Shares transferred		115,000		
Less: Annual exemptions 2003/04	3,000			
2002/03	3,000	6,000	109,000*	–
Estate at death:				
Free estate		221,000		
Settled property – Richard's settlement		55,000	276,000	40,000**
			385,000	40,000**

(** 385,000 – 285,000 = 100,000 @ 40%)

*   This will have been a potentially exempt transfer when it was made, but becomes a chargeable transfer since death occurred within seven years. No tax is payable, however, because it is below the nil threshold.

Tax of £40,000 on estate is payable as follows:

By trustees of settled property

$$\frac{55,000}{276,000} \times £40,000 \qquad\qquad 7,971$$

By personal representatives

$$\frac{221,000}{276,000} \times £40,000 \qquad\qquad 32,029$$

£ 40,000

Explanatory Notes

Reversionary interests

1.   A reversionary interest in a settlement is excluded property whether it is transferred in lifetime or on death unless it was acquired for a consideration, or unless it is one to which the settlor or his spouse/civil partner is beneficially entitled (or for interests acquired on or after 10 March 1981, has been at any time beneficially entitled (s 48)). Accordingly the value of the reversion in this example is excluded from Lawrie's estate for inheritance tax purposes.

For detailed notes on excluded property see Example 3.

2. The reason for excluding reversionary interests from a person's estate for inheritance tax purposes was that the capital value of the settlement (as distinct from the value of the right to receive the income for the time being) is included in the estate of the person presently entitled to receive the income for interests in possession created before 22 March 2006 and for some interests in possession created after that date.

    For other interests in possession created on or after 22 March 2006, the settlement is subject to a separate charging regime based upon the value of the trust property and, therefore, it is still unnecessary to tax reversionary interests.

Quick succession relief

3. The settled property does not give rise to quick succession relief on the death of Alan since it was *not* chargeable on the death of Lawrie (see Examples 53 and 55).

    The settlement made by Richard granted a life interest to Alan and a reversion to Lawrie.

    That made by Lawrie granted a life interest to Gladys with reversion to John.

    The fund left by Richard therefore devolves as follows:

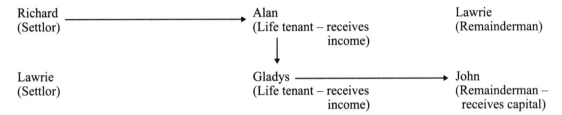

    Lawrie therefore never had an interest in the income of the settlement made by Richard and was therefore not chargeable to inheritance tax on the transfer of the reversion on his death. This passed as part of his estate from which Gladys is to enjoy the income for her life and will not be chargeable to inheritance tax until Gladys's interest in the fund ceases (ordinarily upon her death). On Alan's death on 31 December 2006, however, the trust fund created by Richard is reduced by inheritance tax of £7,971, reducing the value in the estate of Lawrie from which Gladys is to enjoy the income. It does not reduce the inheritance tax payable on Lawrie's death, because the trust fund is excluded property.

Treatment of debts in deceased's estate

4. Debts may be deducted from the chargeable estate if they are:

    (i)   Reasonable funeral expenses, including the cost of a tombstone (s 172).

    (ii) Liabilities imposed by law or incurred for a consideration in money or money's worth (including income and other taxes) (s 5(3), (5)).

    (iii) Liabilities for inheritance tax providing they are paid from the estate (ss 5(4) and 174(2)).

    A debt may not be deducted, however, to the extent that the creditor has received gifts from the deceased (FA 1986 s 103). For details see Example 20.

    The amount due to the turf accountant is not incurred for consideration in money or money's worth and cannot therefore be deducted in arriving at the chargeable estate of Lawrie.

Powers over trust property

5. The inheritance tax treatment of powers over trust property had become uncertain following the decision of the Court of Appeal in Melville v CIR (2001). The case concerned a scheme to obtain capital gains tax gifts holdover relief under TCGA 1992 s 260. In order for the relief to be available, the gift had to be a chargeable transfer for inheritance tax (see Example 50 explanatory note 3). The donor therefore made the gift to a discretionary trust. The aim was, however, to obtain the capital gains relief without attracting a large amount of inheritance tax. This was achieved by giving the

settlor the power, after 90 days, to direct the trustees to exercise various powers, including the power to direct them to transfer all or part of the fund back to him. Since the settlor could effectively revoke the trust after 90 days, the value of the power (and hence the chargeable transfer) was claimed to be the income arising in the 90 day period. The Revenue argued that the power was not 'property' for inheritance tax, being similar to that of a reversionary interest, and should therefore be ignored, so that the value transferred was the full value of the property transferred into the trust. The Court of Appeal found in the taxpayer's favour. Although this decision enabled the taxpayer to avoid capital gains tax, it had adverse inheritance tax implications, in particular for offshore trusts.

The position was amended by FA 2002 s 119, which provides that the definition of 'property' in IHTA 1984 s 272 does not include a 'settlement power'. A settlement power is defined in new s 47A as 'any power over, or exercisable (whether directly or indirectly) in relation to, settled property or a settlement'. To prevent the revised provisions being used for tax avoidance, s 55A provides that someone who *purchases* a settlement power will be treated as making a transfer of value equal to the decrease in value of his estate as a result of the transfer, and no exemptions will be available against the transfer. The revised provisions apply for transfers of value on or after 17 April 2002, but the definitions of settlement power and property are deemed to apply in relation to deaths before that date (to avoid adverse effects of the Melville decision).

The trustees of a discretionary settlement made on 1 November 1966 make the following appointments under powers given to them in the settlement, the cumulative transfers in the ten years prior to 1 November 1996 being £181,000.

(i)   1 July 1999   £40,000   cash to A absolutely

(ii)   1 April 2006   £60,000   cash to the settlor's wife

All the beneficiaries are domiciled and resident in the United Kingdom.

Any tax payable is to be paid by the beneficiaries.

(a)   Calculate the inheritance tax payable (if any) as a result of each of the above appointments and also the amount payable on the ten year anniversaries up to and including 1 November 2006.

The value of relevant property on 31 October 1996 was £162,000 and on 31 October 2006 £290,000.

(b)   If the original settlor added £15,000 to the original settlement on 1 November 2002 (at which time his gross chargeable transfers for the seven years to that date amounted to £215,000 including the £15,000 then transferred) calculate the revised tax liabilities assuming that the value of relevant property at 31 October 2006 was £306,000, including the addition to the settlement which was valued at £16,000 on that date.

The payment of £60,000 to the settlor's wife on 1 April 2006 is to be deemed to be wholly attributable to the funds in the original settlement.

(a) **Inheritance tax position of settlement made 1 November 1966**

	Gross £	Tax £
1 November 1996		
Ten yearly charge (see explanatory notes 3 and 4):		
Distributions in previous ten years (ie amounts subject to exit charges)	181,000	–
Value of relevant property on 31 October 1996	162,000	28,600*
	343,000	28,600*

Actual rate is 30% of effective rate

$$\frac{28,600}{162,000} \times 30\% = 5.296\%$$

Tax payable by trustees is £162,000 x 5.296% = £8,580

* Tax is calculated on 1996/97 scale
   (343,000 – 200,000 = 143,000 @ 20%)

1 July 1999
   Exit charge – on distribution to A
   Amount chargeable = £40,000
   Actual rate at previous ten year anniversary recomputed
   for change of rates
   1999/2000 scale 343,000 – 231,000 = 112,000 @ 20% = £22,400

Actual rate is 30% of effective rate

$$\frac{22,400}{162,000} \times 30\% = 4.15\%$$

Number of complete quarters between 1 November 1996
and 30 June 1999 = 10

Tax payable by A

$$£40,000 \times 4.15\% \times \frac{10}{40} = £415$$

1 April 2006
   Exit charge – on distribution to settlor's wife
   Amount chargeable = £60,000
   Actual rate at previous ten year anniversary recomputed
   for change of rates
   2005/06 scale 343,000 – 275,000 = 68,000 @ 20% = £13,600

Actual rate is 30% of effective rate

$$\frac{13,600}{162,000} \times 30\% = 2.52\%$$

Number of complete quarters between 1 November 1996
and 31 March 2006 = 37

Tax payable by settlor's wife

$$£60,000 \times 2.52\% \times \frac{37}{40} = £1,398$$

	Gross £	Tax £

1 November 2006

    Ten yearly charge

    Distributions in previous ten years (ie between

	Gross £	Tax £
1 November 1996 and 31 October 2006)	100,000	–
Value of relevant property on 31 October 2006	290,000	21,000**
	390,000	21,000**

    (** 390,000 – 285,000 = 105,000 @ 20%)

    Actual rate is 30% of effective rate

$$\frac{21,000}{290,000} \times 30\% = 2.17\%$$

    Tax payable by trustees is £290,000 x 2.17% = £6,293

(b)   **Additions to existing settlement**

1 November 2002

    Recalculation of distributions at previous ten year
    anniversary because of addition to property in the
    settlement:

Distributions in ten years to 31 October 1996			181,000
Value of relevant property at 31 October 1996	162,000		
Value of property added 1 November 2002	15,000	177,000	
		358,000	

1 April 2006

    Exit charge – on distribution to settlor's wife

    Amount chargeable = £60,000

    Revised rate at previous ten year anniversary following addition to
      settlement, using 2005/06 scale:

      358,000 – 275,000 = 83,000 @ 20% = £16,600

    Actual rate is 30% of effective rate

$$\frac{16,600}{177,000} \times 30\% = 2.814\%$$

    Number of complete quarters between 1 November 1996
    and 31 March 2006 = 37

    Tax payable by settlor's wife

$$£60,000 \times 2.814\% \times \frac{37}{40} = £1,562$$

	Gross £	Tax £
1 November 2006		
Ten yearly charge (see explanatory note 7)		
Distributions in previous ten years subject to an exit charge	100,000	–
Chargeable transfers made by settlor in seven years preceding addition to settlement (215,000 – 15,000)	200,000	3,000*
	300,000	3,000
Value of relevant property on 31 October 2005	306,000	61,200
	606,000	64,200†

(* 300,000 – 285,000 = 15,000 @ 20% = £3,000)
(† 606,000 – 285,000 = 321,000 @ 20% = £64,200)

Actual rate is 30% of effective rate

$$\frac{61,200}{306,000} \times 30\% = 6\%$$

proportionately reduced where relevant property added in previous ten years.

Tax payable by trustees:

		£
On relevant property held for preceding ten years (£306,000 – £16,000) = £290,000 @ 6%		17,400
On relevant property added 1 November 2002		
£16,000 @ 6% x $\frac{16}{40}$ (see explanatory note 7)		384
		£ 17,784

Explanatory Notes

Discretionary settlement — deemed chargeable transfers

1.   Where a settlement has an interest in possession which was created before 22 March 2006, the person with that interest is deemed to be beneficially entitled to the underlying assets, and chargeable transfers affecting his interest are deemed to be made by him (s 49).

This is also the case for subsequent interests in possession if they are:

(a)   an immediate post-death interest;

(b)   a disabled person's interest (broadly an interest in possession for a person incapable of looking after their affairs because of mental disorder, or a person in receipt of an attendance allowance or a disability living allowance); or

(c)   a transitional serial interest (IHTA 1984 s 49(1A)).

See Example 52.

In other cases this deemed ownership cannot apply, nor can the trustees make transfers of value or chargeable transfers. They are, however, deemed to make chargeable transfers when they make capital distributions.

Pre 27 March 1974 discretionary settlements

2. Where a settlement without an interest in possession was created before 27 March 1974 it has an inheritance tax accumulation of its own commencing at nil on 27 March 1974 (s 66(6b)). The rules for such settlements were changed from 9 March 1982. Under the old rules, tax was charged by taking into account 'distribution payments', which broadly meant capital distributions, although the term was more widely defined. From 9 March 1982 tax is charged at ten yearly intervals and also when property leaves the settlement, as detailed below.

Ten yearly charge

3. On the tenth anniversary of the creation of the settlement and every subsequent tenth anniversary (but not before 1 April 1983) a charge to inheritance tax arises. This is known as the principal or 'ten yearly' charge (s 64).

    The charge is made on any *relevant property* held in the trust at the anniversary. This means property in which there is no interest in possession (subject to certain exclusions – see note 8). See note 9 re reducing the tax on relevant property that has not been relevant property throughout the ten year period.

    The trust is deemed to make a notional transfer immediately before the anniversary, having previously made chargeable transfers of a specified amount, and *one half* the normal scale rate in force at the date of the charge is used to arrive at the tax on the transfer. There is no grossing up (s 64). The rate of tax charged on the relevant property in the trust is 30% of the effective rate of tax on the notional transfer. With the current half scale rate of 20% this gives a maximum charging rate of 6% (see note 11 re business or agricultural property relief and the instalment option).

    The rules for arriving at both the notional transfer and the previous transfers are different for pre 27 March 1974 trusts and trusts made on or after that date. For the detailed rules relating to post 26 March 1974 trusts see Example 60.

Cumulative transfers at ten year anniversary

4. For pre 27 March 1974 trusts, the inheritance tax accumulation at the anniversary date will normally only show transfers occurring during the preceding ten years. Those transfers will comprise:

    (a) At the first ten year anniversary, distribution payments (as defined under the old rules) up to 8 March 1982. These are not included at later ten year anniversaries.

    (b) The amounts on which exit charges have been made under s 65 (see notes 5 and 6).

    Thus the charge in 2006 uses the exit charges of the preceding ten years:

	£
1 July 1999	40,000
1 April 2006	60,000
	100,000

    These previous transfers are cumulated with the relevant property in the trust at the anniversary to compute the tax at one half normal rates on the notional transfer and arrive at the effective rate. The tax charge on the relevant property is then at 30% of the effective rate (s 66). In each case the tax is calculated at the rates in force at the date of the charge.

    Special rules apply when property has been added to the settlement during the ten year period. These are detailed in note 7.

Exit charges

5. In addition to the 10 yearly charge (explanatory notes 3 and 4) a charge to inheritance tax arises when property in a settlement ceases to be relevant property (s 65). This charge is known as the exit charge. If the tax is payable out of the relevant property remaining in the trust, the distribution is

grossed up using the rate of tax payable on the distribution (ie after reducing it under note 6 below, if appropriate, according to the complete quarters since the last ten year anniversary) (s 65(2)). (For an illustration of grossing up see Example 60.) The method of computing exit charges occurring after the first post 1 April 1983 ten year anniversary of the settlement is the same for both pre 27 March 1974 settlements and settlements made on or after that date.

6.   The charge on distributions after the first ten year anniversary is found by using the rate of tax computed at the previous ten year anniversary (but where the scale of rates has been reduced the rate deemed to have applied at that anniversary is recalculated using the revised scales (Sch 2.3), as shown in part (a) of the example). The exit charge rate is arrived at by applying to that previous rate the fraction x/40 where x is the number of complete quarters in the period since the previous ten year anniversary (s 69). If, therefore, the distribution occurs at the anniversary, or within three months thereafter, no exit charge is payable. The charge is levied on the difference between the value of relevant property before the distribution and its value thereafter. Thus the 'loss to the donor' principle applies to discretionary settlements. The maximum rate for an exit charge is 5.85%, ie 6% (maximum rate at previous ten year anniversary) x 39/40.

Special rules apply where property has been added to a settlement since the date of the last ten year charge (see note 7).

Added property

7.   Where property has been added to a pre 27 March 1974 settlement after 8 March 1982 as a result of a chargeable transfer by the settlor, then on the occasion of the following ten year anniversary the inheritance tax accumulation is deemed to commence with the distributions subject to an exit charge in the previous ten years, plus the aggregate of the values transferred by the settlor in the seven years preceding the date of the addition to the settlement disregarding transfers made on that day. Where two or more additions have been made then the higher of the two (or more) possible figures will be used (s 67(4)). Thus a modest addition to an existing settlement can give rise to a substantial increase in the tax payable. In the example the ten yearly charge on 1 November 2006 would increase from £6,300 to £17,784 if £15,000 was added to the settlement on 1 November 2002.

Although the total value of relevant property added in the previous ten years is chargeable to tax and is added to the accumulation to arrive at the rate of tax, the rate of tax chargeable on that added property is reduced by one-fortieth for each complete quarter before the date that the property became relevant property. In the example the property was added after six years (24 quarters) and therefore tax was payable on the added property of £16,000 @ 6% x 16/40 = £384; being a charge for the last four of the ten years (16 quarters) (s 66(2)).

In addition to affecting the subsequent ten year charge the addition will also increase the exit charge on any distribution occurring after its settlement. This is because it is necessary both for pre and post 27 March 1974 settlements to recompute the tax rate on the previous ten year anniversary by including in the calculation the value of property added subsequently as though it were relevant property at that time (s 69(2), (3)). This is illustrated by the difference in rates in part (b) of the example in relation to the distribution on 1 April 2006 to the settlor's wife where the tax increased from £1,398 to £1,562.

If the £60,000 paid to the settlor's wife on 1 April 2006 had come partly from the original settlement and partly from the added property then two separate computations would be required. The fraction applicable to the added property will not take into account the complete quarters (since the date of the previous anniversary) occurring before the day that the property was added (ss 68(3), 69(4)).

Thus, assuming that £54,000 came from the original settlement and £6,000 from the added property, the computation would be:

1 April 2006   £
    Exit charge – on distribution to settlor's wife
    Original property = £54,000
    Revised rate at previous ten year anniversary 2.814%
    Number of complete quarters = 37
    Tax payable:

$$£54,000 \ \times \ 2.814\% \ \times \ \frac{37}{40} \ = \qquad\qquad\qquad 1,405$$

    Added property – £6,000
    Complete quarters 1 November 1996 to 1 November 2002 = 24

$$\text{Appropriate fraction is} \qquad \frac{37-24}{40} = \frac{13}{40}$$

    Tax payable:

$$£6,000 \ \times \ 2.814\% \ \times \ \frac{13}{40} \ = \qquad\qquad\qquad 54$$

$$\overline{1,459}$$

Where there is no indication as to whether a distribution is paid out of the original property or added property, it is treated as coming out of each proportionately.

Property will be deemed to have been added if the settlor makes any chargeable transfer which results in the value of the property in the settlement increasing, unless it can be shown that the transfer was not primarily intended to increase the value of the settlement and the actual increase was not more than 5% of its original value (s 67(2)).

Meaning of 'relevant property'

8.   Relevant property is defined in s 58 as settled property in which there is an interest in possession created on or after 22 March 2006 other than:

    1.   An immediate post-death interest

    2.   A disabled person's interest (broadly an interest in possession for a person incapable of looking after their affairs because of mental disorder, or a person in receipt of an attendance allowance or a disability living allowance) or

    3.   A transitional serial interest

or there is no qualifying interest in possession, other than:

  (i)   Charitable trusts

  (ii)   Property held on accumulation and maintenance trusts (see Example 64) set up before 22 March 2006 or trusts for a bereaved minor

  (iii)   Maintenance funds for historic buildings etc

  (iv)   Pension funds

  (v)   Employee and newspaper trusts unless there is a post 22 March 2006 interest possession and the interest in possession is—

    –   not an immediate post-death interest,

    –   not a disabled person's interest, and

    –   not a transitional serial interest.

(vi)   Trade or professional compensation funds

(vii)   Protective trusts where the discretionary trust was triggered before 12 April 1978

(viii) Privileged trusts for disabled persons where funds were settled before 10 March 1981

(ix)   Excluded property.

9.   If property in a settlement has not been relevant property throughout the whole of the period then the charge on that property will not take into account the complete quarters (since the date of the previous anniversary) occurring before the day that the property became relevant property (s 68(3)). See Example 61 for an illustration of this point.

Conversion of relevant property into non-relevant property

10. An exit charge can (and in certain cases does) arise if trustees convert relevant property into property that is not relevant property. Such a charge is prevented in most instances, however, by specific provisions. Thus there is no exit charge when property ceases to be relevant property because it is transferred to an employee trust (subject to detailed conditions – see s 75), or is held for an unlimited period for charitable purposes, or becomes the property of a national body such as a museum or the National Trust, or a political party or a non-profit making body (s 76). This is subject to the proviso that the property does not cease to be used for the purposes of the body concerned.

Although an exit charge does not arise when a distribution is made from a charitable trust if it is for that purpose, a special charge is made under s 70 on the cessation of the trust or on a non-privileged distribution. This is calculated by reference to the time that the property has been held (but not before 13 March 1975) and is the sum of

0.25% for each of the first forty quarters
0.20% for each of the next forty quarters
0.15% for each of the next forty quarters
0.10% for each of the next forty quarters
0.05% for each of the next forty quarters

Thus the maximum rate of 30% cannot apply until 2025.

If the trust pays the tax then the amount must be grossed up.

Instalment option

11. It should be noted that where inheritance tax is payable on property eligible for the instalment option, that option is available to trustees of a settlement, provided that the property remains in the settlement (s 227(1)(c)). For details of property eligible see Example 5 at explanatory note 5. If the property is business or agricultural property qualifying for 50% relief, the 6% maximum rate of charge for discretionary trusts is effectively 3% on that property, and when paid by instalments over ten years this becomes 0.3% a year.

Nicholas Carraway, whose gross chargeable transfers in the preceding seven years totalled £100,000 and who had no available annual exemptions, settled a sum of £100,000 on 6 April 1987 in a discretionary trust, personally paying the inheritance tax of £24,667 chargeable on the scale at that time.

On 21 September 1989 the trustees made a distribution of £4,000 to A, subject to payment of tax out of that amount.

On 1 April 1991 the trustees made a distribution of £6,000 to B, subject to payment of tax out of that amount.

The market value of the trust fund on 5 April 1997 was £150,000.

On 27 May 2001 the trustees made a distribution of £20,000 to C, paying the tax out of the remainder of the settled fund.

The market value of the trust fund on 5 April 2007 was £300,000.

On 10 October 2010 the trustees made a final distribution of £330,000 to D, subject to payment of tax out of that amount.

Compute the inheritance tax payable on each chargeable occasion.

Assume for this purpose that the inheritance tax legislation remains unchanged for later years.

Also assume that the 2009/10 rates will continue into 2010/11.

Tax position of settlement (settlor having paid the tax on the settlement)

Initial value of settlement = £100,000

Inheritance tax – effective rate (originally calculated using FA 1987 scale but revised using 1989/90 scale to calculate tax on distribution 21 September 1989):

	Gross £	Tax £
Settlor's previous transfers within seven years before commencement of settlement	100,000	–
Initial value of settlement	100,000	16,400*
	200,000	16,400*

(* 200,000 – 118,000 = 82,000 @ 20%)

Actual rate is 30% of effective rate

$$\frac{16,400}{100,000} \times 30\% = 4.92\%$$

21 September 1989

    Exit charge on distribution to A

    Amount chargeable = £4,000

    Actual rate applicable at formation of settlement
      (revised using 1989/90 lifetime scale) – 4.92%

    Number of complete quarters between 6 April 1987
      and 21 September 1989 = 9

    Tax payable by A out of the distribution

$$£4,000 \times 4.92\% \times \frac{9}{40} = \underline{£44}$$

1 April 1991

    Exit charge on distribution to B

    Amount chargeable – £6,000

    Actual rate applicable at formation of settlement
      (revised using 1990/91 lifetime scale):

    200,000 – 128,000 = 72,000 @ 20% = £14,400

    Actual rate is 30% of effective rate

$$\frac{14,400}{100,000} \times 30\% = 4.32\%$$

    Number of complete quarters between 6 April 1987
      and 31 March 1991 = 15

    Tax payable by B out of the distribution

$$£6,000 \times 4.32\% \times \frac{15}{40} = \underline{£97}$$

	Gross £	Tax using FA 1997 scale £
6 April 1997		
Ten yearly charge (using one half of rate at 6.4.97)		
Settlor's previous transfers within seven years before commencement of settlement	100,000	
Distributions subject to exit charges in previous ten years (£4,000 + £6,000)	10,000	
	110,000	–
Value of relevant property – 5 April 1997	150,000	9,000**
	260,000	9,000**

(** 260,000 – 215,000 = 45,000 @ 20%)

Actual rate is 30% of effective rate

$$\frac{9,000}{150,000} \times 30\% = 1.8\%$$

Tax payable by trustees is £150,000 x 1.8% = £2,700

27 May 2001

Exit charge on distribution to C
Actual rate at previous ten year anniversary
(revised using 2001/02 lifetime scale):

260,000 – 242,000 = 18,000 @ 20% = £3,600

Actual rate is 30% of effective rate

$$\frac{3,600}{150,000} \times 30\% = 0.72\%$$

Number of complete quarters between 6 April 1997 and
26 May 2001 = 16

Rate of exit charge applicable

$$0.72\% \times \frac{16}{40} = 0.288\%$$

Distribution (net) – £20,000

Gross equivalent thereof £20,000 x $\dfrac{100}{99.712}$ = £20,058

Exit charge payable by trustees £20,058 x 0.288% = £58

6 April 2007		
Ten yearly charge (using one half of rate at 6.4.07)		
Settlor's previous transfers within seven years before commencement of settlement	100,000	
Distributions in preceding ten years subject to an exit charge	20,058	
	120,058	–
Value of relevant property – 5 April 2007	300,000	24,011†
	420,058	24,011†

(† 420,058 – 300,000 = 120,058 @ 20%)

Actual rate is 30% of effective rate

$$\frac{24{,}011}{300{,}000} \times 30\% = 2.401\%$$

Tax payable by trustees is £300,000 x 2.401% = £7,203

10 October 2010

Exit charge on distribution to D

Amount chargeable – £330,000

Actual rate at previous ten year anniversary revised using 2010/11 lifetime scale:

420,058 – 325,000 = 95,058 @ 20% = £19,011

Actual rate is 30% of effective rate

$$\frac{19{,}011}{300{,}000} \times 30\% = 2.401\%$$

Number of complete quarters between 6 April 2007 and 9 October 2010 = 14

Tax payable by trustees on final distribution

$$£330{,}000 \times 1.901\% \times \frac{14}{40} = £2{,}196$$

Explanatory Notes

Ten yearly charge on post 26 March 1974 discretionary settlements

1. The rules relating to discretionary settlements were amended from 9 March 1982. Those relating to pre 27 March 1974 settlements are dealt with in Example 59.

2. A charge arises under the 1982 legislation on each tenth anniversary of the settlement. This charge is applied to the *relevant property* held in the trust at the anniversary date, without grossing up (s 64).

    Relevant property used to mean (ie before 22 March 2006) property without an interest in possession. It is defined in detail in Example 59 explanatory note 9.

    For post 26 March 1974 settlements the charge is arrived at as follows (s 66):

    (a) The settlement is deemed to make a notional transfer immediately before the anniversary comprising:

        (i)   the value of the relevant property immediately before the anniversary, ie its value on the day before the anniversary

        (ii) the value immediately after it became comprised in the settlement of any property which was not then relevant property and has not subsequently become relevant property whilst remaining comprised in the settlement (eg where part of the settled property has always been subject to an interest in possession)

        (iii) the value of the property in any related settlement at the time the related settlement commenced (s 66). A related settlement is a settlement made by the same settlor and commencing on the same day (excluding settlements in which all the property is held without time limit for charitable purposes) (s 62). (Such a settlement might originally be a potentially exempt transfer but might then become chargeable because of the donor's death within seven years.)

    (b) The notional transfer in (a) is added to the notional previous transfers to arrive at the effective rate of tax on the notional transfer in (a) (i).

The notional previous transfers are:

(i) Any chargeable transfers made by the settlor in the seven years prior to the creation of the settlement (excluding transfers made on the day the settlement commenced), except where (e) below applies. (It should be noted that if any potentially exempt transfers made before the transfer into settlement become chargeable because of the donor's death within seven years, this will affect the cumulative total of chargeable transfers. This could happen before or after the date of the ten year charge, and if it was after, the ten year charge would have to be recomputed accordingly.)

(ii) In the case of the first ten year anniversary if it occurred before 9 March 1992, any distribution payments made under the old rules before 9 March 1982 and within the ten years before the anniversary.

(iii) Any amounts on which exit charges have been levied under s 65 within the previous ten years (see note 4).

To compute the tax charge one half of the normal rate of tax is used.

(c) Having arrived at the effective rate of tax on the notional transfer, take 30% of that effective rate to arrive at the actual rate (unless the chargeable relevant property had not been relevant property throughout the ten year period, in which case the rate on such property is further reduced by 1/40th for each complete quarter that had elapsed in the ten year period before the property became relevant property). At current rates this gives a maximum charging rate of 6% (or 3% on property that qualifies for 50% business or agricultural property relief, further reduced to 0.3% a year if the instalment option is available – see Example 5 explanatory note 5).

(d) Apply the *rate* arrived at in (c) above to the *relevant property* in the trust at the anniversary, ie to the property at (a) (i) above. Note that the effect of including (a) (ii) and (iii) in the notional transfer is to give a higher cumulative total and thus possibly a higher tax rate, but the charge is levied on the relevant property (a) (i) only.

(e) Where property has been added to the settlement within the previous ten years then although the charge on that property is proportionately reduced as indicated in (c) above, the settlor's previous cumulative transfers at (b) (i) become the chargeable transfers made by him in the seven years preceding the addition to the settlement, if that gives a higher total. Where more than one addition has taken place then either the commencement date or any one of the addition dates is used, whichever gives the highest cumulative total for the previous seven years (s 67).

Where the total used is at one of the addition dates then it is possible that this total will include transfers to the settlement. This would result in a transfer being included twice, eg if the addition was made less than seven years after the commencement of the settlement, the settlor's seven year cumulative total at the date of the addition will include the original chargeable transfer on the creation of the settlement, and (unless it has been the subject of an exit charge) that property will also form part of the relevant property in the settlement (ie included at (a) (i) above). In such circumstances the seven year cumulative total is reduced by the net amount put into the settlement.

Similarly that seven year cumulative total may include the value of property which has ceased to be relevant property at the date of the ten year charge and has been the subject of an exit charge under s 65 (ie included at (b) (iii) above). Then the seven year cumulative total is reduced by the value attributable to the property subject to that exit charge (s 67(3)(b), (5)).

A double counting relief also applies where property has been the subject of an exit charge (eg on the creation of an interest in possession within the last ten years) but has since become relevant property again. Thus its value would appear both as relevant property (under (a)(i) above) and also as property on which an exit charge had been levied in the last ten years (under (b)(iii) above). In such circumstances the latter amount is reduced by the smaller of:

the value at the time of the exit charge; or

the value on the day before the ten year anniversary (s 67(b)).

3. Under the pre 9 March 1982 rules, a proportional periodic charge was payable annually where trustees were not resident in the UK but this charge was abolished when the rules were changed. Any unused tax credit arising from the payment of such annual charges is available against *any* payments under the revised rules, ie both ten yearly charges and exit charges (s 85).

Exit charges

4. A further charge to inheritance tax arises when property in a settlement ceases to be relevant property. This is known as the 'exit charge'. For both pre and post 27 March 1974 settlements where a ten yearly charge has already been made, the exit charge is calculated by using the rate of tax computed at the previous ten year anniversary, recalculated using one half of the scale in force at the date of the distribution (if lower). This charge is further reduced by applying the fraction of x/40 where x is the number of *complete* quarters in the period since the preceding ten year anniversary (s 69) (no charge therefore arising if the distribution is made within the first three months after the anniversary, since x would be nil). The value transferred is the difference between the value of relevant property before the distribution and its value after the distribution. Thus the 'loss to the donor' principle applies and grossing up is necessary if the trustees pay the tax (see note 6). Special rules apply when property has been added to a settlement since the date of the last ten year charge (s 69). For details see Example 59 at explanatory note 8.

Exit charge before first ten year anniversary

5. Where an exit charge arises before the first anniversary to which a ten year charge applies then for post 26 March 1974 settlements the rate of tax is 30% of the effective rate, reduced by applying the fraction of x/40 where x is the number of *complete* quarters in the period since the creation of the settlement (and again no charge arises on a distribution in the first three months after the creation of the settlement since x is nil) (s 68(2)).

The effective rate of tax is found by applying one half of the rates of inheritance tax then applicable to a notional chargeable transfer which is the sum of:

(a) the value of all the property in the settlement, whether it is relevant property or not, immediately after the settlement commenced.

(b) the value of the property in any related settlement immediately after it commenced.

(c) the value of any added property at the time of its addition to the settlement. (This includes accumulated income that has been treated as an accretion to capital, the date of addition being the date that the accumulation was so treated.)

and assumes previous chargeable transfers equal to any chargeable transfers made by the settlor in the seven years prior to the day on which the settlement was created. Note that the charge may be affected if potentially exempt transfers become part of the settlor's cumulative chargeable transfers because he died within seven years of making them. Various problems arise in respect of a settlor's premature death within seven years of making a settlement. These include additional tax being due when the original transfer to settlement was at lifetime rates, or a failed PET made by the settlor prior to the set up of the settlement increasing the tax on the transfer which created the settlement.

If a gift into settlement was free from IHT because of the availability of BPR or APR, and the property involved was subsequently disposed of, the trustees should have replaced it with other agricultural or business property so as to shelter any charge within IHTA 1984 ss 113B and 118.

The problems can be illustrated in this brief example:

A always used up his annual exemption by a gift of £3,000 to his nephew on 20 May each year. A died on 1 May 2006.

On 1 May 2000 A gave his daughter £65,000
On 12 June 2001 he gave his son £100,000
On 1 September 2003, he set up a discretionary settlement with funds of £291,000, paying the tax due.

Original IHT position:

Gifts to son and daughter – PETs

Set up of discretionary trust

This is a chargeable transfer of £291,000. A has a nil cumulative total and the nil rate band for 2003/04 was £255,000. The excess of £36,000 is grossed up as tax is paid by the settlor (36,000 x 100/80 = 45,000).

Chargeable transfer (gross)	£300,000
Tax paid by settlor (300,000 – 255,000 = 45,000 @ 20%)	£9,000

On subsequent death of Mr A

PETs to son and daughter

Transfers of £100,000 to his son and £65,000 to his daughter are within Mr A's nil rate band for 2006/07 so no further tax payable. The cumulative total of transfers is however now increased to £165,000.

Transfer to discretionary trust

	£
Chargeable transfer to trust	300,000
Cumulative transfers	165,000
	465,000
Tax at death rate (465,000 – 285,000 @ 40%)	72,000
Less: paid in 2003/04	9,000
Additional tax payable by trustees	63,000

If the settlor's death occurs before a distribution out of the trust, the charge on the distribution is calculated accordingly. If the settlor dies after the distribution is made the exit charge may be increased and additional tax will then be payable. This is because any failed PETs on death will increase the amount of the settlor's previous transfers in the seven years before the commencement of the settlement.

The effect of the settlor's death on occasions of charge is considered in more detail in Example 62. The rate so calculated is applied to the relevant property leaving the settlement using the 'loss to the donor' principle.

If the property was not relevant property throughout the period since the settlement commenced the rate of tax on that property is reduced according to the complete quarters that had expired before it became relevant property.

Grossing up

6. If the exit charge is paid by the donee then no grossing up is necessary (s 65(2)(a)) but if the tax is paid by the settlement then the chargeable amount must be grossed up (s 65(2)(b)). In the example the distributions to A, B and D did not require any grossing up as they paid the tax out

of the distribution. C, however, received £20,000 after payment of tax. The fund has therefore been reduced by £20,000 plus the tax thereon £58, a total transfer of £20,058.

This is calculated by using the formula of:

$$\text{Net transfer } \times \frac{100}{(100 - \text{rate of tax})} = \text{gross transfer}$$

In this example the rate of tax is 0.288% and therefore the calculation is:

$$£20,000 \times \frac{100}{(100 - 0.288)} = £20,058$$

Tax planning

7. Although the treatment of discretionary trusts is complex, they have a useful role to play in tax planning.

    If a settlor has not made any chargeable transfers, nor used his annual exemptions, he can presently transfer assets to the value of £291,000 into a discretionary trust without paying either inheritance tax or capital gains tax (since the holdover relief in TCGA 1992 s 260 is available on *chargeable* transfers, whether any inheritance tax is payable on those transfers or not). Any transfers out of the trust in the first ten years will then not attract tax (subject to what is said below about business and agricultural property). Care needs to be taken, however, if the settlor has already made potentially exempt transfers, because a liability on the transfer to the trust could then arise if he died within seven years, and also on distributions out of the trust.

    Furthermore, now that all lifetime transfers into trust are subject to the relevant property regime it will be appropriate in many cases for trusts to maintain the flexibility of discretionary trusts rather than be constrained by the use of interest in possession settlements or accumulation and maintenance trusts.

    If the property transferred into trust qualifies for 100% or 50% business or agricultural relief, this increases the amount that can be transferred without tax being payable, subject to what is said above about potentially exempt transfers. Distributions of the business or agricultural property out of the trust also qualify for the relief (providing the trustees have owned the property for two years). There is, however, a particular problem where distributions are made out of the trust within the first ten years, because the whole of the value of the business or agricultural property is taken into account in calculating the initial value of the settlement (see note 5(a) above), so any exit charges on distributions within the first *ten* years are based on the full value of the property when settled. For further details see Example 62 at explanatory note 5.

Spouse as discretionary beneficiary

8. It is possible to include a spouse/civil partner as one of the discretionary beneficiaries, thus ensuring that property is not left directly to the surviving spouse/civil partner to swell that spouse's/civil partner's own estate.

    For example: Mr and Mrs Forster have estates in their sole names of £301,000 and £282,000 respectively. In addition they own a freehold house as joint tenants valued at £400,000. Their wills each leave all of their estate to the other (or to their only child in the case of the second spouse to die). They have not made any lifetime gifts. Their potential liability to inheritance tax is:

	£
On first death:	
Inter-spouse transfer – exempt	nil
On second death:	
Estate of Mr Forster	301,000
Estate of Mrs Forster	282,000
House	400,000
	983,000

Tax thereon (983,000 – 285,000 = 698,000 @ 40%) = £279,200

If, however, their wills were amended to provide for an amount equal to the nil band for inheritance tax to devolve upon a discretionary settlement, from which spouse, child and, say, grandchildren could benefit, with the residue of the estate devolving on the spouse, then the nil rate band of the spouse dying first would be utilised, viz:

	£
On first death (say Mr Forster)	
Free assets	301,000
Pecuniary legacy to discretionary trust	285,000
Residue to spouse	16,000
½ share of house (passes to spouse by survivorship)	200,000
Exempt transfer	216,000
Value of Estate	
Own assets	301,000
½ share of house	200,000
	501,000
Less: exempt transfer	216,000
Chargeable estate	285,000
Covered by nil threshold.	
On Mrs Forster's death	
Own assets	282,000
Residue from husband's estate	16,000
House	400,000
	698,000

Tax thereon (698,000 – 285,000 = 413,000 @ 40%) = £165,200

Thus taking both deaths together the discretionary trust will at the time of the second death save inheritance tax equal to the value of the nil rate band on the first death (£285,000 @ 40% = £114,000). Provided the value in the discretionary trust does not increase faster than the rate of increase of the nil rate band, no further tax will be payable on capital distributions from the trust. The surviving spouse will be able to have use of the income (and capital) of the trust with the agreement of the trustees (but distributions must not be made with in first three months – see note 9 below). The income of the trust will be subject to income tax at 40% but this will be recoverable to the extent that it exceeds the beneficiary's personal tax liability if the income is distributed (see Example 47 for further details).

Distributions within two years after death

9.   If a discretionary trust is created by will, distributions out of it within two years after the death are treated as having been made under the will (IHTA 1984 s 144) rather than being treated as amounts on which an exit charge is payable. This is a very useful provision enabling maximum flexibility to be

built into a will so that the estate may be distributed taking into account the situation at the time of the death, rather than having to review the will regularly to ensure that its provisions are still appropriate.

To be within the provisions of s 144, the distribution must be one on which tax would otherwise be chargeable. It must not therefore occur within the first three months after death, because exit charges do not apply to such distributions (see note 5). In the case of Frankland v CIR (CA 1997), within three months after the creation of a discretionary trust by will, the trust property was transferred to a trust in which the surviving spouse had a life interest. The intention was to avoid the inheritance tax on the death estate through the substitution of an exempt spouse transfer for the taxable transfer to the discretionary trust. It was held that s 144 did not apply because there would have been no exit charge on the transfer to the life interest trust.

10. Where distributions of assets from a discretionary trust within two years after death are treated as made at death as indicated in note 9 above, the capital gains tax position must be considered if the assets are liable to that tax and have increased in value since death. The capital gains tax gifts holdover relief of TCGA 1992 s 260 only applies if the transfer is chargeable to inheritance tax (see Example 50 explanatory note 3), which it is not where IHTA 1984 s 144 applies. Capital gains tax cannot therefore be held over unless the assets qualify for business gifts holdover relief under TCGA 1992 s 165 (as to which see Example 50 part A(d)). See Example 50 explanatory note 5 for a way in which capital gains tax may be avoided.

On 6 June 1994 H, who had made no previous transfers of value, settled £80,000 on himself for life, with remainder to his wife, W, for life, with remainder on her death on discretionary trusts for the benefit of their children and grandchildren.

H died on 5 May 1995 when his own assets were valued at £90,000.

His cumulative chargeable transfers at that date were £95,000.

By his will he left all his property to his children equally.

His wife, W, died on 4 April 1998 leaving assets valued at £184,000.

By her will she settled £50,000 cash on discretionary charitable trusts without limit of time, and the residue to her brother for life with remainder to his children.

She had made chargeable transfers of value totalling £103,750, all less than seven years before her death.

The settled fund from her husband's death was valued at £110,000 upon her death.

On 8 August 2000 the trustees appointed £30,000 gross to the eldest child, William, for life with remainder to his children who attained 18 or being daughters sooner married, whom failing to revert to the trust fund.

On 10 April 2003 William and his wife (who had no children) were killed in a car accident.

After payment of inheritance tax and other expenses in connection with his death, the fund appointed to William, which then fell back into the settlement created on 6 June 1994, was valued at only £24,000.

The rest of the property in that settlement was valued at that date at £96,000.

The recombined settlement may be taken to have the following values:

As at 5 June 2004   £113,640
As at 4 May 2005   £125,410
As at 3 April 2008   £157,624

Calculate the inheritance tax payable in connection with the appointment on 8 August 2000 and on the first ten year anniversary.

(So far as future events are concerned assume that the law set out in IHTA 1984 does not change.)

61.2 DISCRETIONARY SETTLEMENT — RELATED SETTLEMENTS, PROPERTY LEAVING AND REVERTING TO SETTLEMENT

6 June 1994   –   H settles £80,000 on himself for life
                  –   No inheritance tax payable as no loss to his estate.

5 May 1995   –   H dies, settlement passes to spouse for life – exempt transfer.

4 April 1998   –   W dies, and is deemed settlor of discretionary trust dated 6 June 1994.

		Gross	Tax on 1997/98 scale
Tax position of deemed settlor W at date of her death, 4 April 1998		£	£
Cumulative transfers in seven years to date of death		103,750	–
Free estate on death	184,000		
Less: Charitable settlement (exempt)	50,000		
	134,000		
Interest in possession in husband's 1994 settlement	110,000	244,000	53,100*
		347,750	53,100*

(* 347,750 – 215,000 = 132,750 @ 40%)

Inheritance tax payable:

£

By personal representatives $\dfrac{134,000}{244,000}$ x £53,100 =   29,161

By trustees of settlement $\dfrac{110,000}{244,000}$ x £53,100 =   23,939

                                          53,100

Initial value of related settlement (W's 1998 will settlement)

Free estate	184,000
Less: to charitable trusts	50,000
	134,000
Less: IHT payable by personal representatives	29,161
	£ 104,839

Initial value of discretionary settlement (ie value at time it was deemed to commence)

Value of fund in which W had an interest in possession at her death	110,000
Less: IHT payable by trustees	23,939
	£ 86,061

8 August 2000 – Exit charge on creation of life interest for William		Gross	Tax on 2000/01 scale
		£	£
Settlor's seven year cumulative total at time settlement deemed to commence		103,750	–
Notional transfer			
Initial value of settlement	86,061		
Initial value of related settlement	104,839		
Initial value of added property	nil	190,900	12,130*
		294,650	12,130*

(* 294,650 – 234,000 = 60,650 @ 20%)

Actual rate is 30% of effective rate

$$\frac{12,130}{190,900} \times 30\% = 1.91\%$$

Quarters since settlement deemed to commence

4 April 1998 to 8 August 2000 = 9 quarters

Tax payable:

$$1.91\% \times \frac{9}{40} \times £30,000 = \underline{£129}$$

6 June 2004 ten year charge

	£
Assumed cumulative total:	
Settlor's 7 year cumulative total at time settlement deemed to commence	103,750
Exit charges in last 10 years	30,000
	133,750

Less: Amount included in £133,750 and also reflected in value of relevant property of £113,640 below

$$\frac{{}^*24,000}{{}^*24,000 + {}^{**}96,000} \times £113,640 \quad \text{(Value of fund at 10 year anniversary)} \qquad 22,728$$

	111,022

*   Property reverting on death of William
** Value of rest of property at that time

	£
Assumed transfer at 10 year anniversary:	
Relevant property	113,640
Initial value of related settlement	104,839
	218,479

	Gross £	Tax on 2004/05 scale £
Assumed cumulative total	111,022	nil
Assumed transfer at 10 year anniversary	218,479	13,300*
	329,501	13,300*

(* 329,501 – 263,000 = 66,501 @ 20%)

Actual rate is 30% of effective rate

$$\frac{13,300}{218,479} \times 30\% = 1.826\%$$

Appropriate fraction:

Original settlement (4/5 x 113,640) (ie $\dfrac{96,000}{24,000 + 96,000}$ calculation above) = £90,912

Complete quarters until property becomes relevant property

6 June 1994 to 4 April 1998 = 15 quarters reduction
Appropriate fraction – 25/40ths

Property returning to settlement (1/5 x 113,640) (ie $\dfrac{24{,}000}{24{,}000 + 96{,}000}$ calculation above) = £22,728

Complete quarters prior to property last becoming relevant property
6 June 1994 to 10 April 2003 = 35 quarters reduction
Appropriate fraction – 5/40ths

Tax payable:	£
Original settlement 1.826% x 25/40 x 90,912	1,038
Returned property 1.826% x 5/40 x 22,728	52

Value of settlement at		
10 year anniversary	£ 113,640	1,090

Explanatory Notes

Settlement on self

1.   A transfer of value normally occurs when a person transfers property to a settlement.

    However, if the settlor retains an interest in possession in the property in the settlement then there is no loss to his estate and therefore no transfer of value.

    If the property subsequently forms part of a discretionary settlement, or the interest in possession passes to anyone other than the settlor or his spouse, then the settlor or spouse (whoever last had the interest in possession) is deemed to have created a separate settlement at that time (unless the original settlement was made before 27 March 1974) (s 80).

    Accordingly the discretionary settlement is not deemed to be made until W dies, since until then she had an interest in possession, being entitled as of right to the income.

Related settlements

2.   Any other settlements created at the time of W's death would normally be related settlements (s 62(1)).

    However the charitable trust is not regarded as related as the assets are held for charitable purposes without limit of time (s 62(2)) – see Example 60 explanatory note 2(a)(iii).

    Furthermore the transfer to the charitable trust is an exempt transfer (s 23) thus reducing the estate chargeable on W's death.

    The inheritance tax payable on the settlement is met by the trustees, thus reducing the initial value of the discretionary settlement from £110,000 to £86,061.

Exit charges

3.   The effective rate of tax on an exit depends upon whether the distribution occurs before the first 10 year anniversary (s 68) or after that date (s 69).

    Although the settlement was deemed to be created by the death of W, the anniversary date is fixed by s 61 as being the 10th anniversary of the date when the original settlement commenced (s 61(2)).

4.   For the purpose of computing the assumed cumulative total and notional transfer, the date of the deemed creation of the settlement applies and accordingly the settlement commences with W's 7 year cumulative total immediately prior to her death, the settlement created by her will becoming a related settlement.

5.   Because the property was not relevant property throughout the whole of the period since the settlement was created, s 68(3) applies and only the period from the deemed creation (4 April 1998) to date of distribution (8 August 2000) is used to compute the appropriate fraction.

Ten yearly charge

6. On the 10th anniversary of the settlement (6 June 2004) s 66 applies.

    As the property subject to the exit charge (distribution to William) is also included in the value of relevant property (because of the death of William and his wife and the consequent reversion of the property to the discretionary settlement), the assumed cumulative total is reduced by the lower of:

    (a) the exit charge £30,000; or

    (b) the proportionate value at the 10 year anniversary of the property which has reverted

    (s 66(5)).

    At the time the property reverted to the settlement it was valued at £24,000 and the other property in the settlement at £96,000.

    Accordingly $\dfrac{24,000}{120,000}$ of the value at 6 June 2004 relates to the exit to William, ie:

    $\frac{1}{5}$ x £113,640 = £22,728.

7. The charge at the 10 year anniversary is reduced by the number of complete quarters prior to the appropriate date. Again the appropriate fractions reflect the fact that part of the property only became relevant property on 4 April 1998, and part last reverted to the settlement on 10 April 2003 (s 66(2)).

8. See Examples 59, 60 and 62 for further details of discretionary trusts.

On 6 June 1996 Smith retired from the family farming partnership which had commenced twenty years earlier when he had taken his brother and their sons into partnership.

His cumulative chargeable transfers at that date were £158,352 arising out of transfers of value made in late 1989, and he had not yet made any potentially exempt transfers.

At the time of his retirement he transferred the freehold interest in one of his farms, valued at £100,000, which had been leased for the last 10 years to a non-family tenant farmer, to the trustees of a discretionary settlement he created in favour of the children of his brother, who had recently been killed in a farming accident for which Smith felt some moral responsibility. He agreed to pay any inheritance tax due.

At the same time he settled £100,000 of the cash due to him from the partnership on a second discretionary settlement in favour of his own children.

The trustees of this settlement paid any inheritance tax due.

On 5 May 1997 Smith added £24,000 in cash to the brother's children's settlement (on which the trustees are to pay the inheritance tax due).

On 6 May 1997 Smith gave his own children £195,000 in cash.

On 1 January 1998 the trustees of the brother's children's settlement appointed £18,000 to the late brother's eldest son.

On 9 September 1999 when the brother's children's settlement consisted of the farm and 12,000 £1 shares in ABC plc, Smith added a further 120,000 £1 shares in ABC plc to that trust and paid the inheritance tax himself.

On 2 February 2002 the trustees of the brother's children's settlement appointed 66,000 shares in ABC plc to the eldest daughter absolutely.

The assets in the brother's children's settlement were:

	Market value of farm	Shares in ABC plc at value for inheritance tax
9 September 1999	£200,000	133⅓p each
2 February 2002	£210,000	150p each
5 June 2006	£300,000	200p each
6 June 2006	£300,000	201¾p each

Calculate the inheritance tax payable by the trustees in connection with the two appointments from the brother's children's settlement and on the first 10 year anniversary of that trust.

Ignore capital gains tax.

Tax position of settlor — Smith

			Gross	Tax (on 1996/97 scale)	Net
Inheritance tax accumulation 6 June 1996			£	£	£
Cumulative transfers to date (1989)			158,352	–	158,352
Brother's children's settlement – Farm		100,000			
Less: Agricultural property relief 50% (see explanatory note 5)		50,000			
		50,000			
Less: Annual exemptions 1996/97	3,000				
1995/96	3,000				
	6,000				
$(** \dfrac{50,000}{150,000} \times £6,000)$		2,000			
Net transfer, grossed up (see explanatory note 4)		48,000	49,588	1,588	48,000
			207,940	1,588	206,352
Own children's settlement – Cash		100,000			
Less: Annual exemption					
$(** \dfrac{100,000}{150,000} \times £6,000)$		4,000	96,000	19,200	76,800
			303,940	20,788*	283,152

(** see explanatory note 1)
(*   303,940 – 200,000 = 103,940 @ 20%)

Tax position of settlements:

Initial value of brother's children's settlement   £ 100,000
Initial value of own children's settlement
(a related settlement – £100,000 less tax £19,200)   £ 80,800

5 May 1997 — Property added to brother's children's settlement

Tax position of settlor — Smith

			Gross	Tax (1997/98 scale)
Inheritance tax accumulation			£	£
Cumulative transfers in last 7 years (303,940 – 158,352)			145,588	–
Added property		24,000		
Less: Annual exemptions 1997/98	3,000			
1996/97	3,000	6,000	18,000	–
			163,588	– *

(* 163,588 – 215,000 = Nil)

Initial value of added property = £24,000

Tax position of brother's children's settlement

1 January 1998

Exit charge on distribution to late brother's eldest son (Note – as farm is not sold the distribution must come from property added on 5 May 1997 and the tax calculation is affected accordingly)

		Gross	Tax (1997/98 scale)
		£	£
Assumed transfer:			
Settlor's 7 year cumulative total at time settlement commenced (s 68(4)(b))		158,352	–
Notional transfer (s 68(4)(a) and (5))			
Initial value of settlement	100,000		
Initial value of related settlement	80,800		
Initial value of added property	24,000	204,800	29,630
(* 363,152 – 215,000 = 148,152 @ 20%)		363,152	29,630*

Effective rate: $\dfrac{29,630}{204,800} \times 100\% = 14.468\%$

Appropriate fraction (s 68(3)):

Quarters since settlement commenced	
6 June 1996 to 1 January 1998	6 quarters
Less: Complete quarters until property added	
6 June 1996 to 5 May 1997	3 quarters
	3

Tax payable on distribution of £18,000:

$14.468\% \times 30\% \times \dfrac{3}{40} \times £18,000 = £59$

9 September 1999 — further added property

Tax position of settlor — Smith

		Gross	Tax (1999/2000 scale)	Net
		£	£	£
Cumulative transfers to date (5 May 1997)		163,588		
Gift to children (6 May 1997) – Potentially exempt		–	163,588	–	163,588
Added property 120,000 shares @ 133⅓p		160,000		
Less: Annual exemptions 1999/2000	3,000			
1998/99	3,000	6,000		
Net transfer				154,000
Grossed up*		175,647	21,647	
		339,235	21,647	317,588

* Cumulative net transfers of £317,588 exceed nil band of £231,000 by £86,586, the gross equivalent of which is 86,586 x 100/80 = £108,235. The tax payable is therefore £21,647 and the grossed up transfer is (154,000 + 21,647 =) £175,647.

Initial value of added property – £ 160,000 (tax paid by settlor)

Tax position of brother's children's settlement

2 February 2002

*Exit charge on distribution to eldest daughter
(Shares deemed to have been appropriated pro-rata
out of property added on 5 May 1997 and 9 September
1999, since the farm is still owned)*

		Gross	*Tax (2001/02 scale)*
		£	£
Assumed transfer:			
Settlor's 7 year cumulative total at time settlement commenced (see explanatory note 9)		158,352	–
Notional transfer			
At 1 January 1998 (above)	204,800		
Initial value of further added property	160,000	364,800	56,230
		523,152	56,230*

(* 523,152 – 242,000 = 281,152 @ 20%)

Effective rate: $\dfrac{56,230}{364,800}$ x 100% = 15.414%

Actual rate is 30% of effective rate, ie 30% x 15.414% = 4.624%
Appropriate fraction:
Quarters since settlement commenced

6 June 1996 to 2 February 2002	22
Less: Complete quarters until first addition (as above)	3
	19

6 June 1996 to 2 February 2002	22
Less: Complete quarters until second addition	
6 June 1996 to 9 September 1999	13
	9

Tax payable on distribution of 66,000 ABC plc shares at £1.50 to daughter – value distributed £99,000:

re 1997 addition (12,000 shares)

$$4.624\% \ \times \ \frac{19}{40} \ \times \ £99,000 \ \times \ \frac{12,000}{132,000} \ = \ 198$$

re 1999 addition (120,000 shares)

$$4.624\% \ \times \ \frac{9}{40} \ \times \ £99,000 \ \times \ \frac{120,000}{132,000} \ = \ 936$$

$$£ \ 1,134$$

6 June 2006 – 10 year charge (see explanatory notes 8, 9 and 10)		*Gross* £	*Tax (2006/07 scale)* £
Assumed cumulative total:			
Settlor's 7 year cumulative total at time settlement commenced (see explanatory notes 9 and 10)		158,352	
Exit charges in previous 10 years			
1 January 1998	18,000		
2 February 2002	99,000	117,000	
		275,352	–
Assumed transfer:			
Relevant property – value as at 5 June 2005			
Farm	300,000		
Less: Agricultural property relief 50%	150,000		
	150,000		
66,000 shares in ABC plc @ 200p	132,000		
	282,000		
Initial value of related settlement	80,800	362,800	70,630*
		638,152	70,630*

(* 638,152 – 285,000 = 353,152 @ 20%)

Effective rate: $\dfrac{70,630}{362,800}$ x 100% = 19.468%

(Note that with the present single rate structure the effective rate will always be 20% if the assumed cumulative total exceeds the nil threshold, and the subsequent calculations are not necessary. It is still, however, necessary to value the respective parts of the settled fund if it has not all been settled for the full ten years.)

Appropriate fraction

    Farm – no reduction (settled for full 10 years)
    Shares – 6/66 added 5 May 1997 = 3 quarters reduction giving 37/40
    Shares – 60/66 added 9 September 1999 = 13 quarters reduction giving 27/40

Inheritance tax payable:

19.468% x 30% x £150,000 (re farm)	8,761
$19.468\% \ \text{x} \ 30\% \ \text{x} \ \dfrac{37}{40} \ \text{x} \ £132,000 \ \text{x} \ \dfrac{6,000}{66,000}$	648
$19.468\% \ \text{x} \ 30\% \ \text{x} \ \dfrac{27}{40} \ \text{x} \ £132,000 \ \text{x} \ \dfrac{60,000}{66,000}$	4,731
	£ 14,140

Explanatory Notes

Same day transfers

1.   Where two transfers are made on the same day, the annual exemptions are divided between the transfers proportionally to the value transferred, even if one of the transfers was a potentially exempt transfer. In this example both transfers are immediately chargeable.

The transfer to the brother's children's settlement is added to the inheritance tax accumulation before the gift to the trustees of Smith's own children's settlement because the tax on the former gift is to be met by Smith, whereas the trustees of his children's settlement are to meet the tax due on that later transfer and the total tax on both gifts would be higher if they were included the other way round (s 266(1)).

Related settlement

2. Because his children's settlement is made on the same day as his settlement on his brother's children it is a related settlement (s 62).

    Although the amount settled by Smith was £100,000, inheritance tax of £19,200 was payable by the trustees, giving an initial value of £80,800 applicable to that related settlement.

3. The tax on the brother's children's settlement is paid by Smith (the settlor) and therefore its initial value remains at £100,000.

4. The chargeable transfer of £48,000 so far as his own inheritance tax accumulation is concerned has to be grossed up since he bears the tax. Thus, on the scale applicable in 1996/97:

	Net		*Gross*
Cumulative transfers to date	158,352		158,352
Balance of nil band	41,648		41,648
	200,000		200,000
	6,352	x $\frac{100}{80}$ =	7,940
	£ 206,352		£ 207,940

giving tax of (7,940 − 6,352 =) £1,588.

Exit charge

5. The rate of tax payable on an exit depends on whether the property leaving the settlement came from the original settlement (or property held at the previous 10 year anniversary) or property added.

    In this example the original settlement in favour of his brother's children was a farm which is still owned throughout the period under consideration so therefore the distributions must always be from the added property.

    Note however that where property has qualified for annual exemptions and/or business or agricultural relief when it was put into the settlement, this is not taken into account in calculating the initial value of the settlement, so any exit charges on distributions within the first ten years are based on the full value of the property when settled, as shown in the example in relation to the exit charge on 1 January 1998 (s 68). If the distribution itself consists of qualifying business or agricultural property, the relief is available in arriving at the value of the distribution (providing the trustees satisfy the conditions for relief). When calculating the ten yearly charge, business or agricultural property relief is taken into account in arriving at the value of the trust property, as shown in the example in the calculation on 6 June 2006 (s 66).

    The rate of agricultural property relief on the transfer of the farm to the settlement in 1996 was 50% for tenanted agricultural property rather than 100% for owner occupied property etc (see Example 25). Where rates of relief increase after a settlement, the increased rate may be taken into account in computing any *additional* liability to inheritance tax resulting from a death within seven years where the date of death is *after* the date of increase. However the increased rate is *not* applied to calculations of the accumulated transfers brought forward where the original chargeable transfer was before the date of increase even if that amount is used to calculate liabilities after that date.

    Agricultural property relief of 50% will be available on 5 June 2006, as the lease was granted prior to 1 September 1995 and vacant possession is not available within twelve months.

Exit charge – rate of tax when property has been added

6.   The effective rate of tax on an exit depends upon whether the distribution occurs before the first 10 year anniversary (in which case s 68 applies) or after the first 10 years (then s 69 applies) (see Example 60 explanatory notes 4 and 5).

In this example the exits are both before the first 10 year anniversary, so the effective rate is calculated by adding a notional transfer to the settlor's 7 year cumulative total at the time the settlement commenced.

The notional transfer is the sum of the initial values of the original settlement, related settlements and added property (including accumulated income treated as an accretion to capital).

The effective rate is reduced to an appropriate fraction comprising the number of complete quarters from the date the settlement commenced to the date of the charge, divided by 40.

However when the property leaving the settlement is not part of the original settlement then the numerator is reduced by the number of complete quarters from the date of settlement to the date the property is added.

The tax payable on the distribution is then 30% of the appropriate fraction of the effective rate.

7.   On the occasion of the second distribution it should be noted that the rate must be recomputed using the inheritance tax rates then applicable (if lower) and, because further property has been added, the notional transfer has been increased.

Provisions to avoid double counting

8.   Where property has been added to the settlement after 8 March 1982 when the law relating to discretionary trusts altered (strictly because 'the settlor has made a chargeable transfer as a result of which the value of the property comprised in the settlement was increased') the rules in s 67 apply when calculating the tax charge on the 10 year anniversary.

The 'assumed cumulative total' to be used includes the highest of the settlor's 7 year cumulative total as at the date the settlement commenced and his 7 year cumulative totals at the time of additions, reduced when appropriate as explained below.

If no reductions were made this procedure might result in double counting, eg if the addition is made less than 7 years after the commencement of the settlement, the settlor's 7 year cumulative total at the date of the addition will include the sum originally settled as well as earlier additions which (unless the property has been the subject of an exit charge) form part or all of the relevant property in the settlement now subject to the 10 year charge. It will also reflect the initial value of any related settlement.

In such circumstances the 7 year cumulation is reduced by so much as is attributable to property whose value is taken into account in the 'assumed transfer' (s 67(5)(a)).

Similarly the 7 year cumulative total at the time of an addition may reflect the value of property which has ceased to be relevant property at the date of the 10 year charge and has been the subject of an exit charge in the previous 10 years. Once again the 7 year cumulation is reduced by the amount attributable to the property in respect of which the exit charge was made (s 67(5)(b)).

Double counting relief also applies where property has been the subject of an exit charge on the creation of an interest in possession within the last 10 years, but has since become relevant property again. Its value would appear both as relevant property and as property on which an exit charge had been levied in the last 10 years. In such circumstances, the latter amount is reduced by the smaller of the value at the time of the exit charge and the value at the time of the 10 year charge (s 67(6)).

9.   (i)   In the example the settlor's 7 year cumulative total at the time of the first addition and the available reduction in calculating the effective rate on the 10 year charge is:

		Cumulative Total £	Available Reduction £
(a)	his 7 year cumulation prior to the creation of the settlement	158,352	–
(b)	relating to the creation of the settlement of which £1,588 is attributable to the tax paid and £48,000 is attributable to relevant property in the settlement at the time of the 10 year charge (the farm)	49,588	48,000
(c)	by reference to the creation of the related (own children's) settlement. Of this sum £19,200 was used by the trustees to pay the tax so that only £76,800 is attributable to the initial value of the related settlement in the 'assumed transfer'	96,000	76,800
		303,940	124,800
Less:	Transfers more than 7 years prior to the date of the addition, ie prior to 6 May 1990		
	1989 transfer	158,352	–
		145,588	124,800

(ii)   The settlor's 7 year cumulative total at the time of the second addition and the available reduction in calculating the effective rate on the 10 year charge is:

		Cumulative Total £	Available Reduction £
(a)	his 7 year cumulation prior to the creation of the settlement	158,352	–
(b)	relating to the creation of the settlement, as in (i) (b) above	49,588	48,000
(c)	by reference to the creation of the related (own children's) settlement, as in (i) (c) above	96,000	76,800
(d)	by reference to the first addition of £24,000. The chargeable £18,000 is therefore attributable to relevant property in the settlement at the time of the 10 year charge or to property that is the subject of the exit charge on 1 January 1998	18,000	18,000
(e)	Gift to children – potentially exempt	–	–
		321,940	142,800
Less:	Transfers more than 7 years prior to date of second addition	158,352	–
		163,588	142,800

See Example 60 explanatory note 2(e) for the reason why the second addition is not included in the assumed cumulative total.

(iii)   The assumed cumulative total is therefore the highest of:

			£	£
(a)	Settlor's 7 year cumulative total prior to the creation of the settlement			158,352
(b)	Settlor's 7 year cumulative total on first addition (see 9(i))	145,588		
	Less: Available reduction	124,800	20,788	
(c)	Settlor's 7 year cumulative total on second addition (see 9(ii))	163,588		
	Less: Available reduction	142,800	20,788	

Accordingly the cumulative total on creation of the settlement is used.

Effect of settlor's death

10.   Note that if Smith had died before 6 May 2004 then the potentially exempt gift of £195,000 to his children would have become chargeable. This would alter the calculation of liability at the time of the second addition (even though death occurred after the tax had been agreed). The 7 year cumulative total would then be:

	Cumulative Total £	Available Reduction £
As 9(ii) (a) to (d) above	321,940	142,800
(e) Gift to children – now chargeable	195,000	–
	516,940	142,800
Less Transfers more than 7 years prior to date of second addition	158,352	–
	358,588	142,800

The assumed cumulative total would therefore be the highest of:

			£	£
(a)	Settlor's 7 year cumulative total prior to the creation of the settlement			158,352
(b)	Settlor's 7 year cumulative total on first addition	145,588		
	Less Available reduction	124,800	20,788	
(c)	Settlor's 7 year cumulative total on second addition	358,588		
	Less Available reduction	142,800	215,788	

This would revise the inheritance tax liability on 2 February 2002 and also on subsequent occasions of charge, such as the 10 year anniversary on 6 June 2006, as follows:

Exit charge 2 February 2002

	Gross £	Tax (2001/02 scale) £
Assumed transfer:		
Settlor's cumulative total as above	215,788	–
Notional transfer (see page 62.4)	364,800	67,717
	580,588	67,717*

(* 580,588 – 242,000 = 338,588 @ 20%)

Actual rate is 30% of the effective rate

$$\frac{67,717}{364,800} \times 100 \times 30\% = 5.569\%$$

Tax payable:

re 1997 addition (12,000 shares)

$$5.569\% \times \frac{19}{40} \times £99,000 \times \frac{12,000}{132,000} = \quad 238$$

re 1999 addition (120,000 shares)

$$5.569\% \times \frac{9}{40} \times £99,000 \times \frac{120,000}{132,000} = 1,127$$

£ 1,365 (previously £1,134)

6 June 2006 – 10 year charge

	Gross £	Tax (on 2006/07 scale) £
Settlor's cumulative total as above	215,788	–
Exit charges in previous 10 years (see page 62.5)	117,000	
	332,788	9,557*
Assumed transfer (see page 62.5)	362,800	72,560
	695,588	82,117

(* 332,788 – 285,000 = 47,788 @ 20%)

Effective rate: $\dfrac{72,560}{362,800} \times 100 = 20\%$

Inheritance tax payable:

20% x 30% x £150,000	9,000
$20\% \times 30\% \times \dfrac{37}{40} \times £132,000 \times \dfrac{6,000}{66,000}$	666
$20\% \times 30\% \times \dfrac{27}{40} \times £132,000 \times \dfrac{60,000}{66,000}$	4,860
	£ 14,526 (previously £14,140)

11. The relevant value of the property comprised in the settlement is its value on the day preceding the 10th anniversary – in this case 5 June 2006 (s 64).

Associated operations

12. If two or more settlements of an identical or substantially similar nature were set up over a short term, HMRC Capital Taxes took the view that the associated operations provisions of s 268 (as to

which see Example 22) would apply. This would have resulted in the settlements being treated as a single settlement set up at the time of the last settlement, with only one nil rate band. In the case of Rysaffe Trustee Co (CI) Ltd v IRC 2002, however, the High Court held that as a matter of general law the creation of five identical settlements must be treated as five separate settlements, not one. It was up to the settlor to determine if he wished to create more than one settlement and the associated operations provisions of s 268 could not apply.

13.   For further notes on discretionary trusts see Examples 59, 60 and 61.

A has a protected life interest within Trustee Act 1925 s 33(1) in a trust fund valued at £250,000 created by his uncle and on 1 July 2002 purported to assign that life interest to his brother. The trustees pointed out that the attempted alienation was ineffective and brought the protected life interest to an end, substituting for it a discretionary trust under which the beneficiaries were A, his wife and their children.

The only previous transfer A had made at that date was £108,000 in respect of a gift in July 1995.

A also has a life interest under his father's will trust.

On 1 May 2005 A sold this life interest to a Reversionary Interest Society for £200,000 – the full market value. The assets of the trust fund were worth £512,000 at that time.

He did not advise the trustees of the fund of the availability of annual inheritance tax exemptions.

On 21 April 2006 A sold his house, then valued at £200,000 on a vacant possession basis, to his daughter D for £160,000 but reserving to himself a lease of the property for 99 years determinable on his death. The value of the lease at that time was £80,000.

On 1 May 2006, before his daughter had paid the £160,000 (although all documentation had been completed), A was killed in a car accident. His other assets totalled £30,000 net.

His uncle's discretionary, formerly protective, trust fund was then valued at £305,000.

By his will, A created a discretionary trust of the whole of his free estate in favour of his children. On 12 March 2008 the trustees appointed a sum of £10,000, free of tax, to a son, S, absolutely.

Calculate:

(a)   the inheritance tax payable as a result of these transactions and consequent upon A's death

(b)   the rate at which inheritance tax will be payable on future appointments out of the discretionary trust created by A's will.

(a) **Inheritance tax accumulation — A**

1 July 2002
Cessation of protected life interest – No transfer of value –
A deemed to retain an interest in possession (s 88(2))

		Gross	Tax on 2005/06 scale
		£	£
1 May 2005			
Cumulative chargeable transfers within previous seven years (ie since 2 May 1998)		–	–
Sale of life interest under father's will trust			
Value of trust fund	512,000		
Less: Amount received	200,000	312,000	7,400*
		312,000	7,400*

(* 312,000 – 275,000 = 37,000 @ 20%)

21 April 2006			
Sale of house to daughter			
Market value	200,000		
Less: Amount receivable	160,000		
	40,000		
Less: Value retained through lease for life	80,000		
	No loss to A	–	
Accumulation at death on 1 May 2006		312,000	

Inheritance tax accumulation — daughter

21 April 2006			
Amount payable for house		160,000	
Less: Value of house to daughter			
Open market value without lease	200,000		
Value of lease	80,000	120,000	
'Gift' to father		40,000	
Less: Annual exemptions 2006/07	3,000		
2005/06	3,000	6,000	
Potentially exempt transfer		34,000	

Death of A — 1 May 2006	£	£
Estate on death		
Net assets	30,000	
Amount due from daughter re house sale	160,000	190,000
Settled property		
Lease for life		
Value of house	200,000	
Less: Amount attributable to consideration received		
(see explanatory note 3) — one half	100,000	100,000
Deemed life interest in protective trust		305,000
		595,000

Inheritance tax due on death

Date of death 1 May 2006

	Gross £	Tax on 2006/07 scale £
On gifts within seven years before death		
Transfers within 7 years before 1 May 2006 (ie on and after 2 May 1999)	–	–
1 May 2005 – sale of life interest	312,000	10,800*
	312,000	10,800*

(* 312,000 – 285,000 = 27,000 @ 40%)

On estate at death

(Nil threshold already exceeded by lifetime transfers)
£595,000 @ 40%   238,000

Tax payable		£
By trustees of father's will trust	10,800	
Less: paid on original transfer	7,400	3,400
By personal representatives:		
$\dfrac{190,000}{595,000}$ x 238,000		76,000
By trustees of protective trust		
$\dfrac{305,000}{595,000}$ x 238,000		122,000
By daughter re house		
$\dfrac{100,000}{595,000}$ x 238,000		40,000

Appointment of £10,000 by the trustees of the will of A to S

12 March 2008 – Appointment is within 2 years after the death and is deemed to have been made by A under his will (s 144). No further tax is payable.

(b)   **Discretionary trust created by A's will**

	£
A's estate	190,000
Less: appointment to son	10,000
	180,000
Less: tax payable by executors	76,000
Net amount transferred to discretionary settlement created by the will	104,000

Rate of tax on distributions before the first ten year anniversary on 1 May 2016

A's seven year cumulative total at *commencement of settlement* (ignoring transfers of value made on that day, that is the transfer of value deemed to have been made on A's death), was £312,000. The position of the settlement is therefore as follows:

	£
Cumulative total of settlor	312,000
Net amount transferred as above	104,000
	416,000

As this is above the threshold the 'effective' rate of tax on distributions is 20%.

If the tax rates have been reduced when the distribution occurs, the 'effective rate' is recalculated using the new reduced rates.

Rate of tax at ten year anniversaries

This is 30% of the 'effective rate' found by assuming a transfer of value equal to the value of the trust fund immediately before the ten year anniversary (ie on 30 April 2016, 30 April 2026 and so on), made by a transferor whose cumulative total is deemed to be £312,000 *plus* the amounts taxed on exit from the discretionary trust in the preceding ten years, using one half the scale current at the date of the ten year anniversary.

If any property subject to the ten year charge was not 'relevant property' throughout the whole of the preceding ten years or was not comprised in the settlement throughout the whole of that period, then in relation to that property alone the 'effective rate' above is reduced by 1/40th for each complete successive quarter which expired before the property became relevant property.

The value charged to tax is the value of the 'relevant property' in the settlement immediately before the anniversary on the appropriate 30 April.

Rate of tax between ten year anniversaries

This is the 'appropriate fraction' (ie N/40 – where 'N' is the number of completed quarters since the last ten year anniversary or since the property became relevant property) of the rate charged on the last ten year anniversary.

If the tax rates have been reduced since the last ten year anniversary, the current lower rates are substituted.

Explanatory Notes

1.   *1 July 2002 – purported assignment to brother*

When A's life interest comes to an end there is no transfer of value because A is deemed to retain his interest in possession (s 88(2)).

2.   *1 May 2005 – sale of life interest*

Although the sale by A of his life interest to the Reversionary Interest Society is a commercial transaction for full value, s 10 does not prevent its being a transfer of value because s 52(2) expressly provides that a transfer of value arises with an allowance for the sale price received, ie a lifetime transfer of £512,000 (the value of the assets comprising the trust fund) less the £200,000 received = £312,000.

The transfer is not a potentially exempt transfer because the interest does not become comprised in the estate of another individual, nor is another individual's estate increased as a result of the transfer, and it therefore falls outside s 3A.

S 57 allows the annual and marriage exemptions to be applied to events on the happening of which tax is chargeable under s 52 (ie the coming to an end during lifetime of interests in possession in settled property) provided the transferor (the person with the interest in possession which came to an end) gives the trustees a formal notice telling them of the availability of the exemption and the extent to which he is making it available.

As no such notice has been given the exemptions are not available to the trustees.

3.   *21 April 2006 – lease for life*

For the purposes of inheritance tax a lease for life is deemed to be a settlement of the property leased – s 43(3). Because the value of the property remains in the estate of A no income tax charge would arise under the pre-owned asset provisions of FA 2004.

Although the lease determinable on A's death was not created by his daughter but reserved by A himself, so that strictly no allowance for the consideration given can be made, in such circumstances the Revenue will nevertheless treat an appropriate part of the total consideration given as referable to the grant of the lease for life.

As the value of A's life interest is £80,000, and the difference between the market value and the amount receivable is £40,000, the relevant portion is one half (s 170).

In so far as the daughter is concerned, far from having purchased the house at an undervalue, she has depleted her own estate in favour of her father when the aggregate of what she has paid him and the value of the lease is taken into account.

Hence the potentially exempt transfer of value in her case.

4.   *1 May 2006 – position on A's death*

On A's death the tax on transfers of value made within the last seven years is recalculated using the full scale rates in force at the date of death and by accumulation with transfers within the seven years preceding each gift.

The difference between the tax calculated on this basis and the tax originally calculated using the lifetime rates in force at the time of the transfer is due from the trustee of A's father's will trust (s 201).

A's own assets on death include the sum of £160,000 due to him from his daughter.

His estate for inheritance tax purposes (defined in s 5(1) as the aggregate of all the property to which he is beneficially entitled – except excluded property) includes the value of the house in which he has a lease for life less the amount attributable to the consideration received in order to prevent double counting. In this example the gifts with reservation rules do not apply as no transfer of value occurred when A sold the house to his daughter.

His chargeable estate also includes the value of the property in the protective trust in which his life interest is deemed to continue (see explanatory note 1).

5.   *12 March 2008 – variation within two years after death*

Example 34 illustrates how s 142 allows beneficiaries within two years after a death to vary the dispositions without that variation being itself a transfer of value, and for the tax payable in connection with the death to be calculated as though the variation had been made by the deceased himself.

Section 144 provides that distributions made within two years after death out of discretionary settlements created by the deceased's will (other than in the first three months after death) are similarly treated as having been made at the time of the death and are not therefore subject to an exit charge. (See Example 60 explanatory note 9 for the position on transfers within the first three months and explanatory note 10 for the interaction of s 144 with capital gains tax.)

The £10,000 appointed by the trustees of A's will to A's son is therefore deemed for the purposes of inheritance tax to have been given to him by his father A under his will and does not give rise to any exit charge under the discretionary trust rules.

Section 144 also provides that distributions out of discretionary settlements within two years after the settlor's death made under s 75 (employee trusts), s 76 (charities, political parties etc) or Sch 4.16(1) (maintenance funds for historic buildings etc) are treated as having been made at the time of death.

6.   See Example 60 for the rules for calculating the rate at which inheritance tax will be payable on appointments after the first 10 year anniversary out of the discretionary trust created by A's will.

A. You receive a letter from a wealthy client:

10 August 2006

Dear William

As you will recall, I had previously intended to transfer £360,000 into an accumulation and maintenance settlement for my minor children. Due to my emergency operation on 20 March 2006 I was unable to do this and when I came out of hospital you advised me that the rules had changed and that accumulation and maintenance settlements are no longer be available.

Due to the uncertainties of the Government's proposals you suggested that I write to you again in the summer.

I recall reading that it is now possible to put assets into trust for children which can be kept until they are 25 (rather than the age of 18 as originally proposed). Is this something that you would recommend? As you know I think it highly irresponsible for any parent to let an 18-year old receive substantial capital; whilst not entirely happy about it, I would be less concerned about my children receiving their entitlement at 25.

If not, what other strategies would you suggest I consider.

Please let me know what reporting requirements and other ongoing tax-related responsibilities this will entail.

Yours sincerely

Bernard

PS As you may recall, Celia, my late wife, left £250,000 on trust for the children in her will. The terms of the trust mean that the children do not get the money until they are 25. Is this trust affected by the recent changes?

B. Another of your clients of more modest means than Bernard wants to know whether there would be any tax advantages if he and his wife transferred funds to their children. The children are aged 15, 12 and 10. Prepare notes on the points to be made to the client.

A. **Accumulation and maintenance settlement**

31 August 2006

Dear Bernard,

Thank you for your letter of 10 August.

Unfortunately, whilst some amendments have been made to the Government's proposals, they have effectively ended the benign tax treatment given to accumulation and maintenance settlements.

If it is any consolation, had you been able to settle the funds before 22 March 2006, the trust would have still been affected by the new rules and thus there would have been a requirement for a beneficiary to receive the trust funds at the age of 18.

You correctly refer to the changes which allow some trusts to retain funds until a child reaches the age of 25 (rather than 18). However, this applies only to certain trusts which were set up under the will of the child's parent (or under the Criminal Injuries Compensation Scheme). Thus, the trust set up by Celia for your children will qualify. Trusts that take advantage of this slight relaxation will suffer from charges when capital is taken from the trust if a beneficiary is over the age of 18. However, this should not be relevant in the case of Celia's trust because the capital in the trust is covered by the nil rate band (currently £285,000) and this tends to increase from year to year. However, I am assuming that Celia made no significant chargeable transfers in the seven years before she died. If that assumption is incorrect, please let me know.

If you wish to make a lifetime gift to your children, you have broadly two options. First, you can make an outright gift (to a bare trust on behalf of your children). This means that they can get the capital as soon as they are 18. Such a gift would constitute a potentially exempt transfer and will escape inheritance tax altogether provided you live for seven years after the gift. In view of your understandable objections to giving 18-year olds substantial sums of money, I would not recommend that you followed this option. However, you should note that it is the most tax-friendly solution.

Alternatively, you can settle the funds into a trust. Since 22 March 2006, the tax treatment has been the same for both interest in possession trusts and those where the trustees have a lot more freedom about paying income and capital to the beneficiaries. In the circumstances I would suggest that you consider using a discretionary trust as that gives you the greatest flexibility in the future.

If you proceed, inheritance tax will be payable at 20% on the funds entering the trust. However, on the basis that you have made no chargeable transfers to date, the first £285,000 will be covered by the nil rate band. The next £6,000 will be covered by your annual exemption for this year and for last year.

Therefore, assuming you were to gift £360,000, the trustees would be required to pay inheritance tax of £13,800 (£354,000 – £285,000 @ 20%).

This tax will be payable (assuming you make the gift before the end of next month) by 30 April 2007. Otherwise, it will be payable six months after the end of the month in which you make the gift.

Further tax will be payable from your estate should you die within seven years of making the gift. This will be payable six months after the end of the month in which you die.

If the tax is not paid on the due date, interest is charged at the rate in force at that time (currently 3%).

This means that even though the trustees will have twelve months in which to report the transfer, the notification will need to be submitted much earlier than that if interest charges are to be avoided.

Initial and ongoing reporting requirements:

In relation to yourself

(i) In addition to the possible requirement for your personal representatives to report the transfer into settlement as detailed above, you will need to include in your tax return for the year ended

5 April 2007 full details of any chargeable assets disposed of in order to raise the funds for the settlement, so that any chargeable gains arising may be calculated.

(ii)   Income arising under the settlement will not affect you in so far as it is accumulated for the benefit of your children but if while the children are under eighteen years of age and unmarried the trustees make any payment for their maintenance, education or benefit the amount so paid will be regarded as your income for tax purposes, and will consequently need to be included in your personal income tax return. You would be entitled to recover any tax paid from the trustees or from the children who receive the income. To the extent that the trust's income consisted of dividend income, there is an increased tax cost of making such payments compared with dividend income received directly (see point (iii) below under the heading In relation to the trustees).

(iii) The same reporting responsibilities will apply if you make any additions to the settlement in future years.

In relation to the trustees

(i)   The trustees should inform HMRC that the settlement has been created and ask for a reference for the settlement.

(ii)   Tax return forms must be prepared and submitted by the trustees for each year ended 5 April. The forms give details of the income of the trust, the trustees' expenses and outgoings, disposals and deemed disposals for capital gains tax purposes, details of any distributions made to the children and may include the calculation of the self-assessed tax liability. The income of an accumulation and maintenance settlement is chargeable at the rates applicable to discretionary trusts, currently 32½% for dividends and 40% for other income. The first £500 of income, plus the amount used for expenses, is charged at 10% for dividends, 20% for other savings income and 22% for any non-savings income.

The capital gains of the accumulation and maintenance settlement will be chargeable at 40% after the deduction of the annual exemption (£4,400 for 2006/07, reduced if you have created more than one settlement).

(iii) If the trustees distribute any income for the maintenance or education of one or more of the children when they are still under eighteen and unmarried, then as stated above, such income will be treated as your income for tax purposes. Even so, the amount of any such income will be declared in the trust tax return and will be included in calculating the income liable at the 32½% and 40% rates. The trustees will deduct tax at 40% from the payments and if the underlying income includes dividends, the dividend credits cannot be taken into account as tax paid by the trustees, thus increasing their tax liability.

(iv)   Inheritance tax will be payable on the 10th anniversary (and every subsequent 10 years) on the value of the trust assets. The top charging rate is currently 6% but the trustees have the benefit of the nil rate band (currently £285,000) before any tax is payable.

(v)   Charges will also be payable by the trustees whenever capital distributions are made by the trust. This basic rate of this charge is 6% although in practice the actual rate will be a lot lower. This is because the calculation takes into account the nil rate band at the time of the distribution. Furthermore, the basic rate of the charge is then multiplied by a top rate of n/40 where n is the number of complete quarters since the last ten-year anniversary (or the creation of the trust).

Therefore no exit charge will be payable during the first 3 months of any 10-year period, and 39/40 of the basic charge will be payable in the final quarter.

In relation to your children

(i)   The children have no reporting responsibility until they reach age eighteen.

(ii)   When income is distributed to your children, this will be shown on their tax returns (which you will complete whilst they are minors).

I shall be happy to discuss any of the above points with you in more detail if you wish, and to assist in the completion of relevant forms.

Yours sincerely,

William

B.   **Transferring funds to infant children**

1.   Where funds are transferred to children under 18, there is little opportunity to obtain any income tax advantages. The funds transfer would be treated for income tax as a settlement. Unless it is covered by one of the exceptions listed below, settlement income that is paid to or would otherwise be treated as the income of a child of the settlor who is under 18 and unmarried is treated as the parent's income and not the child's (ITTOIA 2005 s 629). A settlement includes 'any disposition, trust, covenant, agreement, arrangement or transfer of assets' (s 620).

2.   Each parent may, however, give each such child a capital sum from which not more than £100 gross income arises each year. If income exceeds the limit the whole amount is taxable (s 629(3)).

3.   Before 9 March 1999, there were income tax advantages if the parents arranged for funds for each child to be held under a 'bare trust', under which the child had an absolute right to the property and income, but the trustees (who could be the parents) were the legal owners, effectively holding as the child's nominee. The disadvantage of such trusts was that the child could not be prevented from obtaining legal ownership of the funds at age 18.

       The income tax advantages of bare trusts by parents in favour of their minor children are no longer available for trusts created on or after 9 March 1999. Subject to the de minimis amount of £100 referred to in note 2 above, the income arising will be taxed as that of the parent under s 629.

4.   The changed rules for bare trusts do not alter the capital gains treatment, which treats gains arising as the child's gains against which the annual exemption (currently £8,800) is available, the rates of tax on any gains above that level being 10%, 20% or 40% depending on the child's income. Funds could therefore be invested for the child purely for capital growth, with no income arising. This does not, however, give the former benefits of being able to use the child's personal allowance and lower tax rates against income.

5.   Other possibilities, which also do not make use of the children's allowances and lower tax rates are as follows (see explanatory note 12):

       (a)   National Savings and Investments Children's Bonus Bonds for children under 16.

       (b)   Friendly society policies (with premiums up to £270 per annum).

       (c)   Contributions of up to £2,808 net per child into a personal pension plan. The basic rate tax relief of 22% is added to the amount invested in the plan, so that for a contribution of £2,808 the plan investment would be £3,600.

6.   Where a child aged 16 or 17 opens a cash individual savings account (ISA) with funds provided by the parents then this will be treated as a settlement and the income arising will be taxable on the parent (subject to the de minimis amount of £100) even though income within an ISA is normally tax free.

Explanatory Notes

Payments re settlor's infant, unmarried children

1. The income of discretionary and accumulation settlements is charged at the dividend trust rate (currently 32½%) if it is dividend or similar income (see Example 42 for details) and at the rate applicable to trusts (currently 40%) if it is non-dividend income. These rates do not apply to any amount which is treated as the settlor's income *before* it is distributed (TA 1988 s 686(2)(b)).

    But see the new rules introduced in FA 2005 s 14 as set out on page (vii) in the Summary of Provisions of Finance Act 2005.

    Under FA 2005 s 14 the first £500 of relevant income will not be charged at the special trust tax rates, but will instead be charged at the income tax rate appropriate to the type of income, known as standard rate band. Therefore, if payments are received net of tax (for example, building society interest) up to the limit of the standard rate band, then the trustees will have no further tax to pay.

    HMRC have confirmed that the standard rate band set out in FA 2005 s 14 will apply to trust income *net* of trust management expenses so potentially it will apply to other charges as well.

    Although the management expenses are deducted from the trust income taxed at the lowest rate first, the standard rate band will apply in the order – basic rate income at 22% first, followed by lower rate 20% income and finally dividends at 10%.

    See Examples 42, 47 and 48 for further details on the standard rate band and its interaction with trust expenses and additional liabilities where amounts are distributed.

    Although any payment made by the trustees for the maintenance or education of a child of the settlor who is under 18 and unmarried is deemed to be the settlor's income, it is not so treated *before* the payment is made. The trustees are therefore liable to tax at the 40% rate, and any payments for the children are grossed up at that rate (TA 1988 s 687). See Example 42 under heading *Income taxed as income of settlor* for the effect of the treatment of dividend income on the overall tax charge where dividend income is paid to minor children via a discretionary trust.

Notification of liability to tax

2. Since the trustees are chargeable to income tax on the trust income that arises, they must notify HMRC that they are so liable within six months after the end of the first relevant tax year. This is the same requirement as that of an individual taxpayer and carries a penalty of up to 100% of the tax due in the event of failure to notify (TMA 1970 s 7).

Person becoming absolutely entitled as against the trustees; gifts holdover relief

3. When a person becomes absolutely entitled to trust assets as against the trustees, other than on the death of a life tenant, the assets are deemed to have been disposed of by the trustees at market value for capital gains tax purposes. Any capital gain arising may be held over if the assets are qualifying assets under TCGA 1992 s 165 (see Example 50 part A(d)).

    If the assets are not qualifying assets for TCGA 1992 s 165, there is the possibility of holding over a gain under the provisions of TCGA 1992 s 260, because s 260(2)(d) specifically allows a gain to be held over on a disposal on which inheritance tax is not chargeable by reason of the inheritance tax exemption for accumulation and maintenance settlements where a beneficiary becomes entitled to trust property or a life interest therein, or dies before reaching the specified age (IHTA 1984 s 71(4)). There is, however, a problem here in that if the child becomes entitled to the trust income at eighteen, the inheritance tax exemption applies at that time and the trust becomes an interest in possession trust. If, however, the child is not entitled to the capital until say age 25, the transfer of assets to the child when he reaches that age is no longer within s 71(4) (because the capital supporting the interest in possession is already deemed to belong to the child) and capital gains tax holdover relief under TCGA 1992 s 260 would therefore not be available.

    This will cease to be a problem after 5 April 2008.

Requirements for and advantages of accumulation and maintenance settlements

4. Accumulation and maintenance settlements receive favourable treatment for inheritance tax. To qualify for this treatment, one or more of the beneficiaries must become entitled to the property (or an interest in possession therein) upon their attaining an age not greater than twenty-five years (s 71) and in the meantime the income must be accumulated, or distributed for the maintenance, education or benefit of a beneficiary. The settlement must either terminate as an accumulation and maintenance settlement not more than twenty-five years after its creation, or all the beneficiaries must be children of a common grandparent (s 71(2)).

    If those grandchildren fail to survive, their children or widows/widowers qualify.

    'Children' includes step-children, adopted and illegitimate children.

5. Accumulation and maintenance settlements cannot be established after 21 March 2006. However, those already in existence can continue. Nevertheless, from 6 April 2008, with certain exceptions, the capital must be payable to the beneficiaries when they reach the age of 18. The exceptions (which continue to permit capital, but not just income to be taken up to the age of 25) relate to trusts for bereaved minors set up by a bequest from their parent (or under the Criminal Injuries Compensation Scheme).

    If an accumulation and maintenance settlement ceases to qualify as such, either because all beneficiaries are no longer children of a common grandparent or because of the 25 year rule, the trustees are liable to an inheritance tax charge. Thereafter the normal ten yearly and exit charges apply.

6. If a settlement ceases to be an A&M settlement on 6 April 2008 simply because of the requirement to pay capital by the age of 18, no inheritance tax will be payable on the settlement ceasing to qualify.

Reporting potentially exempt transfers that become chargeable

7. Potentially exempt transfers that become chargeable because of the death of the donor within seven years must be included in the account delivered by the personal representatives, along with details of the deceased's estate (IHTA 1984 s 216). Section 216 also requires potentially exempt transfers to be reported by the donee, the donee being primarily liable for payment of the tax.

Bare trusts

8. Bare trusts used to provide a simple way of enabling children's personal allowances and lower tax rates to be used against funds from the parent, so long as the income merely accumulated for the children's benefit without actually being paid to them. The parents could act as trustees and there thus need be no administration costs.

    The income tax advantages of bare trusts by parents in favour of their children under 18 were blocked by FA 1999 s 64, amending TA 1988 s 660B for trusts created on or after 9 March 1999 or where funds are added on or after that date.

    The advantages continue for bare trusts created by parents before that date providing no funds are added. The tax deducted at source from the accumulated income may be reclaimed to the extent that it exceeds the child's liability, except for dividend credits, which are no longer repayable.

    The revised rules do not prevent bare trusts being created by a parent's will, or by other relatives. It is not, however, possible for a parent to circumvent the rules by creating a bare trust for a relative's or friend's children and for the relative/friend to do the same for his children (ITTOIA 2005 s 620).

9. Property held on a bare trust is in the legal ownership of the trustees and must remain in their ownership if and so long as the beneficiary is a minor (since a minor cannot give a valid receipt). As and when the beneficiary is over 18 he may call for the legal ownership to be transferred to him at any time.

Under self-assessment, trustees are not required to complete tax returns in respect of bare trusts (although they may send a return of *income*, but not capital gains, if they wish – see Example 47 explanatory note 8), and the child must show the income and gains in his own return.

10. Because the property is held for the beneficiary absolutely, it is not settled property for capital gains tax (TCGA 1992 s 60), and any gains are taxable on the beneficiary, so that the full annual exemption (£8,800 for 2006/07) and lower rate bands are available unless used against other gains. This means that bare trusts created by parents could still be tax-efficient if the funds were invested purely for capital growth, with no income arising. Even if some income did arise, the parent would only be in the same income tax position as if income had arisen to the parent directly.

11. Although there is no equivalent to TCGA 1992 s 60 in the income tax legislation, the trustee is effectively only a nominee, so presumably the provisions of TA 1988 s 686A charging tax at the excess of the dividend trust rate of 32½% over the tax credit rate of 10% where a company purchases the trustees' shares (see Example 49 explanatory note 4) do not apply. As far as inheritance tax is concerned, the transfer to the bare trust is a potentially exempt transfer, so that tax will not be payable providing the donor survives the transfer by seven years. In the hands of the beneficiary, the property is not treated as settled property since it is held for him absolutely.

Other tax-efficient ways of benefiting children

12. In addition to creating accumulation and maintenance settlements, which have the inheritance tax advantages outlined in note 4 above, or creating bare trusts that do not produce income but offer capital growth, parents may use funds for the benefit of their children without being caught by the income tax parental settlement rules as follows, as indicated in the example at part B note 5:

    (a) National Savings and Investments Children's Bonus Bonds may be purchased for children under 16 (maximum holding per child £3,000 in latest issue plus holdings in earlier issues). Interest on the bonds is tax-free. They mature at the child's 21st birthday.

    (b) Premiums of up to £270 per annum for each child may be paid on a qualifying friendly society policy. The proceeds of the policy are tax-free and the society does not pay tax on its income and gains in respect of such policies.

    (c) Personal pension contributions of up to £2,808 net, £3,600 gross, per child may be paid each year. The child may not, however, draw any benefits from a pension plan until pension age is reached (age 55 from 2010).

    These tax-efficient payments do not, however, give any opportunity for using the child's personal allowance and lower rates of tax.

You were contacted in September 2006 by the trustees of the Green grandchildren's trust, a trust resident in the UK with UK based trustees. They are concerned about the tax treatment of dividends, tax credits on distributions to beneficiaries and capital gains.

The following details are known:

(1)   The trust's main asset is a 27% shareholding in Green plc, an unquoted UK trading company. The shareholding was acquired by gift in 1987 from the settlor. The shares were worth £850,000 at that time and a gain of £650,000 was held over. The settlor had acquired the shares in 1967. This shareholding is now worth about £2 million. It is anticipated that the company may be floated on the London Stock Exchange in the next year or so, in which case the shares could increase in value to over £5 million.

(2)   The trust's main source of income is dividends from its shareholding in Green plc. Normally about half the dividend is distributed to the beneficiaries.

(3)   The trust is an accumulation and maintenance trust which provides for a grandchild of the settlor to receive a life interest at age 25 with capital distributions subject to trustees' discretion.

(4)   There are currently eight grandchildren with age ranges 19 to 26. It is unlikely that any further beneficiaries will come into existence and the trustees have established eight accounts within the trust for administration purposes. Only two of the beneficiaries work for Green plc. The trustees are under pressure to completely wind up the trust and distribute to the beneficiaries. The trustees have already resolved to fully distribute all retained income within the trust.

(5)   The trust had a brought forward tax credit pool for TA 1988 s 687 purposes of £650,000 at 6 April 1999, being mainly tax at the trust rate on dividends.

The trustees wish to call a meeting with their advisers to consider the best way forward. They would like to understand the effect of the changes on trust income, distributions and gains, in relation to the question whether to retain in the fund or distribute. They also wish to discuss how the FA 2006 changes affect their trust.

Draft technical notes for the meeting with the trustees.

Technical notes for meeting with trustees of Green grandchildren's trust

Tax treatment of dividends from 6 April 1999 to 5 April 2004

1. Before 6 April 1999 dividends carried a repayable tax credit of 25% of the cash dividend (20% of the tax credit inclusive amount), so that a cash dividend of £80 represented a dividend of £100 with a credit of £20, which was repayable to a non-taxpayer. Trust expenses were deducted from net trust income to give the amount available for distribution to beneficiaries.

   A grandchild with a life interest in the trust (ie a grandchild over 25) was (and still is) entitled to the income whether it was distributed or not. If the grandchild's personal allowance covered his income, he could therefore claim repayment of the dividend credit. If the grandchild was a basic rate taxpayer no further tax was payable. A higher rate taxpayer had to pay a further 20% of the tax credit inclusive amount (25% of the cash dividend).

   Where the dividend income was subject to accumulation, it was taxable at the 34% rate applicable to trusts. If any of the dividend income was paid out as maintenance to grandchildren under 25, then since the trust was created by a grandparent rather than a parent, the amount distributed was (and still is) treated as the grandchildren's income, from which tax at 34% had been deducted. Grandchildren not liable to tax would recover the whole of the 34% tax, basic rate taxpayers would recover the difference and higher rate taxpayers would pay an extra 6%.

2. From 6 April 1999 dividend credits are reduced to 1/9th of the cash amount (10% of the tax credit inclusive figure). Trust expenses are deducted from dividend income in priority to other sources of trust income. The dividend tax credits are not repayable. Thus a dividend of £80 carries a non-repayable credit of £9.

   Grandchildren with a life interest will accordingly no longer be able to recover the tax credits. Those liable at the basic rate will still have no further tax to pay and those with income above the basic rate threshold will be liable at the excess of the Schedule F (now dividend) upper rate of 32½% over the tax credit rate of 10%.

3. As far as dividends subject to accumulation were concerned, they were chargeable from 6 April 1999 at a special Schedule F (now dividend) trust rate of 25%. The trustees were left with broadly the same net of tax income as previously, ie:

	Pre 6 April 1999 £	6 April 1999 to 5 April 2004 £
Dividend received	80.00	80.00
Tax credit	20.00	8.89
Trust income	100.00	88.89
Tax at 34%/25%	34.00	22.22
Net of tax income	66.00	66.67

Tax treatment of dividends from 6 April 2004

4. From 6 April 2004 the dividend trust rate for accumulations was increased from 25% to 32½%. This has reduced the amount of income now available for distribution.

	Pre 6 April 2004 £	Post 6 April 2004 £
Dividend received	80.00	80.00
Tax credit	8.89	8.89
Trust income	88.89	88.89
Tax at 25%/32½%	22.22	28.89
Net of tax income	66.67	60.00

Grandchildren with a life interest will continue to receive dividends with a non-repayable tax credit of 10% and to be liable to dividend trust tax of 32½% (less tax credit of 10%) if higher rate taxpayers.

Effect on income available for distribution

5.   Distributions out of the trust to grandchildren under 25 are made net of 40% tax and treated as income of the grandchildren as previously. From 6 April 1999, however, the trustees cannot treat dividend credits as tax already paid in calculating how much of the 40%/34% tax on a distribution has already been accounted for, since they may only include in the tax pool the excess of tax at the dividend trust rate of 32½%/25% over the 10% tax credit rate. The effect is that the maximum distribution out of post 5 April 1999 dividend income is 60% (prior to 6 April 2004 – 66%) of the tax credit *exclusive* amount, eg:

	2003/04 £	2004/05 onwards £
Tax credit exclusive dividend income (net of trust expenses), say	1,800	1,800
Tax credit (1/9)	200	200
Trust gross income	2,000	2,000
Tax on income (25%/32½%)	500	650
Net income	1,500	1,350
Maximum gross payment to beneficiaries:		
Tax credit *exclusive* dividend	1,800	1,800
Tax thereon @ 34%/40%	612	720
Distributable amount	1,188	1,080
Tax to be paid by trustees:		
Tax on gross income	500	650
Covered by tax credits	200	200
Payable by trustees on income	300	450
Tax on distributions	612	720
Further tax due from trustees	312	270

Although the trustees received £1,800 as income it is not possible to distribute that amount because of the tax due on income. In fact it is not normally possible to distribute all of the net income because of the additional tax due from the trustees on distribution, however that amount may be covered by amounts brought forward within the tax pool.

The whole of the tax deducted from the distributions may be repaid to non-taxpaying beneficiaries. Thus in 2003/04 non-taxpaying beneficiaries could recover tax of £612 and from 2004/05 tax of £720.

Tax pool brought forward

6.   The provisions in note 5 from 6 April 1999 onwards may not apply where there is a tax pool brought forward (£650,000 at 6 April 1999 in the case of the Green grandchildren's trust, although this will have been increased by Schedule F (now dividend) tax paid on dividends received after that date as indicated in note 5). The whole of the brought forward figure, which largely represents dividend credits, is fully available to cover the tax on distributions to the beneficiaries. Thus if the trustees distribute all retained income, the restriction of payments to 60% of the dividends will apply only to the post 5 April 1999 amounts, and even then there may be surplus tax in the tax pool because of earlier changes of rates etc. Any surplus remaining in the tax pool when the last child attains age 25 cannot then be used.

Although making an income distribution would use some of the tax pool brought forward, the benefit would depend on the tax position of the beneficiaries, since if the distribution was chargeable to higher rate tax in the hands of the grandchild, no tax would be repayable to them.

To the extent that trust income has been accumulated and thus forms part of the trust capital, it would be paid over to the beneficiaries as capital and no part of the tax suffered could be recovered nor, on the other hand, would any higher rate tax be payable.

Capital gains if trust wound up

7. The Green plc shareholding is currently worth around £2 million, and may increase to over £5 million if the company is floated on the Stock Exchange. Its base cost for capital gains tax in 1987 was (850,000 less heldover gain 650,000 =) £200,000, so that there will be a substantial capital gain on disposal. The gain will be reduced by indexation allowance on the cost of £200,000 from 1987 to April 1998 and the gain will qualify for taper relief under TCGA 1992 s 2A and Sch A1 for complete years of ownership from 6 April 1998 to the date of disposal.

8. Following changes in FA 2000 s 67, all holdings in unquoted trading companies qualify for the business assets rate of relief. In the case of the Green plc shares the holding qualified for the business assets rate from the outset, ie from 6 April 1998, since the trustees owned the requisite 25% or more of the voting rights (see explanatory notes 5 and 6).

    If Green plc obtains a Stock Exchange listing, the business assets rate of taper relief will still apply on disposal of the holding, providing the trustees still hold 5% of the voting rights. If they do not, then the business assets rate will apply only according to the proportion of the trust income relating to the life interest beneficiaries who are employees of the company, of whom there are two. (For the period from 6 April 1998 to 5 April 2000 such beneficiaries would have had to be *full-time* employees in order for the business assets rate of taper relief to apply by reference to their employment.) The much lower non-business assets rate will apply to the remainder of the gain, the qualifying period of ownership in that event including an extra year since the shares were owned before 17 March 1998.

9. Assuming the conditions for the business assets rate of relief continued to apply, the holding would qualify for taper relief of 75% for a disposal in 2006/07.

10. Taper relief would still apply if the shares were distributed to the beneficiaries rather than being sold. Alternatively business gifts holdover relief under TCGA 1992 s 165 could be claimed in respect of the trustees' gains (providing the shares remained unquoted, or the trustees retained 25% or more of the voting rights), so that the beneficiaries' acquisition costs would be reduced accordingly. The heldover gains would, however, then not be reduced by taper relief. The beneficiaries would be entitled to taper relief when they disposed of the shares based on their period of ownership and the business/non-business status of the shares during that period.

11. If the shares were distributed to the beneficiaries, then following the taper relief changes in FA 2000 s 67, the business assets rate would apply in respect of the period of ownership of all beneficiaries so long as Green plc remained unquoted. If it obtained a Stock Exchange listing, then unless the beneficiary's shareholding was 5% or more (which on an equal distribution of 27% between eight beneficiaries it would not be), the business assets rate in respect of the period from the date the shares became quoted would only apply to a beneficiary who worked for the company. For other beneficiaries their gains on disposal would be apportioned according to the business/non-business periods and the higher rates of taper relief would apply only to the business assets proportion.

Rules for Accumulation and Maintenance Settlements post FA 2006

12. One of the main changes of the 2006 rules is that new A&M settlements cannot be established on or after 22 March 2006 (IHTA 1984 s 71(1A)).

    Furthermore, existing A&M settlements will need to ensure that by 6 April 2008 at least one beneficiary will be beneficially entitled to the capital at the age of 18. This represents two changes:

(i)   It was previously sufficient for an interest in possession to be given whereas now the right to the underlying capital is necessary.

(ii)   There is now a reduction in the maximum age at which this can occur from 25 to 18.

If these new conditions are not met after 5 April 2008, the settlement will be subject to the exit and 10-yearly charges regime.

The 10 year anniversaries will be based on the date the trust was established in 1987 rather than the date the trust property became "relevant property" in 2008.

Explanatory Notes

Treatment of dividend income in discretionary trusts

1.   The basic income tax treatment of discretionary trusts is that in respect of income which the trustees have the power to accumulate, or which may be distributed at their discretion, the trustees are liable to tax under TA 1988 s 686 at the dividend trust rate of 32½% on dividend income and at the 'rate applicable to trusts' of 40% on other income. The tax suffered by the trustees forms a tax pool (TA 1988 s 687), which is available to cover the tax on any distributions to the beneficiaries. From 6 April 2004 only 22½% of the 32½% tax credit on dividends goes into the tax pool, hence the reduced level of possible distribution as indicated in the example.

But see the new rules introduced in FA 2005 s 14 as set out on page (vii) in the Summary of Provisions of Finance Act 2005.

Under FA 2005 s 14 the first £500 of relevant income will not be charged at the special trust tax rates, but will instead be charged at the income tax rate appropriate to the type of income, known as standard rate band. Therefore, if payments are received net of tax (for example, building society interest) up to the limit of the standard rate band, then the trustees will have no further tax to pay.

The Revenue have confirmed that the standard rate band set out in FA 2005 s 14 will apply to trust income *net* of trust management expenses so potentially it will apply to other charges as well.

Although the management expenses are deducted from the trust income taxed at the lowest rate first, the standard rate band will apply in the order – basic rate income at 22% first, followed by lower rate 20% income and finally dividends at 10%.

See Examples 42, 47 and 48 for the details of this provision which applies from 6 April 2005.

2.   In this example, once a grandchild reaches age 25 and becomes entitled to a life interest in the trust, his share of the trust income is taxable on him, whether it is received or retained within the trust. If there is unutilised tax within the pool of tax under TA 1988 s 687 when the last grandchild reaches age 25 the unused amount will be wasted, although this would not be a disadvantage to the extent that capital distributions were then made to grandchildren who would be liable to higher rate tax on income distributions.

Capital gains tax holdover relief and taper relief

3.   There are two holdover reliefs available for capital gains tax, the business assets holdover relief of TCGA 1992 s 165 (see Example 50 part A(d) for the definition of business assets for this purpose) and the holdover relief of TCGA 1992 s 260 for gifts on which inheritance tax is chargeable. Even if inheritance tax is not chargeable, s 260(2)(d) provides that the capital gains holdover relief is still available where a beneficiary becomes entitled to trust property or a life interest therein under IHTA 1984 s 71(4) (accumulation and maintenance trusts). In this example this would only apply in relation to beneficiaries under 25 who had not already attained a life interest (see Example 64 explanatory note 3). So long as the shares remain unquoted, or the trustees retain 25% of the voting rights, however, the Green plc shares will be business assets for TCGA 1992 s 165.

However see pages 35.3 and 50.6–50.7 regarding new sections in FA 2004 restricting gift holdover relief in respect of disposals of assets by trustees of settlor-interested settlements.

4. The introduction of capital gains taper relief in FA 1998 has affected the benefit of making holdover elections, because taper relief is given according to the period of ownership of the *donee*, and the ownership period of the donor is irrelevant. For disposals on or after 6 April 2002, FA 2002 s 46 reduced the business assets taper period, so that the maximum 75% relief is available after two complete years, the relief for one complete year being increased to 50%. If the 75% rate of relief is available, this reduces the trustees' tax rate on gains to 25% of 40% = 10%.

   If the 10% taper relief rate is available on trustees' disposals, it will often be thought preferable for trustees to realise gains themselves and distribute cash to beneficiaries, rather than distributing assets, because the beneficiaries themselves may not qualify for the business assets rate, although if they do, it will take only two years for them to reach the maximum level of entitlement. If they qualified only for the lower non-business assets rate, it would take ten years to reach the maximum, which is 40% rather than 75% as for business assets, and no relief at all is available until there are three complete years of ownership.

5. Before FA 2000, in order for shares held by trustees in trading companies to be business assets for taper relief, the trustees needed to hold 25% or more of the voting rights, or the trustees needed to hold 5% of the voting rights and a beneficiary with a life interest needed to be a *full-time* officer or employee of the company. If the trust qualified only under the second heading, ie 5% voting rights and a full-time working beneficiary with a life interest, then if only some of the beneficiaries had a life interest, the business assets rate applied only according to the proportion of the trust income relating to the life interest beneficiaries (TCGA 1992 Sch A1.8).

6. FA 2000 s 67 changed the taper relief definition of business assets so that it includes *all* unquoted shares in trading companies from 6 April 2000. The conditions for quoted shares to qualify as business assets were also relaxed from that date. Quoted trading company shares held by trusts now qualify as business assets for taper relief if the trustees own 5% or more of the voting rights *or* a beneficiary with a life interest is an officer or employee (full-time or part-time) of the company. The provisions in explanatory note 5 apply where a beneficiary's life interest does not extend to the whole of the trust fund.

   More changes to the taper relief definition of business assets were made by FA 2003 s 160. For details see Example 36 part (a)(ii), which also deals with other taper relief points. See also Example 50 part B.

INDEX

References are to page numbers.